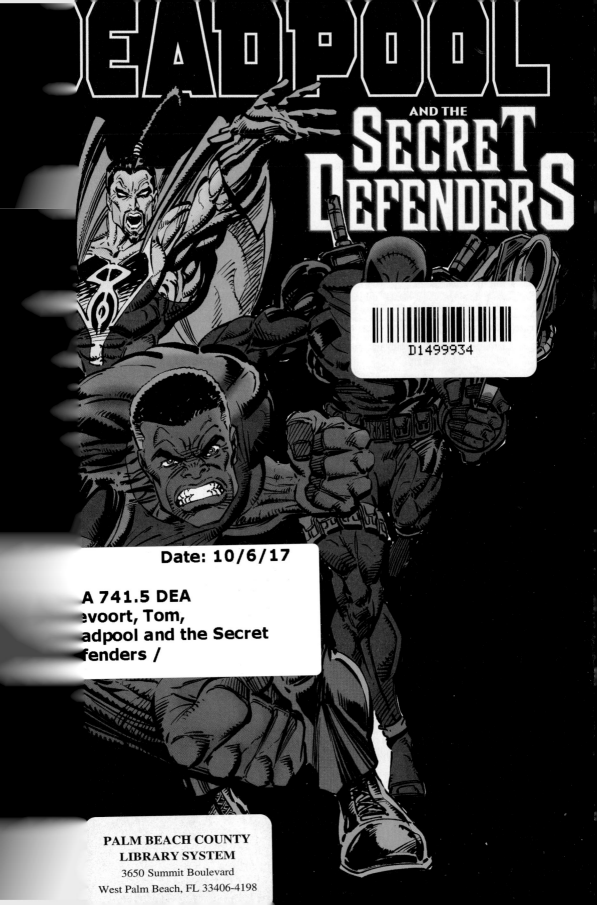

DEADPOOL

AND THE
SECRET
DEFENDERS

DEADPOOL

AND THE
SECRET DEFENDERS

TOM BREVOORT
& MIKE KANTEROVICH
WRITERS

JERRY DeCAIRE &
BILL WYLIE
PENCILERS

TONY DeZUNIGA WITH **DON HUDSON**
INKERS

JOHN KALISZ & JIM HOSTON
COLORISTS

JOHN COSTANZA
LETTERER

LYNAIRE BRUST
ASSISTANT EDITOR

CRAIG ANDERSON
EDITOR

MICHAEL BAIR & MATT MILLA
FRONT COVER ARTISTS

BILL WYLIE
BACK COVER ARTIST

DEADPOOL CREATED BY ROB LIEFELD & FABIAN NICIEZA

COLLECTION EDITOR:
MARK D. BEAZLEY
ASSISTANT EDITOR:
CAITLIN O'CONNELL
ASSOCIATE MANAGING EDITOR:
KATERI WOODY
ASSOCIATE MANAGER, DIGITAL ASSETS:
JOE HOCHSTEIN
SENIOR EDITOR, SPECIAL PROJECTS:
JENNIFER GRÜNWALD

VP PRODUCTION & SPECIAL PROJECTS:
JEFF YOUNGQUIST
RESEARCH & LAYOUT:
JEPH YORK
PRODUCTION:
COLORTEK & JOE FRONTIRRE
BOOK DESIGNER:
JAY BOWEN
SVP PRINT, SALES & MARKETING:
DAVID GABRIEL

EDITOR IN CHIEF:
AXEL ALONSO
CHIEF CREATIVE OFFICER:
JOE QUESADA
PUBLISHER:
DAN BUCKLEY
EXECUTIVE PRODUCER:
ALAN FINE

DEADPOOL AND THE SECRET DEFENDERS. Contains material originally published in magazine form as SECRET DEFENDERS #15-25. First printing 2017. ISBN# 978-1-302-90417-3. Published by MARVEL WORLDWIDE, INC., a subsidiary of MARVEL ENTERTAINMENT, LLC. OFFICE OF PUBLICATION: 135 West 50th Street, New York, NY 10020. Copyright © 2017 MARVEL No similarity between any of the names, characters, persons, and/or institutions in this magazine with those of any living or dead person or institution is intended, and any such similarity which may exist is purely coincidental. **Printed in the U.S.A.** ALAN FINE, President, Marvel Entertainment; DAN BUCKLEY, President, TV, Publishing & Brand Management; JOE QUESADA, Chief Creative Officer; TOM BREVOORT, SVP of Publishing; DAVID BOGART, SVP of Business Affairs & Operations, Publishing & Partnership; C.B. CEBULSKI, VP of Brand Management & Development, Asia; DAVID GABRIEL, SVP of Sales & Marketing, Publishing; JEFF YOUNGQUIST, VP of Production & Special Projects; DAN CARR, Executive Director of Publishing Technology; ALEX MORALES, Director of Publishing Operations; SUSAN CRESPI, Production Manager; STAN LEE, Chairman Emeritus. For information regarding advertising in Marvel Comics or on Marvel.com, please contact Vit DeBellis, Integrated Sales Manager, at vdebellis@marvel.com. For Marvel subscription inquiries, please call 888-511-5480. **Manufactured between 12/23/2016 and 1/30/2017 by LSC COMMUNICATIONS INC., SALEM, VA, USA.**

10 9 8 7 6 5 4 3 2 1

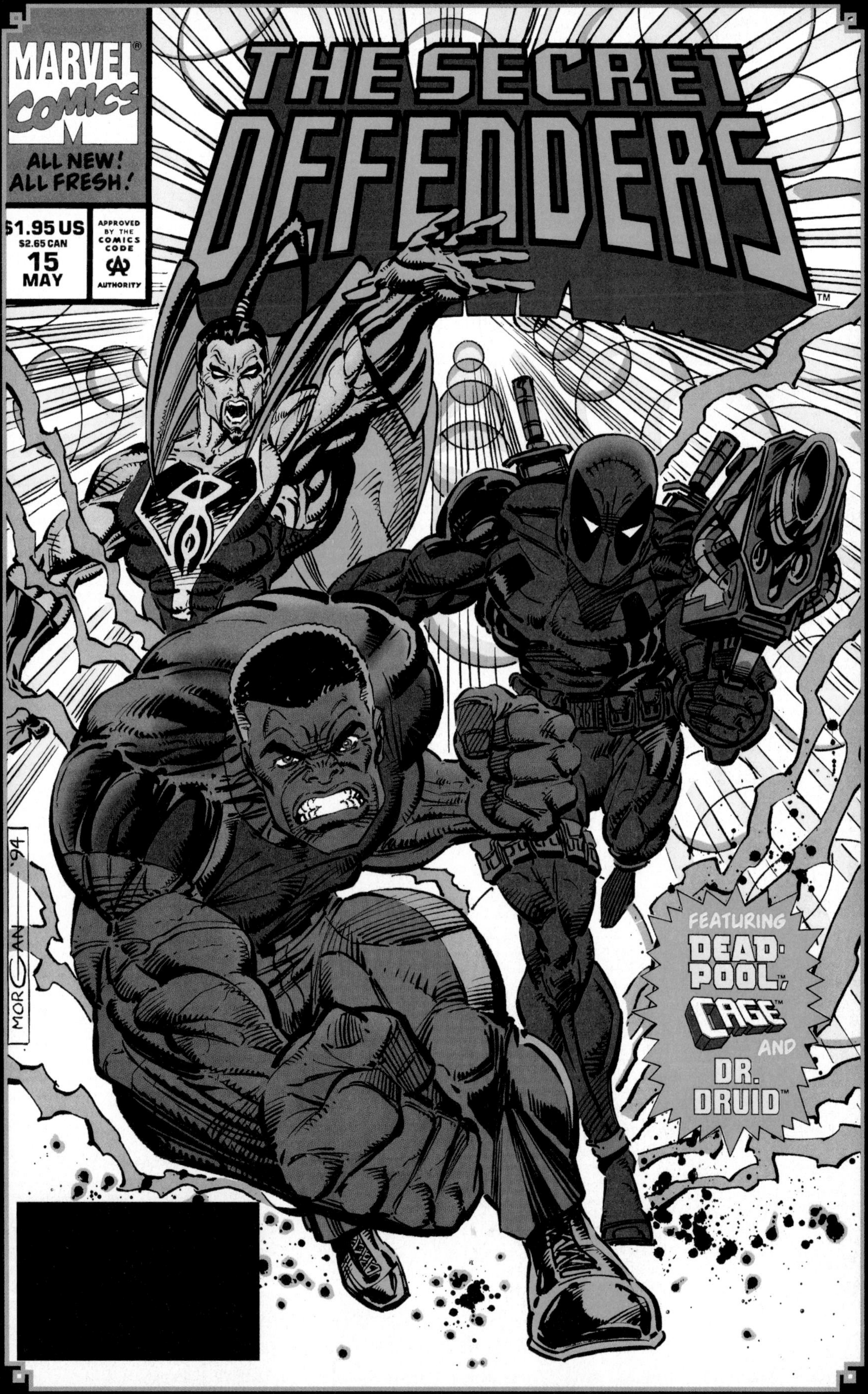
MARVEL®
COMICS
ALL NEW! ALL FRESH!
$1.95 US
$2.65 CAN
15
MAY
APPROVED BY THE COMICS CODE AUTHORITY
THE SECRET DEFENDERS™
MORGAN '94
FEATURING
DEADPOOL,™
CAGE™
AND
DR. DRUID™

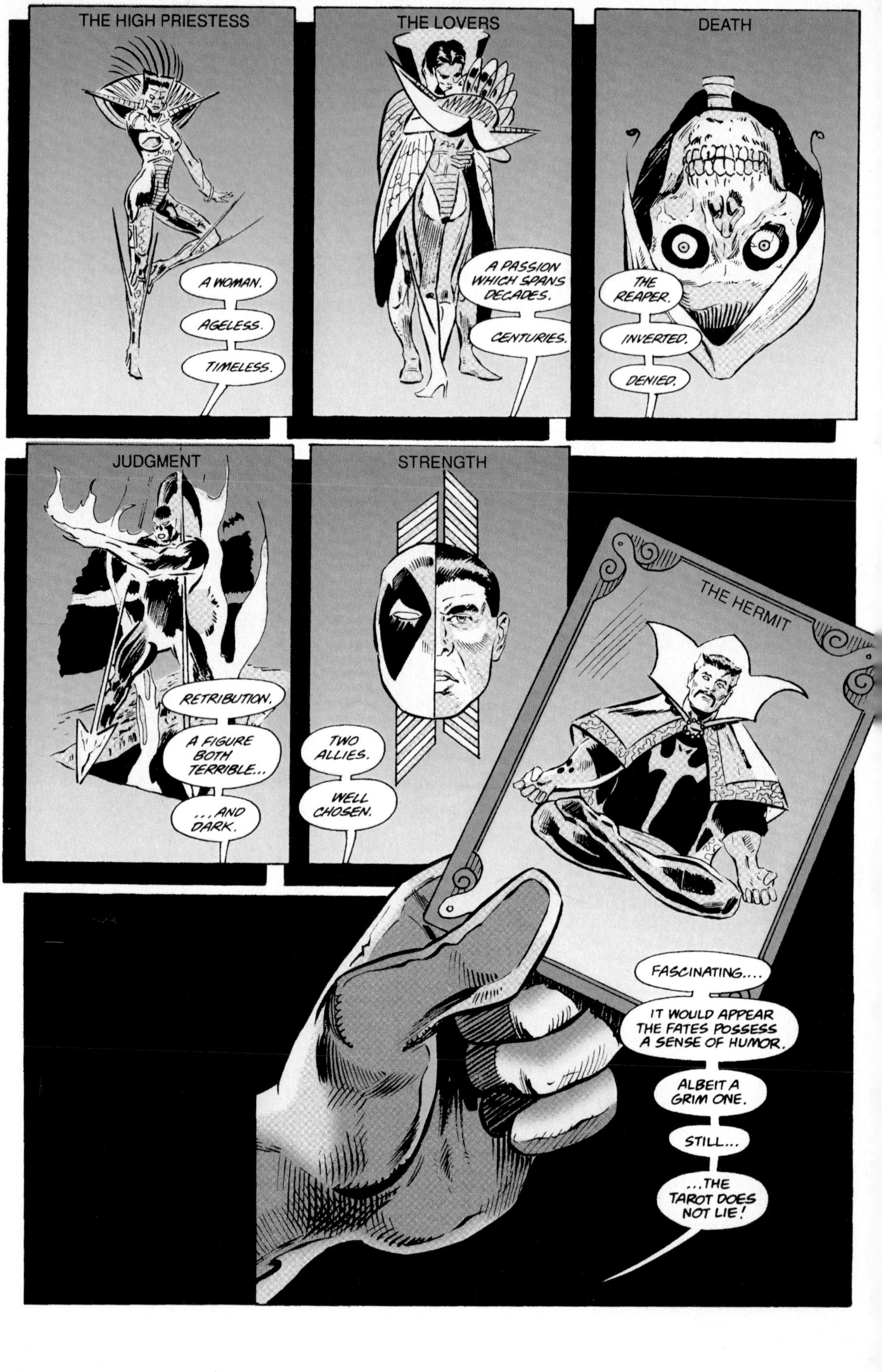
THE HIGH PRIESTESS
A WOMAN.
AGELESS.
TIMELESS.
THE LOVERS
A PASSION WHICH SPANS DECADES.
CENTURIES.
DEATH
THE REAPER.
INVERTED.
DENIED.
JUDGMENT
RETRIBUTION.
A FIGURE BOTH TERRIBLE...
...AND DARK.
STRENGTH
TWO ALLIES.
WELL CHOSEN.
THE HERMIT
FASCINATING....
IT WOULD APPEAR THE FATES POSSESS A SENSE OF HUMOR.
ALBEIT A GRIM ONE.
STILL...
...THE TAROT DOES NOT LIE!

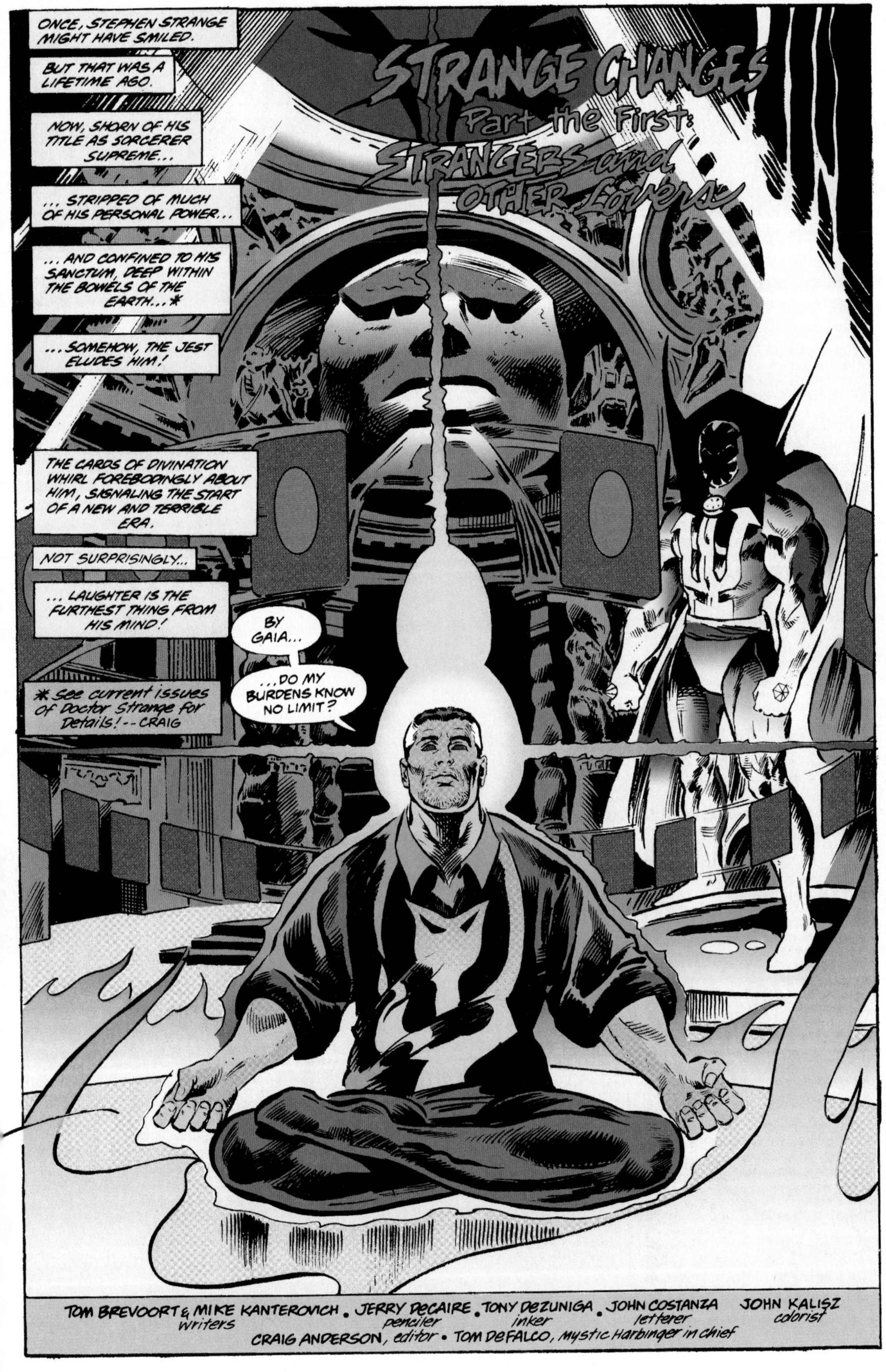
ONCE, STEPHEN STRANGE MIGHT HAVE SMILED.
BUT THAT WAS A LIFETIME AGO.
STRANGE CHANGES
Part the First:
STRANGERS and OTHER Lovers
NOW, SHORN OF HIS TITLE AS SORCERER SUPREME...
... STRIPPED OF MUCH OF HIS PERSONAL POWER...
... AND CONFINED TO HIS SANCTUM, DEEP WITHIN THE BOWELS OF THE EARTH...*
... SOMEHOW, THE JEST ELUDES HIM!
THE CARDS OF DIVINATION WHIRL FOREBODINGLY ABOUT HIM, SIGNALING THE START OF A NEW AND TERRIBLE ERA.
NOT SURPRISINGLY...
... LAUGHTER IS THE FURTHEST THING FROM HIS MIND!
BY GAIA...
...DO MY BURDENS KNOW NO LIMIT?
* See current issues of Doctor Strange for Details! -- CRAIG

TOM BREVOORT & MIKE KANTEROVICH, writers • JERRY DeCAIRE, penciler • TONY DeZUNIGA, inker • JOHN COSTANZA, letterer • JOHN KALISZ, colorist

CRAIG ANDERSON, editor • TOM DeFALCO, mystic Harbinger in chief

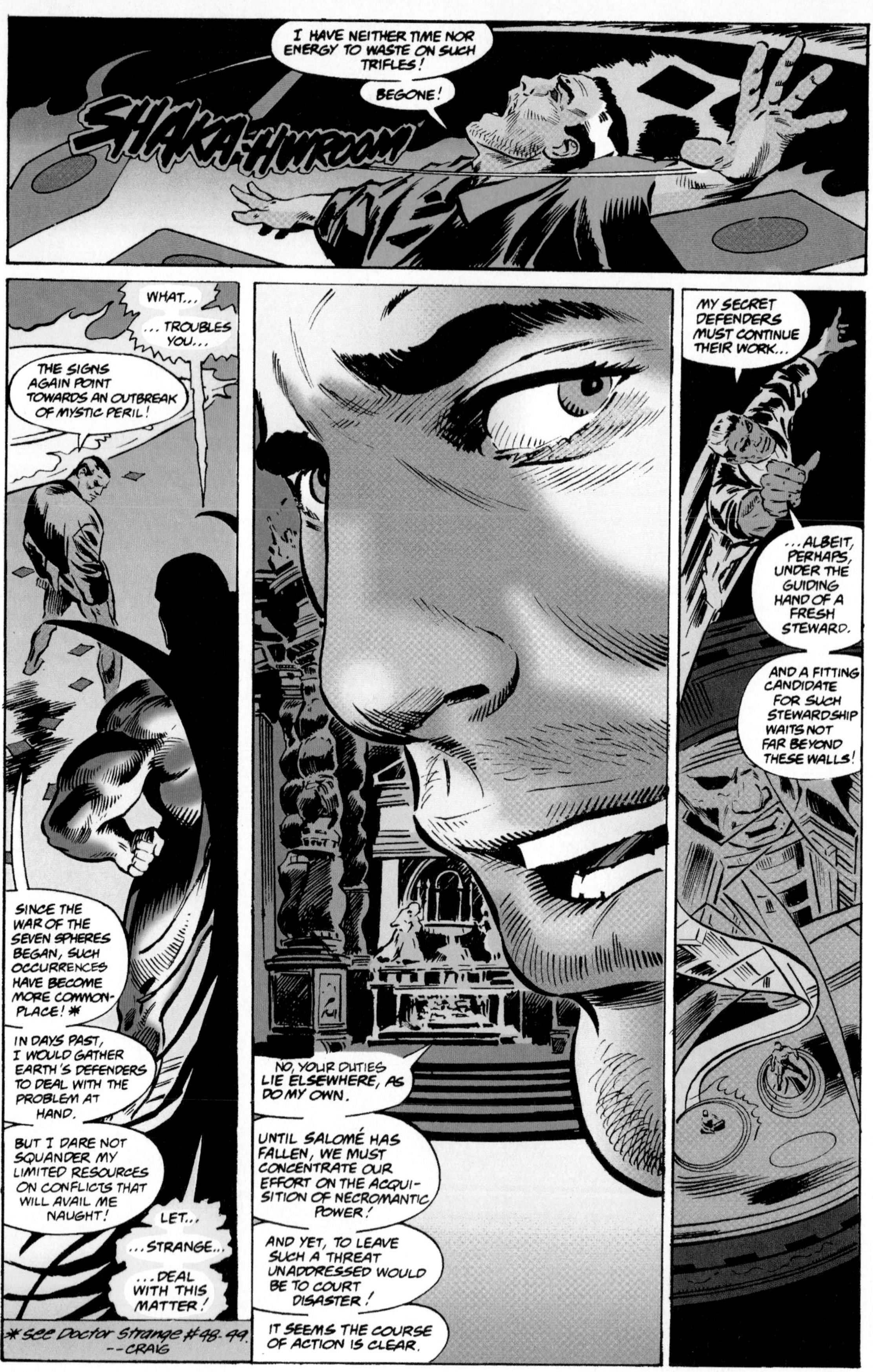

I HAVE NEITHER TIME NOR ENERGY TO WASTE ON SUCH TRIFLES!
BEGONE!
SHAKA-HWROOM
WHAT...
...TROUBLES YOU...
THE SIGNS AGAIN POINT TOWARDS AN OUTBREAK OF MYSTIC PERIL!
SINCE THE WAR OF THE SEVEN SPHERES BEGAN, SUCH OCCURRENCES HAVE BECOME MORE COMMONPLACE! *
IN DAYS PAST, I WOULD GATHER EARTH'S DEFENDERS TO DEAL WITH THE PROBLEM AT HAND.
BUT I DARE NOT SQUANDER MY LIMITED RESOURCES ON CONFLICTS THAT WILL AVAIL ME NAUGHT!
LET...
...STRANGE...
...DEAL WITH THIS MATTER!
* See Doctor Strange #48-49. --CRAIG
NO, YOUR DUTIES LIE ELSEWHERE, AS DO MY OWN.
UNTIL SALOMÉ HAS FALLEN, WE MUST CONCENTRATE OUR EFFORT ON THE ACQUISITION OF NECROMANTIC POWER!
AND YET, TO LEAVE SUCH A THREAT UNADDRESSED WOULD BE TO COURT DISASTER!
IT SEEMS THE COURSE OF ACTION IS CLEAR.
MY SECRET DEFENDERS MUST CONTINUE THEIR WORK...
...ALBEIT, PERHAPS, UNDER THE GUIDING HAND OF A FRESH STEWARD.
AND A FITTING CANDIDATE FOR SUCH STEWARDSHIP WAITS NOT FAR BEYOND THESE WALLS!

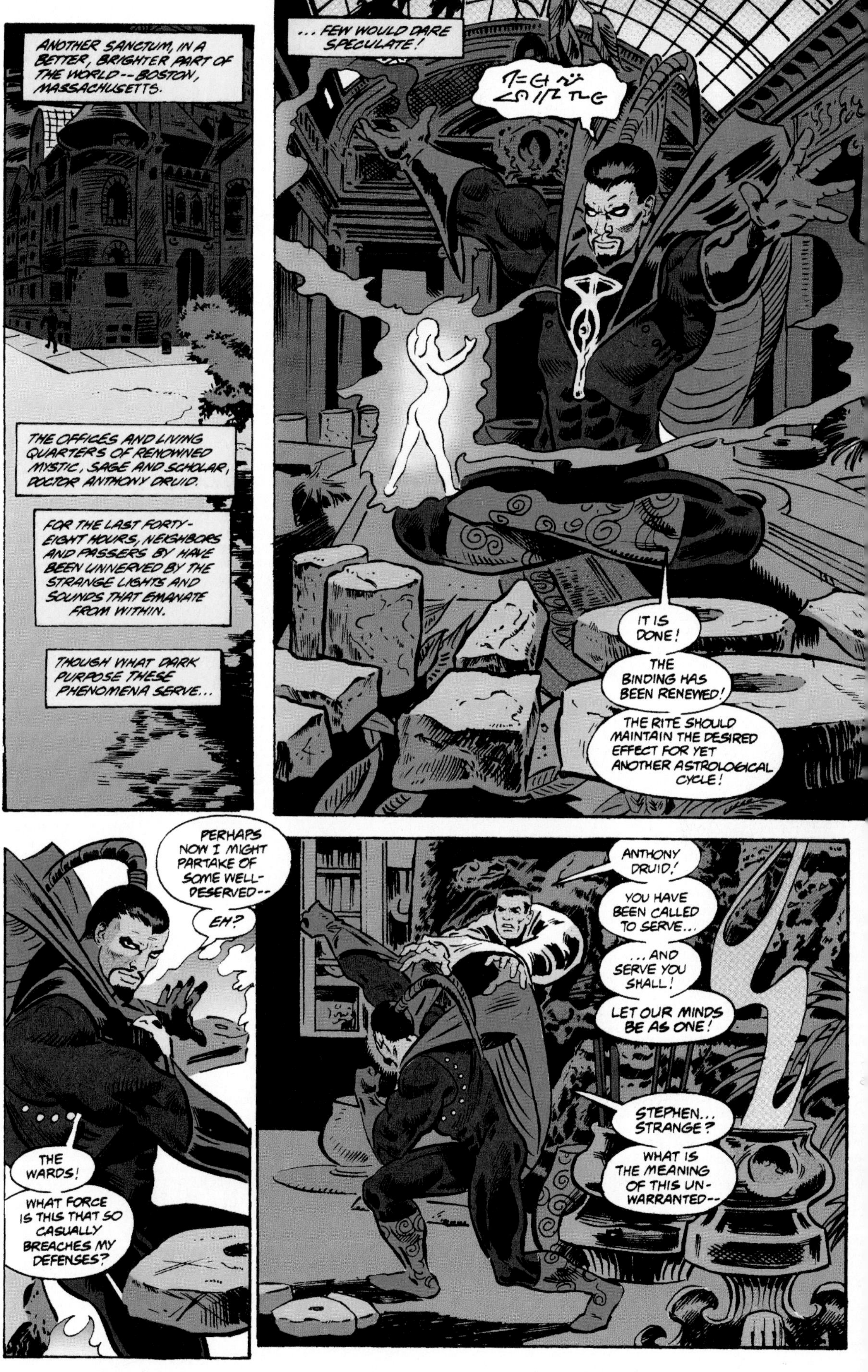
ANOTHER SANCTUM, IN A BETTER, BRIGHTER PART OF THE WORLD -- BOSTON, MASSACHUSETTS.
THE OFFICES AND LIVING QUARTERS OF RENOWNED MYSTIC, SAGE AND SCHOLAR, DOCTOR ANTHONY DRUID.
FOR THE LAST FORTY-EIGHT HOURS, NEIGHBORS AND PASSERS BY HAVE BEEN UNNERVED BY THE STRANGE LIGHTS AND SOUNDS THAT EMANATE FROM WITHIN.
THOUGH WHAT DARK PURPOSE THESE PHENOMENA SERVE...
... FEW WOULD DARE SPECULATE!
IT IS DONE!
THE BINDING HAS BEEN RENEWED!
THE RITE SHOULD MAINTAIN THE DESIRED EFFECT FOR YET ANOTHER ASTROLOGICAL CYCLE!
PERHAPS NOW I MIGHT PARTAKE OF SOME WELL-DESERVED--
EH?
THE WARDS!
WHAT FORCE IS THIS THAT SO CASUALLY BREACHES MY DEFENSES?
ANTHONY DRUID!
YOU HAVE BEEN CALLED TO SERVE...
...AND SERVE YOU SHALL!
LET OUR MINDS BE AS ONE!
STEPHEN... STRANGE?
WHAT IS THE MEANING OF THIS UN-WARRANTED--

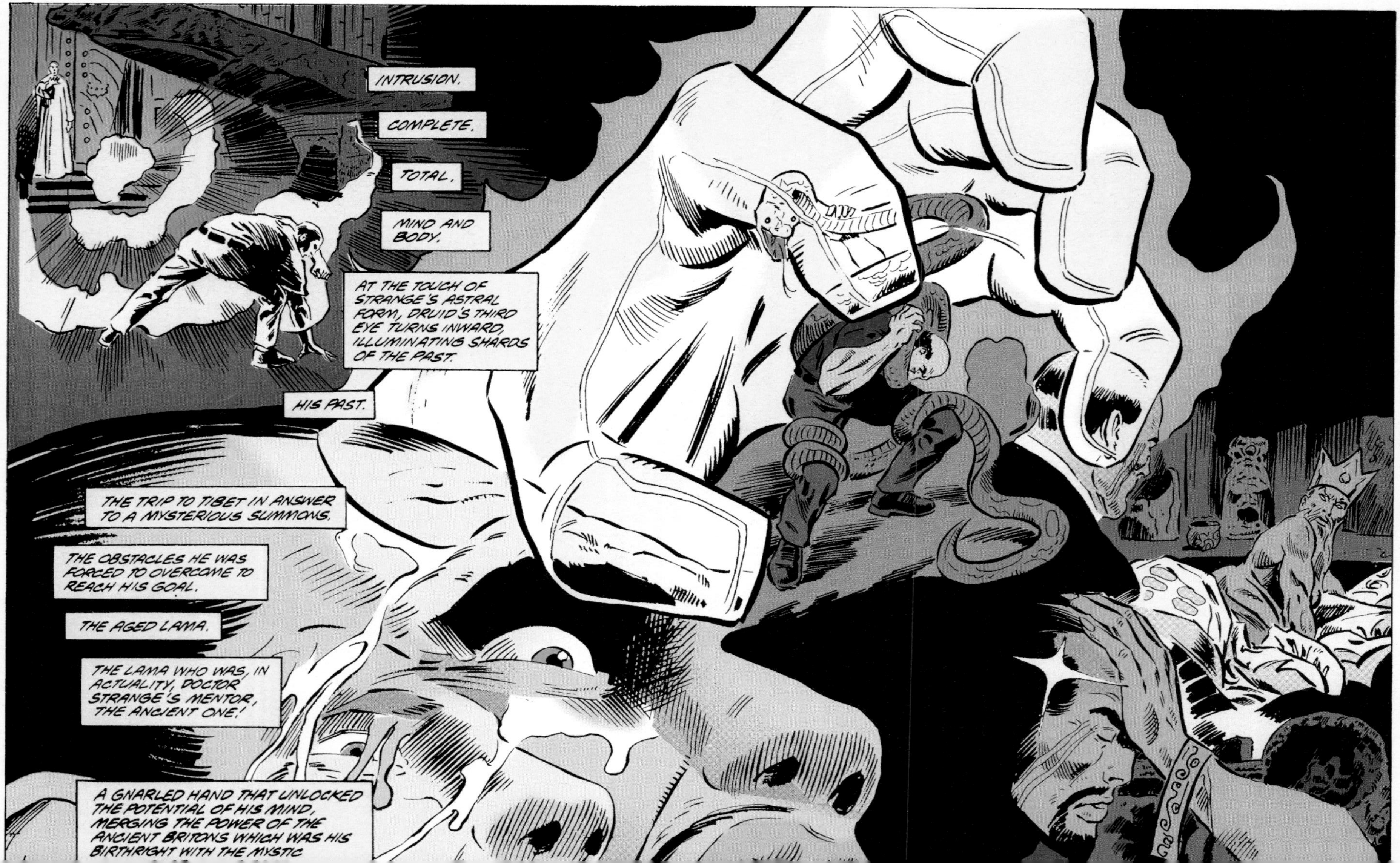
INTRUSION.
COMPLETE.
TOTAL.
MIND AND BODY.
AT THE TOUCH OF STRANGE'S ASTRAL FORM, DRUID'S THIRD EYE TURNS INWARD, ILLUMINATING SHARDS OF THE PAST.
HIS PAST.
THE TRIP TO TIBET IN ANSWER TO A MYSTERIOUS SUMMONS.
THE OBSTACLES HE WAS FORCED TO OVERCOME TO REACH HIS GOAL.
THE AGED LAMA.
THE LAMA WHO WAS, IN ACTUALITY, DOCTOR STRANGE'S MENTOR, THE ANCIENT ONE!
A GNARLED HAND THAT UNLOCKED THE POTENTIAL OF HIS MIND, MERGING THE POWER OF THE ANCIENT BRITONS WHICH WAS HIS BIRTHRIGHT WITH THE MYSTIC

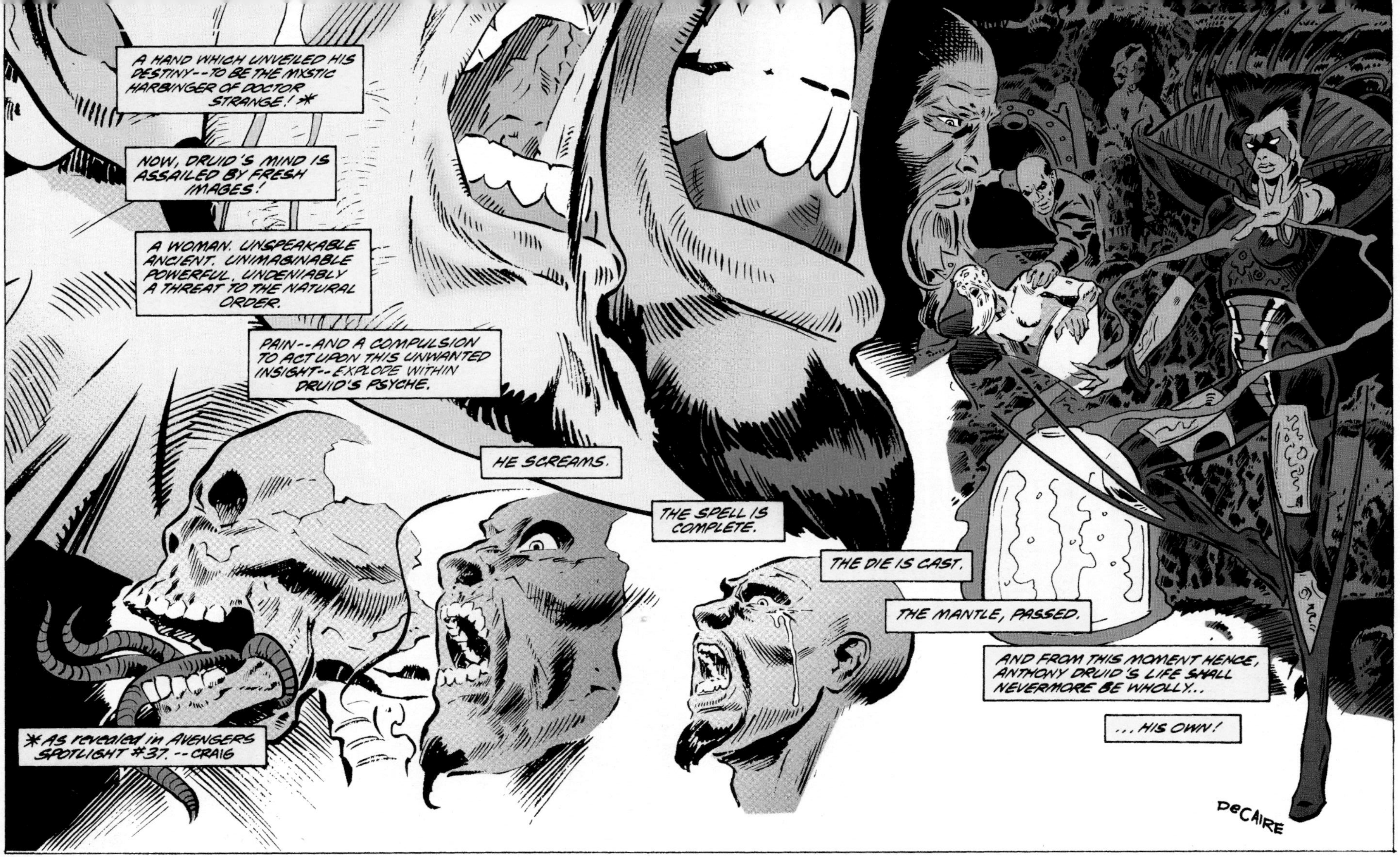

A HAND WHICH UNVEILED HIS DESTINY--TO BE THE MYSTIC HARBINGER OF DOCTOR STRANGE! *
NOW, DRUID'S MIND IS ASSAILED BY FRESH IMAGES!
A WOMAN. UNSPEAKABLE ANCIENT. UNIMAGINABLE POWERFUL. UNDENIABLY A THREAT TO THE NATURAL ORDER.
PAIN--AND A COMPULSION TO ACT UPON THIS UNWANTED INSIGHT--EXPLODE WITHIN DRUID'S PSYCHE.
HE SCREAMS.
THE SPELL IS COMPLETE.
THE DIE IS CAST.
THE MANTLE, PASSED.
AND FROM THIS MOMENT HENCE, ANTHONY DRUID'S LIFE SHALL NEVERMORE BE WHOLLY...
...HIS OWN!
* As revealed in AVENGERS SPOTLIGHT #37. --CRAIG
DeCAIRE

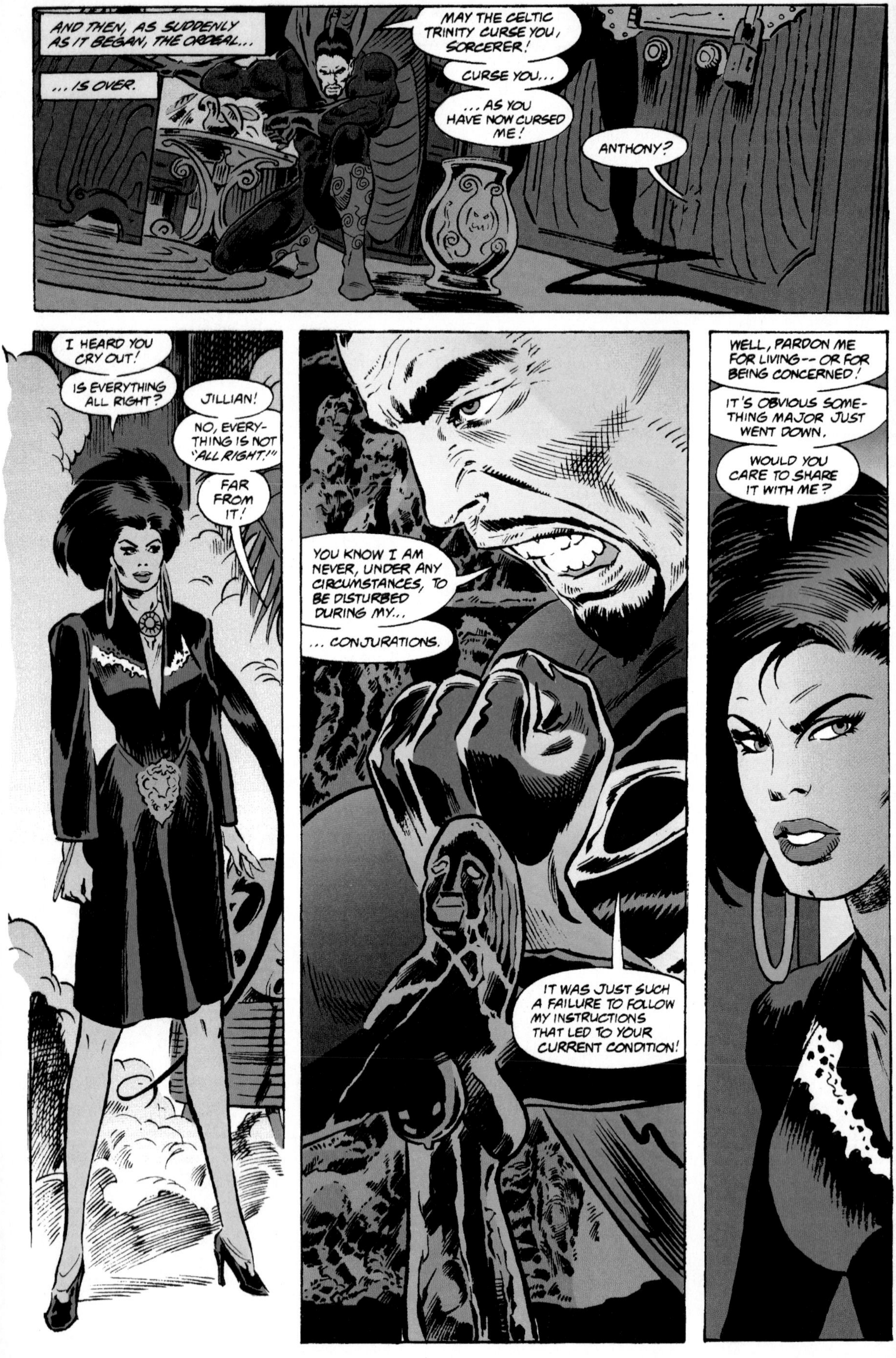
AND THEN, AS SUDDENLY AS IT BEGAN, THE ORDEAL...
... IS OVER.
MAY THE CELTIC TRINITY CURSE YOU, SORCERER!
CURSE YOU...
... AS YOU HAVE NOW CURSED ME!
ANTHONY?
I HEARD YOU CRY OUT!
IS EVERYTHING ALL RIGHT?
JILLIAN!
NO, EVERYTHING IS NOT "ALL RIGHT!"
FAR FROM IT!
YOU KNOW I AM NEVER, UNDER ANY CIRCUMSTANCES, TO BE DISTURBED DURING MY...
... CONJURATIONS.
IT WAS JUST SUCH A FAILURE TO FOLLOW MY INSTRUCTIONS THAT LED TO YOUR CURRENT CONDITION!
WELL, PARDON ME FOR LIVING-- OR FOR BEING CONCERNED!
IT'S OBVIOUS SOMETHING MAJOR JUST WENT DOWN.
WOULD YOU CARE TO SHARE IT WITH ME?

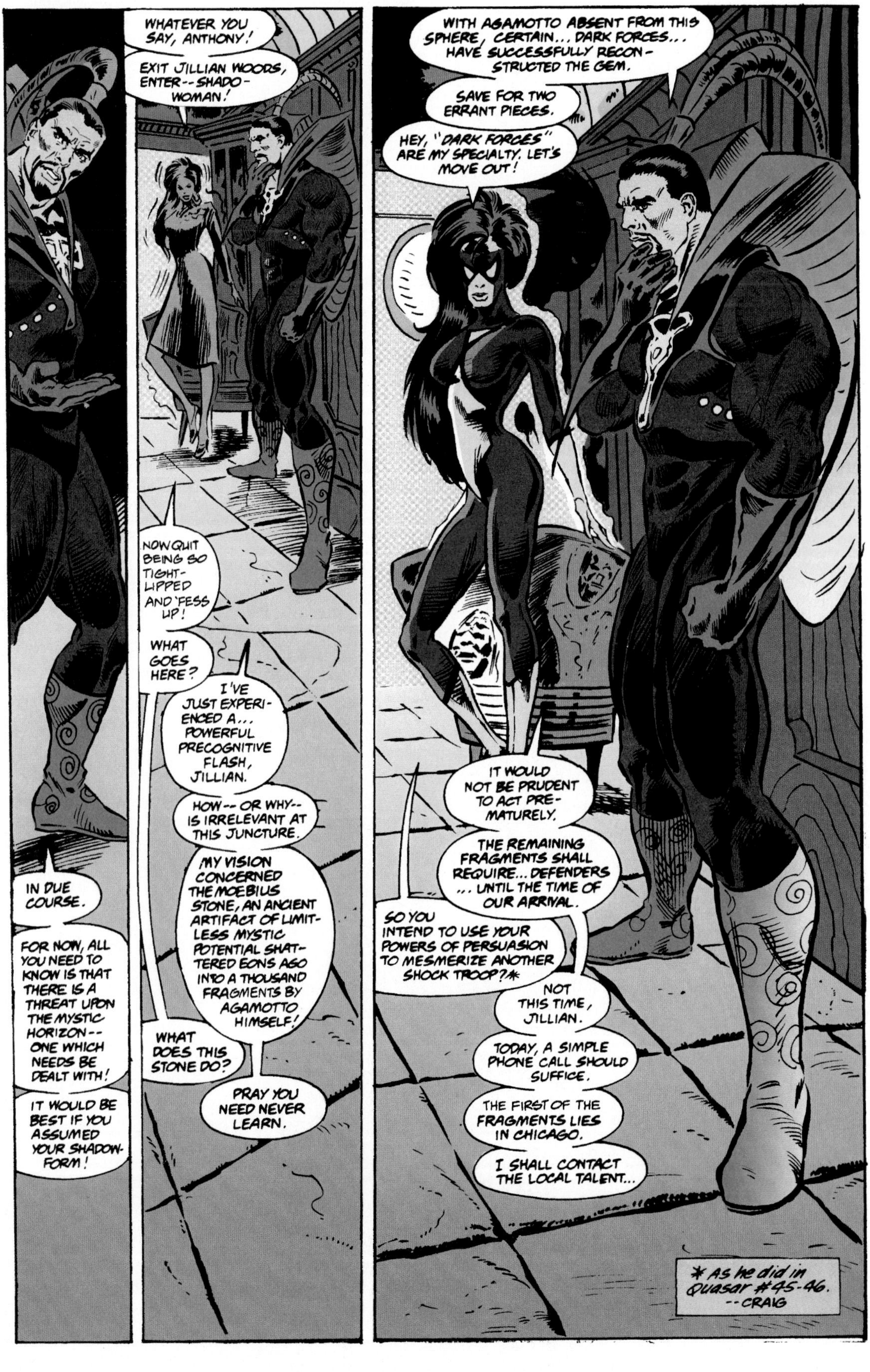
IN DUE COURSE.
FOR NOW, ALL YOU NEED TO KNOW IS THAT THERE IS A THREAT UPON THE MYSTIC HORIZON -- ONE WHICH NEEDS BE DEALT WITH!
IT WOULD BE BEST IF YOU ASSUMED YOUR SHADOW-FORM!
WHATEVER YOU SAY, ANTHONY!
EXIT JILLIAN WOODS, ENTER--SHADO-WOMAN!
NOW QUIT BEING SO TIGHT-LIPPED AND 'FESS UP!
WHAT GOES HERE?
I'VE JUST EXPERIENCED A... POWERFUL PRECOGNITIVE FLASH, JILLIAN.
HOW -- OR WHY -- IS IRRELEVANT AT THIS JUNCTURE.
MY VISION CONCERNED THE MOEBIUS STONE, AN ANCIENT ARTIFACT OF LIMITLESS MYSTIC POTENTIAL SHATTERED EONS AGO INTO A THOUSAND FRAGMENTS BY AGAMOTTO HIMSELF!
WHAT DOES THIS STONE DO?
PRAY YOU NEED NEVER LEARN.
WITH AGAMOTTO ABSENT FROM THIS SPHERE, CERTAIN... DARK FORCES... HAVE SUCCESSFULLY RECONSTRUCTED THE GEM.
SAVE FOR TWO ERRANT PIECES.
HEY, "DARK FORCES" ARE MY SPECIALTY. LET'S MOVE OUT!
IT WOULD NOT BE PRUDENT TO ACT PREMATURELY.
THE REMAINING FRAGMENTS SHALL REQUIRE... DEFENDERS... UNTIL THE TIME OF OUR ARRIVAL.
SO YOU INTEND TO USE YOUR POWERS OF PERSUASION TO MESMERIZE ANOTHER SHOCK TROOP?*
NOT THIS TIME, JILLIAN.
TODAY, A SIMPLE PHONE CALL SHOULD SUFFICE.
THE FIRST OF THE FRAGMENTS LIES IN CHICAGO.
I SHALL CONTACT THE LOCAL TALENT...
* As he did in Quasar #45-46. --CRAIG

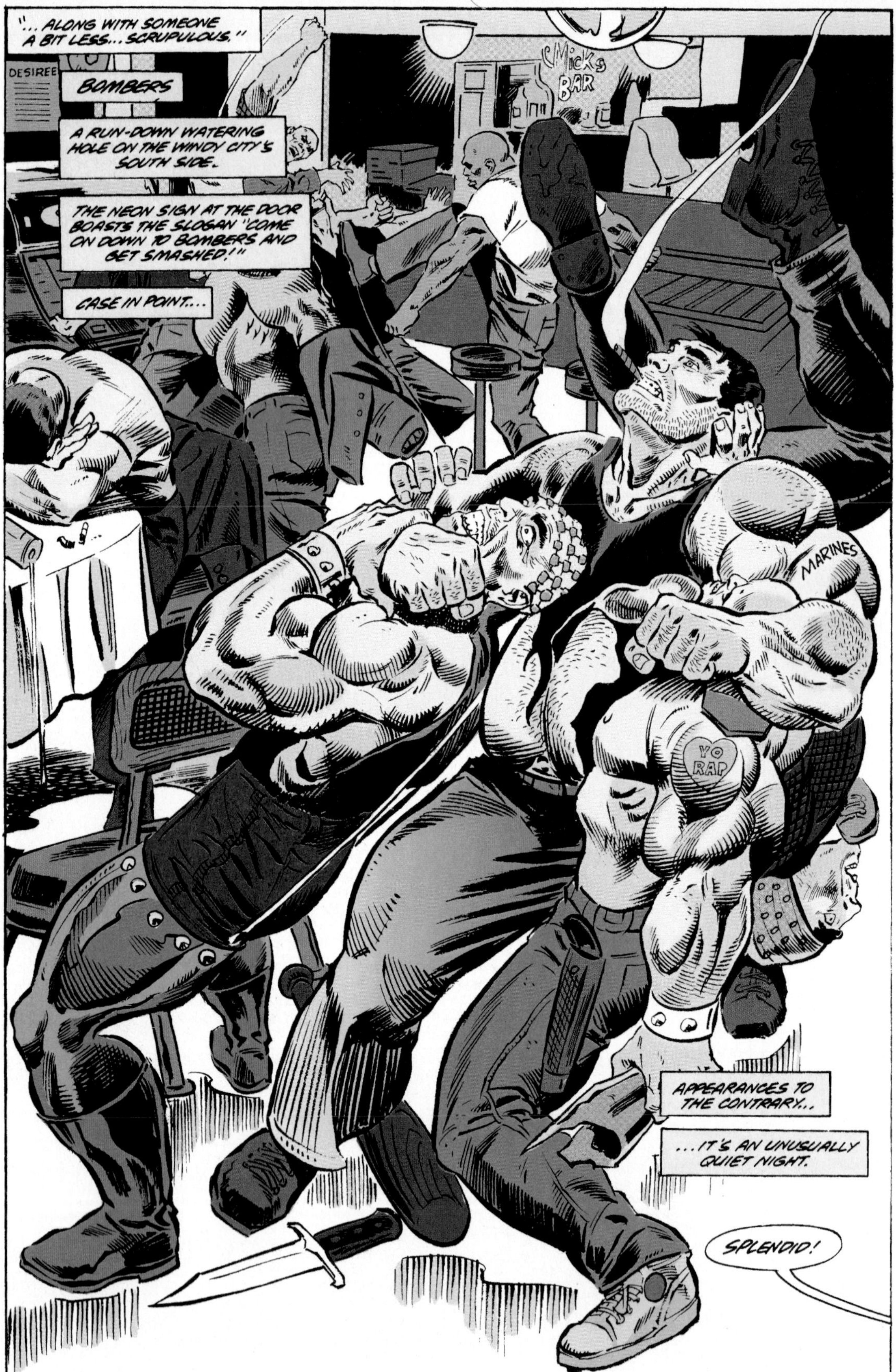
"...ALONG WITH SOMEONE A BIT LESS... SCRUPULOUS."
DESIREE
BOMBERS
A RUN-DOWN WATERING HOLE ON THE WINDY CITY'S SOUTH SIDE.
THE NEON SIGN AT THE DOOR BOASTS THE SLOGAN "COME ON DOWN TO BOMBERS AND GET SMASHED!"
CASE IN POINT...
Mick's BAR
MARINES
YO RAP
APPEARANCES TO THE CONTRARY...
...IT'S AN UNUSUALLY QUIET NIGHT.
SPLENDID!

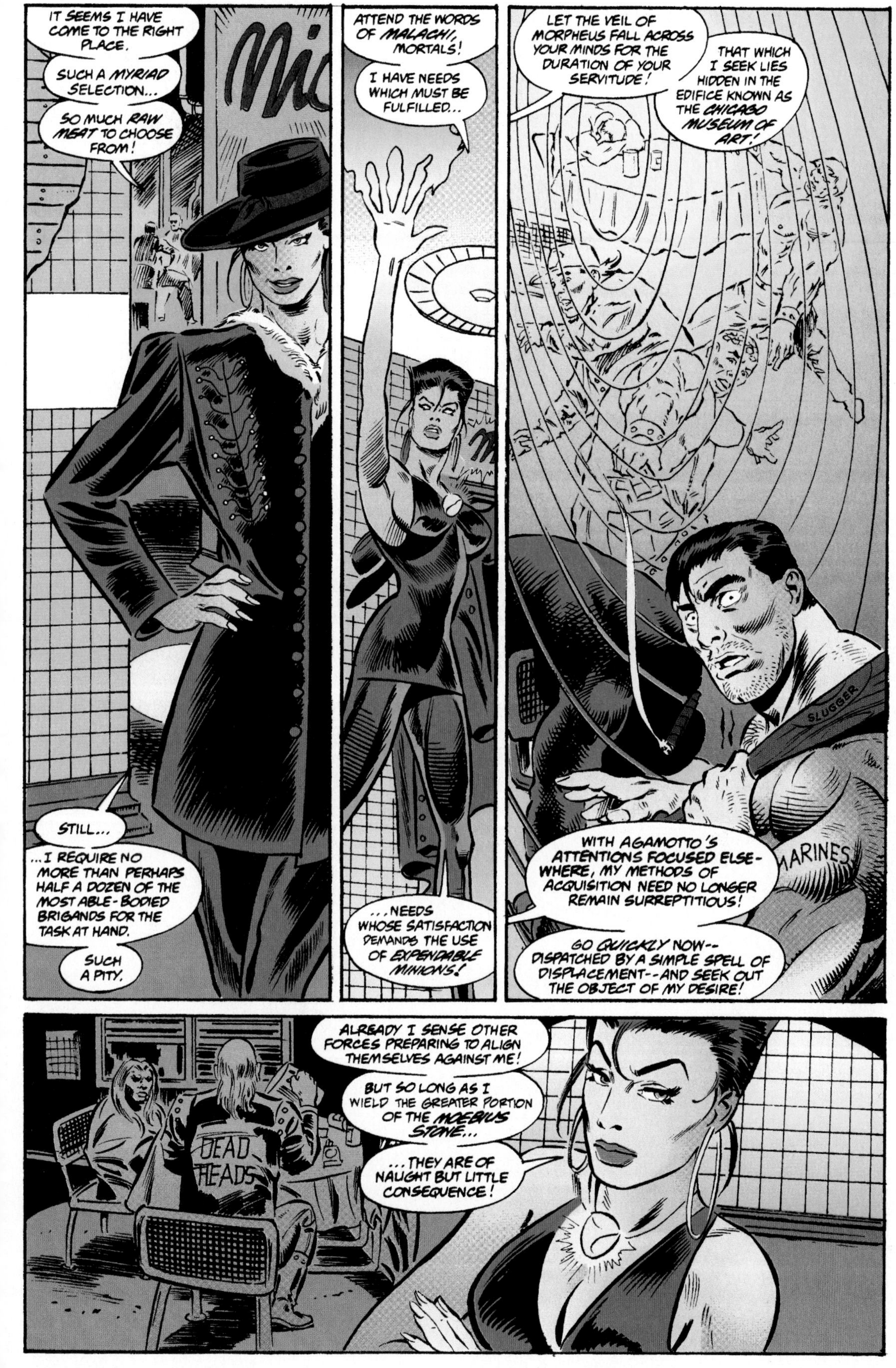
IT SEEMS I HAVE COME TO THE RIGHT PLACE.
SUCH A MYRIAD SELECTION...
SO MUCH RAW MEAT TO CHOOSE FROM!
STILL...
...I REQUIRE NO MORE THAN PERHAPS HALF A DOZEN OF THE MOST ABLE-BODIED BRIGANDS FOR THE TASK AT HAND.
SUCH A PITY.
ATTEND THE WORDS OF MALACHI, MORTALS!
I HAVE NEEDS WHICH MUST BE FULFILLED...
...NEEDS WHOSE SATISFACTION DEMANDS THE USE OF EXPENDABLE MINIONS!
LET THE VEIL OF MORPHEUS FALL ACROSS YOUR MINDS FOR THE DURATION OF YOUR SERVITUDE!
THAT WHICH I SEEK LIES HIDDEN IN THE EDIFICE KNOWN AS THE CHICAGO MUSEUM OF ART!
SLUGGER
MARINES
WITH AGAMOTTO'S ATTENTIONS FOCUSED ELSE-WHERE, MY METHODS OF ACQUISITION NEED NO LONGER REMAIN SURREPTITIOUS!
GO QUICKLY NOW--DISPATCHED BY A SIMPLE SPELL OF DISPLACEMENT--AND SEEK OUT THE OBJECT OF MY DESIRE!
DEAD HEADS
ALREADY I SENSE OTHER FORCES PREPARING TO ALIGN THEMSELVES AGAINST ME!
BUT SO LONG AS I WIELD THE GREATER PORTION OF THE MOEBIUS STONE...
...THEY ARE OF NAUGHT BUT LITTLE CONSEQUENCE!

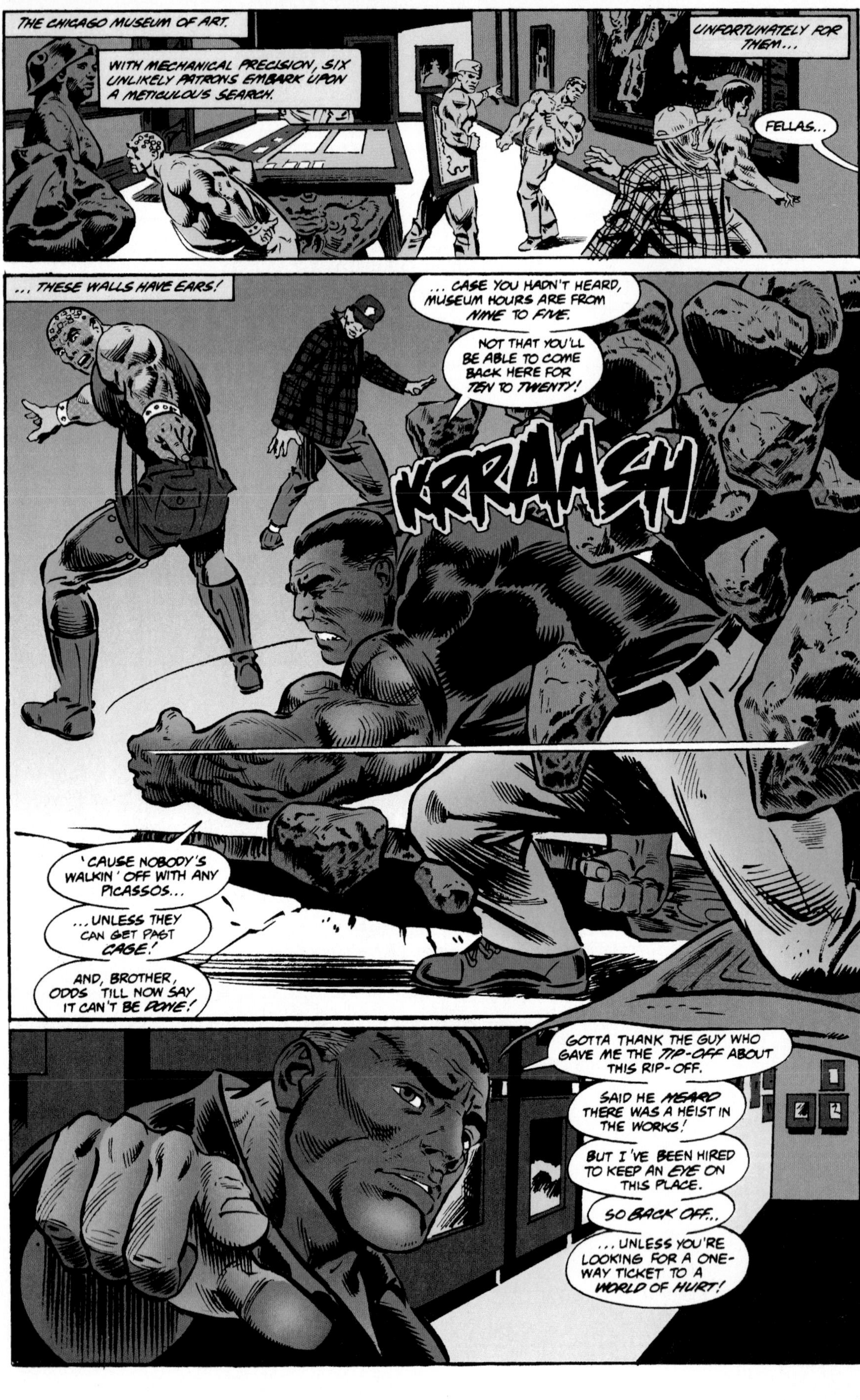
THE CHICAGO MUSEUM OF ART.
WITH MECHANICAL PRECISION, SIX UNLIKELY PATRONS EMBARK UPON A METICULOUS SEARCH.
UNFORTUNATELY FOR THEM...
FELLAS...
... THESE WALLS HAVE EARS!
... CASE YOU HADN'T HEARD, MUSEUM HOURS ARE FROM NINE TO FIVE.
NOT THAT YOU'LL BE ABLE TO COME BACK HERE FOR TEN TO TWENTY!
KRRAAASH
'CAUSE NOBODY'S WALKIN' OFF WITH ANY PICASSOS...
... UNLESS THEY CAN GET PAST CAGE!
AND, BROTHER, ODDS 'TILL NOW SAY IT CAN'T BE DONE!
GOTTA THANK THE GUY WHO GAVE ME THE TIP-OFF ABOUT THIS RIP-OFF.
SAID HE HEARD THERE WAS A HEIST IN THE WORKS!
BUT I'VE BEEN HIRED TO KEEP AN EYE ON THIS PLACE.
SO BACK OFF...
... UNLESS YOU'RE LOOKING FOR A ONE-WAY TICKET TO A WORLD OF HURT!

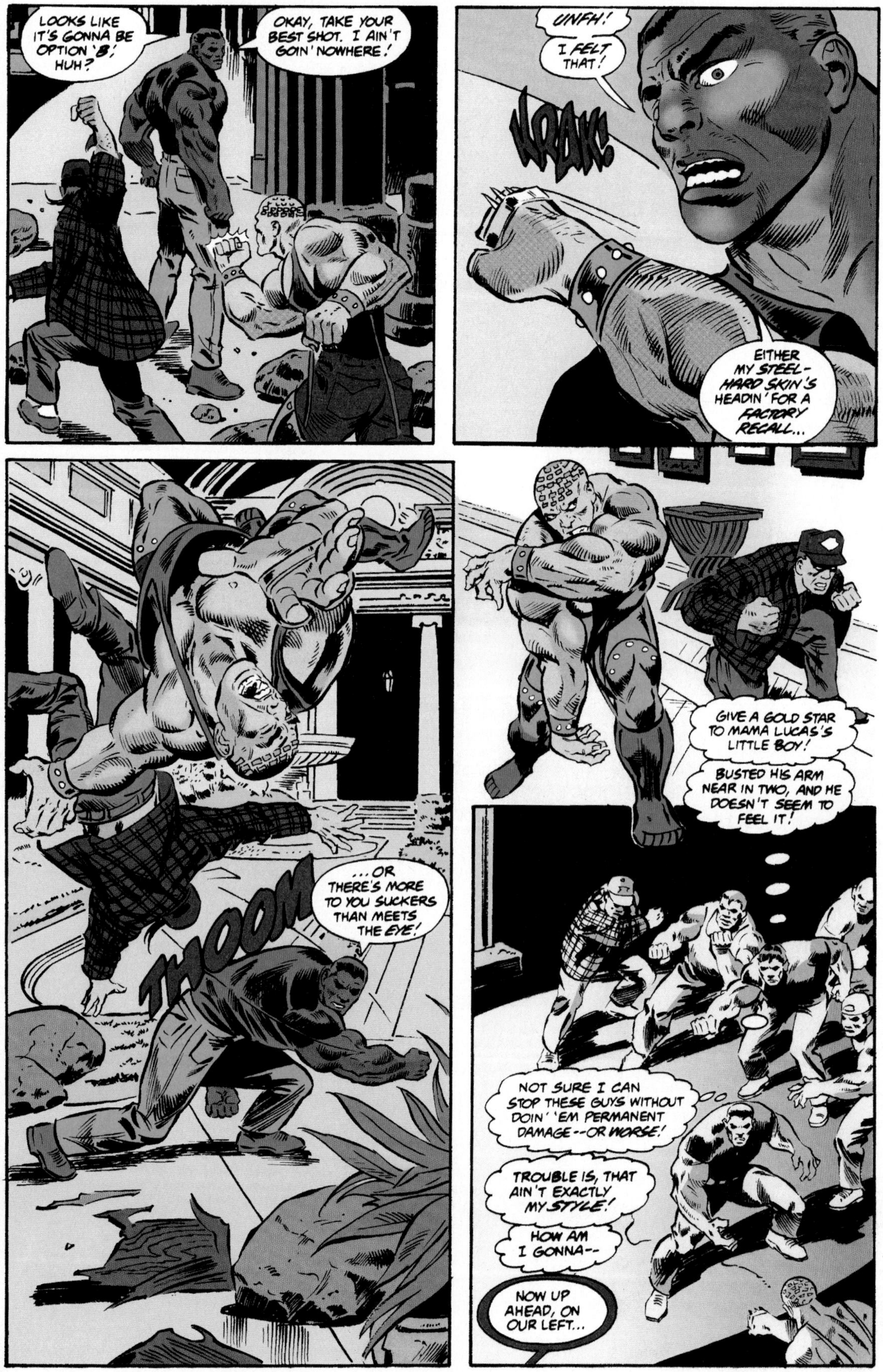

LOOKS LIKE IT'S GONNA BE OPTION 'B', HUH?
OKAY, TAKE YOUR BEST SHOT. I AIN'T GOIN' NOWHERE!
UNFH!
I FELT THAT!
KRAK!
EITHER MY STEEL-HARD SKIN'S HEADIN' FOR A FACTORY RECALL...
...OR THERE'S MORE TO YOU SUCKERS THAN MEETS THE EYE!
THOOM
GIVE A GOLD STAR TO MAMA LUCAS'S LITTLE BOY!
BUSTED HIS ARM NEAR IN TWO, AND HE DOESN'T SEEM TO FEEL IT!
NOT SURE I CAN STOP THESE GUYS WITHOUT DOIN' 'EM PERMANENT DAMAGE--OR WORSE!
TROUBLE IS, THAT AIN'T EXACTLY MY STYLE!
HOW AM I GONNA--
NOW UP AHEAD, ON OUR LEFT...

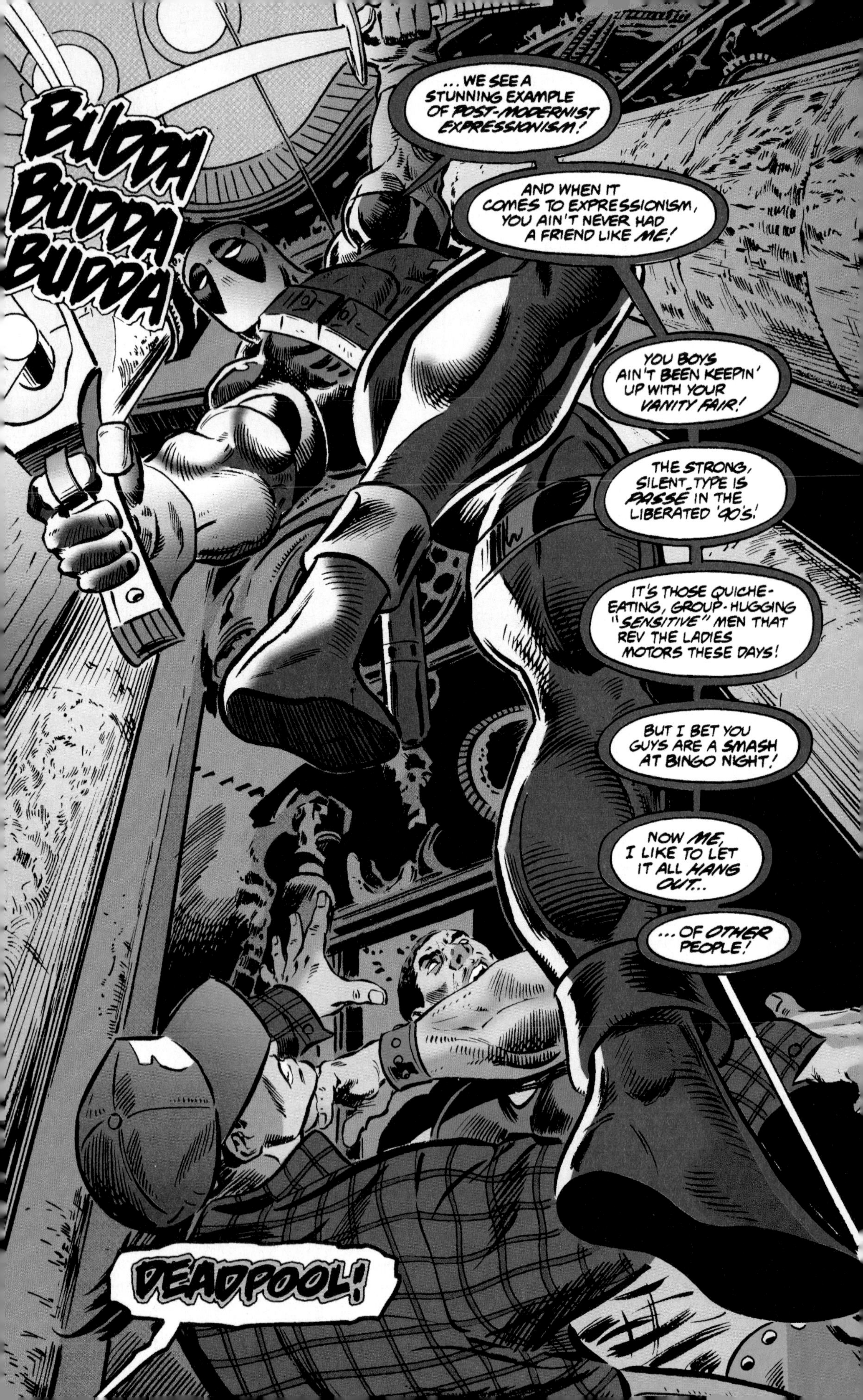
BUDDA BUDDA BUDDA
...WE SEE A STUNNING EXAMPLE OF POST-MODERNIST EXPRESSIONISM!
AND WHEN IT COMES TO EXPRESSIONISM, YOU AIN'T NEVER HAD A FRIEND LIKE ME!
YOU BOYS AIN'T BEEN KEEPIN' UP WITH YOUR VANITY FAIR!
THE STRONG, SILENT TYPE IS PASSÉ IN THE LIBERATED '90'S!
IT'S THOSE QUICHE-EATING, GROUP-HUGGING "SENSITIVE" MEN THAT REV THE LADIES MOTORS THESE DAYS!
BUT I BET YOU GUYS ARE A SMASH AT BINGO NIGHT!
NOW ME, I LIKE TO LET IT ALL HANG OUT...
...OF OTHER PEOPLE!
DEADPOOL!

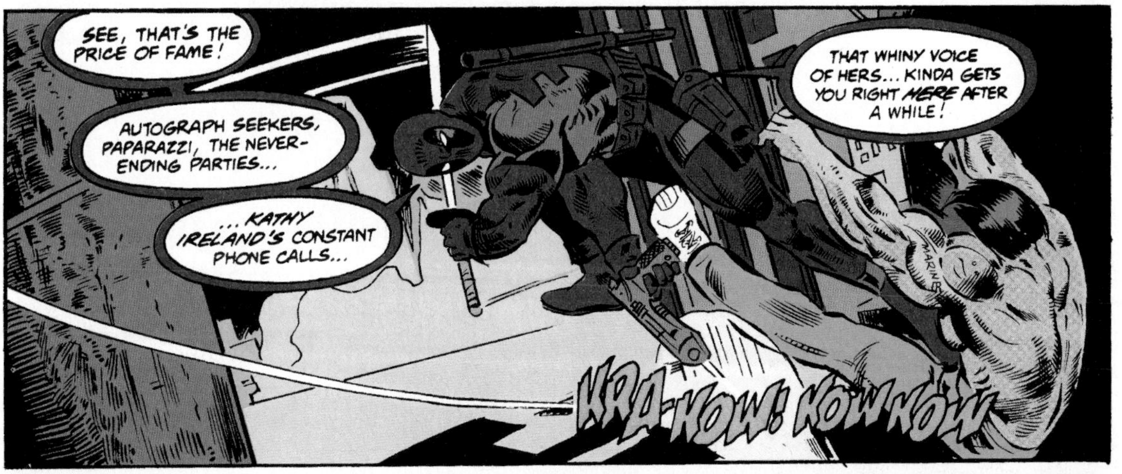
SEE, THAT'S THE PRICE OF FAME!
AUTOGRAPH SEEKERS, PAPARAZZI, THE NEVER-ENDING PARTIES...
...KATHY IRELAND'S CONSTANT PHONE CALLS...
THAT WHINY VOICE OF HERS... KINDA GETS YOU RIGHT HERE AFTER A WHILE!
KRA-KOW! KOW KOW

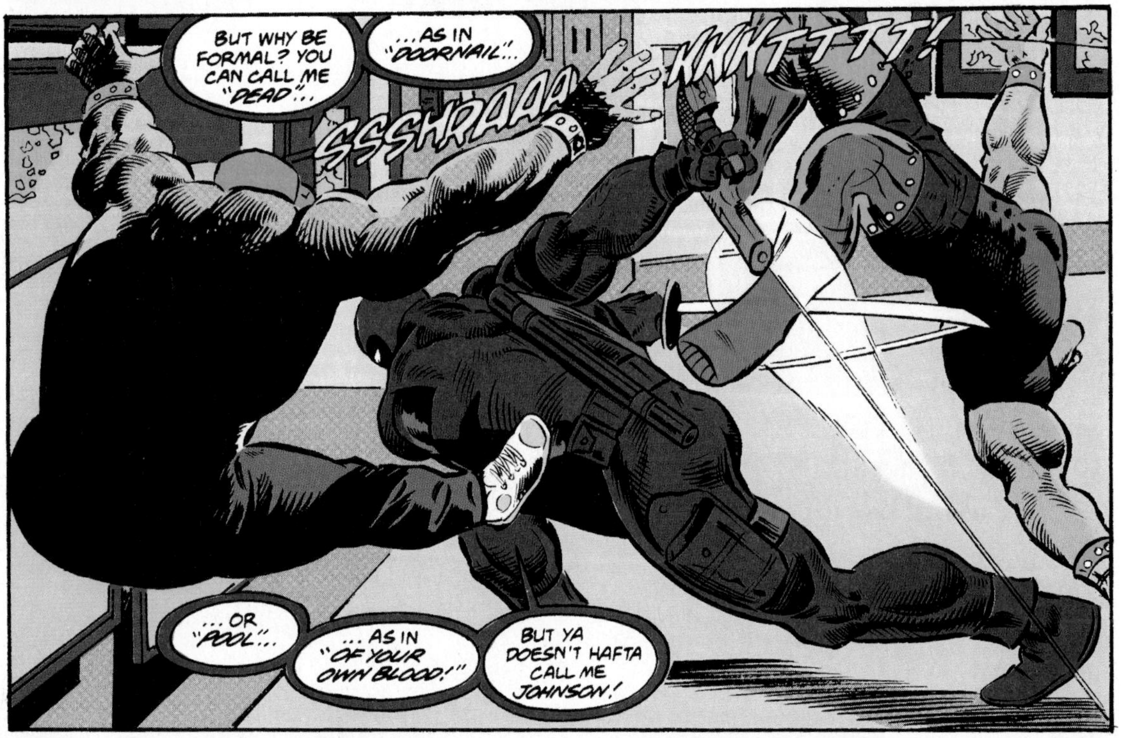
BUT WHY BE FORMAL? YOU CAN CALL ME "DEAD"...
...AS IN "DOORNAIL"...
KKKTTTTT!
SSSHRAAA
...OR "POOL"...
...AS IN "OF YOUR OWN BLOOD!"
BUT YA DOESN'T HAFTA CALL ME JOHNSON!

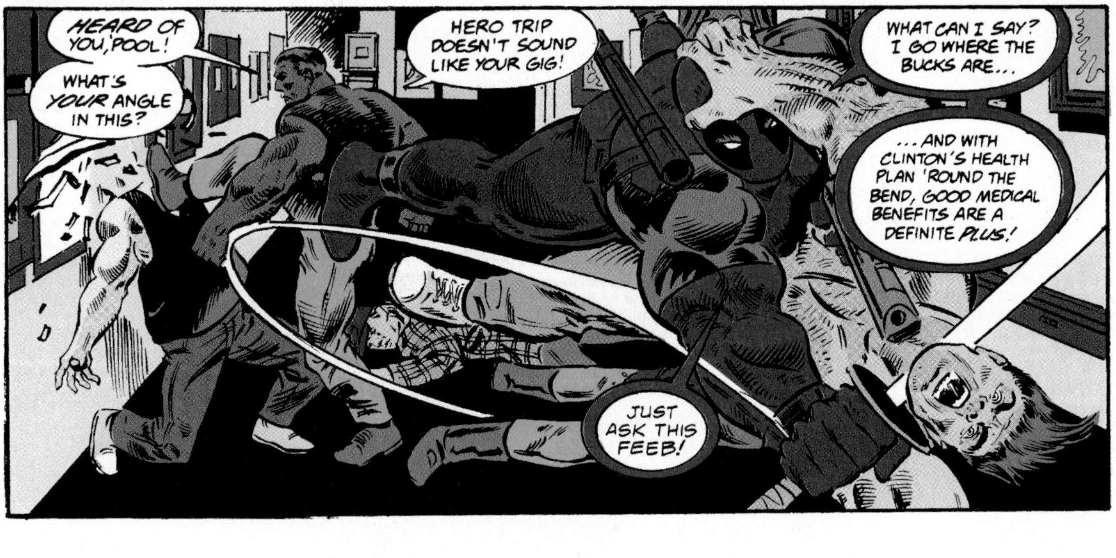
HEARD OF YOU, POOL!
WHAT'S YOUR ANGLE IN THIS?
HERO TRIP DOESN'T SOUND LIKE YOUR GIG!
WHAT CAN I SAY? I GO WHERE THE BUCKS ARE...
...AND WITH CLINTON'S HEALTH PLAN 'ROUND THE BEND, GOOD MEDICAL BENEFITS ARE A DEFINITE PLUS!
JUST ASK THIS FEEB!

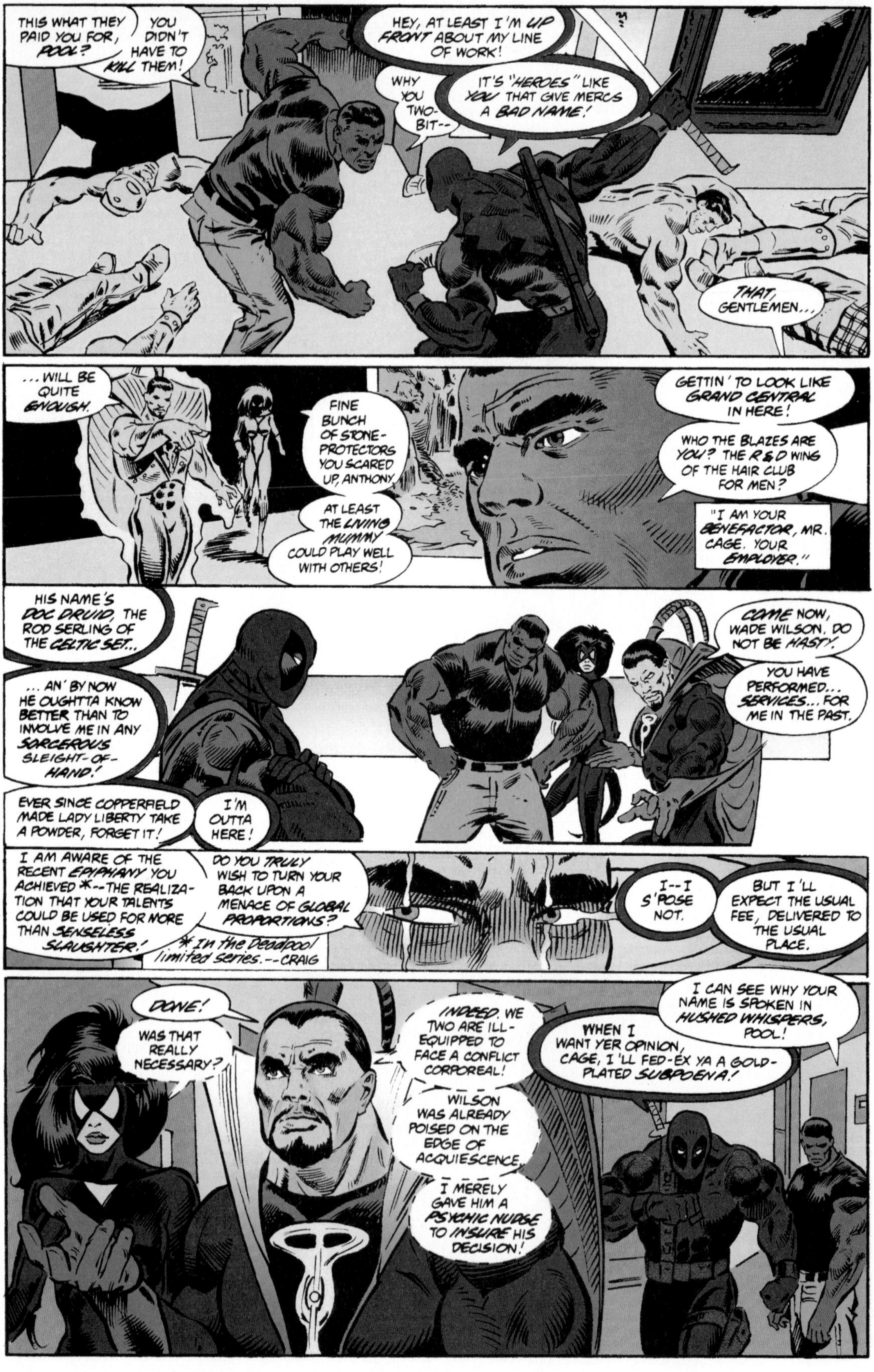
THIS WHAT THEY PAID YOU FOR, POOL?
YOU DIDN'T HAVE TO KILL THEM!
HEY, AT LEAST I'M UP FRONT ABOUT MY LINE OF WORK!
IT'S "HEROES" LIKE YOU THAT GIVE MERCS A BAD NAME!
WHY YOU TWO-BIT--
THAT, GENTLEMEN...
...WILL BE QUITE ENOUGH.
FINE BUNCH OF STONE-PROTECTORS YOU SCARED UP, ANTHONY.
AT LEAST THE LIVING MUMMY COULD PLAY WELL WITH OTHERS!
GETTIN' TO LOOK LIKE GRAND CENTRAL IN HERE!
WHO THE BLAZES ARE YOU? THE R&D WING OF THE HAIR CLUB FOR MEN?
"I AM YOUR BENEFACTOR, MR. CAGE. YOUR EMPLOYER."
HIS NAME'S DOC DRUID, THE ROD SERLING OF THE CELTIC SET...
...AN' BY NOW HE OUGHTTA KNOW BETTER THAN TO INVOLVE ME IN ANY SORCEROUS SLEIGHT-OF-HAND!
EVER SINCE COPPERFIELD MADE LADY LIBERTY TAKE A POWDER, FORGET IT!
I'M OUTTA HERE!
COME NOW, WADE WILSON. DO NOT BE HASTY.
YOU HAVE PERFORMED... SERVICES... FOR ME IN THE PAST.
I AM AWARE OF THE RECENT EPIPHANY YOU ACHIEVED *--THE REALIZATION THAT YOUR TALENTS COULD BE USED FOR MORE THAN SENSELESS SLAUGHTER.
* In the Deadpool limited series. --CRAIG
DO YOU TRULY WISH TO TURN YOUR BACK UPON A MENACE OF GLOBAL PROPORTIONS?
I--I S'POSE NOT.
BUT I'LL EXPECT THE USUAL FEE, DELIVERED TO THE USUAL PLACE.
DONE!
WAS THAT REALLY NECESSARY?
INDEED. WE TWO ARE ILL-EQUIPPED TO FACE A CONFLICT CORPOREAL!
WILSON WAS ALREADY POISED ON THE EDGE OF ACQUIESCENCE.
I MERELY GAVE HIM A PSYCHIC NUDGE TO INSURE HIS DECISION!
I CAN SEE WHY YOUR NAME IS SPOKEN IN HUSHED WHISPERS, POOL!
WHEN I WANT YER OPINION, CAGE, I'LL FED-EX YA A GOLD-PLATED SUBPOENA!

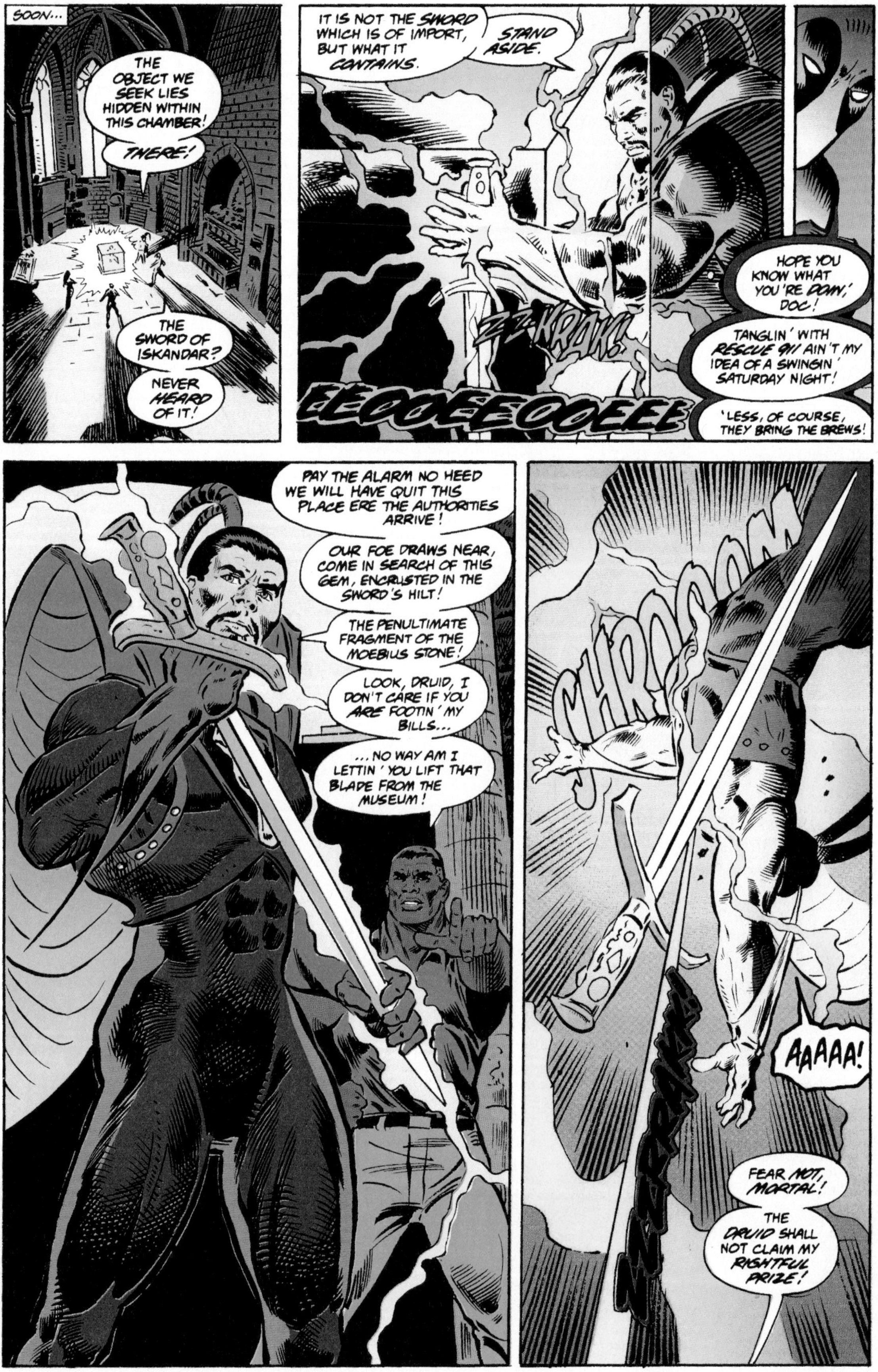
SOON...
THE OBJECT WE SEEK LIES HIDDEN WITHIN THIS CHAMBER!
THERE!
THE SWORD OF ISKANDAR?
NEVER HEARD OF IT!
IT IS NOT THE SWORD WHICH IS OF IMPORT, BUT WHAT IT CONTAINS.
STAND ASIDE.
ZZ-KRAK!
EEOOEEOOEEE
HOPE YOU KNOW WHAT YOU'RE DOIN', DOC!
TANGLIN' WITH RESCUE 911 AIN'T MY IDEA OF A SWINGIN' SATURDAY NIGHT!
'LESS, OF COURSE, THEY BRING THE BREWS!
PAY THE ALARM NO HEED WE WILL HAVE QUIT THIS PLACE ERE THE AUTHORITIES ARRIVE!
OUR FOE DRAWS NEAR, COME IN SEARCH OF THIS GEM, ENCRUSTED IN THE SWORD'S HILT!
THE PENULTIMATE FRAGMENT OF THE MOEBIUS STONE!
LOOK, DRUID, I DON'T CARE IF YOU ARE FOOTIN' MY BILLS...
...NO WAY AM I LETTIN' YOU LIFT THAT BLADE FROM THE MUSEUM!
CHROOOOM
AAAAA!
FEAR NOT, MORTAL!
THE DRUID SHALL NOT CLAIM MY RIGHTFUL PRIZE!

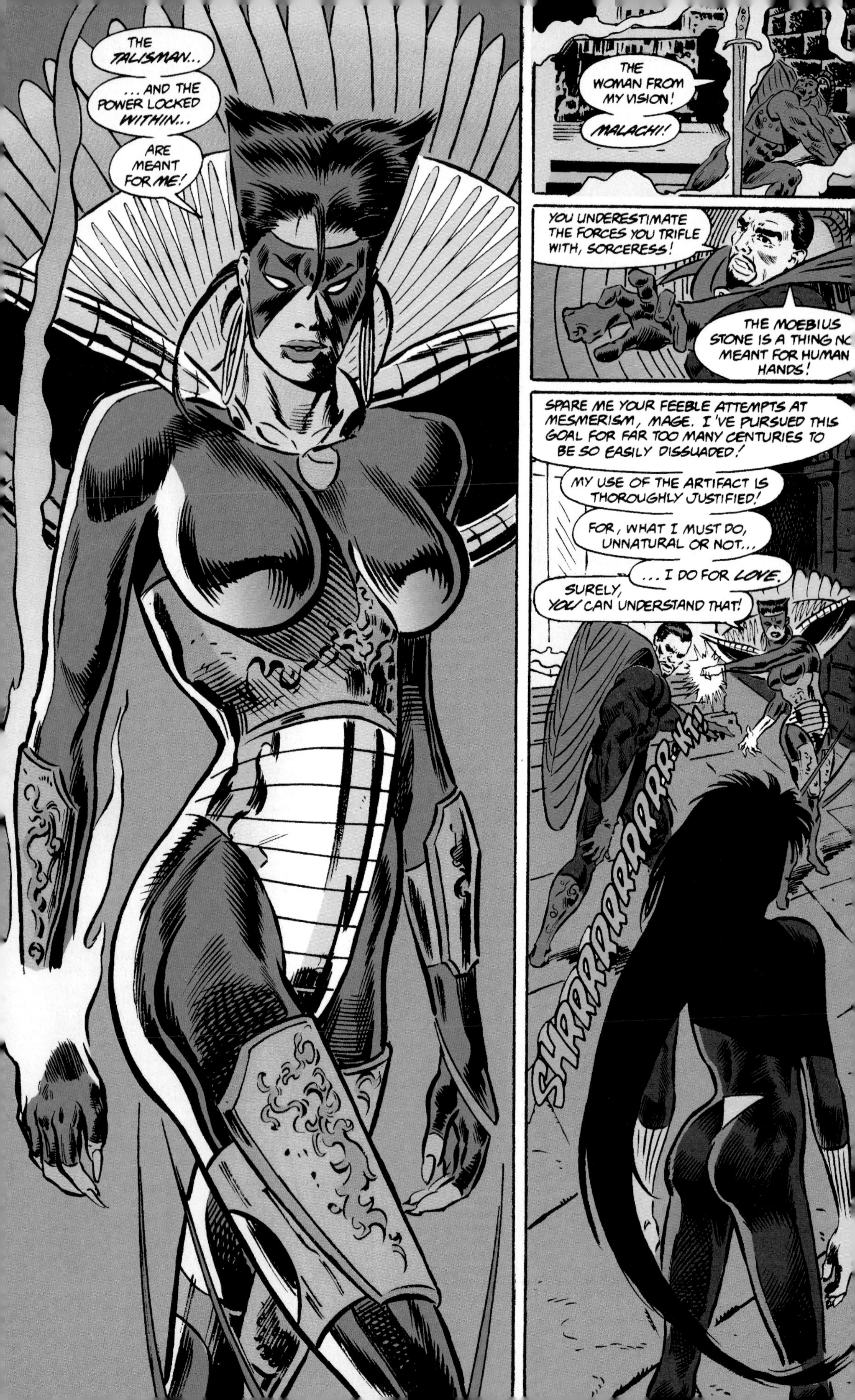
THE TALISMAN...
...AND THE POWER LOCKED WITHIN...
ARE MEANT FOR ME!
THE WOMAN FROM MY VISION!
MALACHI!
YOU UNDERESTIMATE THE FORCES YOU TRIFLE WITH, SORCERESS!
THE MOEBIUS STONE IS A THING NO MEANT FOR HUMAN HANDS!
SPARE ME YOUR FEEBLE ATTEMPTS AT MESMERISM, MAGE. I'VE PURSUED THIS GOAL FOR FAR TOO MANY CENTURIES TO BE SO EASILY DISSUADED!
MY USE OF THE ARTIFACT IS THOROUGHLY JUSTIFIED!
FOR, WHAT I MUST DO, UNNATURAL OR NOT...
...I DO FOR LOVE.
SURELY, YOU CAN UNDERSTAND THAT!
SHRRRRRRRRR-K!!

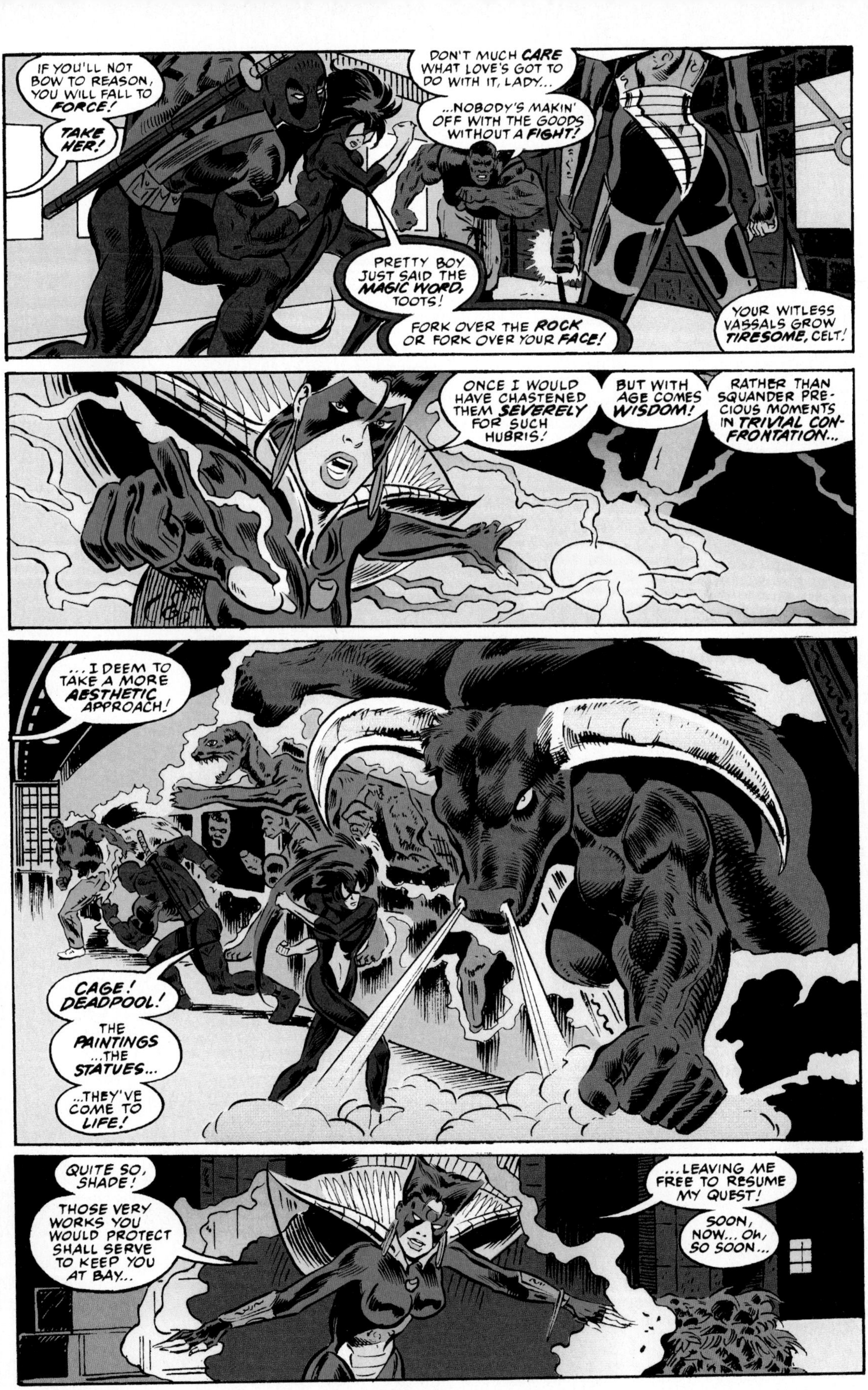
IF YOU'LL NOT BOW TO REASON, YOU WILL FALL TO FORCE!
TAKE HER!
DON'T MUCH CARE WHAT LOVE'S GOT TO DO WITH IT, LADY...
...NOBODY'S MAKIN' OFF WITH THE GOODS WITHOUT A FIGHT!
PRETTY BOY JUST SAID THE MAGIC WORD, TOOTS!
FORK OVER THE ROCK OR FORK OVER YOUR FACE!
YOUR WITLESS VASSALS GROW TIRESOME, CELT!
ONCE I WOULD HAVE CHASTENED THEM SEVERELY FOR SUCH HUBRIS!
BUT WITH AGE COMES WISDOM!
RATHER THAN SQUANDER PRECIOUS MOMENTS IN TRIVIAL CONFRONTATION...
...I DEEM TO TAKE A MORE AESTHETIC APPROACH!
CAGE! DEADPOOL!
THE PAINTINGS ...THE STATUES...
...THEY'VE COME TO LIFE!
QUITE SO, SHADE!
THOSE VERY WORKS YOU WOULD PROTECT SHALL SERVE TO KEEP YOU AT BAY...
...LEAVING ME FREE TO RESUME MY QUEST!
SOON, NOW... OH, SO SOON...

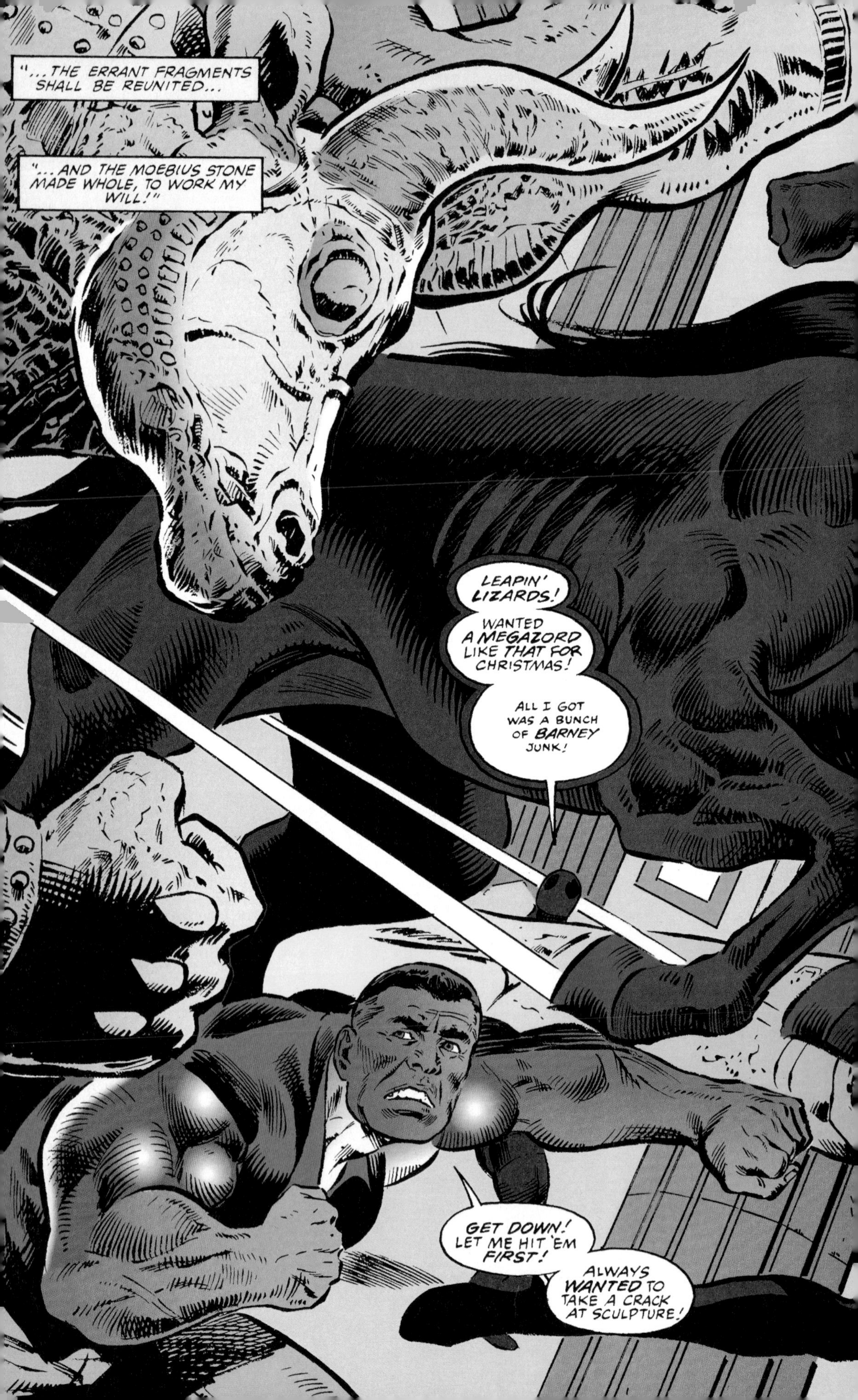
"...THE ERRANT FRAGMENTS SHALL BE REUNITED...
"...AND THE MOEBIUS STONE MADE WHOLE, TO WORK MY WILL!"
LEAPIN' LIZARDS!
WANTED A MEGAZORD LIKE THAT FOR CHRISTMAS!
ALL I GOT WAS A BUNCH OF BARNEY JUNK!
GET DOWN! LET ME HIT 'EM FIRST!
ALWAYS WANTED TO TAKE A CRACK AT SCULPTURE!

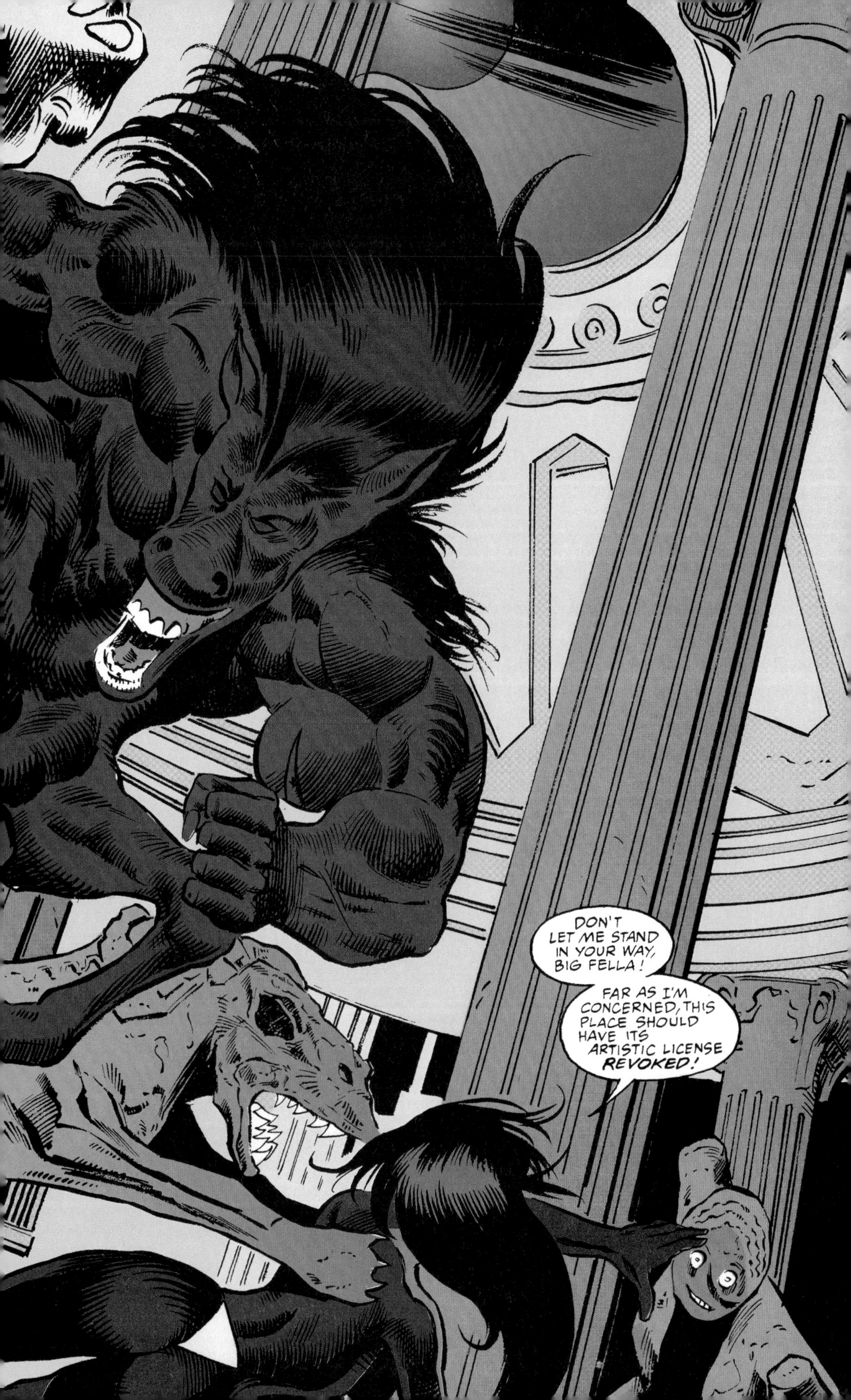
DON'T LET ME STAND IN YOUR WAY, BIG FELLA!
FAR AS I'M CONCERNED, THIS PLACE SHOULD HAVE ITS ARTISTIC LICENSE REVOKED!

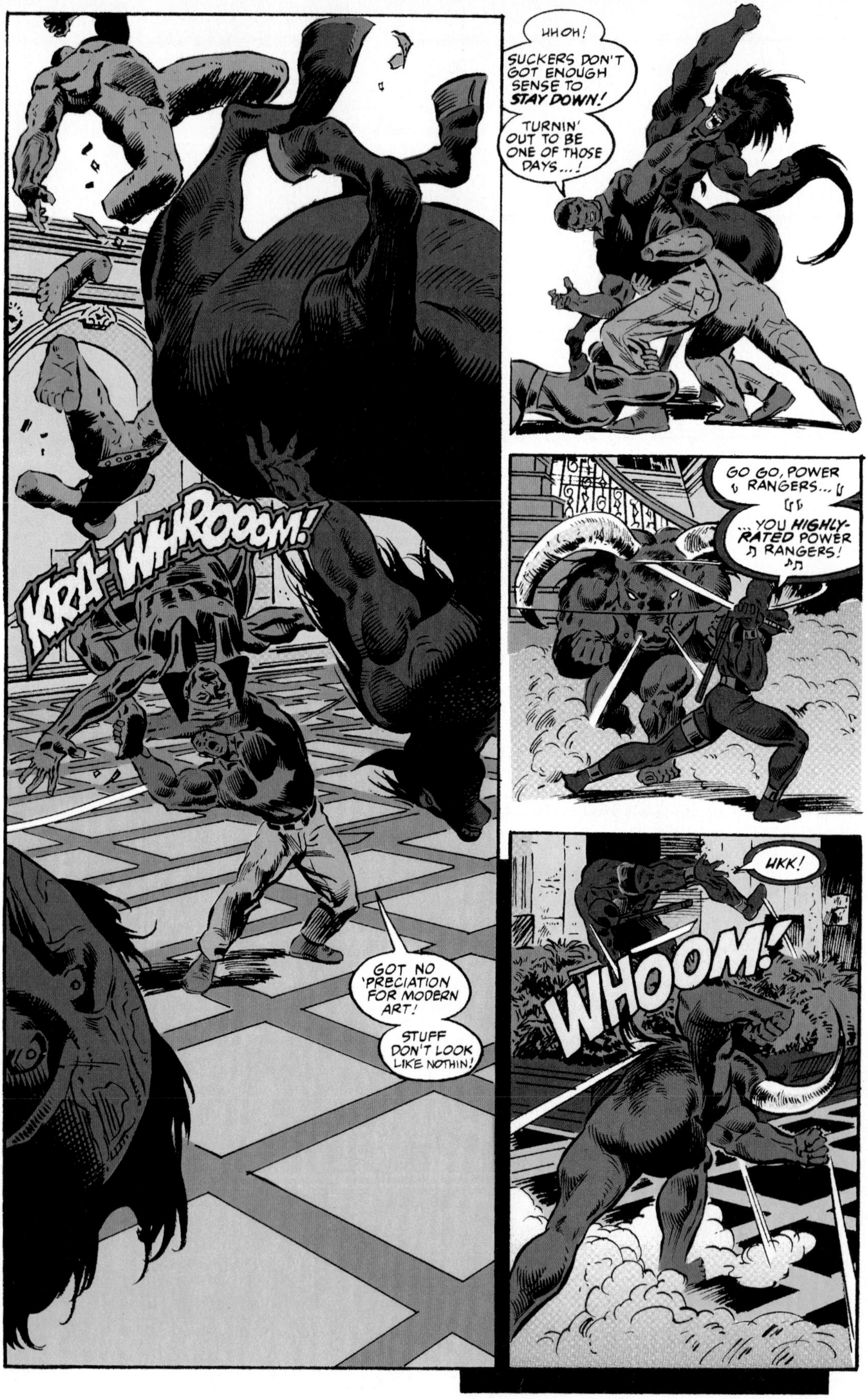
UHOH!
SUCKERS DON'T GOT ENOUGH SENSE TO STAY DOWN!
TURNIN' OUT TO BE ONE OF THOSE DAYS...!
KRA-WHROOOM!
GOT NO 'PRECIATION FOR MODERN ART!
STUFF DON'T LOOK LIKE NOTHIN!
GO GO, POWER RANGERS...
...YOU HIGHLY-RATED POWER RANGERS!
UKK!
WHOOM!

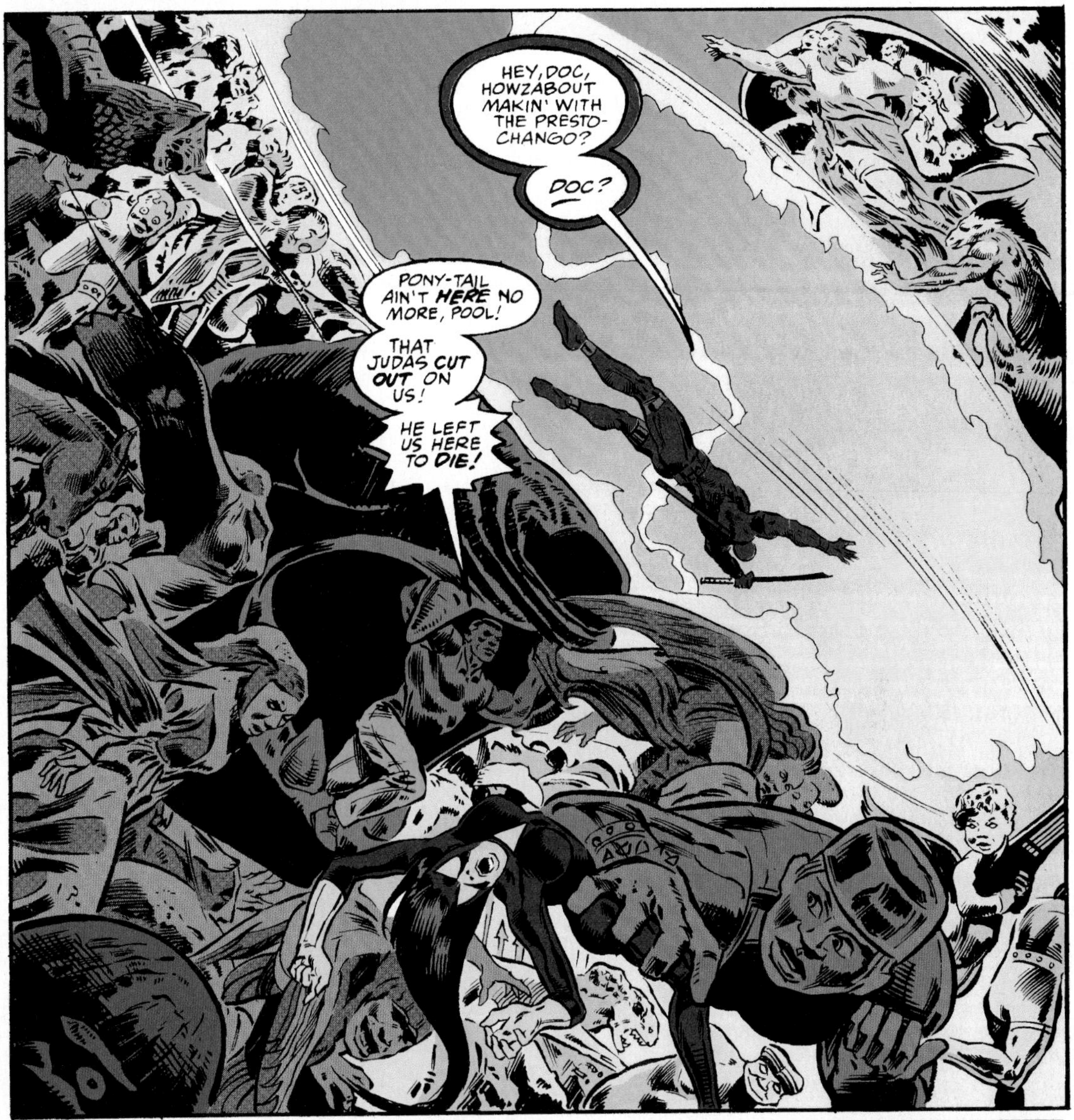
HEY, DOC, HOWZABOUT MAKIN' WITH THE PRESTO-CHANGO?
DOC?
PONY-TAIL AIN'T HERE NO MORE, POOL!
THAT JUDAS CUT OUT ON US!
HE LEFT US HERE TO DIE!

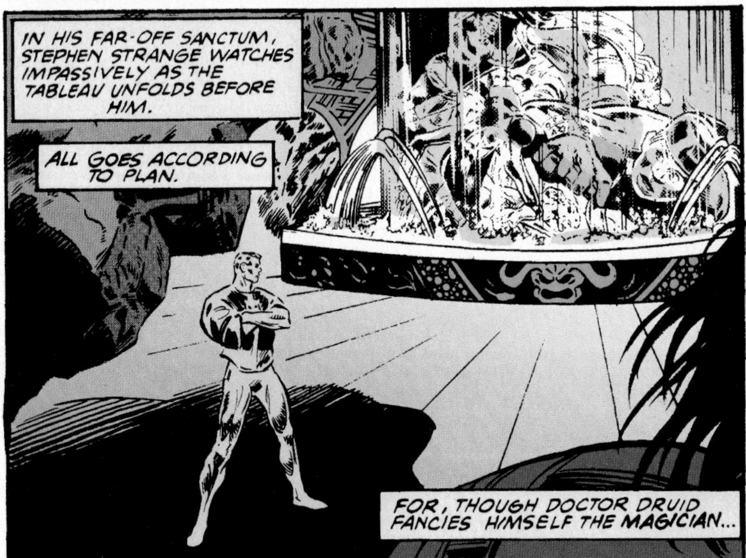
IN HIS FAR-OFF SANCTUM, STEPHEN STRANGE WATCHES IMPASSIVELY AS THE TABLEAU UNFOLDS BEFORE HIM.
ALL GOES ACCORDING TO PLAN.
FOR, THOUGH DOCTOR DRUID FANCIES HIMSELF THE MAGICIAN...

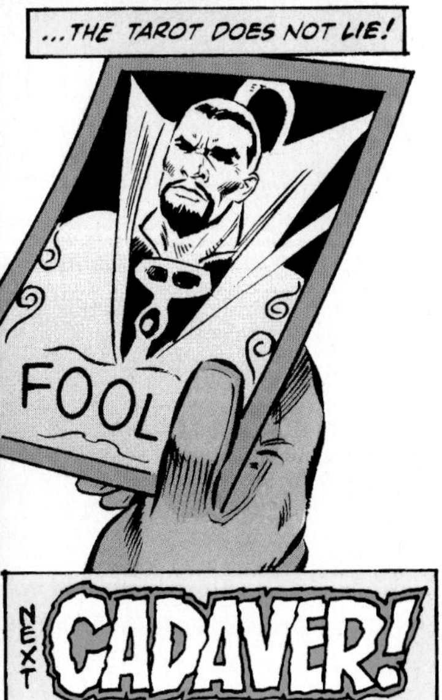
...THE TAROT DOES NOT LIE!
FOOL
NEXT
CADAVER!

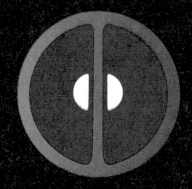

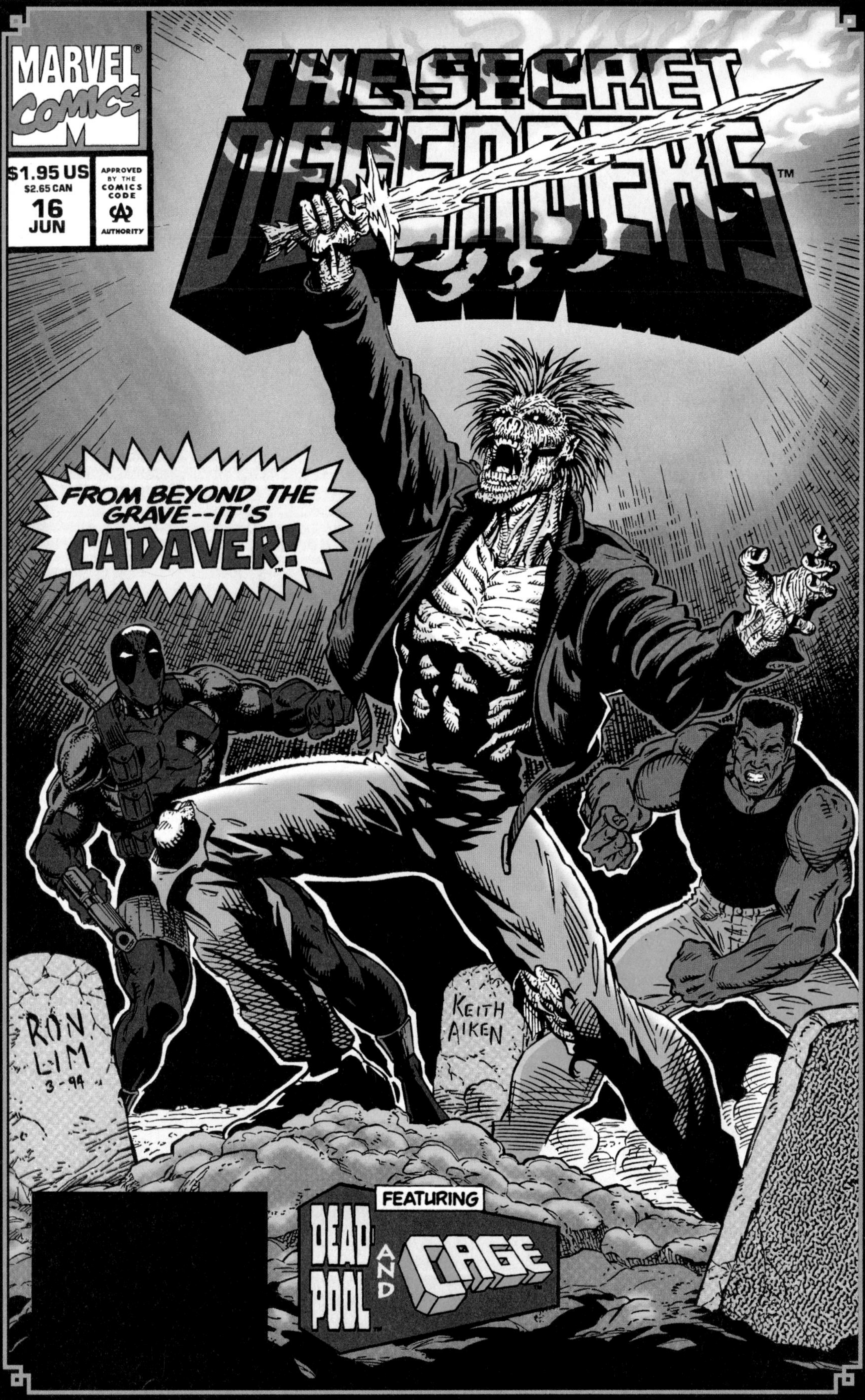
MARVEL COMICS
$1.95 US
$2.65 CAN
16
JUN
APPROVED BY THE COMICS CODE AUTHORITY
THE SECRET DEFENDERS
FROM BEYOND THE GRAVE--IT'S CADAVER!
RON LIM 3-94
KEITH AIKEN
FEATURING
DEAD POOL AND CAGE

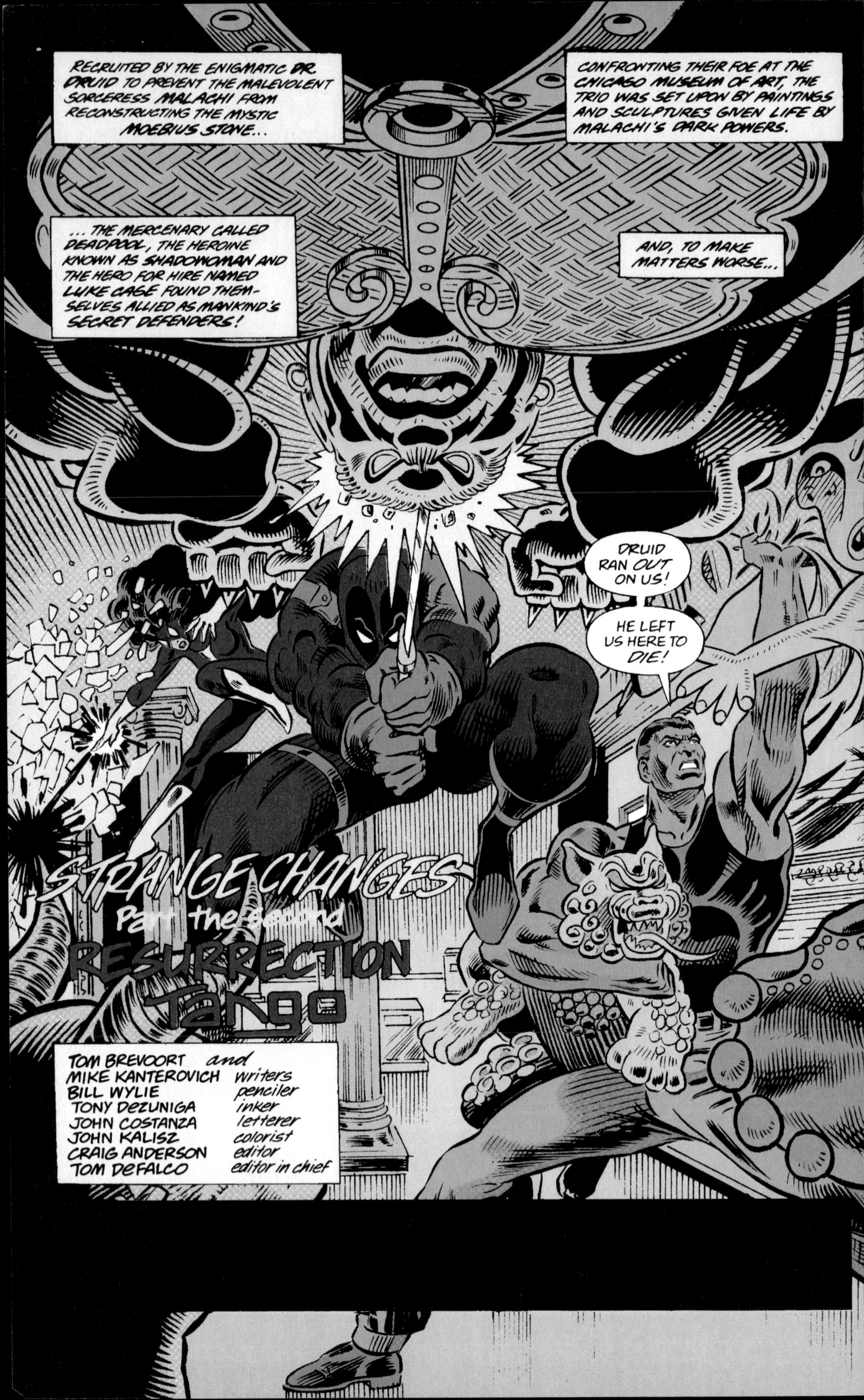
RECRUITED BY THE ENIGMATIC DR. DRUID TO PREVENT THE MALEVOLENT SORCERESS MALACHI FROM RECONSTRUCTING THE MYSTIC MOEBIUS STONE...
... THE MERCENARY CALLED DEADPOOL, THE HEROINE KNOWN AS SHADOWOMAN AND THE HERO FOR HIRE NAMED LUKE CAGE FOUND THEMSELVES ALLIED AS MANKIND'S SECRET DEFENDERS!
CONFRONTING THEIR FOE AT THE CHICAGO MUSEUM OF ART, THE TRIO WAS SET UPON BY PAINTINGS AND SCULPTURES GIVEN LIFE BY MALACHI'S DARK POWERS.
AND, TO MAKE MATTERS WORSE...
DRUID RAN OUT ON US!
HE LEFT US HERE TO DIE!
STRANGE CHANGES
Part the Second
RESURRECTION TANGO
TOM BREVOORT and MIKE KANTEROVICH writers
BILL WYLIE penciler
TONY DEZUNIGA inker
JOHN COSTANZA letterer
JOHN KALISZ colorist
CRAIG ANDERSON editor
TOM DEFALCO editor in chief

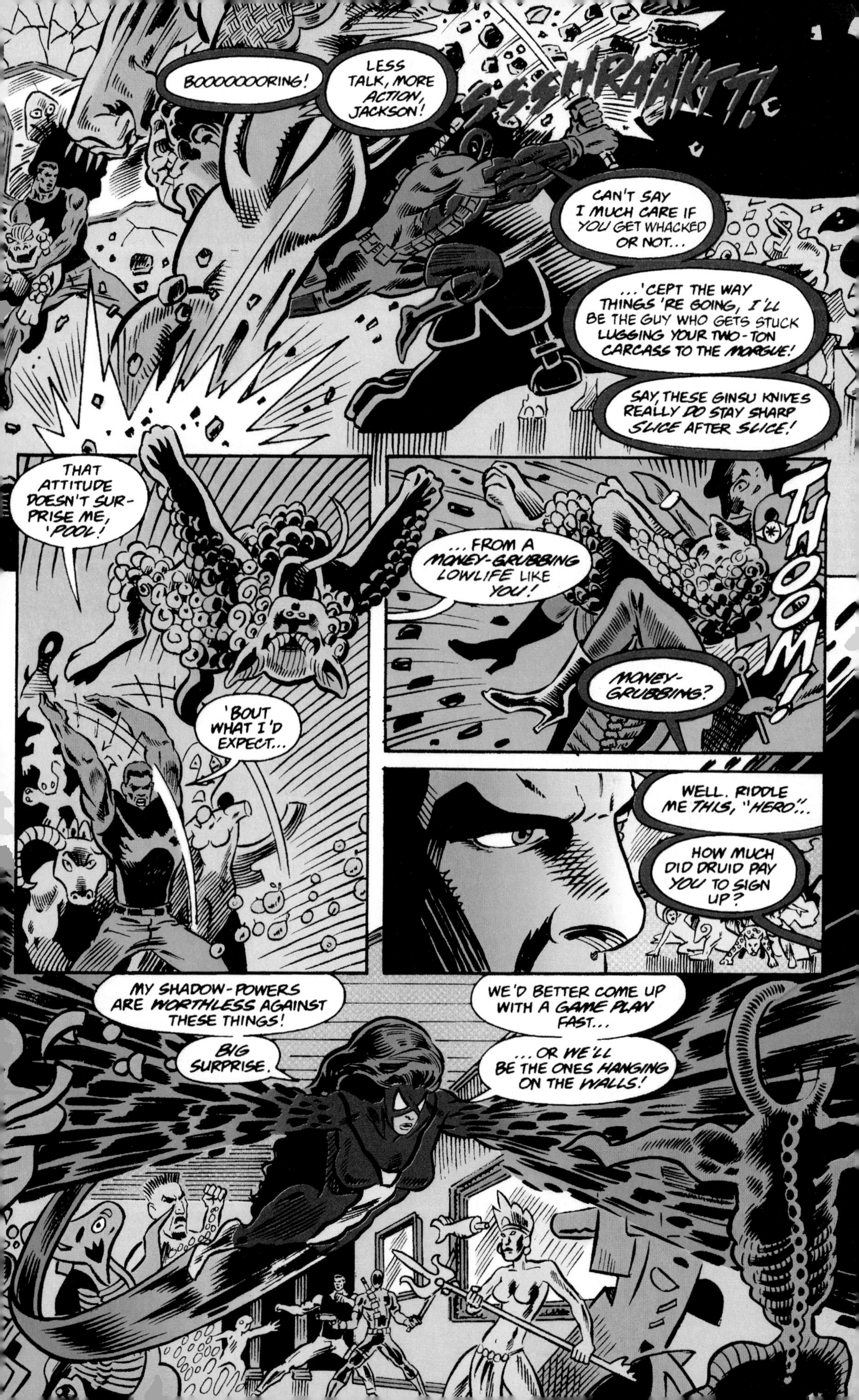
BOOOOOOORING!
LESS TALK, MORE ACTION, JACKSON!
SSSHRAAKTT!
CAN'T SAY I MUCH CARE IF YOU GET WHACKED OR NOT...
...'CEPT THE WAY THINGS 'RE GOING, I'LL BE THE GUY WHO GETS STUCK LUGGING YOUR TWO-TON CARCASS TO THE MORGUE!
SAY, THESE GINSU KNIVES REALLY DO STAY SHARP SLICE AFTER SLICE!
THAT ATTITUDE DOESN'T SURPRISE ME, 'POOL!
'BOUT WHAT I'D EXPECT...
...FROM A MONEY-GRUBBING LOWLIFE LIKE YOU!
THOOOM!
MONEY-GRUBBING?
WELL. RIDDLE ME THIS, "HERO"...
HOW MUCH DID DRUID PAY YOU TO SIGN UP?
MY SHADOW-POWERS ARE WORTHLESS AGAINST THESE THINGS!
BIG SURPRISE.
WE'D BETTER COME UP WITH A GAME PLAN FAST...
...OR WE'LL BE THE ONES HANGING ON THE WALLS!

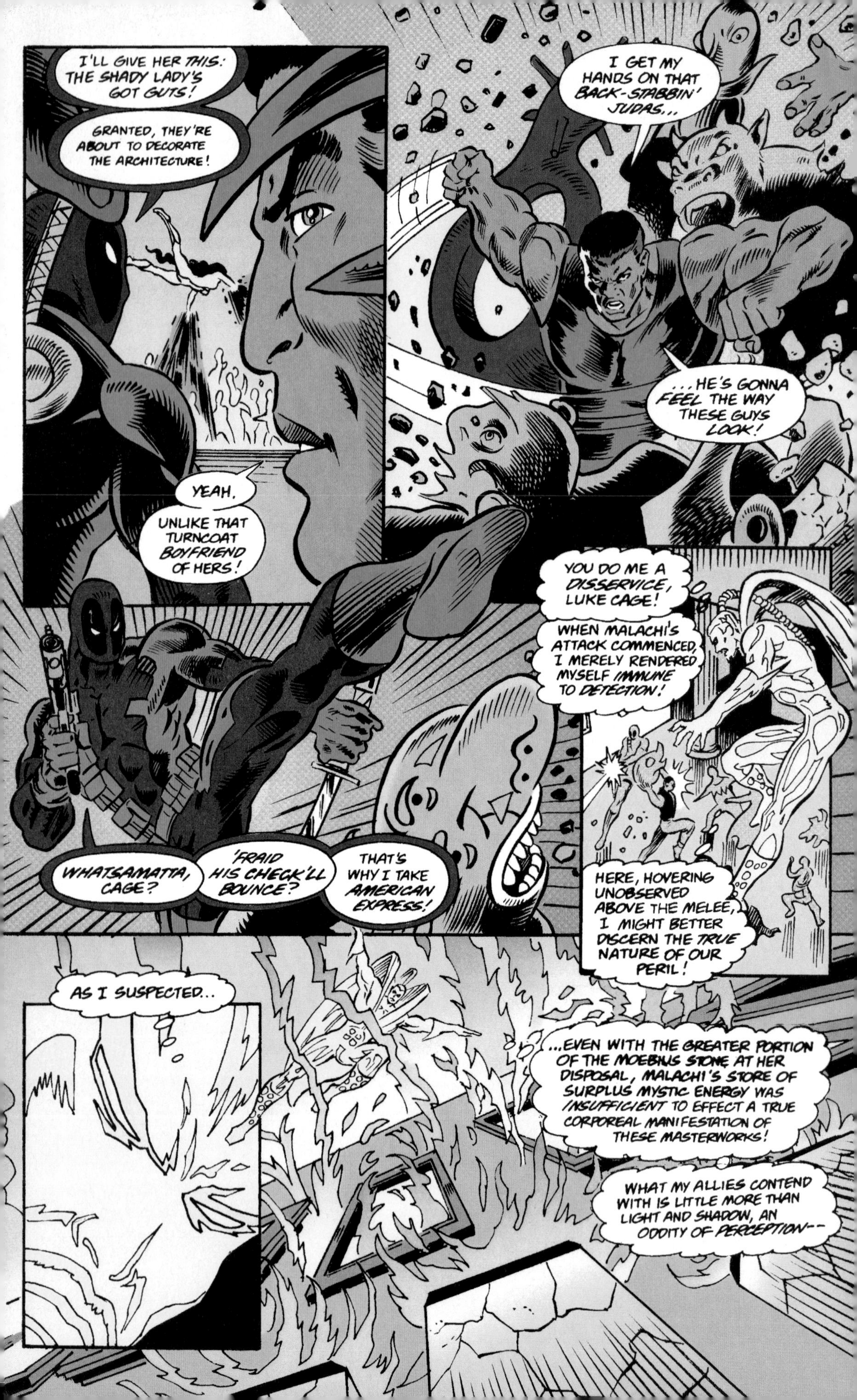
I'LL GIVE HER THIS: THE SHADY LADY'S GOT GUTS!
GRANTED, THEY'RE ABOUT TO DECORATE THE ARCHITECTURE!
YEAH.
UNLIKE THAT TURNCOAT BOYFRIEND OF HERS!
I GET MY HANDS ON THAT BACK-STABBIN' JUDAS...
...HE'S GONNA FEEL THE WAY THESE GUYS LOOK!
WHATSAMATTA, CAGE?
'FRAID HIS CHECK'LL BOUNCE?
THAT'S WHY I TAKE AMERICAN EXPRESS!
YOU DO ME A DISSERVICE, LUKE CAGE!
WHEN MALACHI'S ATTACK COMMENCED, I MERELY RENDERED MYSELF IMMUNE TO DETECTION!
HERE, HOVERING UNOBSERVED ABOVE THE MELEE, I MIGHT BETTER DISCERN THE TRUE NATURE OF OUR PERIL!
AS I SUSPECTED...
...EVEN WITH THE GREATER PORTION OF THE MOEBIUS STONE AT HER DISPOSAL, MALACHI'S STORE OF SURPLUS MYSTIC ENERGY WAS INSUFFICIENT TO EFFECT A TRUE CORPOREAL MANIFESTATION OF THESE MASTERWORKS!
WHAT MY ALLIES CONTEND WITH IS LITTLE MORE THAN LIGHT AND SHADOW, AN ODDITY OF PERCEPTION--

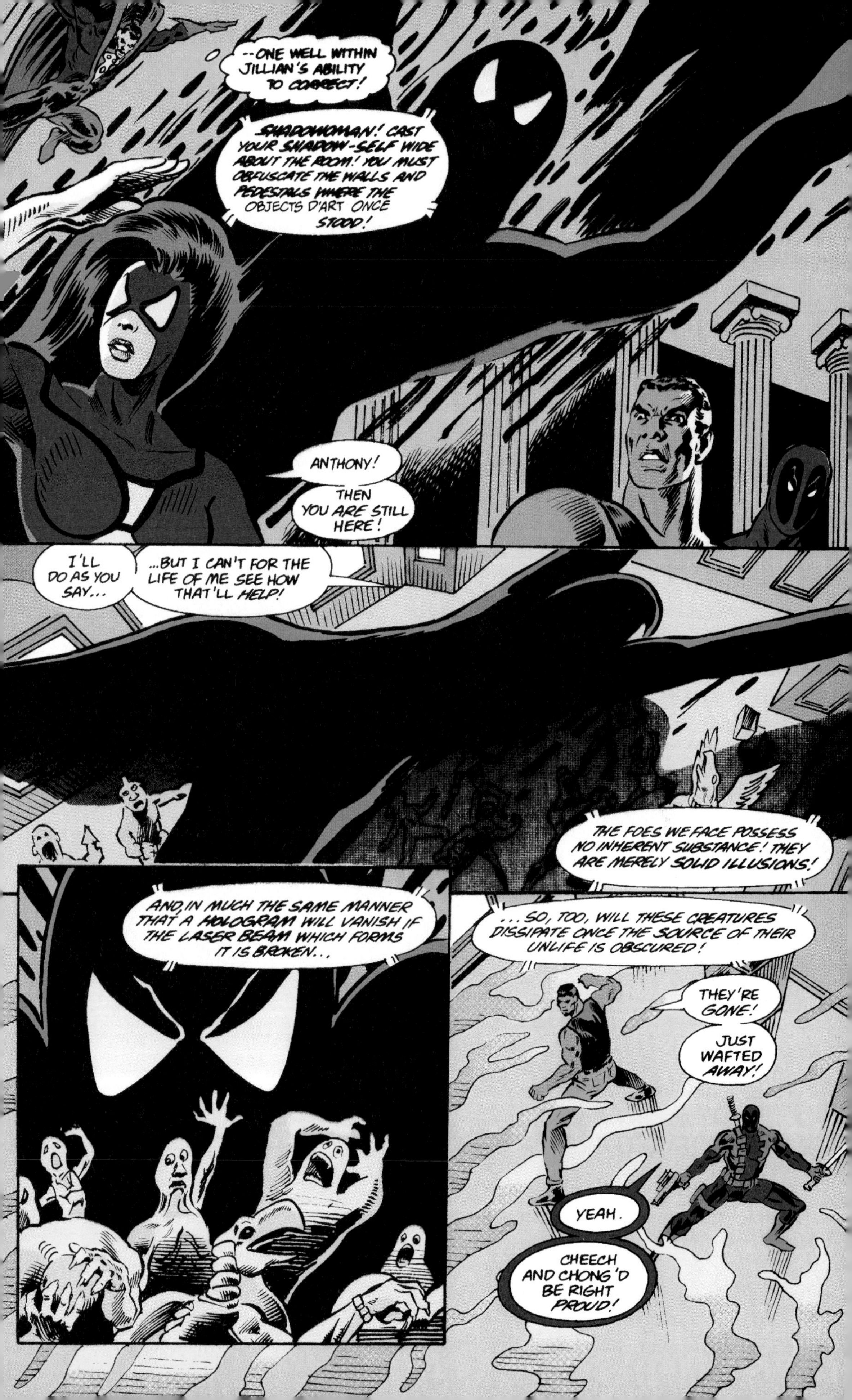
--ONE WELL WITHIN JILLIAN'S ABILITY TO CORRECT!
SHADOWOMAN! CAST YOUR SHADOW-SELF WIDE ABOUT THE ROOM! YOU MUST OBFUSCATE THE WALLS AND PEDESTALS WHERE THE OBJECTS D'ART ONCE STOOD!
ANTHONY!
THEN YOU ARE STILL HERE!
I'LL DO AS YOU SAY...
...BUT I CAN'T FOR THE LIFE OF ME SEE HOW THAT'LL HELP!
THE FOES WE FACE POSSESS NO INHERENT SUBSTANCE! THEY ARE MERELY SOLID ILLUSIONS!
AND, IN MUCH THE SAME MANNER THAT A HOLOGRAM WILL VANISH IF THE LASER BEAM WHICH FORMS IT IS BROKEN...
...SO, TOO, WILL THESE CREATURES DISSIPATE ONCE THE SOURCE OF THEIR UNLIFE IS OBSCURED!
THEY'RE GONE!
JUST WAFTED AWAY!
YEAH.
CHEECH AND CHONG'D BE RIGHT PROUD!

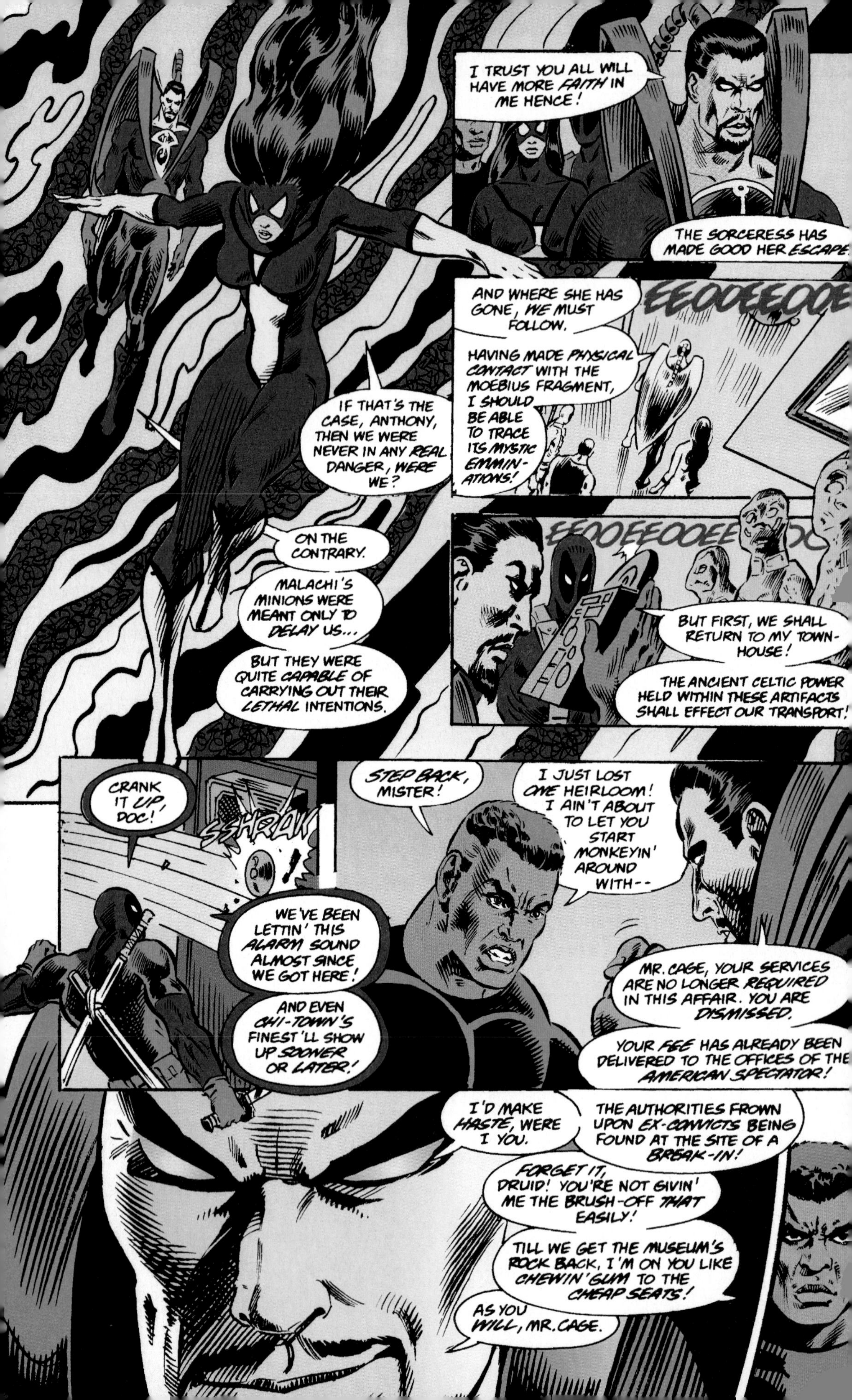
I TRUST YOU ALL WILL HAVE MORE FAITH IN ME HENCE!
THE SORCERESS HAS MADE GOOD HER ESCAPE
AND WHERE SHE HAS GONE, WE MUST FOLLOW.
HAVING MADE PHYSICAL CONTACT WITH THE MOEBIUS FRAGMENT, I SHOULD BE ABLE TO TRACE ITS MYSTIC EMMINATIONS!
EEOOEEEOOE
IF THAT'S THE CASE, ANTHONY, THEN WE WERE NEVER IN ANY REAL DANGER, WERE WE?
ON THE CONTRARY.
MALACHI'S MINIONS WERE MEANT ONLY TO DELAY US...
BUT THEY WERE QUITE CAPABLE OF CARRYING OUT THEIR LETHAL INTENTIONS.
EEOOEEEOOEE
BUT FIRST, WE SHALL RETURN TO MY TOWN-HOUSE!
THE ANCIENT CELTIC POWER HELD WITHIN THESE ARTIFACTS SHALL EFFECT OUR TRANSPORT!
CRANK IT UP, DOC!
SSHRAK!
WE'VE BEEN LETTIN' THIS ALARM SOUND ALMOST SINCE WE GOT HERE!
AND EVEN CHI-TOWN'S FINEST'LL SHOW UP SOONER OR LATER!
STEP BACK, MISTER!
I JUST LOST ONE HEIRLOOM! I AIN'T ABOUT TO LET YOU START MONKEYIN' AROUND WITH--
MR. CAGE, YOUR SERVICES ARE NO LONGER REQUIRED IN THIS AFFAIR. YOU ARE DISMISSED.
YOUR FEE HAS ALREADY BEEN DELIVERED TO THE OFFICES OF THE AMERICAN SPECTATOR!
I'D MAKE HASTE, WERE I YOU.
THE AUTHORITIES FROWN UPON EX-CONVICTS BEING FOUND AT THE SITE OF A BREAK-IN!
FORGET IT, DRUID! YOU'RE NOT GIVIN' ME THE BRUSH-OFF THAT EASILY!
TILL WE GET THE MUSEUM'S ROCK BACK, I'M ON YOU LIKE CHEWIN' GUM TO THE CHEAP SEATS!
AS YOU WILL, MR. CAGE.

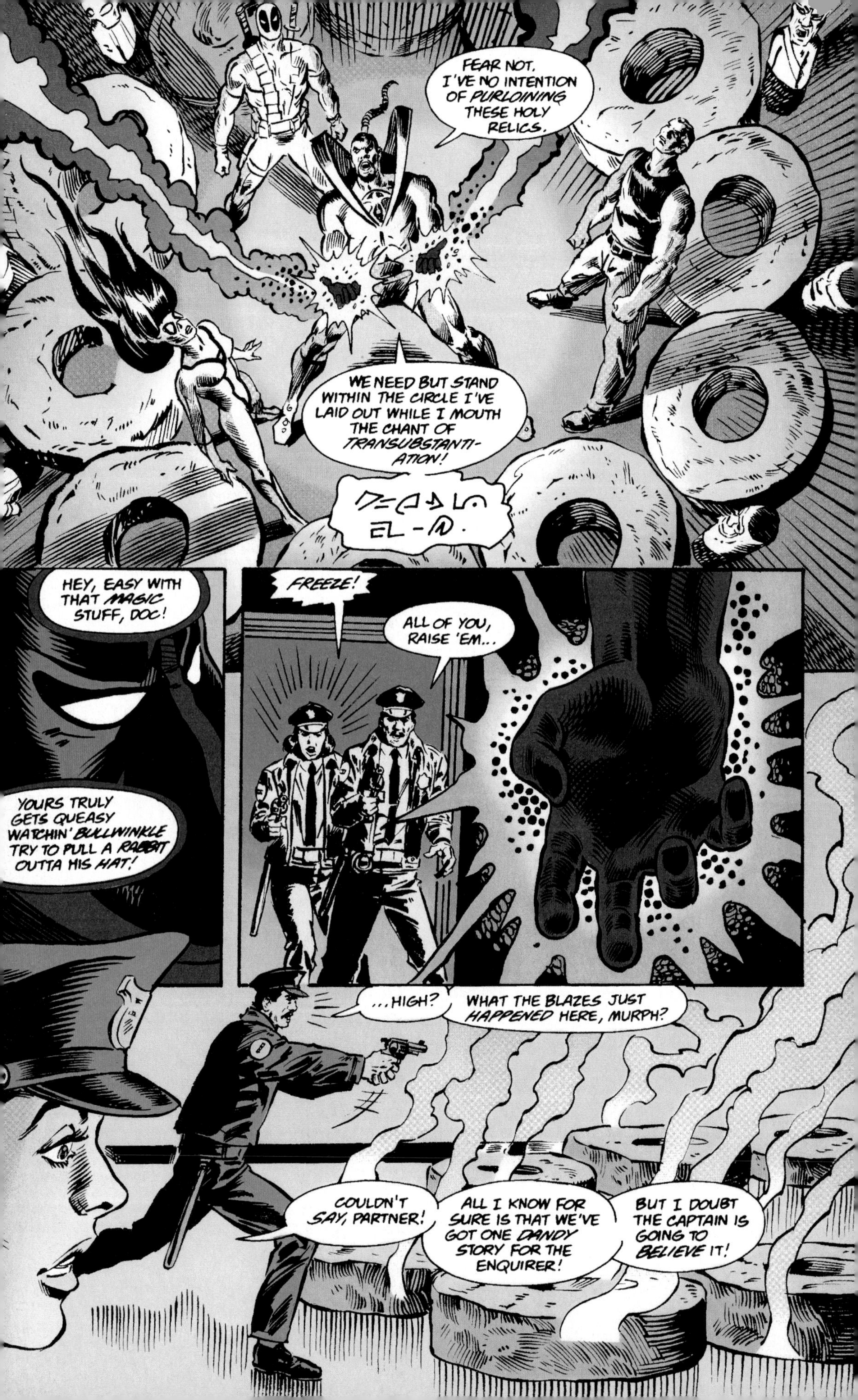
FEAR NOT. I'VE NO INTENTION OF PURLOINING THESE HOLY RELICS.
WE NEED BUT STAND WITHIN THE CIRCLE I'VE LAID OUT WHILE I MOUTH THE CHANT OF TRANSUBSTANTI-ATION!
HEY, EASY WITH THAT MAGIC STUFF, DOC!
YOURS TRULY GETS QUEASY WATCHIN' BULLWINKLE TRY TO PULL A RABBIT OUTTA HIS HAT!
FREEZE!
ALL OF YOU, RAISE 'EM...
...HIGH?
WHAT THE BLAZES JUST HAPPENED HERE, MURPH?
COULDN'T SAY, PARTNER!
ALL I KNOW FOR SURE IS THAT WE'VE GOT ONE DANDY STORY FOR THE ENQUIRER!
BUT I DOUBT THE CAPTAIN IS GOING TO BELIEVE IT!

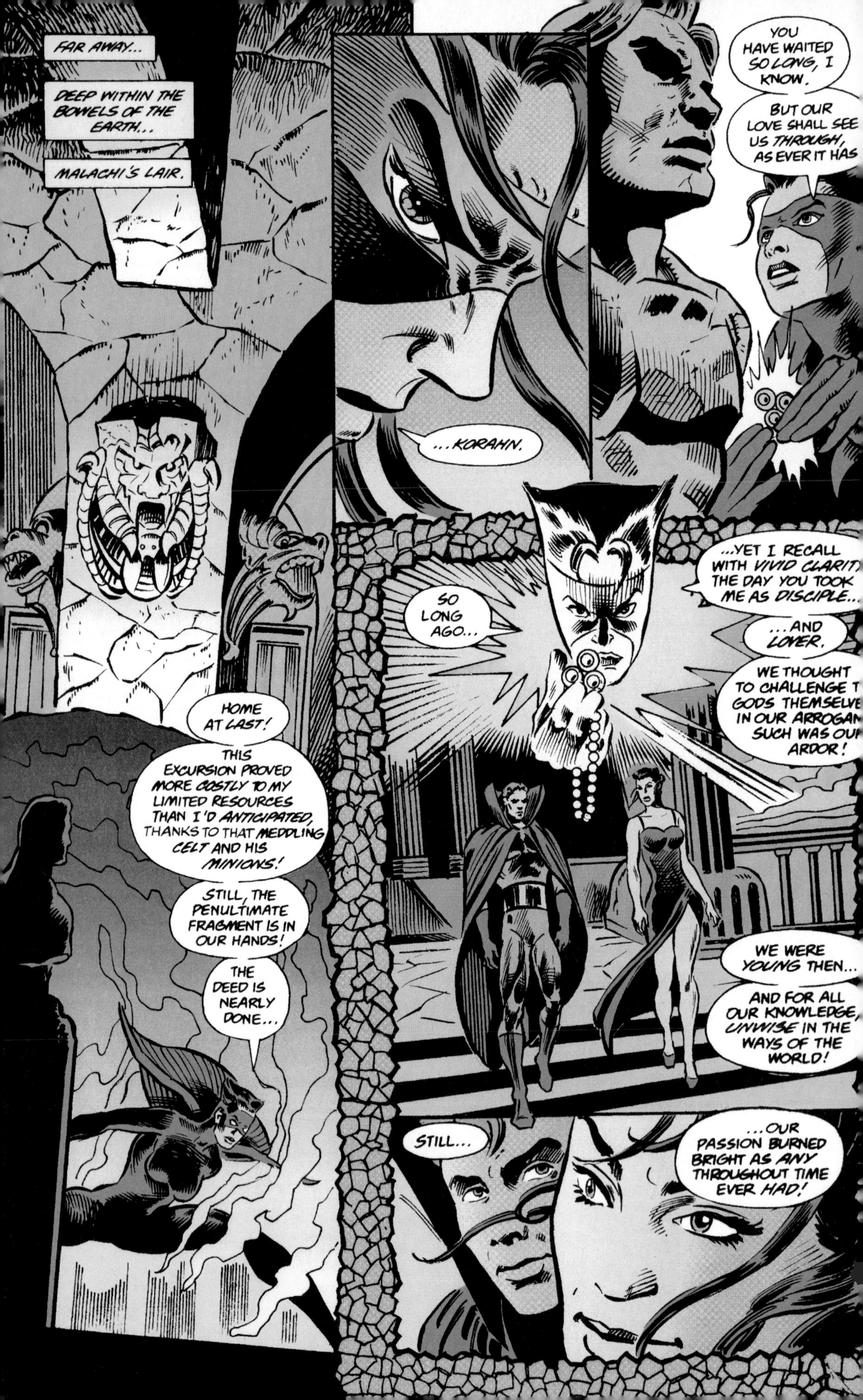
FAR AWAY...
DEEP WITHIN THE BOWELS OF THE EARTH...
MALACHI'S LAIR.
HOME AT LAST!
THIS EXCURSION PROVED MORE COSTLY TO MY LIMITED RESOURCES THAN I'D ANTICIPATED, THANKS TO THAT MEDDLING CELT AND HIS MINIONS!
STILL, THE PENULTIMATE FRAGMENT IS IN OUR HANDS!
THE DEED IS NEARLY DONE...
...KORAHN.
YOU HAVE WAITED SO LONG, I KNOW.
BUT OUR LOVE SHALL SEE US THROUGH, AS EVER IT HAS
SO LONG AGO...
...YET I RECALL WITH VIVID CLARIT THE DAY YOU TOOK ME AS DISCIPLE...
...AND LOVER.
WE THOUGHT TO CHALLENGE T GODS THEMSELVE IN OUR ARROGAN SUCH WAS OU ARDOR!
WE WERE YOUNG THEN...
AND FOR ALL OUR KNOWLEDGE, UNWISE IN THE WAYS OF THE WORLD!
STILL...
...OUR PASSION BURNED BRIGHT AS ANY THROUGHOUT TIME EVER HAD!

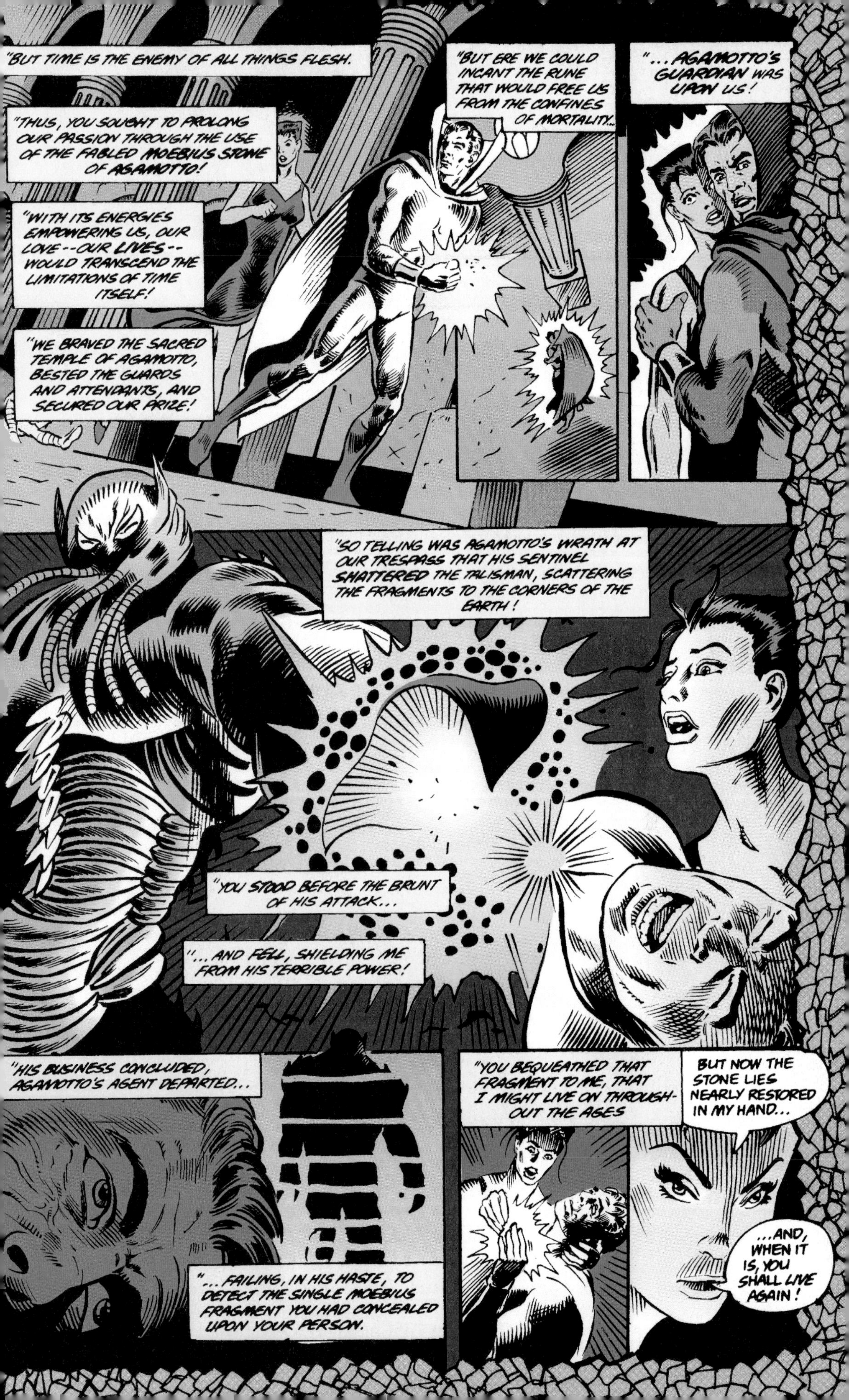
"BUT TIME IS THE ENEMY OF ALL THINGS FLESH.
"THUS, YOU SOUGHT TO PROLONG OUR PASSION THROUGH THE USE OF THE FABLED MOEBIUS STONE OF AGAMOTTO!
"WITH ITS ENERGIES EMPOWERING US, OUR LOVE--OUR LIVES--WOULD TRANSCEND THE LIMITATIONS OF TIME ITSELF!
"WE BRAVED THE SACRED TEMPLE OF AGAMOTTO, BESTED THE GUARDS AND ATTENDANTS, AND SECURED OUR PRIZE!
"BUT ERE WE COULD INCANT THE RUNE THAT WOULD FREE US FROM THE CONFINES OF MORTALITY...
"...AGAMOTTO'S GUARDIAN WAS UPON US!
"SO TELLING WAS AGAMOTTO'S WRATH AT OUR TRESPASS THAT HIS SENTINEL SHATTERED THE TALISMAN, SCATTERING THE FRAGMENTS TO THE CORNERS OF THE EARTH!
"YOU STOOD BEFORE THE BRUNT OF HIS ATTACK...
"...AND FELL, SHIELDING ME FROM HIS TERRIBLE POWER!
"HIS BUSINESS CONCLUDED, AGAMOTTO'S AGENT DEPARTED...
"...FAILING, IN HIS HASTE, TO DETECT THE SINGLE MOEBIUS FRAGMENT YOU HAD CONCEALED UPON YOUR PERSON.
"YOU BEQUEATHED THAT FRAGMENT TO ME, THAT I MIGHT LIVE ON THROUGH-OUT THE AGES
BUT NOW THE STONE LIES NEARLY RESTORED IN MY HAND...
...AND, WHEN IT IS, YOU SHALL LIVE AGAIN!

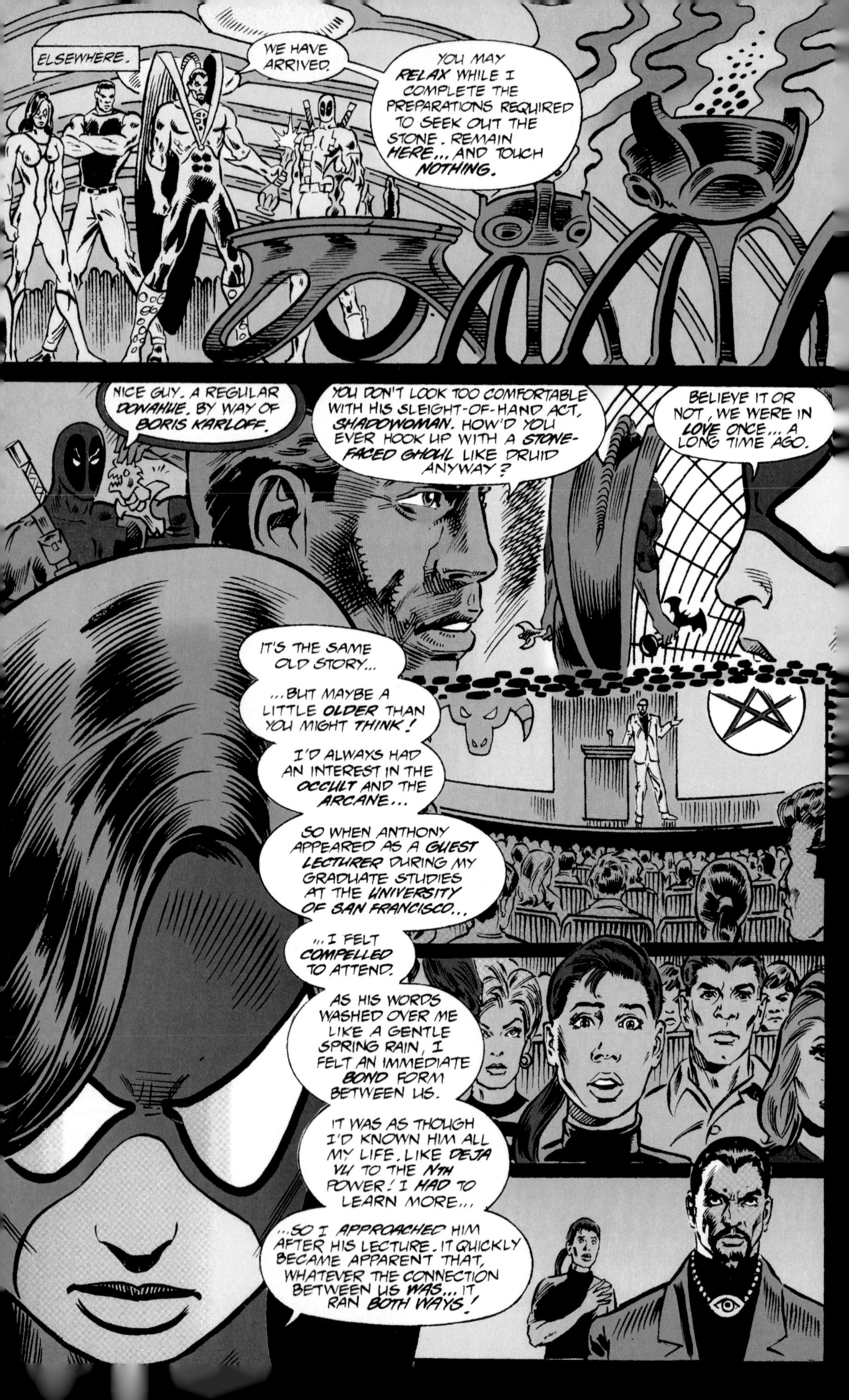
ELSEWHERE.
WE HAVE ARRIVED.
YOU MAY RELAX WHILE I COMPLETE THE PREPARATIONS REQUIRED TO SEEK OUT THE STONE. REMAIN HERE... AND TOUCH NOTHING.
NICE GUY. A REGULAR DONAHUE. BY WAY OF BORIS KARLOFF.
YOU DON'T LOOK TOO COMFORTABLE WITH HIS SLEIGHT-OF-HAND ACT, SHADOWOMAN. HOW'D YOU EVER HOOK UP WITH A STONE-FACED GHOUL LIKE DRUID ANYWAY?
BELIEVE IT OR NOT, WE WERE IN LOVE ONCE... A LONG TIME AGO.
IT'S THE SAME OLD STORY...
...BUT MAYBE A LITTLE OLDER THAN YOU MIGHT THINK!
I'D ALWAYS HAD AN INTEREST IN THE OCCULT AND THE ARCANE...
SO WHEN ANTHONY APPEARED AS A GUEST LECTURER DURING MY GRADUATE STUDIES AT THE UNIVERSITY OF SAN FRANCISCO...
...I FELT COMPELLED TO ATTEND.
AS HIS WORDS WASHED OVER ME LIKE A GENTLE SPRING RAIN, I FELT AN IMMEDIATE BOND FORM BETWEEN US.
IT WAS AS THOUGH I'D KNOWN HIM ALL MY LIFE. LIKE DEJA VU TO THE NTH POWER! I HAD TO LEARN MORE...
...SO I APPROACHED HIM AFTER HIS LECTURE. IT QUICKLY BECAME APPARENT THAT, WHATEVER THE CONNECTION BETWEEN US WAS... IT RAN BOTH WAYS!

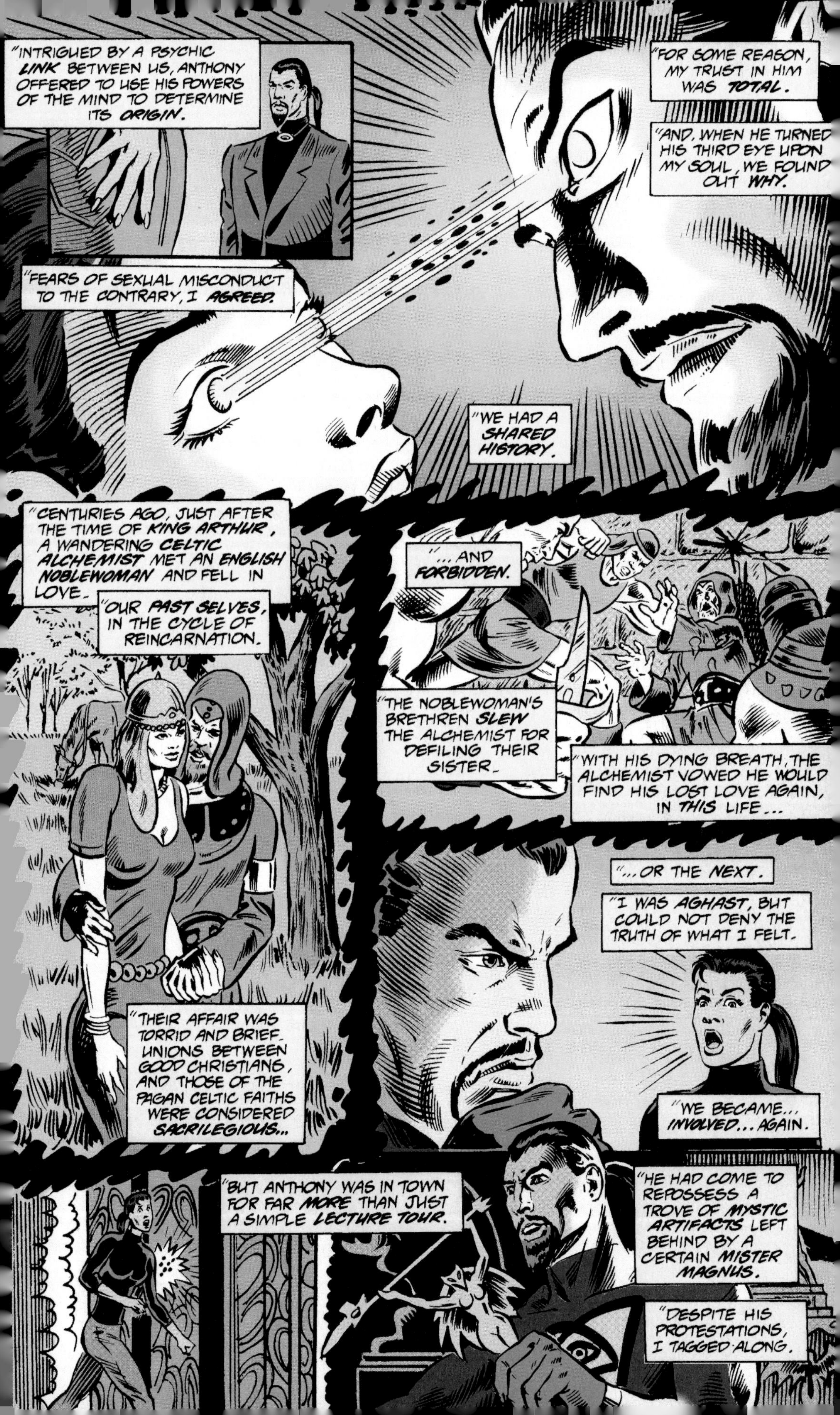
"INTRIGUED BY A PSYCHIC LINK BETWEEN US, ANTHONY OFFERED TO USE HIS POWERS OF THE MIND TO DETERMINE ITS ORIGIN.
"FOR SOME REASON, MY TRUST IN HIM WAS TOTAL.
"AND, WHEN HE TURNED HIS THIRD EYE UPON MY SOUL, WE FOUND OUT WHY.
"FEARS OF SEXUAL MISCONDUCT TO THE CONTRARY, I AGREED.
"WE HAD A SHARED HISTORY.
"CENTURIES AGO, JUST AFTER THE TIME OF KING ARTHUR, A WANDERING CELTIC ALCHEMIST MET AN ENGLISH NOBLEWOMAN AND FELL IN LOVE.
"OUR PAST SELVES, IN THE CYCLE OF REINCARNATION.
"THEIR AFFAIR WAS TORRID AND BRIEF. UNIONS BETWEEN GOOD CHRISTIANS, AND THOSE OF THE PAGAN CELTIC FAITHS WERE CONSIDERED SACRILEGIOUS...
"...AND FORBIDDEN.
"THE NOBLEWOMAN'S BRETHREN SLEW THE ALCHEMIST FOR DEFILING THEIR SISTER.
"WITH HIS DYING BREATH, THE ALCHEMIST VOWED HE WOULD FIND HIS LOST LOVE AGAIN, IN THIS LIFE...
"...OR THE NEXT.
"I WAS AGHAST, BUT COULD NOT DENY THE TRUTH OF WHAT I FELT.
"WE BECAME... INVOLVED... AGAIN.
"BUT ANTHONY WAS IN TOWN FOR FAR MORE THAN JUST A SIMPLE LECTURE TOUR.
"HE HAD COME TO REPOSSESS A TROVE OF MYSTIC ARTIFACTS LEFT BEHIND BY A CERTAIN MISTER MAGNUS.
"DESPITE HIS PROTESTATIONS, I TAGGED ALONG.

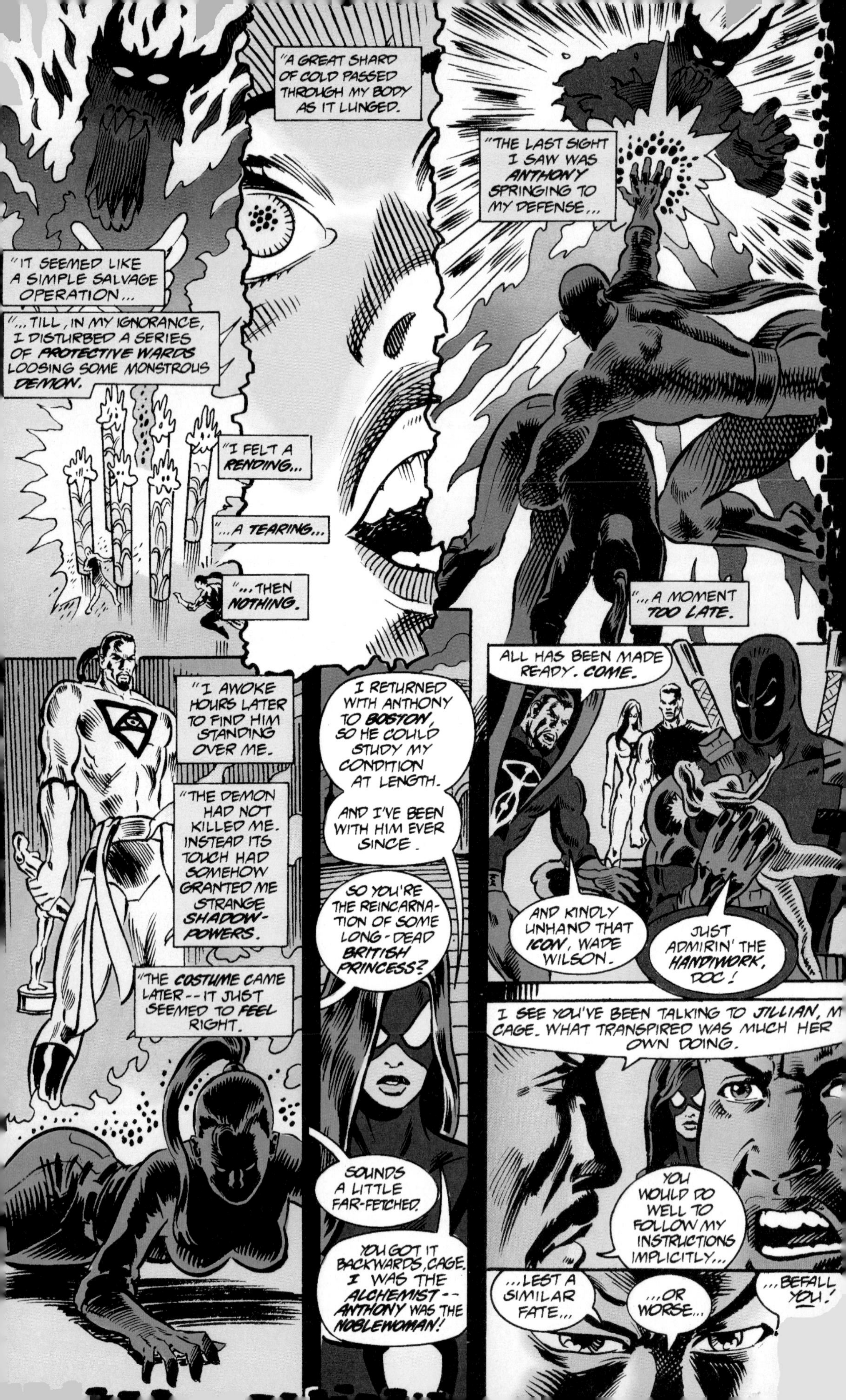
"A GREAT SHARD OF COLD PASSED THROUGH MY BODY AS IT LUNGED.
"THE LAST SIGHT I SAW WAS ANTHONY SPRINGING TO MY DEFENSE...
"IT SEEMED LIKE A SIMPLE SALVAGE OPERATION...
"...TILL, IN MY IGNORANCE, I DISTURBED A SERIES OF PROTECTIVE WARDS LOOSING SOME MONSTROUS DEMON.
"I FELT A RENDING...
"...A TEARING...
"...THEN NOTHING.
"...A MOMENT TOO LATE.
"I AWOKE HOURS LATER TO FIND HIM STANDING OVER ME.
"THE DEMON HAD NOT KILLED ME. INSTEAD ITS TOUCH HAD SOMEHOW GRANTED ME STRANGE SHADOW-POWERS.
"THE COSTUME CAME LATER--IT JUST SEEMED TO FEEL RIGHT.
I RETURNED WITH ANTHONY TO BOSTON, SO HE COULD STUDY MY CONDITION AT LENGTH.
AND I'VE BEEN WITH HIM EVER SINCE.
SO YOU'RE THE REINCARNATION OF SOME LONG-DEAD BRITISH PRINCESS?
SOUNDS A LITTLE FAR-FETCHED.
YOU GOT IT BACKWARDS, CAGE. I WAS THE ALCHEMIST--ANTHONY WAS THE NOBLEWOMAN!
ALL HAS BEEN MADE READY. COME.
AND KINDLY UNHAND THAT ICON, WADE WILSON.
JUST ADMIRIN' THE HANDIWORK, DOC!
I SEE YOU'VE BEEN TALKING TO JILLIAN, M CAGE. WHAT TRANSPIRED WAS MUCH HER OWN DOING.
YOU WOULD DO WELL TO FOLLOW MY INSTRUCTIONS IMPLICITLY...
...LEST A SIMILAR FATE...
...OR WORSE...
...BEFALL YOU!

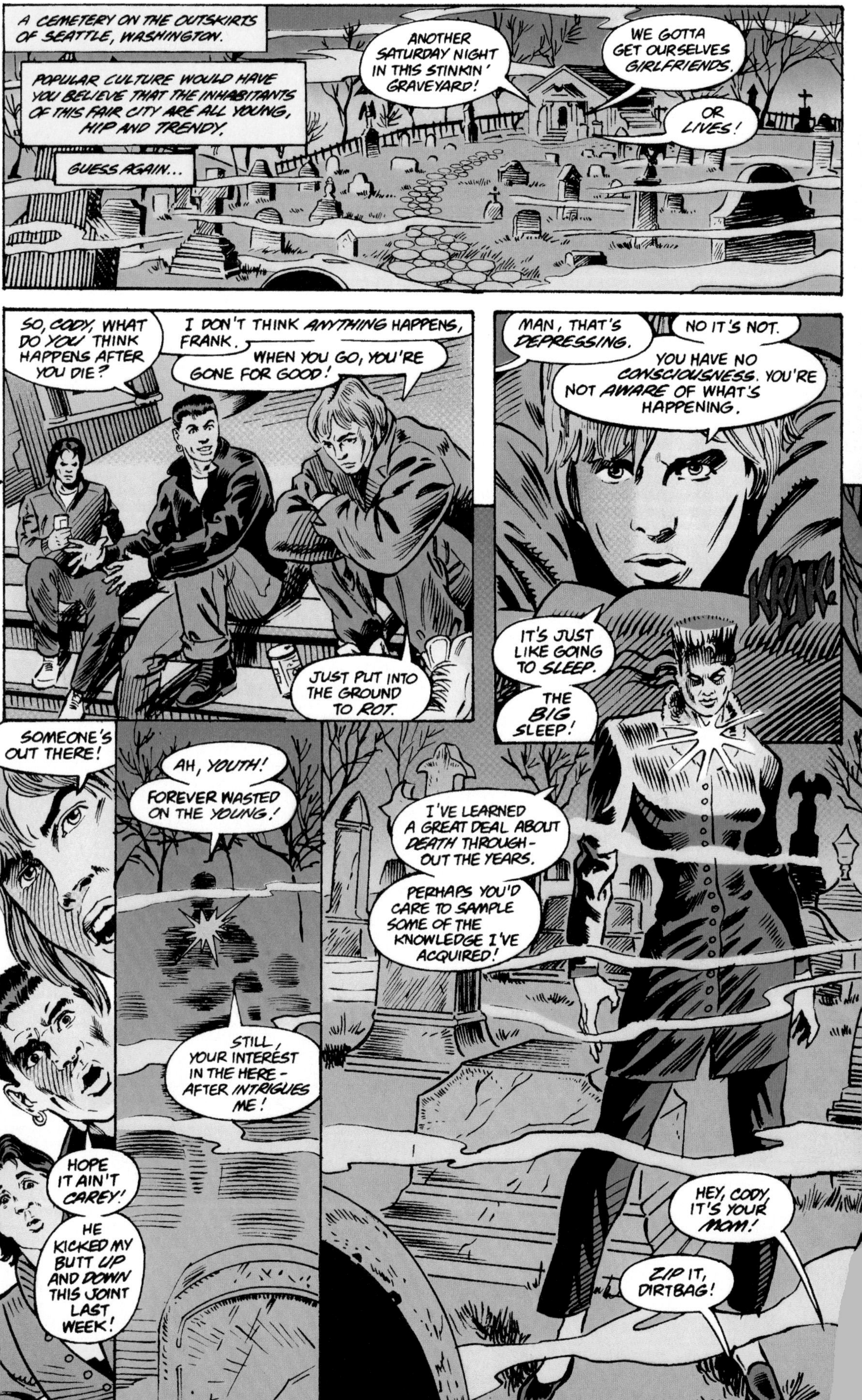

A CEMETERY ON THE OUTSKIRTS OF SEATTLE, WASHINGTON.
POPULAR CULTURE WOULD HAVE YOU BELIEVE THAT THE INHABITANTS OF THIS FAIR CITY ARE ALL YOUNG, HIP AND TRENDY.
GUESS AGAIN...
ANOTHER SATURDAY NIGHT IN THIS STINKIN' GRAVEYARD!
WE GOTTA GET OURSELVES GIRLFRIENDS.
OR LIVES!
SO, CODY, WHAT DO YOU THINK HAPPENS AFTER YOU DIE?
I DON'T THINK ANYTHING HAPPENS, FRANK.
WHEN YOU GO, YOU'RE GONE FOR GOOD!
JUST PUT INTO THE GROUND TO ROT.
MAN, THAT'S DEPRESSING.
NO IT'S NOT.
YOU HAVE NO CONSCIOUSNESS. YOU'RE NOT AWARE OF WHAT'S HAPPENING.
IT'S JUST LIKE GOING TO SLEEP.
THE BIG SLEEP!
KRAK!
SOMEONE'S OUT THERE!
AH, YOUTH!
FOREVER WASTED ON THE YOUNG!
STILL, YOUR INTEREST IN THE HERE-AFTER INTRIGUES ME!
I'VE LEARNED A GREAT DEAL ABOUT DEATH THROUGH-OUT THE YEARS.
PERHAPS YOU'D CARE TO SAMPLE SOME OF THE KNOWLEDGE I'VE ACQUIRED!
HOPE IT AIN'T CAREY!
HE KICKED MY BUTT UP AND DOWN THIS JOINT LAST WEEK!
HEY, CODY, IT'S YOUR MOM!
ZIP IT, DIRTBAG!

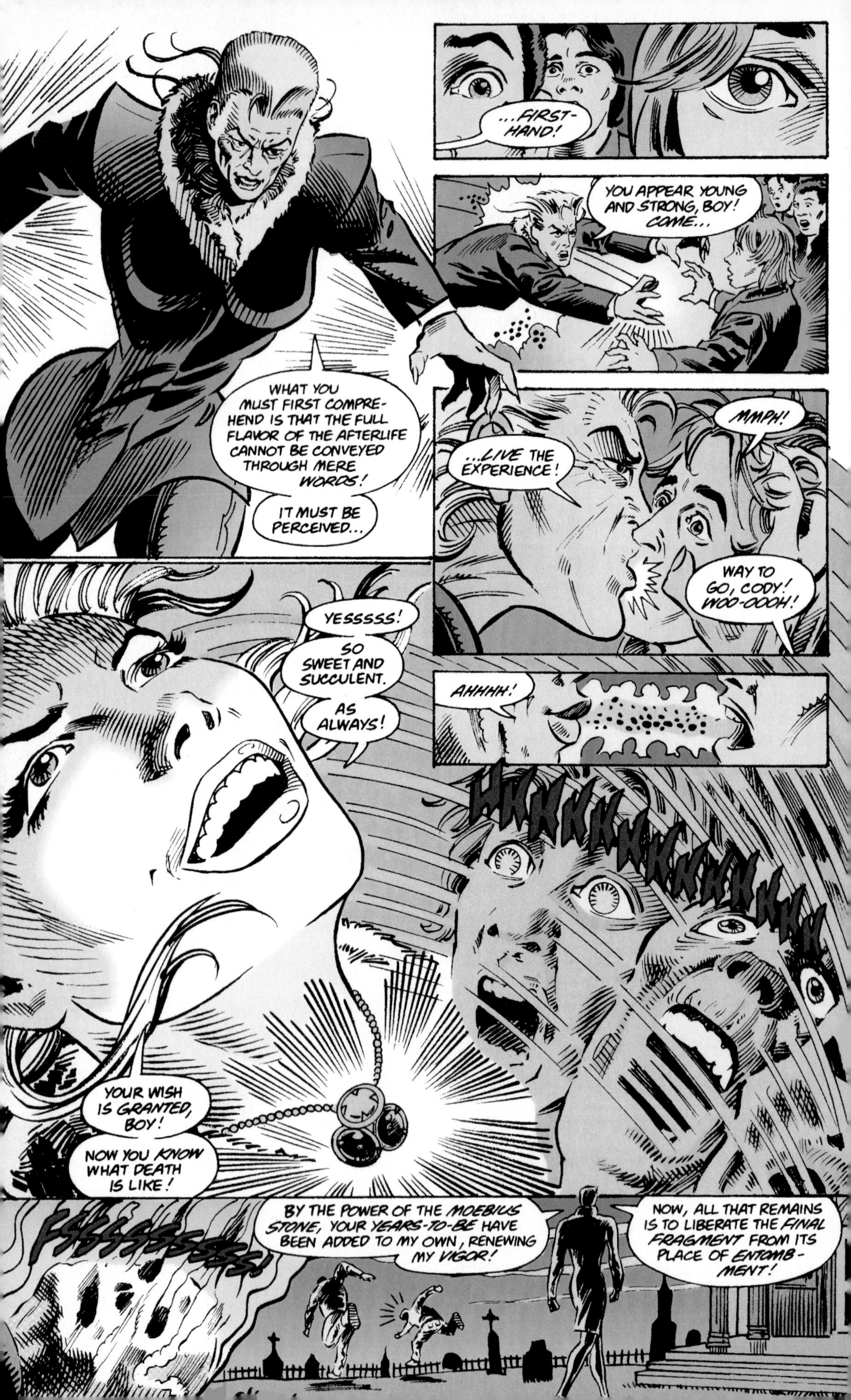

WHAT YOU MUST FIRST COMPREHEND IS THAT THE FULL FLAVOR OF THE AFTERLIFE CANNOT BE CONVEYED THROUGH MERE WORDS!
IT MUST BE PERCEIVED...
...FIRST-HAND!
YOU APPEAR YOUNG AND STRONG, BOY! COME...
...LIVE THE EXPERIENCE!
MMPH!
WAY TO GO, CODY! WOO-OOOH!
AHHHH!
YESSSSS!
SO SWEET AND SUCCULENT.
AS ALWAYS!
HHHNKKKKKKKKKKKKK
YOUR WISH IS GRANTED, BOY!
NOW YOU KNOW WHAT DEATH IS LIKE!
FSSSSSSSSSS!
BY THE POWER OF THE MOEBIUS STONE, YOUR YEARS-TO-BE HAVE BEEN ADDED TO MY OWN, RENEWING MY VIGOR!
NOW, ALL THAT REMAINS IS TO LIBERATE THE FINAL FRAGMENT FROM ITS PLACE OF ENTOMB-MENT!

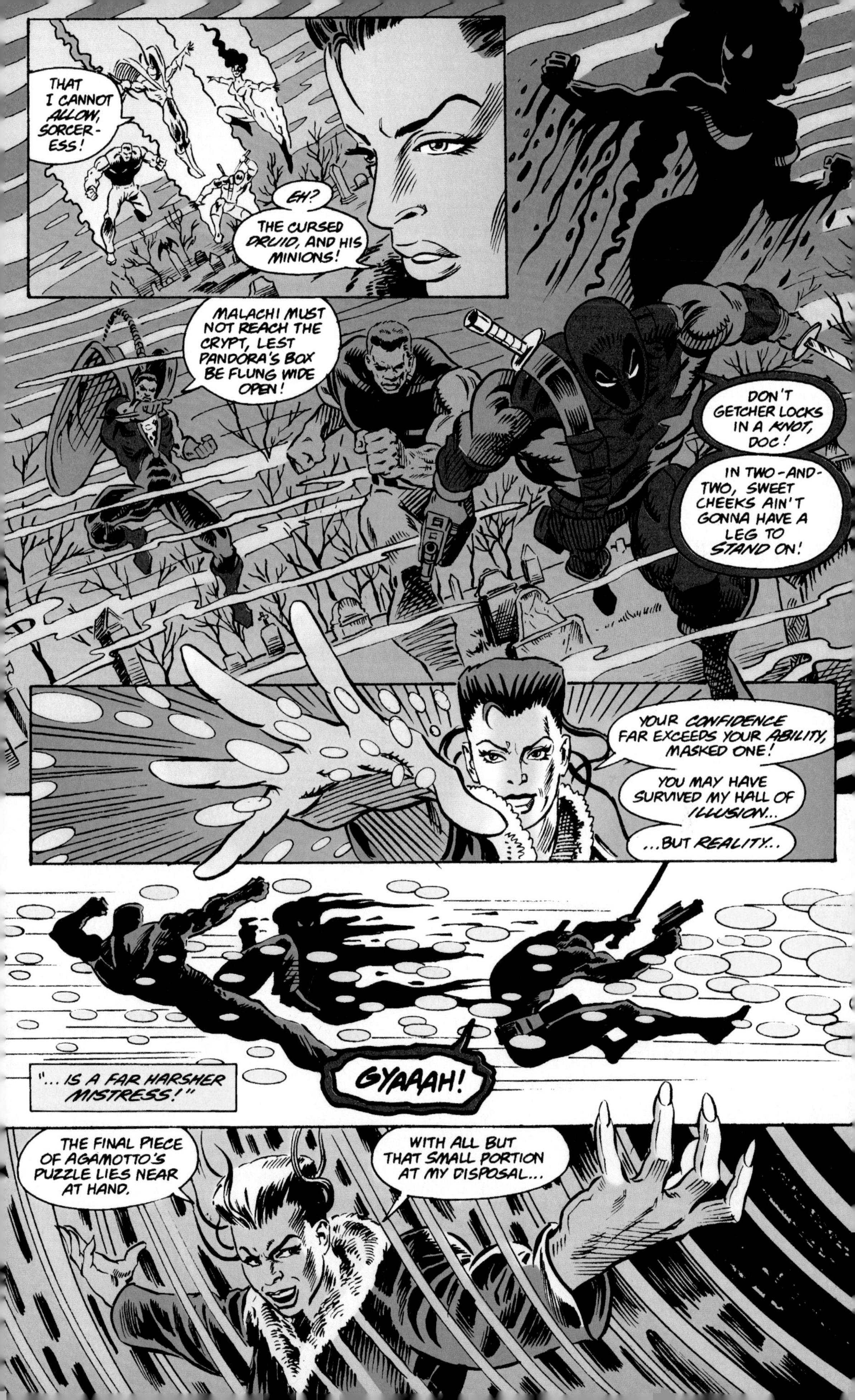
THAT I CANNOT ALLOW, SORCERESS!
EH?
THE CURSED DRUID, AND HIS MINIONS!
MALACHI MUST NOT REACH THE CRYPT, LEST PANDORA'S BOX BE FLUNG WIDE OPEN!
DON'T GETCHER LOCKS IN A KNOT, DOC!
IN TWO-AND-TWO, SWEET CHEEKS AIN'T GONNA HAVE A LEG TO STAND ON!
YOUR CONFIDENCE FAR EXCEEDS YOUR ABILITY, MASKED ONE!
YOU MAY HAVE SURVIVED MY HALL OF ILLUSION...
...BUT REALITY...
"...IS A FAR HARSHER MISTRESS!"
GYAAAH!
THE FINAL PIECE OF AGAMOTTO'S PUZZLE LIES NEAR AT HAND.
WITH ALL BUT THAT SMALL PORTION AT MY DISPOSAL...

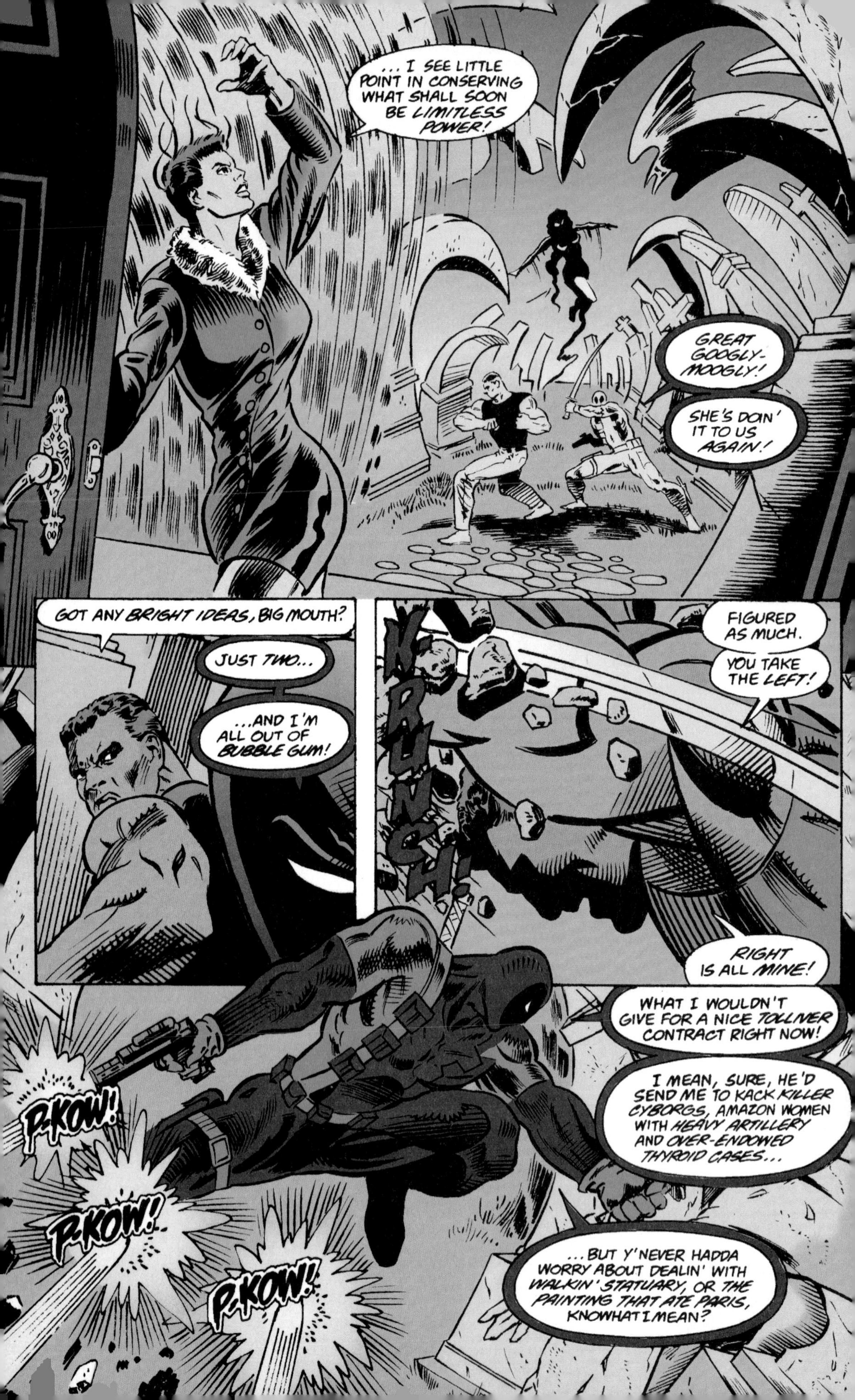
...I SEE LITTLE POINT IN CONSERVING WHAT SHALL SOON BE LIMITLESS POWER!
GREAT GOOGLY-MOOGLY!
SHE'S DOIN' IT TO US AGAIN!
GOT ANY BRIGHT IDEAS, BIG MOUTH?
JUST TWO...
...AND I'M ALL OUT OF BUBBLE GUM!
KRUNCH!
FIGURED AS MUCH.
YOU TAKE THE LEFT!
RIGHT IS ALL MINE!
WHAT I WOULDN'T GIVE FOR A NICE TOLLIVER CONTRACT RIGHT NOW!
I MEAN, SURE, HE'D SEND ME TO KACK KILLER CYBORGS, AMAZON WOMEN WITH HEAVY ARTILLERY AND OVER-ENDOWED THYROID CASES...
P-KOW!
P-KOW!
P-KOW!
...BUT Y'NEVER HADDA WORRY ABOUT DEALIN' WITH WALKIN' STATUARY, OR THE PAINTING THAT ATE PARIS, KNOWHATIMEAN?

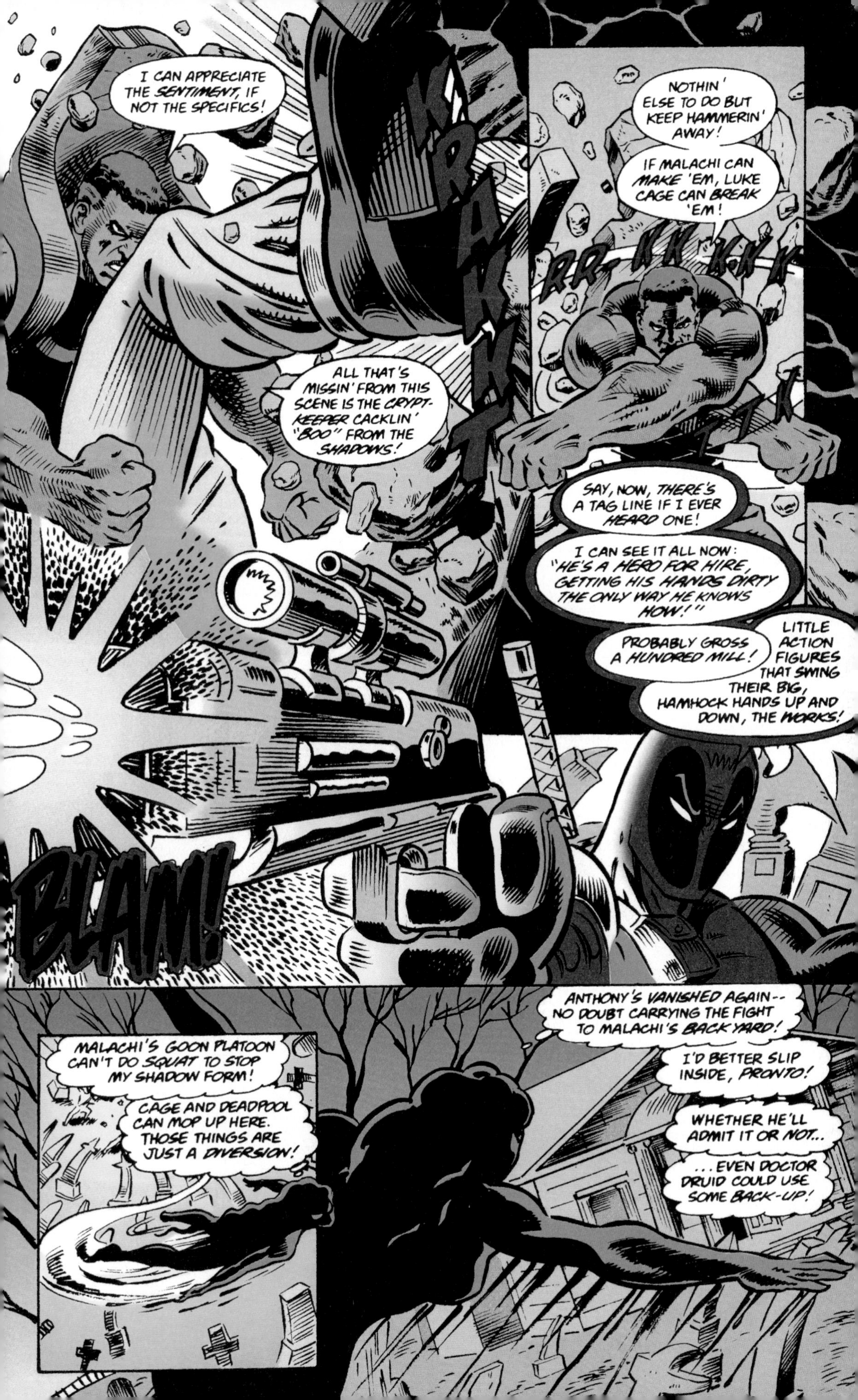
I CAN APPRECIATE THE SENTIMENT, IF NOT THE SPECIFICS!
KRAKKT
NOTHIN' ELSE TO DO BUT KEEP HAMMERIN' AWAY!
IF MALACHI CAN MAKE 'EM, LUKE CAGE CAN BREAK 'EM!
RR-KKKKK
ALL THAT'S MISSIN' FROM THIS SCENE IS THE CRYPT-KEEPER CACKLIN' "BOO" FROM THE SHADOWS!
SAY, NOW, THERE'S A TAG LINE IF I EVER HEARD ONE!
I CAN SEE IT ALL NOW: "HE'S A HERO FOR HIRE, GETTING HIS HANDS DIRTY THE ONLY WAY HE KNOWS HOW!"
PROBABLY GROSS A HUNDRED MILL!
LITTLE ACTION FIGURES THAT SWING THEIR BIG, HAMHOCK HANDS UP AND DOWN, THE WORKS!
BLAM!
ANTHONY'S VANISHED AGAIN-- NO DOUBT CARRYING THE FIGHT TO MALACHI'S BACK YARD!
I'D BETTER SLIP INSIDE, PRONTO!
WHETHER HE'LL ADMIT IT OR NOT...
...EVEN DOCTOR DRUID COULD USE SOME BACK-UP!
MALACHI'S GOON PLATOON CAN'T DO SQUAT TO STOP MY SHADOW FORM!
CAGE AND DEADPOOL CAN MOP UP HERE. THOSE THINGS ARE JUST A DIVERSION!

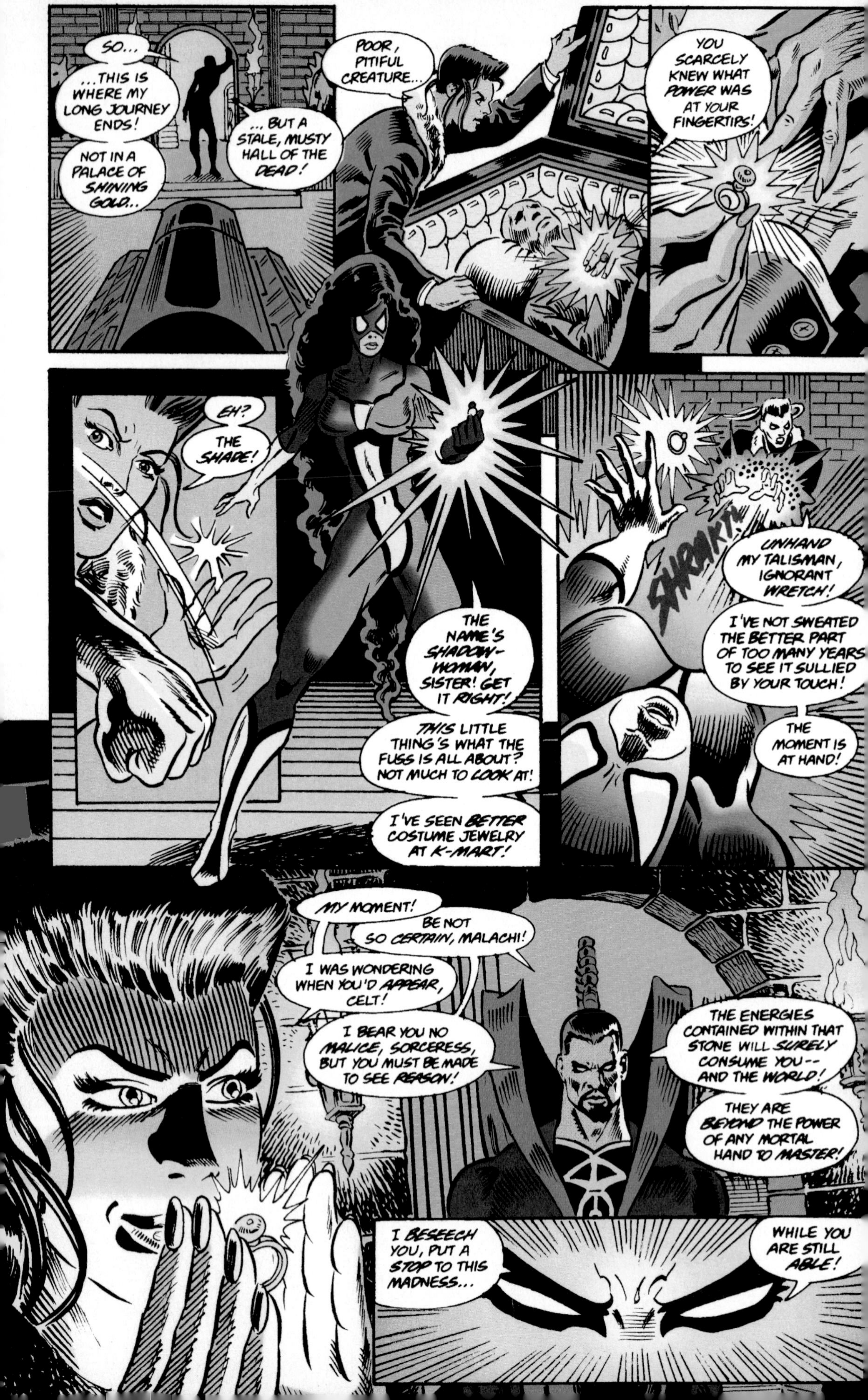
SO...
...THIS IS WHERE MY LONG JOURNEY ENDS!
NOT IN A PALACE OF SHINING GOLD...
..., BUT A STALE, MUSTY HALL OF THE DEAD!
POOR, PITIFUL CREATURE...
YOU SCARCELY KNEW WHAT POWER WAS AT YOUR FINGERTIPS!
EH? THE SHADE!
THE NAME'S SHADOW-WOMAN, SISTER! GET IT RIGHT!
THIS LITTLE THING'S WHAT THE FUSS IS ALL ABOUT? NOT MUCH TO LOOK AT!
I'VE SEEN BETTER COSTUME JEWELRY AT K-MART!
SHRAKT!
UNHAND MY TALISMAN, IGNORANT WRETCH!
I'VE NOT SWEATED THE BETTER PART OF TOO MANY YEARS TO SEE IT SULLIED BY YOUR TOUCH!
THE MOMENT IS AT HAND!
MY MOMENT!
BE NOT SO CERTAIN, MALACHI!
I WAS WONDERING WHEN YOU'D APPEAR, CELT!
I BEAR YOU NO MALICE, SORCERESS, BUT YOU MUST BE MADE TO SEE REASON!
THE ENERGIES CONTAINED WITHIN THAT STONE WILL SURELY CONSUME YOU-- AND THE WORLD!
THEY ARE BEYOND THE POWER OF ANY MORTAL HAND TO MASTER!
I BESEECH YOU, PUT A STOP TO THIS MADNESS...
WHILE YOU ARE STILL ABLE!

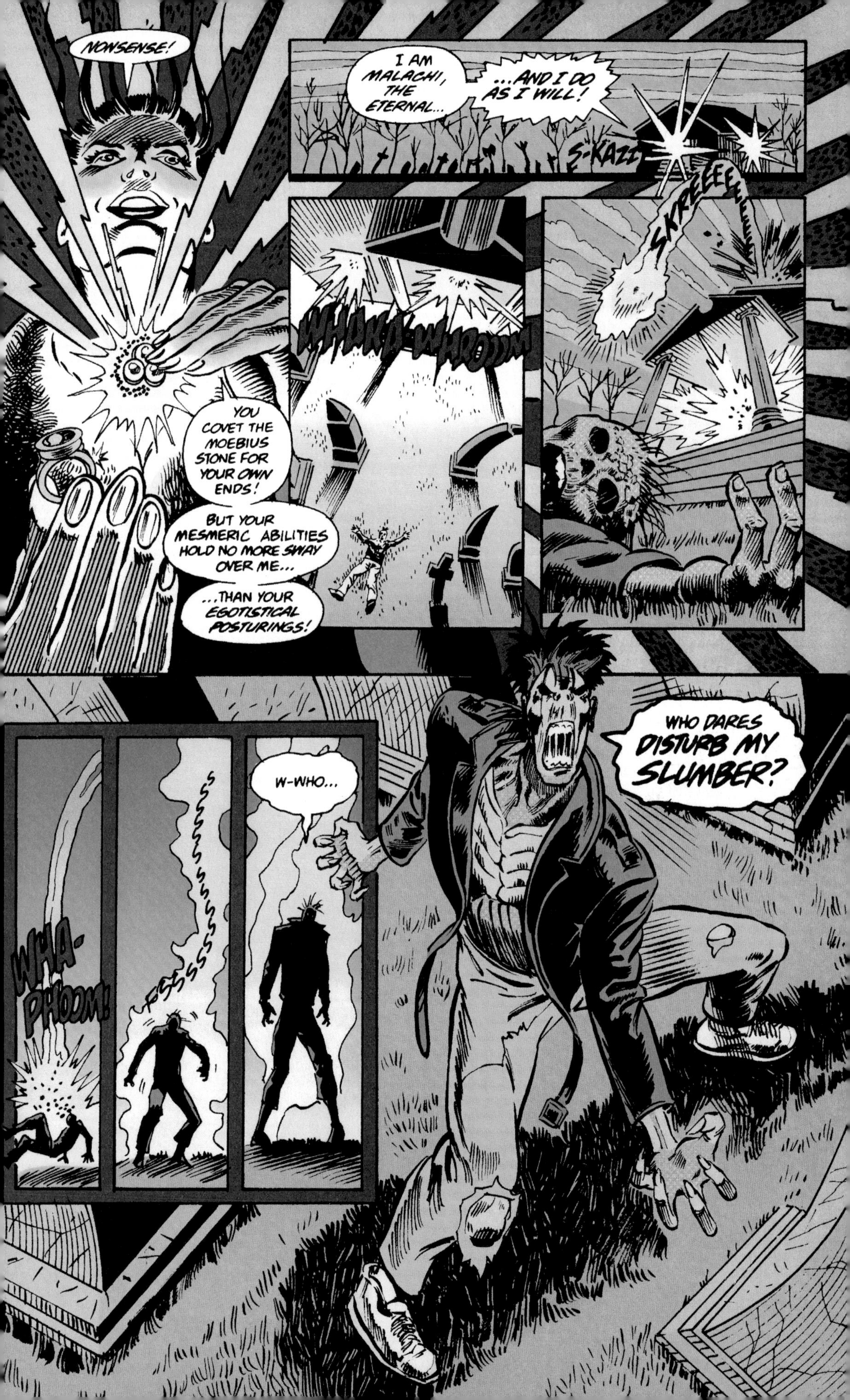
NONSENSE!
I AM MALACHI, THE ETERNAL...
...AND I DO AS I WILL!
S-KAZZ
YOU COVET THE MOEBIUS STONE FOR YOUR OWN ENDS!
BUT YOUR MESMERIC ABILITIES HOLD NO MORE SWAY OVER ME...
...THAN YOUR EGOTISTICAL POSTURINGS!
WHUD-WHROOM
SKREEEE
WHA-PHOOM!
FSSSSSS
W-WHO...
WHO DARES DISTURB MY SLUMBER?

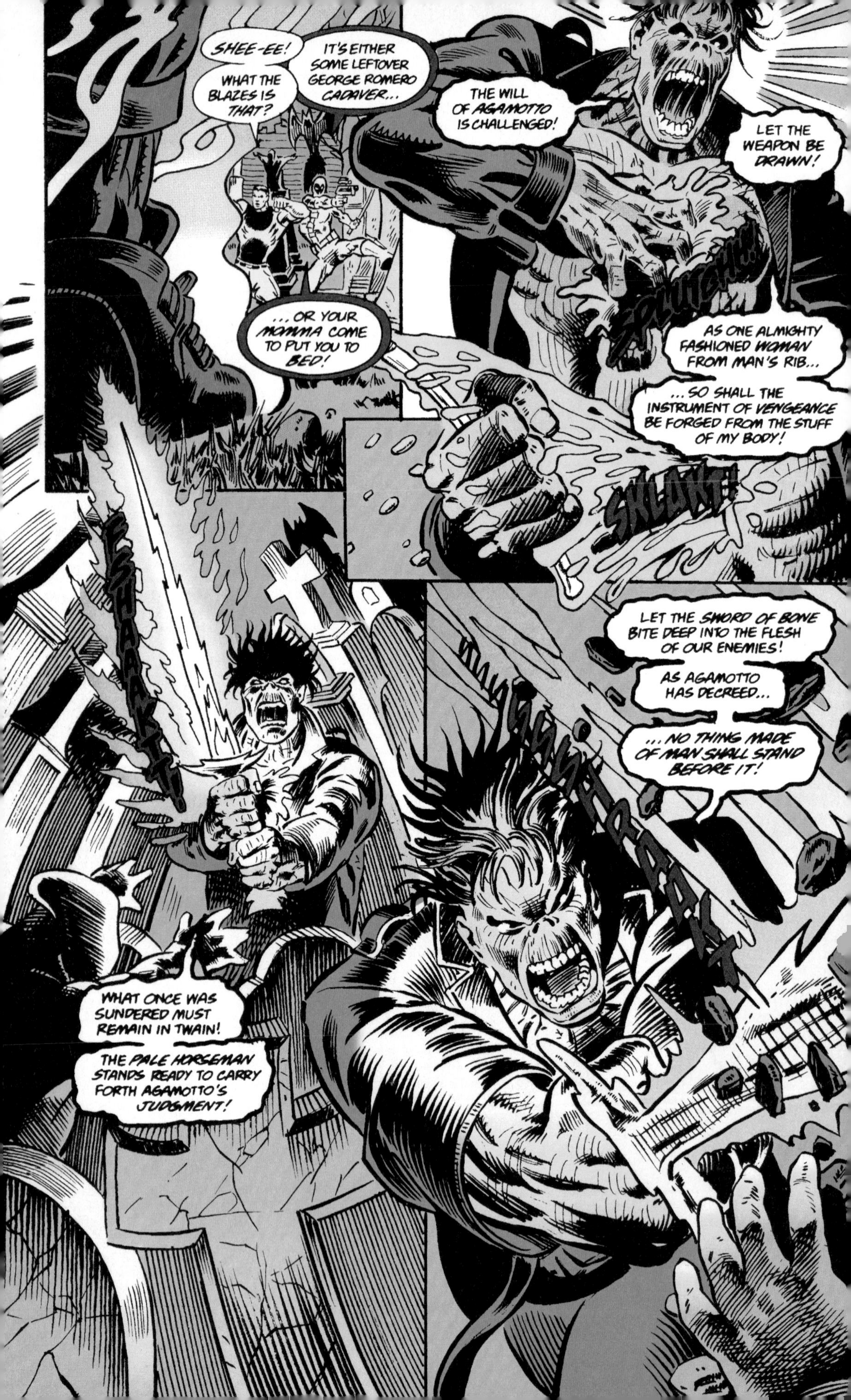
SHEE-EE!
WHAT THE BLAZES IS THAT?
IT'S EITHER SOME LEFTOVER GEORGE ROMERO CADAVER...
...OR YOUR MOMMA COME TO PUT YOU TO BED!
THE WILL OF AGAMOTTO IS CHALLENGED!
LET THE WEAPON BE DRAWN!
SPLUTCH!!
AS ONE ALMIGHTY FASHIONED WOMAN FROM MAN'S RIB...
...SO SHALL THE INSTRUMENT OF VENGEANCE BE FORGED FROM THE STUFF OF MY BODY!
SKLORT!
FSHAAKT!
LET THE SWORD OF BONE BITE DEEP INTO THE FLESH OF OUR ENEMIES!
AS AGAMOTTO HAS DECREED...
...NO THING MADE OF MAN SHALL STAND BEFORE IT!
WHAT ONCE WAS SUNDERED MUST REMAIN IN TWAIN!
THE PALE HORSEMAN STANDS READY TO CARRY FORTH AGAMOTTO'S JUDGMENT!

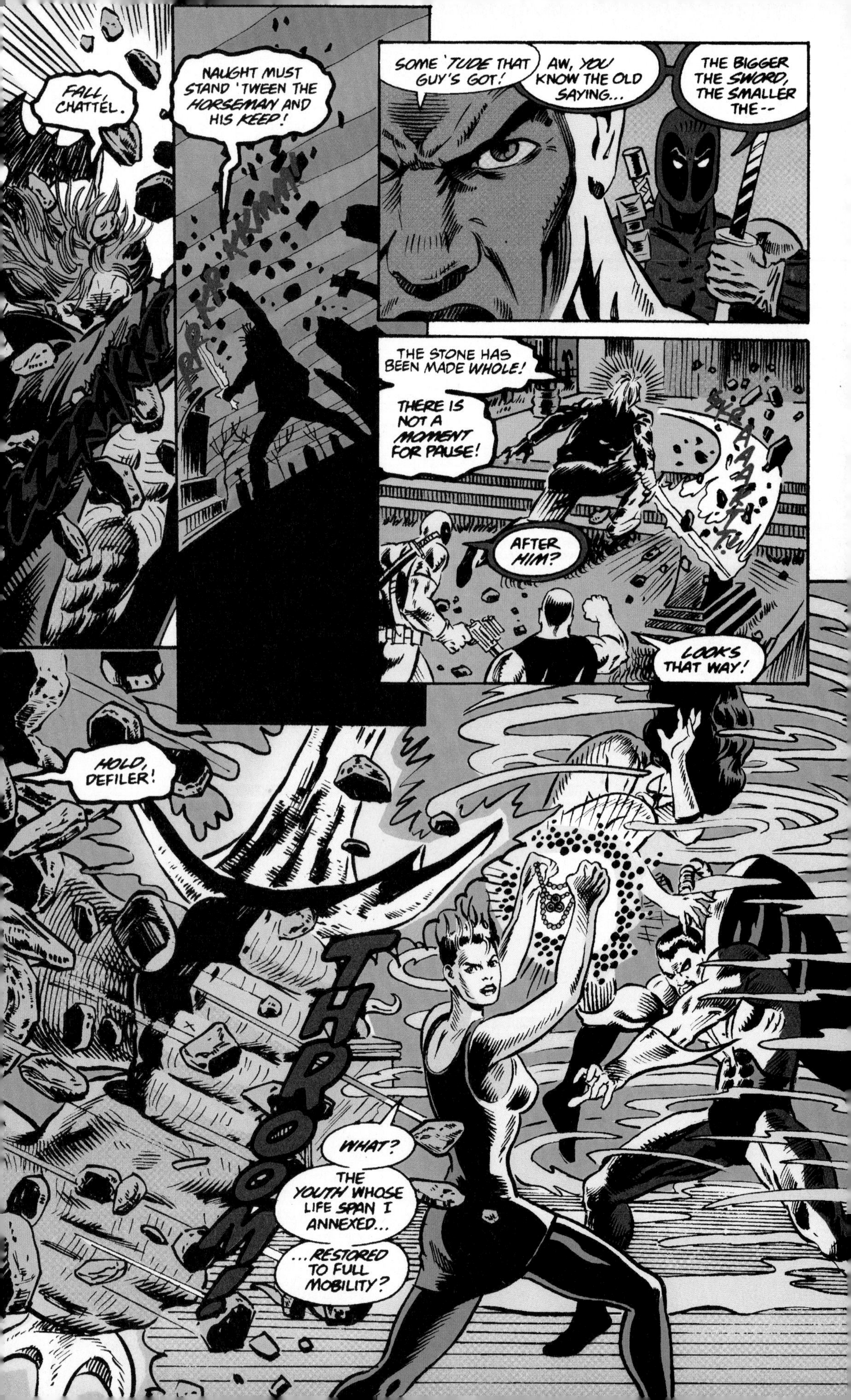
FALL, CHATTEL.
NAUGHT MUST STAND 'TWEEN THE HORSEMAN AND HIS KEEP!
SOME 'TUDE THAT GUY'S GOT!
AW, YOU KNOW THE OLD SAYING...
THE BIGGER THE SWORD, THE SMALLER THE--
THE STONE HAS BEEN MADE WHOLE!
THERE IS NOT A MOMENT FOR PAUSE!
AFTER HIM?
LOOKS THAT WAY!
HOLD, DEFILER!
THROOOOM!
WHAT?
THE YOUTH WHOSE LIFE SPAN I ANNEXED...
...RESTORED TO FULL MOBILITY?

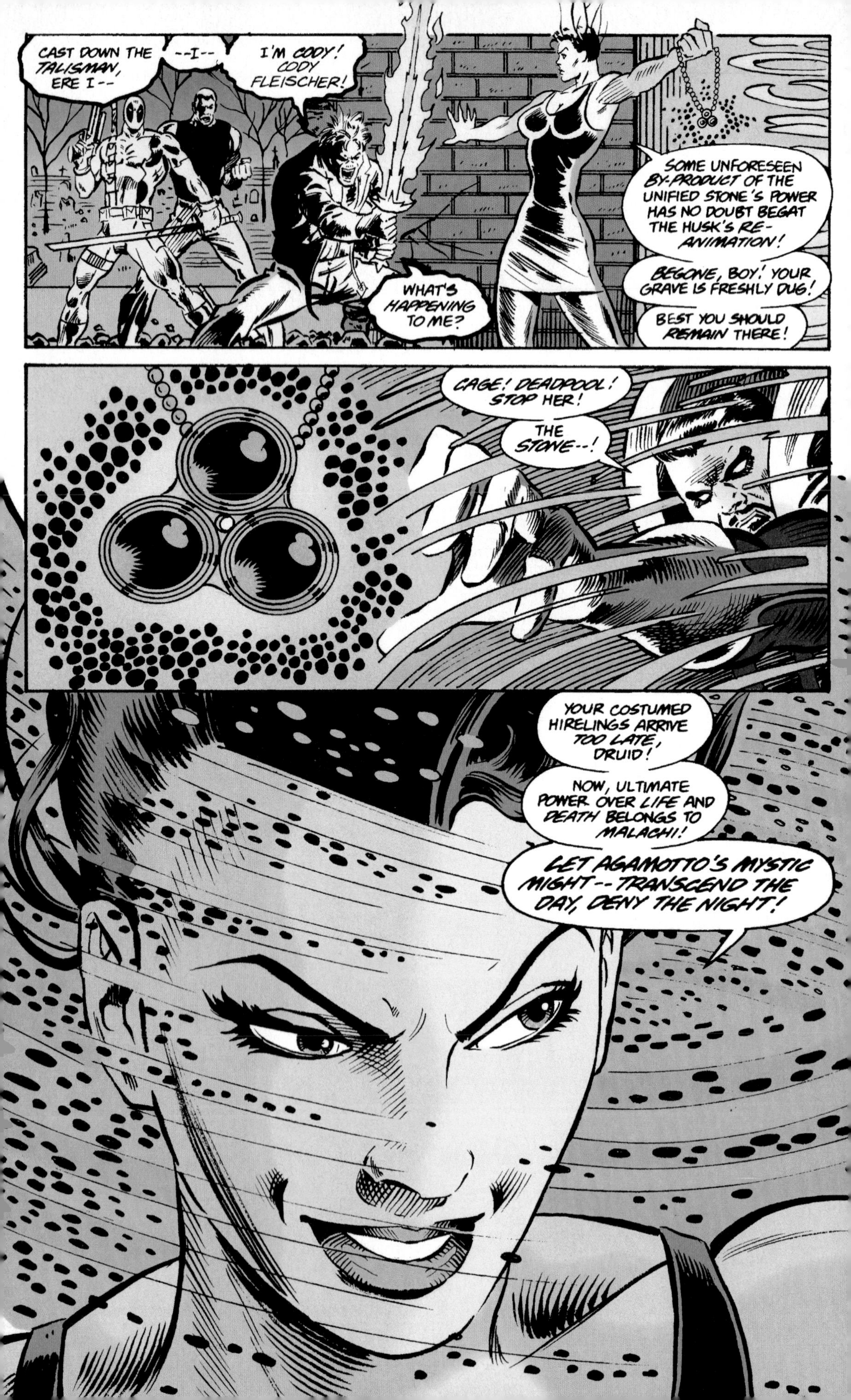
CAST DOWN THE TALISMAN, ERE I --
--I--
I'M CODY! CODY FLEISCHER!
SOME UNFORESEEN BY-PRODUCT OF THE UNIFIED STONE'S POWER HAS NO DOUBT BEGAT THE HUSK'S RE-ANIMATION!
BEGONE, BOY! YOUR GRAVE IS FRESHLY DUG!
BEST YOU SHOULD REMAIN THERE!
WHAT'S HAPPENING TO ME?
CAGE! DEADPOOL! STOP HER!
THE STONE--!
YOUR COSTUMED HIRELINGS ARRIVE TOO LATE, DRUID!
NOW, ULTIMATE POWER OVER LIFE AND DEATH BELONGS TO MALACHI!
LET AGAMOTTO'S MYSTIC MIGHT--TRANSCEND THE DAY, DENY THE NIGHT!

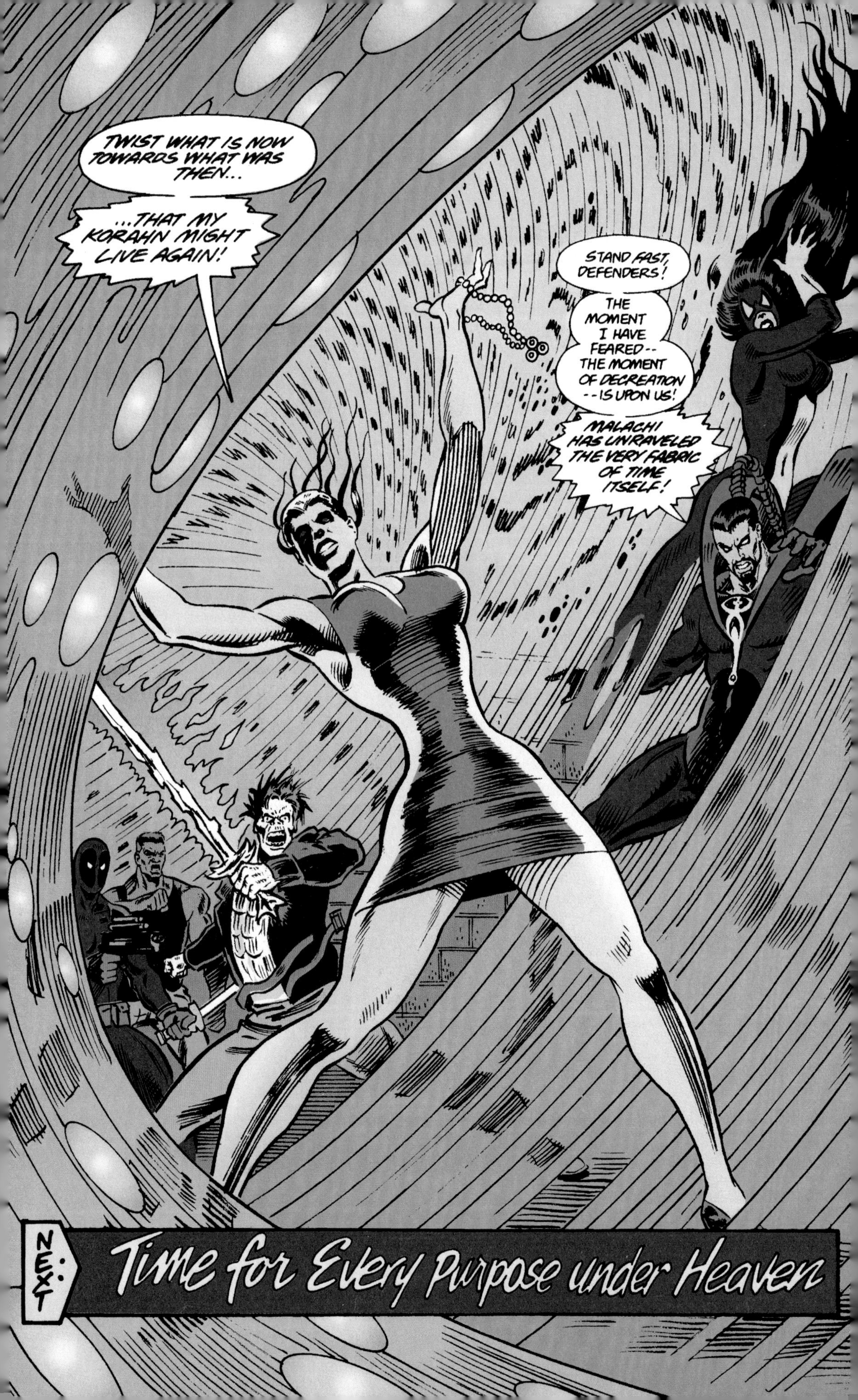
TWIST WHAT IS NOW TOWARDS WHAT WAS THEN...
...THAT MY KORAHN MIGHT LIVE AGAIN!
STAND FAST, DEFENDERS!
THE MOMENT I HAVE FEARED-- THE MOMENT OF DECREATION --IS UPON US!
MALACHI HAS UNRAVELED THE VERY FABRIC OF TIME ITSELF!
NEXT: Time for Every Purpose under Heaven

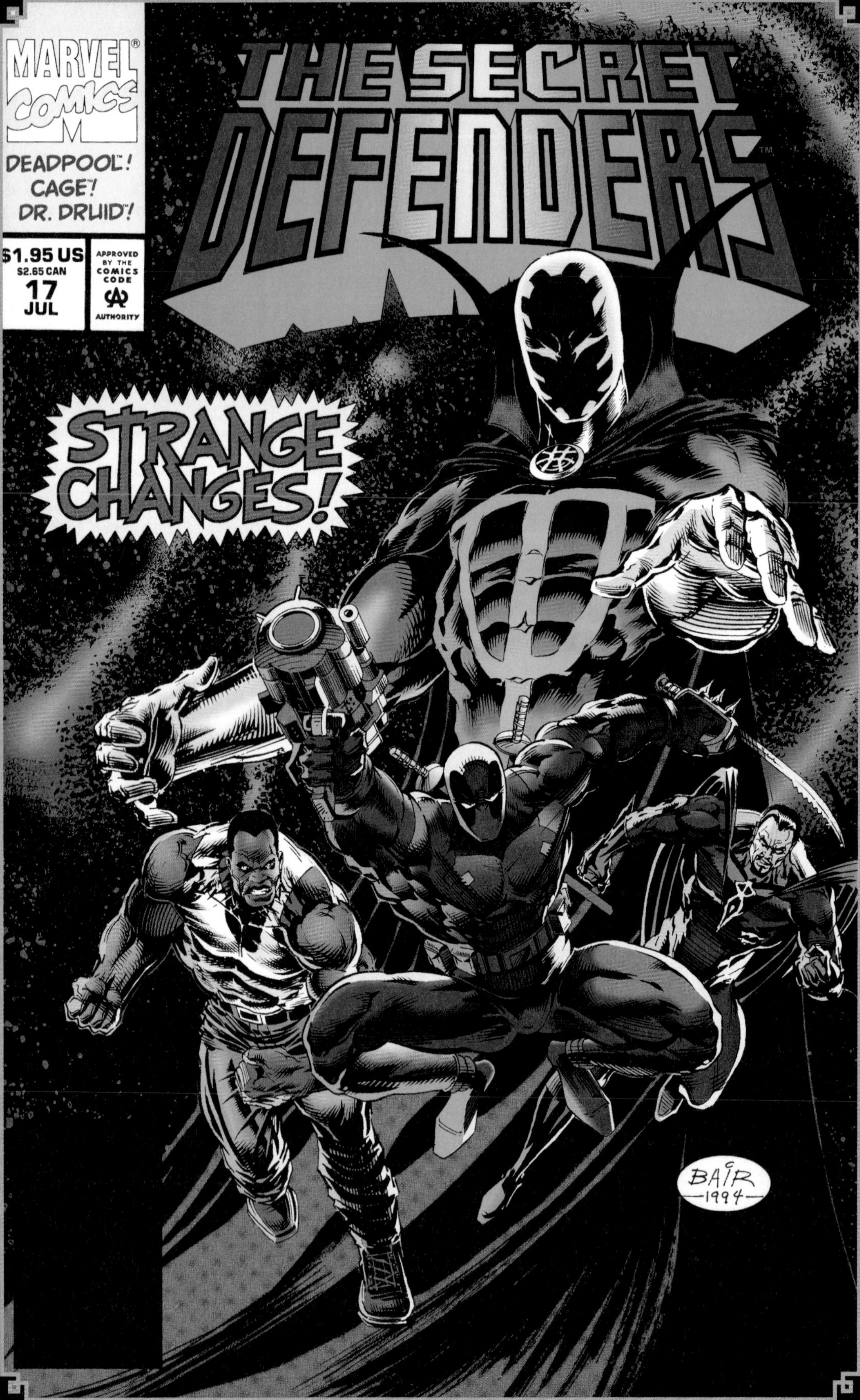
MARVEL® COMICS
THE SECRET DEFENDERS™
DEADPOOL™! CAGE™! DR. DRUID™!
$1.95 US $2.65 CAN 17 JUL
APPROVED BY THE COMICS CODE AUTHORITY
STRANGE CHANGES!
BAIR 1994

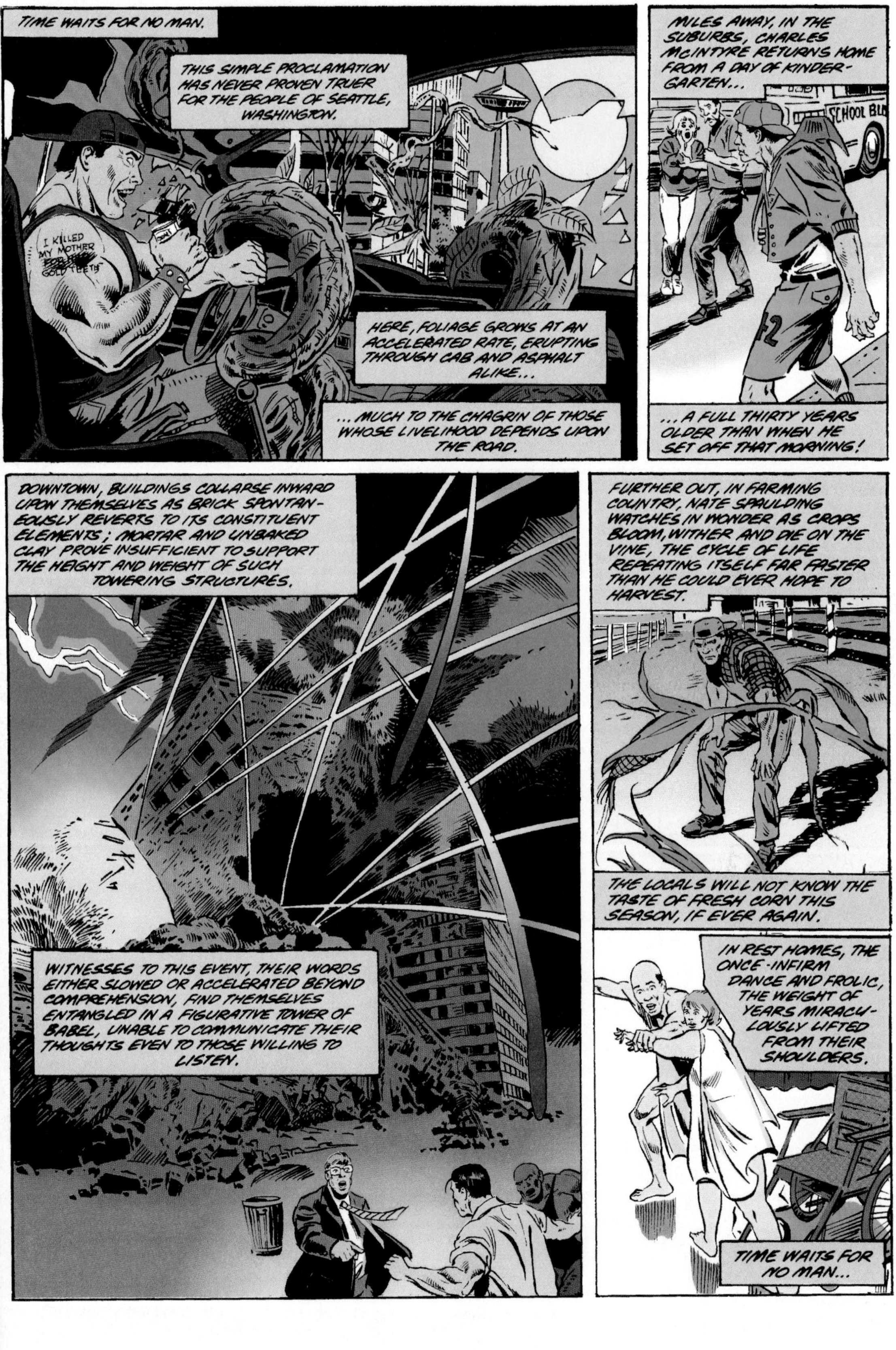

TIME WAITS FOR NO MAN.
THIS SIMPLE PROCLAMATION HAS NEVER PROVEN TRUER FOR THE PEOPLE OF SEATTLE, WASHINGTON.
HERE, FOLIAGE GROWS AT AN ACCELERATED RATE, ERUPTING THROUGH CAB AND ASPHALT ALIKE...
...MUCH TO THE CHAGRIN OF THOSE WHOSE LIVELIHOOD DEPENDS UPON THE ROAD.
MILES AWAY, IN THE SUBURBS, CHARLES McINTYRE RETURNS HOME FROM A DAY OF KINDER-GARTEN...
...A FULL THIRTY YEARS OLDER THAN WHEN HE SET OFF THAT MORNING!
DOWNTOWN, BUILDINGS COLLAPSE INWARD UPON THEMSELVES AS BRICK SPONTAN-EOUSLY REVERTS TO ITS CONSTITUENT ELEMENTS; MORTAR AND UNBAKED CLAY PROVE INSUFFICIENT TO SUPPORT THE HEIGHT AND WEIGHT OF SUCH TOWERING STRUCTURES.
WITNESSES TO THIS EVENT, THEIR WORDS EITHER SLOWED OR ACCELERATED BEYOND COMPREHENSION, FIND THEMSELVES ENTANGLED IN A FIGURATIVE TOWER OF BABEL, UNABLE TO COMMUNICATE THEIR THOUGHTS EVEN TO THOSE WILLING TO LISTEN.
FURTHER OUT, IN FARMING COUNTRY, NATE SPAULDING WATCHES IN WONDER AS CROPS BLOOM, WITHER AND DIE ON THE VINE, THE CYCLE OF LIFE REPEATING ITSELF FAR FASTER THAN HE COULD EVER HOPE TO HARVEST.
THE LOCALS WILL NOT KNOW THE TASTE OF FRESH CORN THIS SEASON, IF EVER AGAIN.
IN REST HOMES, THE ONCE-INFIRM DANCE AND FROLIC, THE WEIGHT OF YEARS MIRACU-LOUSLY LIFTED FROM THEIR SHOULDERS.
TIME WAITS FOR NO MAN...

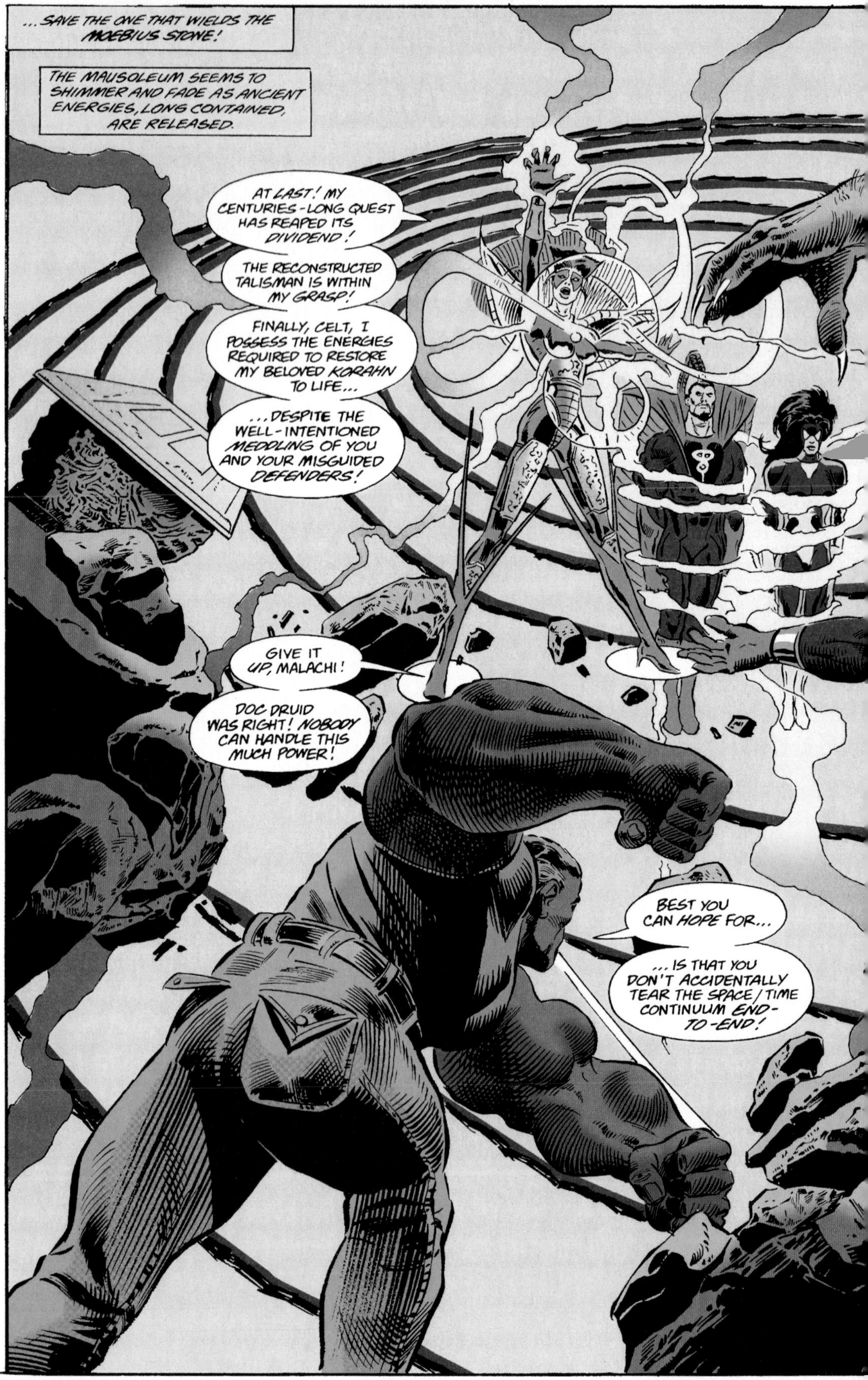
...SAVE THE ONE THAT WIELDS THE MOEBIUS STONE!
THE MAUSOLEUM SEEMS TO SHIMMER AND FADE AS ANCIENT ENERGIES, LONG CONTAINED, ARE RELEASED.
AT LAST! MY CENTURIES-LONG QUEST HAS REAPED ITS DIVIDEND!
THE RECONSTRUCTED TALISMAN IS WITHIN MY GRASP!
FINALLY, CELT, I POSSESS THE ENERGIES REQUIRED TO RESTORE MY BELOVED KORAHN TO LIFE...
...DESPITE THE WELL-INTENTIONED MEDDLING OF YOU AND YOUR MISGUIDED DEFENDERS!
GIVE IT UP, MALACHI!
DOC DRUID WAS RIGHT! NOBODY CAN HANDLE THIS MUCH POWER!
BEST YOU CAN HOPE FOR...
...IS THAT YOU DON'T ACCIDENTALLY TEAR THE SPACE/TIME CONTINUUM END-TO-END!

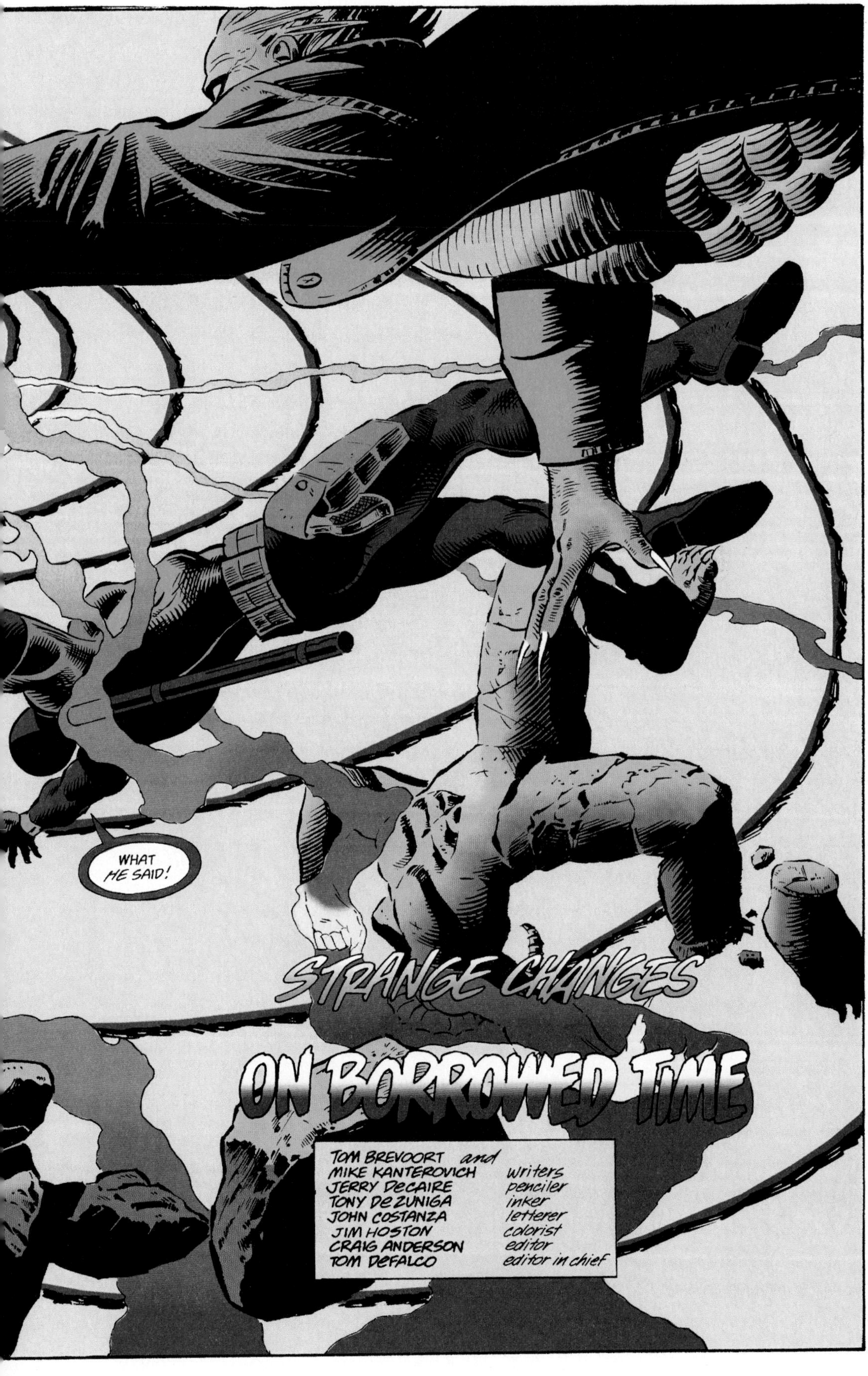
WHAT ME SAID!
STRANGE CHANGES
ON BORROWED TIME
TOM BREVOORT and MIKE KANTEROVICH writers
JERRY DECAIRE penciler
TONY DEZUNIGA inker
JOHN COSTANZA letterer
JIM HOSTON colorist
CRAIG ANDERSON editor
TOM DEFALCO editor in chief

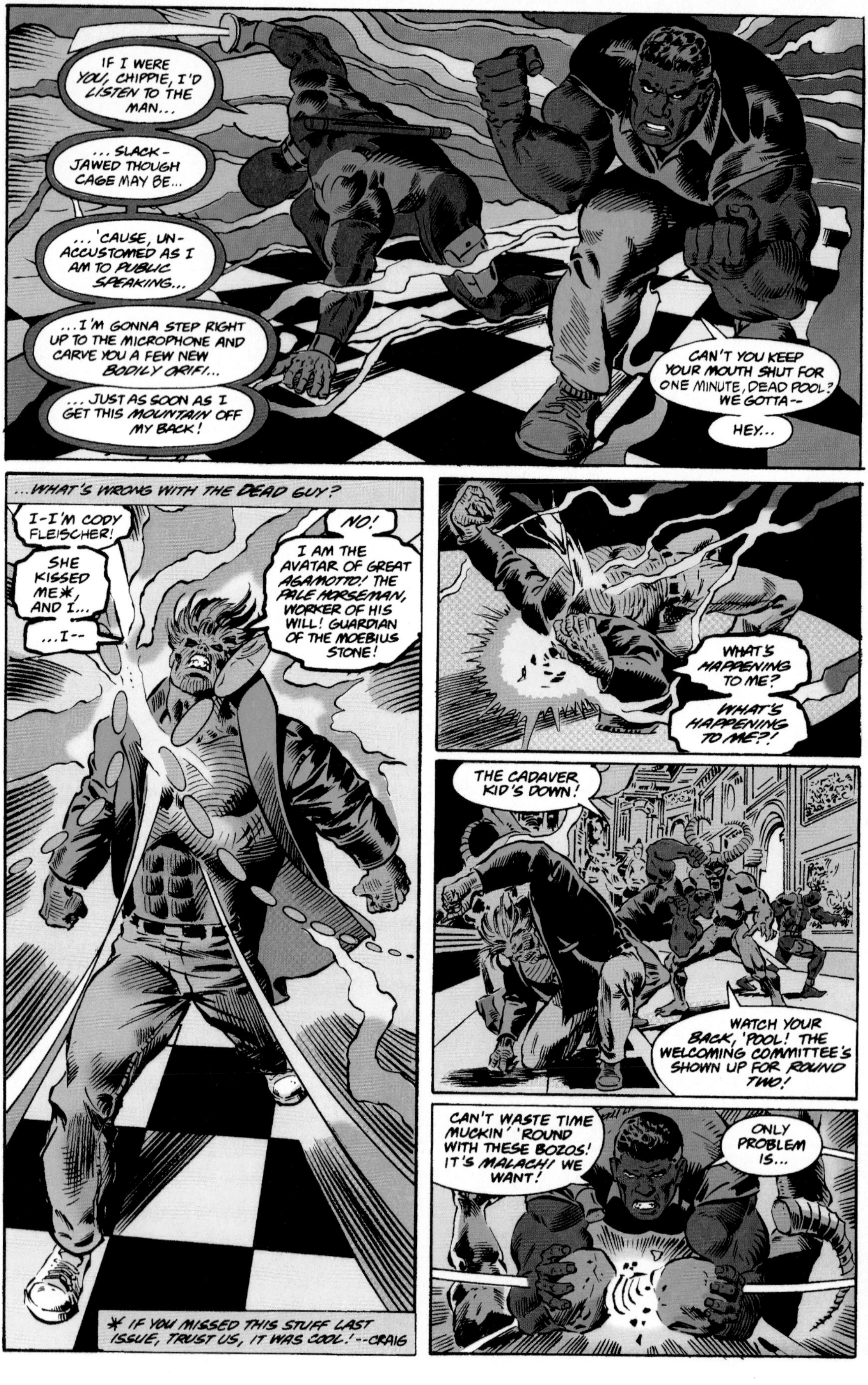
IF I WERE YOU, CHIPPIE, I'D LISTEN TO THE MAN...
...SLACK-JAWED THOUGH CAGE MAY BE...
...'CAUSE, UN-ACCUSTOMED AS I AM TO PUBLIC SPEAKING...
...I'M GONNA STEP RIGHT UP TO THE MICROPHONE AND CARVE YOU A FEW NEW BODILY ORIFI...
...JUST AS SOON AS I GET THIS MOUNTAIN OFF MY BACK!
CAN'T YOU KEEP YOUR MOUTH SHUT FOR ONE MINUTE, DEAD POOL? WE GOTTA--
HEY...
...WHAT'S WRONG WITH THE DEAD GUY?
I-I'M CODY FLEISCHER!
SHE KISSED ME*, AND I...
...I--
NO!
I AM THE AVATAR OF GREAT AGAMOTTO! THE PALE HORSEMAN, WORKER OF HIS WILL! GUARDIAN OF THE MOEBIUS STONE!
* IF YOU MISSED THIS STUFF LAST ISSUE, TRUST US, IT WAS COOL! --CRAIG
WHAT'S HAPPENING TO ME?
WHAT'S HAPPENING TO ME?!
THE CADAVER KID'S DOWN!
WATCH YOUR BACK, 'POOL! THE WELCOMING COMMITTEE'S SHOWN UP FOR ROUND TWO!
CAN'T WASTE TIME MUCKIN' 'ROUND WITH THESE BOZOS! IT'S MALACHI WE WANT!
ONLY PROBLEM IS...

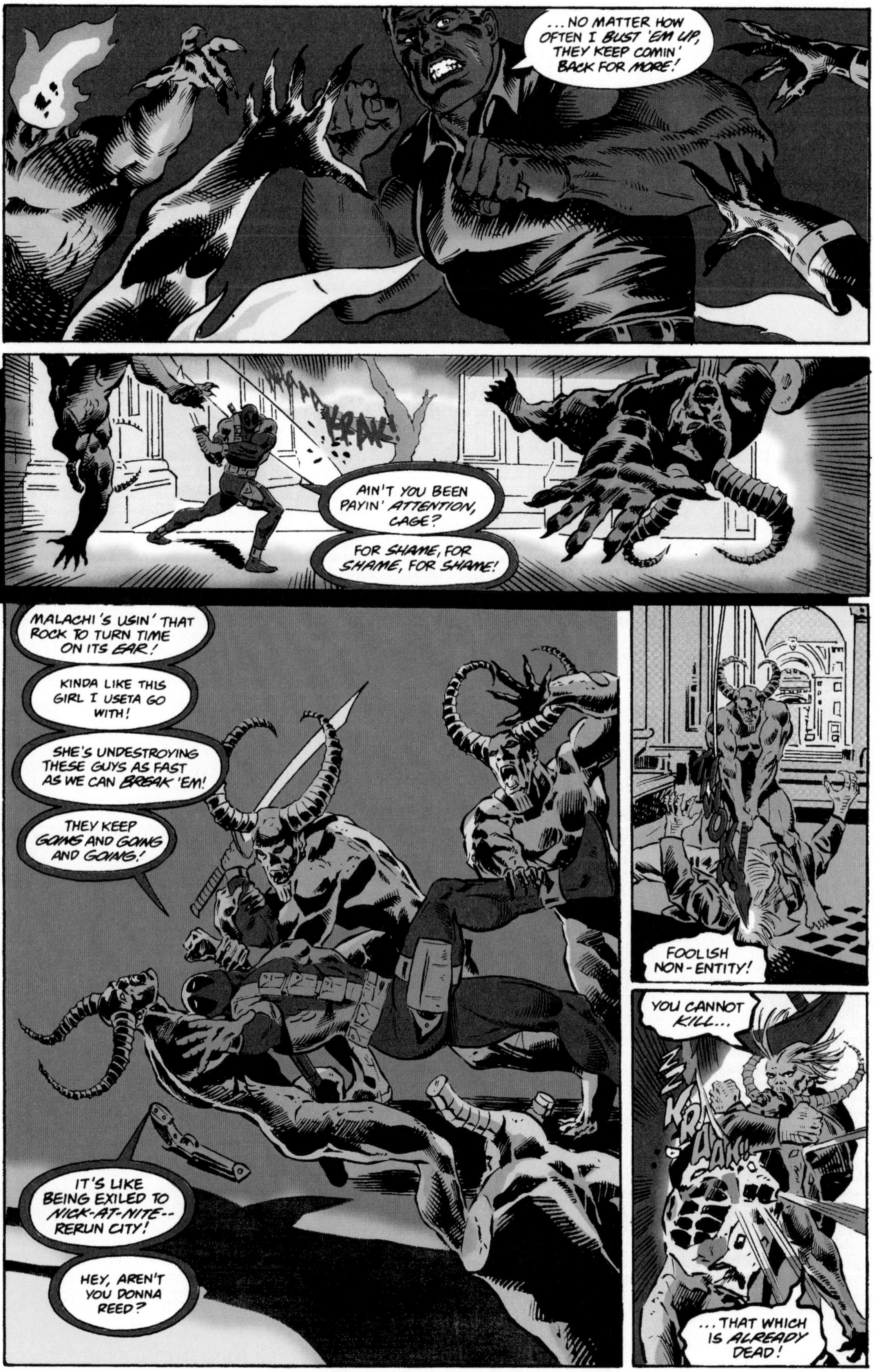
...NO MATTER HOW OFTEN I BUST 'EM UP, THEY KEEP COMIN' BACK FOR MORE!
KRAK!
AIN'T YOU BEEN PAYIN' ATTENTION, CAGE?
FOR SHAME, FOR SHAME, FOR SHAME!
MALACHI'S USIN' THAT ROCK TO TURN TIME ON ITS EAR!
KINDA LIKE THIS GIRL I USETA GO WITH!
SHE'S UNDESTROYING THESE GUYS AS FAST AS WE CAN BREAK 'EM!
THEY KEEP GOING AND GOING AND GOING!
IT'S LIKE BEING EXILED TO NICK-AT-NITE-- RERUN CITY!
HEY, AREN'T YOU DONNA REED?
FOOLISH NON-ENTITY!
YOU CANNOT KILL...
...THAT WHICH IS ALREADY DEAD!

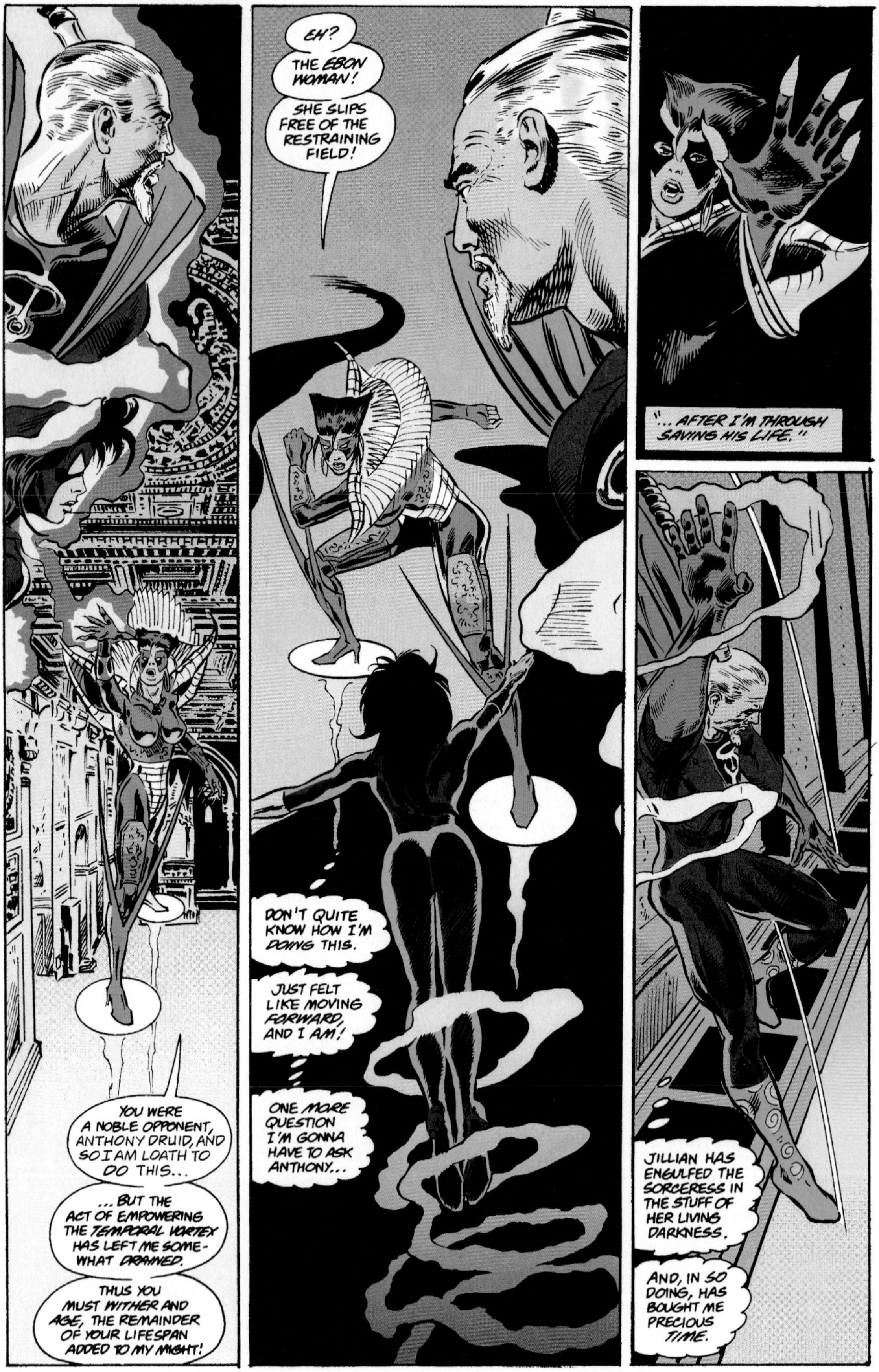

YOU WERE A NOBLE OPPONENT, ANTHONY DRUID, AND SO I AM LOATH TO DO THIS...
...BUT THE ACT OF EMPOWERING THE TEMPORAL VORTEX HAS LEFT ME SOME-WHAT DRAINED.
THUS YOU MUST WITHER AND AGE, THE REMAINDER OF YOUR LIFESPAN ADDED TO MY MIGHT!
EH?
THE EBON WOMAN!
SHE SLIPS FREE OF THE RESTRAINING FIELD!
DON'T QUITE KNOW HOW I'M DOING THIS.
JUST FELT LIKE MOVING FORWARD, AND I AM!
ONE MORE QUESTION I'M GONNA HAVE TO ASK ANTHONY...
"...AFTER I'M THROUGH SAVING HIS LIFE."
JILLIAN HAS ENGULFED THE SORCERESS IN THE STUFF OF HER LIVING DARKNESS.
AND, IN SO DOING, HAS BOUGHT ME PRECIOUS TIME.

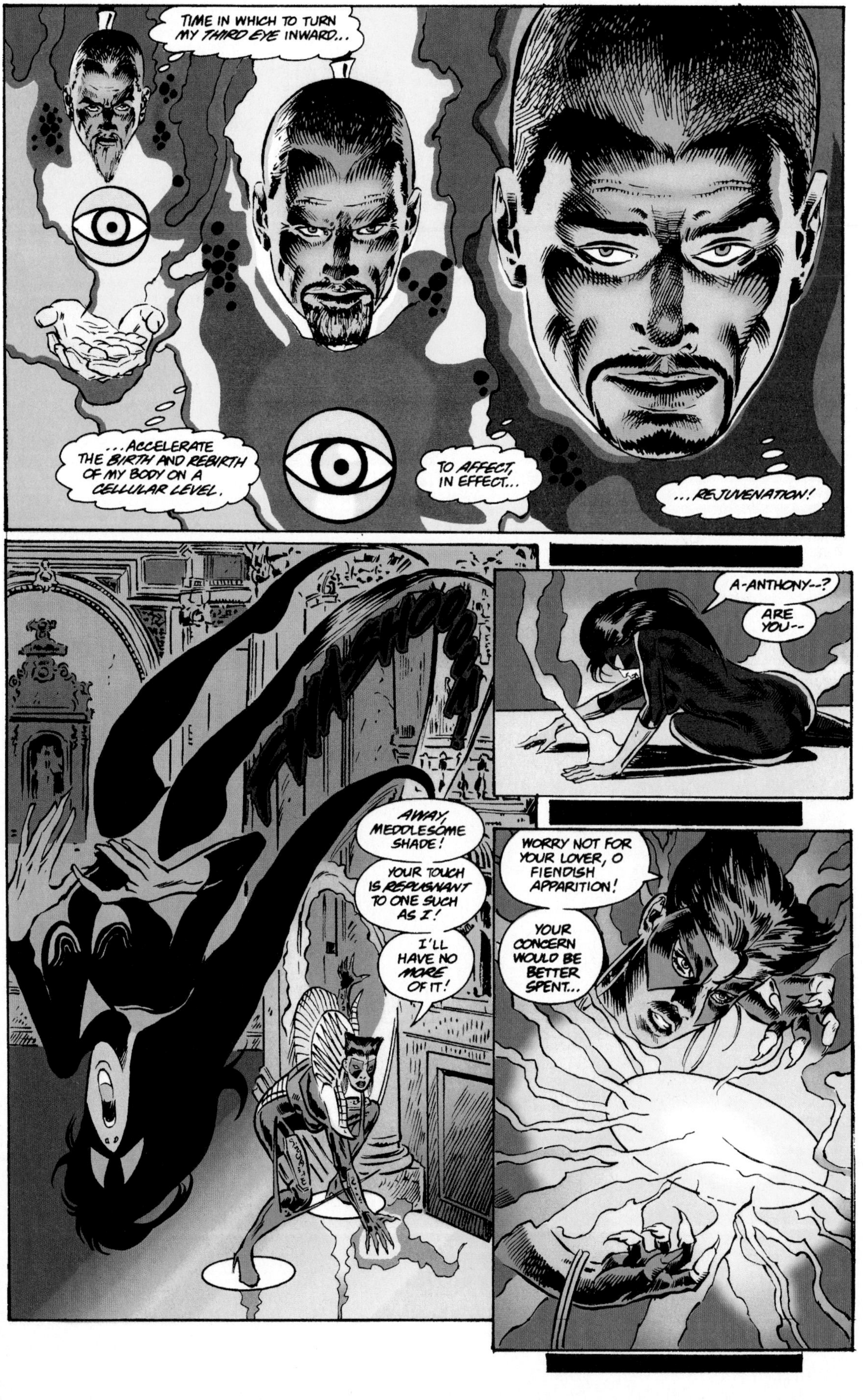
TIME IN WHICH TO TURN MY THIRD EYE INWARD...
...ACCELERATE THE BIRTH AND REBIRTH OF MY BODY ON A CELLULAR LEVEL.
TO AFFECT, IN EFFECT...
...REJUVENATION!
[redacted]
A-ANTHONY--?
ARE YOU--
[redacted]
AWAY, MEDDLESOME SHADE!
YOUR TOUCH IS REPUGNANT TO ONE SUCH AS I!
I'LL HAVE NO MORE OF IT!
WORRY NOT FOR YOUR LOVER, O FIENDISH APPARITION!
YOUR CONCERN WOULD BE BETTER SPENT...
[redacted]

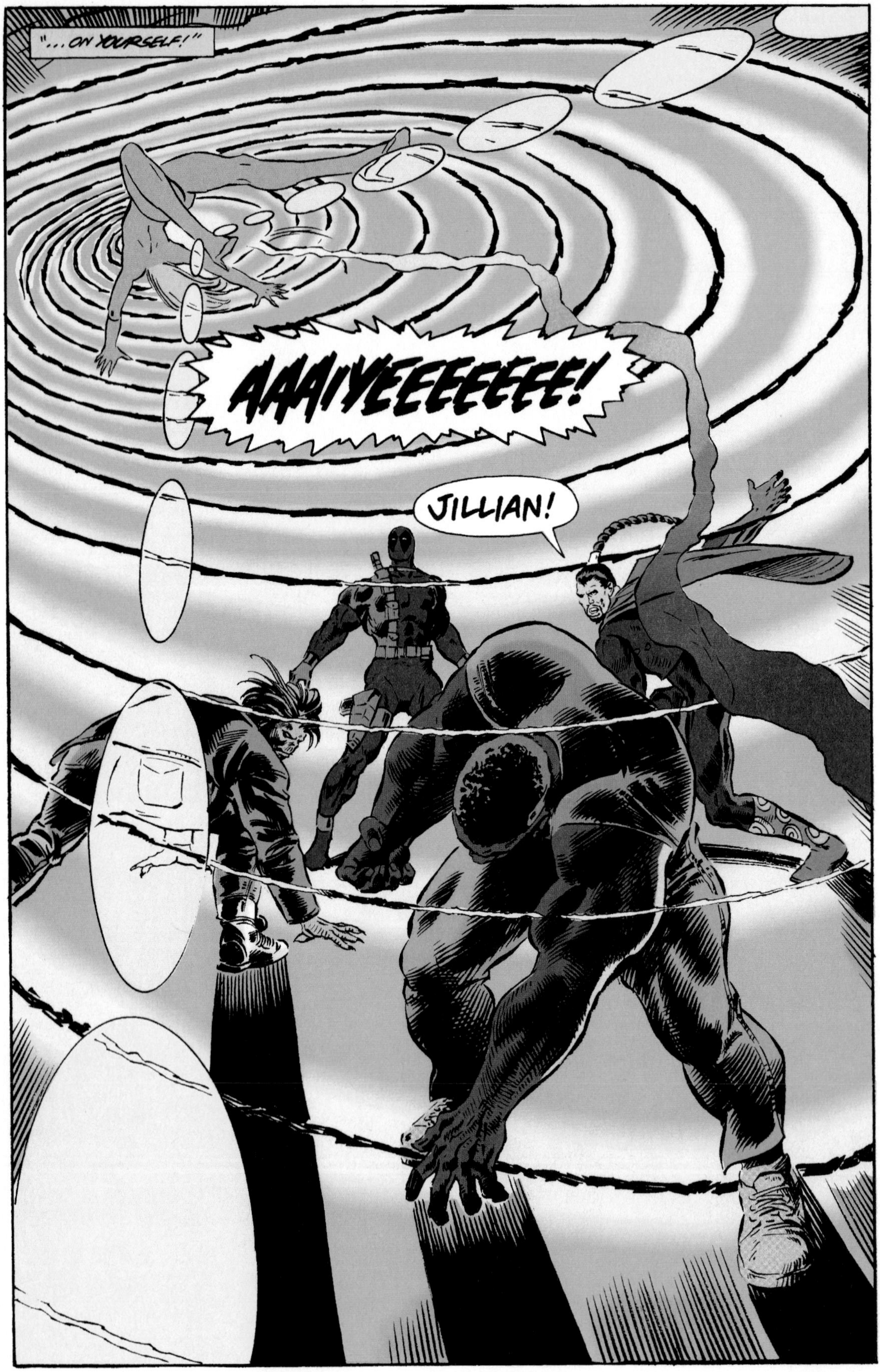
"...ON YOURSELF!"
AAAIYEEEEEEEE!
JILLIAN!

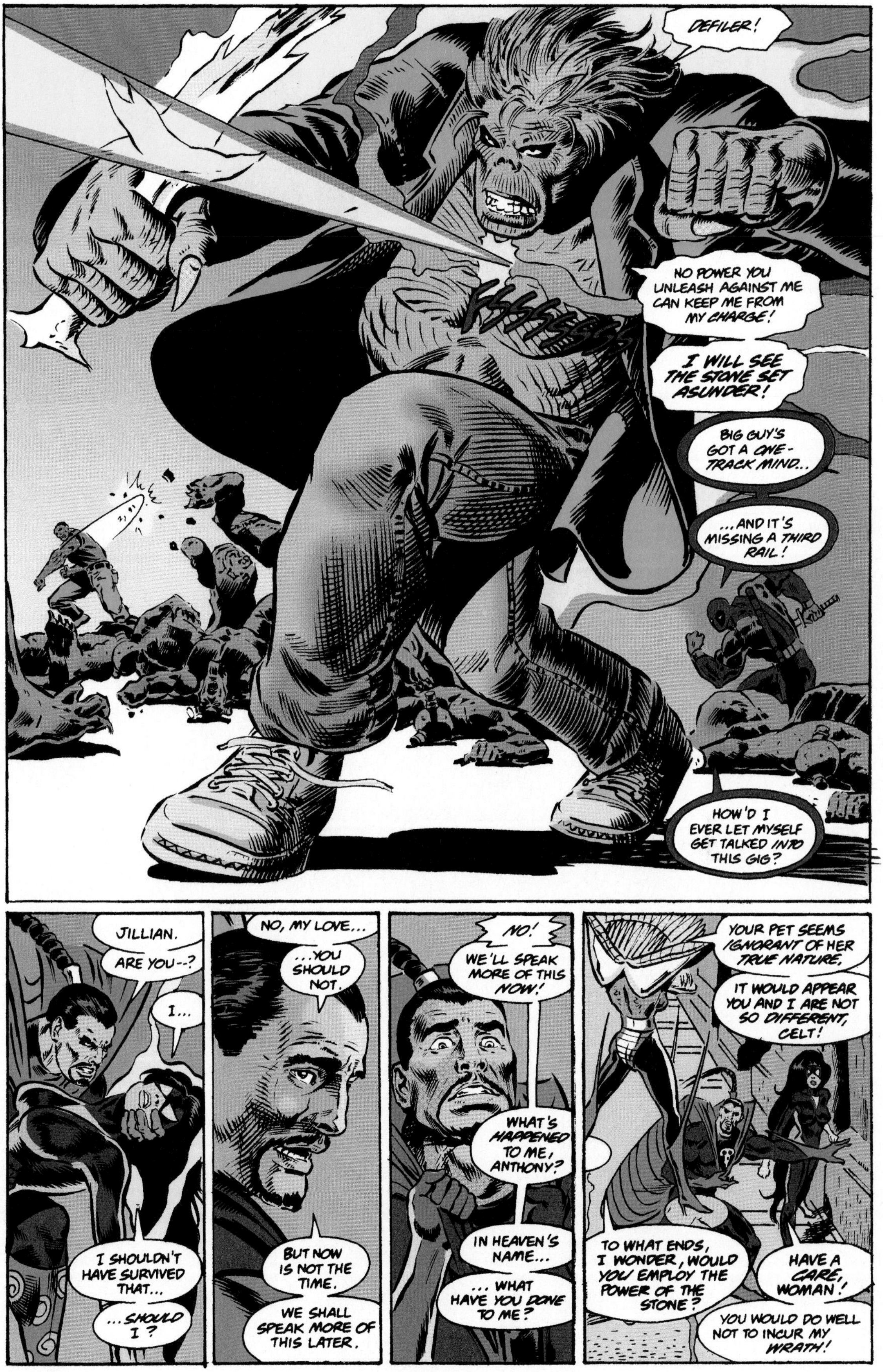
DEFILER!
FSSSSSSS
NO POWER YOU UNLEASH AGAINST ME CAN KEEP ME FROM MY CHARGE!
I WILL SEE THE STONE SET ASUNDER!
BIG GUY'S GOT A ONE-TRACK MIND...
...AND IT'S MISSING A THIRD RAIL!
HOW'D I EVER LET MYSELF GET TALKED INTO THIS GIG?
JILLIAN.
ARE YOU--?
I...
I SHOULDN'T HAVE SURVIVED THAT...
...SHOULD I?
NO, MY LOVE...
...YOU SHOULD NOT.
BUT NOW IS NOT THE TIME.
WE SHALL SPEAK MORE OF THIS LATER.
NO!
WE'LL SPEAK MORE OF THIS NOW!
WHAT'S HAPPENED TO ME, ANTHONY?
IN HEAVEN'S NAME...
... WHAT HAVE YOU DONE TO ME?
YOUR PET SEEMS IGNORANT OF HER TRUE NATURE.
IT WOULD APPEAR YOU AND I ARE NOT SO DIFFERENT, CELT!
TO WHAT ENDS, I WONDER, WOULD YOU EMPLOY THE POWER OF THE STONE?
HAVE A CARE, WOMAN!
YOU WOULD DO WELL NOT TO INCUR MY WRATH!

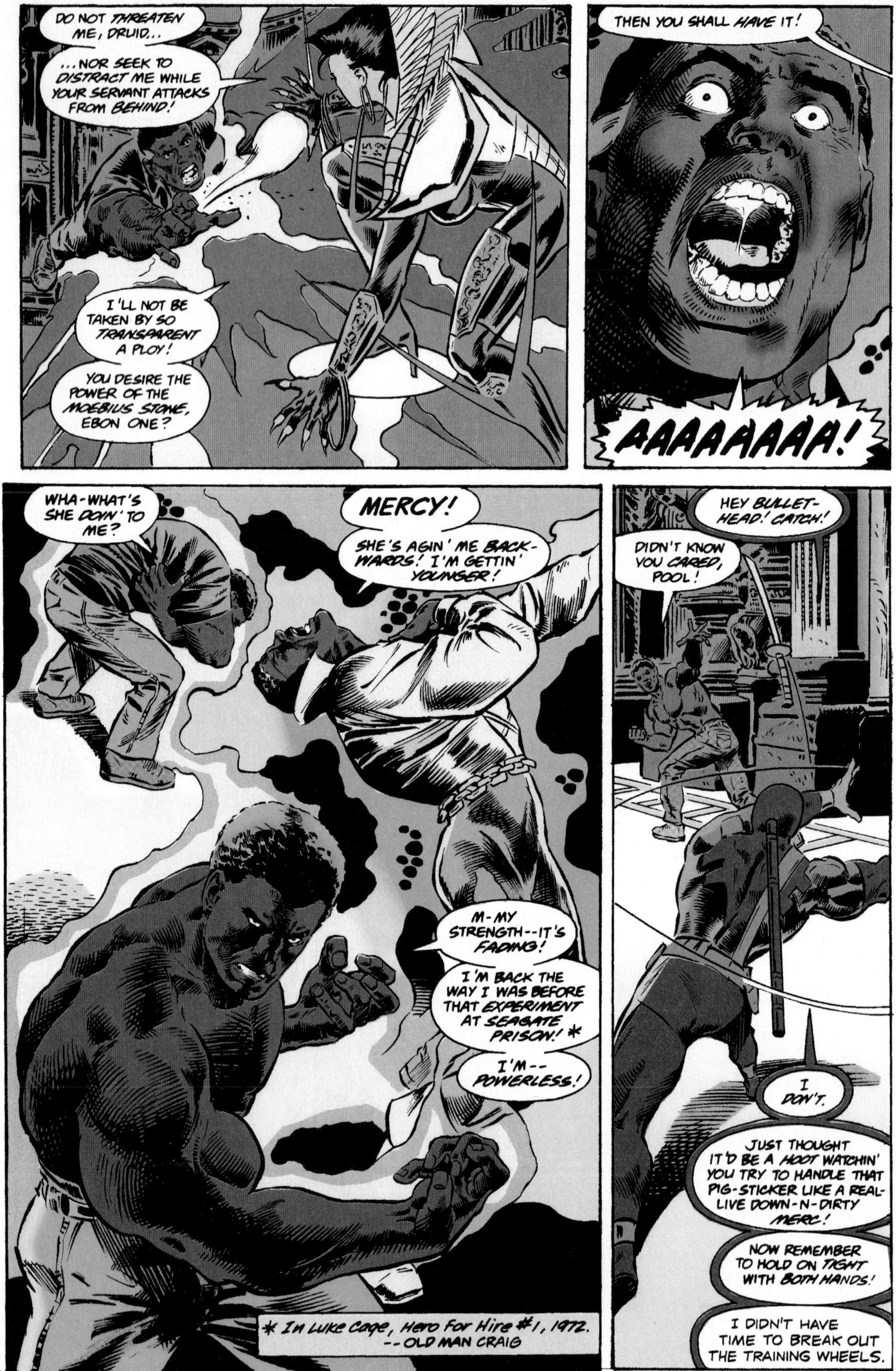

DO NOT THREATEN ME, DRUID...
...NOR SEEK TO DISTRACT ME WHILE YOUR SERVANT ATTACKS FROM BEHIND!
I'LL NOT BE TAKEN BY SO TRANSPARENT A PLOY!
YOU DESIRE THE POWER OF THE MOEBIUS STONE, EBON ONE?
THEN YOU SHALL HAVE IT!
AAAAAAAA!
WHA-WHAT'S SHE DOIN' TO ME?
MERCY!
SHE'S AGIN' ME BACKWARDS! I'M GETTIN' YOUNGER!
M-MY STRENGTH--IT'S FADING!
I'M BACK THE WAY I WAS BEFORE THAT EXPERIMENT AT SEAGATE PRISON! *
I'M--POWERLESS!
* In Luke Cage, Hero For Hire #1, 1972. --OLD MAN CRAIG
HEY BULLET-HEAD! CATCH!
DIDN'T KNOW YOU CARED, POOL!
I DON'T.
JUST THOUGHT IT'D BE A HOOT WATCHIN' YOU TRY TO HANDLE THAT PIG-STICKER LIKE A REAL-LIVE DOWN-N-DIRTY MERC!
NOW REMEMBER TO HOLD ON TIGHT WITH BOTH HANDS!
I DIDN'T HAVE TIME TO BREAK OUT THE TRAINING WHEELS.

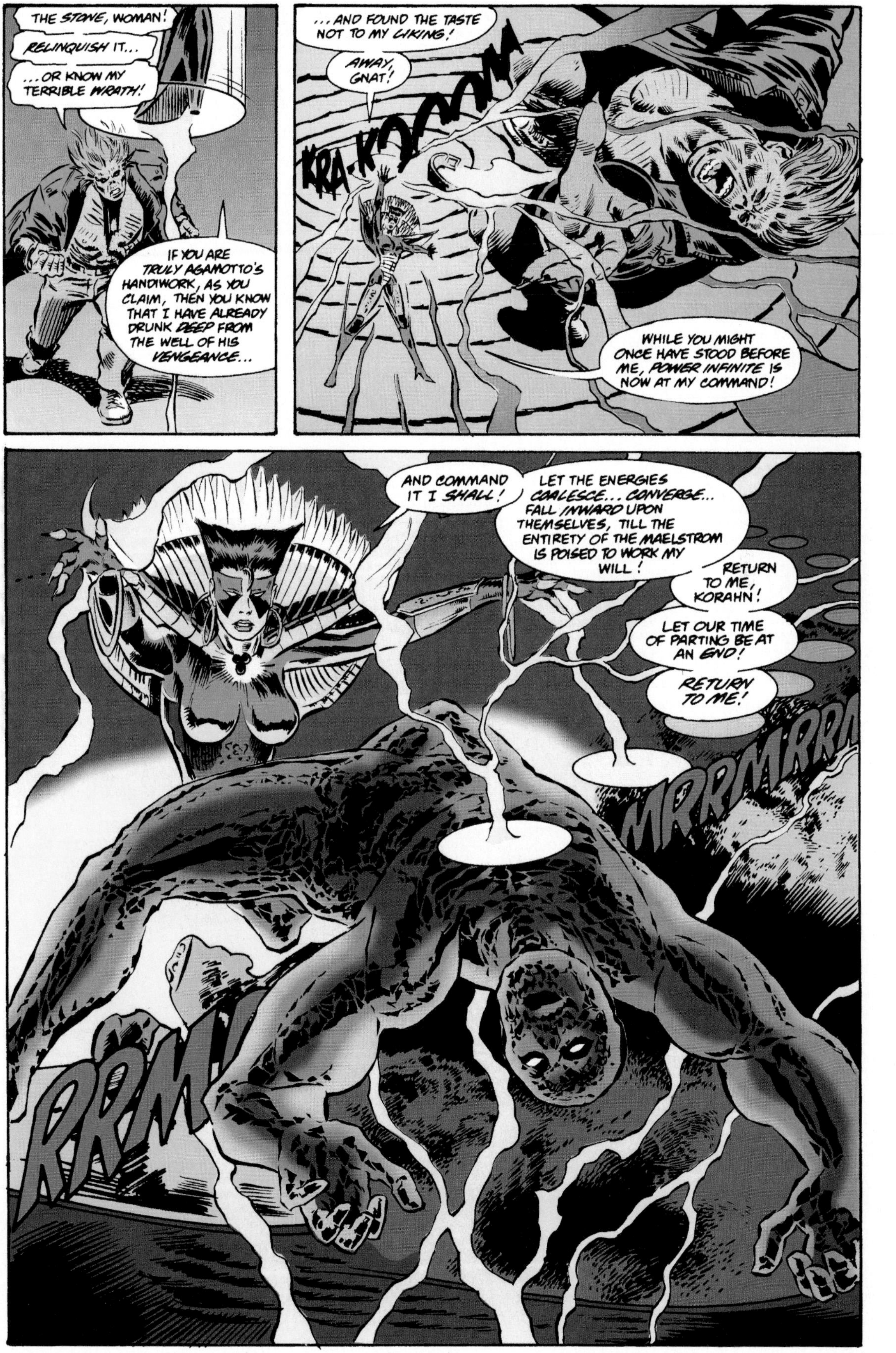

THE STONE, WOMAN!
RELINQUISH IT...
...OR KNOW MY TERRIBLE WRATH!
IF YOU ARE TRULY AGAMOTTO'S HANDIWORK, AS YOU CLAIM, THEN YOU KNOW THAT I HAVE ALREADY DRUNK DEEP FROM THE WELL OF HIS VENGEANCE...
...AND FOUND THE TASTE NOT TO MY LIKING!
AWAY, GNAT!
KRA-KOOOM
WHILE YOU MIGHT ONCE HAVE STOOD BEFORE ME, POWER INFINITE IS NOW AT MY COMMAND!
AND COMMAND IT I SHALL!
LET THE ENERGIES COALESCE... CONVERGE... FALL INWARD UPON THEMSELVES, TILL THE ENTIRETY OF THE MAELSTROM IS POISED TO WORK MY WILL!
RETURN TO ME, KORAHN!
LET OUR TIME OF PARTING BE AT AN END!
RETURN TO ME!
MRRMRRM
RRM

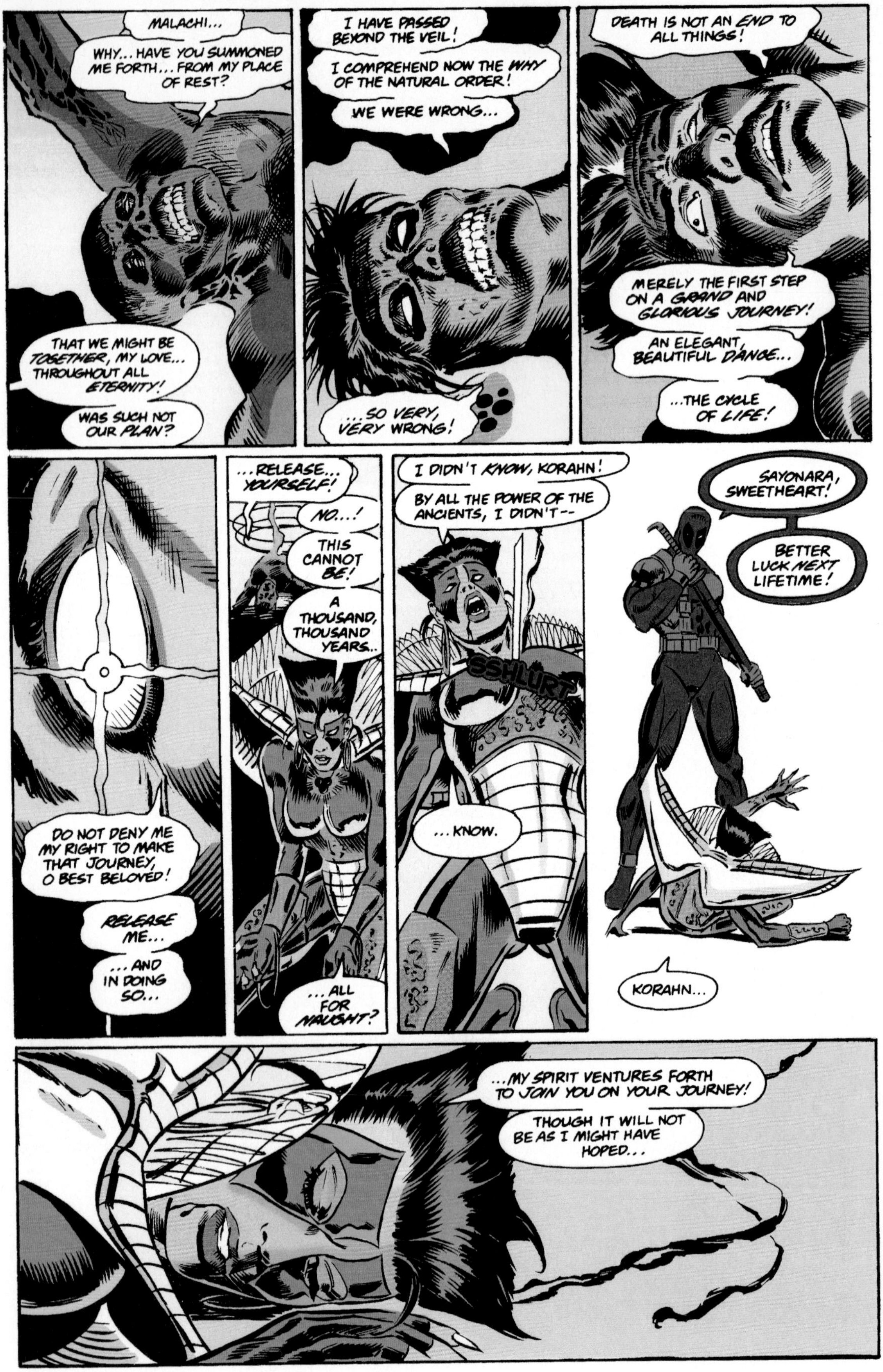
MALACHI...
WHY... HAVE YOU SUMMONED ME FORTH... FROM MY PLACE OF REST?
THAT WE MIGHT BE TOGETHER, MY LOVE... THROUGHOUT ALL ETERNITY!
WAS SUCH NOT OUR PLAN?
I HAVE PASSED BEYOND THE VEIL!
I COMPREHEND NOW THE WHY OF THE NATURAL ORDER!
WE WERE WRONG...
...SO VERY, VERY WRONG!
DEATH IS NOT AN END TO ALL THINGS!
MERELY THE FIRST STEP ON A GRAND AND GLORIOUS JOURNEY!
AN ELEGANT, BEAUTIFUL DANCE...
...THE CYCLE OF LIFE!
DO NOT DENY ME MY RIGHT TO MAKE THAT JOURNEY, O BEST BELOVED!
RELEASE ME...
...AND IN DOING SO...
...RELEASE... YOURSELF!
NO...!
THIS CANNOT BE!
A THOUSAND, THOUSAND YEARS...
...ALL FOR NAUGHT?
I DIDN'T KNOW, KORAHN!
BY ALL THE POWER OF THE ANCIENTS, I DIDN'T--
SSHLURT
...KNOW.
SAYONARA, SWEETHEART!
BETTER LUCK NEXT LIFETIME!
KORAHN...
...MY SPIRIT VENTURES FORTH TO JOIN YOU ON YOUR JOURNEY!
THOUGH IT WILL NOT BE AS I MIGHT HAVE HOPED...

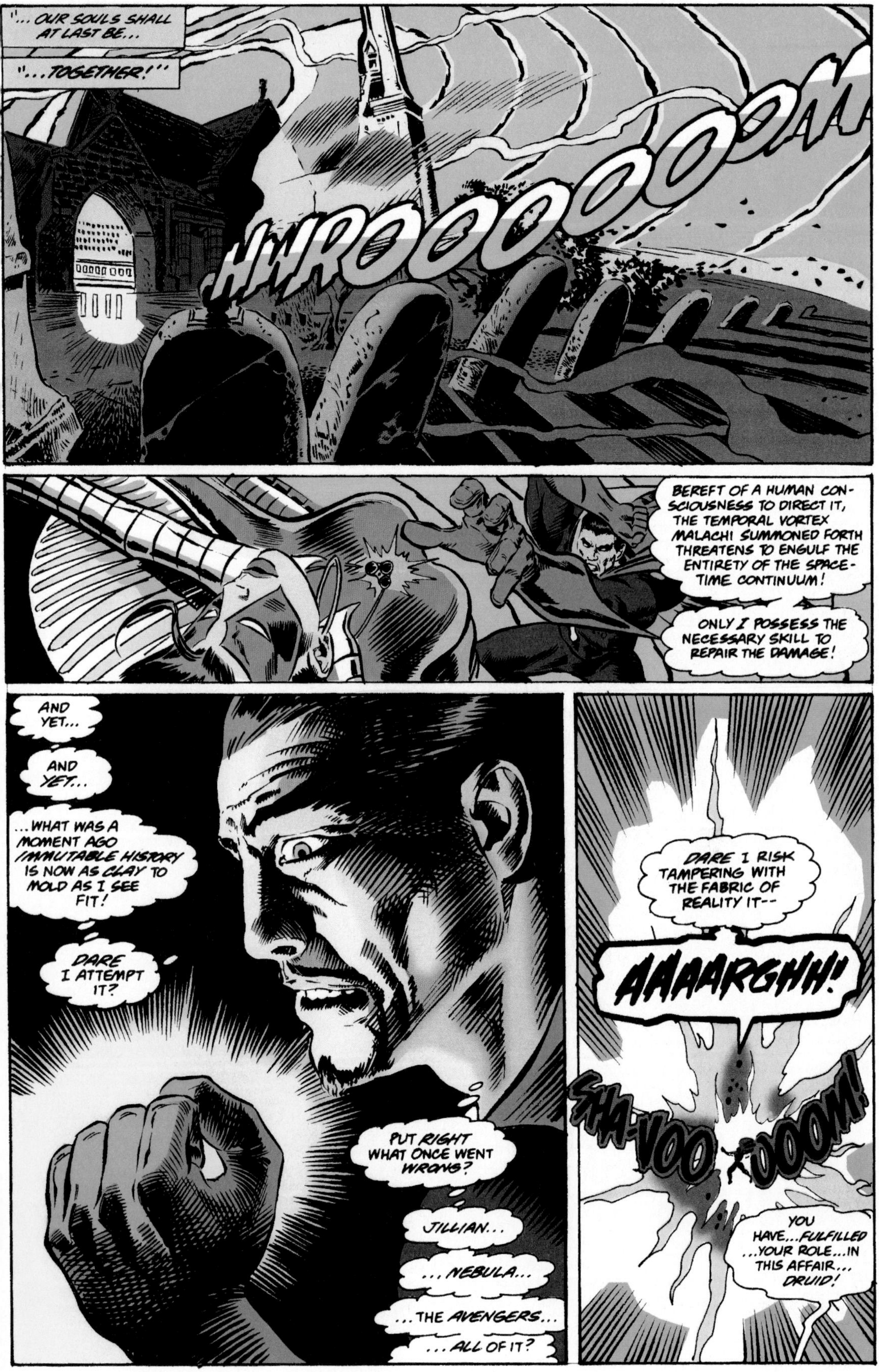
"... OUR SOULS SHALL AT LAST BE...
"...TOGETHER!"
HWROOOOOOOOAAAA
BEREFT OF A HUMAN CONSCIOUSNESS TO DIRECT IT, THE TEMPORAL VORTEX MALACHI SUMMONED FORTH THREATENS TO ENGULF THE ENTIRETY OF THE SPACE-TIME CONTINUUM!
ONLY I POSSESS THE NECESSARY SKILL TO REPAIR THE DAMAGE!
AND YET...
AND YET...
...WHAT WAS A MOMENT AGO IMMUTABLE HISTORY IS NOW AS CLAY TO MOLD AS I SEE FIT!
DARE I ATTEMPT IT?
PUT RIGHT WHAT ONCE WENT WRONG?
JILLIAN...
...NEBULA...
...THE AVENGERS...
...ALL OF IT?
DARE I RISK TAMPERING WITH THE FABRIC OF REALITY IT--
AAAARGHH!
SHA-VOOOOOM!
YOU HAVE...FULFILLED ...YOUR ROLE...IN THIS AFFAIR... DRUID!

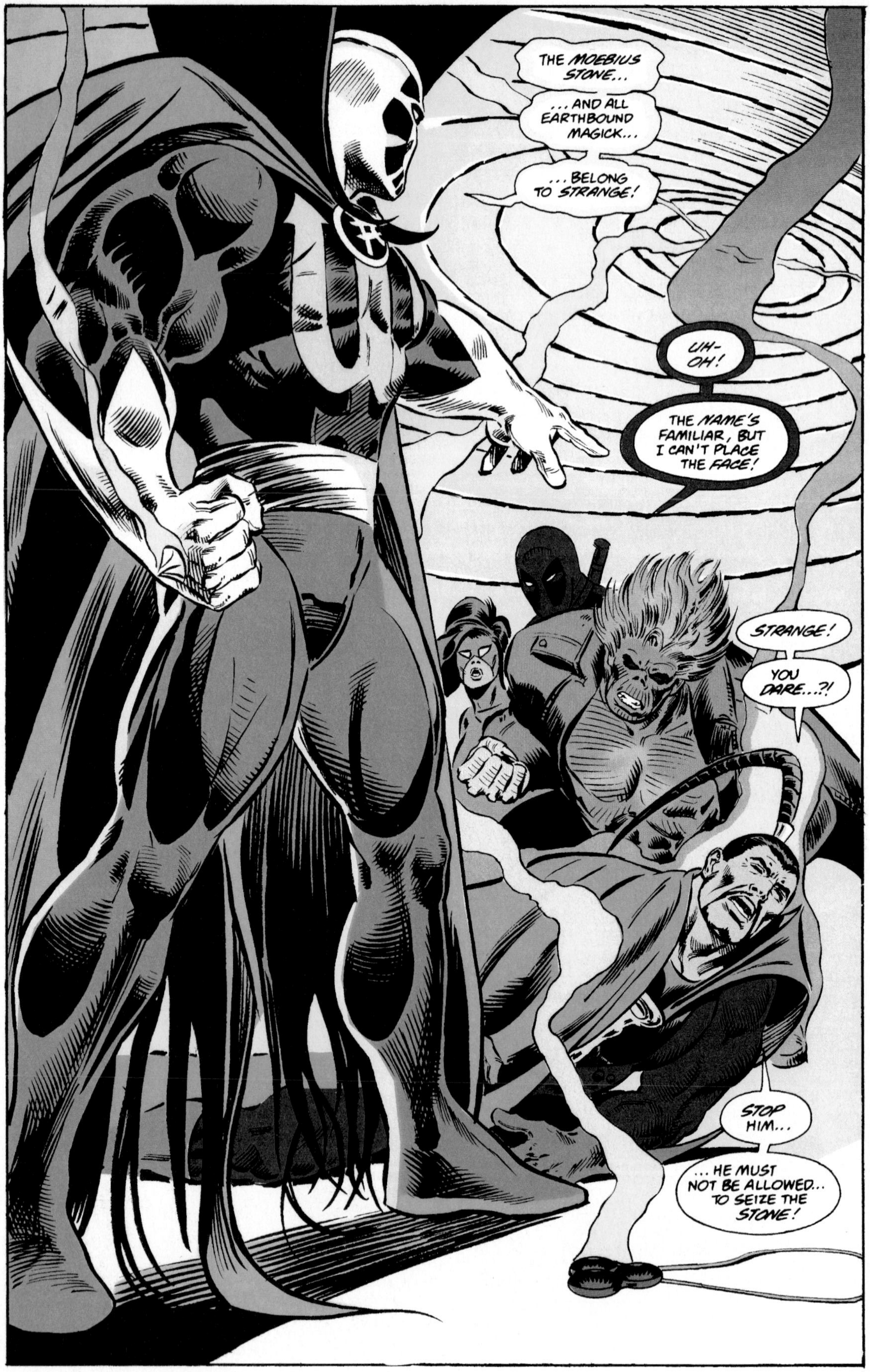
THE MOEBIUS STONE...
...AND ALL EARTHBOUND MAGICK...
...BELONG TO STRANGE!
UH-OH!
THE NAME'S FAMILIAR, BUT I CAN'T PLACE THE FACE!
STRANGE!
YOU DARE...?!
STOP HIM...
...HE MUST NOT BE ALLOWED... TO SEIZE THE STONE!

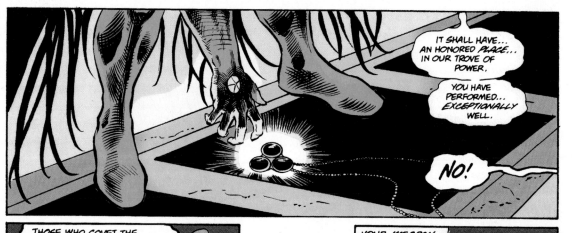

IT SHALL HAVE... AN HONORED *PLACE*... IN OUR TROVE OF POWER.

YOU HAVE PERFORMED... *EXCEPTIONALLY* WELL.

NO!

THOSE WHO COVET THE TREASURES OF AGAMOTTO...

...NEED FIRST CONQUER THE *PALE HORSEMAN!*

AN INTERESTING... DISPLAY, CORPSE...

...BUT *INEFFECTUAL.*

THOUGH A CURIOSITY...

...YOU ARE OF LITTLE IMPORT...

...TO *STRANGE!*

SISSHUUUUUUUUUTTTT

FWOOM

YOUR *WEAPON,* HOWEVER...

...IS *ANOTHER* MATTER.

IT, TOO, BURNS WITH... *AETHERIC FIRE...*

...AND SHOULD PROVE...A WORTHY ADDITION TO--

AAAAA-- THE SWORD... REBELS AT MY TOUCH!

SHAKA-KROOOOOOOM!

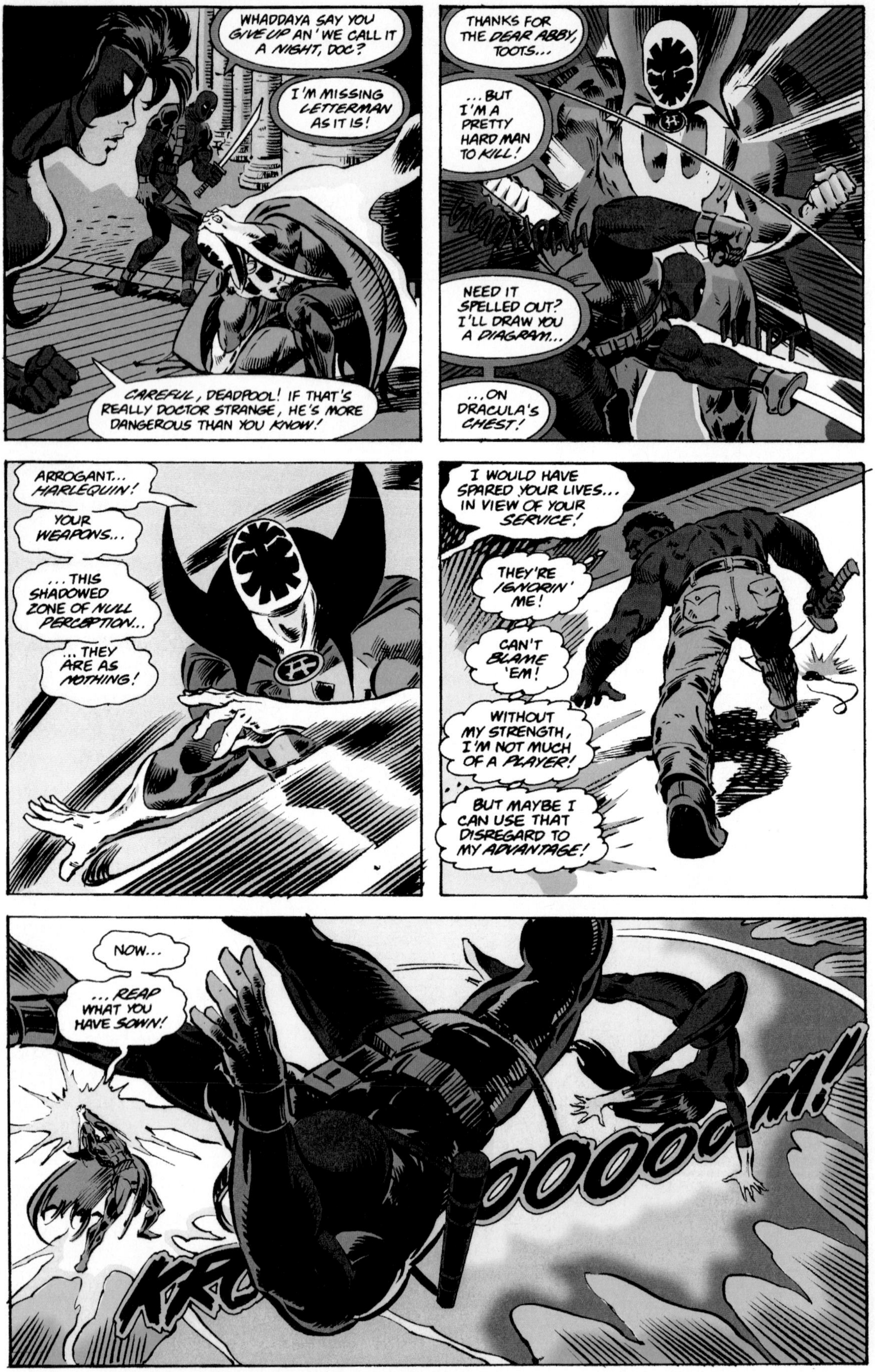
WHADDAYA SAY YOU GIVE UP AN' WE CALL IT A NIGHT, DOC?
I'M MISSING LETTERMAN AS IT IS!
CAREFUL, DEADPOOL! IF THAT'S REALLY DOCTOR STRANGE, HE'S MORE DANGEROUS THAN YOU KNOW!
THANKS FOR THE DEAR ABBY, TOOTS...
...BUT I'M A PRETTY HARD MAN TO KILL!
NEED IT SPELLED OUT? I'LL DRAW YOU A DIAGRAM...
...ON DRACULA'S CHEST!
ARROGANT... HARLEQUIN!
YOUR WEAPONS...
...THIS SHADOWED ZONE OF NULL PERCEPTION...
...THEY ARE AS NOTHING!
I WOULD HAVE SPARED YOUR LIVES... IN VIEW OF YOUR SERVICE!
THEY'RE IGNORIN' ME!
CAN'T BLAME 'EM!
WITHOUT MY STRENGTH, I'M NOT MUCH OF A PLAYER!
BUT MAYBE I CAN USE THAT DISREGARD TO MY ADVANTAGE!
NOW...
...REAP WHAT YOU HAVE SOWN!

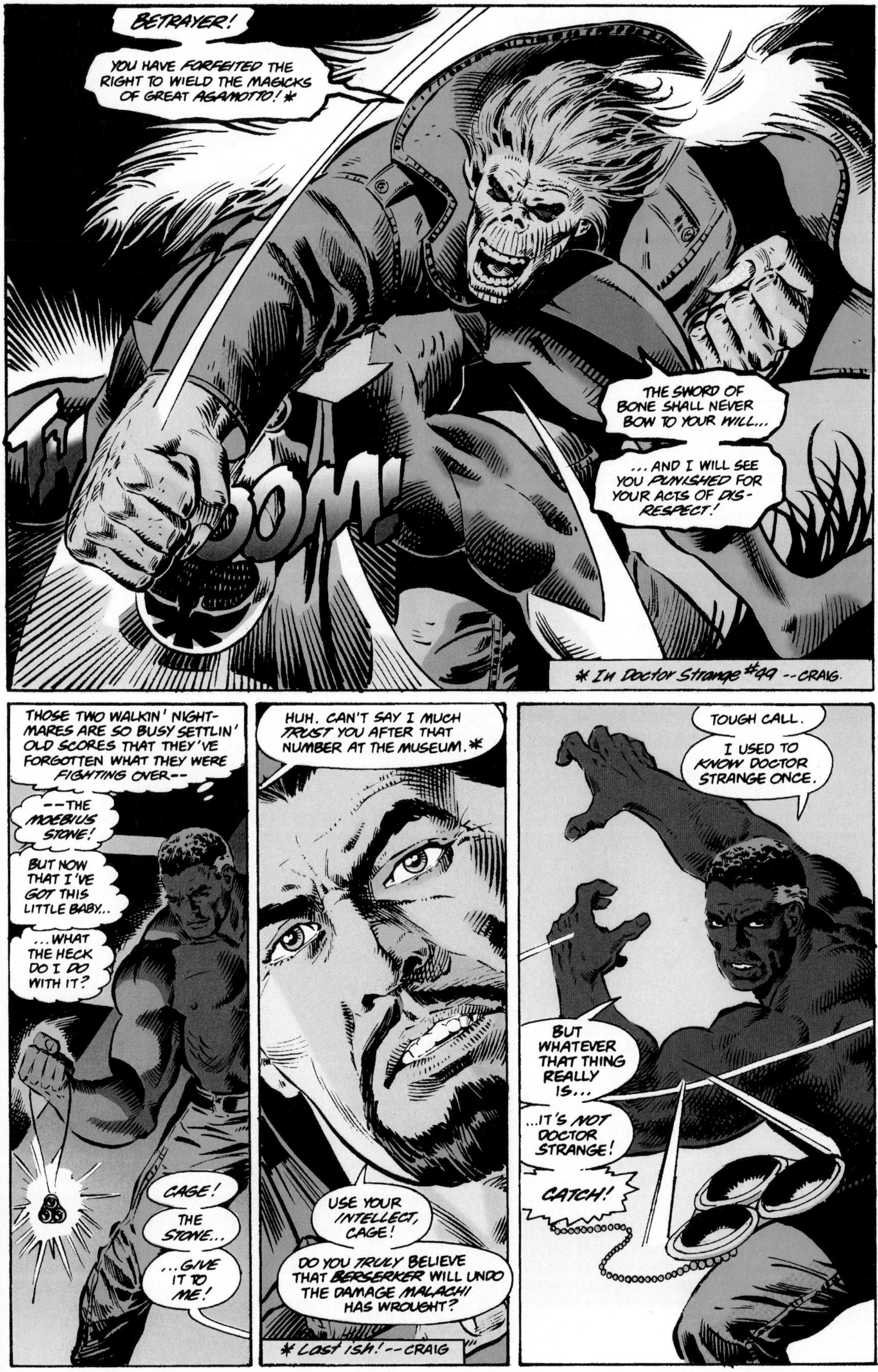

BETRAYER!
YOU HAVE FORFEITED THE RIGHT TO WIELD THE MAGICKS OF GREAT AGAMOTTO! *
THE SWORD OF BONE SHALL NEVER BOW TO YOUR WILL...
...AND I WILL SEE YOU PUNISHED FOR YOUR ACTS OF DIS-RESPECT!
* In Doctor Strange #49 --CRAIG.
THOSE TWO WALKIN' NIGHT-MARES ARE SO BUSY SETTLIN' OLD SCORES THAT THEY'VE FORGOTTEN WHAT THEY WERE FIGHTING OVER--
--THE MOEBIUS STONE!
BUT NOW THAT I'VE GOT THIS LITTLE BABY...
...WHAT THE HECK DO I DO WITH IT?
CAGE!
THE STONE...
...GIVE IT TO ME!
HUH. CAN'T SAY I MUCH TRUST YOU AFTER THAT NUMBER AT THE MUSEUM. *
USE YOUR INTELLECT, CAGE!
DO YOU TRULY BELIEVE THAT BERSERKER WILL UNDO THE DAMAGE MALACHI HAS WROUGHT?
* Last ish! --CRAIG
TOUGH CALL.
I USED TO KNOW DOCTOR STRANGE ONCE.
BUT WHATEVER THAT THING REALLY IS...
...IT'S NOT DOCTOR STRANGE!
CATCH!

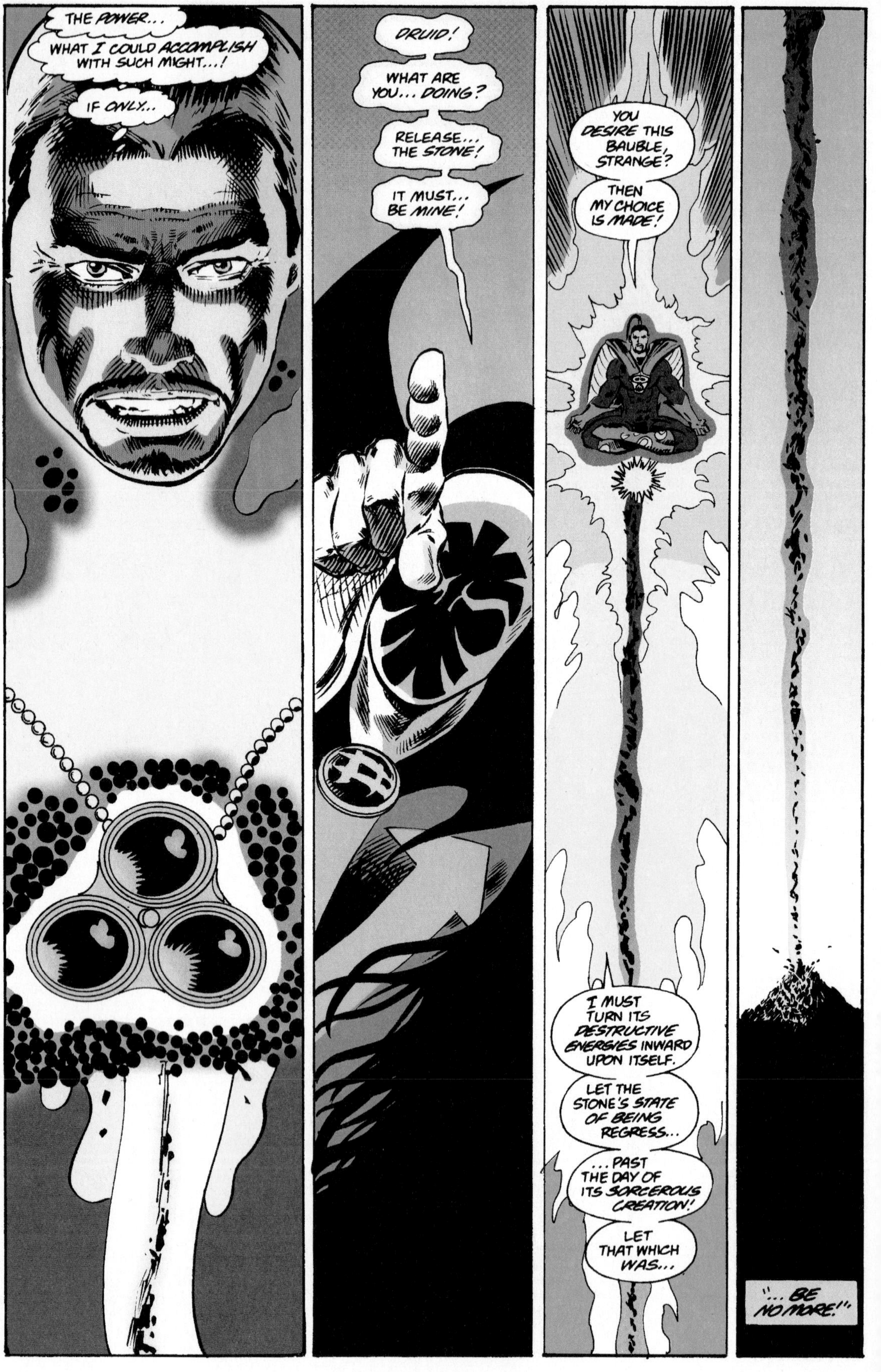
THE POWER...
WHAT I COULD ACCOMPLISH WITH SUCH MIGHT...!
IF ONLY...
DRUID!
WHAT ARE YOU... DOING?
RELEASE... THE STONE!
IT MUST... BE MINE!
YOU DESIRE THIS BAUBLE, STRANGE?
THEN MY CHOICE IS MADE!
I MUST TURN ITS DESTRUCTIVE ENERGIES INWARD UPON ITSELF.
LET THE STONE'S STATE OF BEING REGRESS...
...PAST THE DAY OF ITS SORCEROUS CREATION!
LET THAT WHICH WAS...
"... BE NO MORE!"

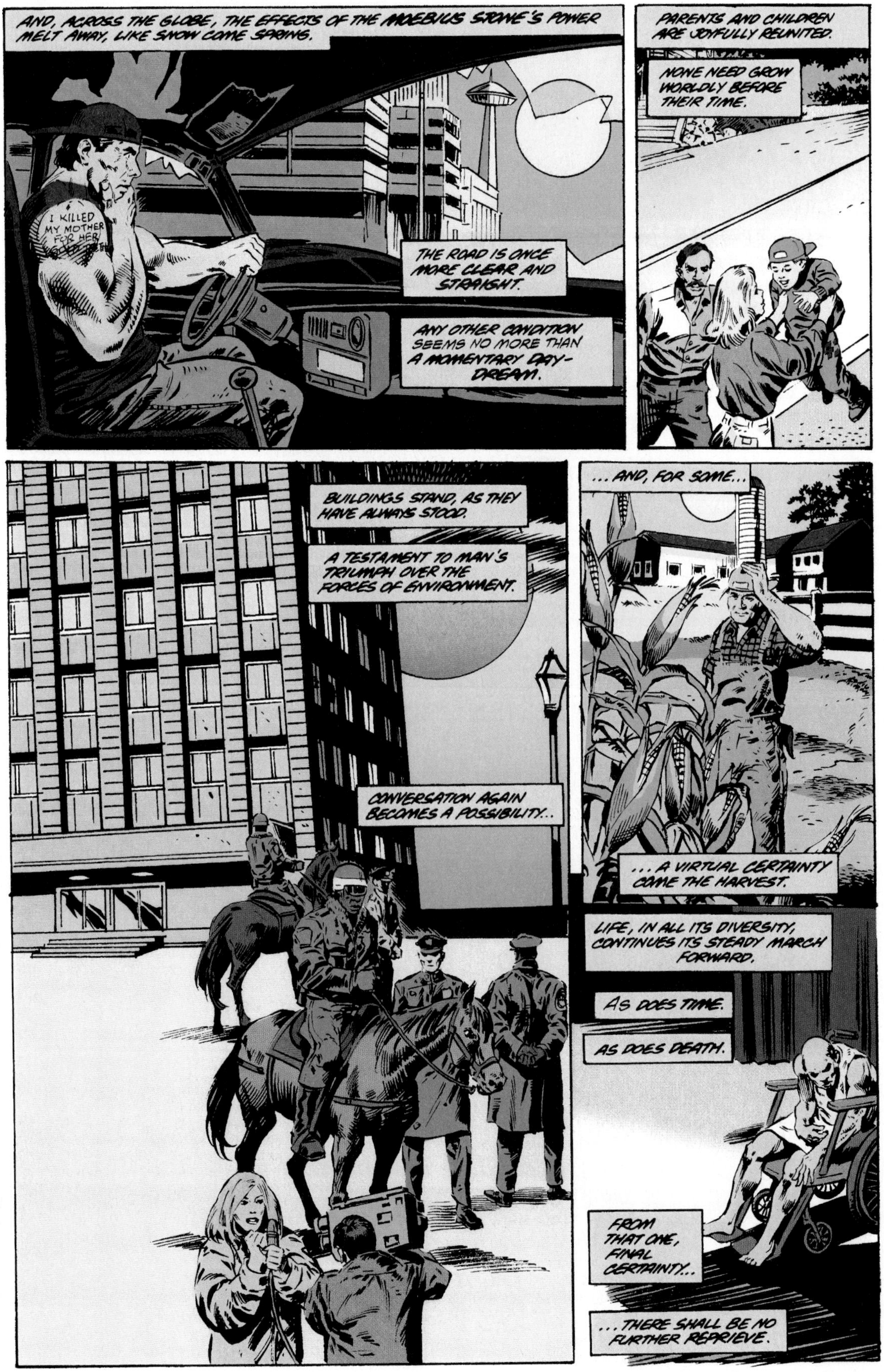
AND, ACROSS THE GLOBE, THE EFFECTS OF THE MOEBIUS STONE'S POWER MELT AWAY, LIKE SNOW COME SPRING.
I KILLED MY MOTHER FOR HER
THE ROAD IS ONCE MORE CLEAR AND STRAIGHT.
ANY OTHER CONDITION SEEMS NO MORE THAN A MOMENTARY DAY-DREAM.
PARENTS AND CHILDREN ARE JOYFULLY REUNITED.
NONE NEED GROW WORLDLY BEFORE THEIR TIME.
BUILDINGS STAND, AS THEY HAVE ALWAYS STOOD.
A TESTAMENT TO MAN'S TRIUMPH OVER THE FORCES OF ENVIRONMENT.
CONVERSATION AGAIN BECOMES A POSSIBILITY...
... AND, FOR SOME...
... A VIRTUAL CERTAINTY COME THE HARVEST.
LIFE, IN ALL ITS DIVERSITY, CONTINUES ITS STEADY MARCH FORWARD.
AS DOES TIME.
AS DOES DEATH.
FROM THAT ONE, FINAL CERTAINTY...
... THERE SHALL BE NO FURTHER REPRIEVE.

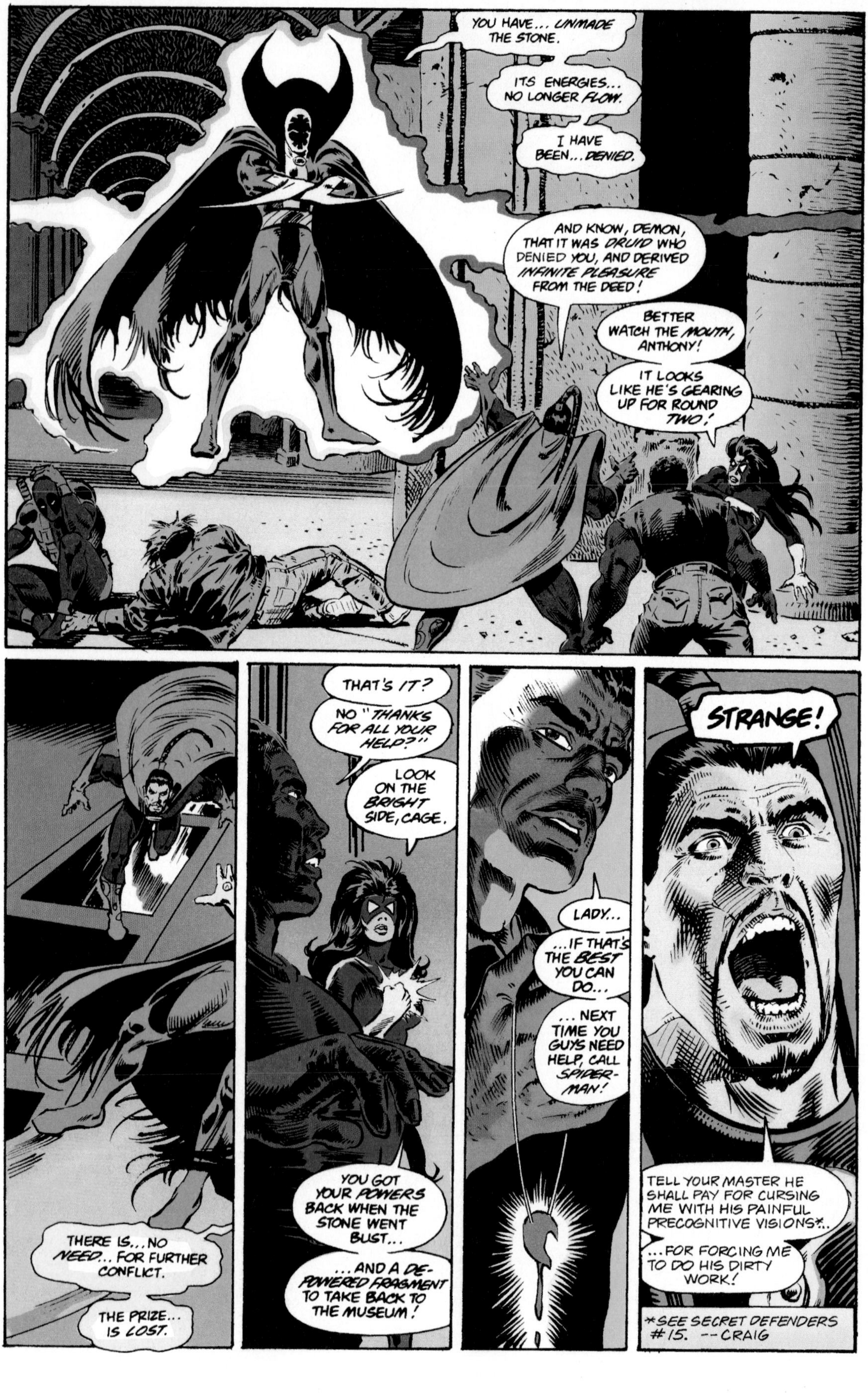

YOU HAVE... UNMADE THE STONE.
ITS ENERGIES... NO LONGER FLOW.
I HAVE BEEN... DENIED.
AND KNOW, DEMON, THAT IT WAS DRUID WHO DENIED YOU, AND DERIVED INFINITE PLEASURE FROM THE DEED!
BETTER WATCH THE MOUTH, ANTHONY!
IT LOOKS LIKE HE'S GEARING UP FOR ROUND TWO!
THERE IS... NO NEED... FOR FURTHER CONFLICT.
THE PRIZE... IS LOST.
THAT'S IT?
NO "THANKS FOR ALL YOUR HELP?"
LOOK ON THE BRIGHT SIDE, CAGE.
YOU GOT YOUR POWERS BACK WHEN THE STONE WENT BUST...
...AND A DE-POWERED FRAGMENT TO TAKE BACK TO THE MUSEUM!
LADY...
...IF THAT'S THE BEST YOU CAN DO...
... NEXT TIME YOU GUYS NEED HELP, CALL SPIDER-MAN!
STRANGE!
TELL YOUR MASTER HE SHALL PAY FOR CURSING ME WITH HIS PAINFUL PRECOGNITIVE VISIONS*...
...FOR FORCING ME TO DO HIS DIRTY WORK!
*SEE SECRET DEFENDERS #15. --CRAIG

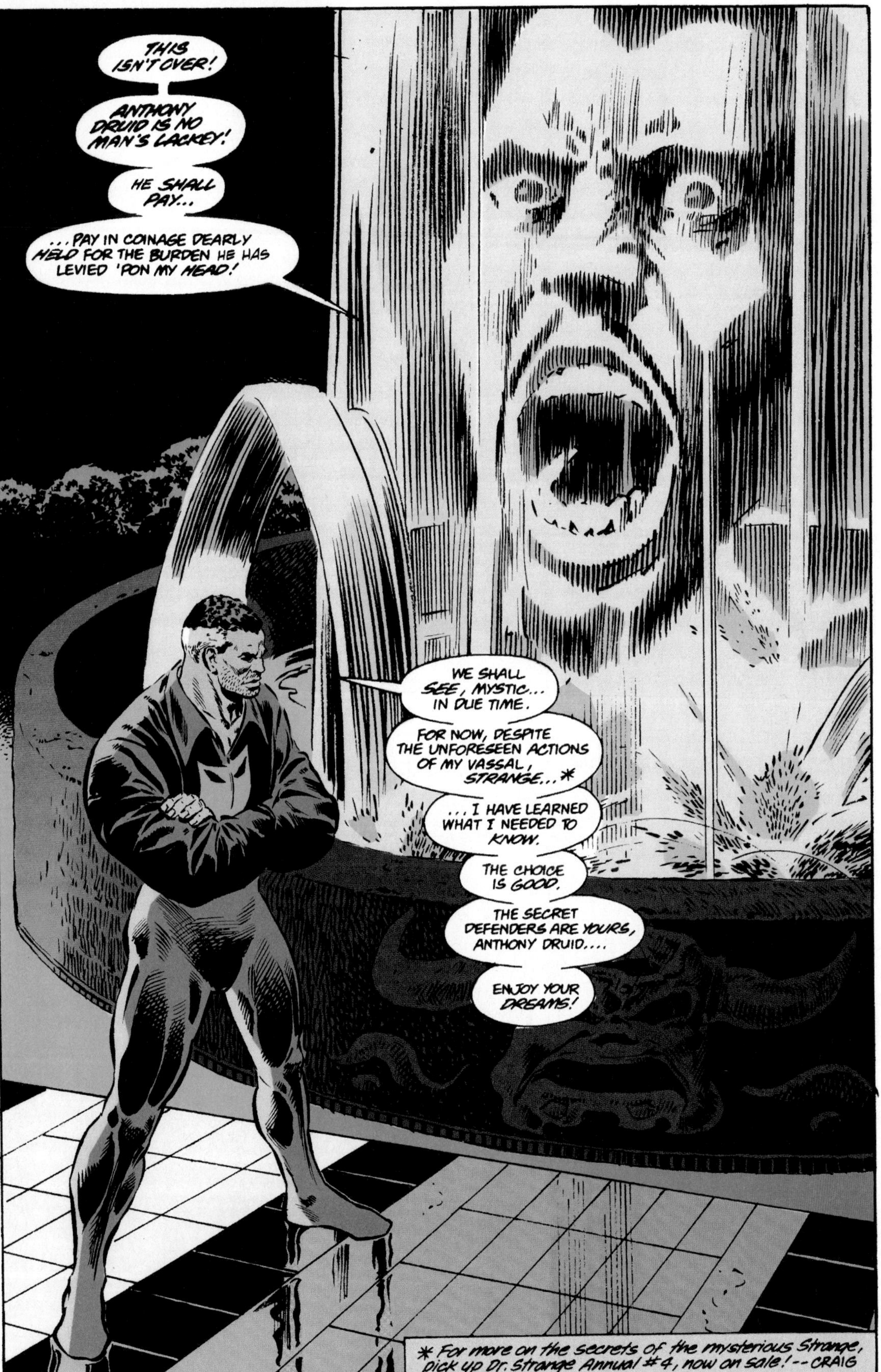
THIS ISN'T OVER!
ANTHONY DRUID IS NO MAN'S LACKEY!
HE SHALL PAY...
...PAY IN COINAGE DEARLY HELD FOR THE BURDEN HE HAS LEVIED 'PON MY HEAD!
WE SHALL SEE, MYSTIC... IN DUE TIME.
FOR NOW, DESPITE THE UNFORESEEN ACTIONS OF MY VASSAL, STRANGE...*
...I HAVE LEARNED WHAT I NEEDED TO KNOW.
THE CHOICE IS GOOD.
THE SECRET DEFENDERS ARE YOURS, ANTHONY DRUID....
ENJOY YOUR DREAMS!
* For more on the secrets of the mysterious Strange, pick up Dr. Strange Annual #4, now on sale! --CRAIG

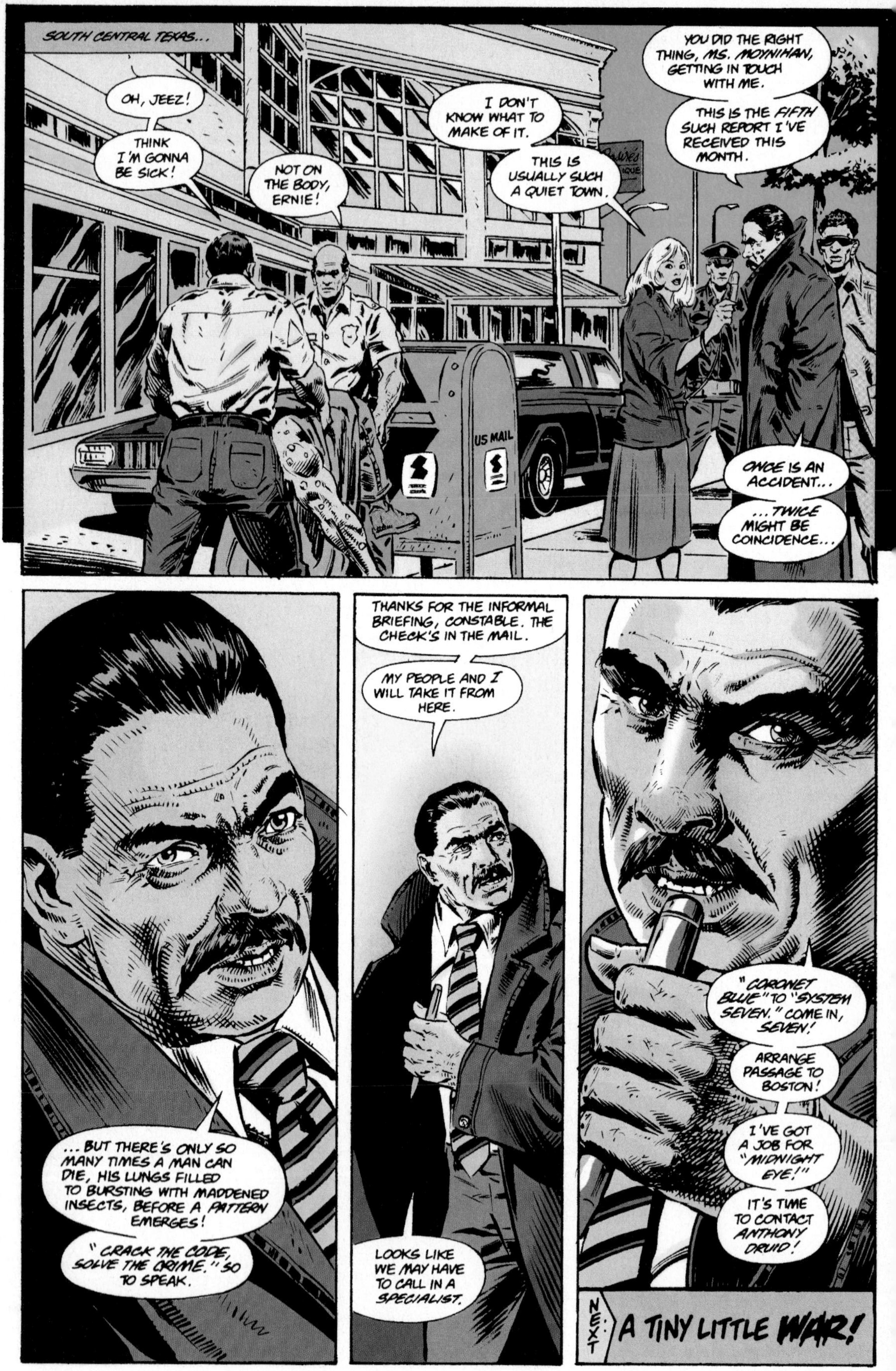
SOUTH CENTRAL TEXAS...
OH, JEEZ!
THINK I'M GONNA BE SICK!
NOT ON THE BODY, ERNIE!
I DON'T KNOW WHAT TO MAKE OF IT.
THIS IS USUALLY SUCH A QUIET TOWN.
YOU DID THE RIGHT THING, MS. MOYNIHAN, GETTING IN TOUCH WITH ME.
THIS IS THE FIFTH SUCH REPORT I'VE RECEIVED THIS MONTH.
US MAIL
ONCE IS AN ACCIDENT...
...TWICE MIGHT BE COINCIDENCE...
...BUT THERE'S ONLY SO MANY TIMES A MAN CAN DIE, HIS LUNGS FILLED TO BURSTING WITH MADDENED INSECTS, BEFORE A PATTERN EMERGES!
"CRACK THE CODE, SOLVE THE CRIME." SO TO SPEAK.
THANKS FOR THE INFORMAL BRIEFING, CONSTABLE. THE CHECK'S IN THE MAIL.
MY PEOPLE AND I WILL TAKE IT FROM HERE.
LOOKS LIKE WE MAY HAVE TO CALL IN A SPECIALIST.
"CORONET BLUE" TO "SYSTEM SEVEN." COME IN, SEVEN!
ARRANGE PASSAGE TO BOSTON!
I'VE GOT A JOB FOR "MIDNIGHT EYE!"
IT'S TIME TO CONTACT ANTHONY DRUID!
NEXT: A TINY LITTLE WAR!

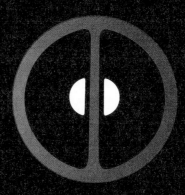

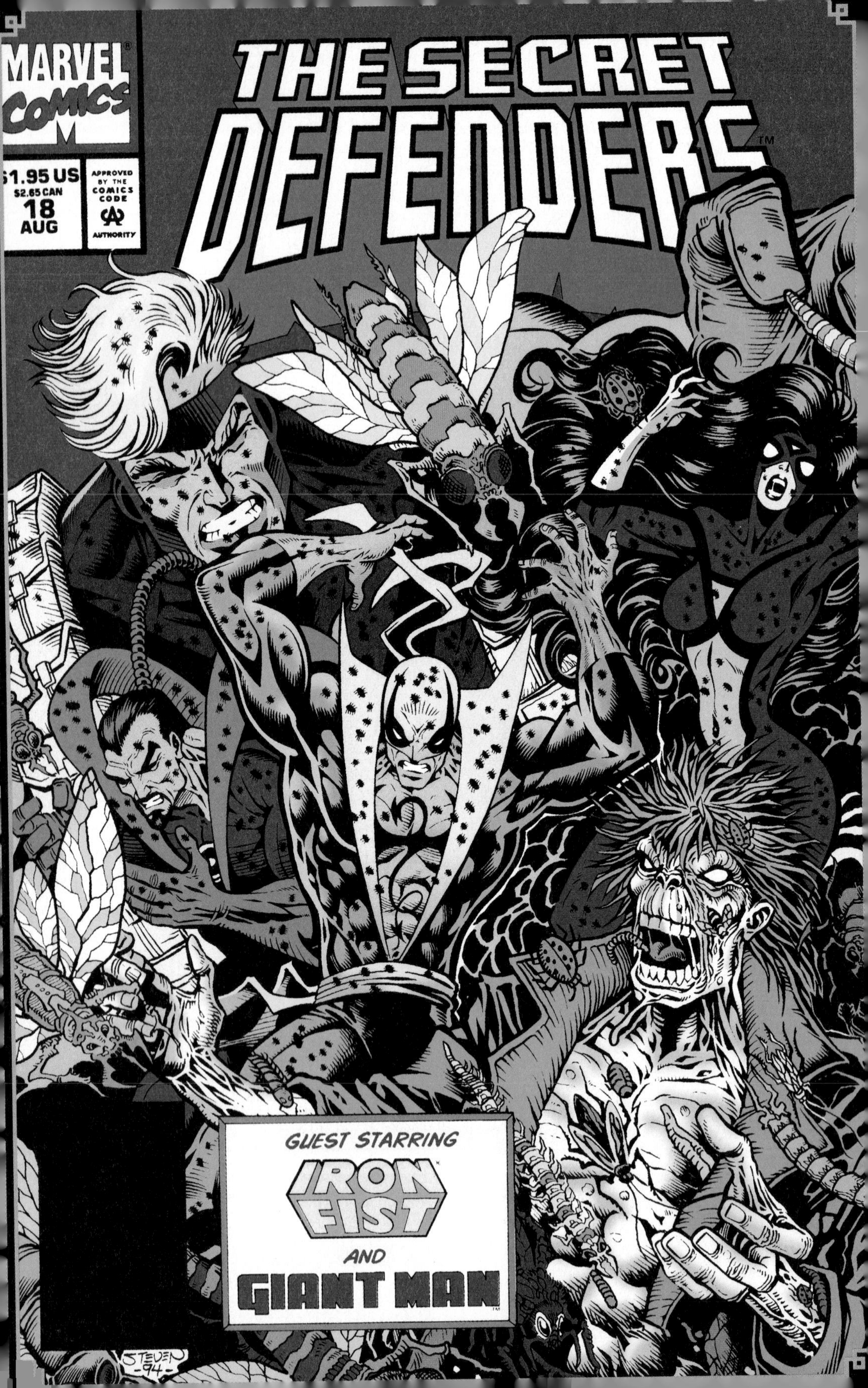

MARVEL COMICS
THE SECRET DEFENDERS™
$1.95 US
$2.65 CAN
18
AUG
APPROVED BY THE COMICS CODE AUTHORITY
GUEST STARRING
IRON FIST™
AND
GIANT MAN™
STEVEN -94-

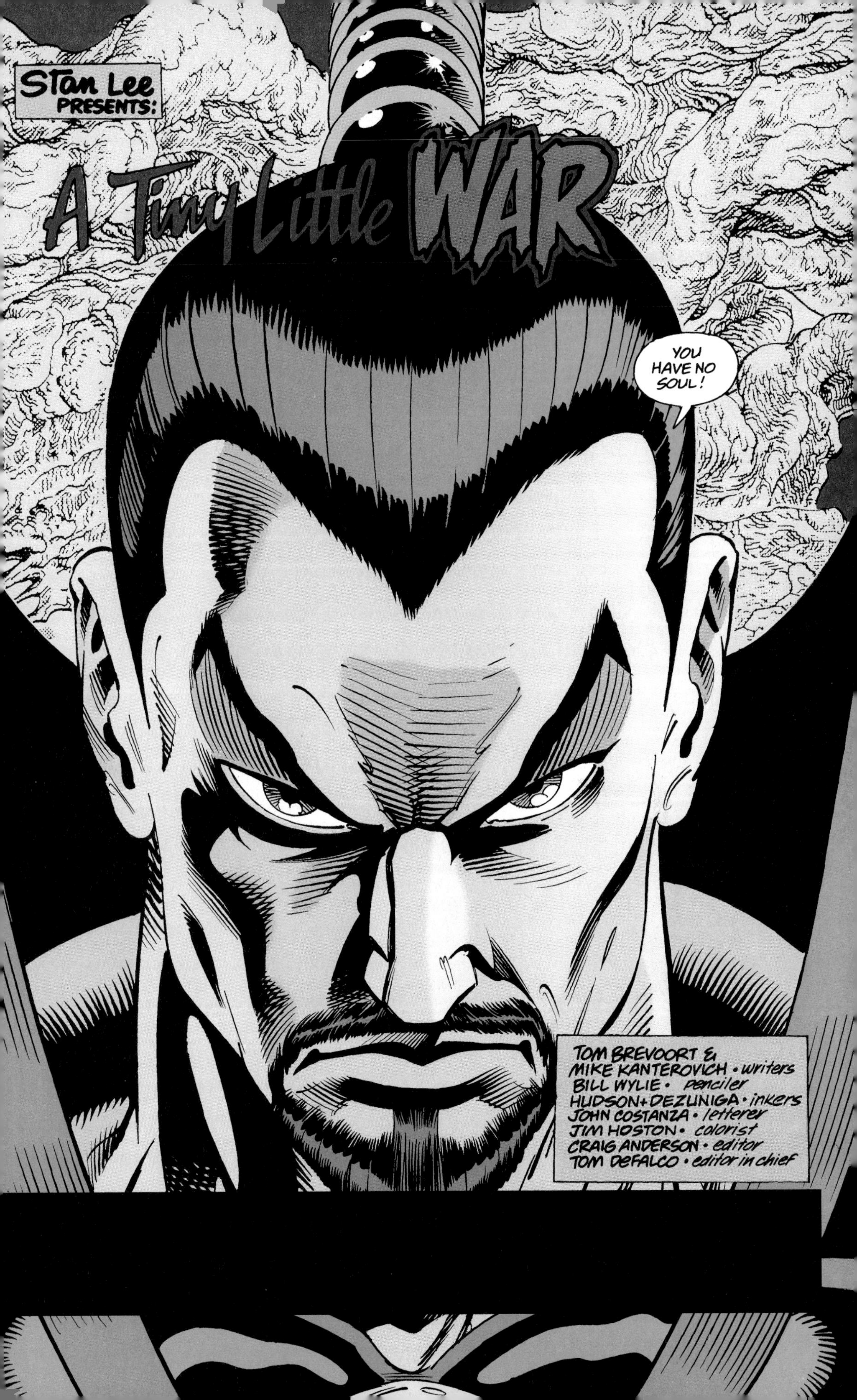

Stan Lee PRESENTS:
A Tiny Little WAR
YOU HAVE NO SOUL!
TOM BREVOORT & MIKE KANTEROVICH • writers
BILL WYLIE • penciler
HUDSON + DEZUNIGA • inkers
JOHN COSTANZA • letterer
JIM HOSTON • colorist
CRAIG ANDERSON • editor
TOM DEFALCO • editor in chief
[redacted]

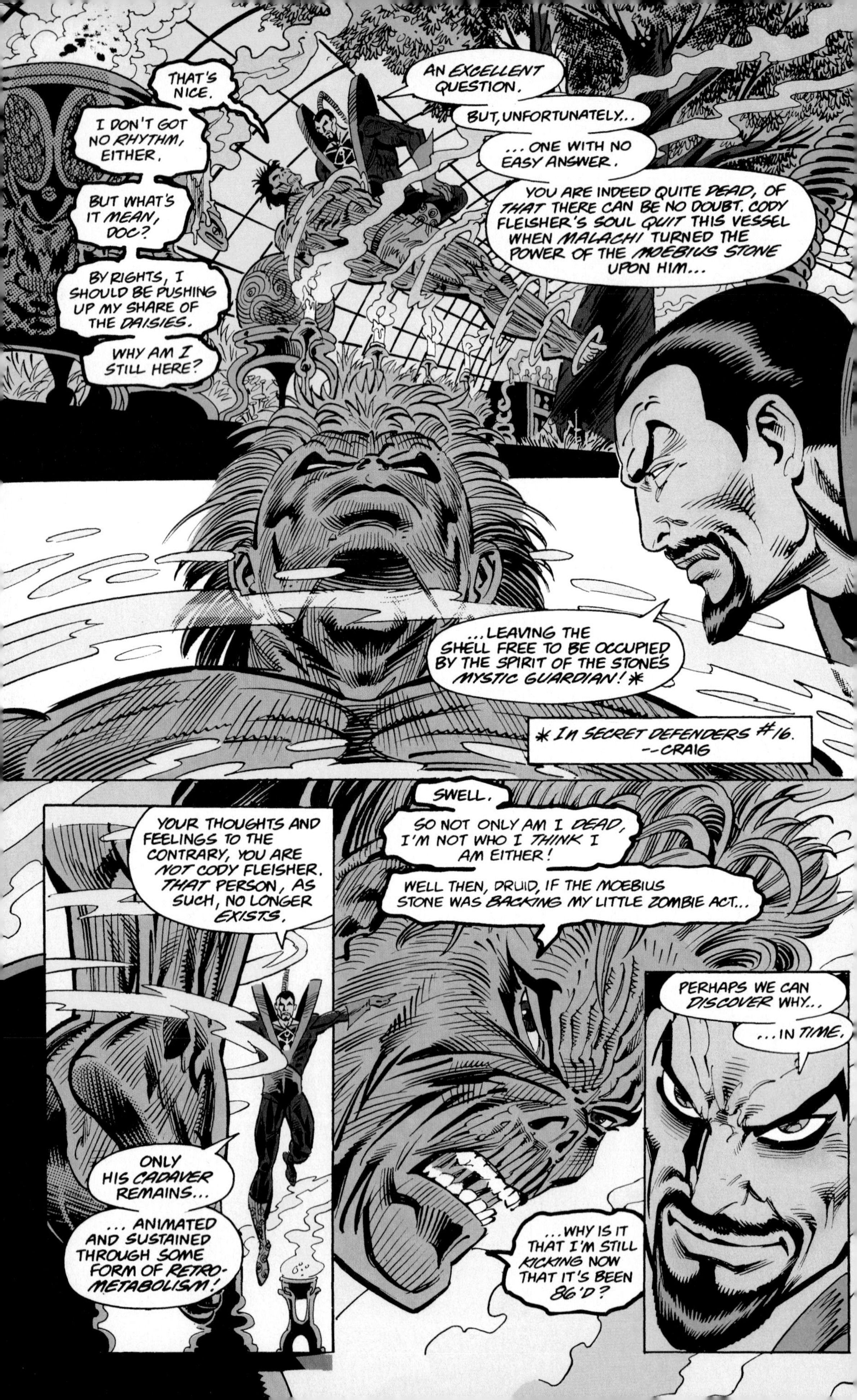

THAT'S NICE.
I DON'T GOT NO RHYTHM, EITHER.
BUT WHAT'S IT MEAN, DOC?
BY RIGHTS, I SHOULD BE PUSHING UP MY SHARE OF THE DAISIES.
WHY AM I STILL HERE?
AN EXCELLENT QUESTION.
BUT, UNFORTUNATELY...
... ONE WITH NO EASY ANSWER.
YOU ARE INDEED QUITE DEAD, OF THAT THERE CAN BE NO DOUBT. CODY FLEISHER'S SOUL QUIT THIS VESSEL WHEN MALACHI TURNED THE POWER OF THE MOEBIUS STONE UPON HIM...
...LEAVING THE SHELL FREE TO BE OCCUPIED BY THE SPIRIT OF THE STONE'S MYSTIC GUARDIAN! *
* In SECRET DEFENDERS #16. --CRAIG
YOUR THOUGHTS AND FEELINGS TO THE CONTRARY, YOU ARE NOT CODY FLEISHER. THAT PERSON, AS SUCH, NO LONGER EXISTS.
SWELL.
SO NOT ONLY AM I DEAD, I'M NOT WHO I THINK I AM EITHER!
WELL THEN, DRUID, IF THE MOEBIUS STONE WAS BACKING MY LITTLE ZOMBIE ACT...
ONLY HIS CADAVER REMAINS...
... ANIMATED AND SUSTAINED THROUGH SOME FORM OF RETRO-METABOLISM!
...WHY IS IT THAT I'M STILL KICKING NOW THAT IT'S BEEN 86'D?
PERHAPS WE CAN DISCOVER WHY...
...IN TIME.

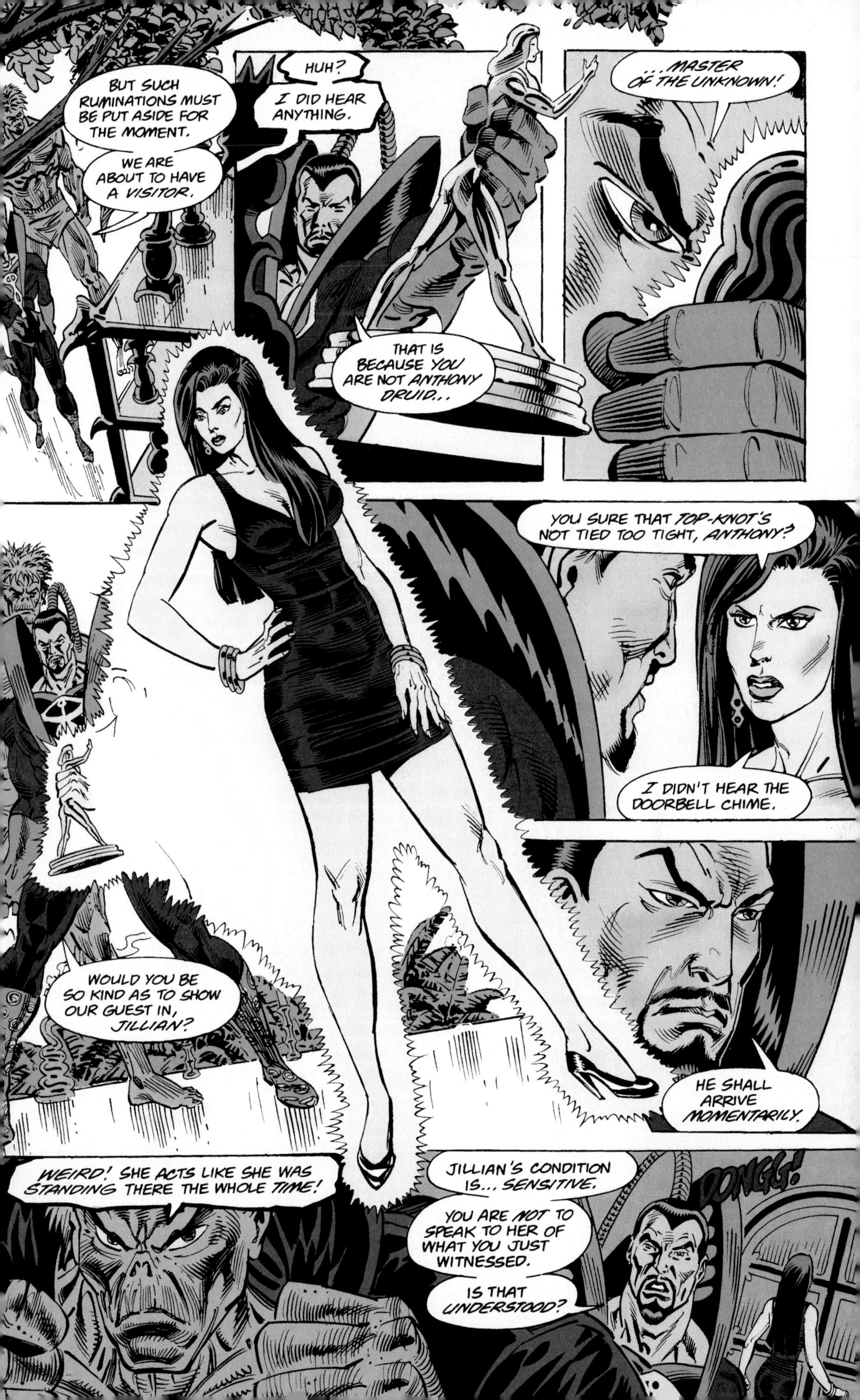
BUT SUCH RUMINATIONS MUST BE PUT ASIDE FOR THE MOMENT.
WE ARE ABOUT TO HAVE A VISITOR.
HUH?
I DID HEAR ANYTHING.
THAT IS BECAUSE YOU ARE NOT ANTHONY DRUID...
...MASTER OF THE UNKNOWN!
WOULD YOU BE SO KIND AS TO SHOW OUR GUEST IN, JILLIAN?
YOU SURE THAT TOP-KNOT'S NOT TIED TOO TIGHT, ANTHONY?
I DIDN'T HEAR THE DOORBELL CHIME.
HE SHALL ARRIVE MOMENTARILY.
WEIRD! SHE ACTS LIKE SHE WAS STANDING THERE THE WHOLE TIME!
JILLIAN'S CONDITION IS... SENSITIVE.
YOU ARE NOT TO SPEAK TO HER OF WHAT YOU JUST WITNESSED.
IS THAT UNDERSTOOD?
DONGG!

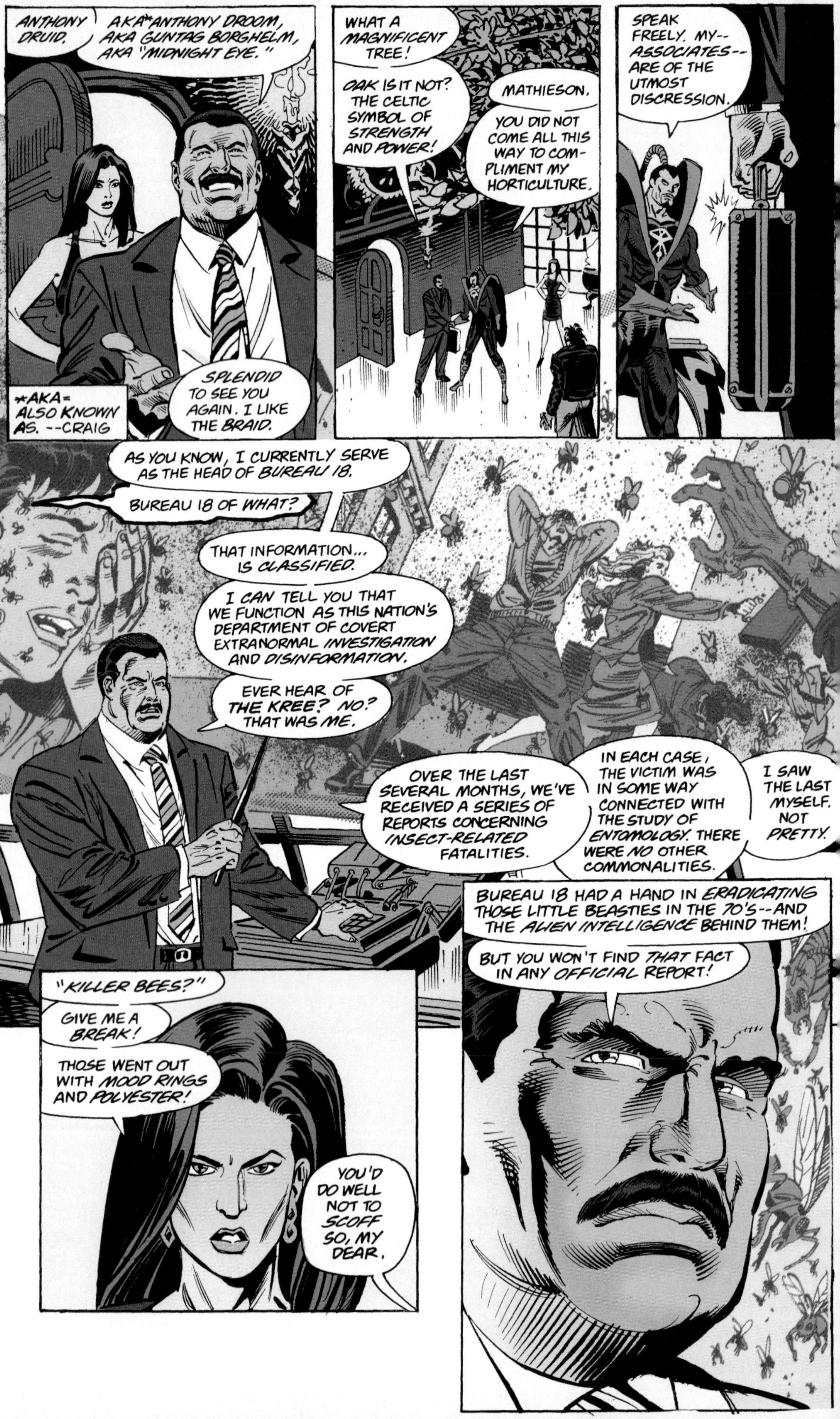
ANTHONY DRUID.
AKA* ANTHONY DROOM, AKA GUNTAG BORGHELM, AKA "MIDNIGHT EYE."
*AKA= ALSO KNOWN AS. --CRAIG
SPLENDID TO SEE YOU AGAIN. I LIKE THE BRAID.
WHAT A MAGNIFICENT TREE!
OAK IS IT NOT? THE CELTIC SYMBOL OF STRENGTH AND POWER!
MATHIESON.
YOU DID NOT COME ALL THIS WAY TO COMPLIMENT MY HORTICULTURE.
SPEAK FREELY. MY-- ASSOCIATES-- ARE OF THE UTMOST DISCRESSION.
AS YOU KNOW, I CURRENTLY SERVE AS THE HEAD OF BUREAU 18.
BUREAU 18 OF WHAT?
THAT INFORMATION... IS CLASSIFIED.
I CAN TELL YOU THAT WE FUNCTION AS THIS NATION'S DEPARTMENT OF COVERT EXTRANORMAL INVESTIGATION AND DISINFORMATION.
EVER HEAR OF THE KREE? NO? THAT WAS ME.
OVER THE LAST SEVERAL MONTHS, WE'VE RECEIVED A SERIES OF REPORTS CONCERNING INSECT-RELATED FATALITIES.
IN EACH CASE, THE VICTIM WAS IN SOME WAY CONNECTED WITH THE STUDY OF ENTOMOLOGY. THERE WERE NO OTHER COMMONALITIES.
I SAW THE LAST MYSELF. NOT PRETTY.
"KILLER BEES?"
GIVE ME A BREAK!
THOSE WENT OUT WITH MOOD RINGS AND POLYESTER!
YOU'D DO WELL NOT TO SCOFF SO, MY DEAR.
BUREAU 18 HAD A HAND IN ERADICATING THOSE LITTLE BEASTIES IN THE 70'S--AND THE ALIEN INTELLIGENCE BEHIND THEM!
BUT YOU WON'T FIND THAT FACT IN ANY OFFICIAL REPORT!

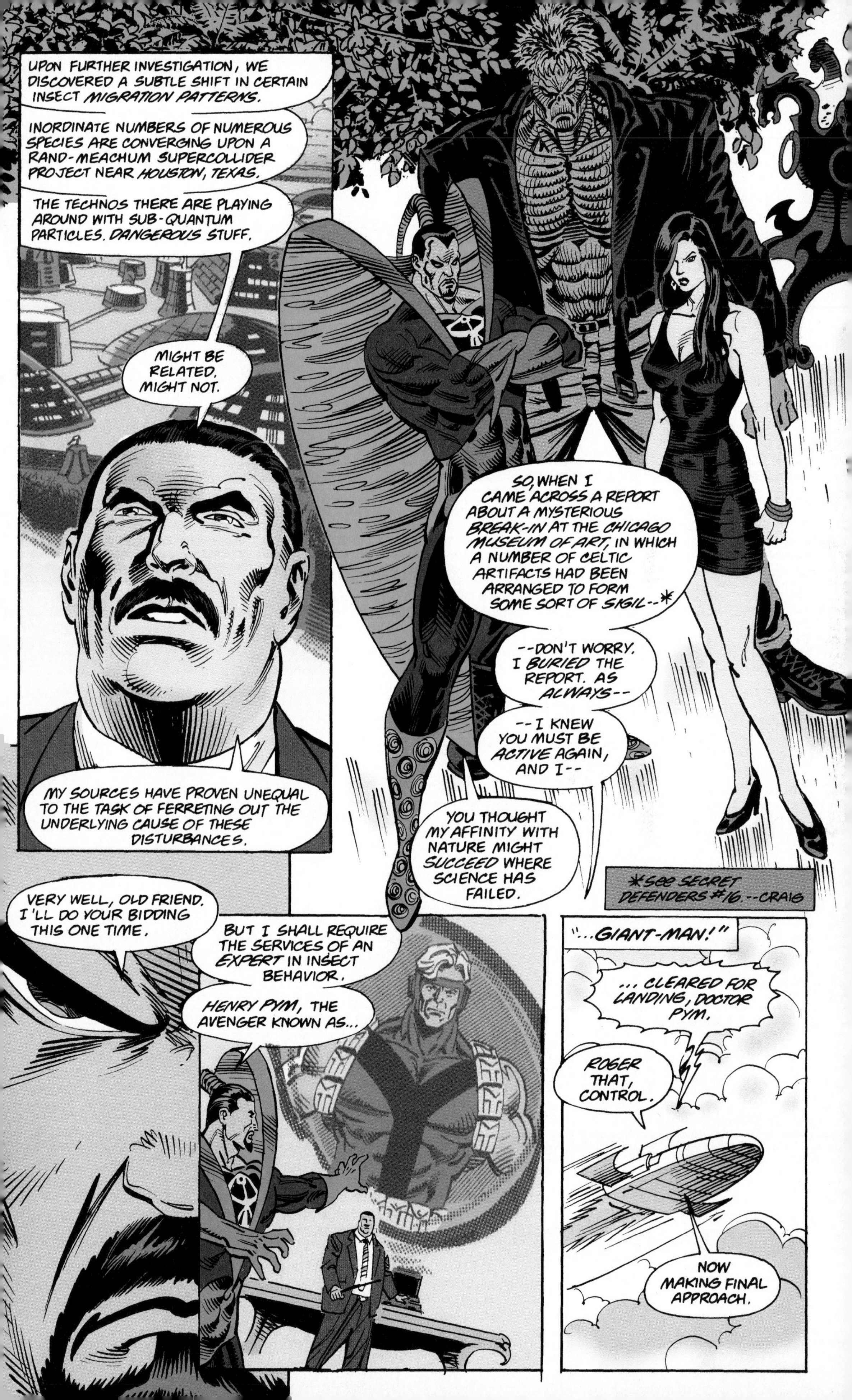
UPON FURTHER INVESTIGATION, WE DISCOVERED A SUBTLE SHIFT IN CERTAIN INSECT MIGRATION PATTERNS.
INORDINATE NUMBERS OF NUMEROUS SPECIES ARE CONVERGING UPON A RAND-MEACHUM SUPERCOLLIDER PROJECT NEAR HOUSTON, TEXAS.
THE TECHNOS THERE ARE PLAYING AROUND WITH SUB-QUANTUM PARTICLES. DANGEROUS STUFF.
MIGHT BE RELATED, MIGHT NOT.
MY SOURCES HAVE PROVEN UNEQUAL TO THE TASK OF FERRETING OUT THE UNDERLYING CAUSE OF THESE DISTURBANCES.
SO, WHEN I CAME ACROSS A REPORT ABOUT A MYSTERIOUS BREAK-IN AT THE CHICAGO MUSEUM OF ART, IN WHICH A NUMBER OF CELTIC ARTIFACTS HAD BEEN ARRANGED TO FORM SOME SORT OF SIGIL--*
--DON'T WORRY. I BURIED THE REPORT. AS ALWAYS--
--I KNEW YOU MUST BE ACTIVE AGAIN, AND I--
YOU THOUGHT MY AFFINITY WITH NATURE MIGHT SUCCEED WHERE SCIENCE HAS FAILED.
*See SECRET DEFENDERS #16. --CRAIG
VERY WELL, OLD FRIEND. I'LL DO YOUR BIDDING THIS ONE TIME.
BUT I SHALL REQUIRE THE SERVICES OF AN EXPERT IN INSECT BEHAVIOR.
HENRY PYM, THE AVENGER KNOWN AS...
"...GIANT-MAN!"
... CLEARED FOR LANDING, DOCTOR PYM.
ROGER THAT, CONTROL.
NOW MAKING FINAL APPROACH.

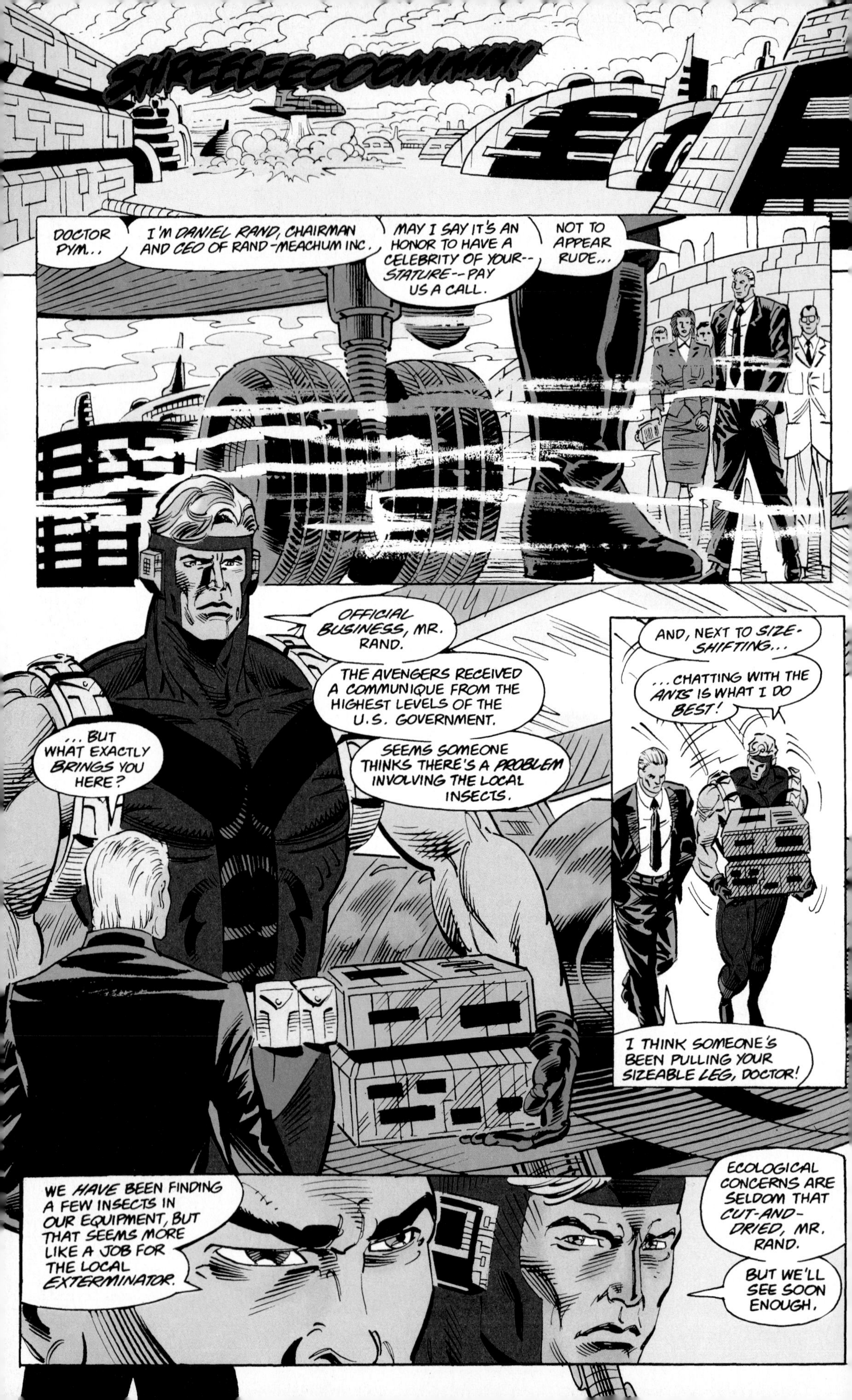
SHREEEEEEOOOMMMM!
DOCTOR PYM...
I'M DANIEL RAND, CHAIRMAN AND CEO OF RAND-MEACHUM INC.
MAY I SAY IT'S AN HONOR TO HAVE A CELEBRITY OF YOUR-- STATURE--PAY US A CALL.
NOT TO APPEAR RUDE...
...BUT WHAT EXACTLY BRINGS YOU HERE?
OFFICIAL BUSINESS, MR. RAND.
THE AVENGERS RECEIVED A COMMUNIQUE FROM THE HIGHEST LEVELS OF THE U.S. GOVERNMENT.
SEEMS SOMEONE THINKS THERE'S A PROBLEM INVOLVING THE LOCAL INSECTS.
AND, NEXT TO SIZE-SHIFTING...
...CHATTING WITH THE ANTS IS WHAT I DO BEST!
I THINK SOMEONE'S BEEN PULLING YOUR SIZEABLE LEG, DOCTOR!
WE HAVE BEEN FINDING A FEW INSECTS IN OUR EQUIPMENT, BUT THAT SEEMS MORE LIKE A JOB FOR THE LOCAL EXTERMINATOR.
ECOLOGICAL CONCERNS ARE SELDOM THAT CUT-AND-DRIED, MR. RAND.
BUT WE'LL SEE SOON ENOUGH.

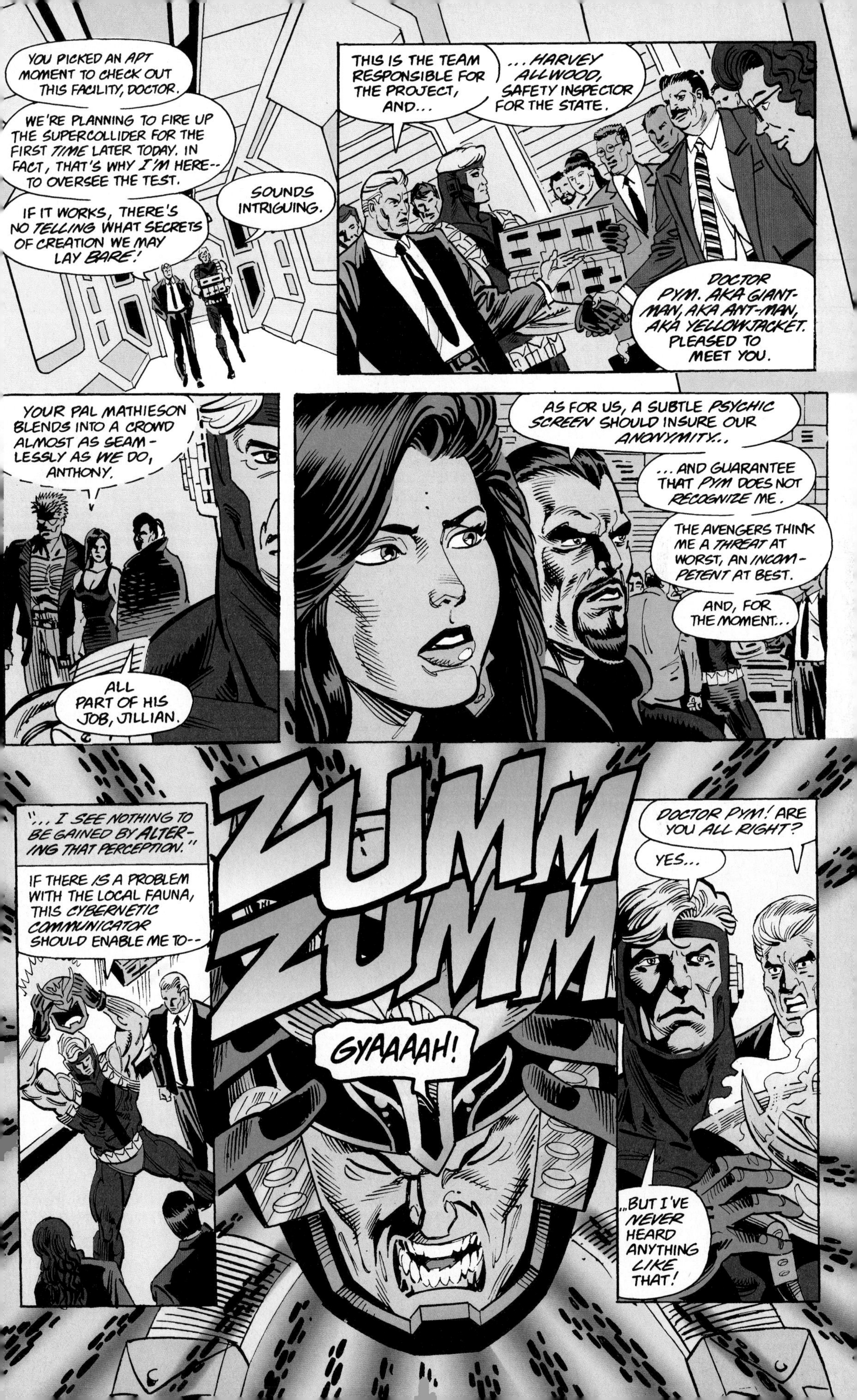
YOU PICKED AN APT MOMENT TO CHECK OUT THIS FACILITY, DOCTOR.
WE'RE PLANNING TO FIRE UP THE SUPERCOLLIDER FOR THE FIRST TIME LATER TODAY. IN FACT, THAT'S WHY I'M HERE-- TO OVERSEE THE TEST.
IF IT WORKS, THERE'S NO TELLING WHAT SECRETS OF CREATION WE MAY LAY BARE!
SOUNDS INTRIGUING.
THIS IS THE TEAM RESPONSIBLE FOR THE PROJECT, AND...
...HARVEY ALLWOOD, SAFETY INSPECTOR FOR THE STATE.
DOCTOR PYM. AKA GIANT-MAN, AKA ANT-MAN, AKA YELLOWJACKET. PLEASED TO MEET YOU.
YOUR PAL MATHIESON BLENDS INTO A CROWD ALMOST AS SEAM-LESSLY AS WE DO, ANTHONY.
ALL PART OF HIS JOB, JILLIAN.
AS FOR US, A SUBTLE PSYCHIC SCREEN SHOULD INSURE OUR ANONYMITY...
...AND GUARANTEE THAT PYM DOES NOT RECOGNIZE ME.
THE AVENGERS THINK ME A THREAT AT WORST, AN INCOM-PETENT AT BEST.
AND, FOR THE MOMENT...
"...I SEE NOTHING TO BE GAINED BY ALTER-ING THAT PERCEPTION."
IF THERE IS A PROBLEM WITH THE LOCAL FAUNA, THIS CYBERNETIC COMMUNICATOR SHOULD ENABLE ME TO--
ZUMM ZUMM
GYAAAAH!
DOCTOR PYM! ARE YOU ALL RIGHT?
YES...
...BUT I'VE NEVER HEARD ANYTHING LIKE THAT!

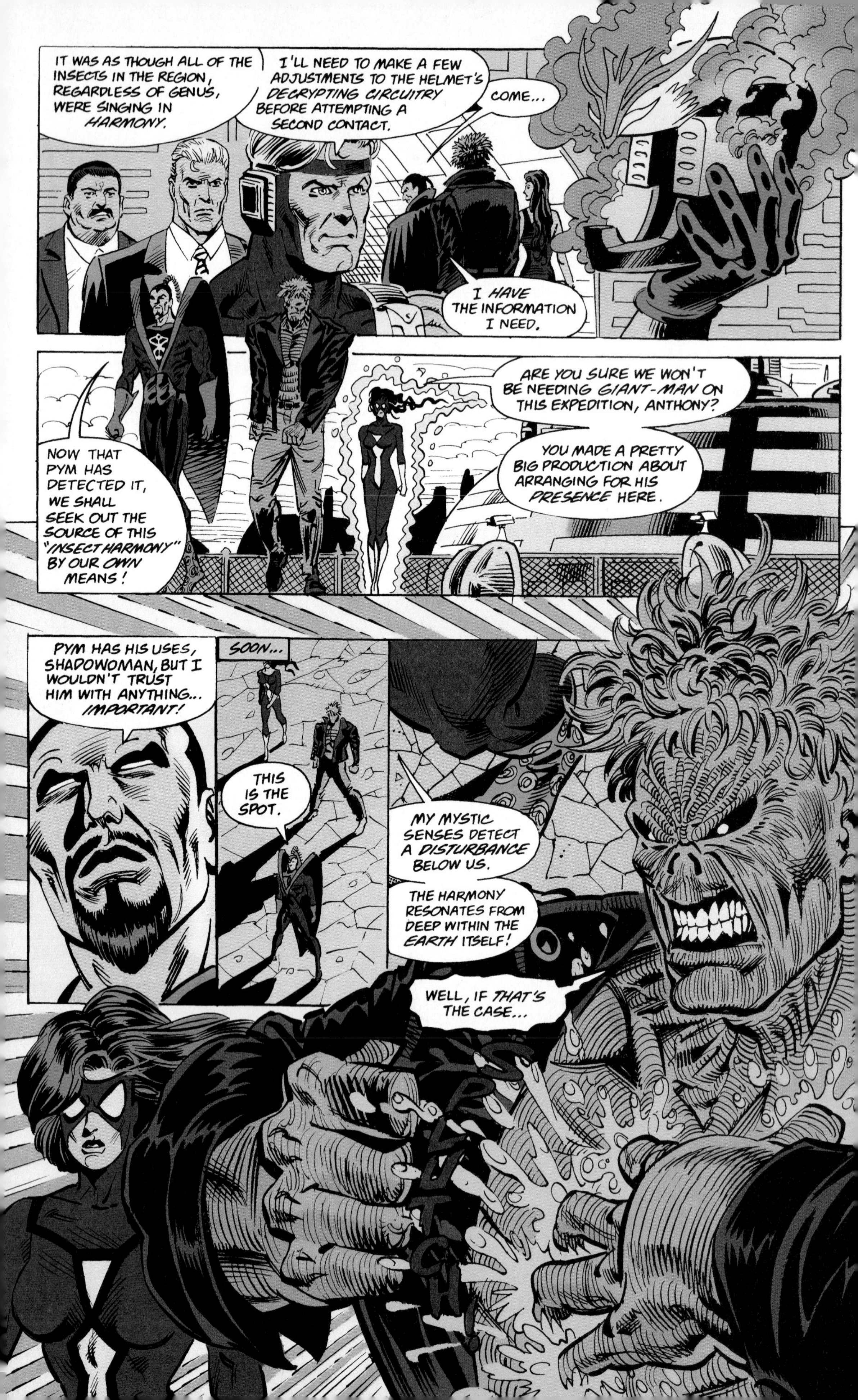
IT WAS AS THOUGH ALL OF THE INSECTS IN THE REGION, REGARDLESS OF GENUS, WERE SINGING IN HARMONY.
I'LL NEED TO MAKE A FEW ADJUSTMENTS TO THE HELMET'S DECRYPTING CIRCUITRY BEFORE ATTEMPTING A SECOND CONTACT.
COME...
I HAVE THE INFORMATION I NEED.
NOW THAT PYM HAS DETECTED IT, WE SHALL SEEK OUT THE SOURCE OF THIS "INSECT HARMONY" BY OUR OWN MEANS!
ARE YOU SURE WE WON'T BE NEEDING GIANT-MAN ON THIS EXPEDITION, ANTHONY?
YOU MADE A PRETTY BIG PRODUCTION ABOUT ARRANGING FOR HIS PRESENCE HERE.
PYM HAS HIS USES, SHADOWOMAN, BUT I WOULDN'T TRUST HIM WITH ANYTHING... IMPORTANT!
SOON...
THIS IS THE SPOT.
MY MYSTIC SENSES DETECT A DISTURBANCE BELOW US.
THE HARMONY RESONATES FROM DEEP WITHIN THE EARTH ITSELF!
WELL, IF THAT'S THE CASE...

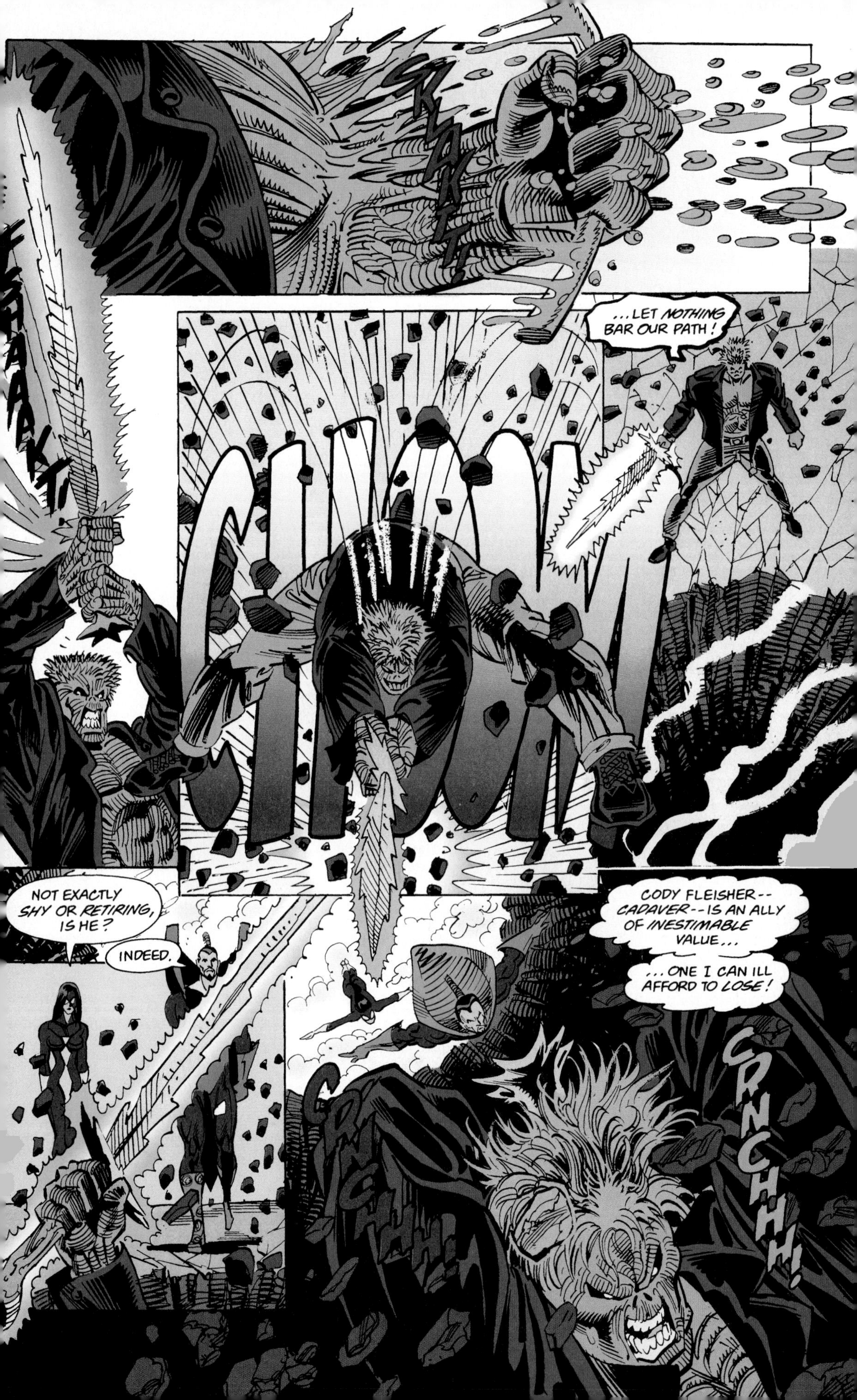
SKLAKT
THHAAKT!
...LET NOTHING BAR OUR PATH!
CHOOM
NOT EXACTLY SHY OR RETIRING, IS HE?
INDEED.
CODY FLEISHER--CADAVER--IS AN ALLY OF INESTIMABLE VALUE...
...ONE I CAN ILL AFFORD TO LOSE!
CRNCHHH!

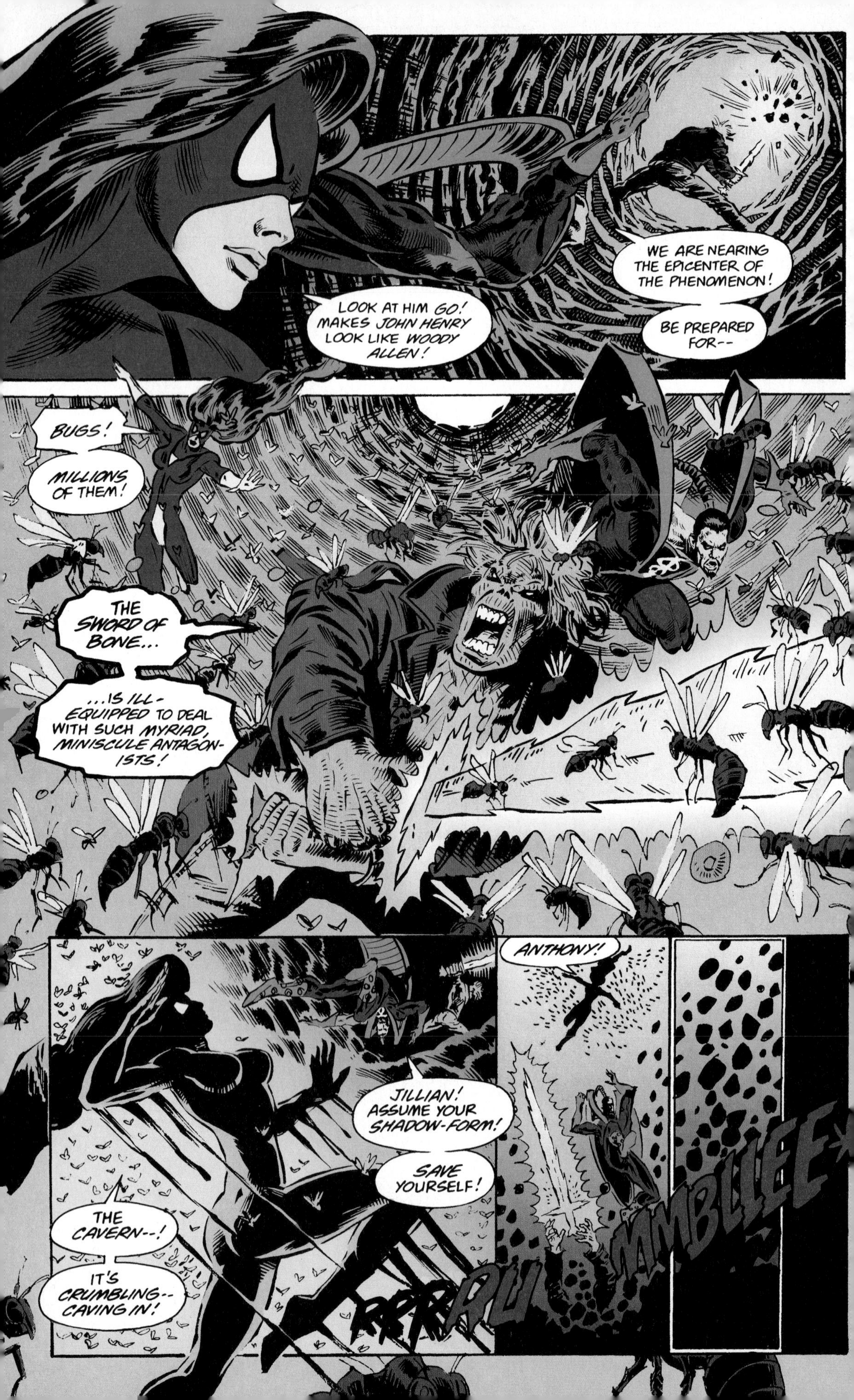
LOOK AT HIM GO! MAKES JOHN HENRY LOOK LIKE WOODY ALLEN!
WE ARE NEARING THE EPICENTER OF THE PHENOMENON!
BE PREPARED FOR--
BUGS!
MILLIONS OF THEM!
THE SWORD OF BONE...
...IS ILL-EQUIPPED TO DEAL WITH SUCH MYRIAD, MINISCULE ANTAGONISTS!
JILLIAN! ASSUME YOUR SHADOW-FORM!
SAVE YOURSELF!
THE CAVERN--!
IT'S CRUMBLING-- CAVING IN!
ANTHONY!
RRRRUUMMBLLEE

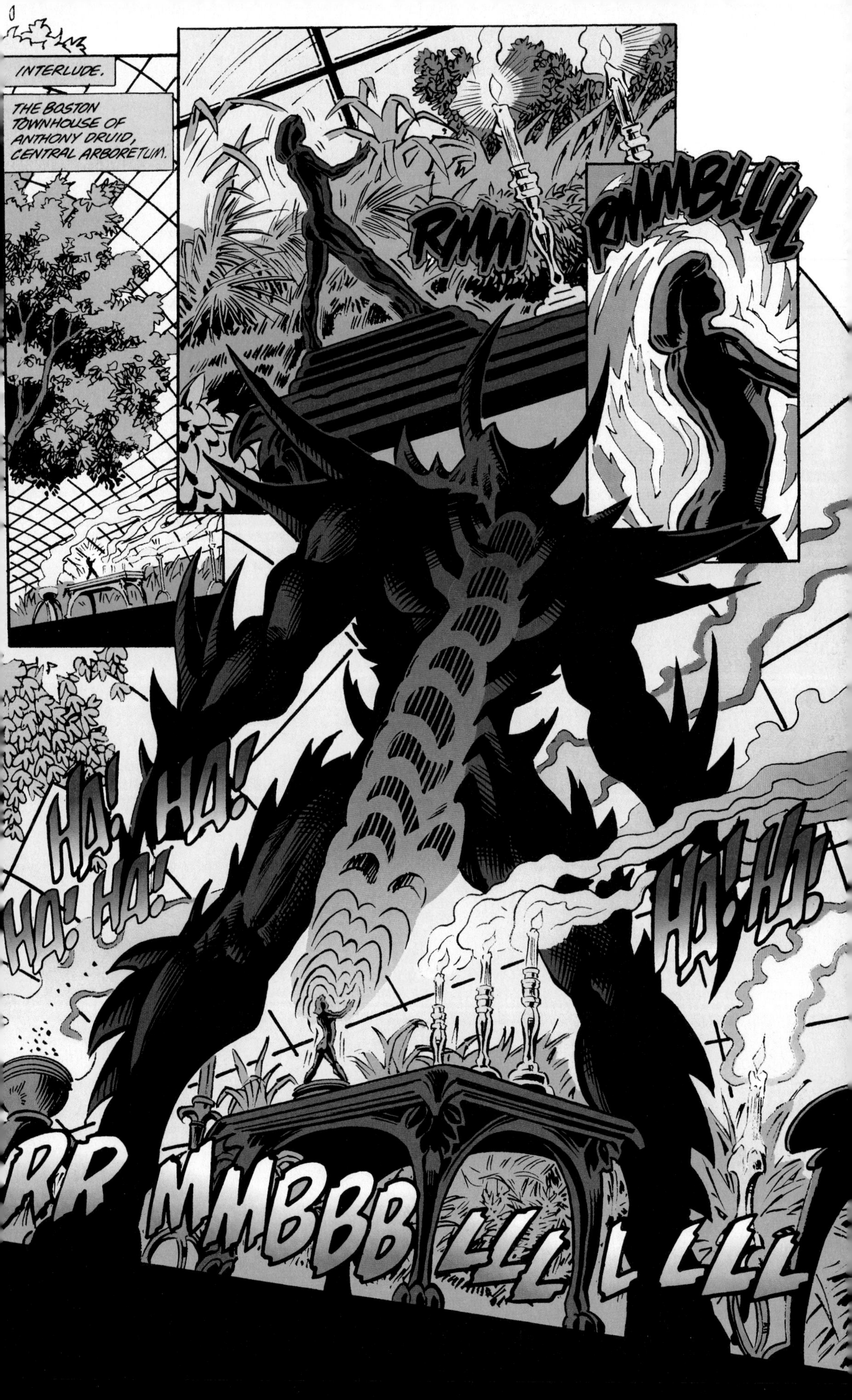
INTERLUDE.
THE BOSTON TOWNHOUSE OF ANTHONY DRUID, CENTRAL ARBORETUM.
RMM RMMBLLLL
HA! HA! HA! HA!
HA! HA!
RR MMBBB LLL LLLL

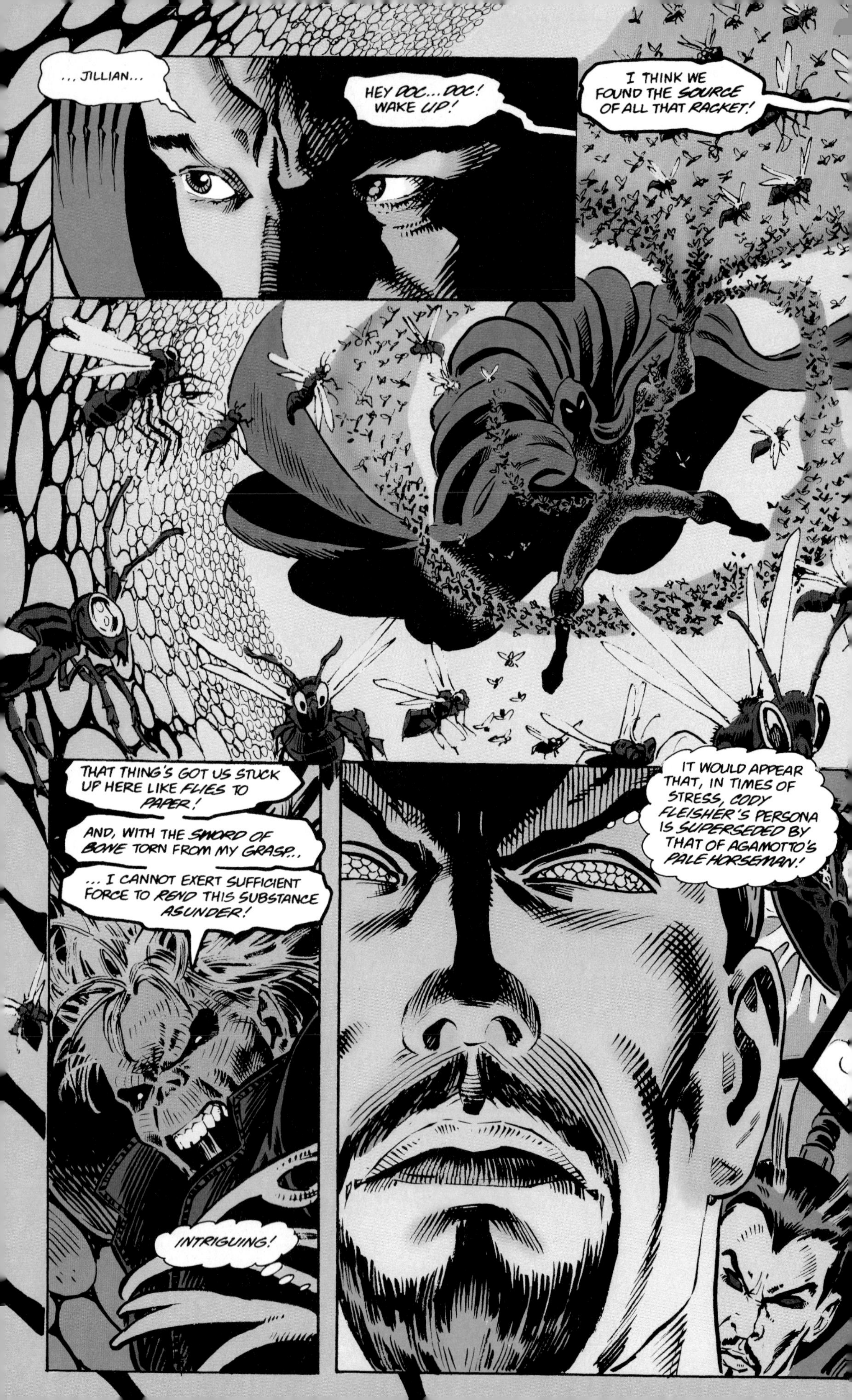

... JILLIAN...
HEY DOC... DOC! WAKE UP!
I THINK WE FOUND THE SOURCE OF ALL THAT RACKET!
THAT THING'S GOT US STUCK UP HERE LIKE FLIES TO PAPER!
AND, WITH THE SWORD OF BONE TORN FROM MY GRASP...
... I CANNOT EXERT SUFFICIENT FORCE TO REND THIS SUBSTANCE ASUNDER!
INTRIGUING!
IT WOULD APPEAR THAT, IN TIMES OF STRESS, CODY FLEISHER'S PERSONA IS SUPERSEDED BY THAT OF AGAMOTTO'S PALE HORSEMAN!

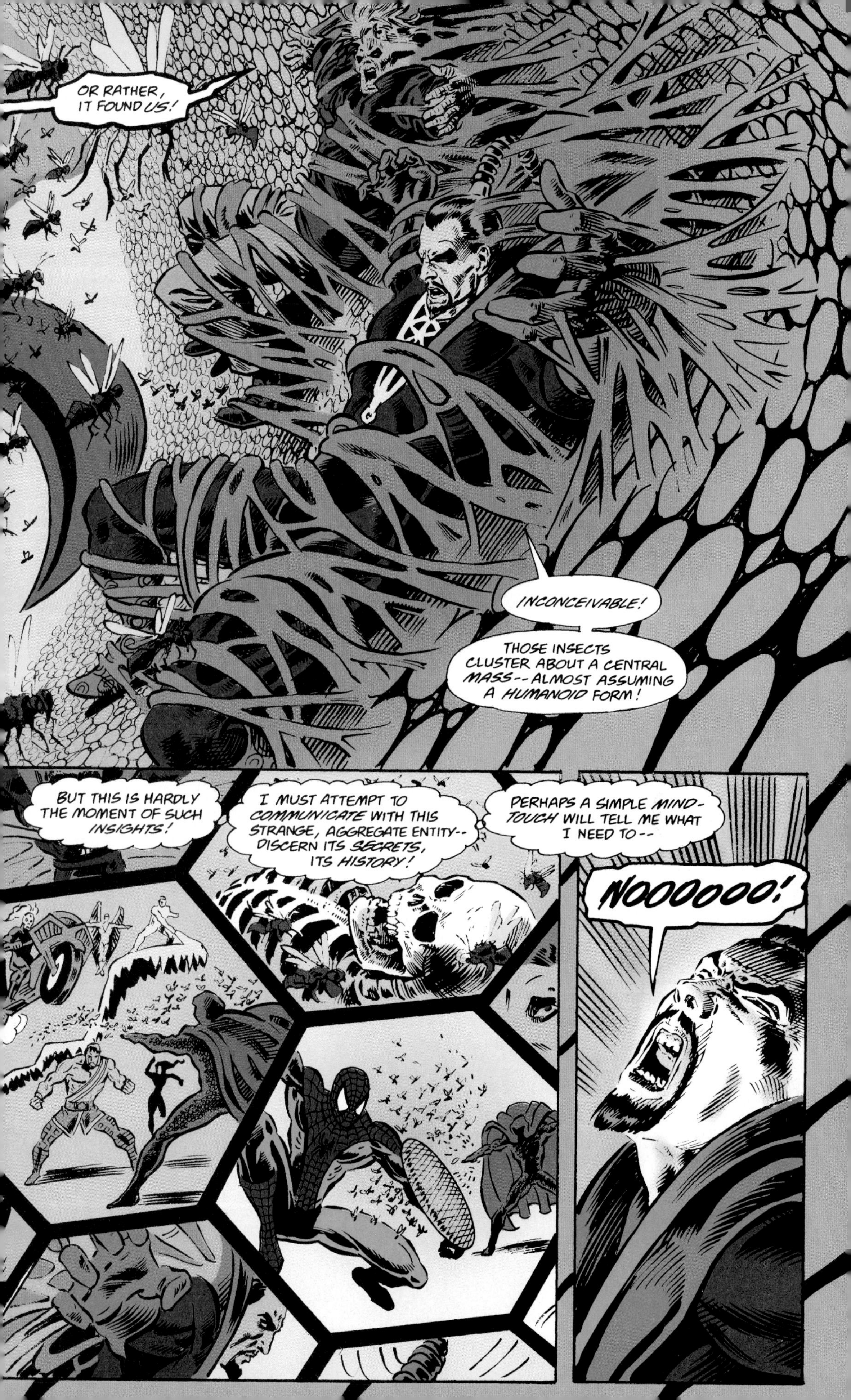

OR RATHER, IT FOUND US!
INCONCEIVABLE!
THOSE INSECTS CLUSTER ABOUT A CENTRAL MASS--ALMOST ASSUMING A HUMANOID FORM!
BUT THIS IS HARDLY THE MOMENT OF SUCH INSIGHTS!
I MUST ATTEMPT TO COMMUNICATE WITH THIS STRANGE, AGGREGATE ENTITY--DISCERN ITS SECRETS, ITS HISTORY!
PERHAPS A SIMPLE MIND-TOUCH WILL TELL ME WHAT I NEED TO--
NOOOOOO!

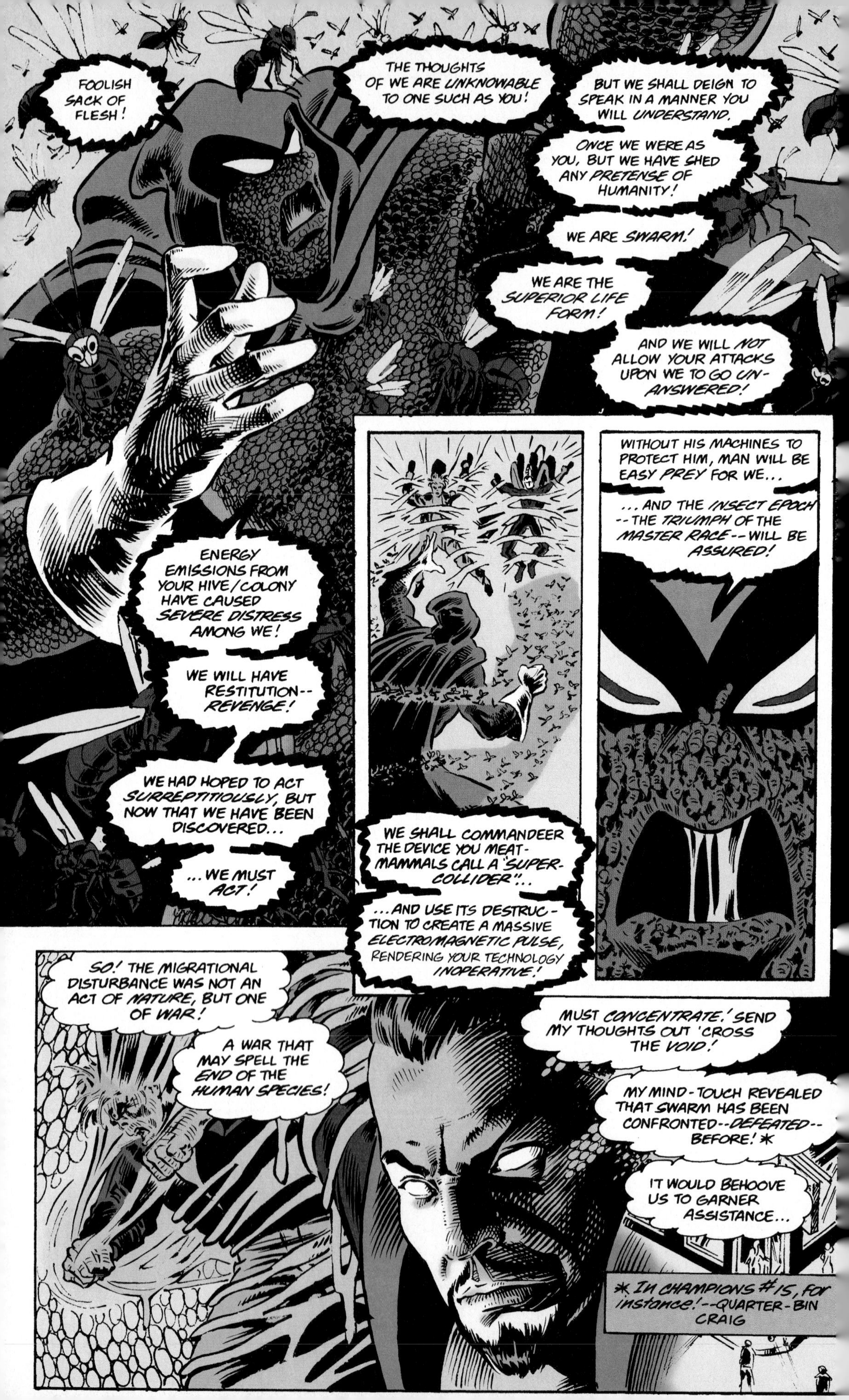
FOOLISH SACK OF FLESH!
THE THOUGHTS OF WE ARE UNKNOWABLE TO ONE SUCH AS YOU!
BUT WE SHALL DEIGN TO SPEAK IN A MANNER YOU WILL UNDERSTAND.
ONCE WE WERE AS YOU, BUT WE HAVE SHED ANY PRETENSE OF HUMANITY!
WE ARE SWARM!
WE ARE THE SUPERIOR LIFE FORM!
AND WE WILL NOT ALLOW YOUR ATTACKS UPON WE TO GO UN-ANSWERED!
ENERGY EMISSIONS FROM YOUR HIVE/COLONY HAVE CAUSED SEVERE DISTRESS AMONG WE!
WE WILL HAVE RESTITUTION--REVENGE!
WE HAD HOPED TO ACT SURREPTITIOUSLY, BUT NOW THAT WE HAVE BEEN DISCOVERED...
...WE MUST ACT!
WE SHALL COMMANDEER THE DEVICE YOU MEAT-MAMMALS CALL A "SUPER-COLLIDER"...
...AND USE ITS DESTRUCTION TO CREATE A MASSIVE ELECTROMAGNETIC PULSE, RENDERING YOUR TECHNOLOGY INOPERATIVE!
WITHOUT HIS MACHINES TO PROTECT HIM, MAN WILL BE EASY PREY FOR WE...
...AND THE INSECT EPOCH--THE TRIUMPH OF THE MASTER RACE--WILL BE ASSURED!
SO! THE MIGRATIONAL DISTURBANCE WAS NOT AN ACT OF NATURE, BUT ONE OF WAR!
A WAR THAT MAY SPELL THE END OF THE HUMAN SPECIES!
MUST CONCENTRATE! SEND MY THOUGHTS OUT 'CROSS THE VOID!
MY MIND-TOUCH REVEALED THAT SWARM HAS BEEN CONFRONTED--DEFEATED--BEFORE! *
IT WOULD BEHOOVE US TO GARNER ASSISTANCE...
* In CHAMPIONS #15, for instance!--QUARTER-BIN CRAIG

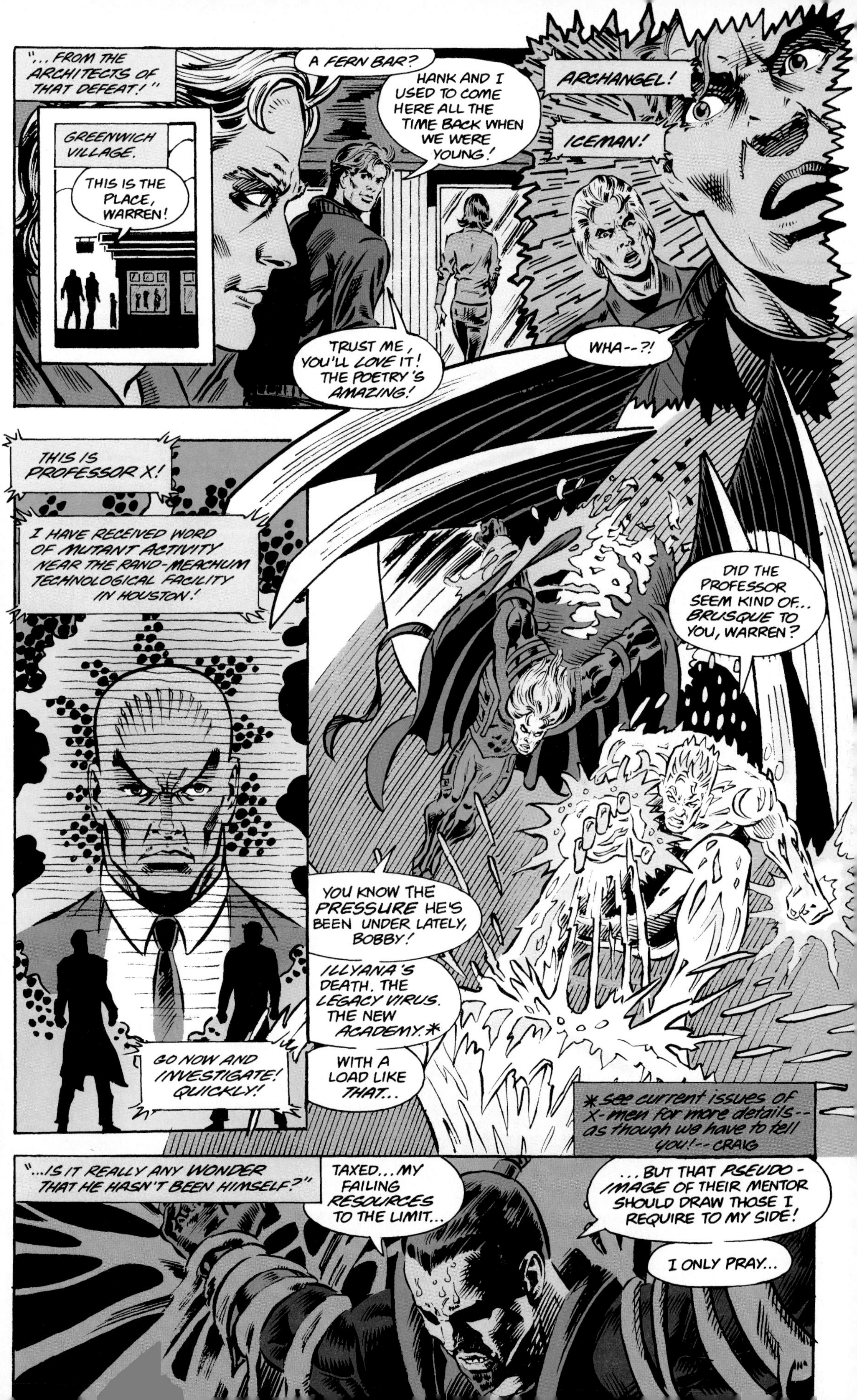
"...FROM THE ARCHITECTS OF THAT DEFEAT!"
GREENWICH VILLAGE.
THIS IS THE PLACE, WARREN!
A FERN BAR?
HANK AND I USED TO COME HERE ALL THE TIME BACK WHEN WE WERE YOUNG!
TRUST ME, YOU'LL LOVE IT! THE POETRY'S AMAZING!
ARCHANGEL!
ICEMAN!
WHA--?!
THIS IS PROFESSOR X!
I HAVE RECEIVED WORD OF MUTANT ACTIVITY NEAR THE RAND-MEACHUM TECHNOLOGICAL FACILITY IN HOUSTON!
GO NOW AND INVESTIGATE! QUICKLY!
DID THE PROFESSOR SEEM KIND OF... BRUSQUE TO YOU, WARREN?
YOU KNOW THE PRESSURE HE'S BEEN UNDER LATELY, BOBBY!
ILLYANA'S DEATH. THE LEGACY VIRUS. THE NEW ACADEMY.*
WITH A LOAD LIKE THAT...
*see current issues of X-men for more details-- as though we have to tell you!--CRAIG
"...IS IT REALLY ANY WONDER THAT HE HASN'T BEEN HIMSELF?"
TAXED... MY FAILING RESOURCES TO THE LIMIT...
...BUT THAT PSEUDO-IMAGE OF THEIR MENTOR SHOULD DRAW THOSE I REQUIRE TO MY SIDE!
I ONLY PRAY...

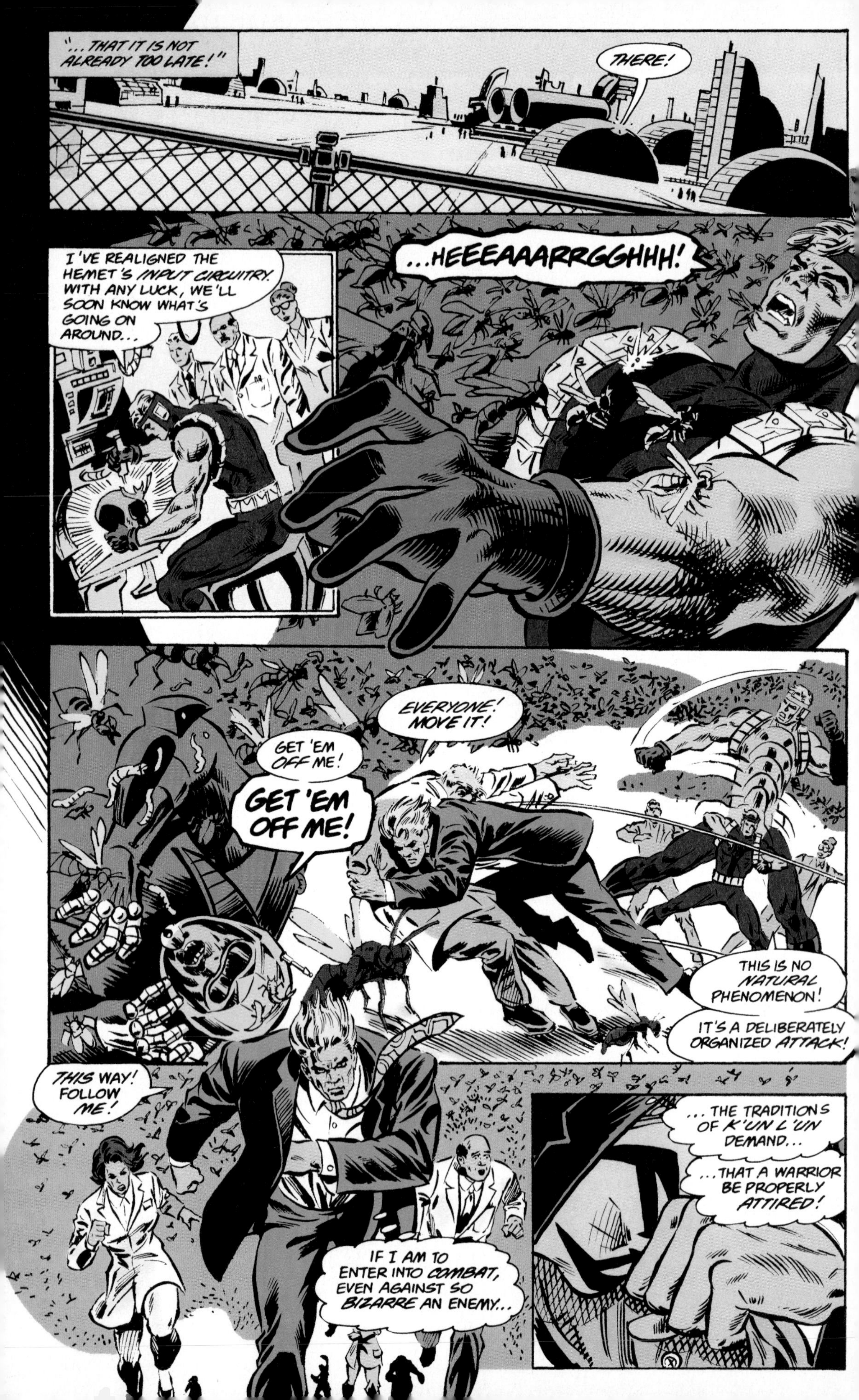
"...THAT IT IS NOT ALREADY TOO LATE!"
THERE!
I'VE REALIGNED THE HEMET'S INPUT CIRCUITRY. WITH ANY LUCK, WE'LL SOON KNOW WHAT'S GOING ON AROUND...
...HEEEAAARRGGHHH!
EVERYONE! MOVE IT!
GET 'EM OFF ME!
GET 'EM OFF ME!
THIS IS NO NATURAL PHENOMENON!
IT'S A DELIBERATELY ORGANIZED ATTACK!
THIS WAY! FOLLOW ME!
IF I AM TO ENTER INTO COMBAT, EVEN AGAINST SO BIZARRE AN ENEMY...
...THE TRADITIONS OF K'UN L'UN DEMAND...
...THAT A WARRIOR BE PROPERLY ATTIRED!

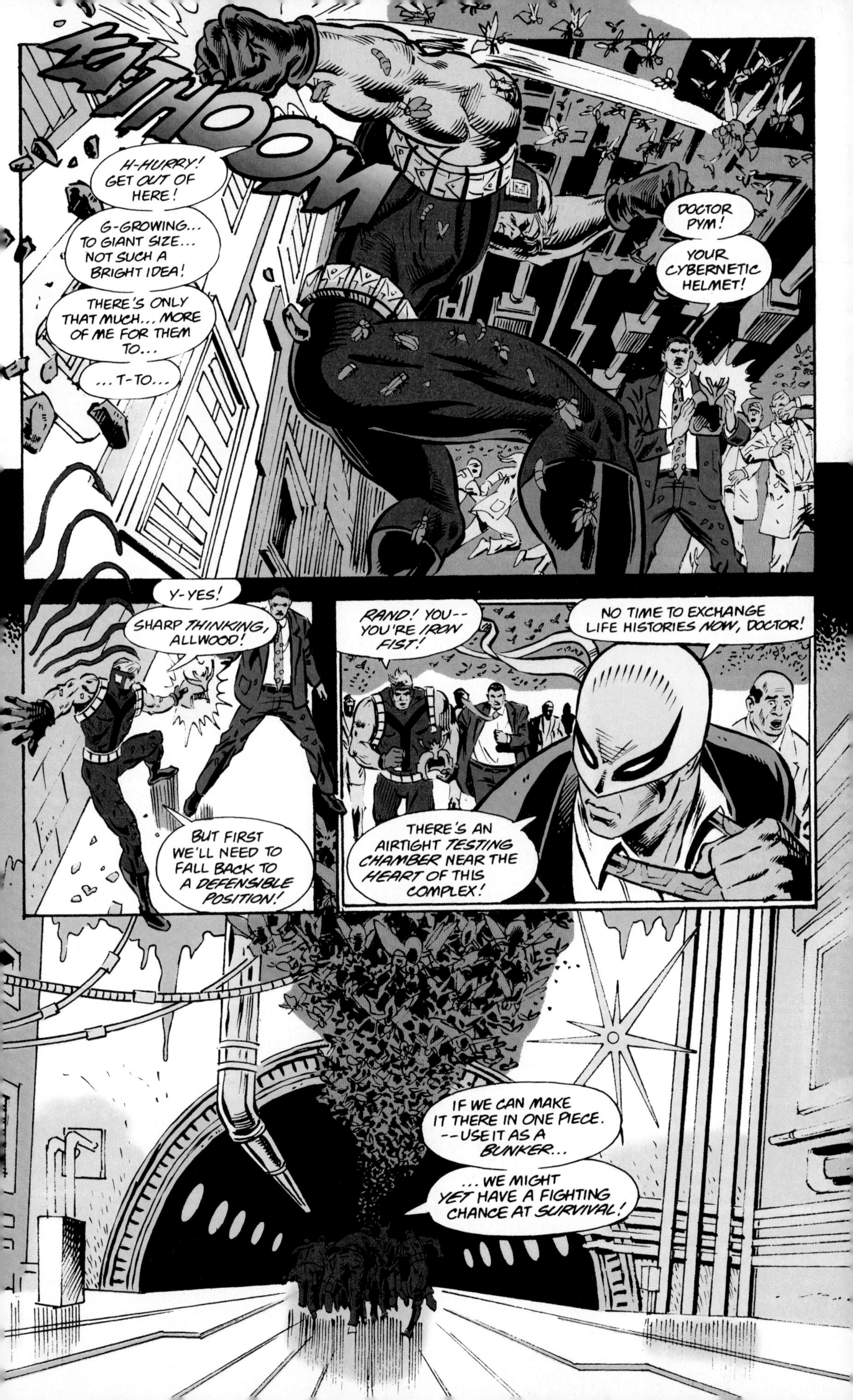
H-HURRY! GET OUT OF HERE!
G-GROWING... TO GIANT SIZE... NOT SUCH A BRIGHT IDEA!
THERE'S ONLY THAT MUCH... MORE OF ME FOR THEM TO...
... T-TO...
DOCTOR PYM!
YOUR CYBERNETIC HELMET!
Y-YES!
SHARP THINKING, ALLWOOD!
BUT FIRST WE'LL NEED TO FALL BACK TO A DEFENSIBLE POSITION!
RAND! YOU-- YOU'RE IRON FIST!
NO TIME TO EXCHANGE LIFE HISTORIES NOW, DOCTOR!
THERE'S AN AIRTIGHT TESTING CHAMBER NEAR THE HEART OF THIS COMPLEX!
IF WE CAN MAKE IT THERE IN ONE PIECE. --USE IT AS A BUNKER...
... WE MIGHT YET HAVE A FIGHTING CHANCE AT SURVIVAL!

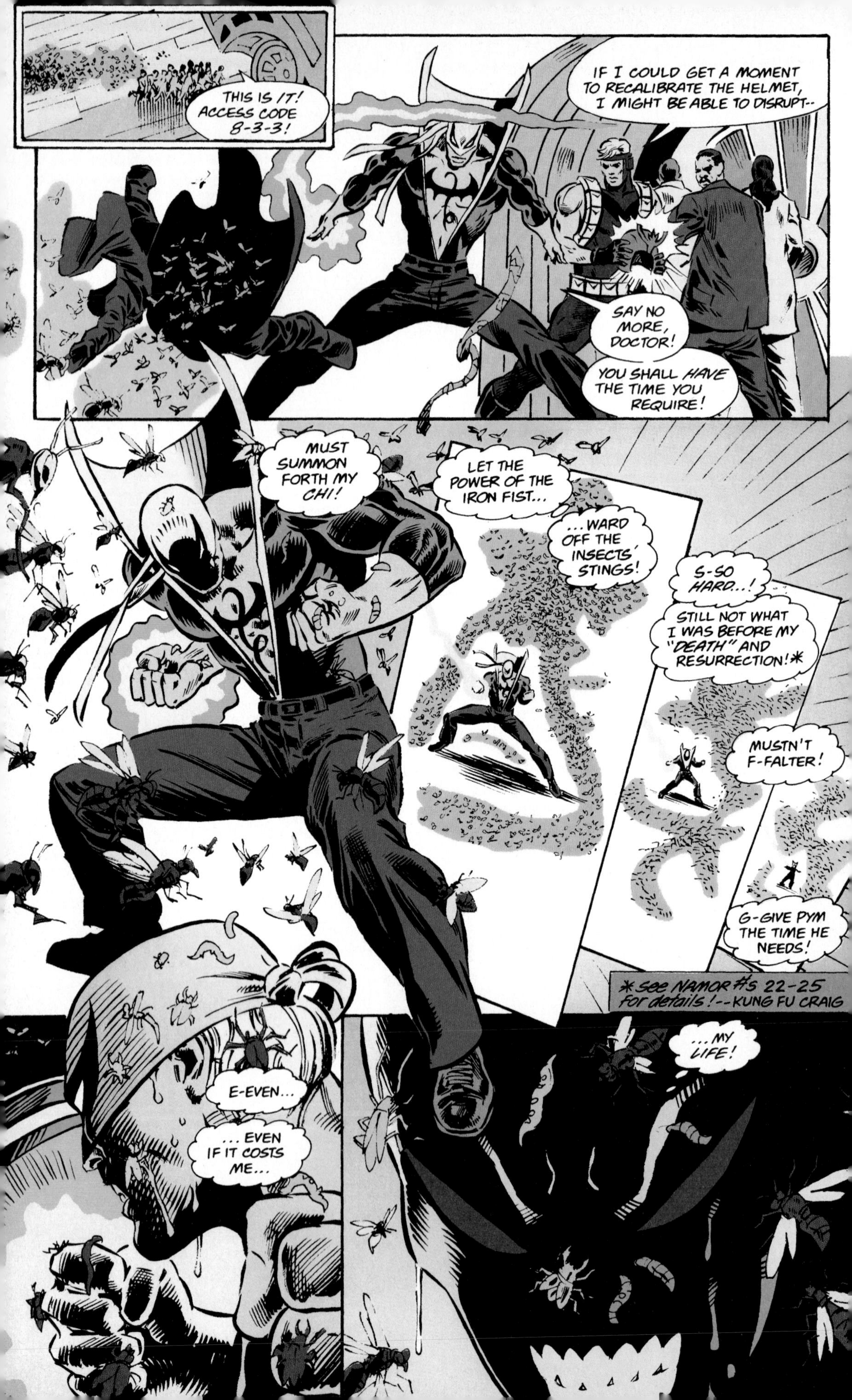

THIS IS IT! ACCESS CODE 8-3-3!
IF I COULD GET A MOMENT TO RECALIBRATE THE HELMET, I MIGHT BE ABLE TO DISRUPT--
SAY NO MORE, DOCTOR!
YOU SHALL HAVE THE TIME YOU REQUIRE!
MUST SUMMON FORTH MY CHI!
LET THE POWER OF THE IRON FIST...
...WARD OFF THE INSECTS' STINGS!
S-SO HARD...!
STILL NOT WHAT I WAS BEFORE MY "DEATH" AND RESURRECTION!*
MUSTN'T F-FALTER!
G-GIVE PYM THE TIME HE NEEDS!
*see Namor #s 22-25 for details! --KUNG FU CRAIG
E-EVEN...
...EVEN IF IT COSTS ME...
...MY LIFE!

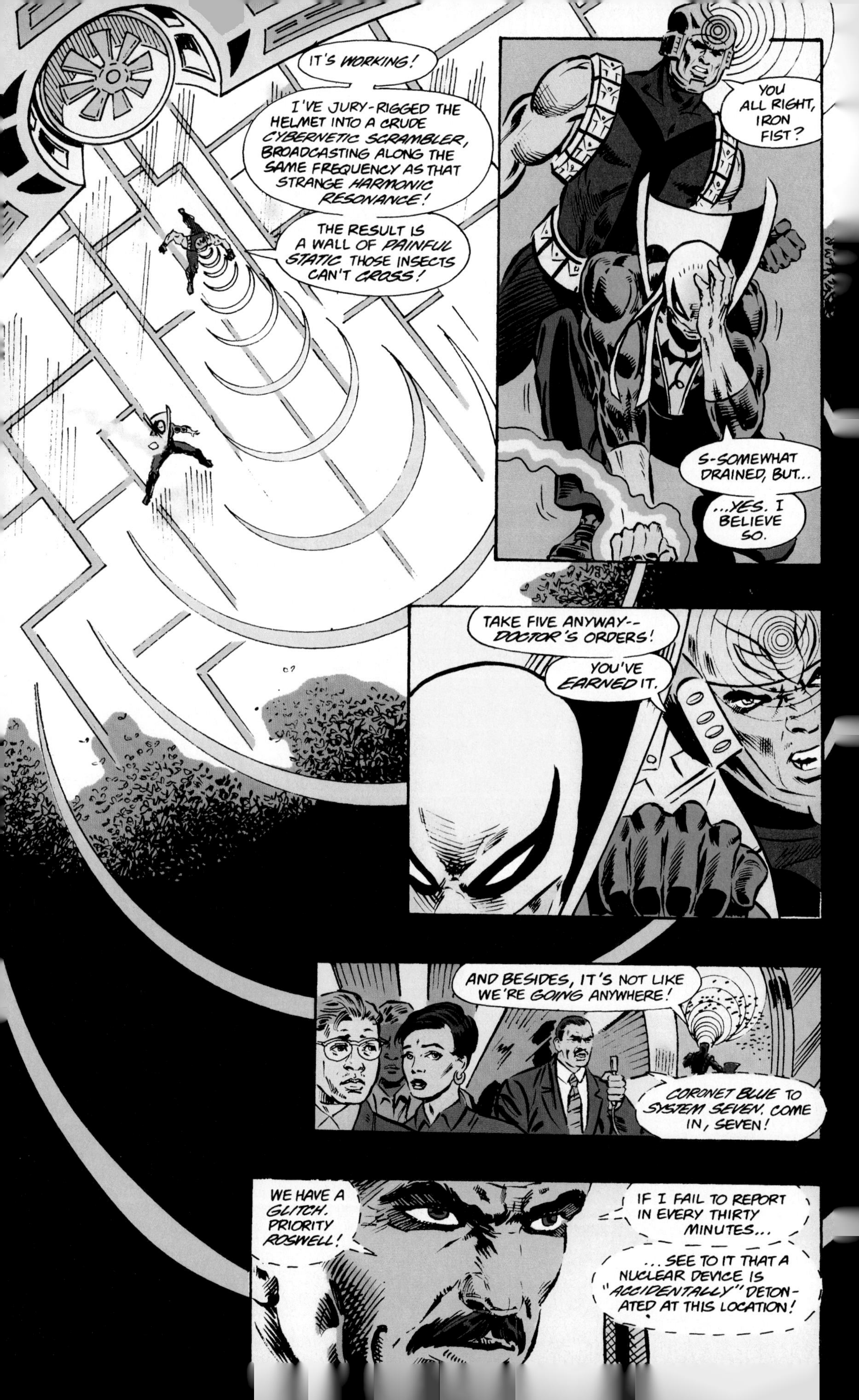
IT'S WORKING!
I'VE JURY-RIGGED THE HELMET INTO A CRUDE CYBERNETIC SCRAMBLER, BROADCASTING ALONG THE SAME FREQUENCY AS THAT STRANGE HARMONIC RESONANCE!
THE RESULT IS A WALL OF PAINFUL STATIC THOSE INSECTS CAN'T CROSS!
YOU ALL RIGHT, IRON FIST?
S-SOMEWHAT DRAINED, BUT...
...YES. I BELIEVE SO.
TAKE FIVE ANYWAY--DOCTOR'S ORDERS!
YOU'VE EARNED IT.
AND BESIDES, IT'S NOT LIKE WE'RE GOING ANYWHERE!
CORONET BLUE TO SYSTEM SEVEN. COME IN, SEVEN!
WE HAVE A GLITCH. PRIORITY ROSWELL!
IF I FAIL TO REPORT IN EVERY THIRTY MINUTES...
...SEE TO IT THAT A NUCLEAR DEVICE IS "ACCIDENTALLY" DETONATED AT THIS LOCATION!

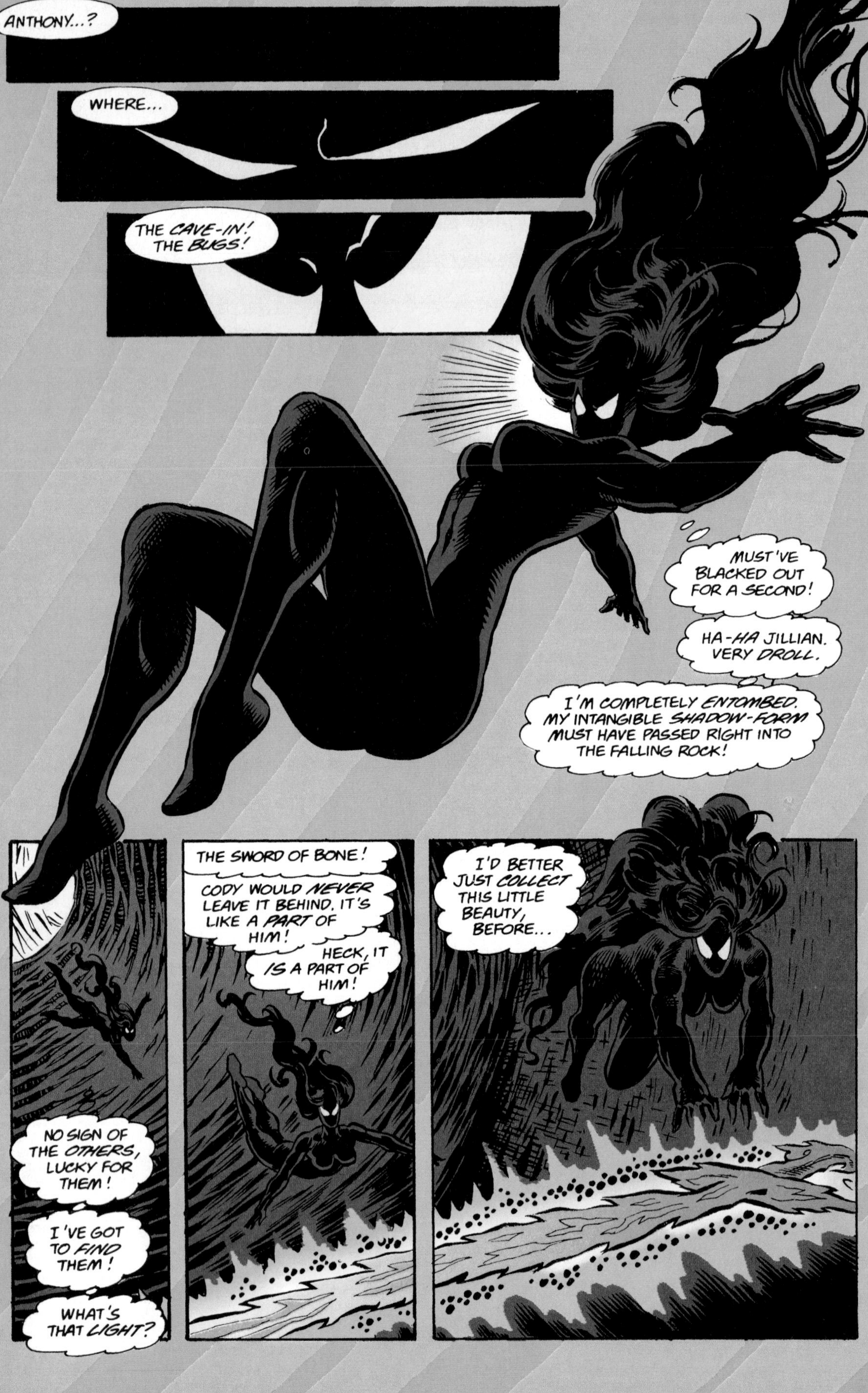
ANTHONY...?
WHERE...
THE CAVE-IN! THE BUGS!
MUST'VE BLACKED OUT FOR A SECOND!
HA-HA JILLIAN. VERY DROLL.
I'M COMPLETELY ENTOMBED. MY INTANGIBLE SHADOW-FORM MUST HAVE PASSED RIGHT INTO THE FALLING ROCK!
NO SIGN OF THE OTHERS, LUCKY FOR THEM!
I'VE GOT TO FIND THEM!
WHAT'S THAT LIGHT?
THE SWORD OF BONE!
CODY WOULD NEVER LEAVE IT BEHIND. IT'S LIKE A PART OF HIM!
HECK, IT IS A PART OF HIM!
I'D BETTER JUST COLLECT THIS LITTLE BEAUTY, BEFORE...

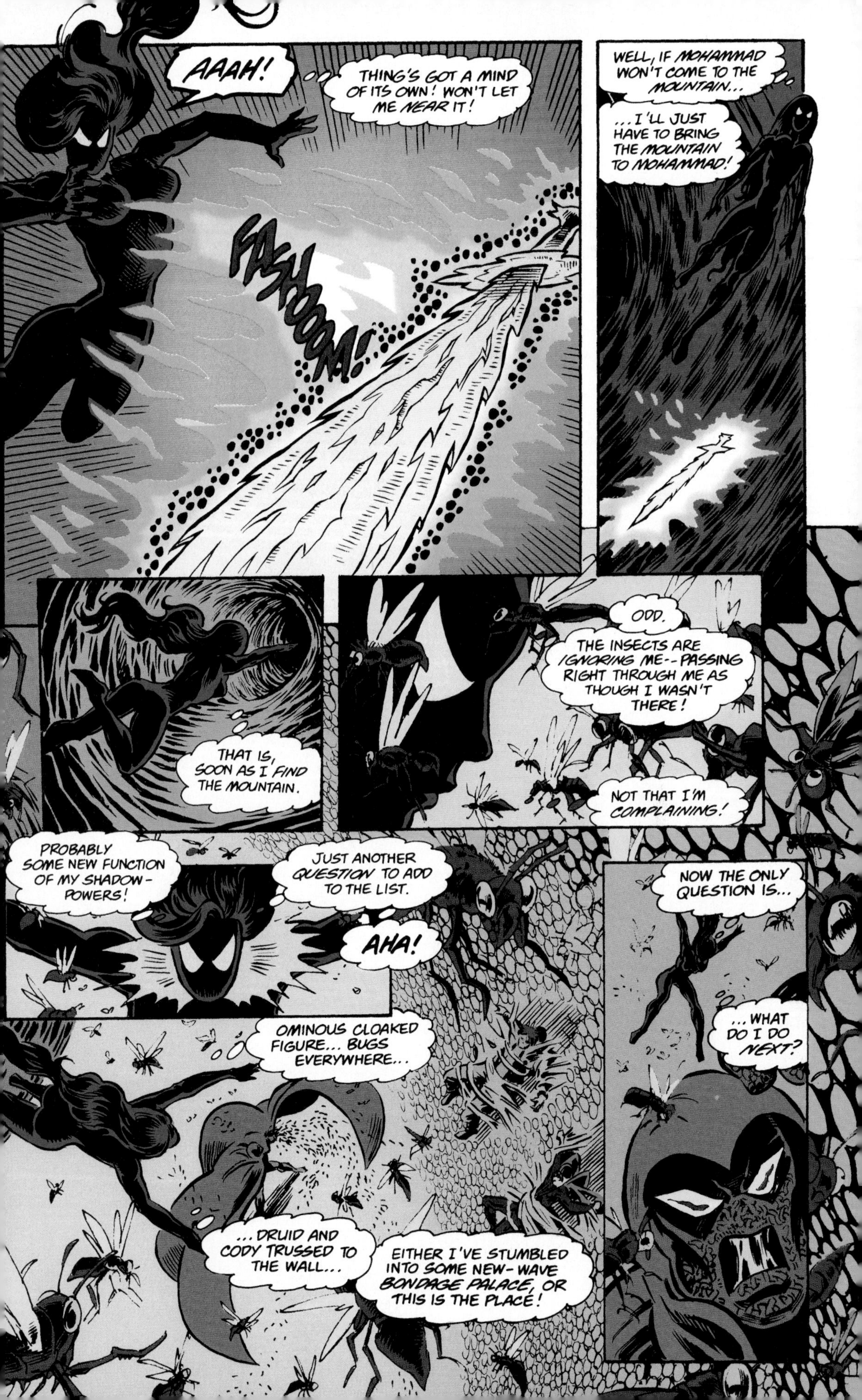
AAAH!
THING'S GOT A MIND OF ITS OWN! WON'T LET ME NEAR IT!
FASHOOOOM!
WELL, IF MOHAMMAD WON'T COME TO THE MOUNTAIN...
...I'LL JUST HAVE TO BRING THE MOUNTAIN TO MOHAMMAD!
THAT IS, SOON AS I FIND THE MOUNTAIN.
ODD.
THE INSECTS ARE IGNORING ME--PASSING RIGHT THROUGH ME AS THOUGH I WASN'T THERE!
NOT THAT I'M COMPLAINING!
PROBABLY SOME NEW FUNCTION OF MY SHADOW-POWERS!
JUST ANOTHER QUESTION TO ADD TO THE LIST.
AHA!
NOW THE ONLY QUESTION IS...
...WHAT DO I DO NEXT?
OMINOUS CLOAKED FIGURE... BUGS EVERYWHERE...
...DRUID AND CODY TRUSSED TO THE WALL...
EITHER I'VE STUMBLED INTO SOME NEW-WAVE BONDAGE PALACE, OR THIS IS THE PLACE!

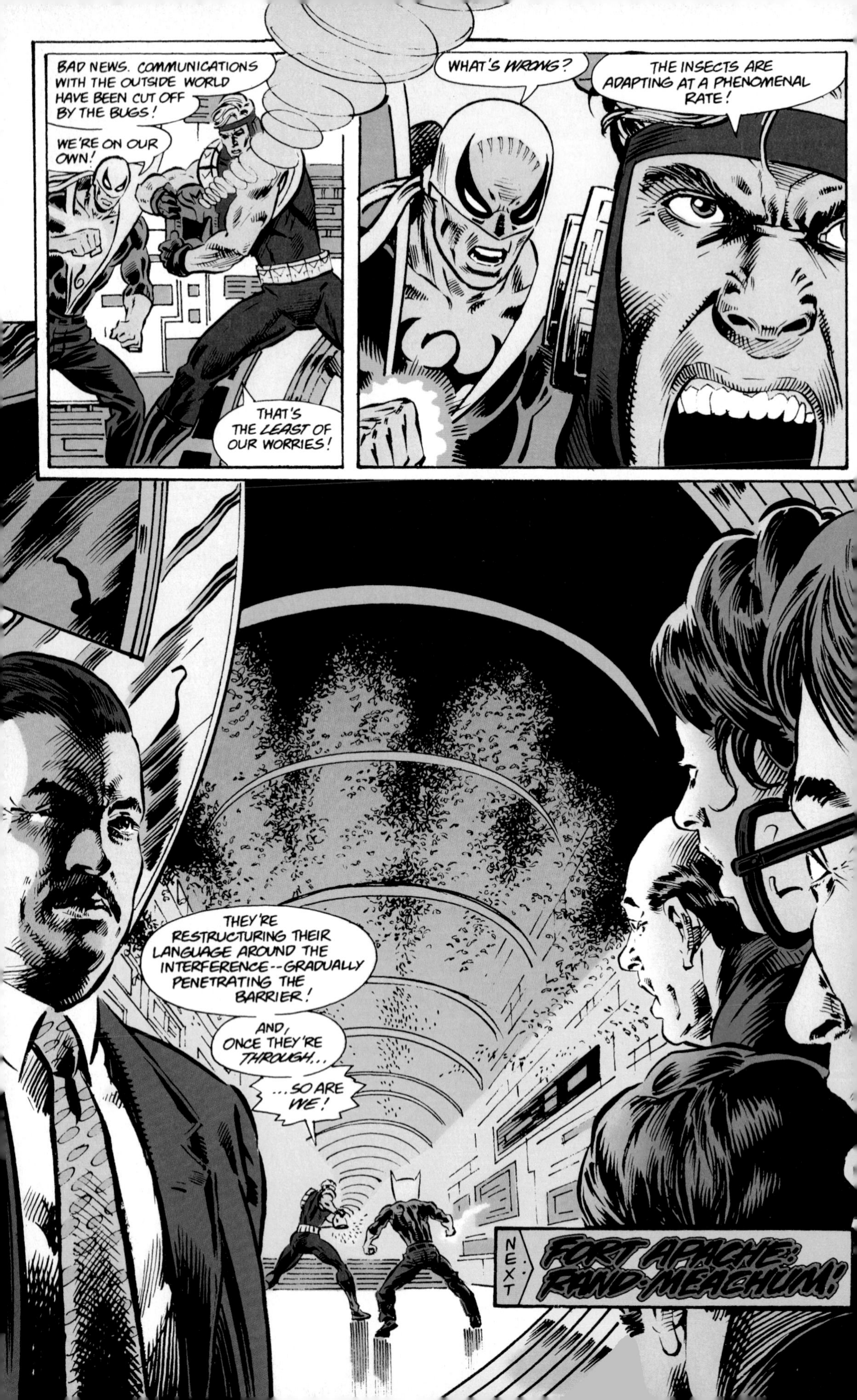
BAD NEWS. COMMUNICATIONS WITH THE OUTSIDE WORLD HAVE BEEN CUT OFF BY THE BUGS!
WE'RE ON OUR OWN!
THAT'S THE LEAST OF OUR WORRIES!
WHAT'S WRONG?
THE INSECTS ARE ADAPTING AT A PHENOMENAL RATE!
THEY'RE RESTRUCTURING THEIR LANGUAGE AROUND THE INTERFERENCE--GRADUALLY PENETRATING THE BARRIER!
AND, ONCE THEY'RE THROUGH...
...SO ARE WE!
NEXT: FORT APACHE: RAND-MEACHUM!

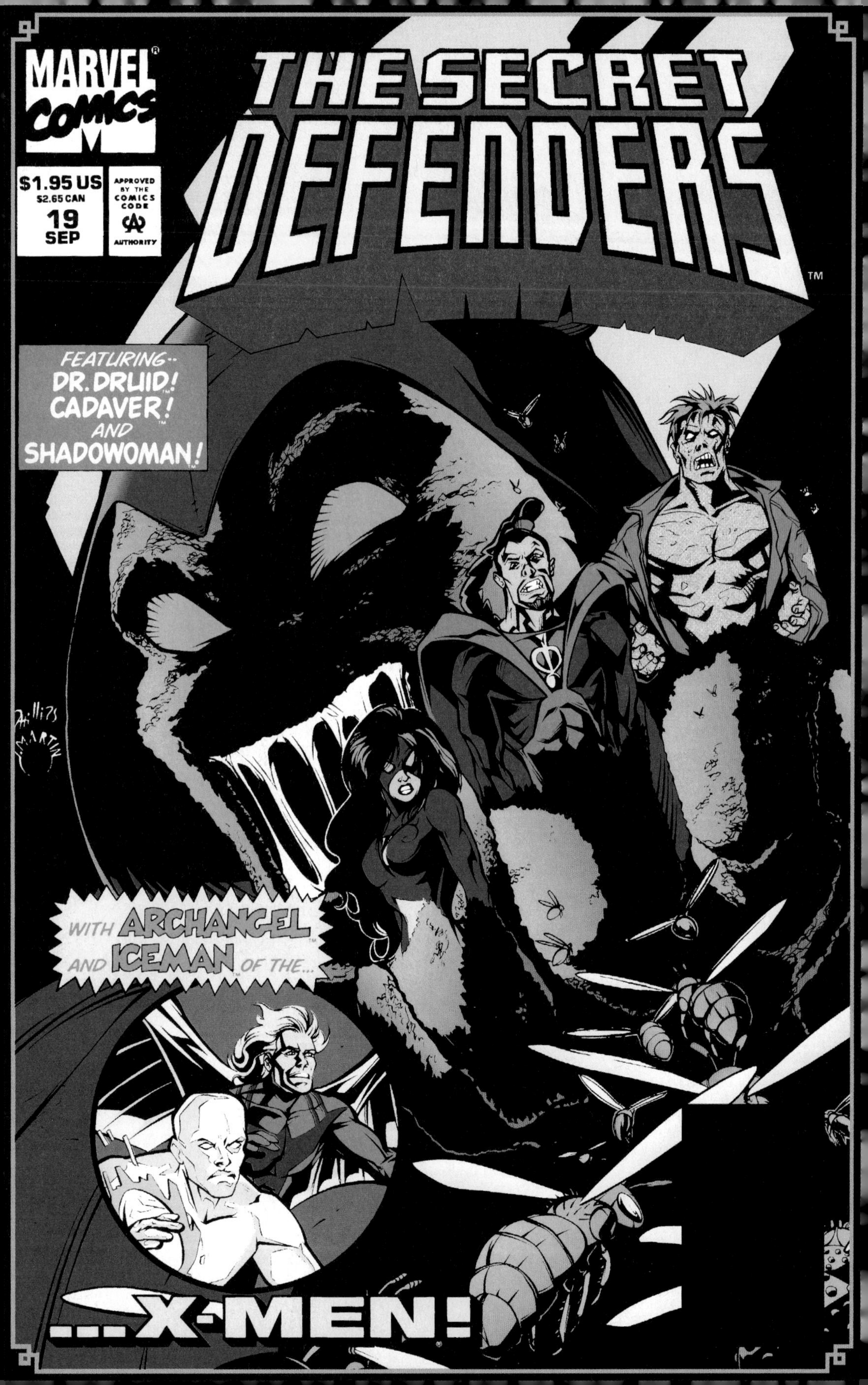

MARVEL COMICS
$1.95 US
$2.65 CAN
19
SEP
APPROVED BY THE COMICS CODE AUTHORITY
THE SECRET DEFENDERS
FEATURING--
DR. DRUID!
CADAVER!
AND
SHADOWOMAN!
WITH ARCHANGEL
AND ICEMAN OF THE...
...X-MEN!

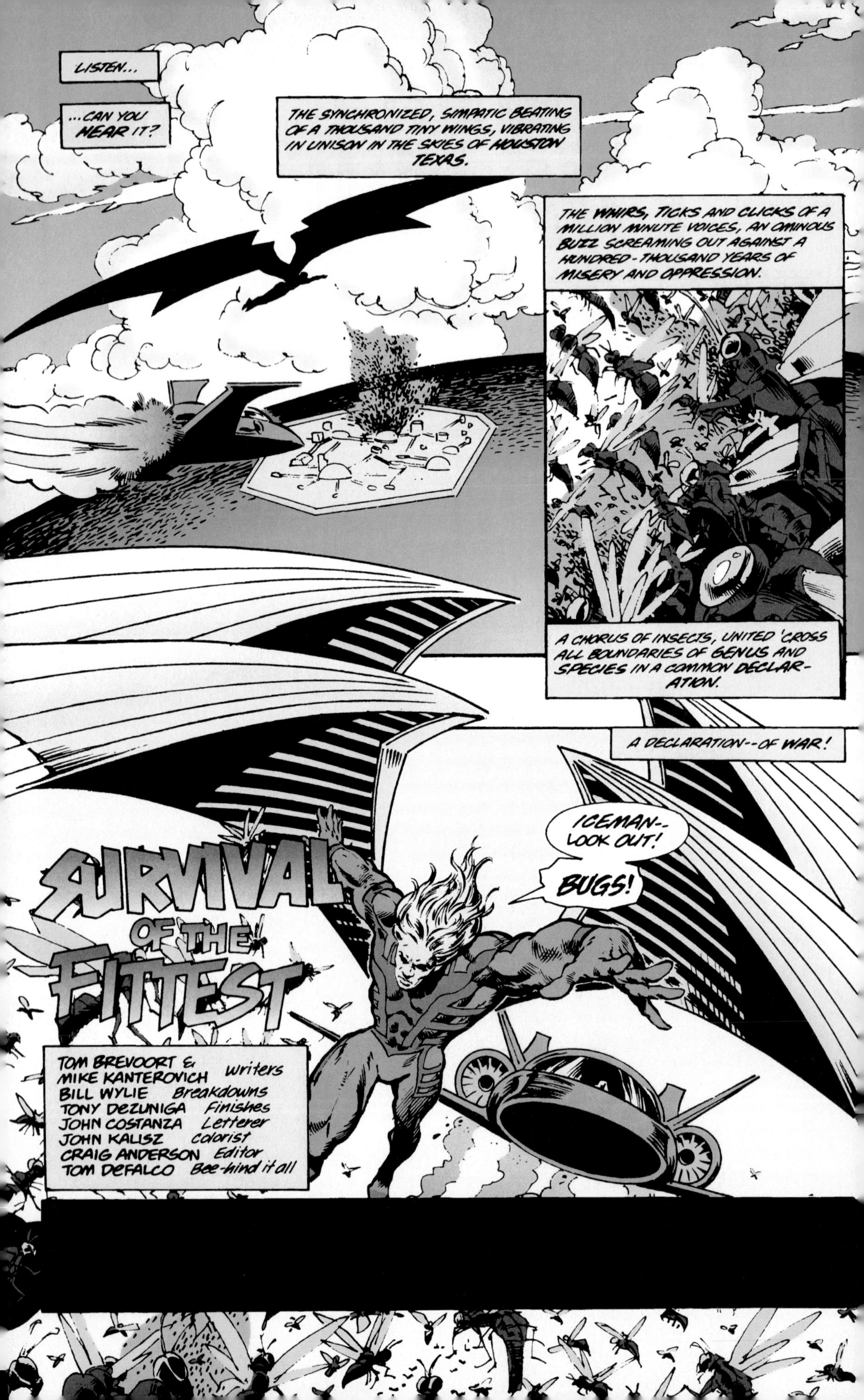
LISTEN...
...CAN YOU HEAR IT?
THE SYNCHRONIZED, SIMPATIC BEATING OF A THOUSAND TINY WINGS, VIBRATING IN UNISON IN THE SKIES OF HOUSTON TEXAS.
THE WHIRS, TICKS AND CLICKS OF A MILLION MINUTE VOICES, AN OMINOUS BUZZ SCREAMING OUT AGAINST A HUNDRED-THOUSAND YEARS OF MISERY AND OPPRESSION.
A CHORUS OF INSECTS, UNITED 'CROSS ALL BOUNDARIES OF GENUS AND SPECIES IN A COMMON DECLARATION.
A DECLARATION--OF WAR!
ICEMAN-- LOOK OUT!
BUGS!
SURVIVAL OF THE FITTEST
TOM BREVOORT & MIKE KANTEROVICH writers
BILL WYLIE Breakdowns
TONY DEZUNIGA Finishes
JOHN COSTANZA Letterer
JOHN KALISZ colorist
CRAIG ANDERSON Editor
TOM DEFALCO Bee-hind it all
[redacted]

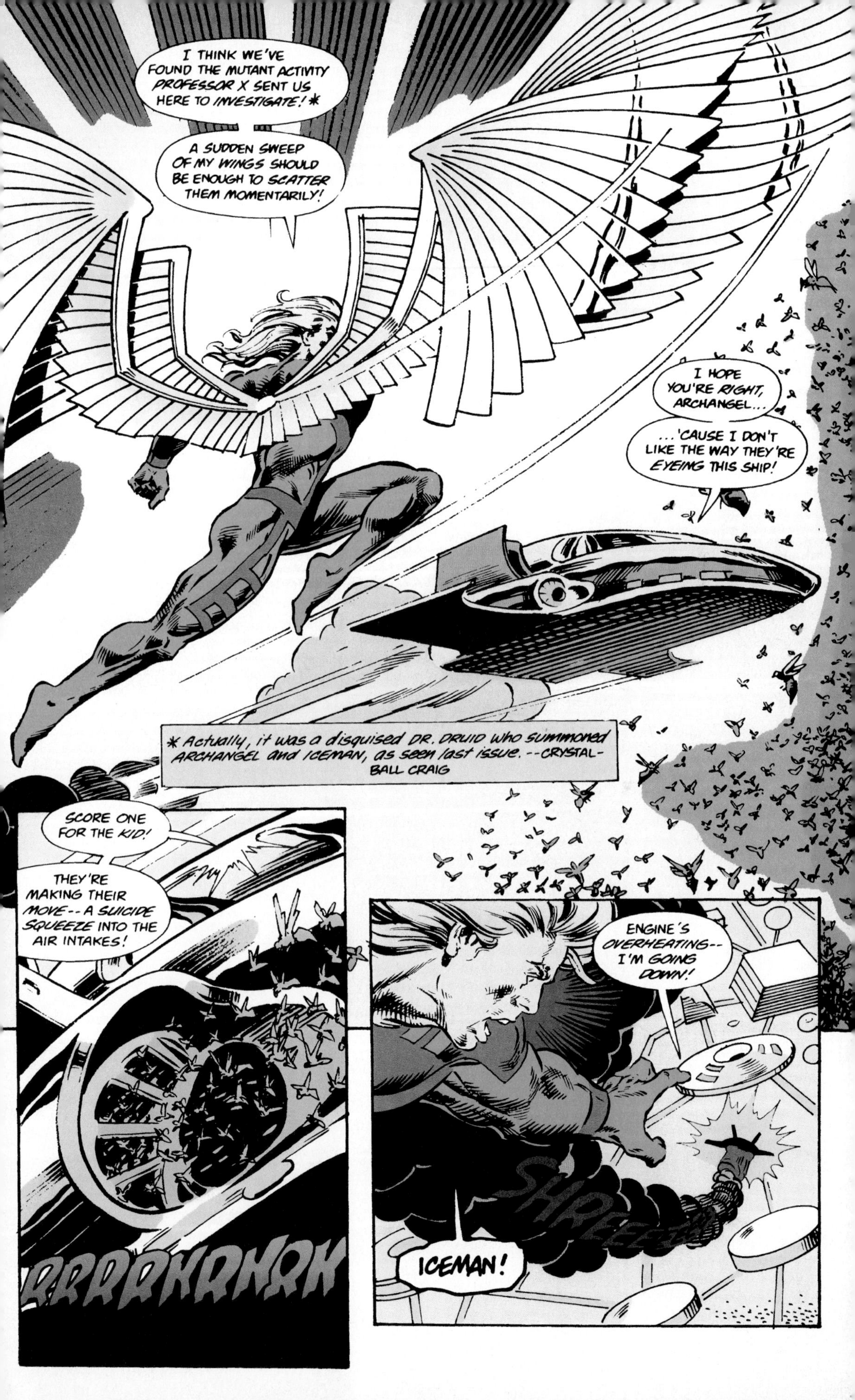
I THINK WE'VE FOUND THE MUTANT ACTIVITY PROFESSOR X SENT US HERE TO INVESTIGATE! *
A SUDDEN SWEEP OF MY WINGS SHOULD BE ENOUGH TO SCATTER THEM MOMENTARILY!
I HOPE YOU'RE RIGHT, ARCHANGEL...
...'CAUSE I DON'T LIKE THE WAY THEY'RE EYEING THIS SHIP!
* Actually, it was a disguised DR. DRUID who summoned ARCHANGEL and ICEMAN, as seen last issue. --CRYSTAL-BALL CRAIG
SCORE ONE FOR THE KID!
THEY'RE MAKING THEIR MOVE--A SUICIDE SQUEEZE INTO THE AIR INTAKES!
RRRRNRNRK
ENGINE'S OVERHEATING--I'M GOING DOWN!
SHREEEE
ICEMAN!

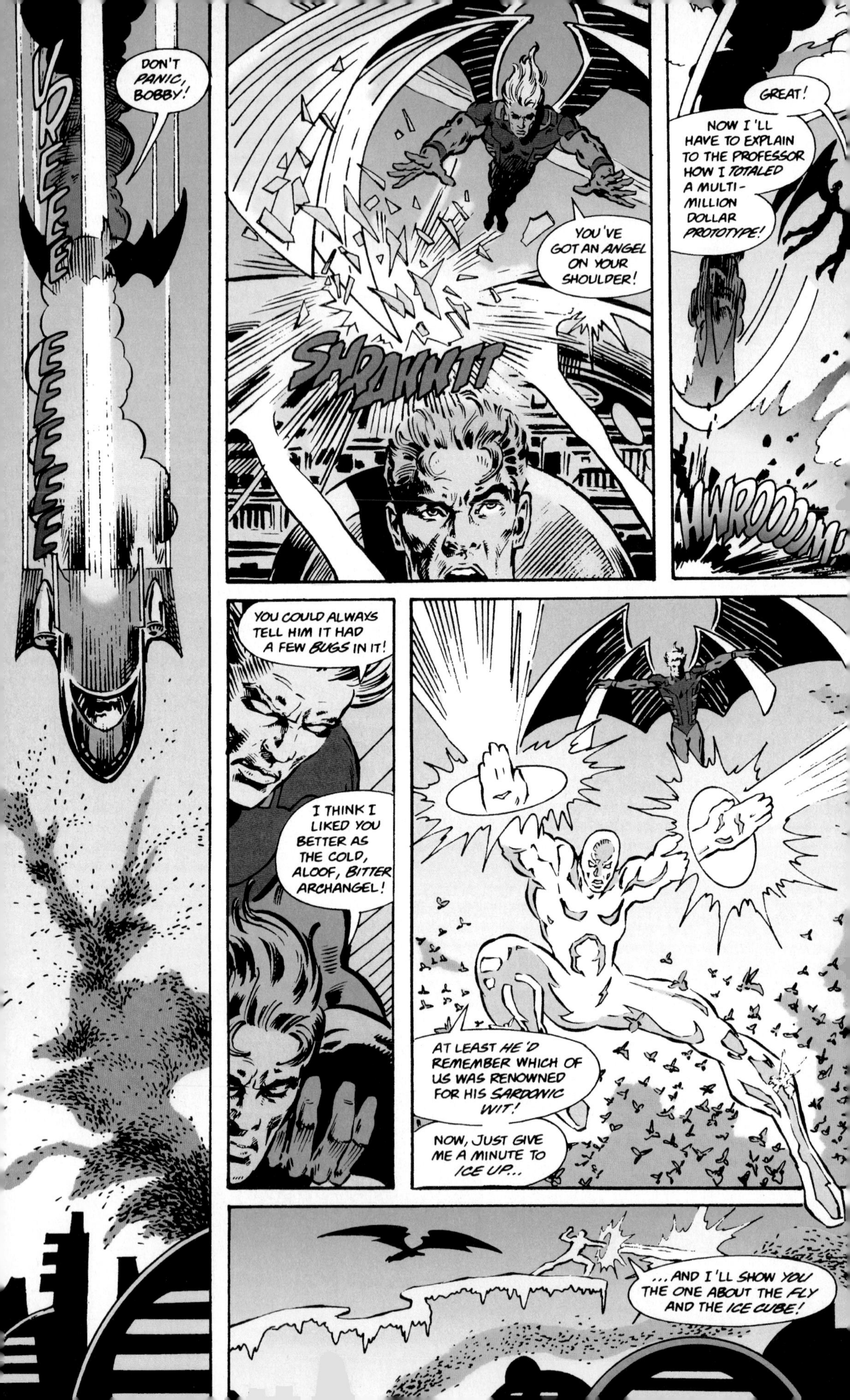
DON'T PANIC, BOBBY!
VREEEEEEEEEEE
YOU'VE GOT AN ANGEL ON YOUR SHOULDER!
SHRAKKTT
GREAT!
NOW I'LL HAVE TO EXPLAIN TO THE PROFESSOR HOW I TOTALED A MULTI-MILLION DOLLAR PROTOTYPE!
HWROOOOM
YOU COULD ALWAYS TELL HIM IT HAD A FEW BUGS IN IT!
I THINK I LIKED YOU BETTER AS THE COLD, ALOOF, BITTER ARCHANGEL!
AT LEAST HE'D REMEMBER WHICH OF US WAS RENOWNED FOR HIS SARDONIC WIT!
NOW, JUST GIVE ME A MINUTE TO ICE UP...
...AND I'LL SHOW YOU THE ONE ABOUT THE FLY AND THE ICE CUBE!

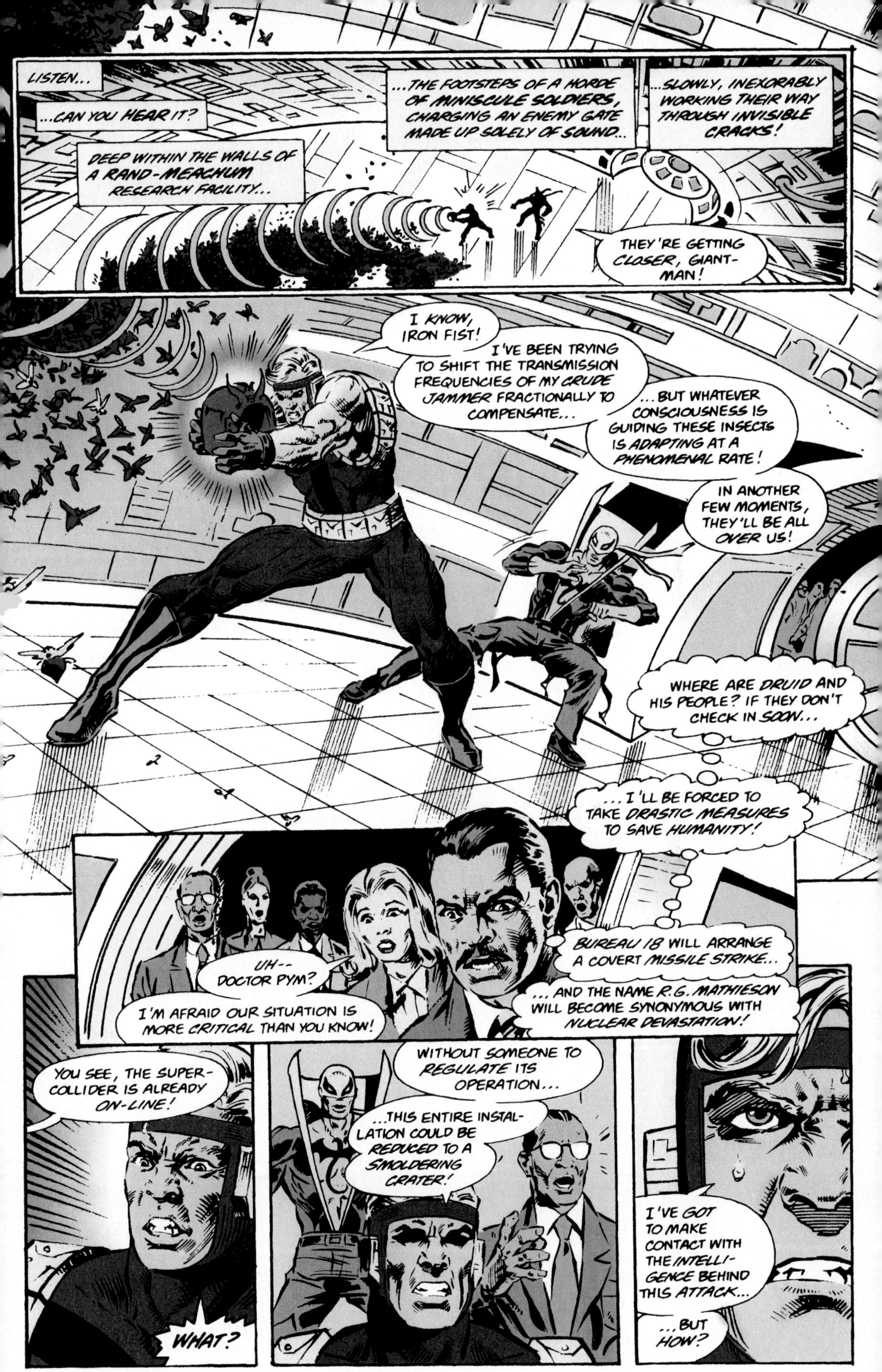
LISTEN...
...CAN YOU HEAR IT?
DEEP WITHIN THE WALLS OF A RAND-MEACHUM RESEARCH FACILITY...
...THE FOOTSTEPS OF A HORDE OF MINISCULE SOLDIERS, CHARGING AN ENEMY GATE MADE UP SOLELY OF SOUND...
...SLOWLY, INEXORABLY WORKING THEIR WAY THROUGH INVISIBLE CRACKS!
THEY'RE GETTING CLOSER, GIANT-MAN!
I KNOW, IRON FIST!
I'VE BEEN TRYING TO SHIFT THE TRANSMISSION FREQUENCIES OF MY CRUDE JAMMER FRACTIONALLY TO COMPENSATE...
...BUT WHATEVER CONSCIOUSNESS IS GUIDING THESE INSECTS IS ADAPTING AT A PHENOMENAL RATE!
IN ANOTHER FEW MOMENTS, THEY'LL BE ALL OVER US!
WHERE ARE DRUID AND HIS PEOPLE? IF THEY DON'T CHECK IN SOON...
...I'LL BE FORCED TO TAKE DRASTIC MEASURES TO SAVE HUMANITY!
BUREAU 18 WILL ARRANGE A COVERT MISSILE STRIKE...
...AND THE NAME R.G. MATHIESON WILL BECOME SYNONYMOUS WITH NUCLEAR DEVASTATION!
UH-- DOCTOR PYM?
I'M AFRAID OUR SITUATION IS MORE CRITICAL THAN YOU KNOW!
YOU SEE, THE SUPER-COLLIDER IS ALREADY ON-LINE!
WHAT?
WITHOUT SOMEONE TO REGULATE ITS OPERATION...
...THIS ENTIRE INSTAL-LATION COULD BE REDUCED TO A SMOLDERING CRATER!
I'VE GOT TO MAKE CONTACT WITH THE INTELLI-GENCE BEHIND THIS ATTACK...
...BUT HOW?

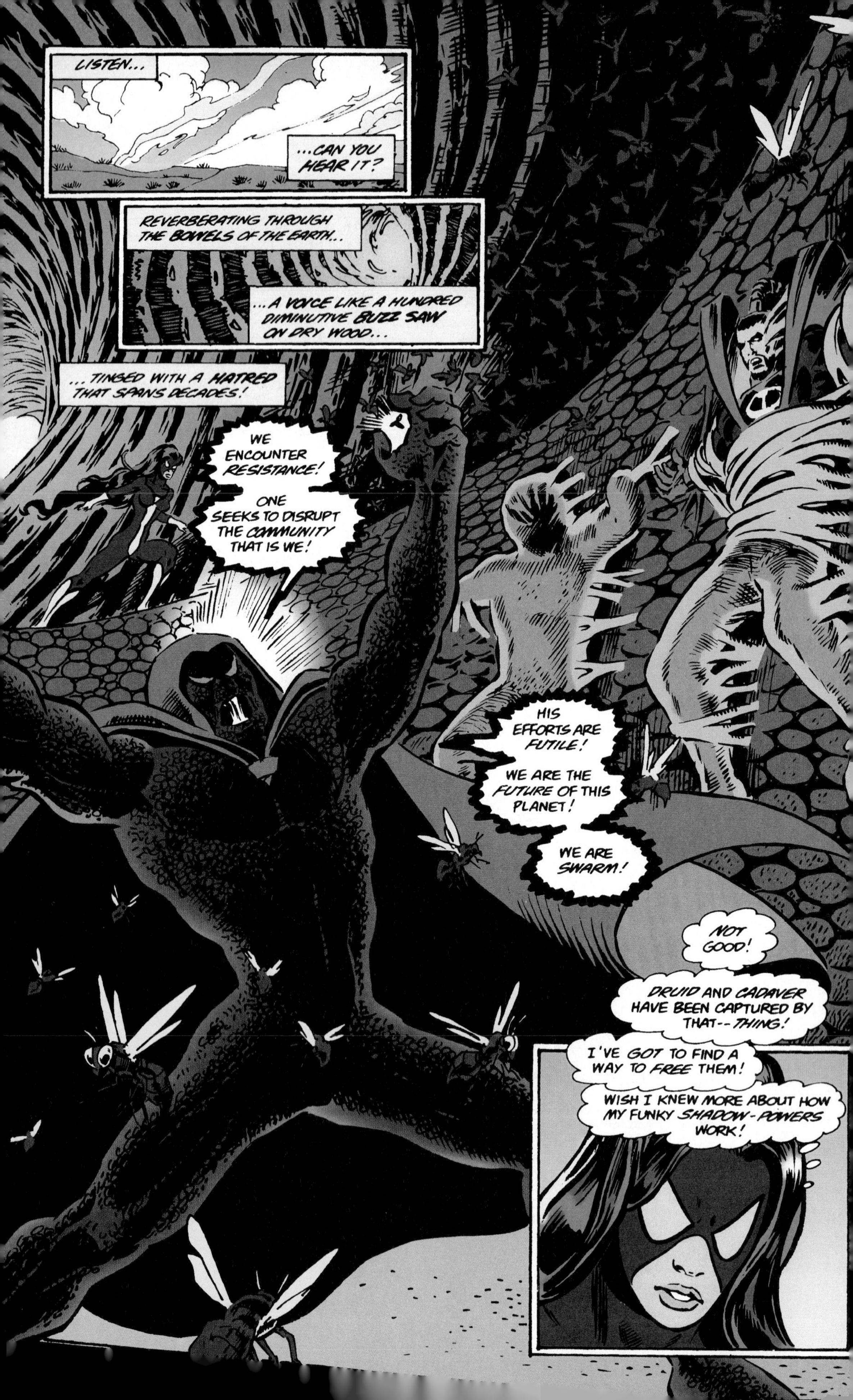
LISTEN...
...CAN YOU HEAR IT?
REVERBERATING THROUGH THE BOWELS OF THE EARTH...
...A VOICE LIKE A HUNDRED DIMINUTIVE BUZZ SAW ON DRY WOOD...
...TINGED WITH A HATRED THAT SPANS DECADES!
WE ENCOUNTER RESISTANCE!
ONE SEEKS TO DISRUPT THE COMMUNITY THAT IS WE!
HIS EFFORTS ARE FUTILE!
WE ARE THE FUTURE OF THIS PLANET!
WE ARE SWARM!
NOT GOOD!
DRUID AND CADAVER HAVE BEEN CAPTURED BY THAT--THING!
I'VE GOT TO FIND A WAY TO FREE THEM!
WISH I KNEW MORE ABOUT HOW MY FUNKY SHADOW-POWERS WORK!

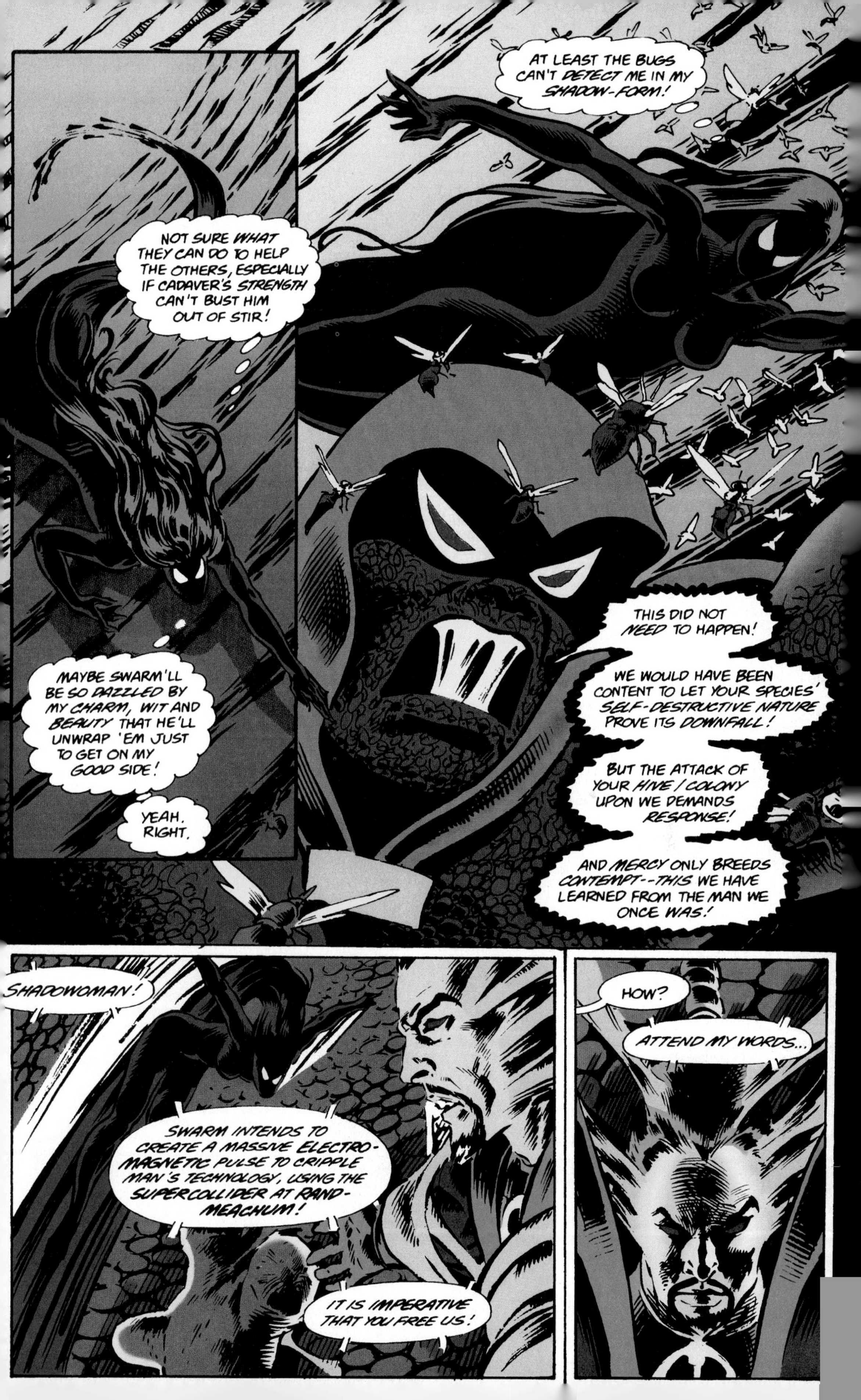
AT LEAST THE BUGS CAN'T DETECT ME IN MY SHADOW-FORM!
NOT SURE WHAT THEY CAN DO TO HELP THE OTHERS, ESPECIALLY IF CADAVER'S STRENGTH CAN'T BUST HIM OUT OF STIR!
MAYBE SWARM'LL BE SO DAZZLED BY MY CHARM, WIT AND BEAUTY THAT HE'LL UNWRAP 'EM JUST TO GET ON MY GOOD SIDE!
YEAH. RIGHT.
THIS DID NOT NEED TO HAPPEN!
WE WOULD HAVE BEEN CONTENT TO LET YOUR SPECIES' SELF-DESTRUCTIVE NATURE PROVE ITS DOWNFALL!
BUT THE ATTACK OF YOUR HIVE / COLONY UPON WE DEMANDS RESPONSE!
AND MERCY ONLY BREEDS CONTEMPT--THIS WE HAVE LEARNED FROM THE MAN WE ONCE WAS!
SHADOWOMAN!
SWARM INTENDS TO CREATE A MASSIVE ELECTRO-MAGNETIC PULSE TO CRIPPLE MAN'S TECHNOLOGY, USING THE SUPERCOLLIDER AT RAND-MEACHUM!
IT IS IMPERATIVE THAT YOU FREE US!
HOW?
ATTEND MY WORDS...

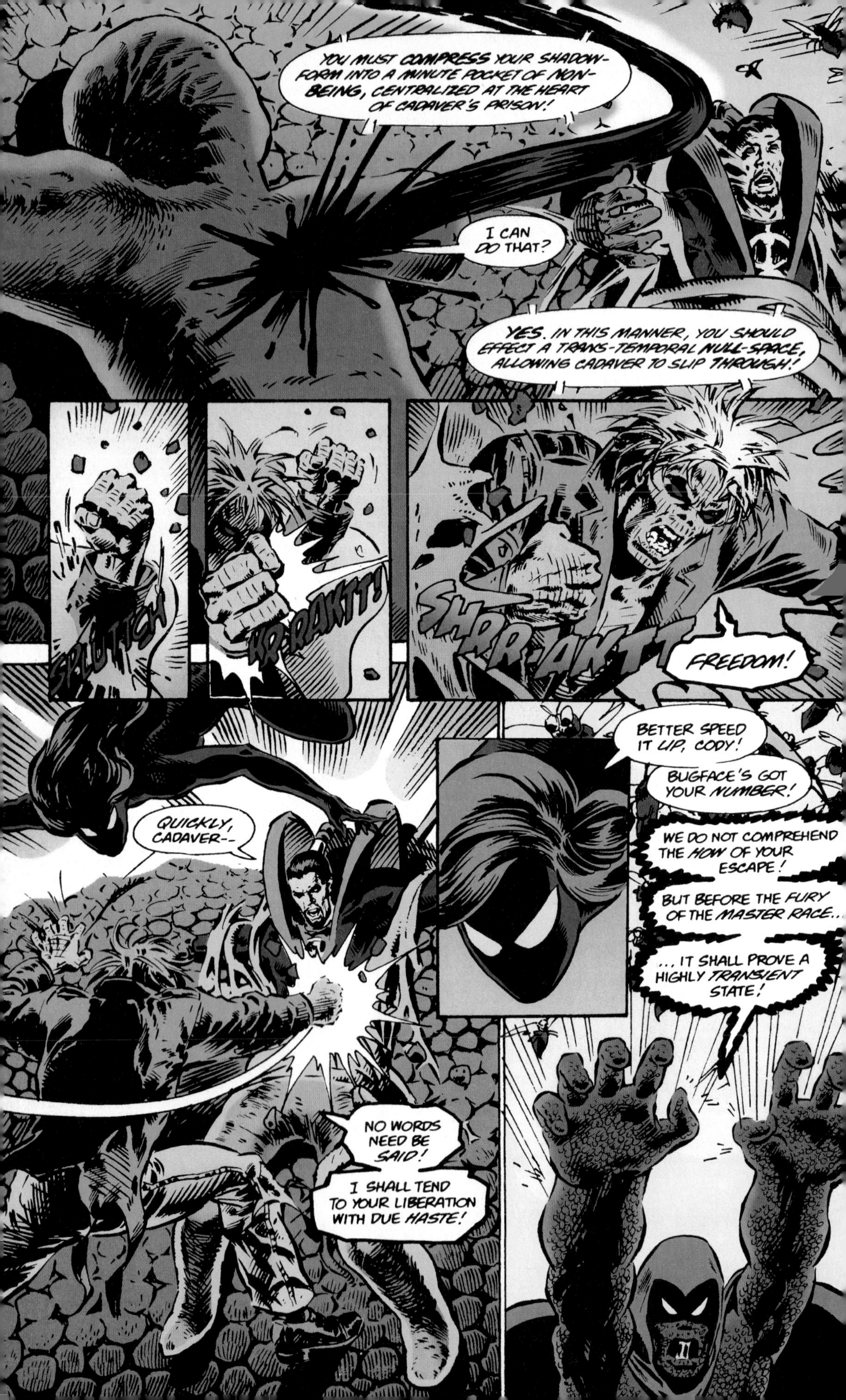
YOU MUST COMPRESS YOUR SHADOW-FORM INTO A MINUTE POCKET OF NON-BEING, CENTRALIZED AT THE HEART OF CADAVER'S PRISON!
I CAN DO THAT?
YES. IN THIS MANNER, YOU SHOULD EFFECT A TRANS-TEMPORAL NULL-SPACE, ALLOWING CADAVER TO SLIP THROUGH!
SPLUTCH
KR-RAKTT!
SHR-R-AKTT
FREEDOM!
QUICKLY, CADAVER--
BETTER SPEED IT UP, CODY!
BUGFACE'S GOT YOUR NUMBER!
WE DO NOT COMPREHEND THE HOW OF YOUR ESCAPE!
BUT BEFORE THE FURY OF THE MASTER RACE...
..., IT SHALL PROVE A HIGHLY TRANSIENT STATE!
NO WORDS NEED BE SAID!
I SHALL TEND TO YOUR LIBERATION WITH DUE HASTE!

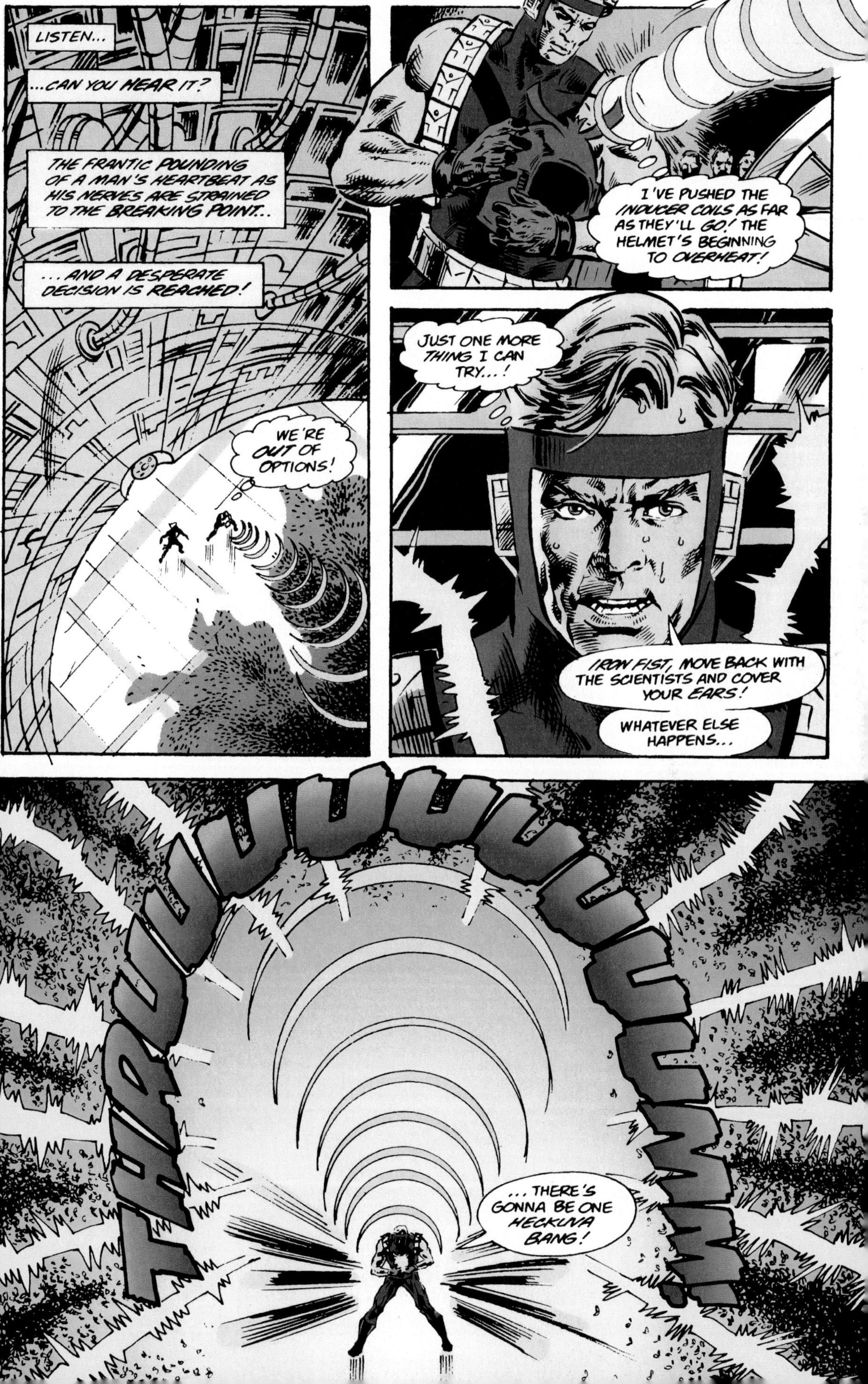
LISTEN...
...CAN YOU HEAR IT?
THE FRANTIC POUNDING OF A MAN'S HEARTBEAT AS HIS NERVES ARE STRAINED TO THE BREAKING POINT...
...AND A DESPERATE DECISION IS REACHED!
I'VE PUSHED THE INDUCER COILS AS FAR AS THEY'LL GO! THE HELMET'S BEGINNING TO OVERHEAT!
WE'RE OUT OF OPTIONS!
JUST ONE MORE THING I CAN TRY...!
IRON FIST, MOVE BACK WITH THE SCIENTISTS AND COVER YOUR EARS!
WHATEVER ELSE HAPPENS...
THRUUUUUUUMMM
...THERE'S GONNA BE ONE HECKUVA BANG!

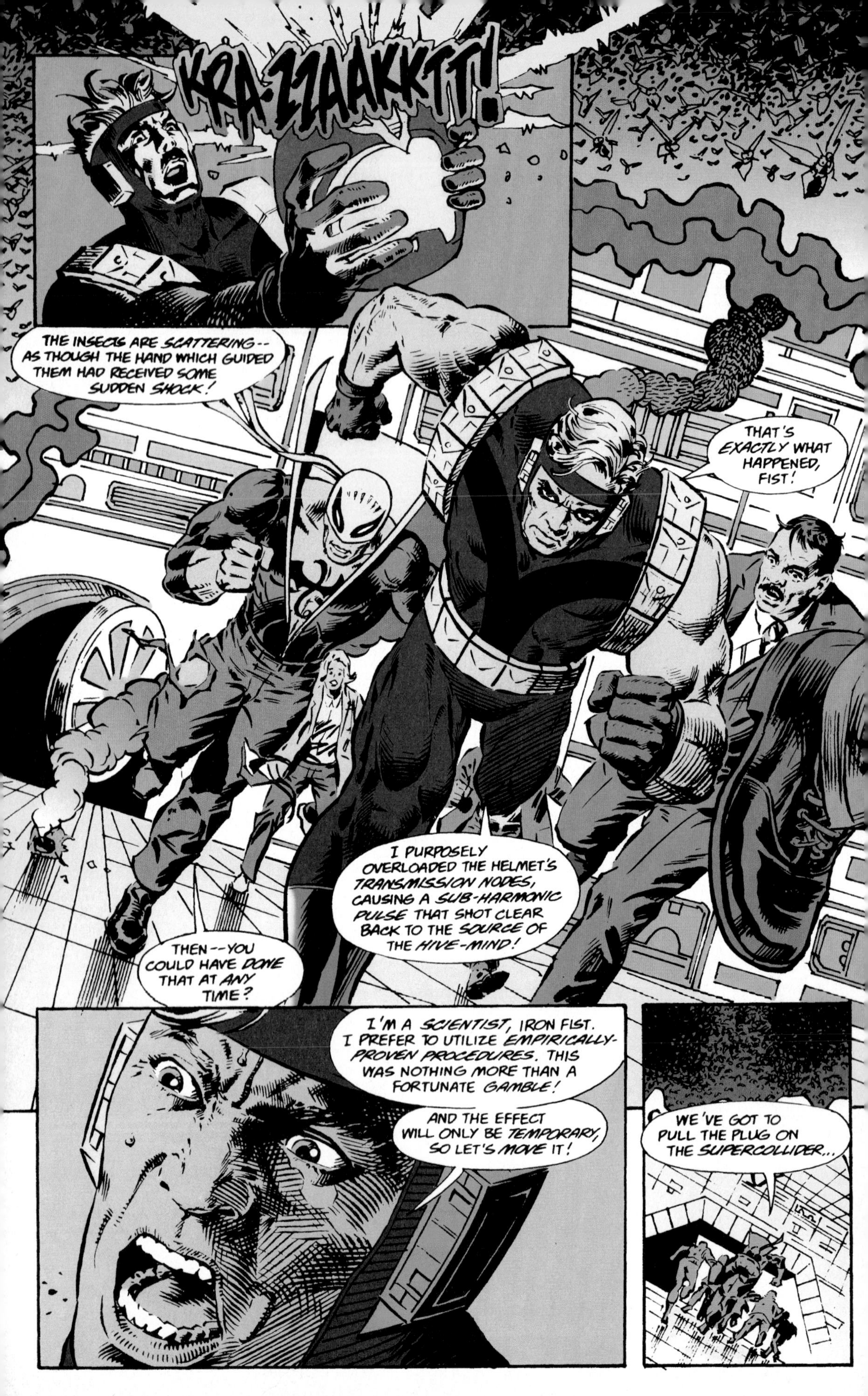
KRA-ZZAAKKTT!
THE INSECTS ARE SCATTERING-- AS THOUGH THE HAND WHICH GUIDED THEM HAD RECEIVED SOME SUDDEN SHOCK!
THAT'S EXACTLY WHAT HAPPENED, FIST!
I PURPOSELY OVERLOADED THE HELMET'S TRANSMISSION NODES, CAUSING A SUB-HARMONIC PULSE THAT SHOT CLEAR BACK TO THE SOURCE OF THE HIVE-MIND!
THEN--YOU COULD HAVE DONE THAT AT ANY TIME?
I'M A SCIENTIST, IRON FIST. I PREFER TO UTILIZE EMPIRICALLY-PROVEN PROCEDURES. THIS WAS NOTHING MORE THAN A FORTUNATE GAMBLE!
AND THE EFFECT WILL ONLY BE TEMPORARY, SO LET'S MOVE IT!
WE'VE GOT TO PULL THE PLUG ON THE SUPERCOLLIDER...

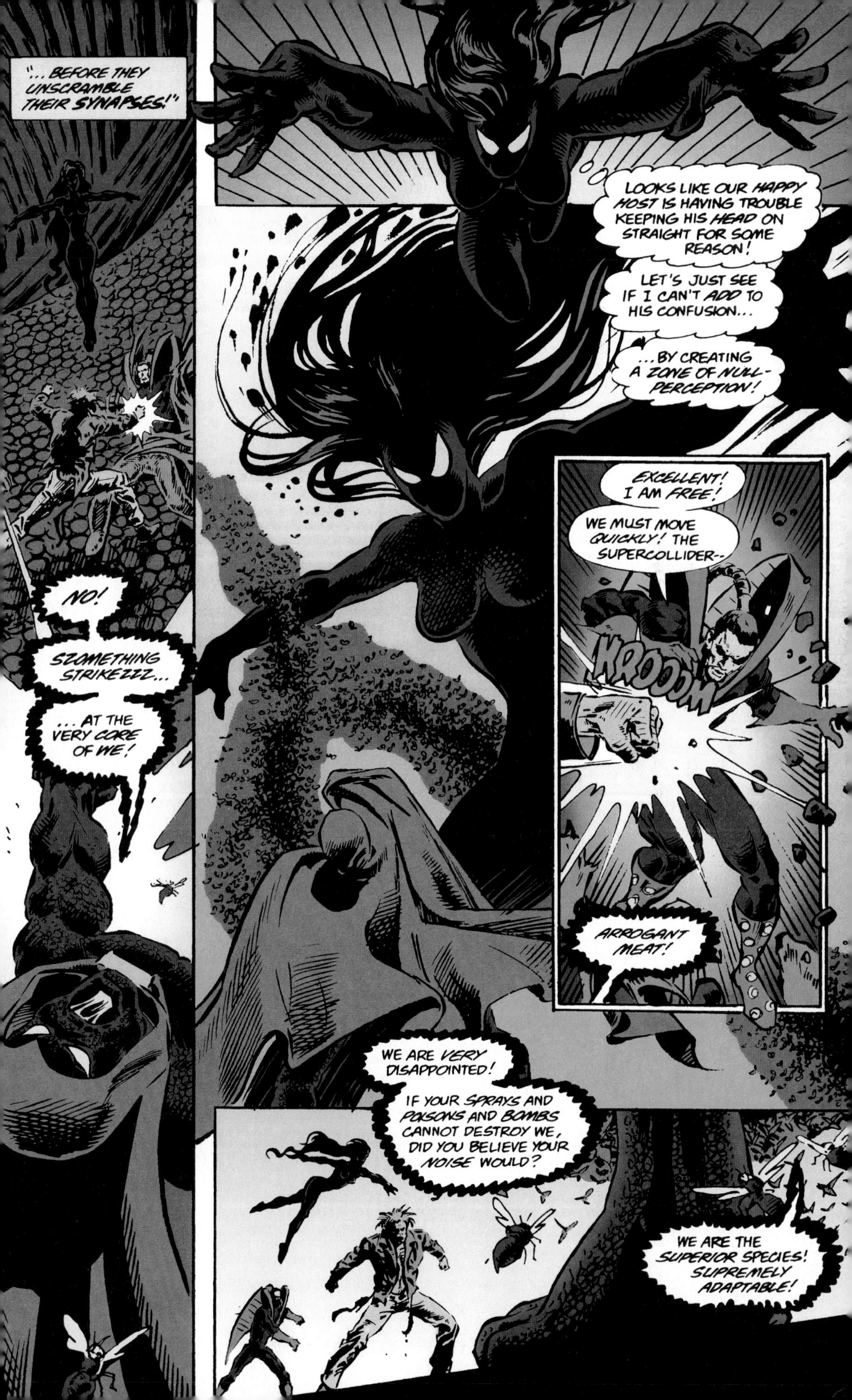
"... BEFORE THEY UNSCRAMBLE THEIR SYNAPSES!"
LOOKS LIKE OUR HAPPY HOST IS HAVING TROUBLE KEEPING HIS HEAD ON STRAIGHT FOR SOME REASON!
LET'S JUST SEE IF I CAN'T ADD TO HIS CONFUSION...
...BY CREATING A ZONE OF NULL-PERCEPTION!
NO!
SZOMETHING STRIKEZZZ...
...AT THE VERY CORE OF WE!
EXCELLENT! I AM FREE!
WE MUST MOVE QUICKLY! THE SUPERCOLLIDER--
KROOOOM
ARROGANT MEAT!
WE ARE VERY DISAPPOINTED!
IF YOUR SPRAYS AND POISONS AND BOMBS CANNOT DESTROY WE, DID YOU BELIEVE YOUR NOISE WOULD?
WE ARE THE SUPERIOR SPECIES! SUPREMELY ADAPTABLE!

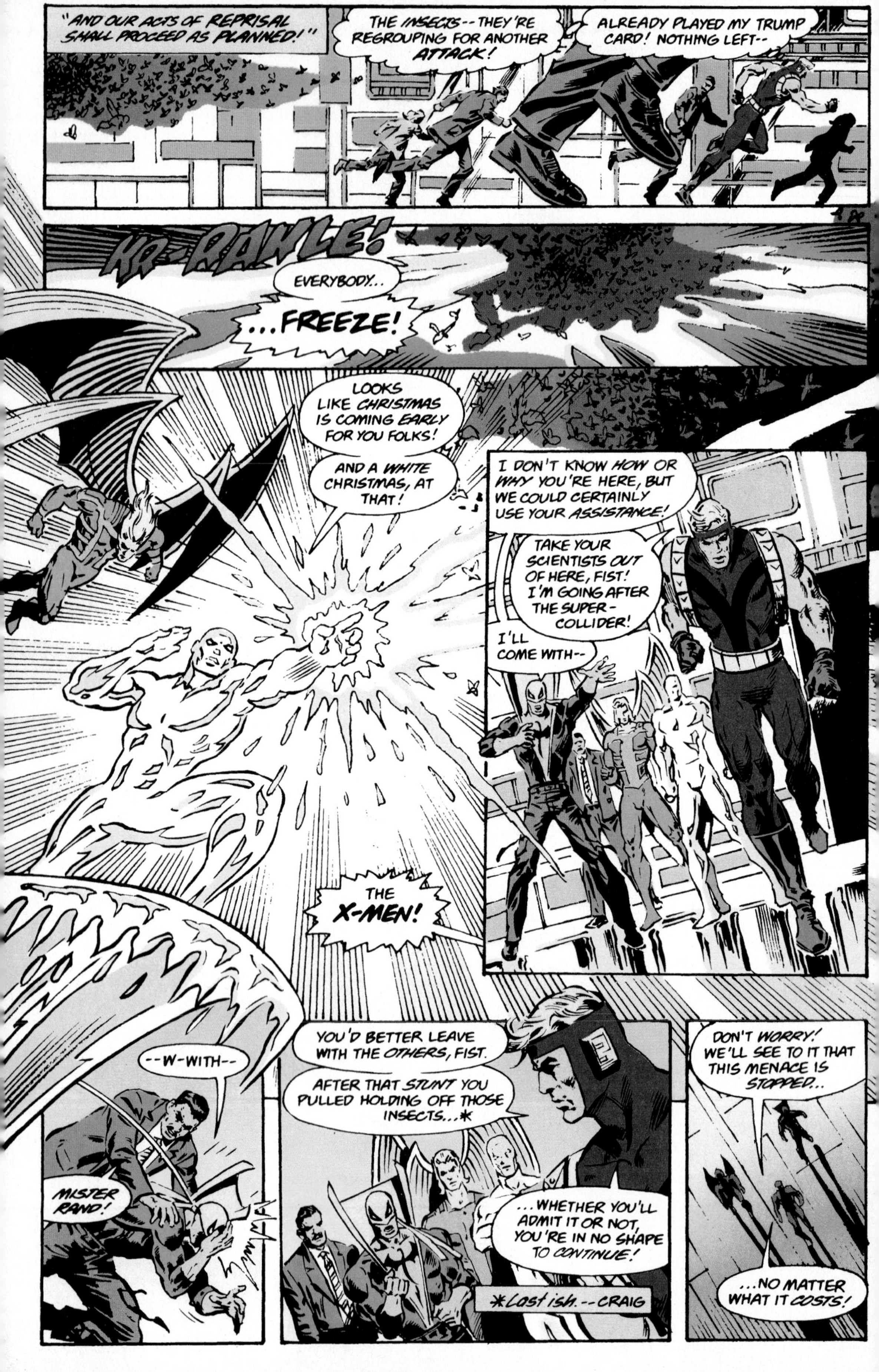
"AND OUR ACTS OF REPRISAL SHALL PROCEED AS PLANNED!"
THE INSECTS-- THEY'RE REGROUPING FOR ANOTHER ATTACK!
ALREADY PLAYED MY TRUMP CARD! NOTHING LEFT--
KRA-RAKLE!
EVERYBODY...
...FREEZE!
LOOKS LIKE CHRISTMAS IS COMING EARLY FOR YOU FOLKS!
AND A WHITE CHRISTMAS, AT THAT!
THE X-MEN!
I DON'T KNOW HOW OR WHY YOU'RE HERE, BUT WE COULD CERTAINLY USE YOUR ASSISTANCE!
TAKE YOUR SCIENTISTS OUT OF HERE, FIST! I'M GOING AFTER THE SUPER-COLLIDER!
I'LL COME WITH--
--W-WITH--
MISTER RAND!
YOU'D BETTER LEAVE WITH THE OTHERS, FIST.
AFTER THAT STUNT YOU PULLED HOLDING OFF THOSE INSECTS...*
...WHETHER YOU'LL ADMIT IT OR NOT, YOU'RE IN NO SHAPE TO CONTINUE!
*Last ish. --CRAIG
DON'T WORRY! WE'LL SEE TO IT THAT THIS MENACE IS STOPPED...
...NO MATTER WHAT IT COSTS!

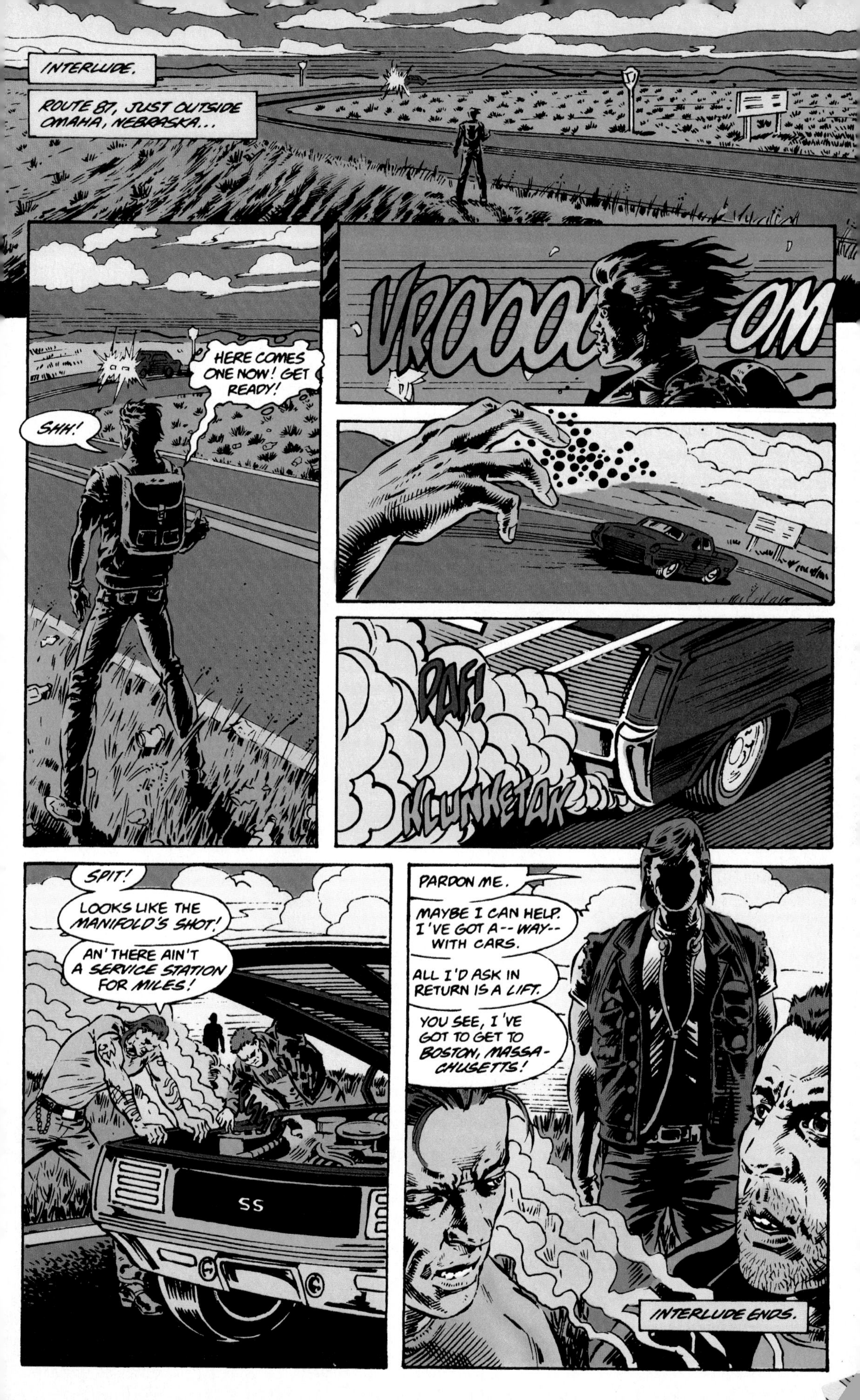
INTERLUDE.
ROUTE 87, JUST OUTSIDE OMAHA, NEBRASKA...
HERE COMES ONE NOW! GET READY!
SHH!
VROOOO OM
PAF!
KLUNKETAK
SPIT!
LOOKS LIKE THE MANIFOLD'S SHOT!
AN' THERE AIN'T A SERVICE STATION FOR MILES!
SS
PARDON ME.
MAYBE I CAN HELP. I'VE GOT A-- WAY-- WITH CARS.
ALL I'D ASK IN RETURN IS A LIFT.
YOU SEE, I'VE GOT TO GET TO BOSTON, MASSACHUSETTS!
INTERLUDE ENDS.

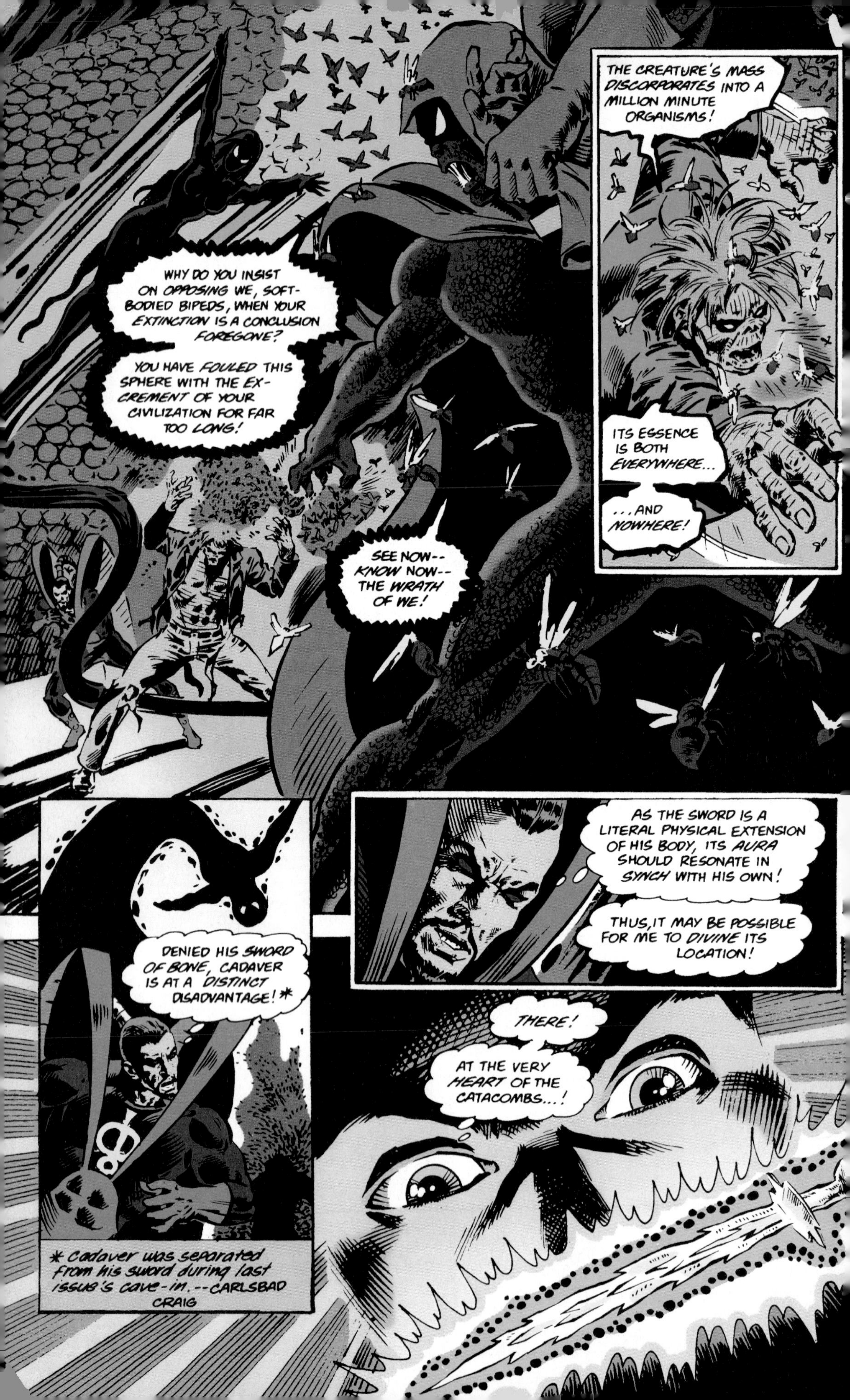
THE CREATURE'S MASS DISCORPORATES INTO A MILLION MINUTE ORGANISMS!
ITS ESSENCE IS BOTH EVERYWHERE...
...AND NOWHERE!
WHY DO YOU INSIST ON OPPOSING WE, SOFT-BODIED BIPEDS, WHEN YOUR EXTINCTION IS A CONCLUSION FOREGONE?
YOU HAVE FOULED THIS SPHERE WITH THE EXCREMENT OF YOUR CIVILIZATION FOR FAR TOO LONG!
SEE NOW--KNOW NOW--THE WRATH OF WE!
DENIED HIS SWORD OF BONE, CADAVER IS AT A DISTINCT DISADVANTAGE!*
* Cadaver was separated from his sword during last issue's cave-in. --CARLSBAD CRAIG
AS THE SWORD IS A LITERAL PHYSICAL EXTENSION OF HIS BODY, ITS AURA SHOULD RESONATE IN SYNCH WITH HIS OWN!
THUS, IT MAY BE POSSIBLE FOR ME TO DIVINE ITS LOCATION!
THERE!
AT THE VERY HEART OF THE CATACOMBS...!

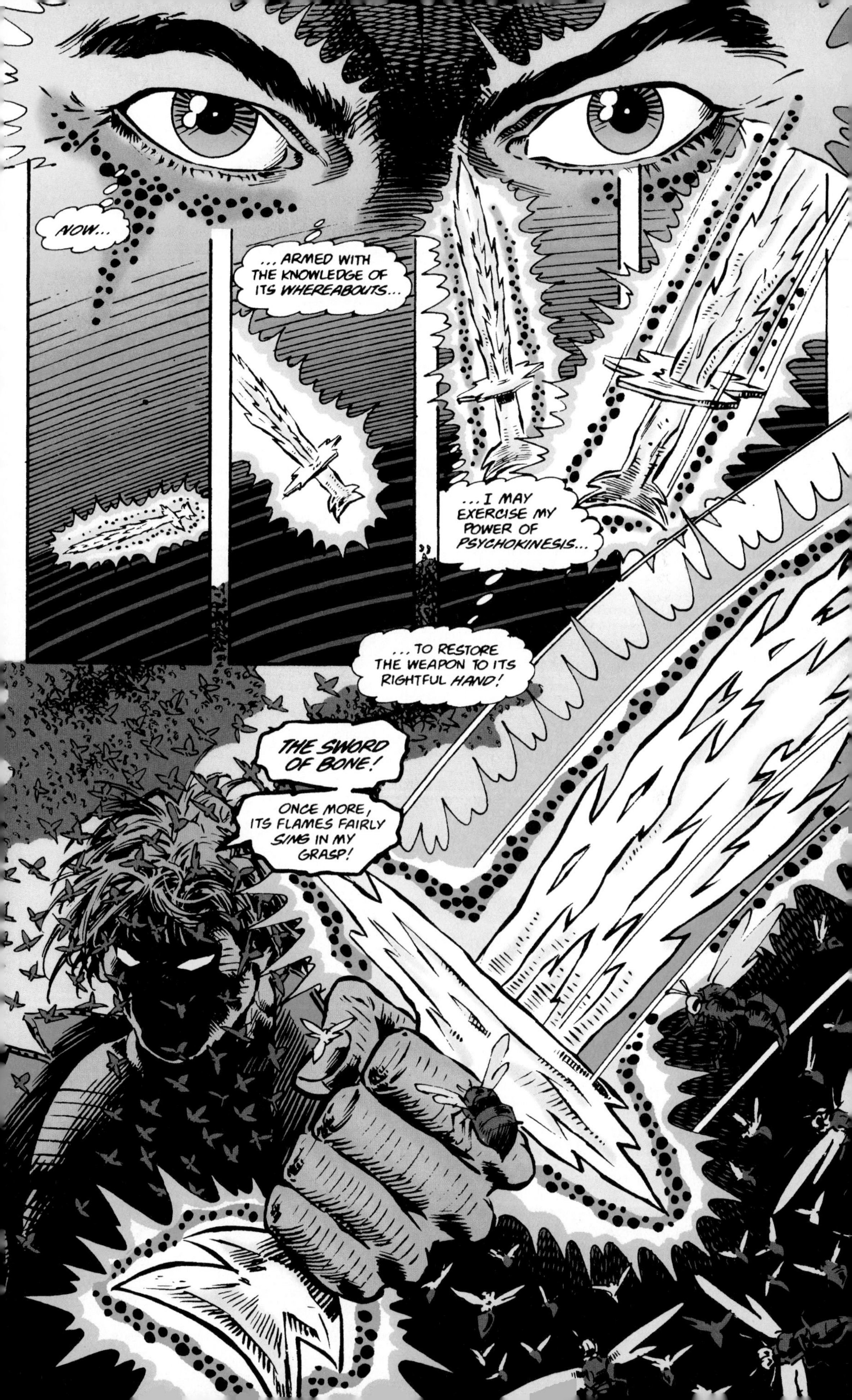
NOW...
...ARMED WITH THE KNOWLEDGE OF ITS WHEREABOUTS...
...I MAY EXERCISE MY POWER OF PSYCHOKINESIS...
...TO RESTORE THE WEAPON TO ITS RIGHTFUL HAND!
THE SWORD OF BONE!
ONCE MORE, ITS FLAMES FAIRLY SING IN MY GRASP!

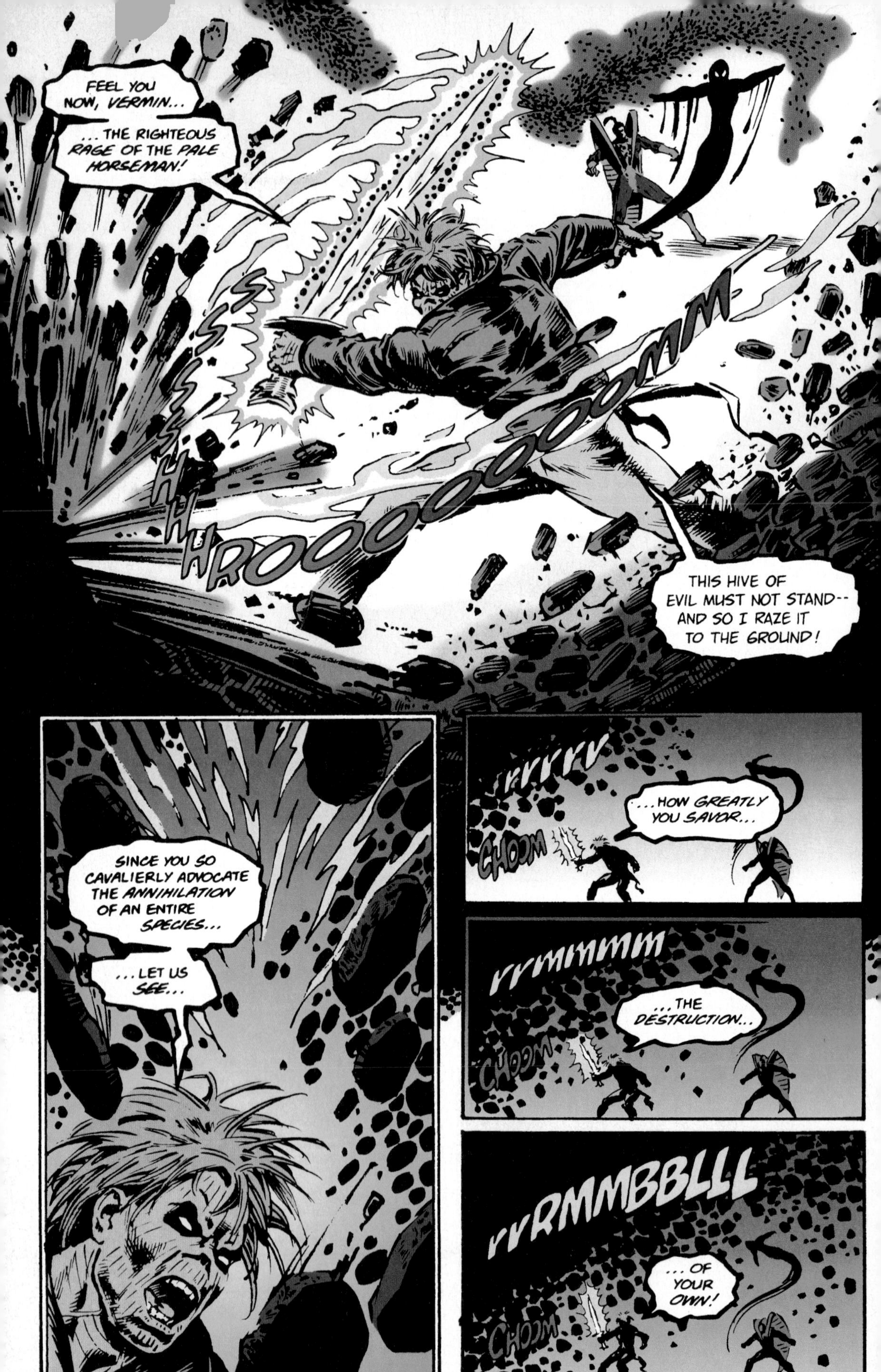
FEEL YOU NOW, VERMIN...
...THE RIGHTEOUS RAGE OF THE PALE HORSEMAN!
SSSHHHHROOOOOOOOOOMM
THIS HIVE OF EVIL MUST NOT STAND-- AND SO I RAZE IT TO THE GROUND!
SINCE YOU SO CAVALIERLY ADVOCATE THE ANNIHILATION OF AN ENTIRE SPECIES...
...LET US SEE...
rrrrrv
CHOOM
...HOW GREATLY YOU SAVOR...
rrmmmmm
CHOOM
...THE DESTRUCTION...
rrRMMBBLLL
CHOOM
...OF YOUR OWN!

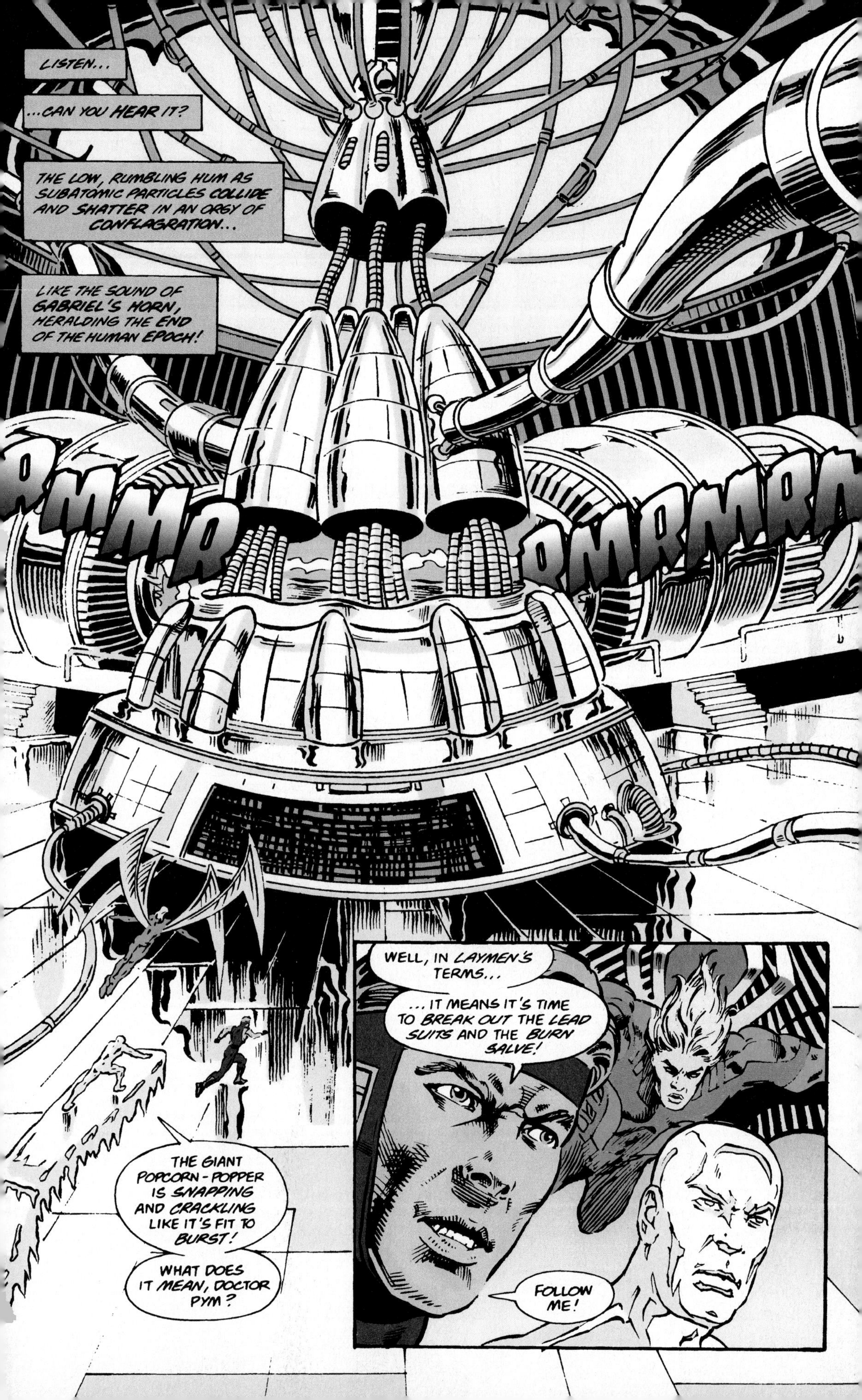
LISTEN...
...CAN YOU HEAR IT?
THE LOW, RUMBLING HUM AS SUBATOMIC PARTICLES COLLIDE AND SHATTER IN AN ORGY OF CONFLAGRATION...
LIKE THE SOUND OF GABRIEL'S HORN, HERALDING THE END OF THE HUMAN EPOCH!
RMMR
RMRMRM
THE GIANT POPCORN-POPPER IS SNAPPING AND CRACKLING LIKE IT'S FIT TO BURST!
WHAT DOES IT MEAN, DOCTOR PYM?
WELL, IN LAYMEN'S TERMS...
...IT MEANS IT'S TIME TO BREAK OUT THE LEAD SUITS AND THE BURN SALVE!
FOLLOW ME!

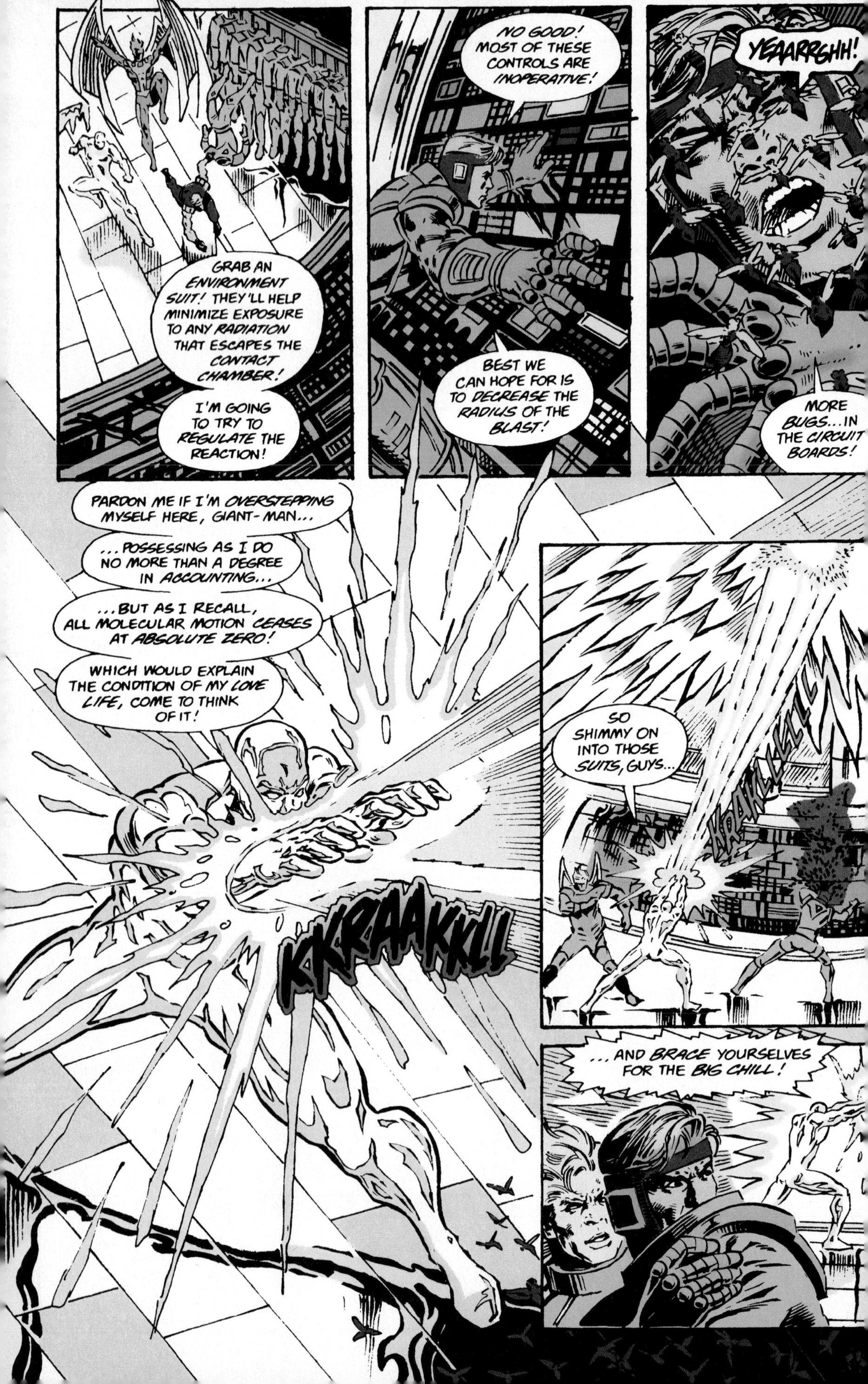
GRAB AN ENVIRONMENT SUIT! THEY'LL HELP MINIMIZE EXPOSURE TO ANY RADIATION THAT ESCAPES THE CONTACT CHAMBER!
I'M GOING TO TRY TO REGULATE THE REACTION!
NO GOOD! MOST OF THESE CONTROLS ARE INOPERATIVE!
BEST WE CAN HOPE FOR IS TO DECREASE THE RADIUS OF THE BLAST!
YEAARRGHH!
MORE BUGS...IN THE CIRCUIT BOARDS!
PARDON ME IF I'M OVERSTEPPING MYSELF HERE, GIANT-MAN...
...POSSESSING AS I DO NO MORE THAN A DEGREE IN ACCOUNTING...
...BUT AS I RECALL, ALL MOLECULAR MOTION CEASES AT ABSOLUTE ZERO!
WHICH WOULD EXPLAIN THE CONDITION OF MY LOVE LIFE, COME TO THINK OF IT!
KKRAAAKKL!
SO SHIMMY ON INTO THOSE SUITS, GUYS...
KRAAKLLLL
...AND BRACE YOURSELVES FOR THE BIG CHILL!

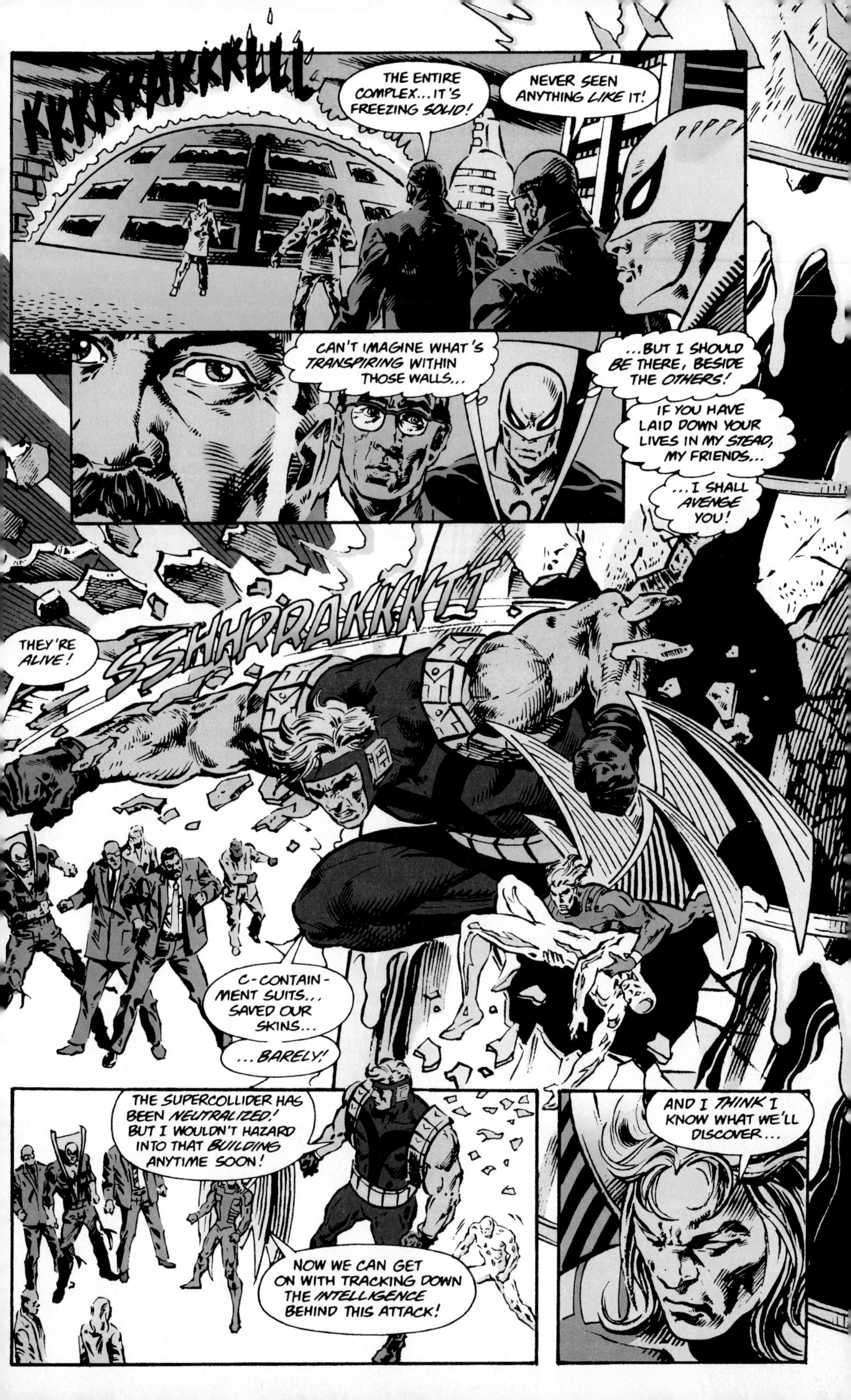
KKKRRAKKKRLLL
THE ENTIRE COMPLEX... IT'S FREEZING SOLID!
NEVER SEEN ANYTHING LIKE IT!
CAN'T IMAGINE WHAT'S TRANSPIRING WITHIN THOSE WALLS...
...BUT I SHOULD BE THERE, BESIDE THE OTHERS!
IF YOU HAVE LAID DOWN YOUR LIVES IN MY STEAD, MY FRIENDS...
...I SHALL AVENGE YOU!
SSHHRRAKKKKTT
THEY'RE ALIVE!
C-CONTAIN-MENT SUITS... SAVED OUR SKINS...
...BARELY!
THE SUPERCOLLIDER HAS BEEN NEUTRALIZED! BUT I WOULDN'T HAZARD INTO THAT BUILDING ANYTIME SOON!
NOW WE CAN GET ON WITH TRACKING DOWN THE INTELLIGENCE BEHIND THIS ATTACK!
AND I THINK I KNOW WHAT WE'LL DISCOVER...

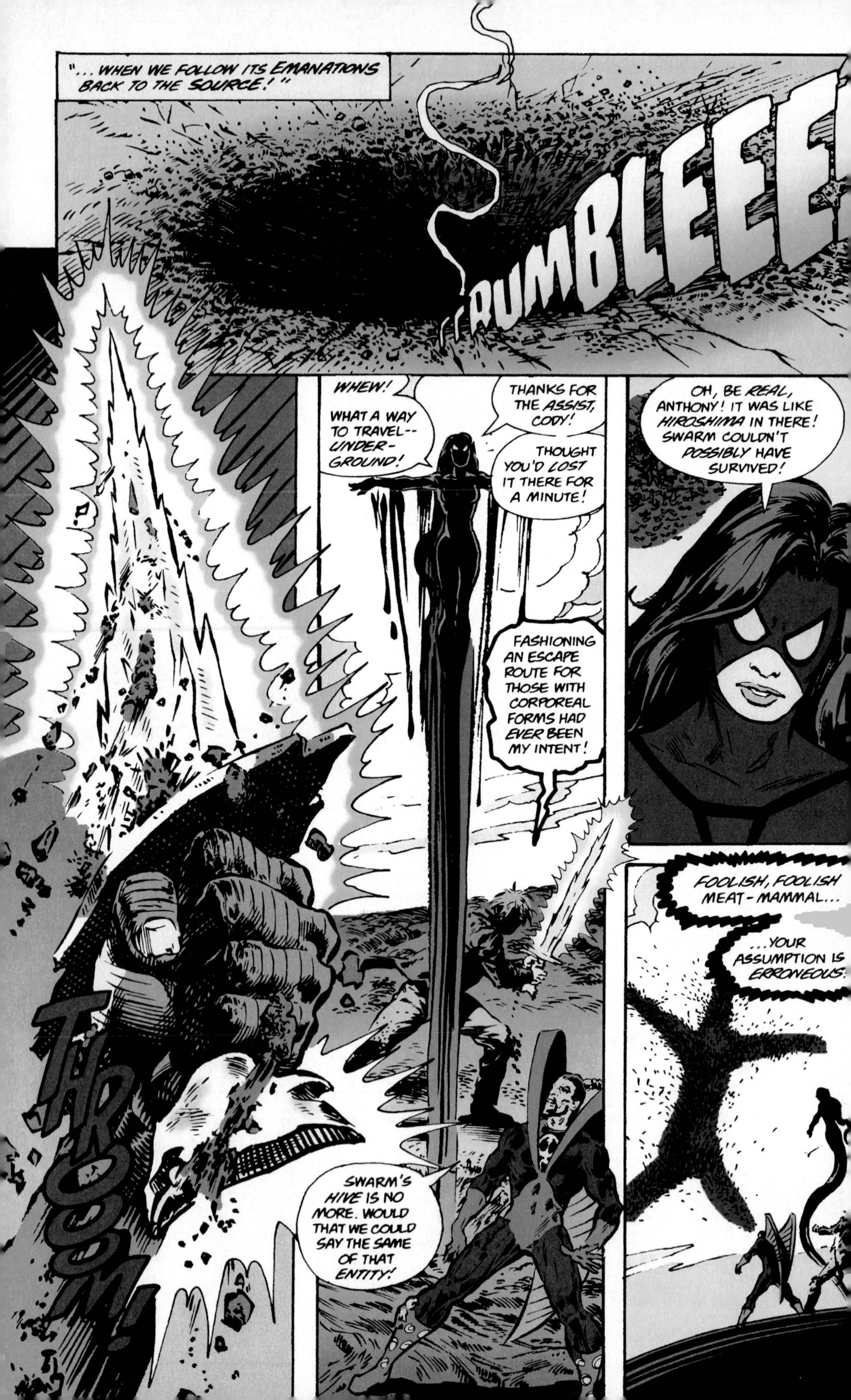
"...WHEN WE FOLLOW ITS EMANATIONS BACK TO THE SOURCE!"
RUMBLEEE
WHEW! WHAT A WAY TO TRAVEL-- UNDER-GROUND!
THANKS FOR THE ASSIST, CODY!
THOUGHT YOU'D LOST IT THERE FOR A MINUTE!
FASHIONING AN ESCAPE ROUTE FOR THOSE WITH CORPOREAL FORMS HAD EVER BEEN MY INTENT!
OH, BE REAL, ANTHONY! IT WAS LIKE HIROSHIMA IN THERE! SWARM COULDN'T POSSIBLY HAVE SURVIVED!
THROOOOM!
SWARM'S HIVE IS NO MORE. WOULD THAT WE COULD SAY THE SAME OF THAT ENTITY!
FOOLISH, FOOLISH MEAT-MAMMAL...
...YOUR ASSUMPTION IS ERRONEOUS!

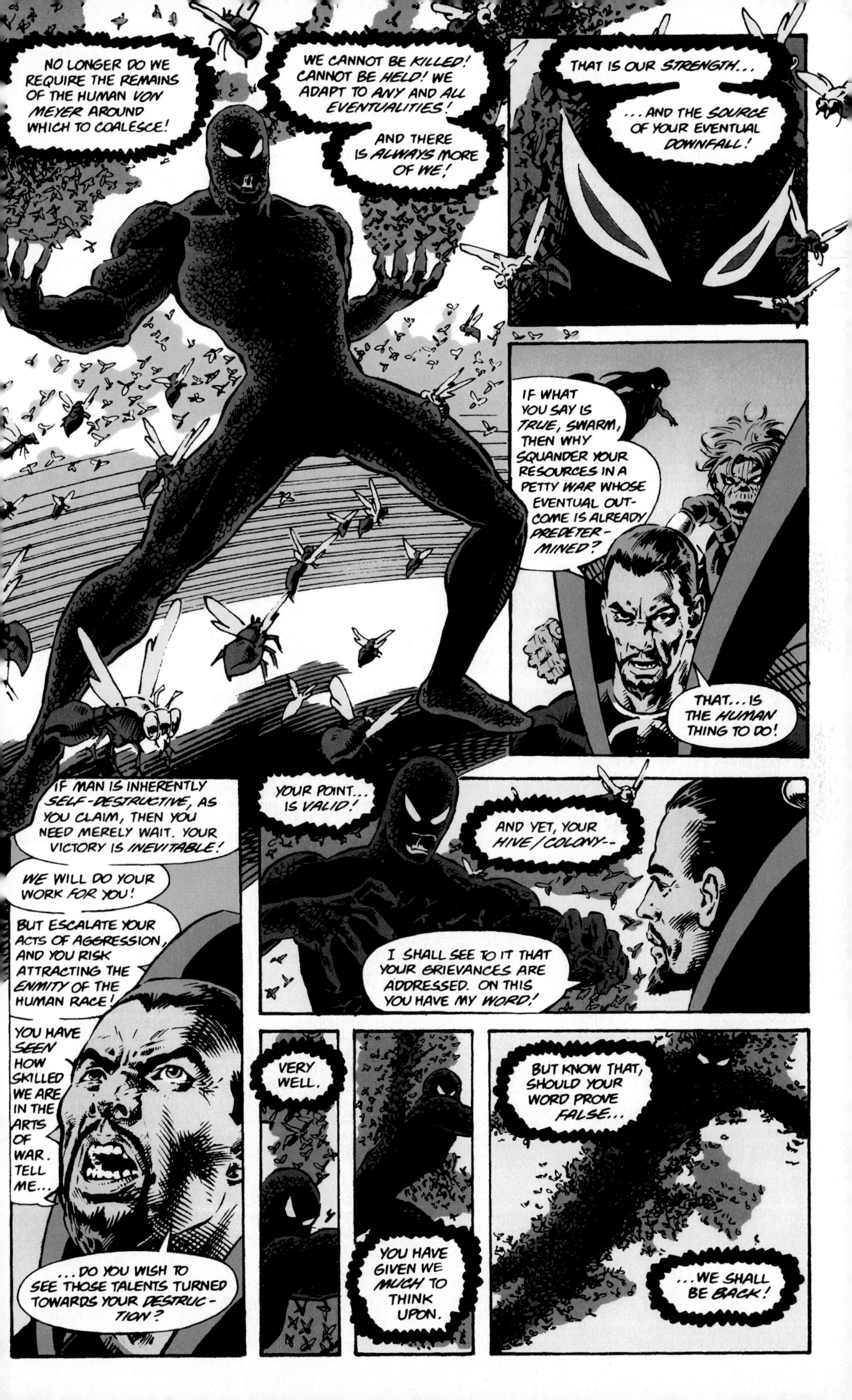
NO LONGER DO WE REQUIRE THE REMAINS OF THE HUMAN VON MEYER AROUND WHICH TO COALESCE!
WE CANNOT BE KILLED! CANNOT BE HELD! WE ADAPT TO ANY AND ALL EVENTUALITIES!
AND THERE IS ALWAYS MORE OF WE!
THAT IS OUR STRENGTH...
...AND THE SOURCE OF YOUR EVENTUAL DOWNFALL!
IF WHAT YOU SAY IS TRUE, SWARM, THEN WHY SQUANDER YOUR RESOURCES IN A PETTY WAR WHOSE EVENTUAL OUTCOME IS ALREADY PREDETERMINED?
THAT... IS THE HUMAN THING TO DO!
IF MAN IS INHERENTLY SELF-DESTRUCTIVE, AS YOU CLAIM, THEN YOU NEED MERELY WAIT. YOUR VICTORY IS INEVITABLE!
WE WILL DO YOUR WORK FOR YOU!
BUT ESCALATE YOUR ACTS OF AGGRESSION, AND YOU RISK ATTRACTING THE ENMITY OF THE HUMAN RACE!
YOU HAVE SEEN HOW SKILLED WE ARE IN THE ARTS OF WAR. TELL ME...
...DO YOU WISH TO SEE THOSE TALENTS TURNED TOWARDS YOUR DESTRUCTION?
YOUR POINT... IS VALID!
AND YET, YOUR HIVE/COLONY--
I SHALL SEE TO IT THAT YOUR GRIEVANCES ARE ADDRESSED. ON THIS YOU HAVE MY WORD!
VERY WELL.
YOU HAVE GIVEN WE MUCH TO THINK UPON.
BUT KNOW THAT, SHOULD YOUR WORD PROVE FALSE...
...WE SHALL BE BACK!

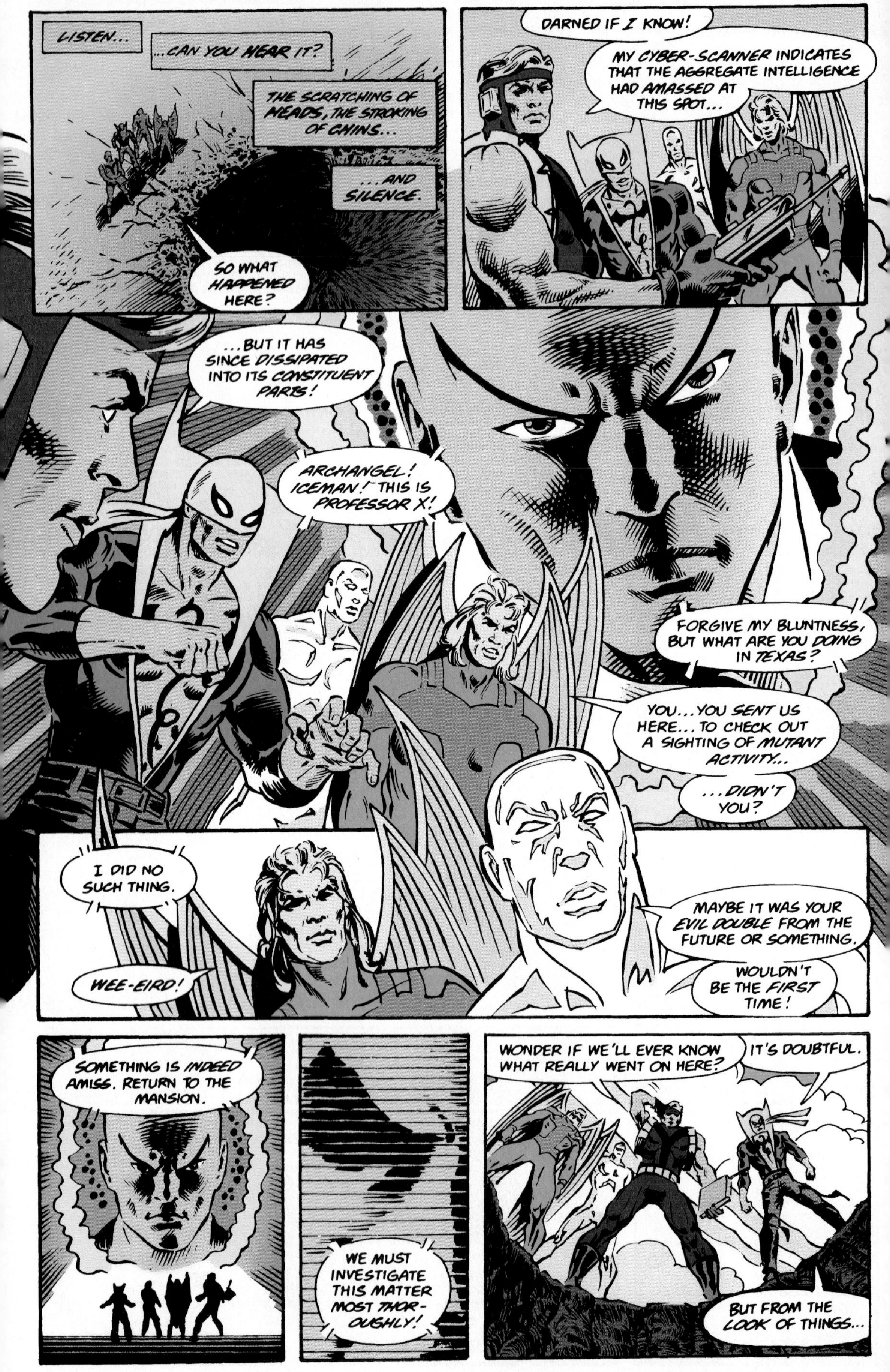
LISTEN...
...CAN YOU HEAR IT?
THE SCRATCHING OF HEADS, THE STROKING OF CHINS...
...AND SILENCE.
SO WHAT HAPPENED HERE?
DARNED IF I KNOW!
MY CYBER-SCANNER INDICATES THAT THE AGGREGATE INTELLIGENCE HAD AMASSED AT THIS SPOT...
...BUT IT HAS SINCE DISSIPATED INTO ITS CONSTITUENT PARTS!
ARCHANGEL! ICEMAN! THIS IS PROFESSOR X!
FORGIVE MY BLUNTNESS, BUT WHAT ARE YOU DOING IN TEXAS?
YOU...YOU SENT US HERE...TO CHECK OUT A SIGHTING OF MUTANT ACTIVITY...
...DIDN'T YOU?
I DID NO SUCH THING.
WEE-EIRD!
MAYBE IT WAS YOUR EVIL DOUBLE FROM THE FUTURE OR SOMETHING.
WOULDN'T BE THE FIRST TIME!
SOMETHING IS INDEED AMISS. RETURN TO THE MANSION.
WE MUST INVESTIGATE THIS MATTER MOST THOROUGHLY!
WONDER IF WE'LL EVER KNOW WHAT REALLY WENT ON HERE?
IT'S DOUBTFUL.
BUT FROM THE LOOK OF THINGS...

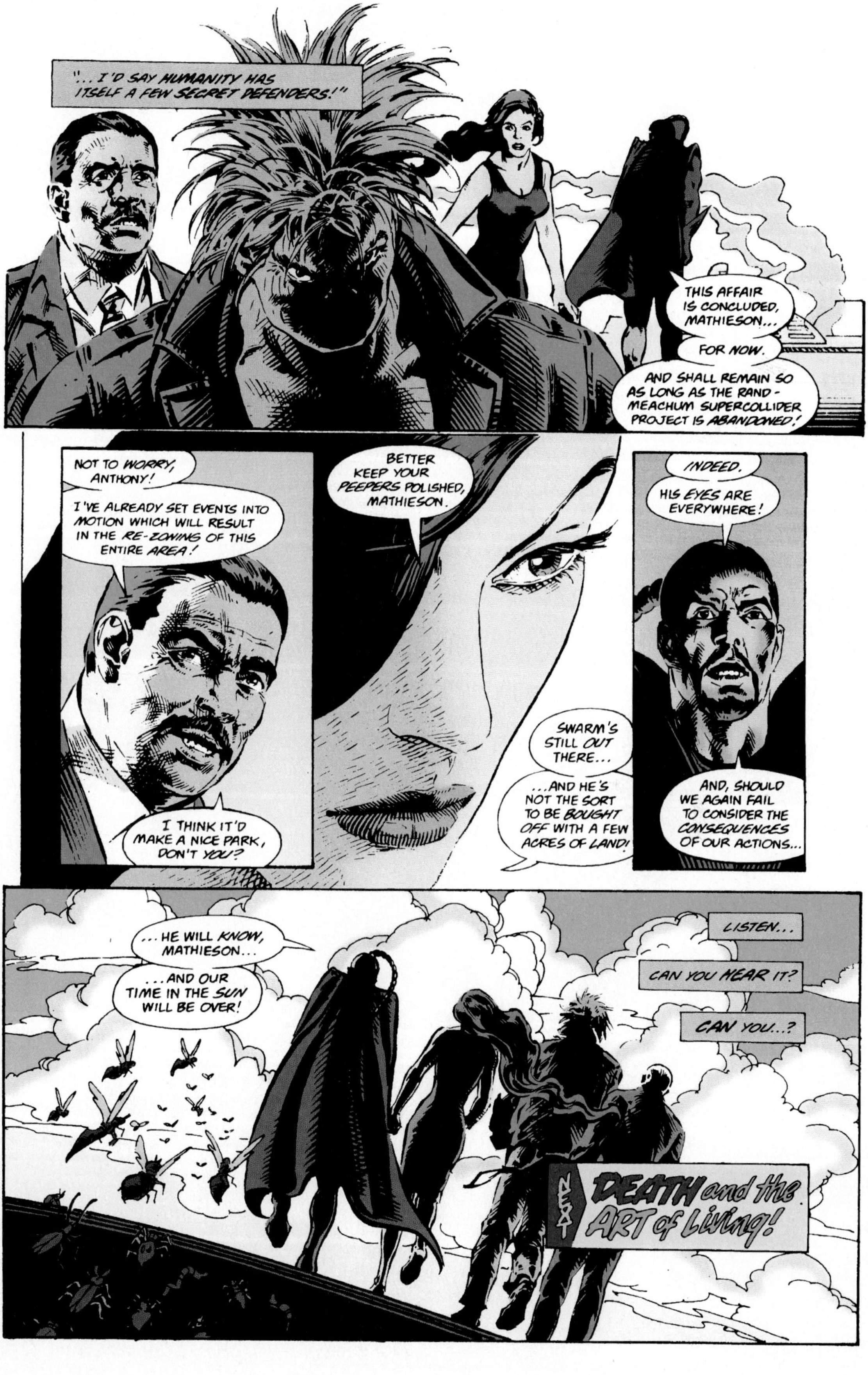
"...I'D SAY HUMANITY HAS ITSELF A FEW SECRET DEFENDERS!"
THIS AFFAIR IS CONCLUDED, MATHIESON...
FOR NOW.
AND SHALL REMAIN SO AS LONG AS THE RAND-MEACHUM SUPERCOLLIDER PROJECT IS ABANDONED!
NOT TO WORRY, ANTHONY!
I'VE ALREADY SET EVENTS INTO MOTION WHICH WILL RESULT IN THE RE-ZONING OF THIS ENTIRE AREA!
I THINK IT'D MAKE A NICE PARK, DON'T YOU?
BETTER KEEP YOUR PEEPERS POLISHED, MATHIESON.
SWARM'S STILL OUT THERE...
...AND HE'S NOT THE SORT TO BE BOUGHT OFF WITH A FEW ACRES OF LAND!
INDEED.
HIS EYES ARE EVERYWHERE!
AND, SHOULD WE AGAIN FAIL TO CONSIDER THE CONSEQUENCES OF OUR ACTIONS...
...HE WILL KNOW, MATHIESON...
...AND OUR TIME IN THE SUN WILL BE OVER!
LISTEN...
CAN YOU HEAR IT?
CAN YOU...?
NEXT
DEATH and the ART of Living!

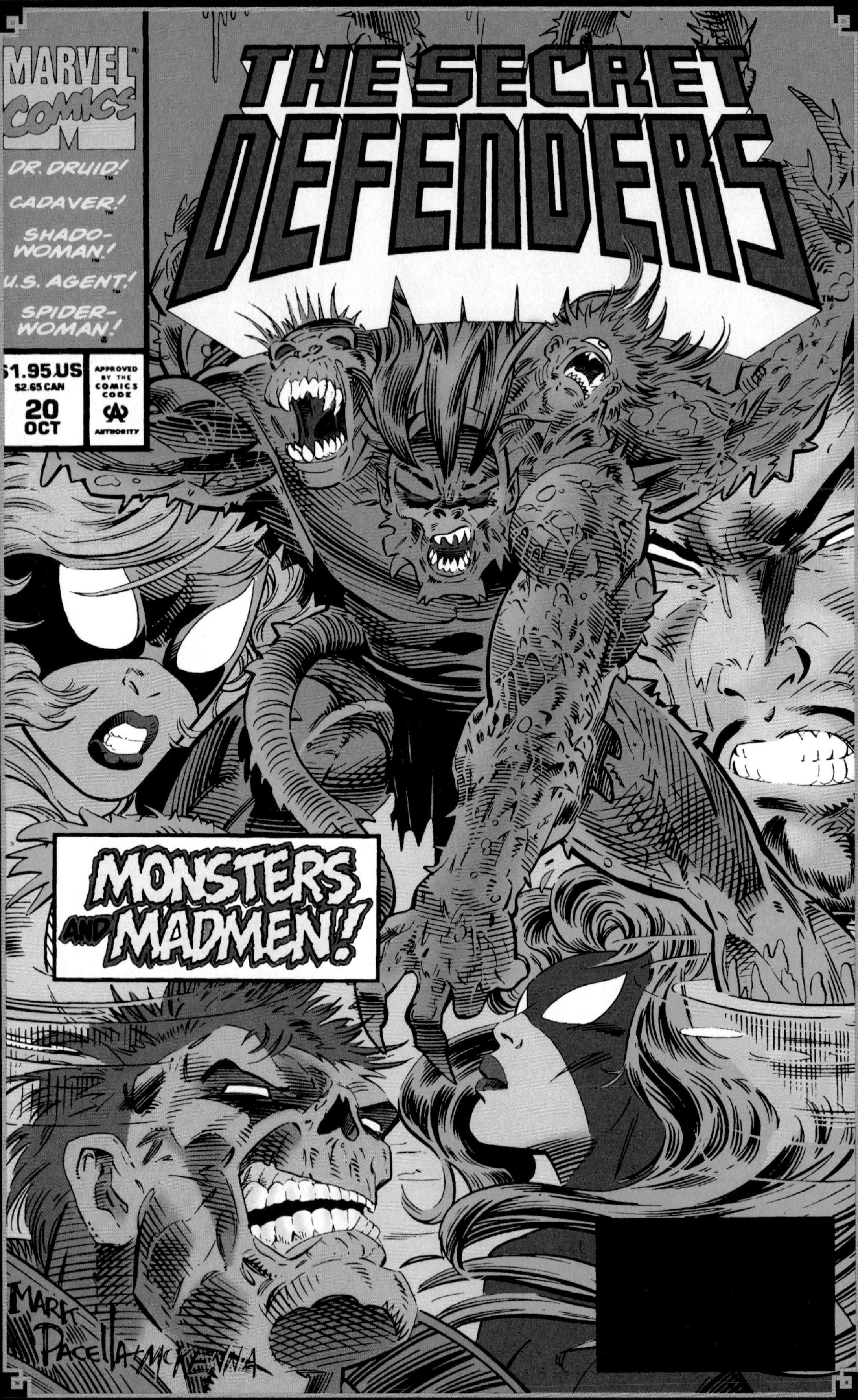
MARVEL COMICS
THE SECRET DEFENDERS
DR. DRUID!
CADAVER!
SHADO-WOMAN!
U.S. AGENT!
SPIDER-WOMAN!
$1.95 US
$2.65 CAN
20
OCT
APPROVED BY THE COMICS CODE AUTHORITY
MONSTERS AND MADMEN!!
MARK PACELLA & MCKENNA

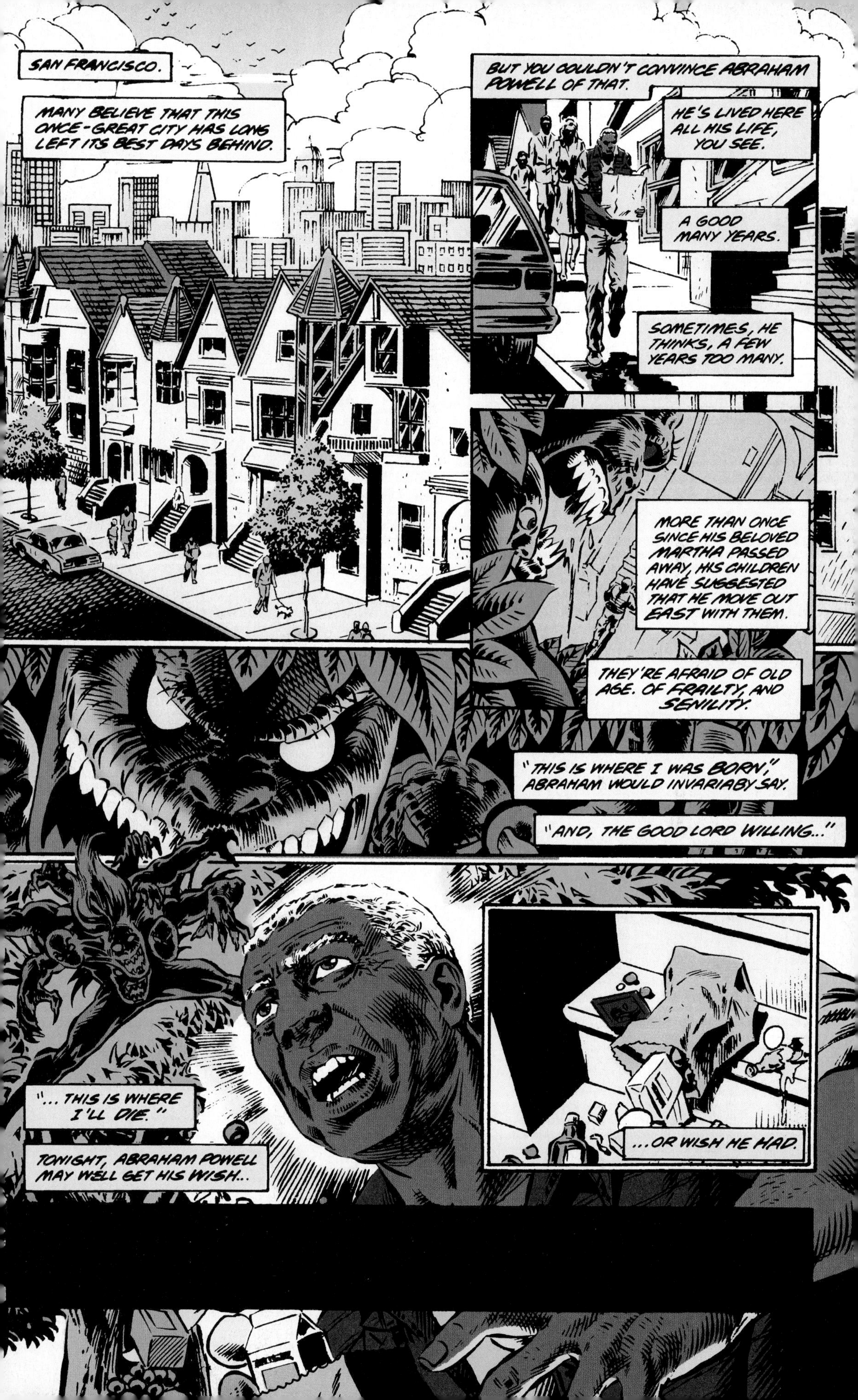
SAN FRANCISCO.
MANY BELIEVE THAT THIS ONCE-GREAT CITY HAS LONG LEFT ITS BEST DAYS BEHIND.
BUT YOU COULDN'T CONVINCE ABRAHAM POWELL OF THAT.
HE'S LIVED HERE ALL HIS LIFE, YOU SEE.
A GOOD MANY YEARS.
SOMETIMES, HE THINKS, A FEW YEARS TOO MANY.
MORE THAN ONCE SINCE HIS BELOVED MARTHA PASSED AWAY, HIS CHILDREN HAVE SUGGESTED THAT HE MOVE OUT EAST WITH THEM.
THEY'RE AFRAID OF OLD AGE. OF FRAILTY, AND SENILITY.
"THIS IS WHERE I WAS BORN," ABRAHAM WOULD INVARIABY SAY.
"AND, THE GOOD LORD WILLING..."
"... THIS IS WHERE I'LL DIE."
...OR WISH HE HAD.
TONIGHT, ABRAHAM POWELL MAY WELL GET HIS WISH...
[redacted]

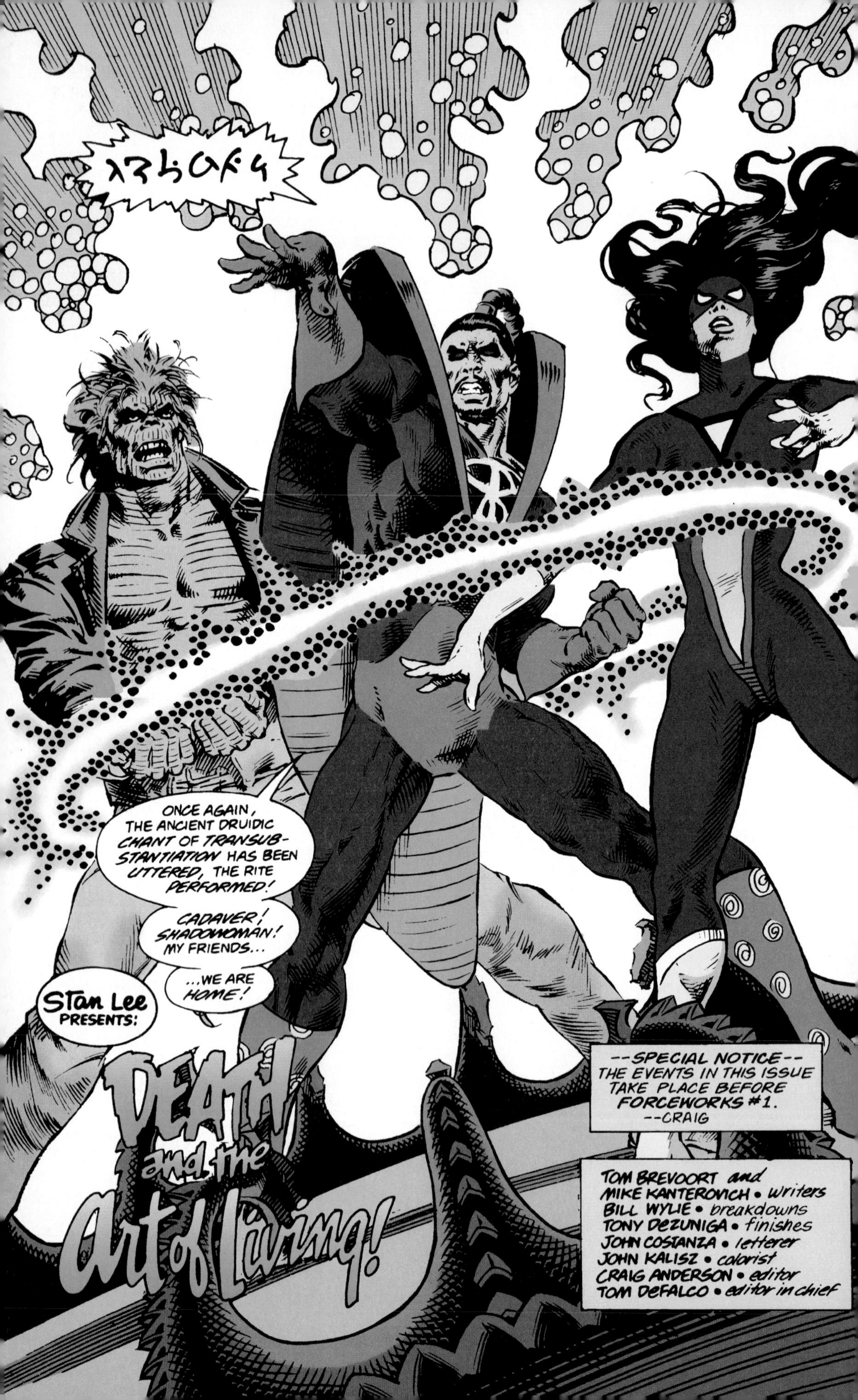

ONCE AGAIN, THE ANCIENT DRUIDIC CHANT OF TRANSUB-STANTIATION HAS BEEN UTTERED, THE RITE PERFORMED!
CADAVER! SHADOWOMAN! MY FRIENDS...
...WE ARE HOME!
STAN LEE PRESENTS:
DEATH and the Art of Living!
--SPECIAL NOTICE-- THE EVENTS IN THIS ISSUE TAKE PLACE BEFORE FORCEWORKS #1. --CRAIG
TOM BREVOORT and MIKE KANTEROVICH • writers
BILL WYLIE • breakdowns
TONY DEZUNIGA • finishes
JOHN COSTANZA • letterer
JOHN KALISZ • colorist
CRAIG ANDERSON • editor
TOM DEFALCO • editor in chief

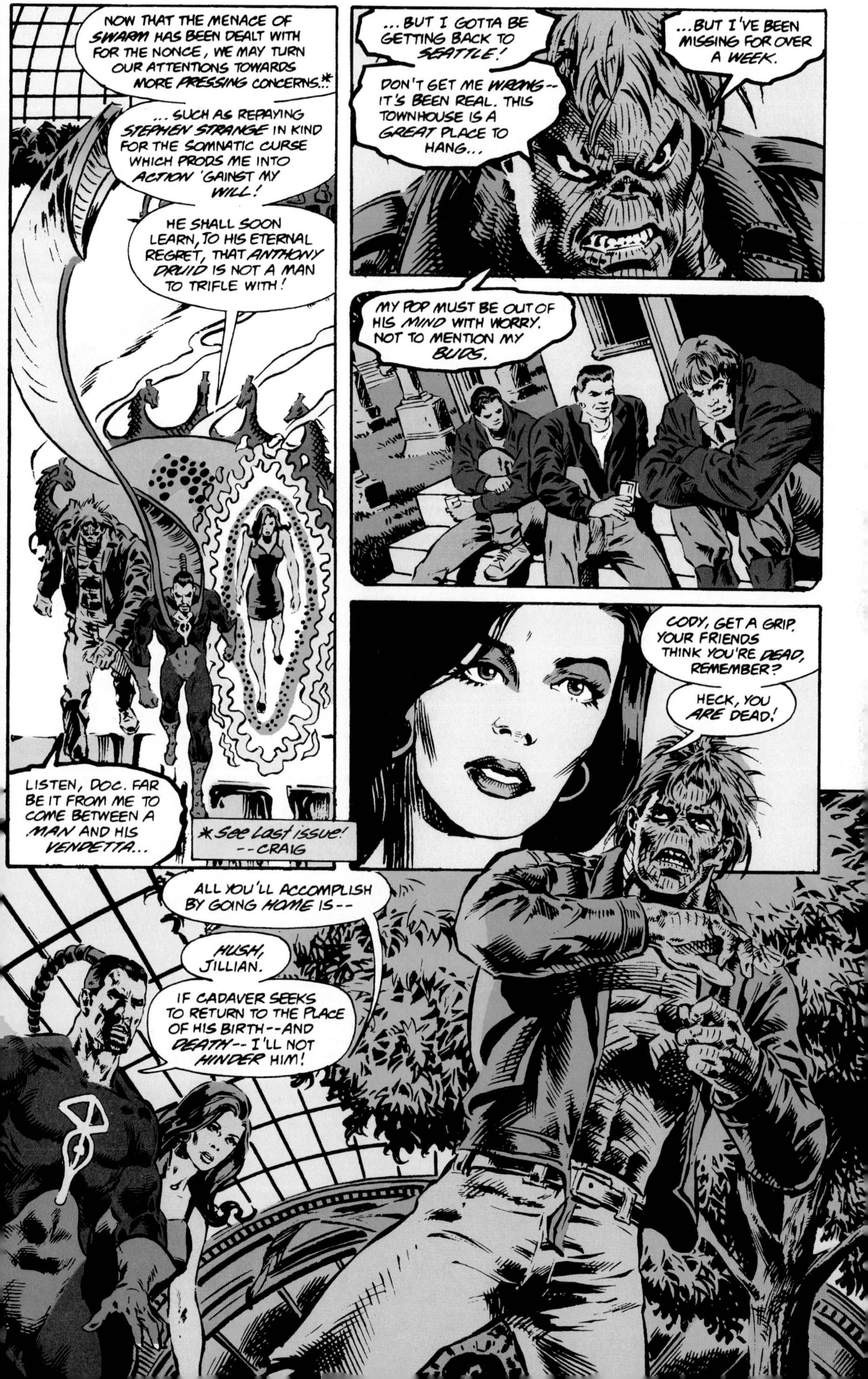
NOW THAT THE MENACE OF SWARM HAS BEEN DEALT WITH FOR THE NONCE, WE MAY TURN OUR ATTENTIONS TOWARDS MORE PRESSING CONCERNS...*
...SUCH AS REPAYING STEPHEN STRANGE IN KIND FOR THE SOMNATIC CURSE WHICH PRODS ME INTO ACTION 'GAINST MY WILL!
HE SHALL SOON LEARN, TO HIS ETERNAL REGRET, THAT ANTHONY DRUID IS NOT A MAN TO TRIFLE WITH!
LISTEN, DOC. FAR BE IT FROM ME TO COME BETWEEN A MAN AND HIS VENDETTA...
* See Last issue! --CRAIG
...BUT I GOTTA BE GETTING BACK TO SEATTLE!
DON'T GET ME WRONG-- IT'S BEEN REAL. THIS TOWNHOUSE IS A GREAT PLACE TO HANG...
...BUT I'VE BEEN MISSING FOR OVER A WEEK.
MY POP MUST BE OUT OF HIS MIND WITH WORRY. NOT TO MENTION MY BUDS.
CODY, GET A GRIP. YOUR FRIENDS THINK YOU'RE DEAD, REMEMBER?
HECK, YOU ARE DEAD!
ALL YOU'LL ACCOMPLISH BY GOING HOME IS--
HUSH, JILLIAN.
IF CADAVER SEEKS TO RETURN TO THE PLACE OF HIS BIRTH--AND DEATH--I'LL NOT HINDER HIM!

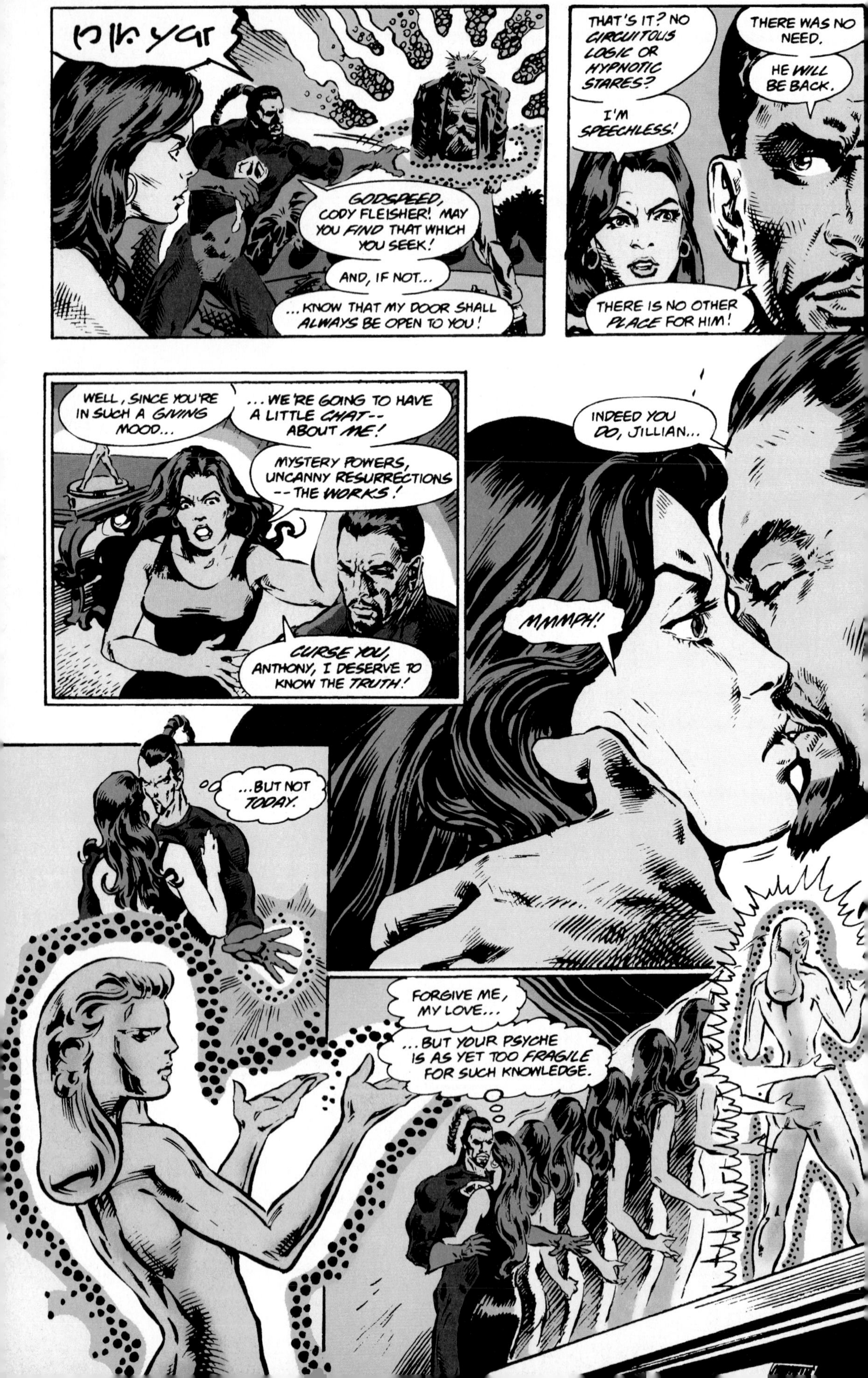

GODSPEED, CODY FLEISHER! MAY YOU FIND THAT WHICH YOU SEEK!
AND, IF NOT...
...KNOW THAT MY DOOR SHALL ALWAYS BE OPEN TO YOU!
THAT'S IT? NO CIRCUITOUS LOGIC OR HYPNOTIC STARES?
I'M SPEECHLESS!
THERE WAS NO NEED.
HE WILL BE BACK.
THERE IS NO OTHER PLACE FOR HIM!
WELL, SINCE YOU'RE IN SUCH A GIVING MOOD...
...WE'RE GOING TO HAVE A LITTLE CHAT-- ABOUT ME!
MYSTERY POWERS, UNCANNY RESURRECTIONS --THE WORKS!
CURSE YOU, ANTHONY, I DESERVE TO KNOW THE TRUTH!
INDEED YOU DO, JILLIAN...
MMMPH!
...BUT NOT TODAY.
FORGIVE ME, MY LOVE...
...BUT YOUR PSYCHE IS AS YET TOO FRAGILE FOR SUCH KNOWLEDGE.

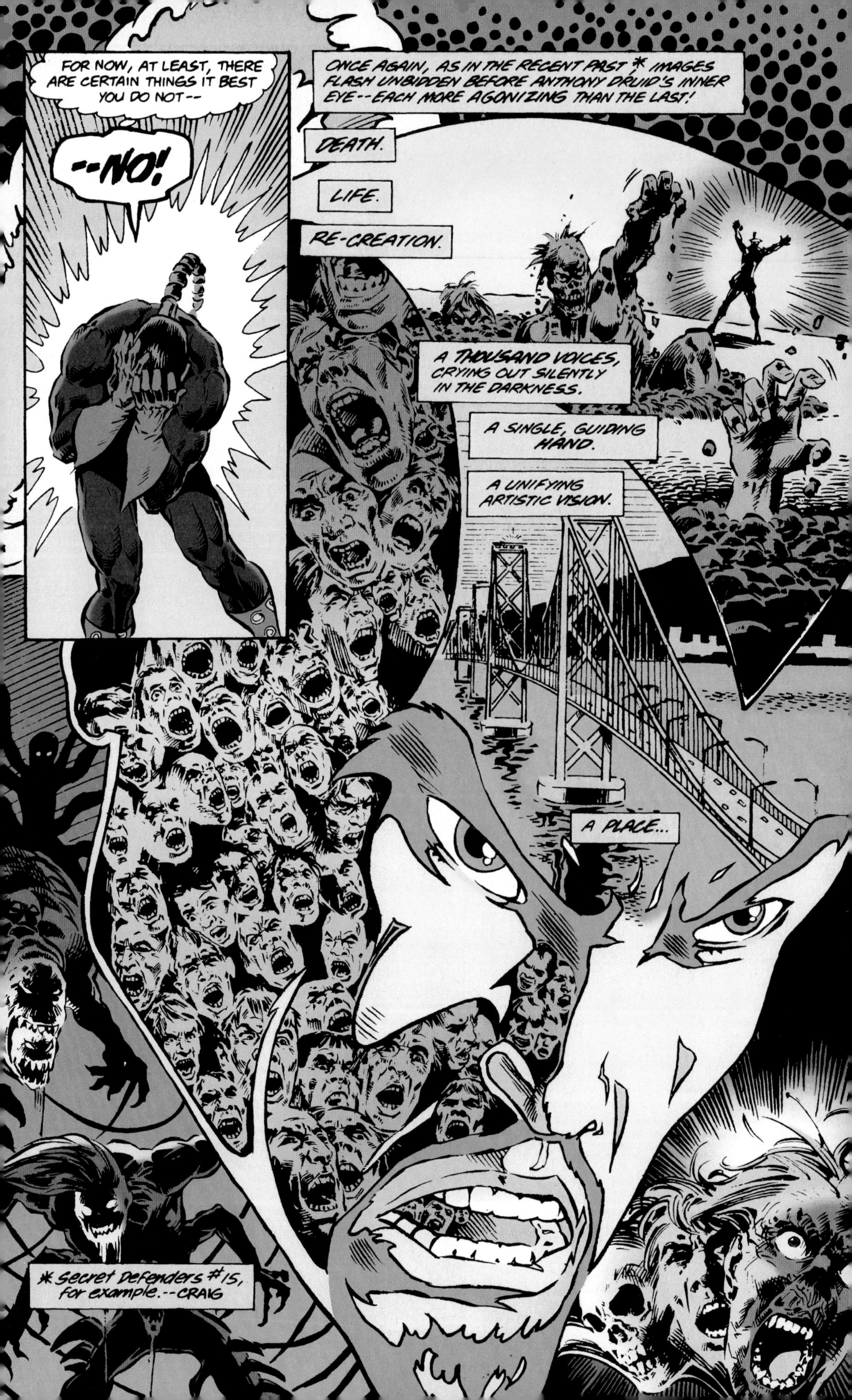

FOR NOW, AT LEAST, THERE ARE CERTAIN THINGS IT BEST YOU DO NOT--
--NO!
ONCE AGAIN, AS IN THE RECENT PAST* IMAGES FLASH UNBIDDEN BEFORE ANTHONY DRUID'S INNER EYE--EACH MORE AGONIZING THAN THE LAST!
DEATH.
LIFE.
RE-CREATION.
A THOUSAND VOICES, CRYING OUT SILENTLY IN THE DARKNESS.
A SINGLE, GUIDING HAND.
A UNIFYING ARTISTIC VISION.
A PLACE...
*Secret Defenders #15, for example.--CRAIG

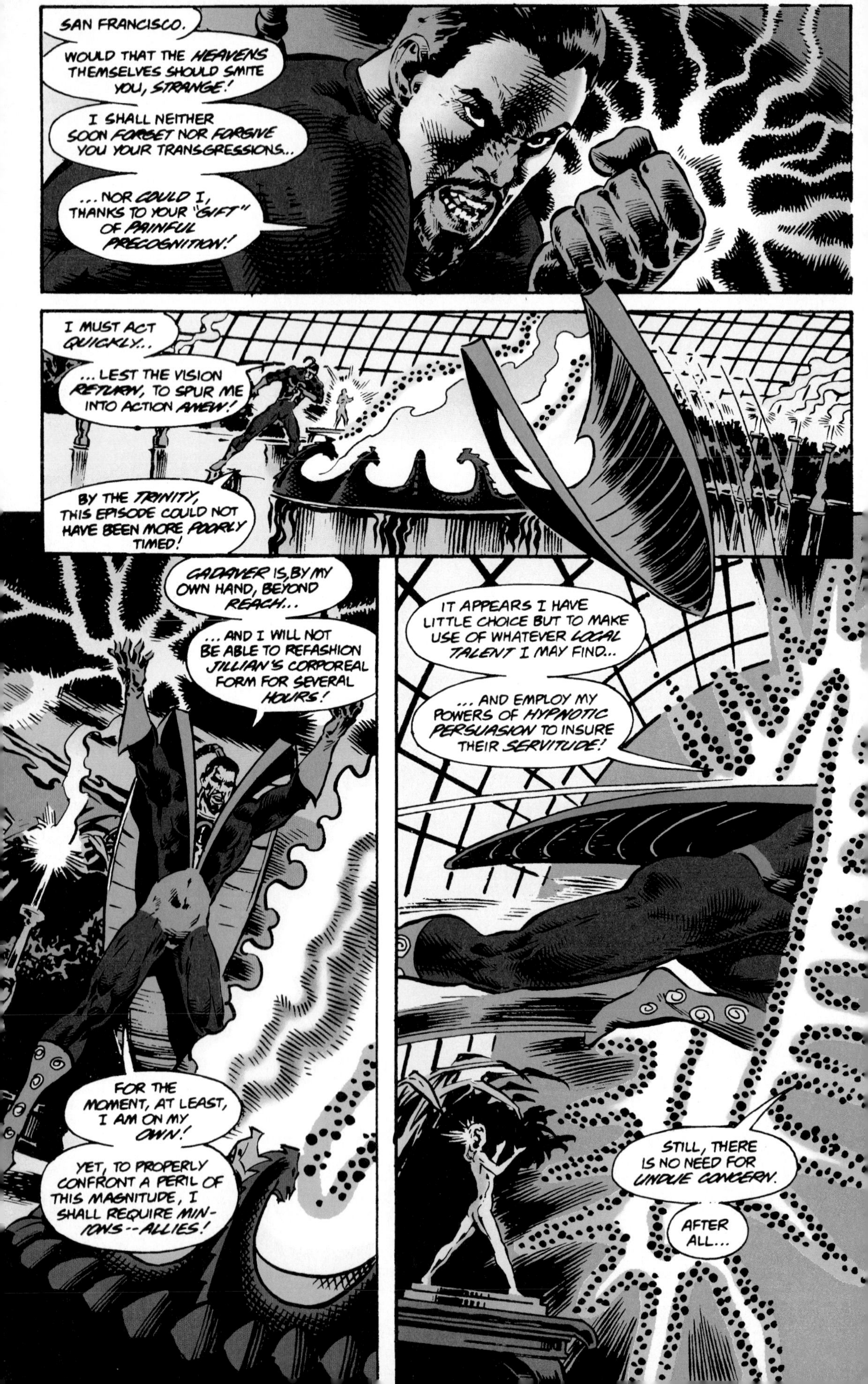
SAN FRANCISCO.
WOULD THAT THE HEAVENS THEMSELVES SHOULD SMITE YOU, STRANGE!
I SHALL NEITHER SOON FORGET NOR FORGIVE YOU YOUR TRANSGRESSIONS...
...NOR COULD I, THANKS TO YOUR "GIFT" OF PAINFUL PRECOGNITION!
I MUST ACT QUICKLY...
...LEST THE VISION RETURN, TO SPUR ME INTO ACTION ANEW!
BY THE TRINITY, THIS EPISODE COULD NOT HAVE BEEN MORE POORLY TIMED!
CADAVER IS, BY MY OWN HAND, BEYOND REACH...
...AND I WILL NOT BE ABLE TO REFASHION JILLIAN'S CORPOREAL FORM FOR SEVERAL HOURS!
FOR THE MOMENT, AT LEAST, I AM ON MY OWN!
YET, TO PROPERLY CONFRONT A PERIL OF THIS MAGNITUDE, I SHALL REQUIRE MIN-IONS--ALLIES!
IT APPEARS I HAVE LITTLE CHOICE BUT TO MAKE USE OF WHATEVER LOCAL TALENT I MAY FIND...
...AND EMPLOY MY POWERS OF HYPNOTIC PERSUASION TO INSURE THEIR SERVITUDE!
STILL, THERE IS NO NEED FOR UNDUE CONCERN.
AFTER ALL...

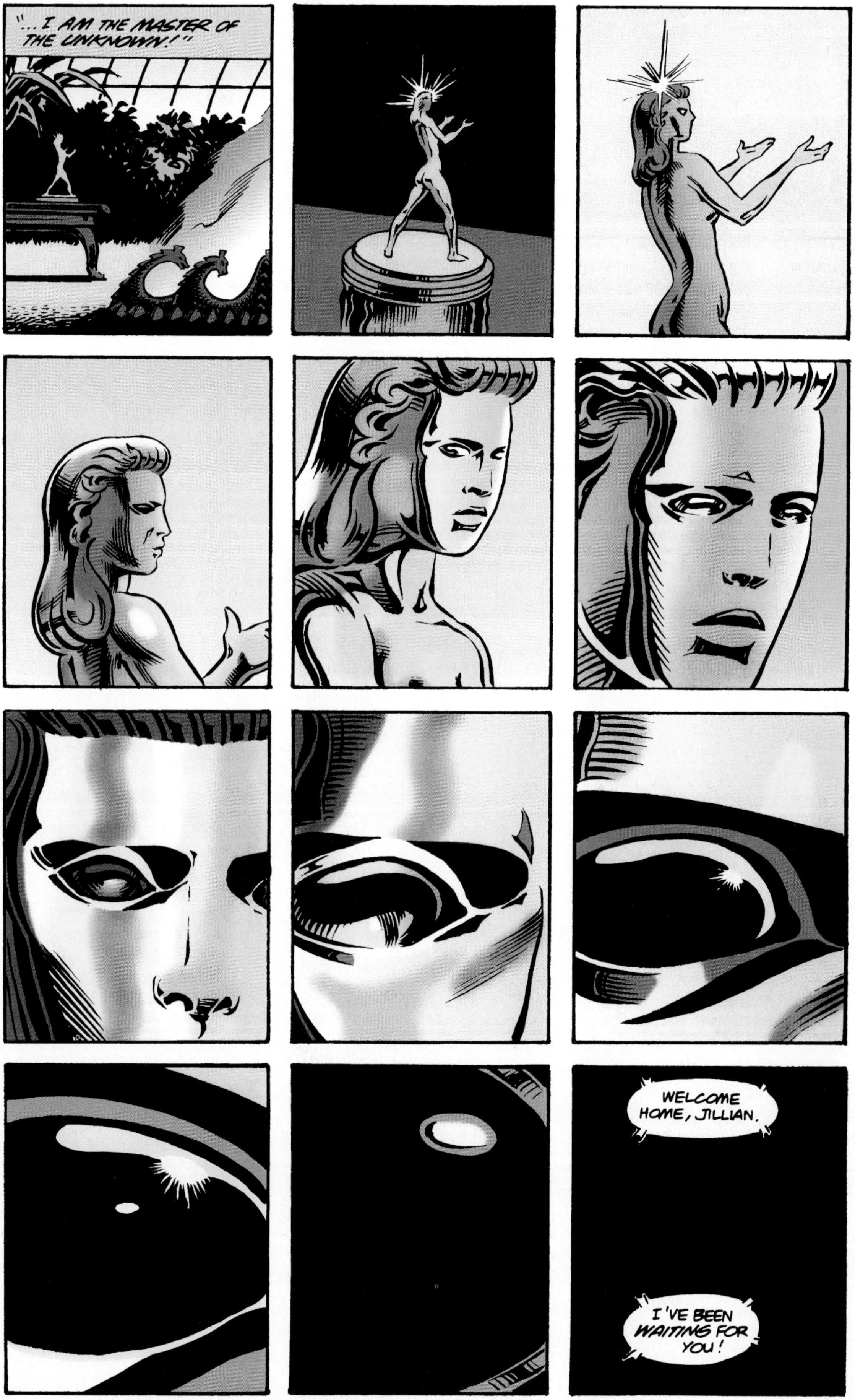
"...I AM THE MASTER OF THE UNKNOWN!"
WELCOME HOME, JILLIAN.
I'VE BEEN WAITING FOR YOU!

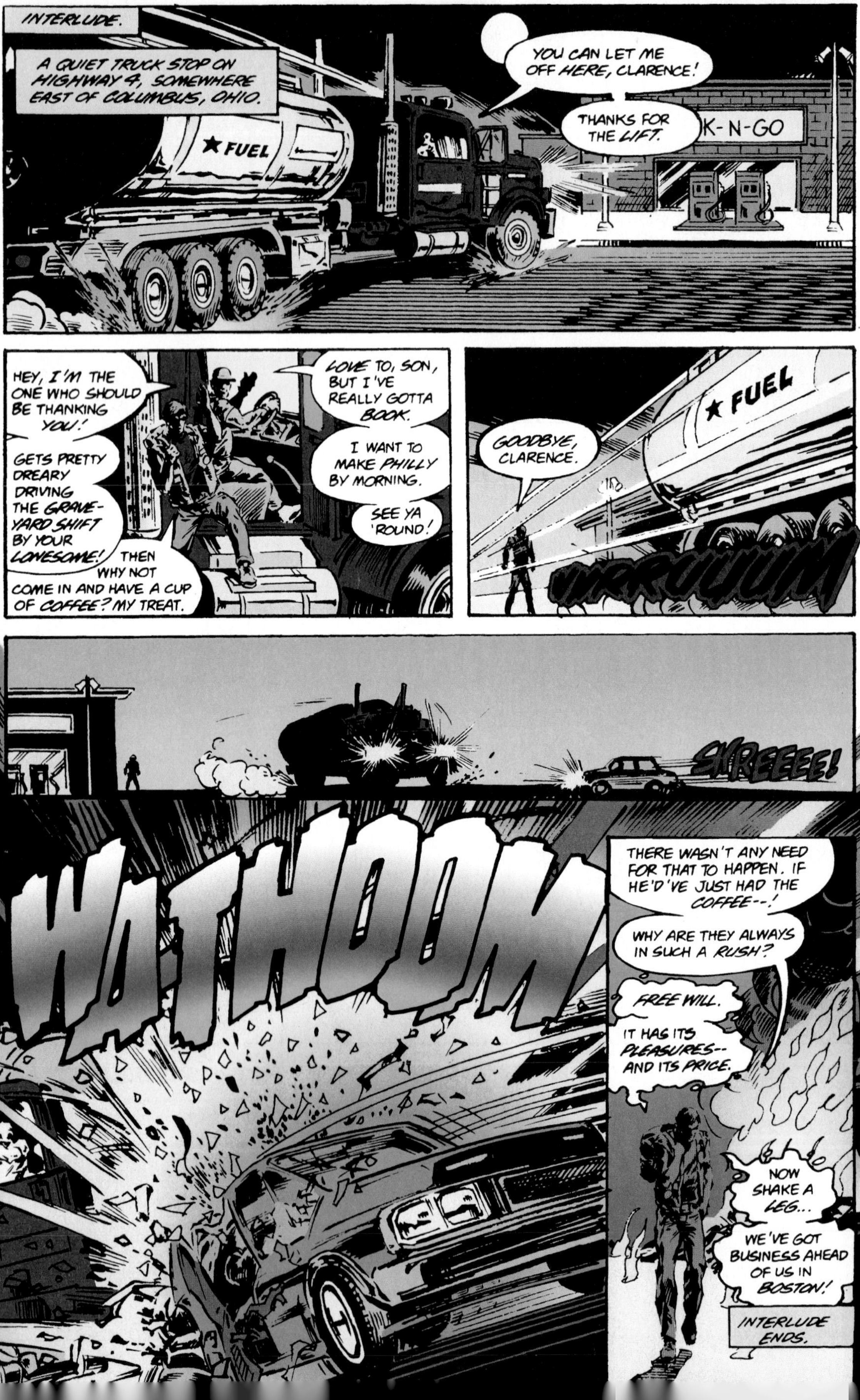
INTERLUDE.
A QUIET TRUCK STOP ON HIGHWAY 4, SOMEWHERE EAST OF COLUMBUS, OHIO.
YOU CAN LET ME OFF HERE, CLARENCE!
THANKS FOR THE LIFT.
K-N-GO
★ FUEL
HEY, I'M THE ONE WHO SHOULD BE THANKING YOU!
GETS PRETTY DREARY DRIVING THE GRAVE-YARD SHIFT BY YOUR LONESOME!
THEN WHY NOT COME IN AND HAVE A CUP OF COFFEE? MY TREAT.
LOVE TO, SON, BUT I'VE REALLY GOTTA BOOK.
I WANT TO MAKE PHILLY BY MORNING.
SEE YA 'ROUND!
★ FUEL
GOODBYE, CLARENCE.
VVRRUUUUM
SKREEEEE!
WA-THOOM!
THERE WASN'T ANY NEED FOR THAT TO HAPPEN. IF HE'D'VE JUST HAD THE COFFEE--!
WHY ARE THEY ALWAYS IN SUCH A RUSH?
FREE WILL.
IT HAS ITS PLEASURES-- AND ITS PRICE.
NOW SHAKE A LEG...
WE'VE GOT BUSINESS AHEAD OF US IN BOSTON!
INTERLUDE ENDS.

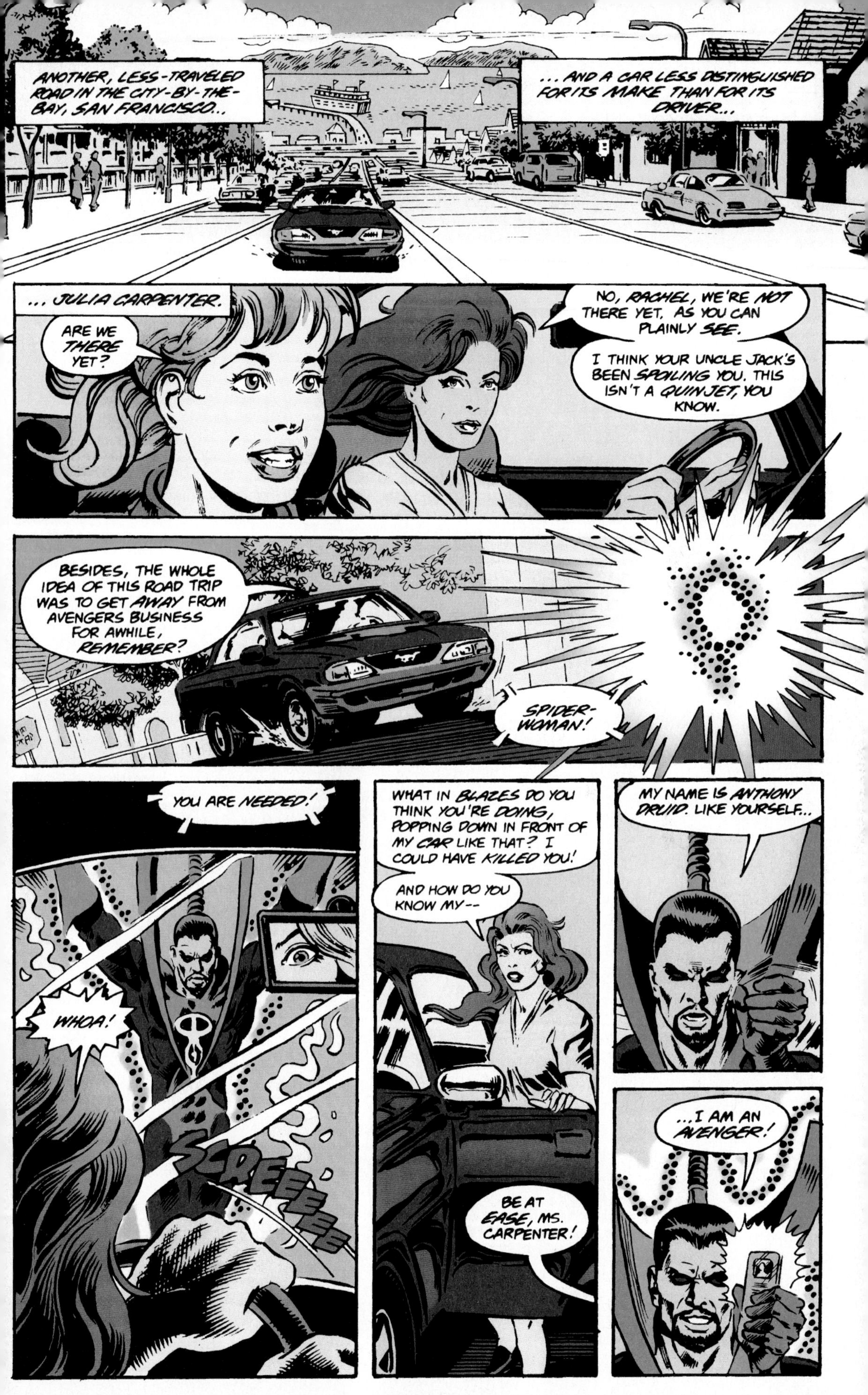
ANOTHER, LESS-TRAVELED ROAD IN THE CITY-BY-THE-BAY, SAN FRANCISCO...
...AND A CAR LESS DISTINGUISHED FOR ITS MAKE THAN FOR ITS DRIVER...
...JULIA CARPENTER.
ARE WE THERE YET?
NO, RACHEL, WE'RE NOT THERE YET, AS YOU CAN PLAINLY SEE.
I THINK YOUR UNCLE JACK'S BEEN SPOILING YOU. THIS ISN'T A QUINJET, YOU KNOW.
BESIDES, THE WHOLE IDEA OF THIS ROAD TRIP WAS TO GET AWAY FROM AVENGERS BUSINESS FOR AWHILE, REMEMBER?
SPIDER-WOMAN!
YOU ARE NEEDED!
WHOA!
SCREEEEEE
WHAT IN BLAZES DO YOU THINK YOU'RE DOING, POPPING DOWN IN FRONT OF MY CAR LIKE THAT? I COULD HAVE KILLED YOU!
AND HOW DO YOU KNOW MY--
BE AT EASE, MS. CARPENTER!
MY NAME IS ANTHONY DRUID. LIKE YOURSELF...
...I AM AN AVENGER!

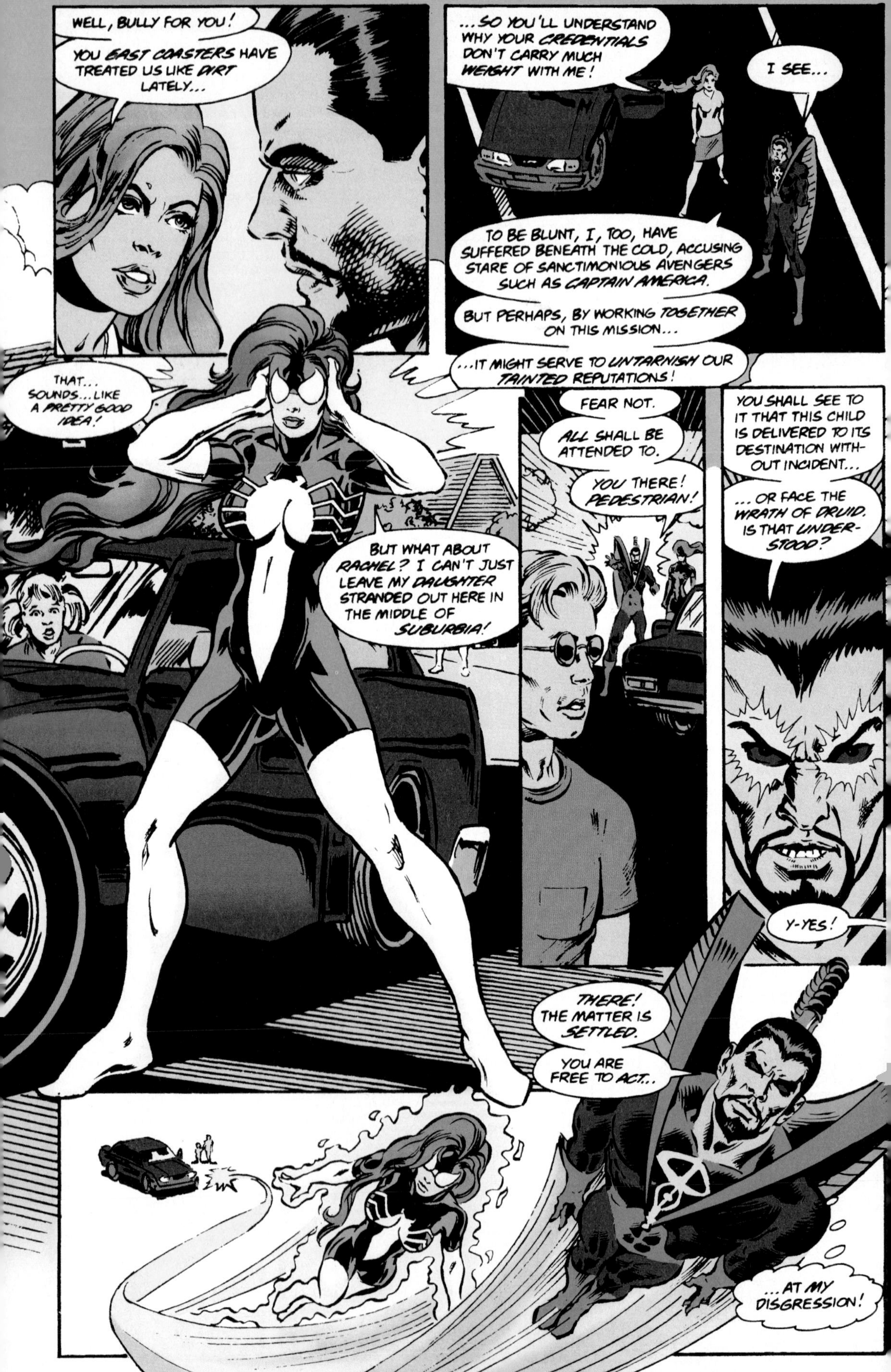
WELL, BULLY FOR YOU!
YOU EAST COASTERS HAVE TREATED US LIKE DIRT LATELY...
...SO YOU'LL UNDERSTAND WHY YOUR CREDENTIALS DON'T CARRY MUCH WEIGHT WITH ME!
I SEE...
TO BE BLUNT, I, TOO, HAVE SUFFERED BENEATH THE COLD, ACCUSING STARE OF SANCTIMONIOUS AVENGERS SUCH AS CAPTAIN AMERICA.
BUT PERHAPS, BY WORKING TOGETHER ON THIS MISSION...
...IT MIGHT SERVE TO UNTARNISH OUR TAINTED REPUTATIONS!
THAT... SOUNDS... LIKE A PRETTY GOOD IDEA!
BUT WHAT ABOUT RACHEL? I CAN'T JUST LEAVE MY DAUGHTER STRANDED OUT HERE IN THE MIDDLE OF SUBURBIA!
FEAR NOT.
ALL SHALL BE ATTENDED TO.
YOU THERE! PEDESTRIAN!
YOU SHALL SEE TO IT THAT THIS CHILD IS DELIVERED TO ITS DESTINATION WITHOUT INCIDENT...
...OR FACE THE WRATH OF DRUID. IS THAT UNDERSTOOD?
Y-YES!
THERE! THE MATTER IS SETTLED.
YOU ARE FREE TO ACT..
...AT MY DISGRESSION!

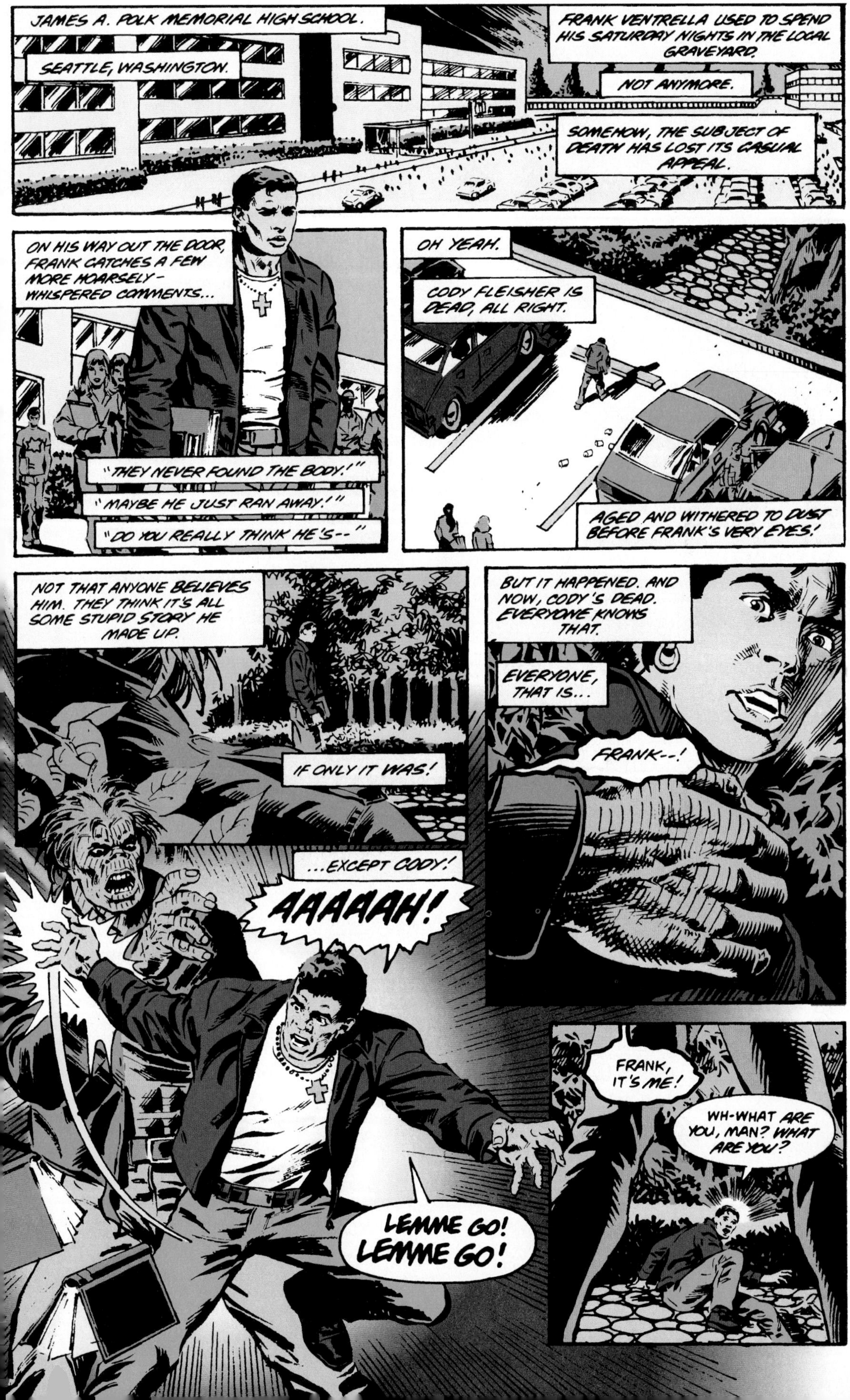

JAMES A. POLK MEMORIAL HIGH SCHOOL.
SEATTLE, WASHINGTON.
FRANK VENTRELLA USED TO SPEND HIS SATURDAY NIGHTS IN THE LOCAL GRAVEYARD.
NOT ANYMORE.
SOMEHOW, THE SUBJECT OF DEATH HAS LOST ITS CASUAL APPEAL.
ON HIS WAY OUT THE DOOR, FRANK CATCHES A FEW MORE HOARSELY-WHISPERED COMMENTS...
"THEY NEVER FOUND THE BODY!"
"MAYBE HE JUST RAN AWAY!"
"DO YOU REALLY THINK HE'S--"
OH YEAH.
CODY FLEISHER IS DEAD, ALL RIGHT.
AGED AND WITHERED TO DUST BEFORE FRANK'S VERY EYES!
NOT THAT ANYONE BELIEVES HIM. THEY THINK IT'S ALL SOME STUPID STORY HE MADE UP.
IF ONLY IT WAS!
BUT IT HAPPENED. AND NOW, CODY'S DEAD. EVERYONE KNOWS THAT.
EVERYONE, THAT IS...
FRANK--!
...EXCEPT CODY!
AAAAAH!
LEMME GO! LEMME GO!
FRANK, IT'S ME!
WH-WHAT ARE YOU, MAN? WHAT ARE YOU?

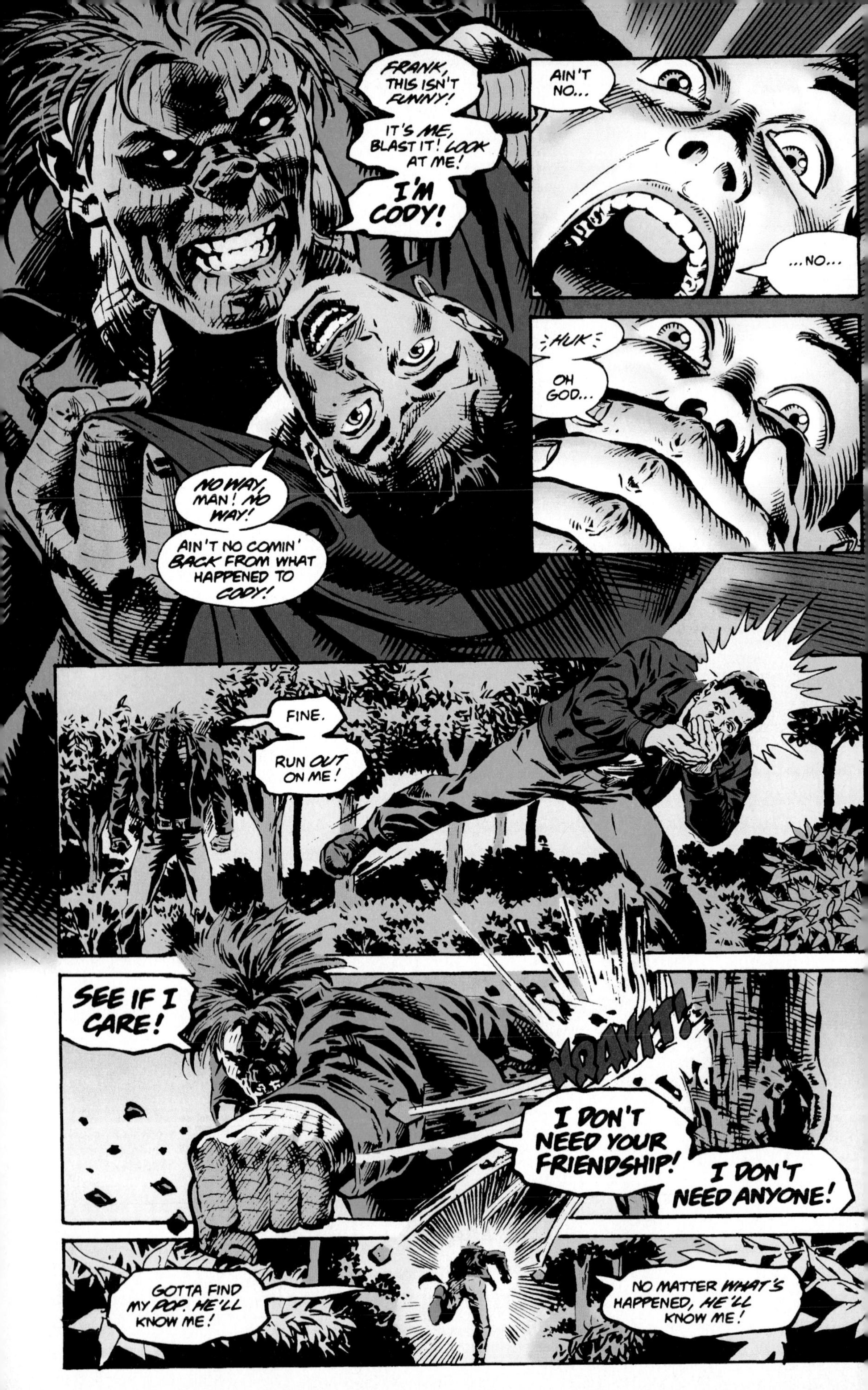
FRANK, THIS ISN'T FUNNY!
IT'S ME, BLAST IT! LOOK AT ME!
I'M CODY!
AIN'T NO...
...NO...
HUK
OH GOD...
NO WAY, MAN! NO WAY!
AIN'T NO COMIN' BACK FROM WHAT HAPPENED TO CODY!
FINE.
RUN OUT ON ME!
SEE IF I CARE!
KRANT!
I DON'T NEED YOUR FRIENDSHIP!
I DON'T NEED ANYONE!
GOTTA FIND MY POP. HE'LL KNOW ME!
NO MATTER WHAT'S HAPPENED, HE'LL KNOW ME!

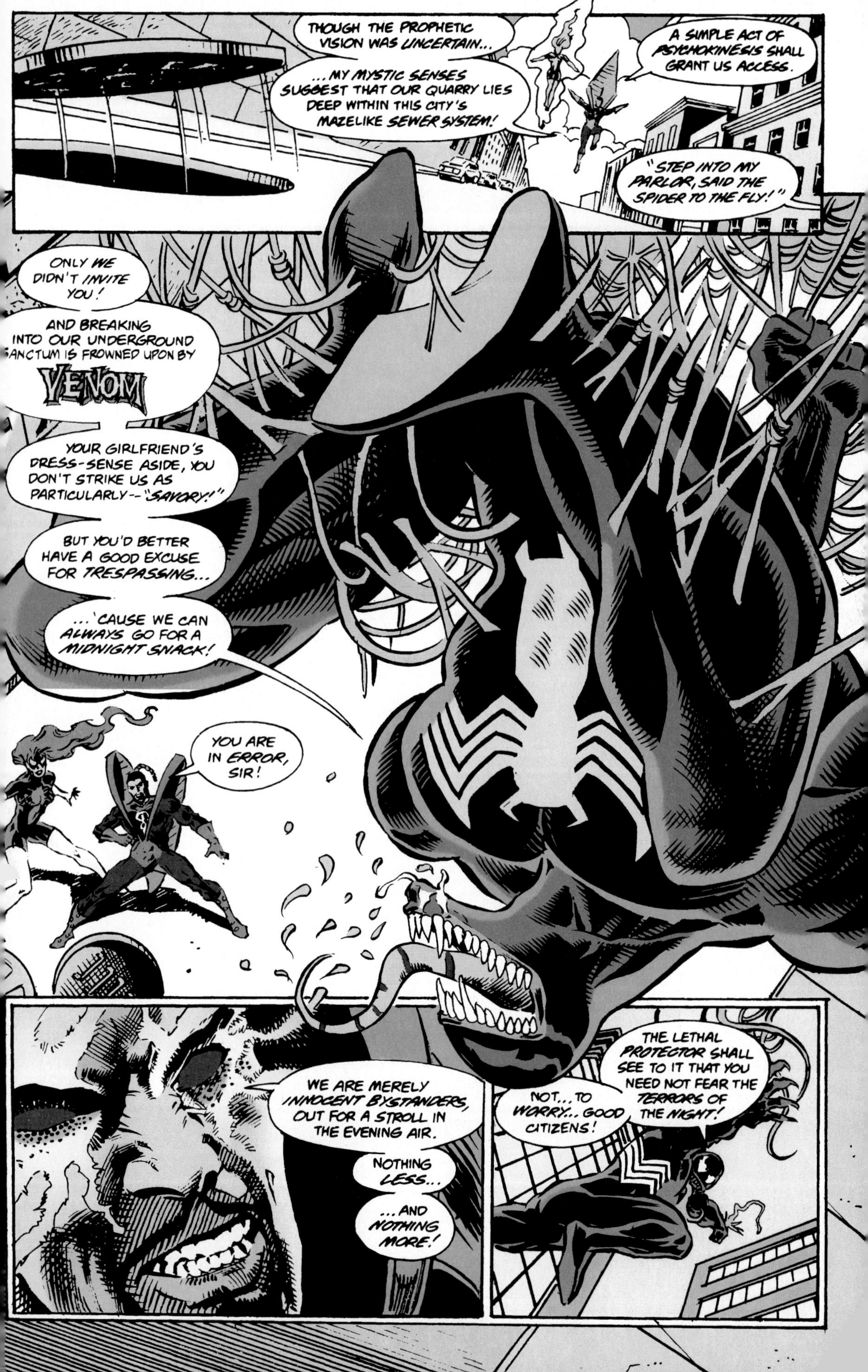
THOUGH THE PROPHETIC VISION WAS UNCERTAIN...
...MY MYSTIC SENSES SUGGEST THAT OUR QUARRY LIES DEEP WITHIN THIS CITY'S MAZELIKE SEWER SYSTEM!
A SIMPLE ACT OF PSYCHOKINESIS SHALL GRANT US ACCESS.
"STEP INTO MY PARLOR, SAID THE SPIDER TO THE FLY!"
ONLY WE DIDN'T INVITE YOU!
AND BREAKING INTO OUR UNDERGROUND SANCTUM IS FROWNED UPON BY
VENOM
YOUR GIRLFRIEND'S DRESS-SENSE ASIDE, YOU DON'T STRIKE US AS PARTICULARLY--"SAVORY!"
BUT YOU'D BETTER HAVE A GOOD EXCUSE FOR TRESPASSING...
...'CAUSE WE CAN ALWAYS GO FOR A MIDNIGHT SNACK!
YOU ARE IN ERROR, SIR!
WE ARE MERELY INNOCENT BYSTANDERS, OUT FOR A STROLL IN THE EVENING AIR.
NOTHING LESS...
...AND NOTHING MORE!
NOT... TO WORRY... GOOD CITIZENS!
THE LETHAL PROTECTOR SHALL SEE TO IT THAT YOU NEED NOT FEAR THE TERRORS OF THE NIGHT!

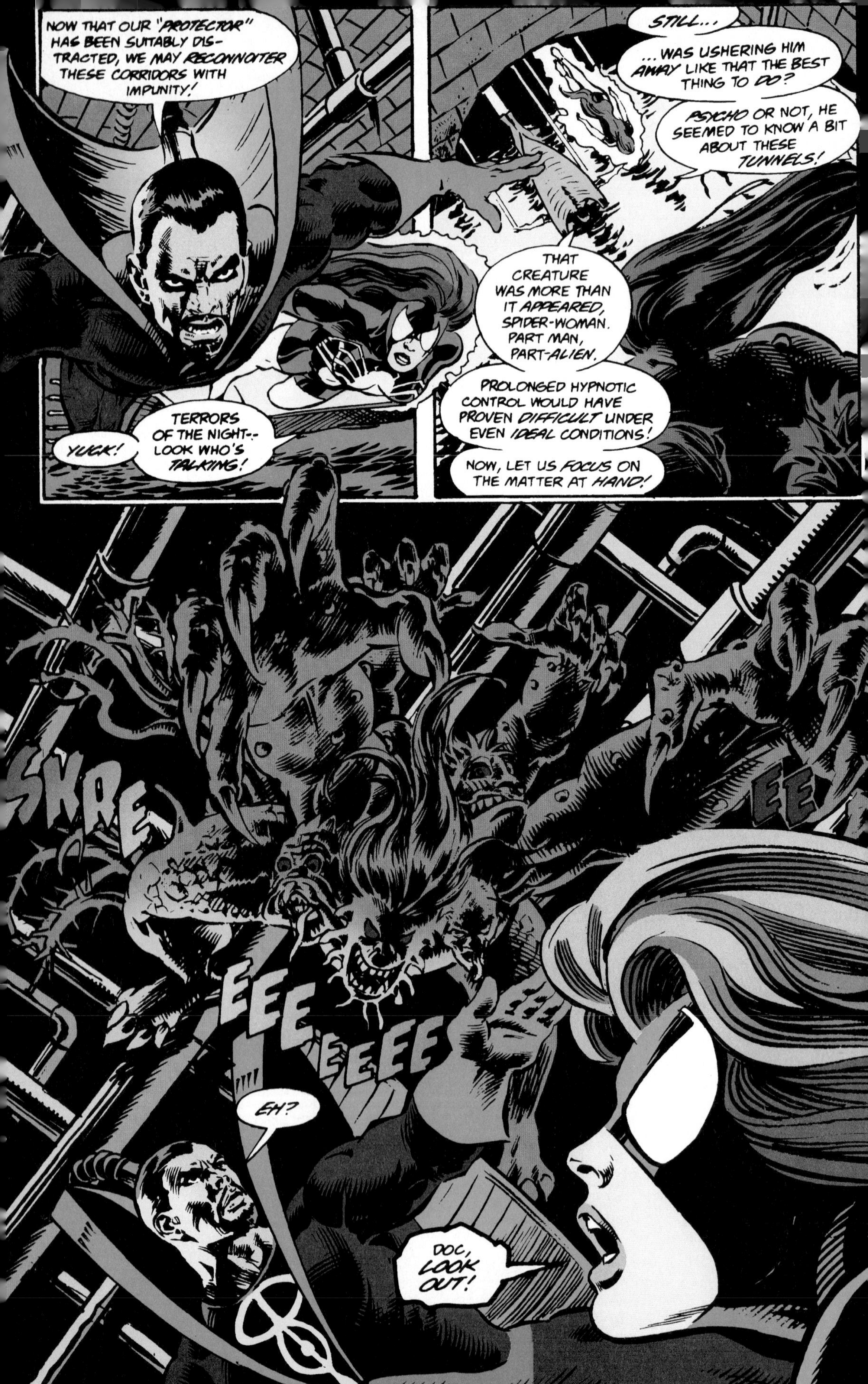
NOW THAT OUR "PROTECTOR" HAS BEEN SUITABLY DISTRACTED, WE MAY RECONNOITER THESE CORRIDORS WITH IMPUNITY!
YUCK!
TERRORS OF THE NIGHT-- LOOK WHO'S TALKING!
STILL...
...WAS USHERING HIM AWAY LIKE THAT THE BEST THING TO DO?
PSYCHO OR NOT, HE SEEMED TO KNOW A BIT ABOUT THESE TUNNELS!
THAT CREATURE WAS MORE THAN IT APPEARED, SPIDER-WOMAN. PART MAN, PART-ALIEN.
PROLONGED HYPNOTIC CONTROL WOULD HAVE PROVEN DIFFICULT UNDER EVEN IDEAL CONDITIONS!
NOW, LET US FOCUS ON THE MATTER AT HAND!
SKRE
EE
EEE
EEEE
EH?
DOC, LOOK OUT!

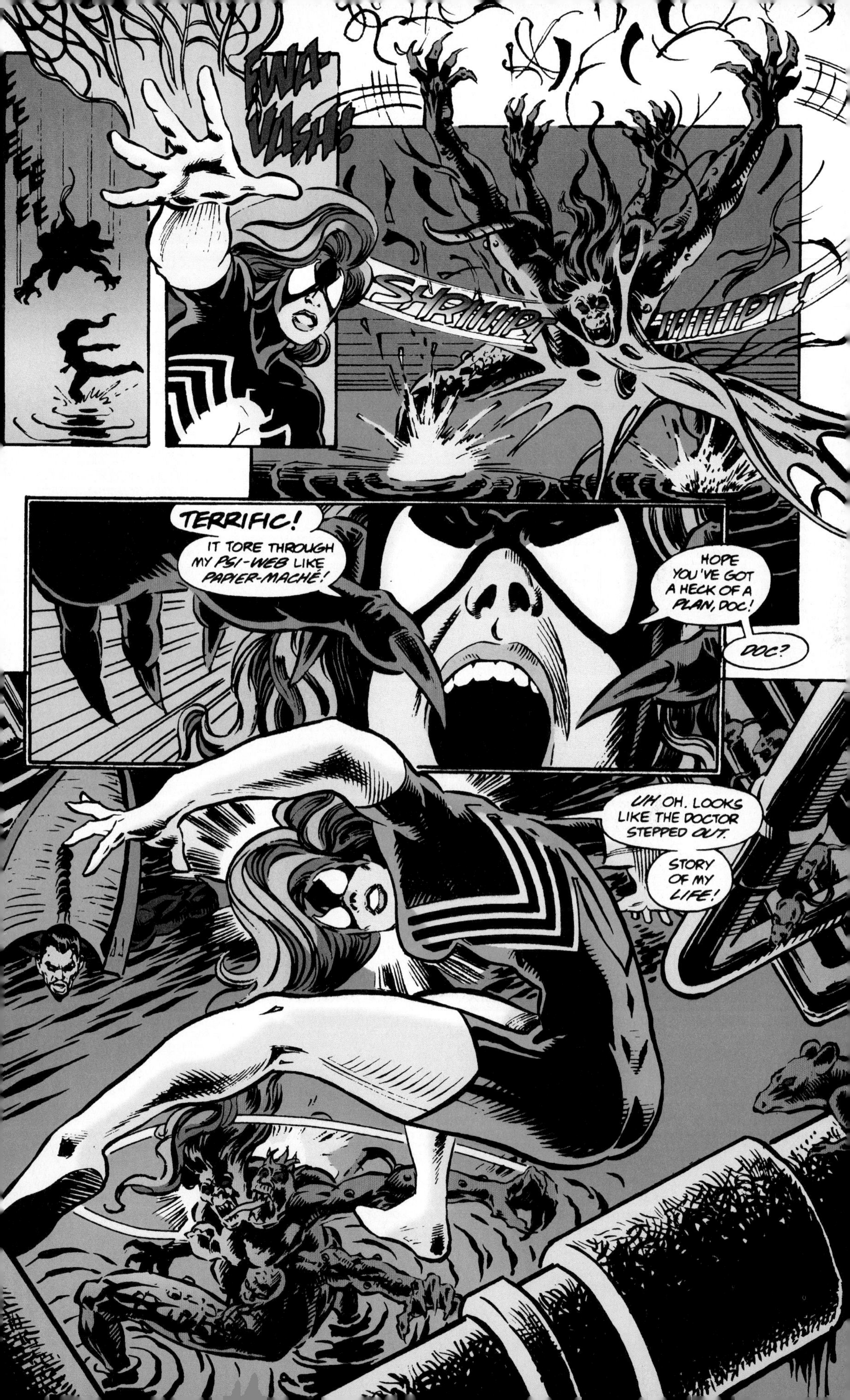

EEEEEE
FWA-VASH!
SHRIIIIPT
THIIIIPT!
TERRIFIC!
IT TORE THROUGH MY PSI-WEB LIKE PAPIER-MACHÉ!
HOPE YOU'VE GOT A HECK OF A PLAN, DOC!
DOC?
UH OH. LOOKS LIKE THE DOCTOR STEPPED OUT.
STORY OF MY LIFE!

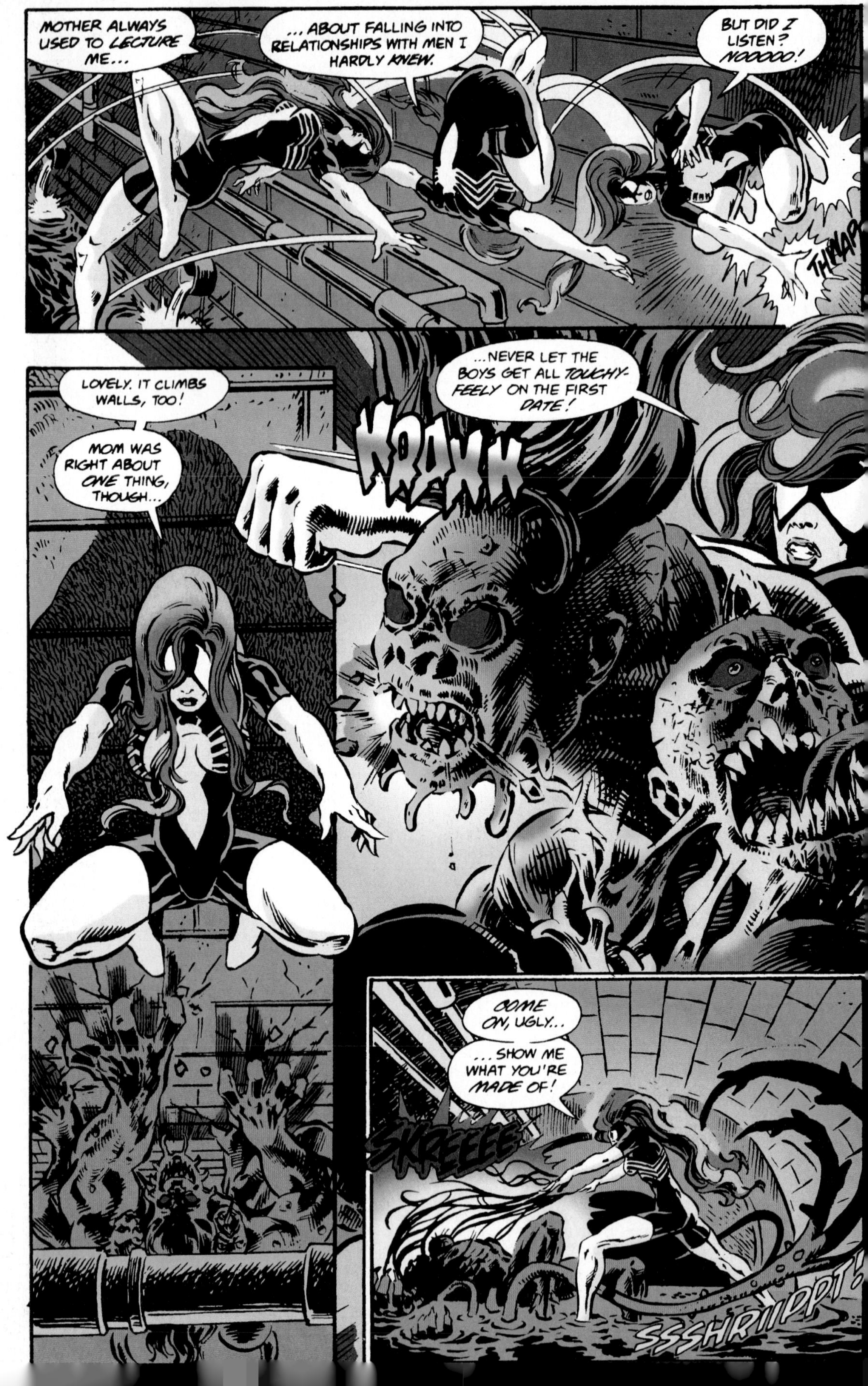
MOTHER ALWAYS USED TO LECTURE ME...
..., ABOUT FALLING INTO RELATIONSHIPS WITH MEN I HARDLY KNEW.
BUT DID I LISTEN? NOOOOO!
THWAP
LOVELY. IT CLIMBS WALLS, TOO!
MOM WAS RIGHT ABOUT ONE THING, THOUGH...
...NEVER LET THE BOYS GET ALL TOUCHY-FEELY ON THE FIRST DATE!
COME ON, UGLY...
...SHOW ME WHAT YOU'RE MADE OF!
SKREEEE
SSSHRIIPPT!

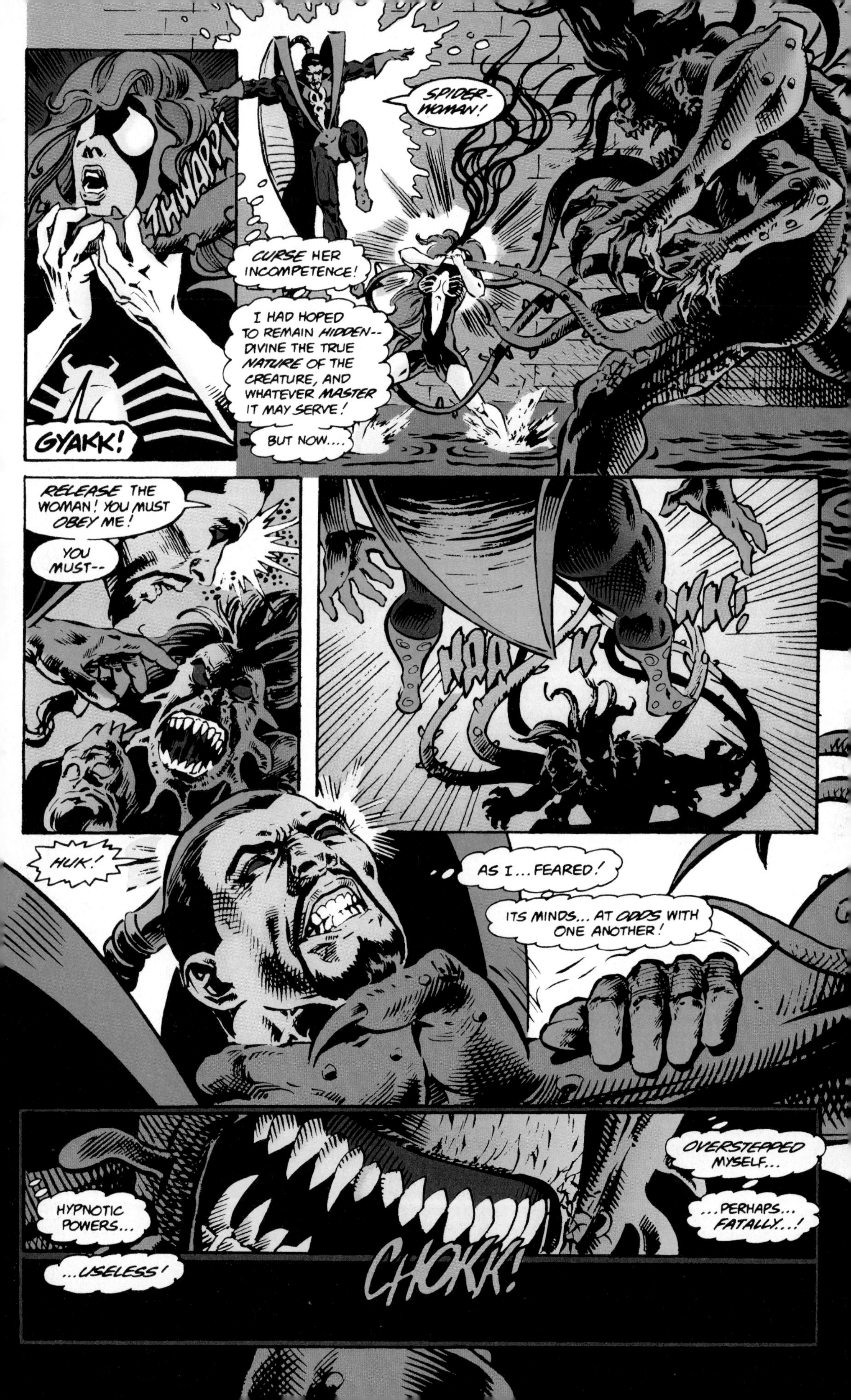
THWAPP!
GYAKK!
SPIDER-WOMAN!
CURSE HER INCOMPETENCE!
I HAD HOPED TO REMAIN HIDDEN-- DIVINE THE TRUE NATURE OF THE CREATURE, AND WHATEVER MASTER IT MAY SERVE!
BUT NOW....
RELEASE THE WOMAN! YOU MUST OBEY ME!
YOU MUST--
HUK!
AS I... FEARED!
ITS MINDS... AT ODDS WITH ONE ANOTHER!
HYPNOTIC POWERS...
...USELESS!
OVERSTEPPED MYSELF...
...PERHAPS... FATALLY...!
CHOKK!

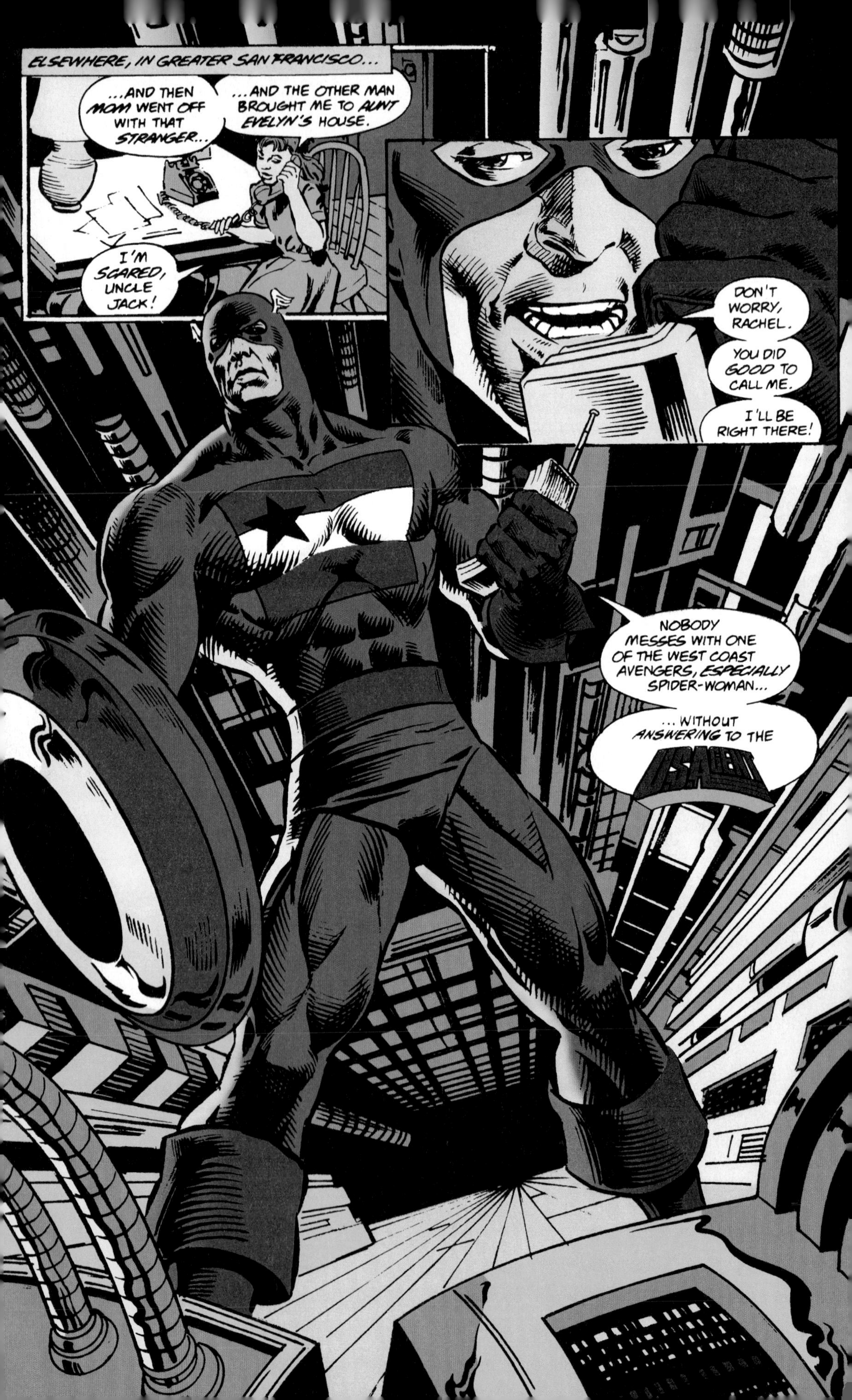
ELSEWHERE, IN GREATER SAN FRANCISCO...
...AND THEN MOM WENT OFF WITH THAT STRANGER...
...AND THE OTHER MAN BROUGHT ME TO AUNT EVELYN'S HOUSE.
I'M SCARED, UNCLE JACK!
DON'T WORRY, RACHEL.
YOU DID GOOD TO CALL ME.
I'LL BE RIGHT THERE!
NOBODY MESSES WITH ONE OF THE WEST COAST AVENGERS, ESPECIALLY SPIDER-WOMAN...
...WITHOUT ANSWERING TO THE
U.S.AGENT

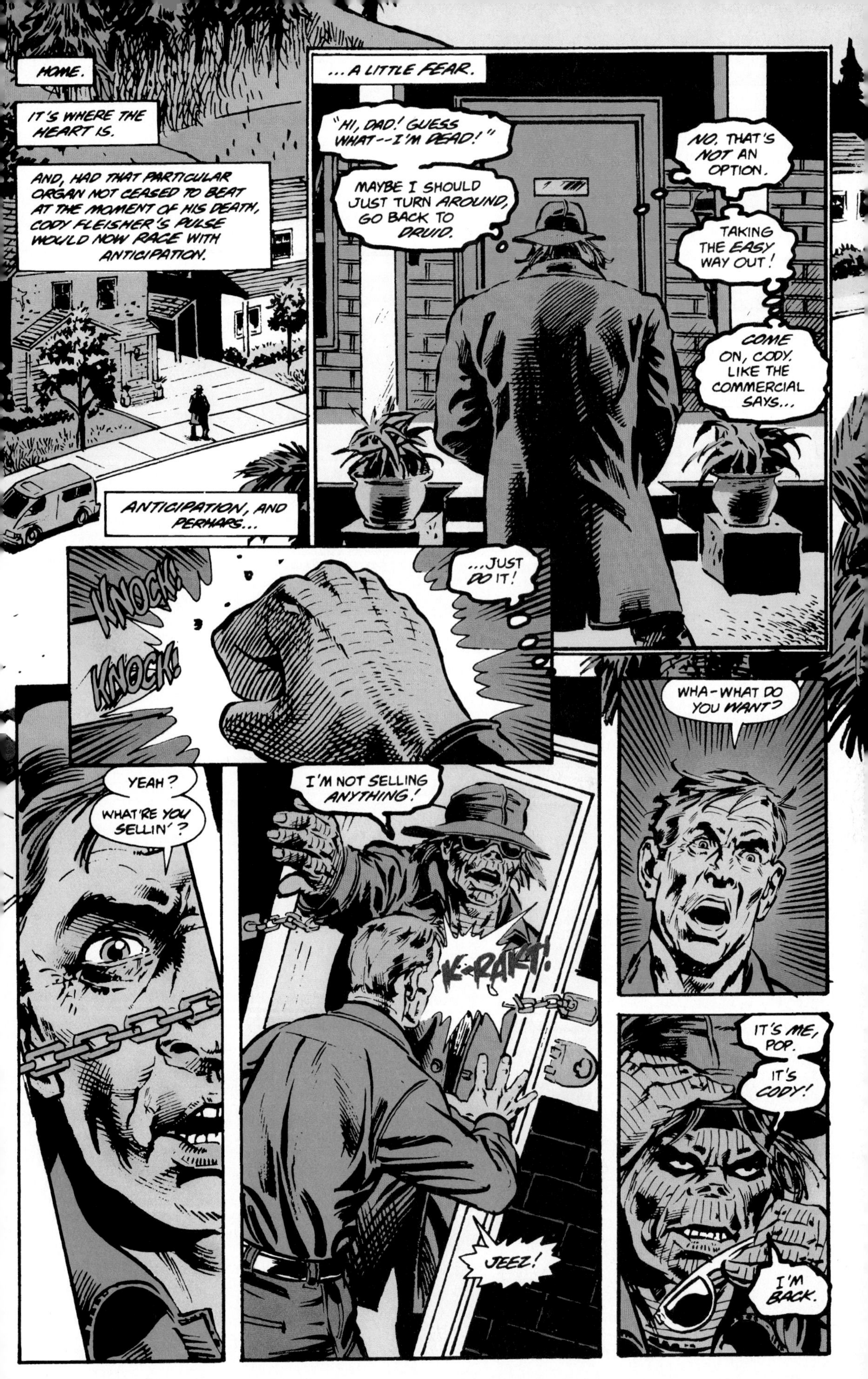
HOME.
IT'S WHERE THE HEART IS.
AND, HAD THAT PARTICULAR ORGAN NOT CEASED TO BEAT AT THE MOMENT OF HIS DEATH, CODY FLEISHER'S PULSE WOULD NOW RACE WITH ANTICIPATION.
ANTICIPATION, AND PERHAPS...
...A LITTLE FEAR.
"HI, DAD! GUESS WHAT--I'M DEAD!"
MAYBE I SHOULD JUST TURN AROUND, GO BACK TO DRUID.
NO. THAT'S NOT AN OPTION.
TAKING THE EASY WAY OUT!
COME ON, CODY. LIKE THE COMMERCIAL SAYS...
...JUST DO IT!
KNOCK!
KNOCK!
YEAH?
WHAT'RE YOU SELLIN'?
I'M NOT SELLING ANYTHING!
K-RAKT!
JEEZ!
WHA-WHAT DO YOU WANT?
IT'S ME, POP.
IT'S CODY!
I'M BACK.

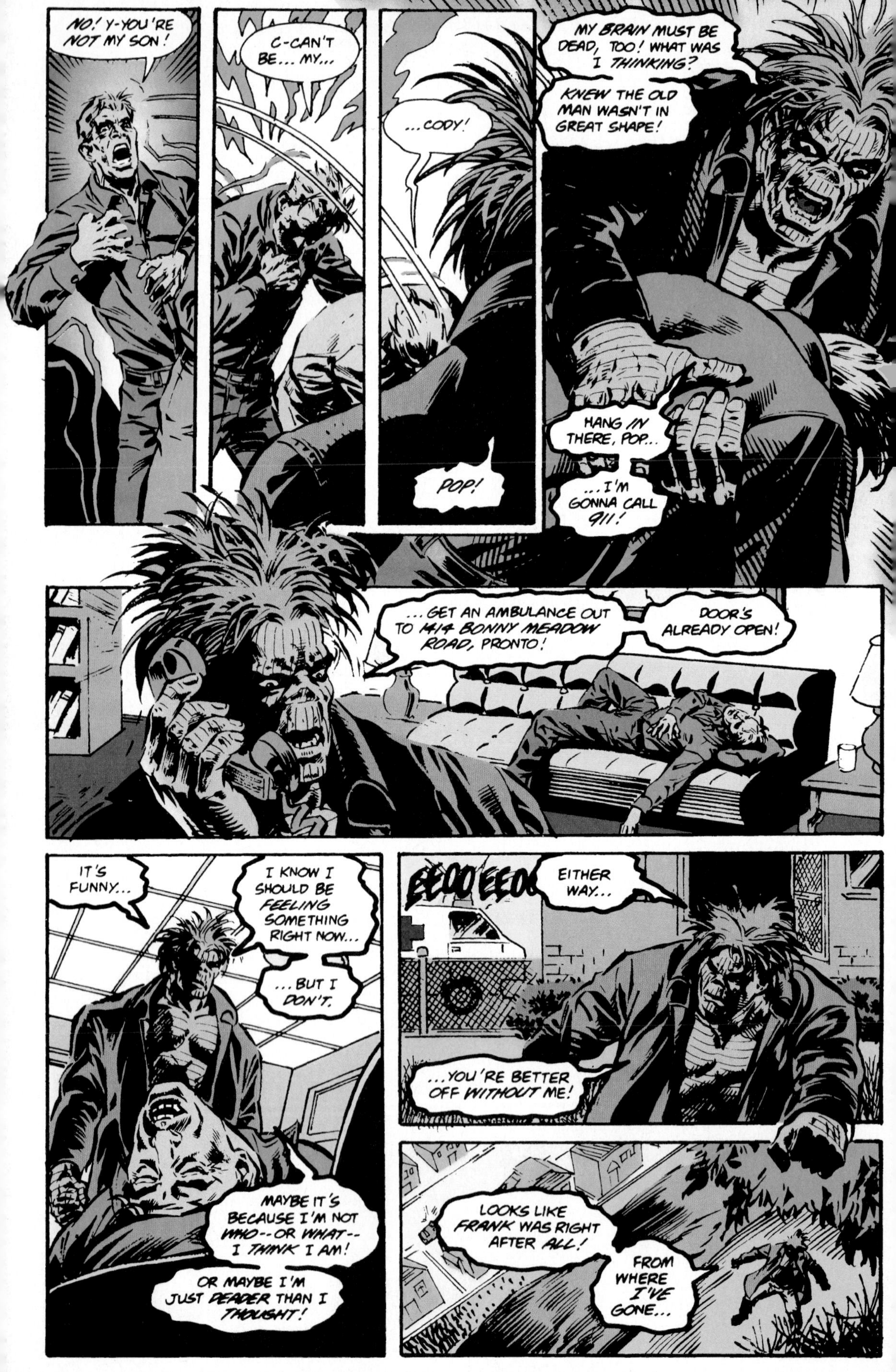
NO! Y-YOU'RE NOT MY SON!
C-CAN'T BE... MY...
...CODY!
POP!
MY BRAIN MUST BE DEAD, TOO! WHAT WAS I THINKING?
KNEW THE OLD MAN WASN'T IN GREAT SHAPE!
HANG IN THERE, POP...
...I'M GONNA CALL 911!
...GET AN AMBULANCE OUT TO 1414 BONNY MEADOW ROAD, PRONTO!
DOOR'S ALREADY OPEN!
IT'S FUNNY...
I KNOW I SHOULD BE FEELING SOMETHING RIGHT NOW...
...BUT I DON'T.
MAYBE IT'S BECAUSE I'M NOT WHO--OR WHAT--I THINK I AM!
OR MAYBE I'M JUST DEADER THAN I THOUGHT!
EEOO EEOO
EITHER WAY...
...YOU'RE BETTER OFF WITHOUT ME!
LOOKS LIKE FRANK WAS RIGHT AFTER ALL!
FROM WHERE I'VE GONE...

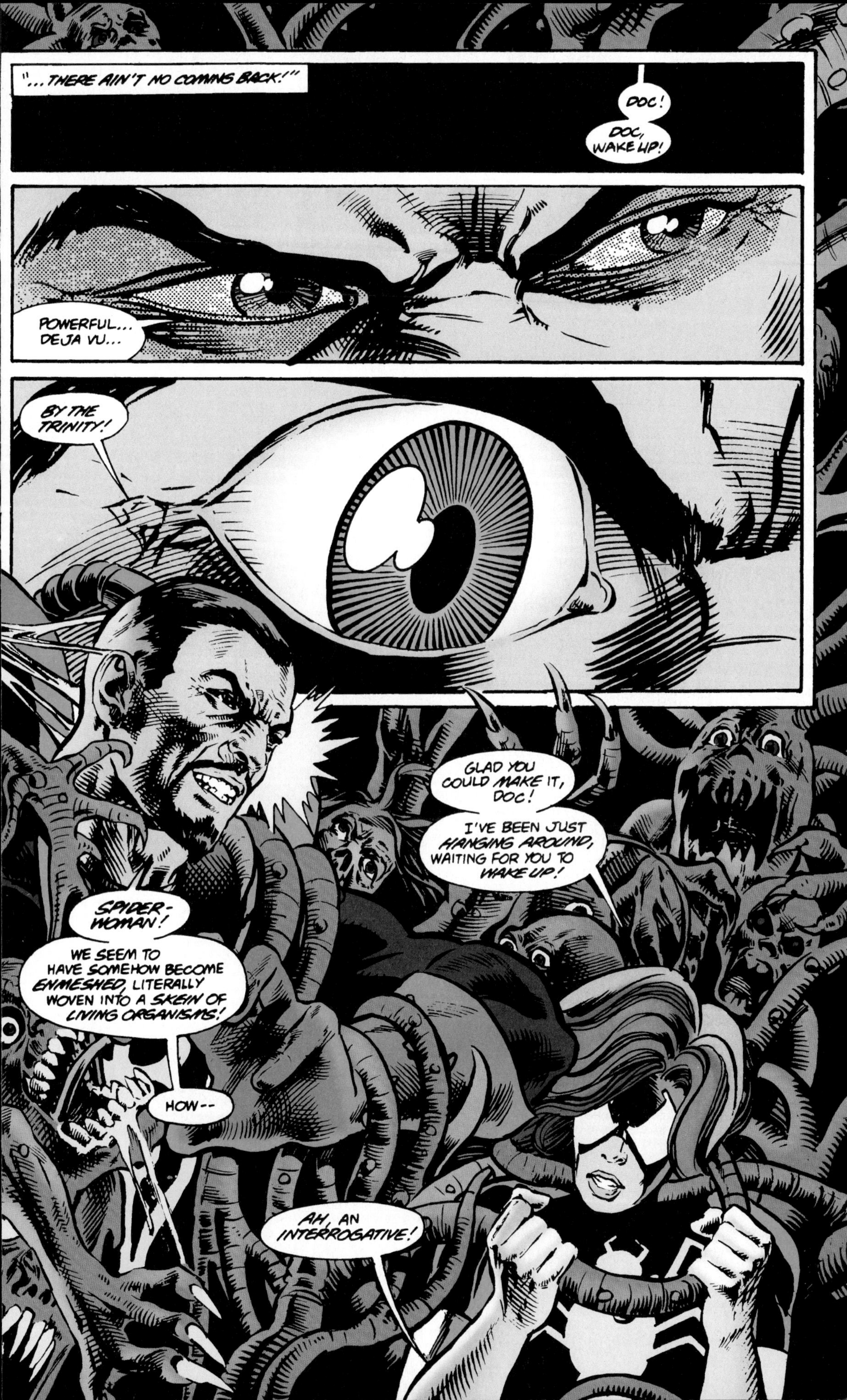
"...THERE AIN'T NO COMING BACK!"
DOC!
DOC, WAKE UP!
POWERFUL... DEJA VU...
BY THE TRINITY!
GLAD YOU COULD MAKE IT, DOC!
I'VE BEEN JUST HANGING AROUND, WAITING FOR YOU TO WAKE UP!
SPIDER-WOMAN!
WE SEEM TO HAVE SOMEHOW BECOME ENMESHED, LITERALLY WOVEN INTO A SKEIN OF LIVING ORGANISMS!
HOW--
AH, AN INTERROGATIVE!

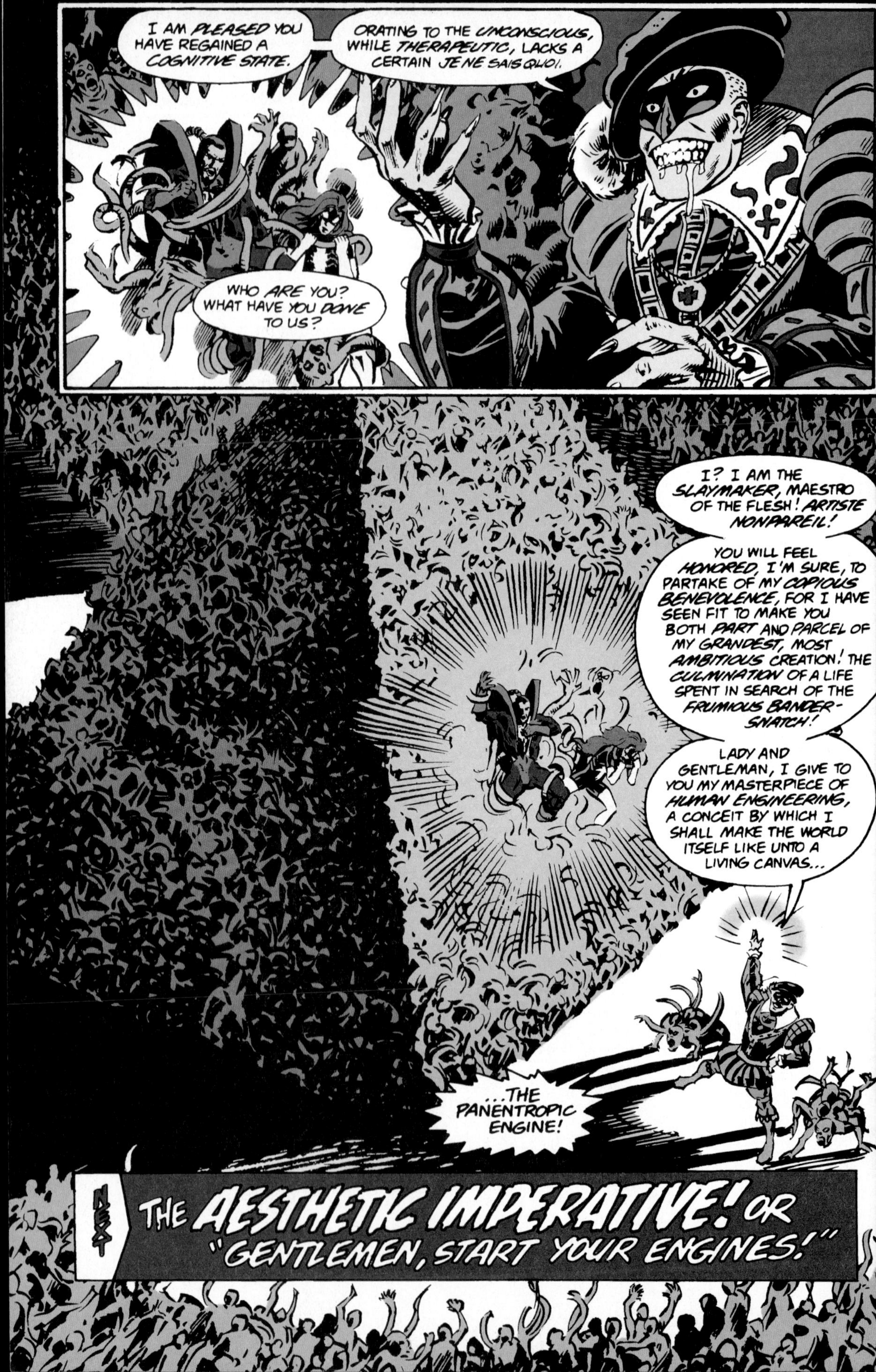
I AM PLEASED YOU HAVE REGAINED A COGNITIVE STATE.
ORATING TO THE UNCONSCIOUS, WHILE THERAPEUTIC, LACKS A CERTAIN JE NE SAIS QUOI.
WHO ARE YOU? WHAT HAVE YOU DONE TO US?
I? I AM THE SLAYMAKER, MAESTRO OF THE FLESH! ARTISTE NONPAREIL!
YOU WILL FEEL HONORED, I'M SURE, TO PARTAKE OF MY COPIOUS BENEVOLENCE, FOR I HAVE SEEN FIT TO MAKE YOU BOTH PART AND PARCEL OF MY GRANDEST, MOST AMBITIOUS CREATION! THE CULMINATION OF A LIFE SPENT IN SEARCH OF THE FRUMIOUS BANDER-SNATCH!
LADY AND GENTLEMAN, I GIVE TO YOU MY MASTERPIECE OF HUMAN ENGINEERING, A CONCEIT BY WHICH I SHALL MAKE THE WORLD ITSELF LIKE UNTO A LIVING CANVAS...
...THE PANENTROPIC ENGINE!
NEXT
THE AESTHETIC IMPERATIVE! OR "GENTLEMEN, START YOUR ENGINES!"

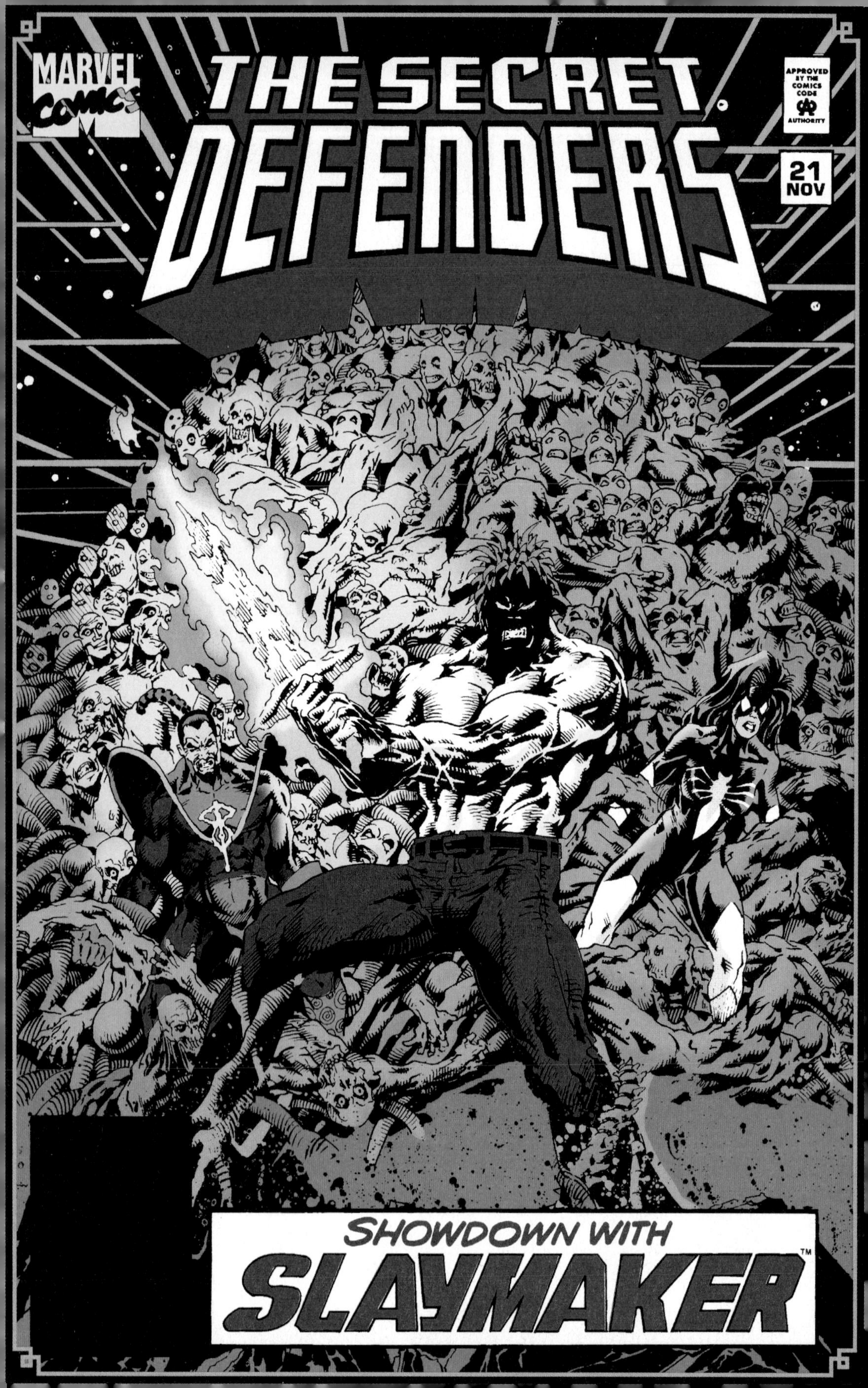
MARVEL COMICS
THE SECRET DEFENDERS
APPROVED BY THE COMICS CODE AUTHORITY
21 NOV
SHOWDOWN WITH
SLAYMAKER™

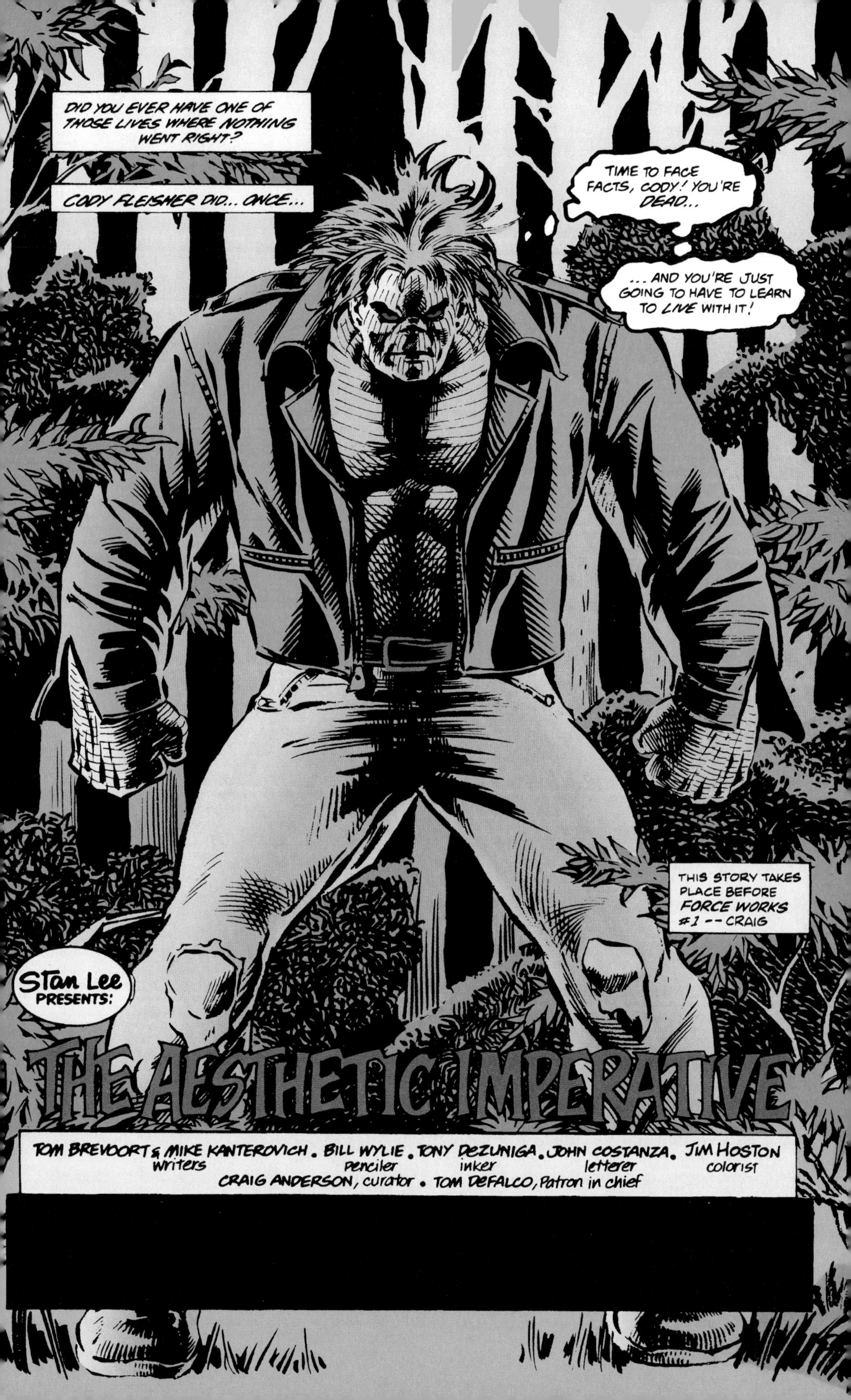

DID YOU EVER HAVE ONE OF THOSE LIVES WHERE NOTHING WENT RIGHT?
CODY FLEISHER DID... ONCE...
TIME TO FACE FACTS, CODY! YOU'RE DEAD...
... AND YOU'RE JUST GOING TO HAVE TO LEARN TO LIVE WITH IT!
THIS STORY TAKES PLACE BEFORE FORCE WORKS #1 -- CRAIG
STAN LEE PRESENTS:
THE AESTHETIC IMPERATIVE
TOM BREVOORT & MIKE KANTEROVICH writers • BILL WYLIE penciler • TONY DEZUNIGA inker • JOHN COSTANZA letterer • JIM HOSTON colorist
CRAIG ANDERSON, curator • TOM DEFALCO, Patron in chief
[redacted]

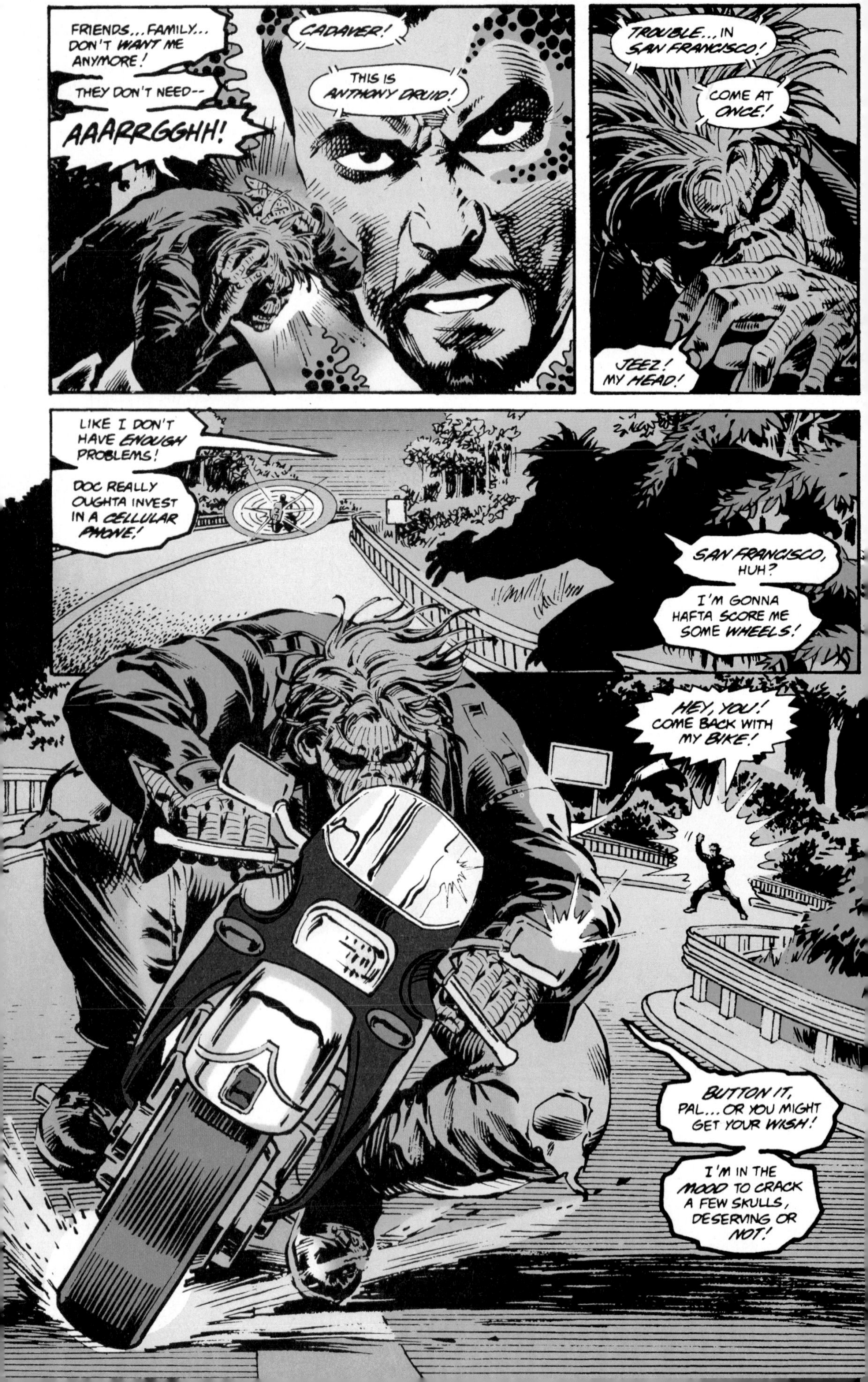
FRIENDS... FAMILY... DON'T WANT ME ANYMORE!
THEY DON'T NEED--
AAAARRGGHH!
CADAVER!
THIS IS ANTHONY DRUID!
TROUBLE... IN SAN FRANCISCO!
COME AT ONCE!
JEEZ! MY HEAD!
LIKE I DON'T HAVE ENOUGH PROBLEMS!
DOC REALLY OUGHTA INVEST IN A CELLULAR PHONE!
SAN FRANCISCO, HUH?
I'M GONNA HAFTA SCORE ME SOME WHEELS!
HEY, YOU! COME BACK WITH MY BIKE!
BUTTON IT, PAL... OR YOU MIGHT GET YOUR WISH!
I'M IN THE MOOD TO CRACK A FEW SKULLS, DESERVING OR NOT!

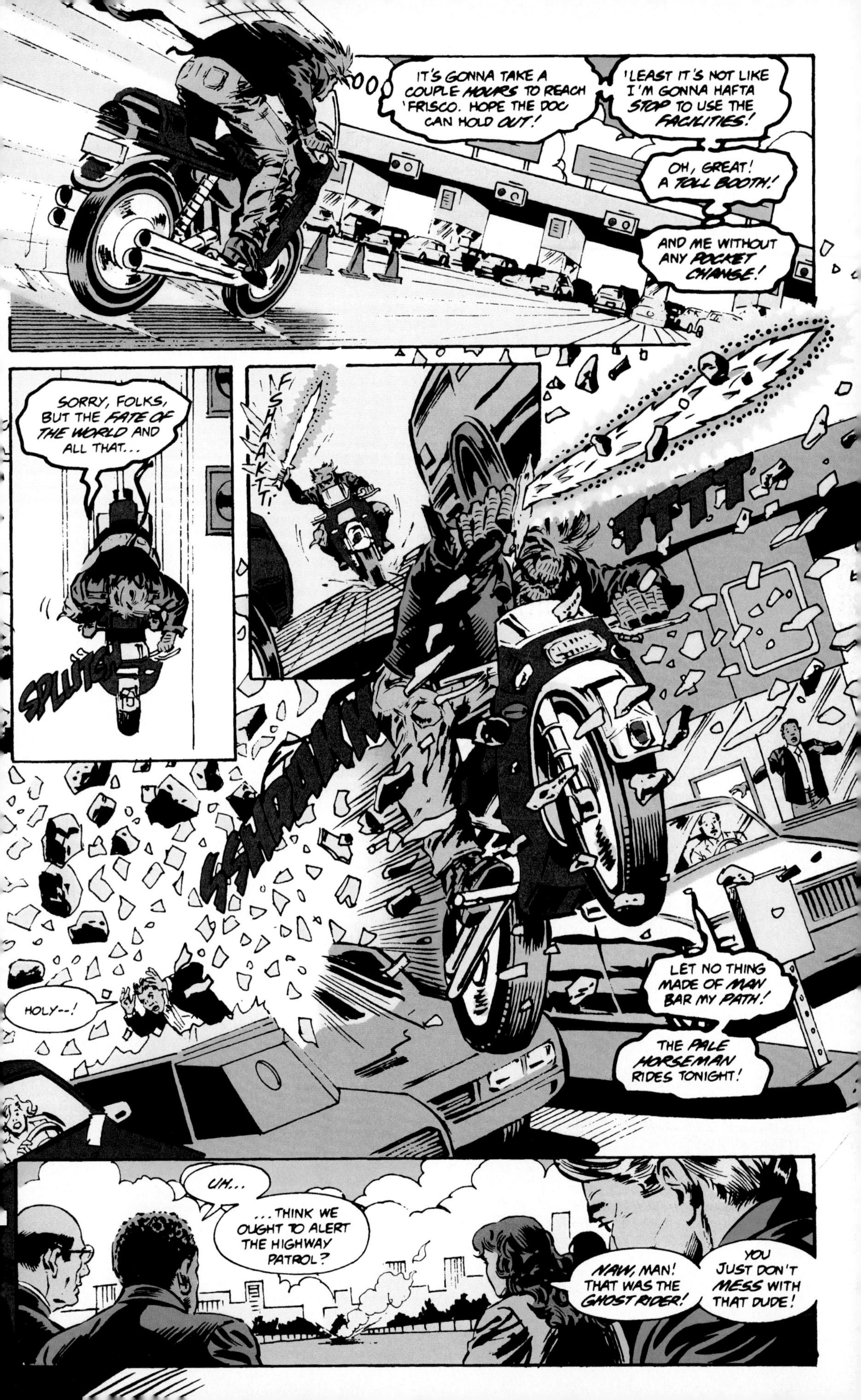
IT'S GONNA TAKE A COUPLE HOURS TO REACH 'FRISCO. HOPE THE DOC CAN HOLD OUT!
'LEAST IT'S NOT LIKE I'M GONNA HAFTA STOP TO USE THE FACILITIES!
OH, GREAT! A TOLL BOOTH!
AND ME WITHOUT ANY POCKET CHANGE!
SORRY, FOLKS, BUT THE FATE OF THE WORLD AND ALL THAT...
SPLUTCH
FSHAAKTT!
TTTT
SHRAKKK
HOLY--!
LET NO THING MADE OF MAN BAR MY PATH!
THE PALE HORSEMAN RIDES TONIGHT!
UH...
...THINK WE OUGHT TO ALERT THE HIGHWAY PATROL?
NAW, MAN! THAT WAS THE GHOST RIDER!
YOU JUST DON'T MESS WITH THAT DUDE!

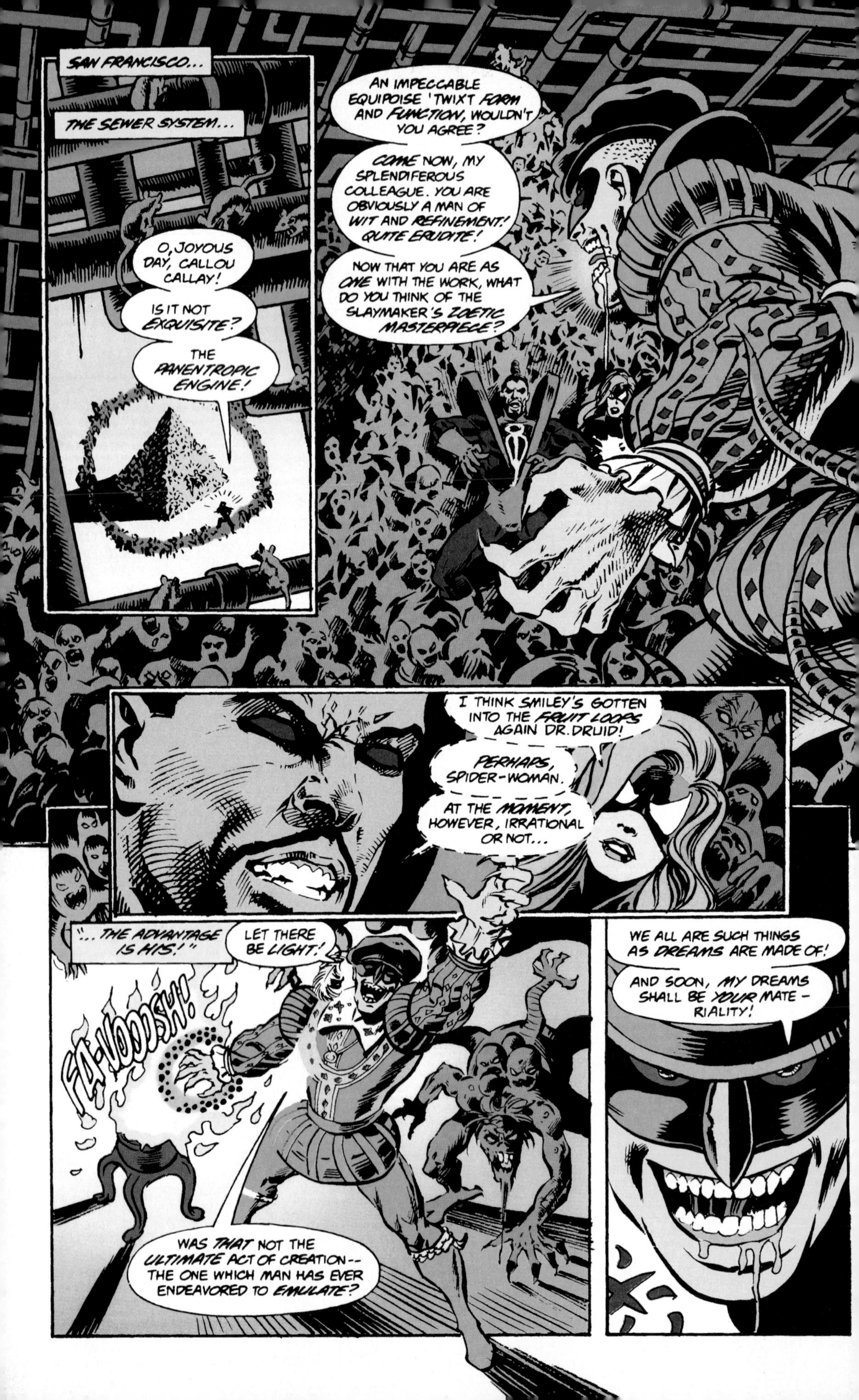
SAN FRANCISCO...
THE SEWER SYSTEM...
O, JOYOUS DAY, CALLOU CALLAY!
IS IT NOT EXQUISITE?
THE PANENTROPIC ENGINE!
AN IMPECCABLE EQUIPOISE 'TWIXT FORM AND FUNCTION, WOULDN'T YOU AGREE?
COME NOW, MY SPLENDIFEROUS COLLEAGUE. YOU ARE OBVIOUSLY A MAN OF WIT AND REFINEMENT! QUITE ERUDITE!
NOW THAT YOU ARE AS ONE WITH THE WORK, WHAT DO YOU THINK OF THE SLAYMAKER'S ZOETIC MASTERPIECE?
I THINK SMILEY'S GOTTEN INTO THE FRUIT LOOPS AGAIN DR. DRUID!
PERHAPS, SPIDER-WOMAN.
AT THE MOMENT, HOWEVER, IRRATIONAL OR NOT...
"...THE ADVANTAGE IS HIS!"
LET THERE BE LIGHT!
FA-VOOOSH!
WAS THAT NOT THE ULTIMATE ACT OF CREATION-- THE ONE WHICH MAN HAS EVER ENDEAVORED TO EMULATE?
WE ALL ARE SUCH THINGS AS DREAMS ARE MADE OF!
AND SOON, MY DREAMS SHALL BE YOUR MATE-RIALITY!

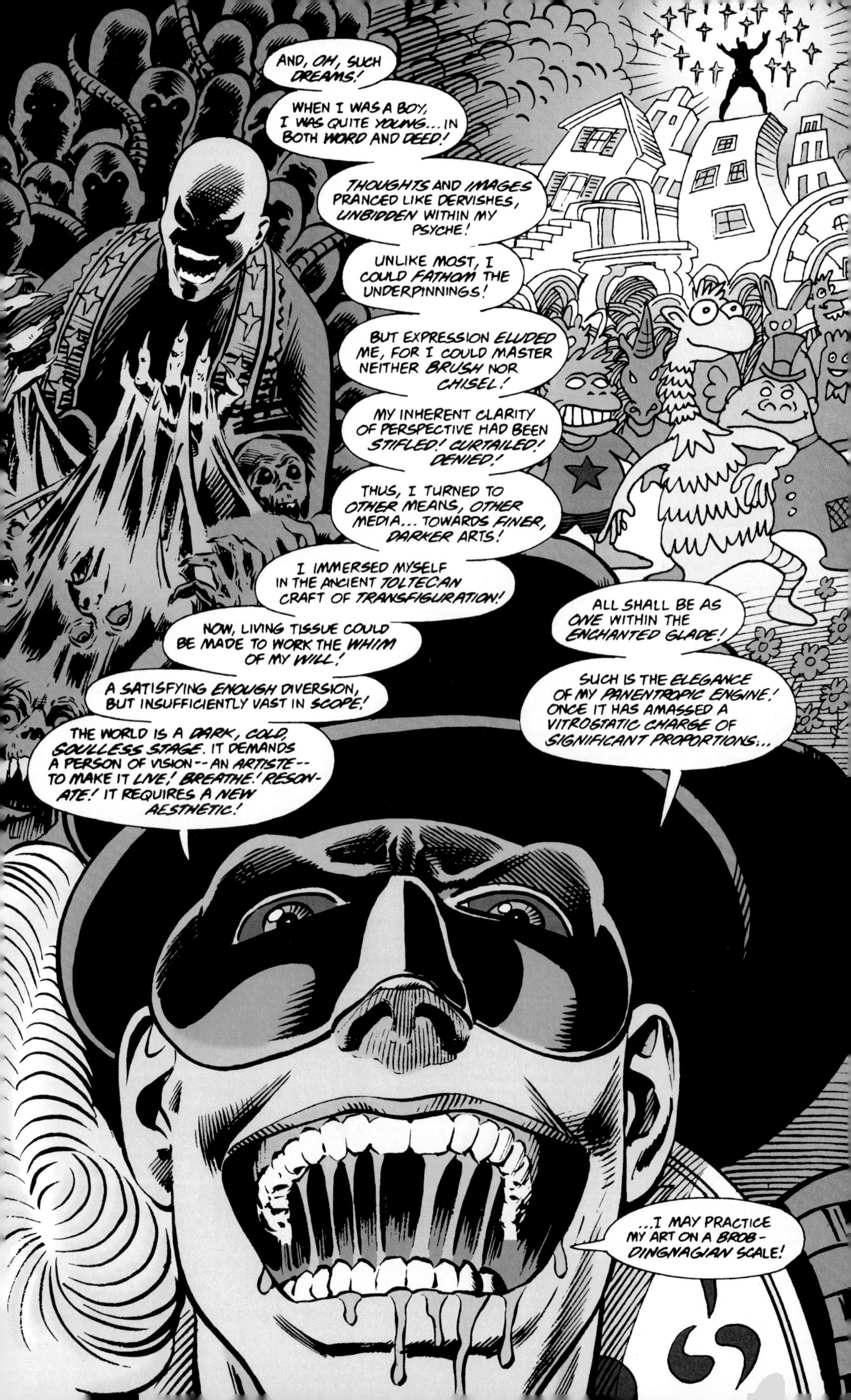
AND, OH, SUCH DREAMS!
WHEN I WAS A BOY, I WAS QUITE YOUNG... IN BOTH WORD AND DEED!
THOUGHTS AND IMAGES PRANCED LIKE DERVISHES, UNBIDDEN WITHIN MY PSYCHE!
UNLIKE MOST, I COULD FATHOM THE UNDERPINNINGS!
BUT EXPRESSION ELUDED ME, FOR I COULD MASTER NEITHER BRUSH NOR CHISEL!
MY INHERENT CLARITY OF PERSPECTIVE HAD BEEN STIFLED! CURTAILED! DENIED!
THUS, I TURNED TO OTHER MEANS, OTHER MEDIA... TOWARDS FINER, DARKER ARTS!
I IMMERSED MYSELF IN THE ANCIENT TOLTECAN CRAFT OF TRANSFIGURATION!
NOW, LIVING TISSUE COULD BE MADE TO WORK THE WHIM OF MY WILL!
A SATISFYING ENOUGH DIVERSION, BUT INSUFFICIENTLY VAST IN SCOPE!
THE WORLD IS A DARK, COLD, SOULLESS STAGE. IT DEMANDS A PERSON OF VISION-- AN ARTISTE-- TO MAKE IT LIVE! BREATHE! RESONATE! IT REQUIRES A NEW AESTHETIC!
ALL SHALL BE AS ONE WITHIN THE ENCHANTED GLADE!
SUCH IS THE ELEGANCE OF MY PANENTROPIC ENGINE! ONCE IT HAS AMASSED A VITROSTATIC CHARGE OF SIGNIFICANT PROPORTIONS...
...I MAY PRACTICE MY ART ON A BROBDINGNAGIAN SCALE!

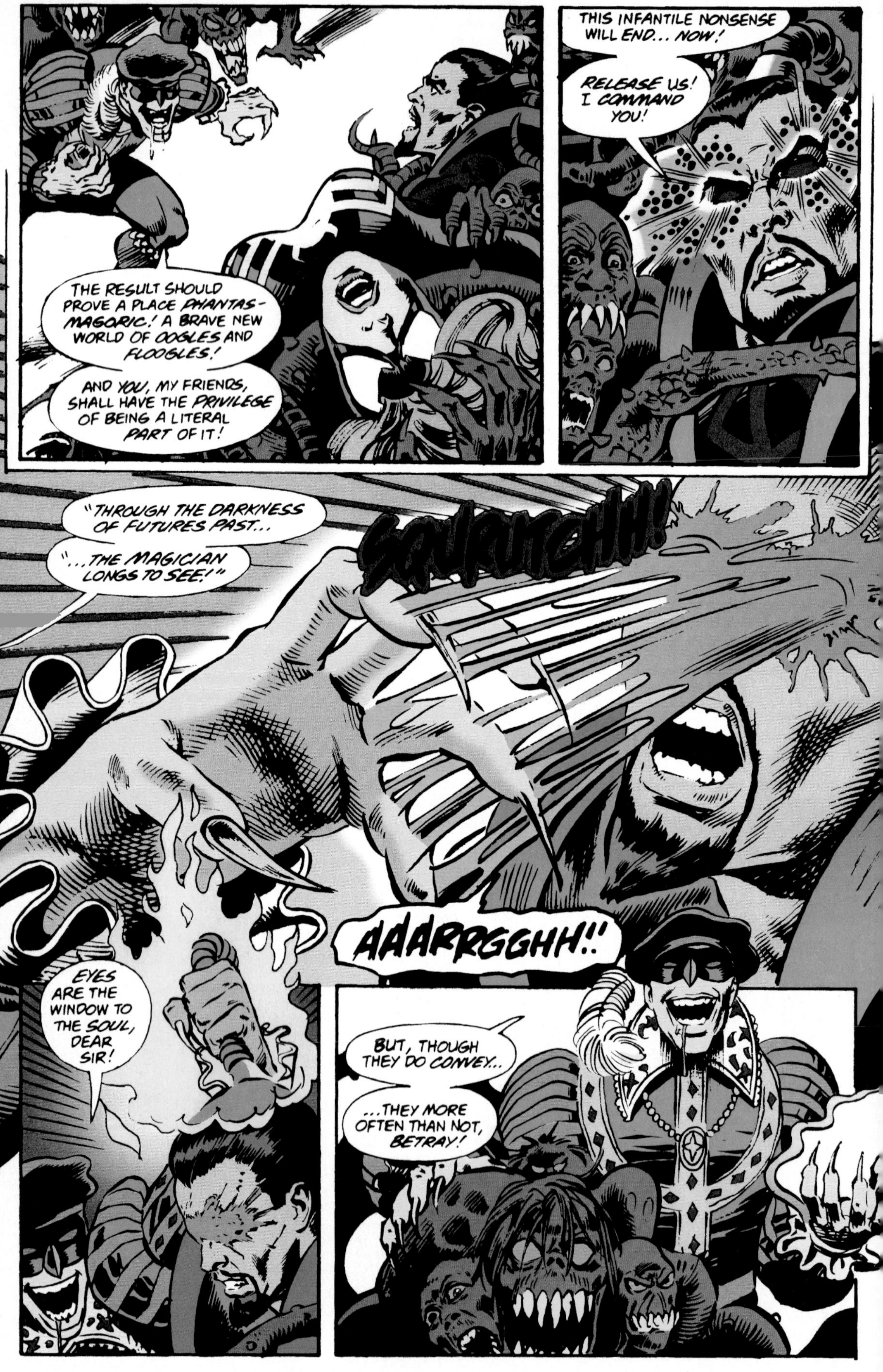
THE RESULT SHOULD PROVE A PLACE PHANTAS-MAGORIC! A BRAVE NEW WORLD OF OOGLES AND FLOOGLES!
AND YOU, MY FRIENDS, SHALL HAVE THE PRIVILEGE OF BEING A LITERAL PART OF IT!
THIS INFANTILE NONSENSE WILL END... NOW!
RELEASE US! I COMMAND YOU!
"THROUGH THE DARKNESS OF FUTURES PAST...
"...THE MAGICIAN LONGS TO SEE!"
SQUUNCHHH!
AAARRGGHH!!
EYES ARE THE WINDOW TO THE SOUL, DEAR SIR!
BUT, THOUGH THEY DO CONVEY...
...THEY MORE OFTEN THAN NOT, BETRAY!

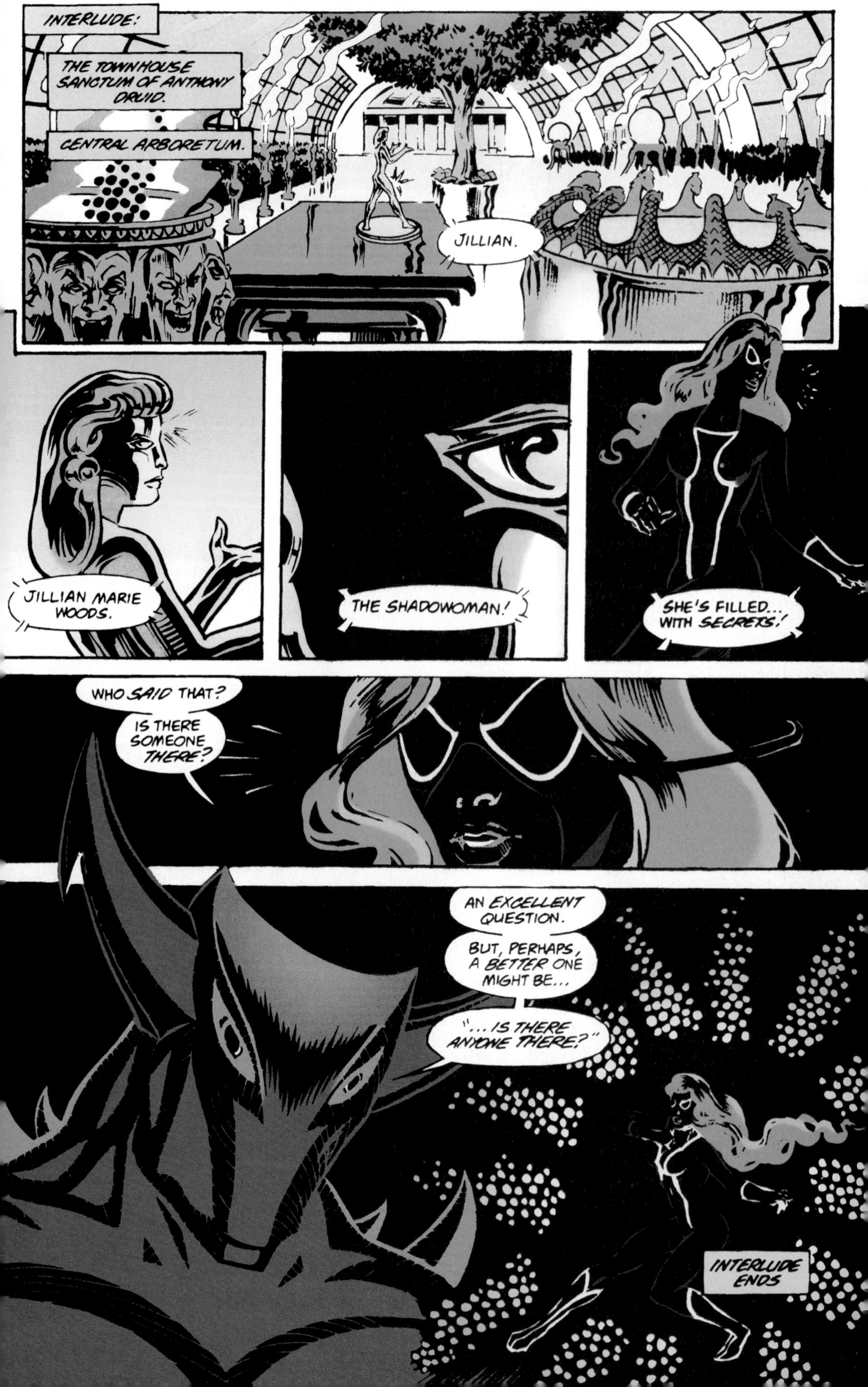
INTERLUDE:
THE TOWNHOUSE SANCTUM OF ANTHONY DRUID.
CENTRAL ARBORETUM.
JILLIAN.
JILLIAN MARIE WOODS.
THE SHADOWOMAN!
SHE'S FILLED... WITH SECRETS!
WHO SAID THAT?
IS THERE SOMEONE THERE?
AN EXCELLENT QUESTION.
BUT, PERHAPS, A BETTER ONE MIGHT BE...
"...IS THERE ANYONE THERE?"
INTERLUDE ENDS

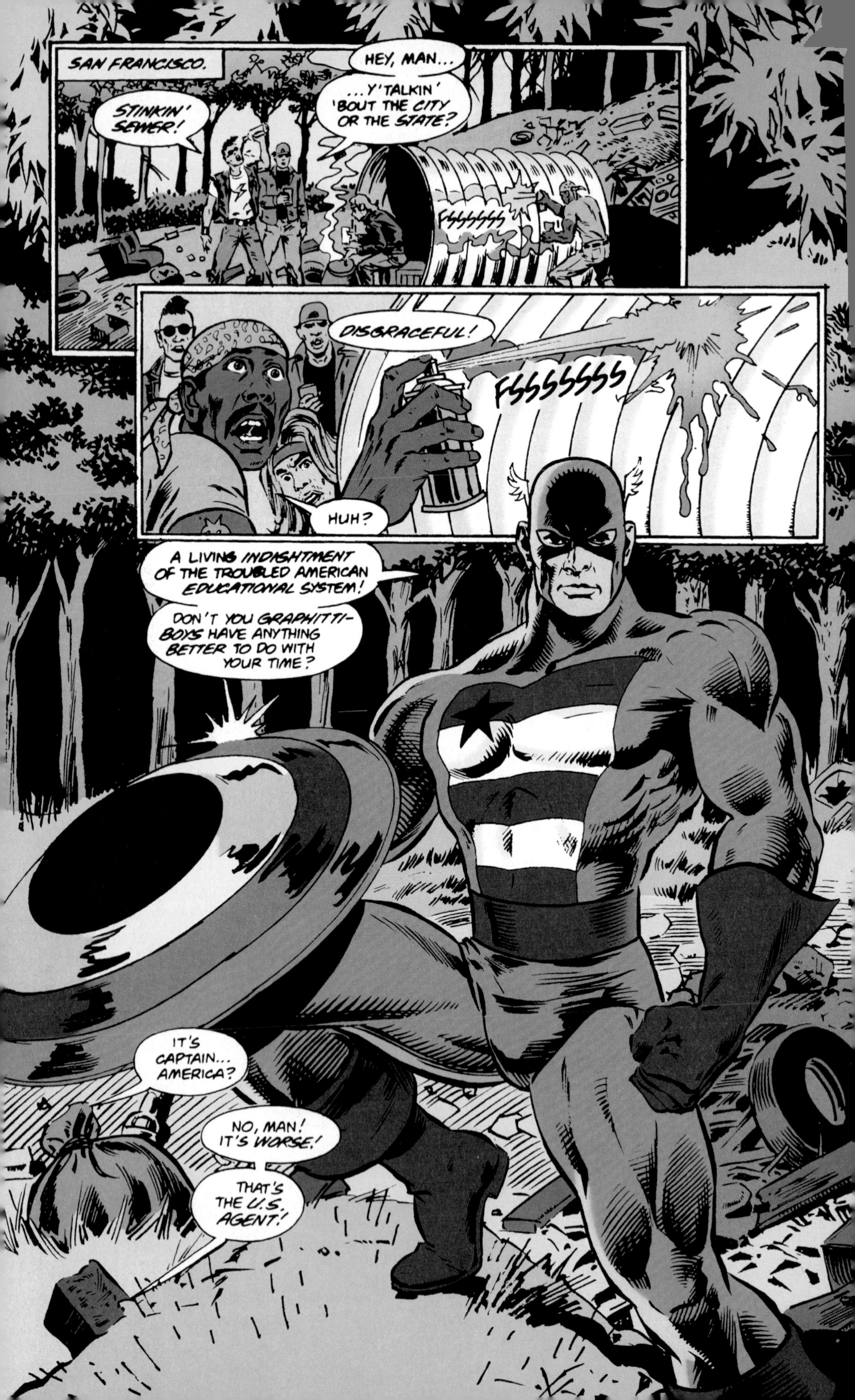
SAN FRANCISCO.
STINKIN' SEWER!
HEY, MAN...
...Y'TALKIN' 'BOUT THE CITY OR THE STATE?
FSSSSSS
DISGRACEFUL!
FSSSSSS
HUH?
A LIVING INDIGHTMENT OF THE TROUBLED AMERICAN EDUCATIONAL SYSTEM!
DON'T YOU GRAPHITTI-BOYS HAVE ANYTHING BETTER TO DO WITH YOUR TIME?
IT'S CAPTAIN... AMERICA?
NO, MAN! IT'S WORSE!
THAT'S THE U.S. AGENT!

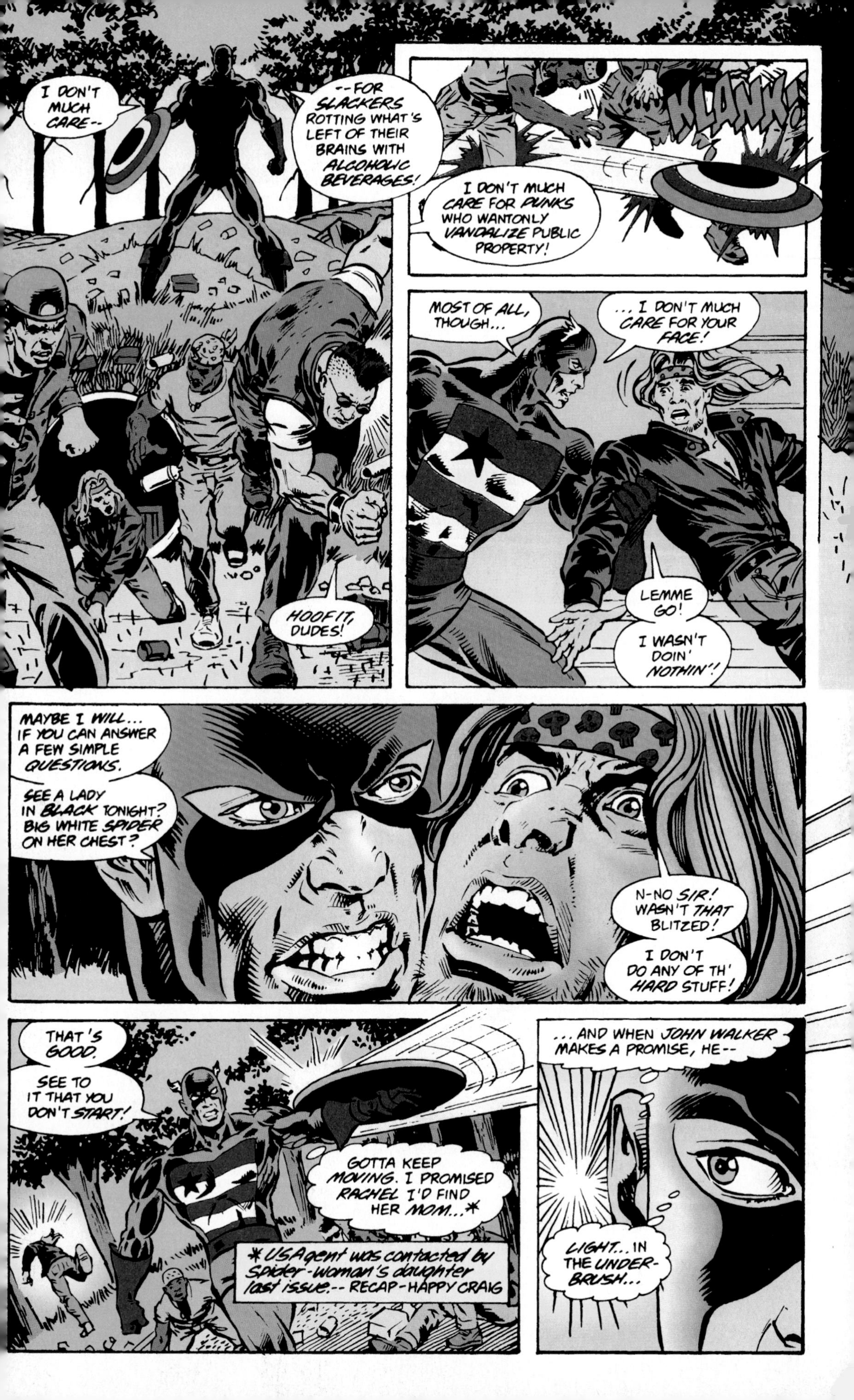
I DON'T MUCH CARE--
--FOR SLACKERS ROTTING WHAT'S LEFT OF THEIR BRAINS WITH ALCOHOLIC BEVERAGES!
KLANK!
I DON'T MUCH CARE FOR PUNKS WHO WANTONLY VANDALIZE PUBLIC PROPERTY!
HOOF IT, DUDES!
MOST OF ALL, THOUGH...
... I DON'T MUCH CARE FOR YOUR FACE!
LEMME GO!
I WASN'T DOIN' NOTHIN'!
MAYBE I WILL... IF YOU CAN ANSWER A FEW SIMPLE QUESTIONS.
SEE A LADY IN BLACK TONIGHT? BIG WHITE SPIDER ON HER CHEST?
N-NO SIR! WASN'T THAT BLITZED!
I DON'T DO ANY OF TH' HARD STUFF!
THAT'S GOOD.
SEE TO IT THAT YOU DON'T START!
GOTTA KEEP MOVING. I PROMISED RACHEL I'D FIND HER MOM...*
*USAgent was contacted by Spider-Woman's daughter last issue.-- RECAP-HAPPY CRAIG
... AND WHEN JOHN WALKER MAKES A PROMISE, HE--
LIGHT... IN THE UNDER-BRUSH...

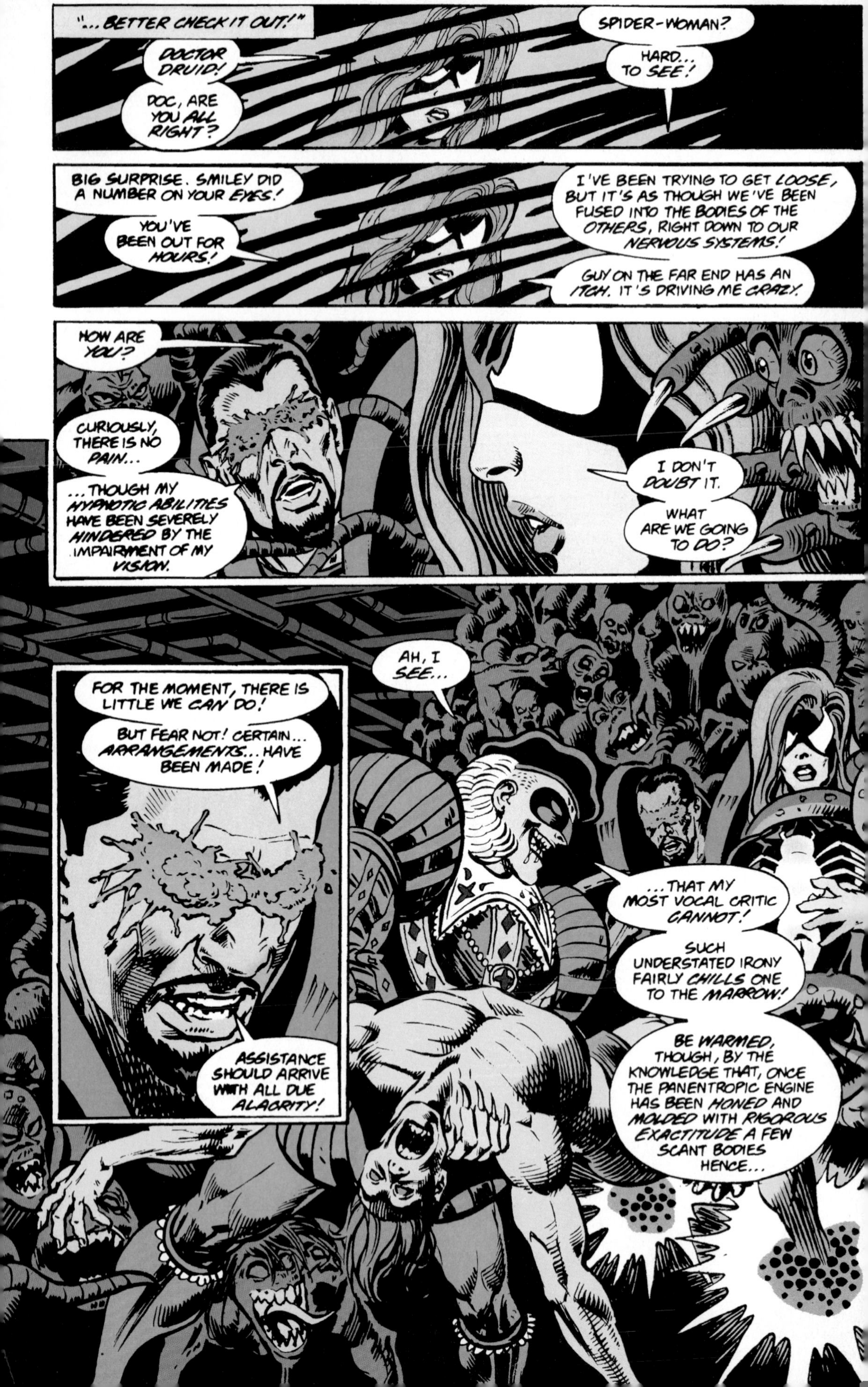

"...BETTER CHECK IT OUT!"
DOCTOR DRUID!
DOC, ARE YOU ALL RIGHT?
SPIDER-WOMAN?
HARD... TO SEE!
BIG SURPRISE. SMILEY DID A NUMBER ON YOUR EYES!
YOU'VE BEEN OUT FOR HOURS!
I'VE BEEN TRYING TO GET LOOSE, BUT IT'S AS THOUGH WE'VE BEEN FUSED INTO THE BODIES OF THE OTHERS, RIGHT DOWN TO OUR NERVOUS SYSTEMS!
GUY ON THE FAR END HAS AN ITCH. IT'S DRIVING ME CRAZY.
HOW ARE YOU?
CURIOUSLY, THERE IS NO PAIN...
...THOUGH MY HYPNOTIC ABILITIES HAVE BEEN SEVERELY HINDERED BY THE IMPAIRMENT OF MY VISION.
I DON'T DOUBT IT.
WHAT ARE WE GOING TO DO?
FOR THE MOMENT, THERE IS LITTLE WE CAN DO!
BUT FEAR NOT! CERTAIN... ARRANGEMENTS... HAVE BEEN MADE!
ASSISTANCE SHOULD ARRIVE WITH ALL DUE ALACRITY!
AH, I SEE...
...THAT MY MOST VOCAL CRITIC CANNOT!
SUCH UNDERSTATED IRONY FAIRLY CHILLS ONE TO THE MARROW!
BE WARMED, THOUGH, BY THE KNOWLEDGE THAT, ONCE THE PANENTROPIC ENGINE HAS BEEN HONED AND MOLDED WITH RIGOROUS EXACTITUDE A FEW SCANT BODIES HENCE...

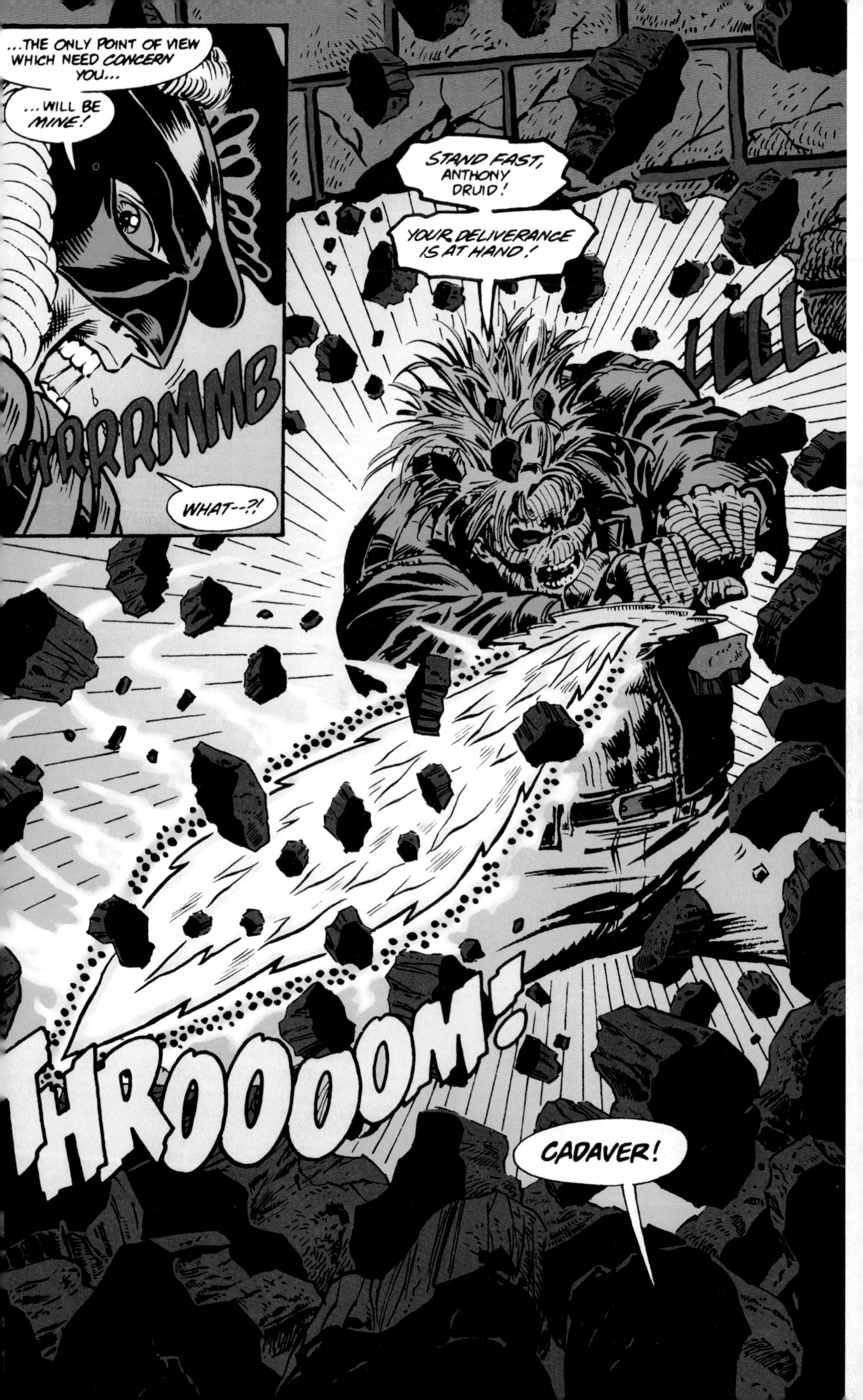
...THE ONLY POINT OF VIEW WHICH NEED CONCERN YOU...
...WILL BE MINE!
RRRRMMMB
WHAT--?!
STAND FAST, ANTHONY DRUID!
YOUR DELIVERANCE IS AT HAND!
LLLL
HROOOOOM!
CADAVER!

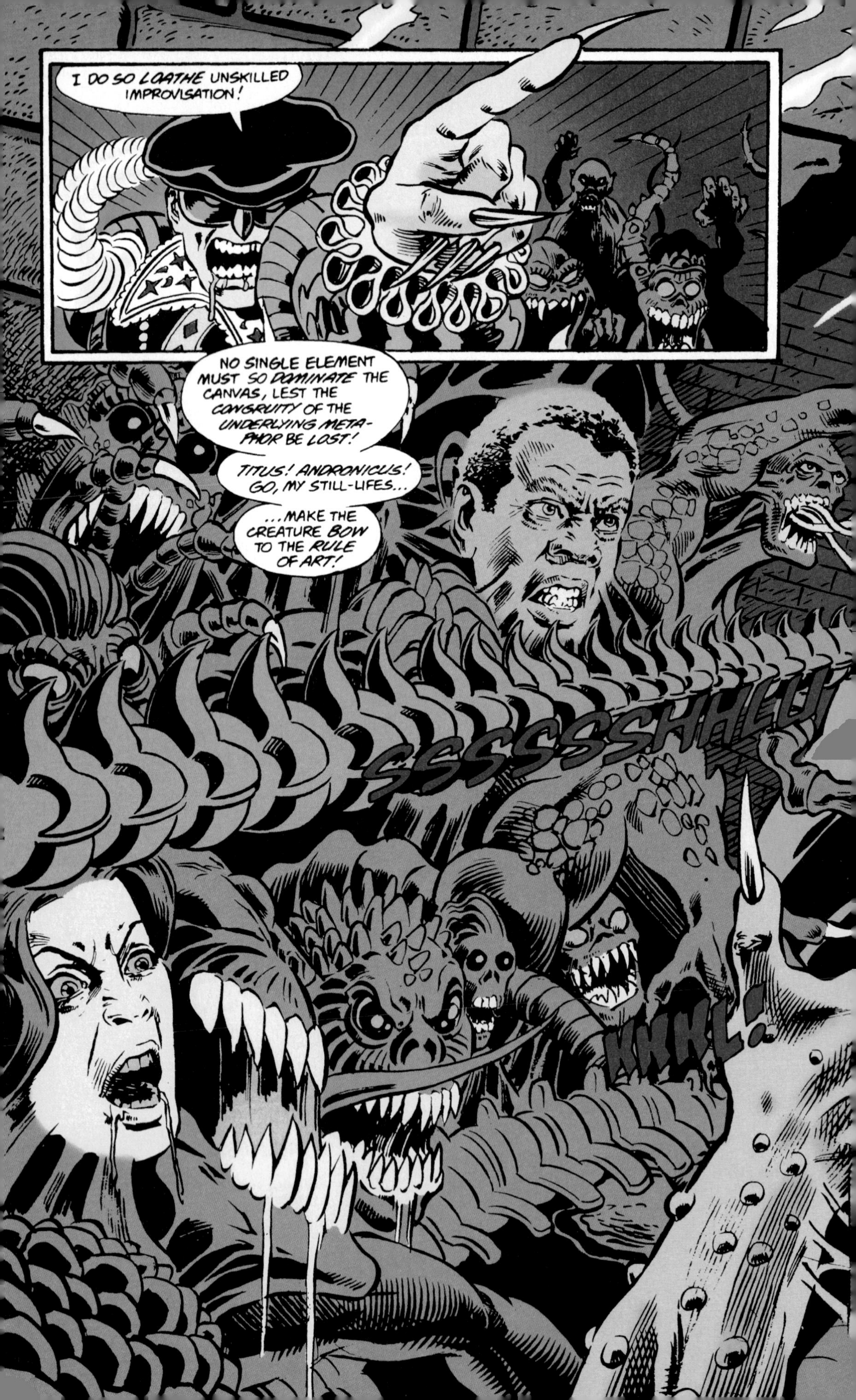

I DO SO LOATHE UNSKILLED IMPROVISATION!
NO SINGLE ELEMENT MUST SO DOMINATE THE CANVAS, LEST THE CONGRUITY OF THE UNDERLYING METAPHOR BE LOST!
TITUS! ANDRONICUS! GO, MY STILL-LIFES...
...MAKE THE CREATURE BOW TO THE RULE OF ART!
SSSSSSHHLU
KKHL!

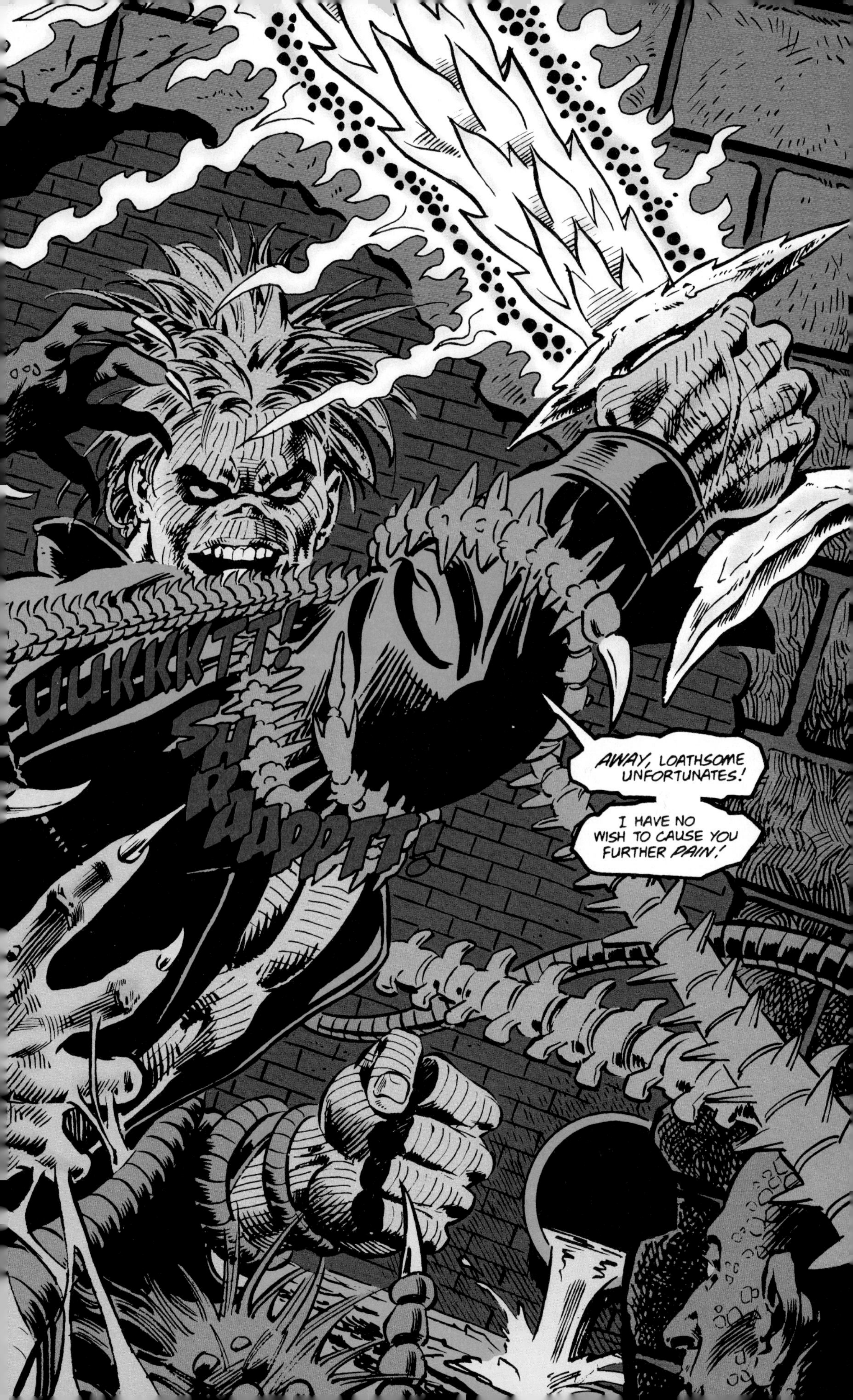
UUKKKTT!
SHRAAPPTT!
AWAY, LOATHSOME UNFORTUNATES!
I HAVE NO WISH TO CAUSE YOU FURTHER PAIN!

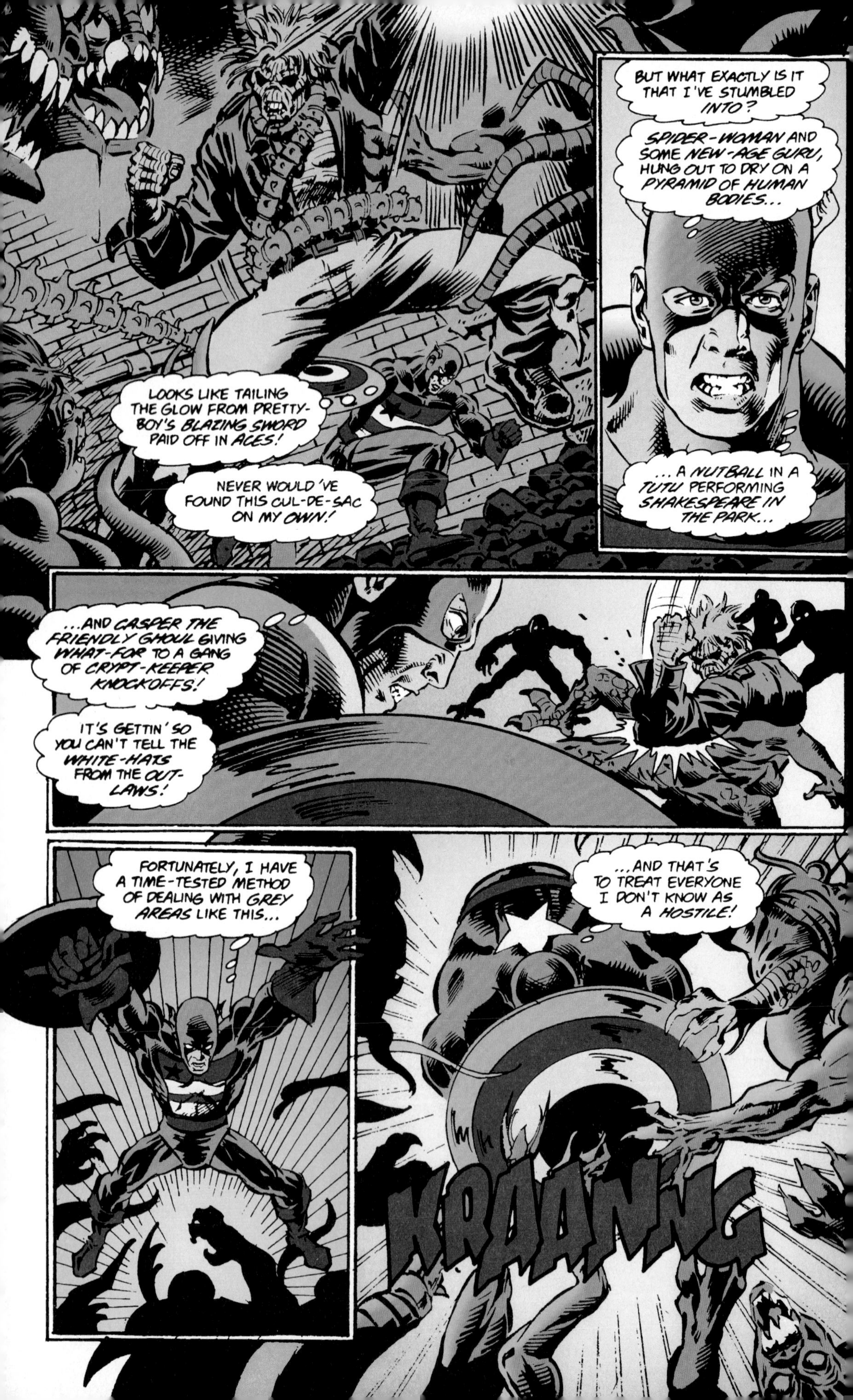
LOOKS LIKE TAILING THE GLOW FROM PRETTY-BOY'S BLAZING SWORD PAID OFF IN ACES!
NEVER WOULD'VE FOUND THIS CUL-DE-SAC ON MY OWN!
BUT WHAT EXACTLY IS IT THAT I'VE STUMBLED INTO?
SPIDER-WOMAN AND SOME NEW-AGE GURU, HUNG OUT TO DRY ON A PYRAMID OF HUMAN BODIES...
...A NUTBALL IN A TUTU PERFORMING SHAKESPEARE IN THE PARK...
...AND CASPER THE FRIENDLY GHOUL GIVING WHAT-FOR TO A GANG OF CRYPT-KEEPER KNOCKOFFS!
IT'S GETTIN' SO YOU CAN'T TELL THE WHITE-HATS FROM THE OUT-LAWS!
FORTUNATELY, I HAVE A TIME-TESTED METHOD OF DEALING WITH GREY AREAS LIKE THIS...
...AND THAT'S TO TREAT EVERYONE I DON'T KNOW AS A HOSTILE!
KRAANNG

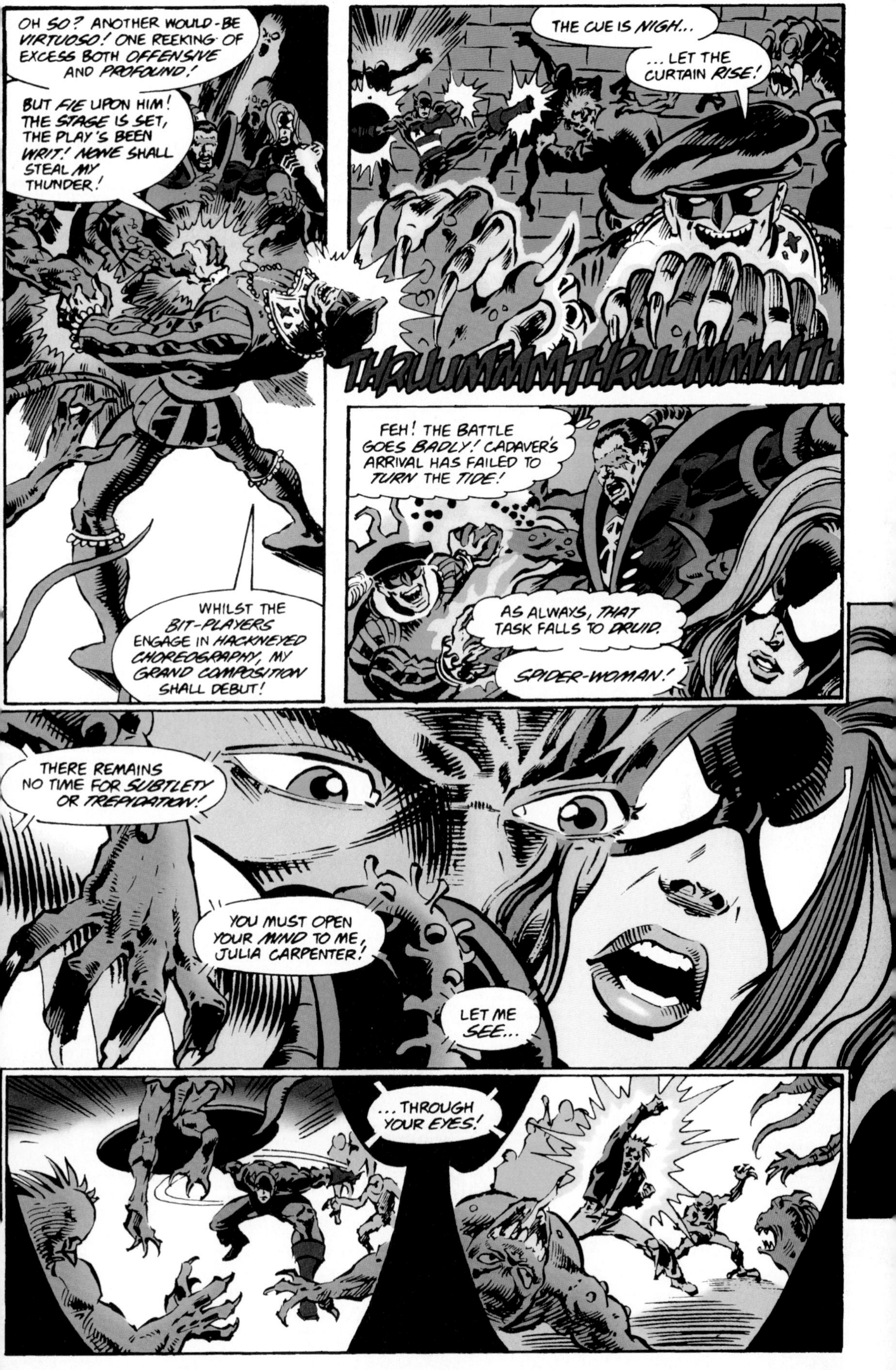
OH SO? ANOTHER WOULD-BE VIRTUOSO! ONE REEKING OF EXCESS BOTH OFFENSIVE AND PROFOUND!
BUT FIE UPON HIM! THE STAGE IS SET, THE PLAY'S BEEN WRIT! NONE SHALL STEAL MY THUNDER!
THE CUE IS NIGH...
...LET THE CURTAIN RISE!
THRUUMMMTHRUUMMMTH
WHILST THE BIT-PLAYERS ENGAGE IN HACKNEYED CHOREOGRAPHY, MY GRAND COMPOSITION SHALL DEBUT!
FEH! THE BATTLE GOES BADLY! CADAVER'S ARRIVAL HAS FAILED TO TURN THE TIDE!
AS ALWAYS, THAT TASK FALLS TO DRUID.
SPIDER-WOMAN!
THERE REMAINS NO TIME FOR SUBTLETY OR TREPIDATION!
YOU MUST OPEN YOUR MIND TO ME, JULIA CARPENTER!
LET ME SEE...
...THROUGH YOUR EYES!

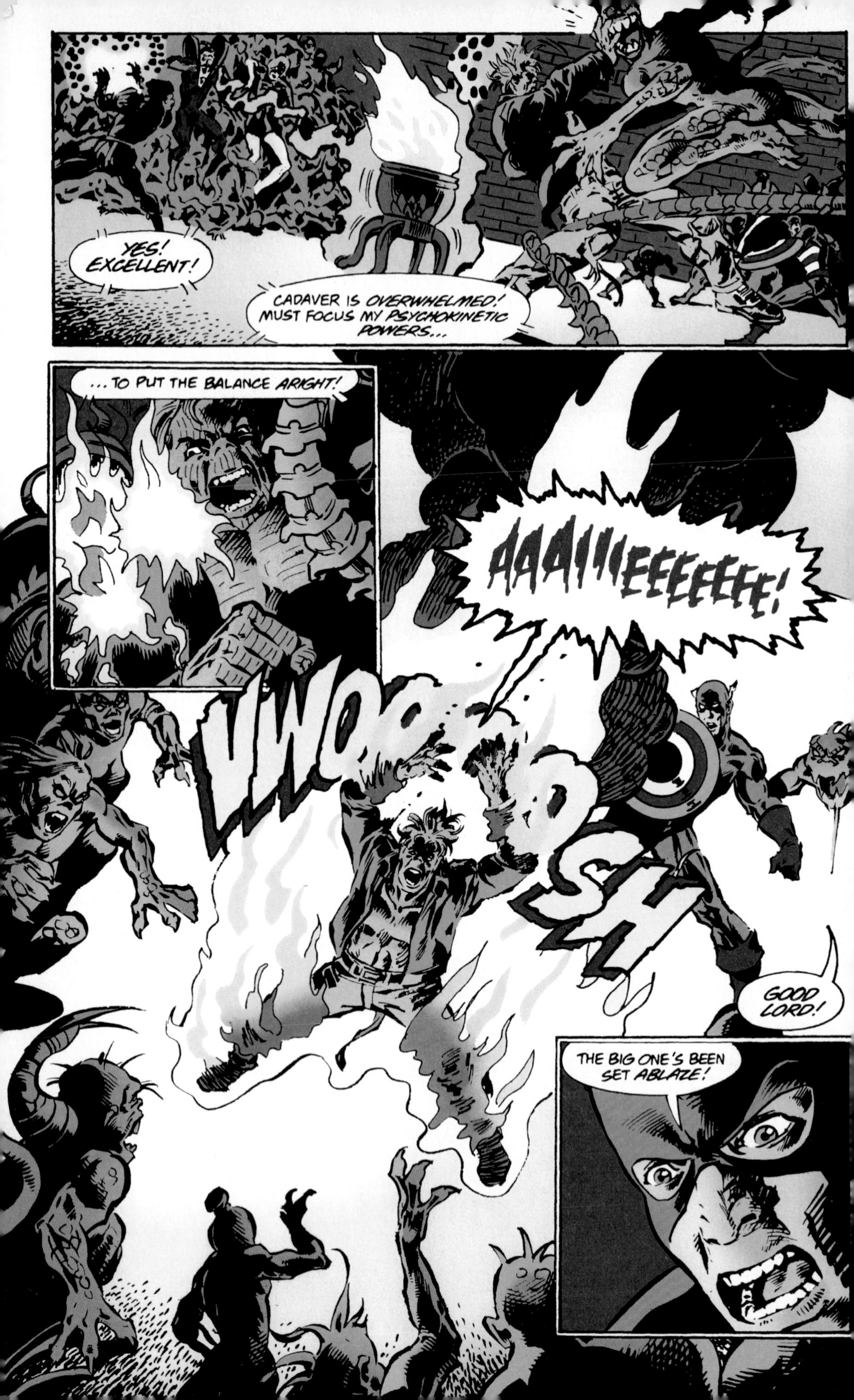
YES! EXCELLENT!
CADAVER IS OVERWHELMED! MUST FOCUS MY PSYCHOKINETIC POWERS...
...TO PUT THE BALANCE ARIGHT!
AAAIIIEEEEEEE!
WOOSH
GOOD LORD!
THE BIG ONE'S BEEN SET ABLAZE!

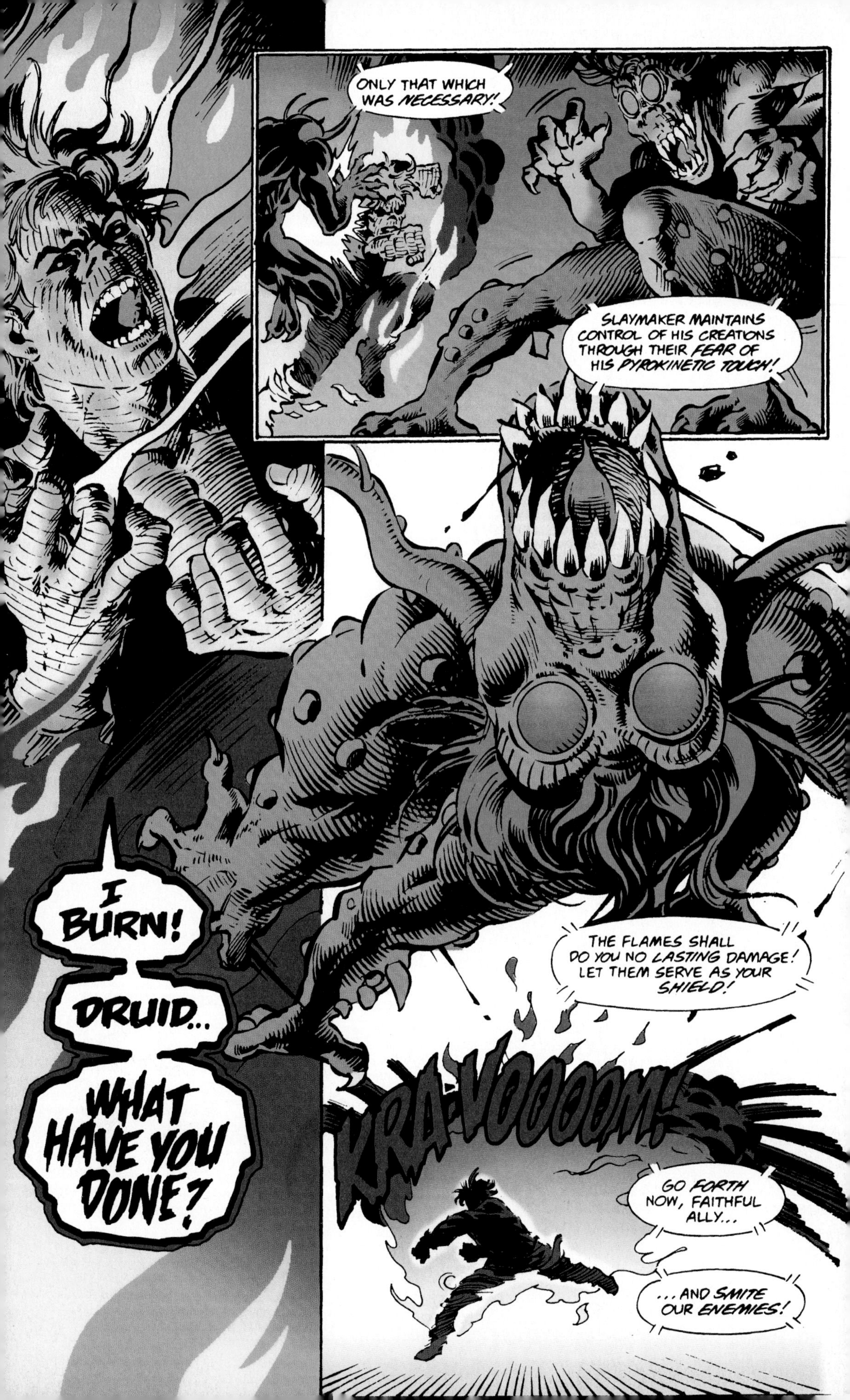
ONLY THAT WHICH WAS NECESSARY!
SLAYMAKER MAINTAINS CONTROL OF HIS CREATIONS THROUGH THEIR FEAR OF HIS PYROKINETIC TOUCH!
I BURN!
DRUID...
WHAT HAVE YOU DONE?
THE FLAMES SHALL DO YOU NO LASTING DAMAGE! LET THEM SERVE AS YOUR SHIELD!
KRA-VOOOOM!
GO FORTH NOW, FAITHFUL ALLY...
...AND SMITE OUR ENEMIES!

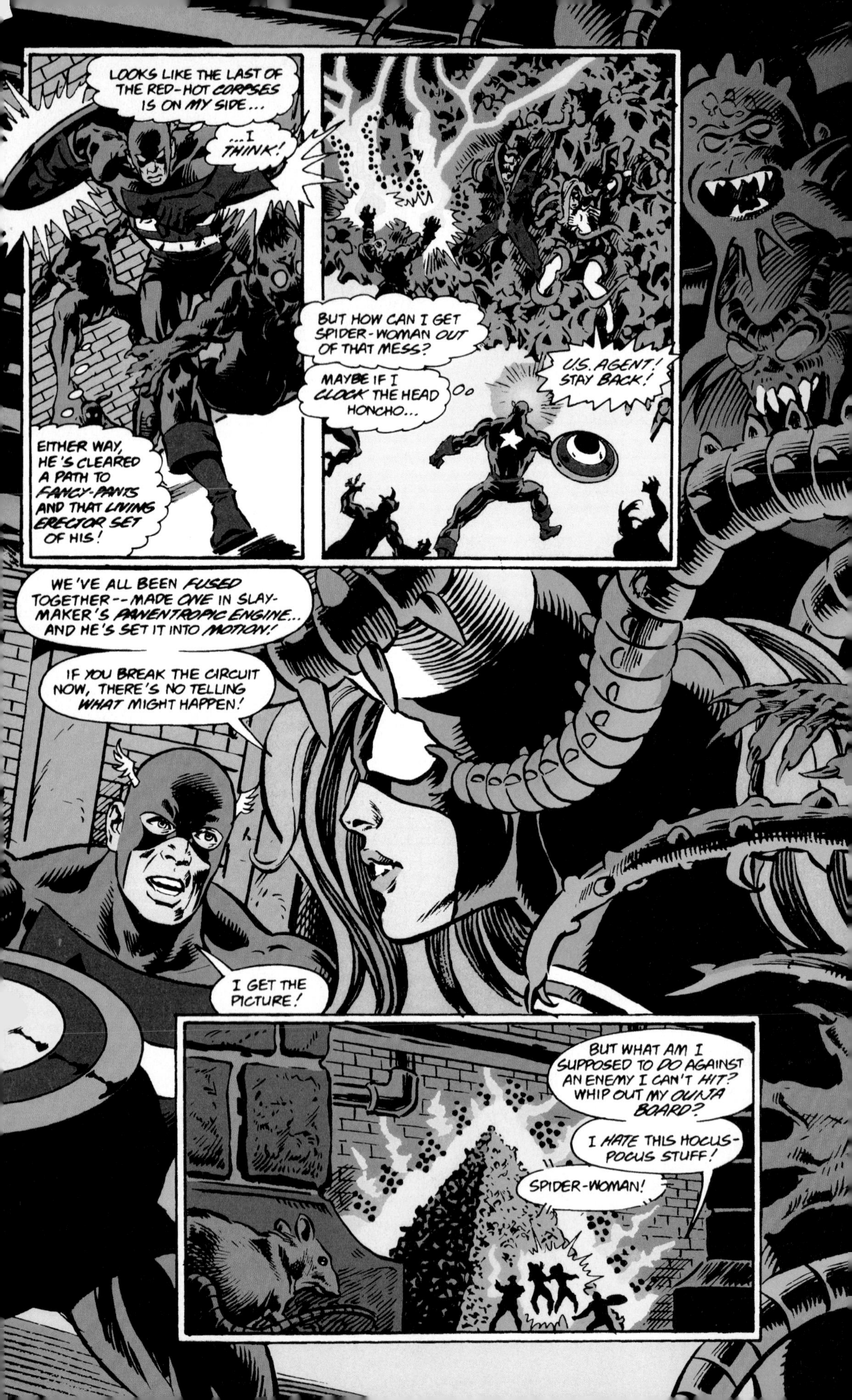
LOOKS LIKE THE LAST OF THE RED-HOT CORPSES IS ON MY SIDE...
...I THINK!
EITHER WAY, HE'S CLEARED A PATH TO FANCY-PANTS AND THAT LIVING ERECTOR SET OF HIS!
BUT HOW CAN I GET SPIDER-WOMAN OUT OF THAT MESS?
MAYBE IF I CLOCK THE HEAD HONCHO...
U.S. AGENT! STAY BACK!
WE'VE ALL BEEN FUSED TOGETHER--MADE ONE IN SLAY-MAKER'S PANENTROPIC ENGINE... AND HE'S SET IT INTO MOTION!
IF YOU BREAK THE CIRCUIT NOW, THERE'S NO TELLING WHAT MIGHT HAPPEN!
I GET THE PICTURE!
BUT WHAT AM I SUPPOSED TO DO AGAINST AN ENEMY I CAN'T HIT? WHIP OUT MY OUIJA BOARD?
I HATE THIS HOCUS-POCUS STUFF!
SPIDER-WOMAN!

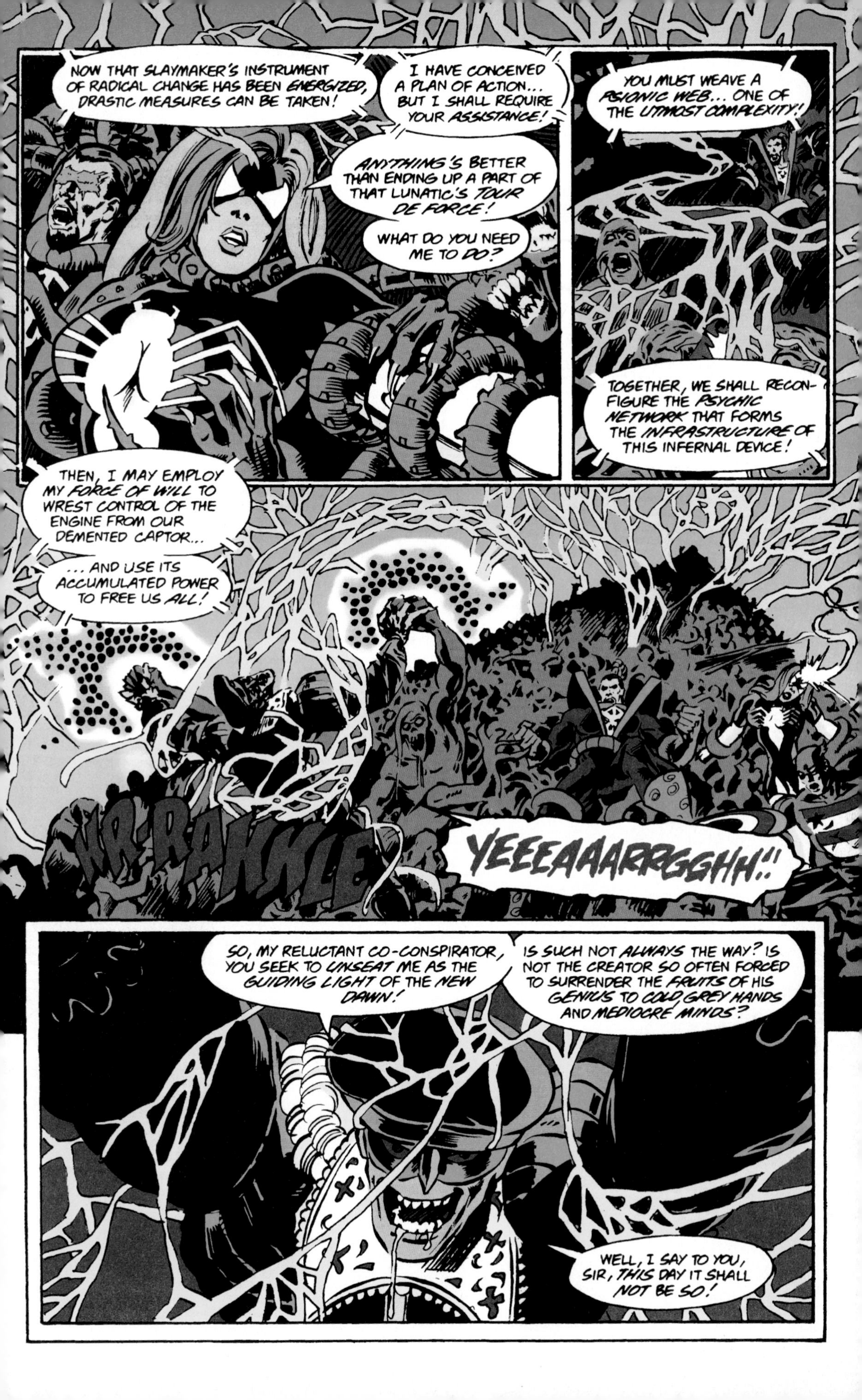
NOW THAT SLAYMAKER'S INSTRUMENT OF RADICAL CHANGE HAS BEEN ENERGIZED, DRASTIC MEASURES CAN BE TAKEN!
I HAVE CONCEIVED A PLAN OF ACTION... BUT I SHALL REQUIRE YOUR ASSISTANCE!
ANYTHING'S BETTER THAN ENDING UP A PART OF THAT LUNATIC'S TOUR DE FORCE!
WHAT DO YOU NEED ME TO DO?
YOU MUST WEAVE A PSIONIC WEB... ONE OF THE UTMOST COMPLEXITY!
TOGETHER, WE SHALL RECONFIGURE THE PSYCHIC NETWORK THAT FORMS THE INFRASTRUCTURE OF THIS INFERNAL DEVICE!
THEN, I MAY EMPLOY MY FORCE OF WILL TO WREST CONTROL OF THE ENGINE FROM OUR DEMENTED CAPTOR...
...AND USE ITS ACCUMULATED POWER TO FREE US ALL!
KR-RAKKLE
YEEEAAARRGGHH!!
SO, MY RELUCTANT CO-CONSPIRATOR, YOU SEEK TO UNSEAT ME AS THE GUIDING LIGHT OF THE NEW DAWN!
IS SUCH NOT ALWAYS THE WAY? IS NOT THE CREATOR SO OFTEN FORCED TO SURRENDER THE FRUITS OF HIS GENIUS TO COLD, GREY HANDS AND MEDIOCRE MINDS?
WELL, I SAY TO YOU, SIR, THIS DAY IT SHALL NOT BE SO!

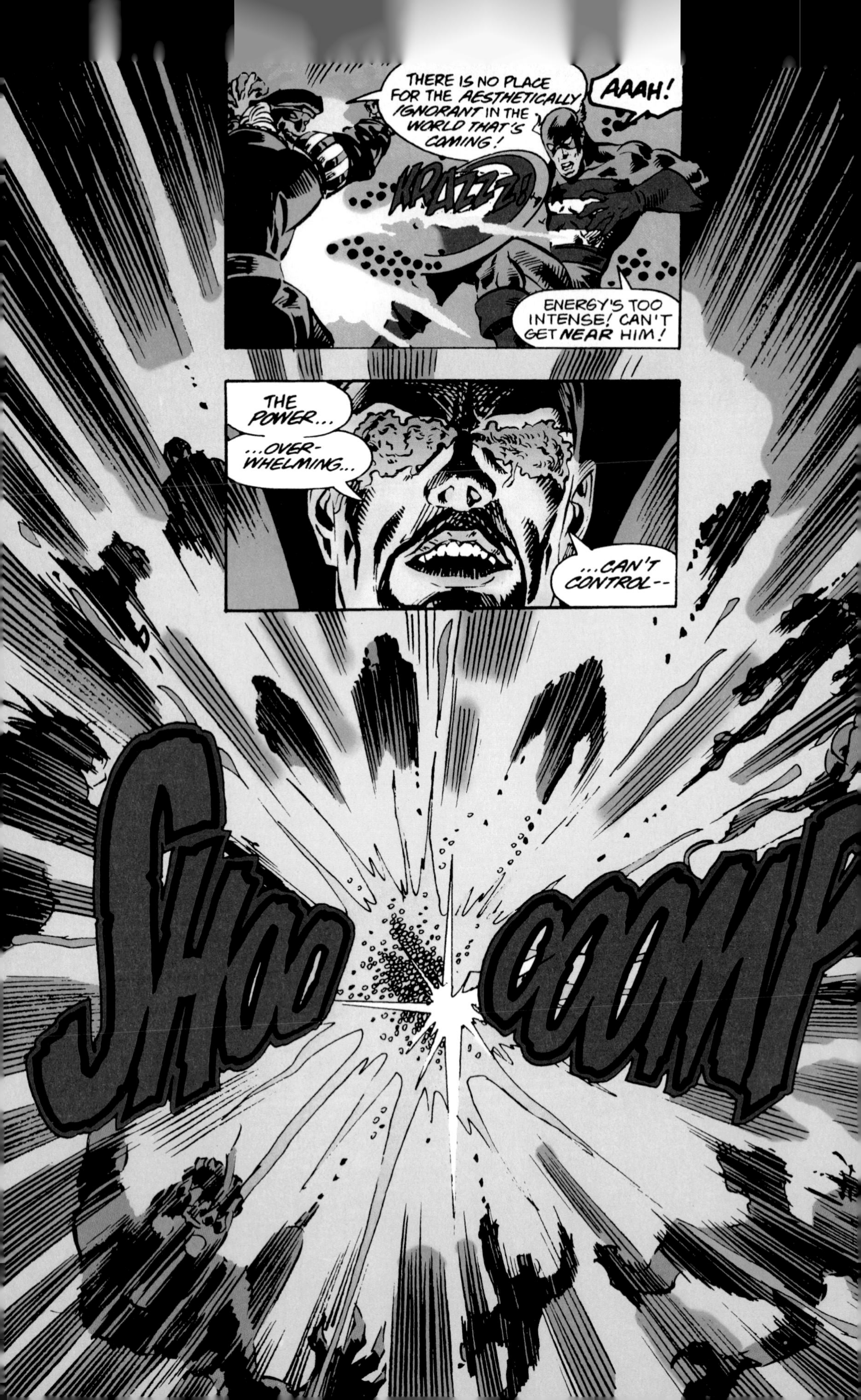
THERE IS NO PLACE FOR THE AESTHETICALLY IGNORANT IN THE WORLD THAT'S COMING!
AAAH!
KRAZZZ
ENERGY'S TOO INTENSE! CAN'T GET NEAR HIM!
THE POWER...
...OVER-WHELMING...
...CAN'T CONTROL--
SHA-COOMP

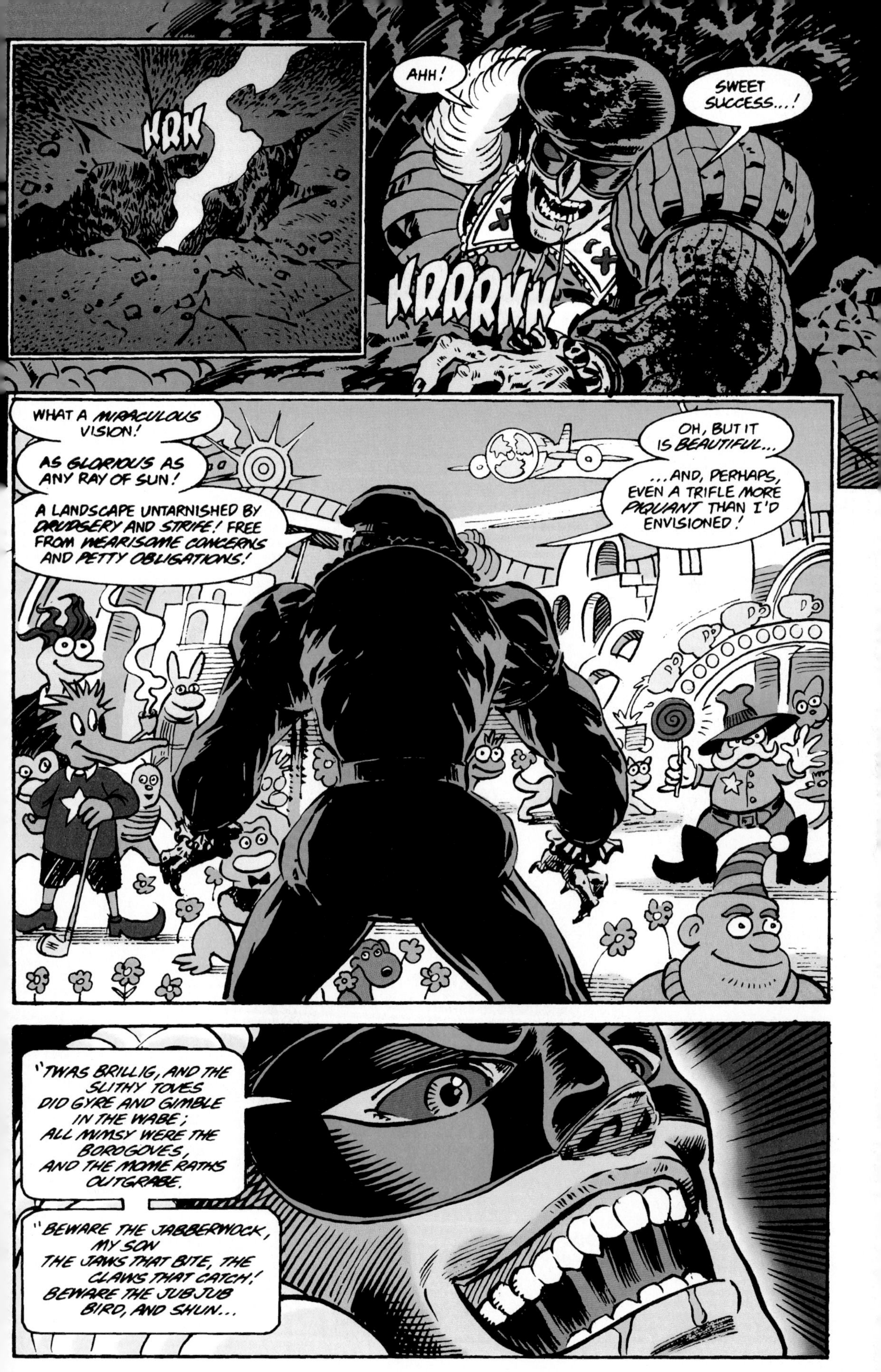
HRN
AHH!
SWEET SUCCESS...!
KRRRKK
WHAT A MIRACULOUS VISION!
AS GLORIOUS AS ANY RAY OF SUN!
A LANDSCAPE UNTARNISHED BY DRUDGERY AND STRIFE! FREE FROM WEARISOME CONCERNS AND PETTY OBLIGATIONS!
OH, BUT IT IS BEAUTIFUL...
...AND, PERHAPS, EVEN A TRIFLE MORE PIQUANT THAN I'D ENVISIONED!
"TWAS BRILLIG, AND THE SLITHY TOVES DID GYRE AND GIMBLE IN THE WABE; ALL MIMSY WERE THE BOROGOVES, AND THE MOME RATHS OUTGRABE.
"BEWARE THE JABBERWOCK, MY SON THE JAWS THAT BITE, THE CLAWS THAT CATCH! BEWARE THE JUBJUB BIRD, AND SHUN...

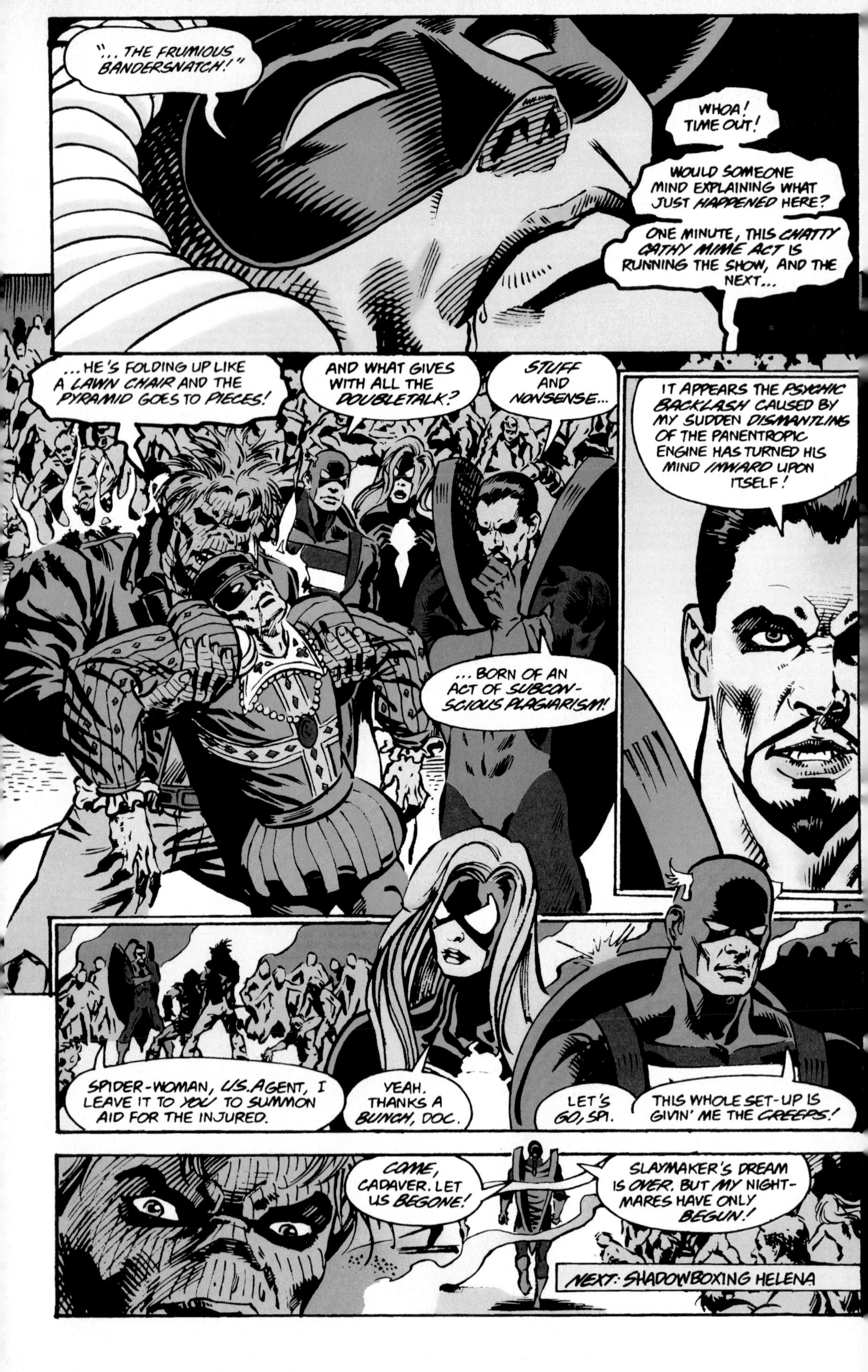
"...THE FRUMIOUS BANDERSNATCH!"
WHOA! TIME OUT!
WOULD SOMEONE MIND EXPLAINING WHAT JUST HAPPENED HERE?
ONE MINUTE, THIS CHATTY CATHY MIME ACT IS RUNNING THE SHOW, AND THE NEXT...
...HE'S FOLDING UP LIKE A LAWN CHAIR AND THE PYRAMID GOES TO PIECES!
AND WHAT GIVES WITH ALL THE DOUBLETALK?
STUFF AND NONSENSE...
...BORN OF AN ACT OF SUBCON-SCIOUS PLAGIARISM!
IT APPEARS THE PSYCHIC BACKLASH CAUSED BY MY SUDDEN DISMANTLING OF THE PANENTROPIC ENGINE HAS TURNED HIS MIND INWARD UPON ITSELF!
SPIDER-WOMAN, U.S. AGENT, I LEAVE IT TO YOU TO SUMMON AID FOR THE INJURED.
YEAH. THANKS A BUNCH, DOC.
LET'S GO, SPI.
THIS WHOLE SET-UP IS GIVIN' ME THE CREEPS!
COME, CADAVER. LET US BEGONE!
SLAYMAKER'S DREAM IS OVER. BUT MY NIGHT-MARES HAVE ONLY BEGUN!
NEXT: SHADOWBOXING HELENA

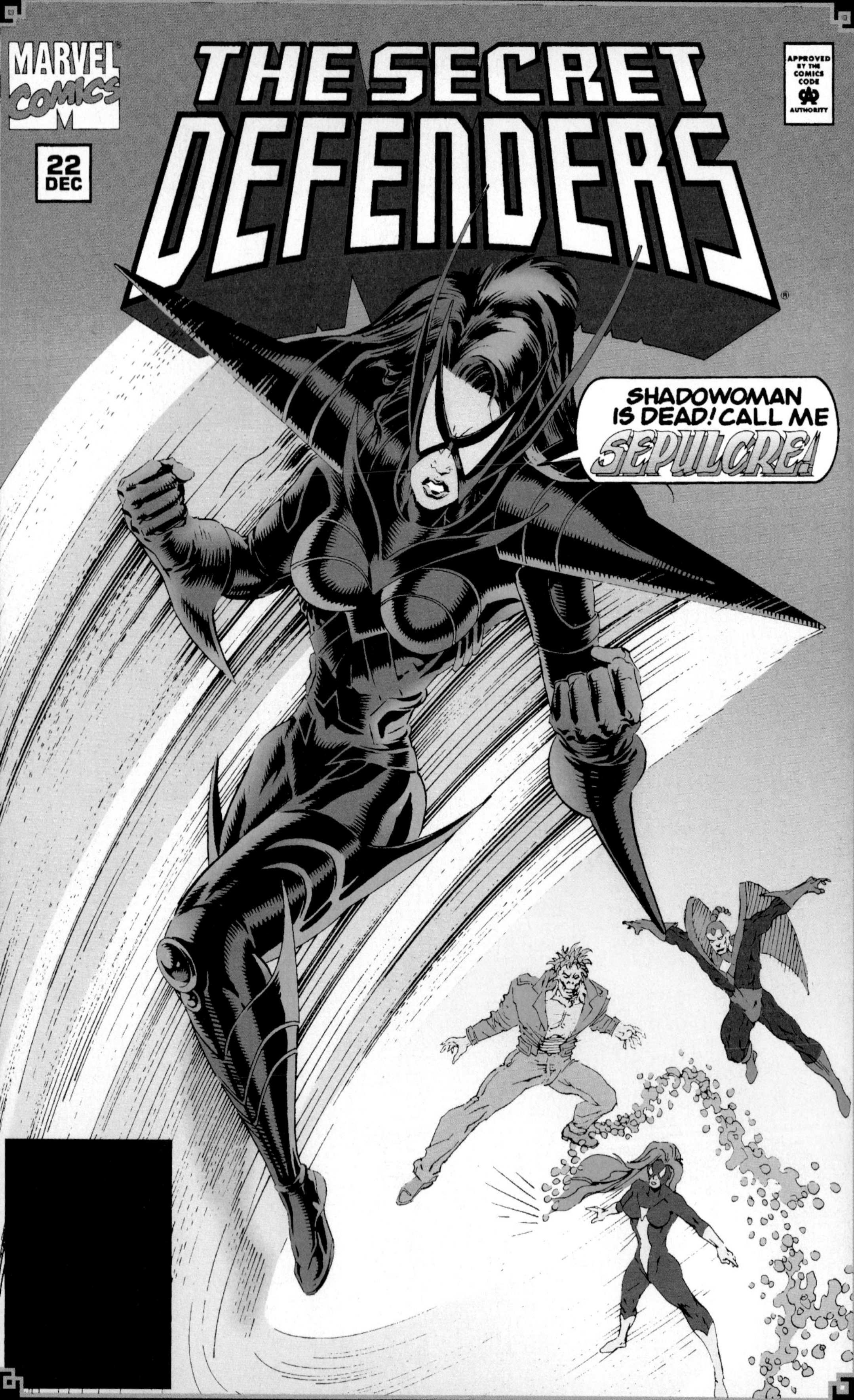
MARVEL COMICS
THE SECRET DEFENDERS
22 DEC
APPROVED BY THE COMICS CODE AUTHORITY
SHADOWOMAN IS DEAD! CALL ME SEPULCRE!

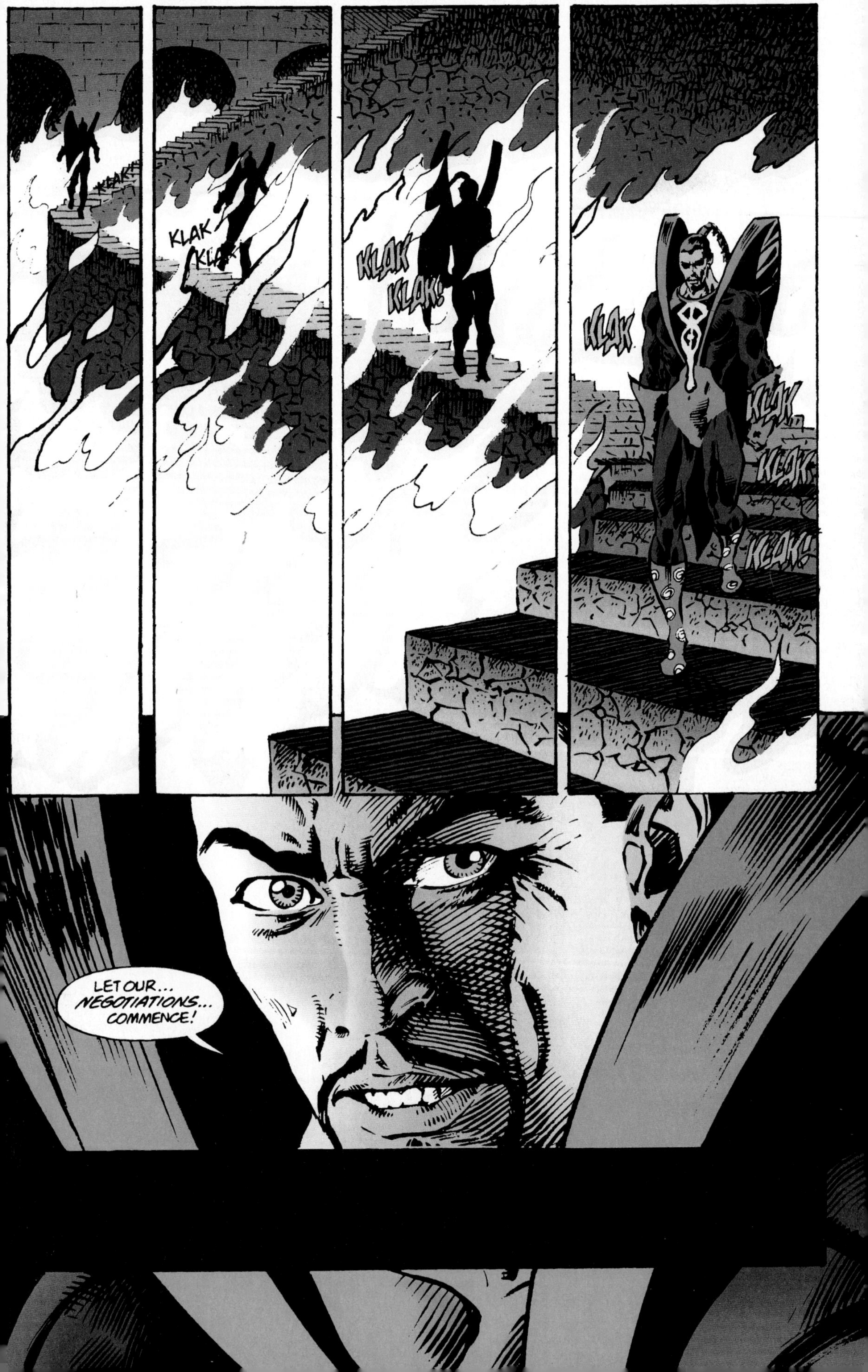
KLAK
KLAK
KLAK
KLAK
KLAK!
KLAK
KLAK
KLAK
KLAK!
LET OUR... NEGOTIATIONS... COMMENCE!

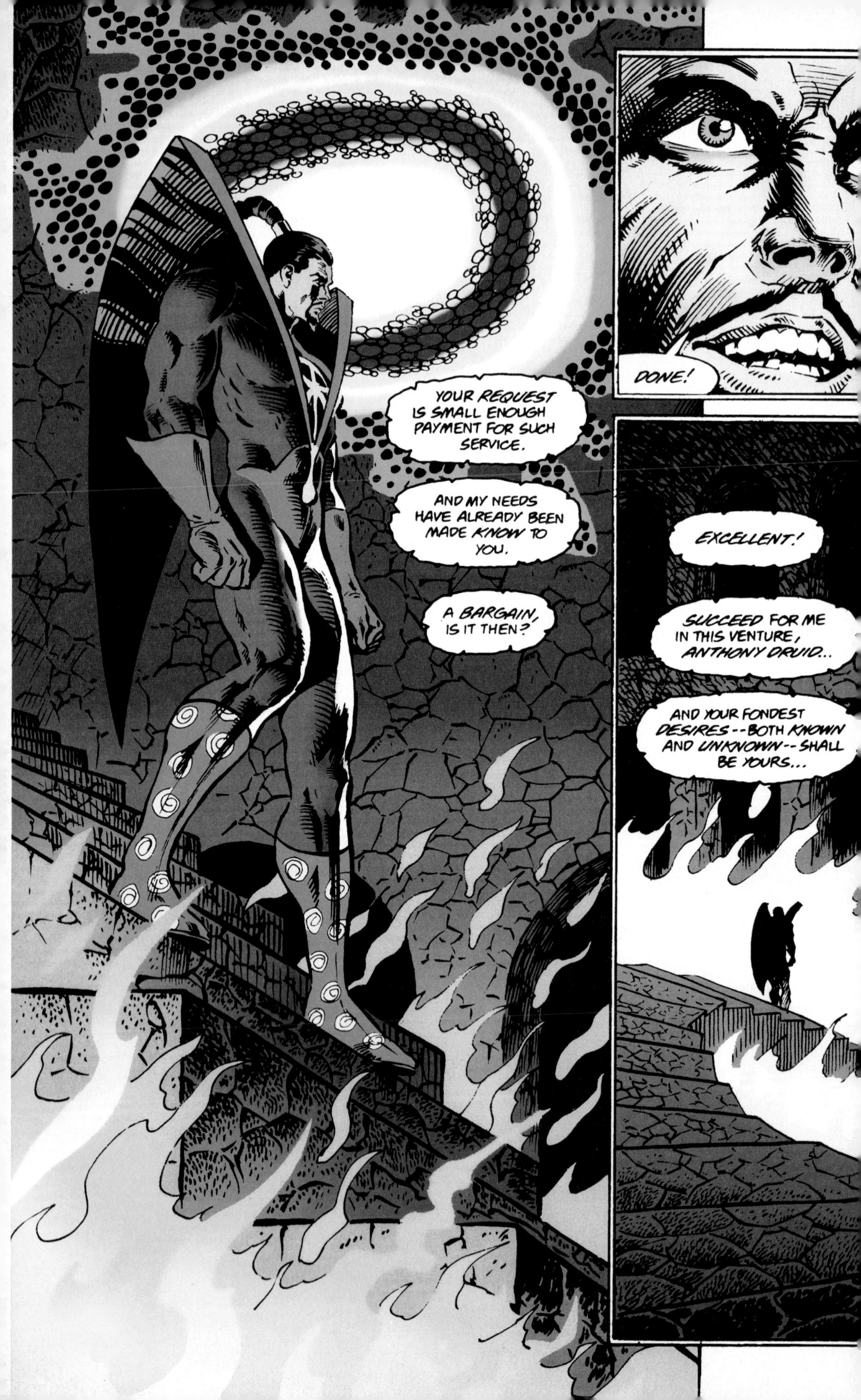

YOUR REQUEST IS SMALL ENOUGH PAYMENT FOR SUCH SERVICE.
AND MY NEEDS HAVE ALREADY BEEN MADE KNOW TO YOU.
A BARGAIN, IS IT THEN?
DONE!
EXCELLENT!
SUCCEED FOR ME IN THIS VENTURE, ANTHONY DRUID...
AND YOUR FONDEST DESIRES--BOTH KNOWN AND UNKNOWN--SHALL BE YOURS...

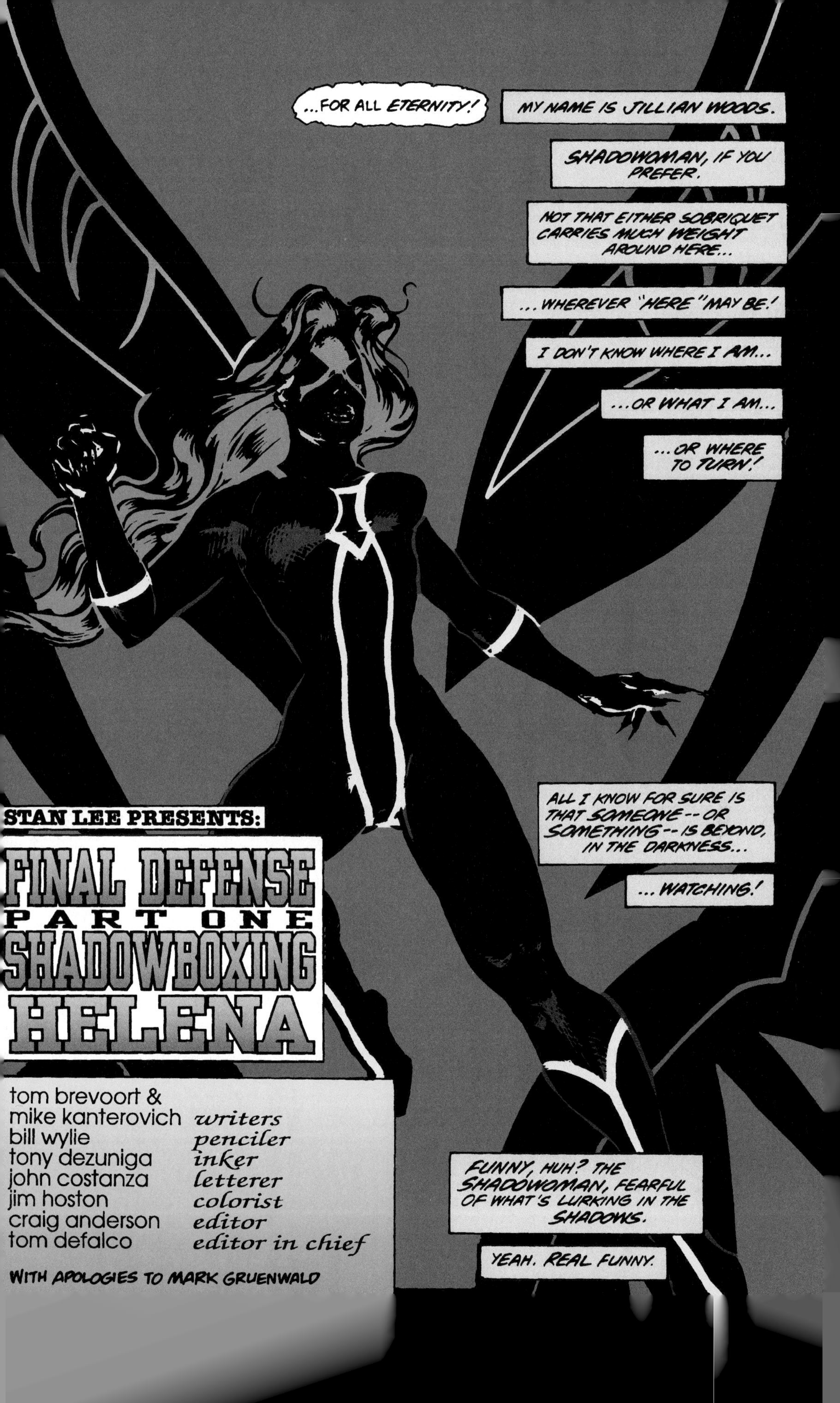

...FOR ALL ETERNITY!
MY NAME IS JILLIAN WOODS.
SHADOWOMAN, IF YOU PREFER.
NOT THAT EITHER SOBRIQUET CARRIES MUCH WEIGHT AROUND HERE...
...WHEREVER "HERE" MAY BE!
I DON'T KNOW WHERE I AM...
...OR WHAT I AM...
...OR WHERE TO TURN!
ALL I KNOW FOR SURE IS THAT SOMEONE -- OR SOMETHING -- IS BEYOND, IN THE DARKNESS...
...WATCHING!
STAN LEE PRESENTS:
FINAL DEFENSE
PART ONE
SHADOWBOXING
HELENA
tom brevoort & mike kanterovich writers
bill wylie penciler
tony dezuniga inker
john costanza letterer
jim hoston colorist
craig anderson editor
tom defalco editor in chief
WITH APOLOGIES TO MARK GRUENWALD
FUNNY, HUH? THE SHADOWOMAN, FEARFUL OF WHAT'S LURKING IN THE SHADOWS.
YEAH. REAL FUNNY.

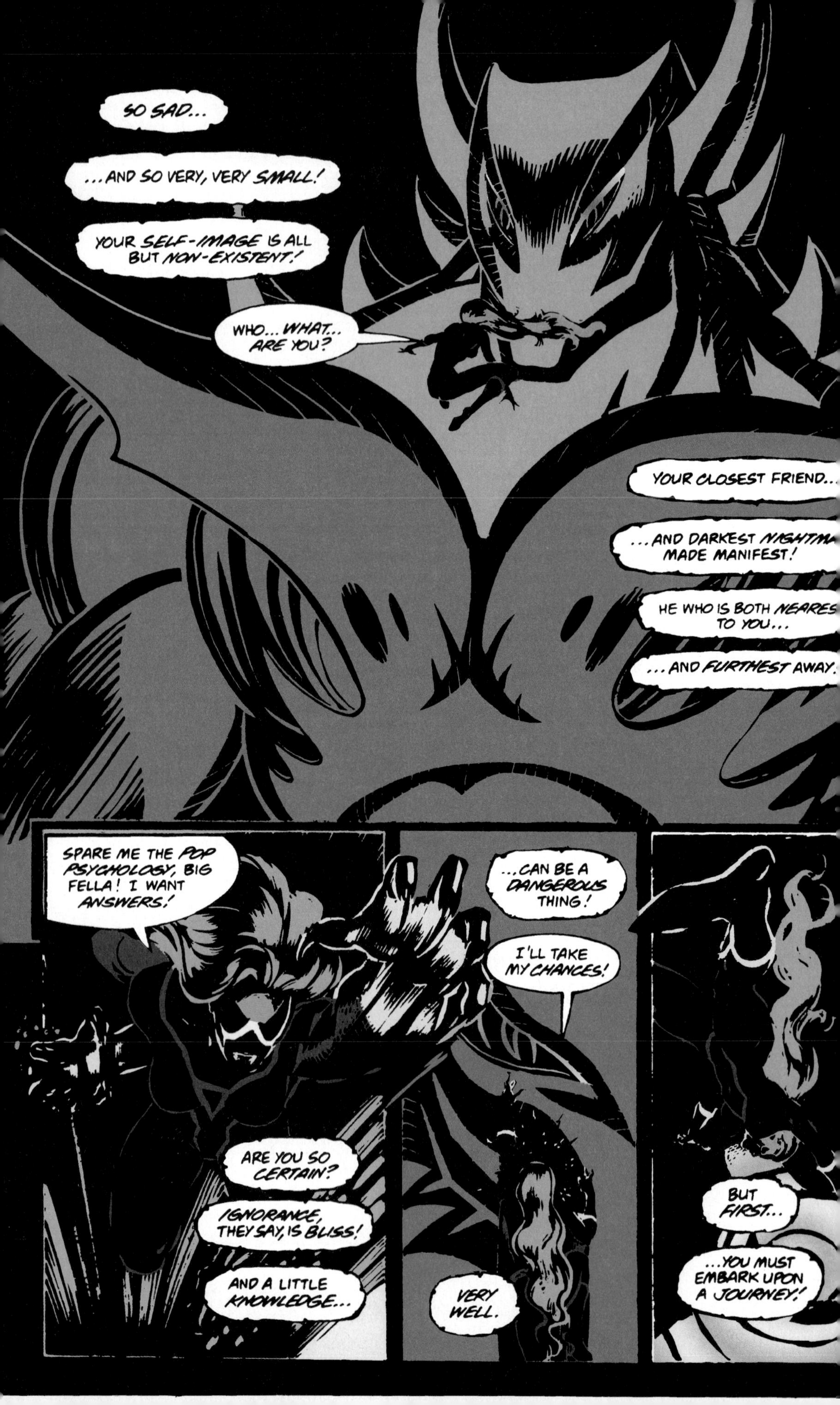
SO SAD...
...AND SO VERY, VERY SMALL!
YOUR SELF-IMAGE IS ALL BUT NON-EXISTENT!
WHO... WHAT... ARE YOU?
YOUR CLOSEST FRIEND...
...AND DARKEST NIGHTMA MADE MANIFEST!
HE WHO IS BOTH NEARES TO YOU...
...AND FURTHEST AWAY.
SPARE ME THE POP PSYCHOLOGY, BIG FELLA! I WANT ANSWERS!
ARE YOU SO CERTAIN?
IGNORANCE, THEY SAY, IS BLISS!
AND A LITTLE KNOWLEDGE...
...CAN BE A DANGEROUS THING!
I'LL TAKE MY CHANCES!
VERY WELL.
BUT FIRST...
...YOU MUST EMBARK UPON A JOURNEY!

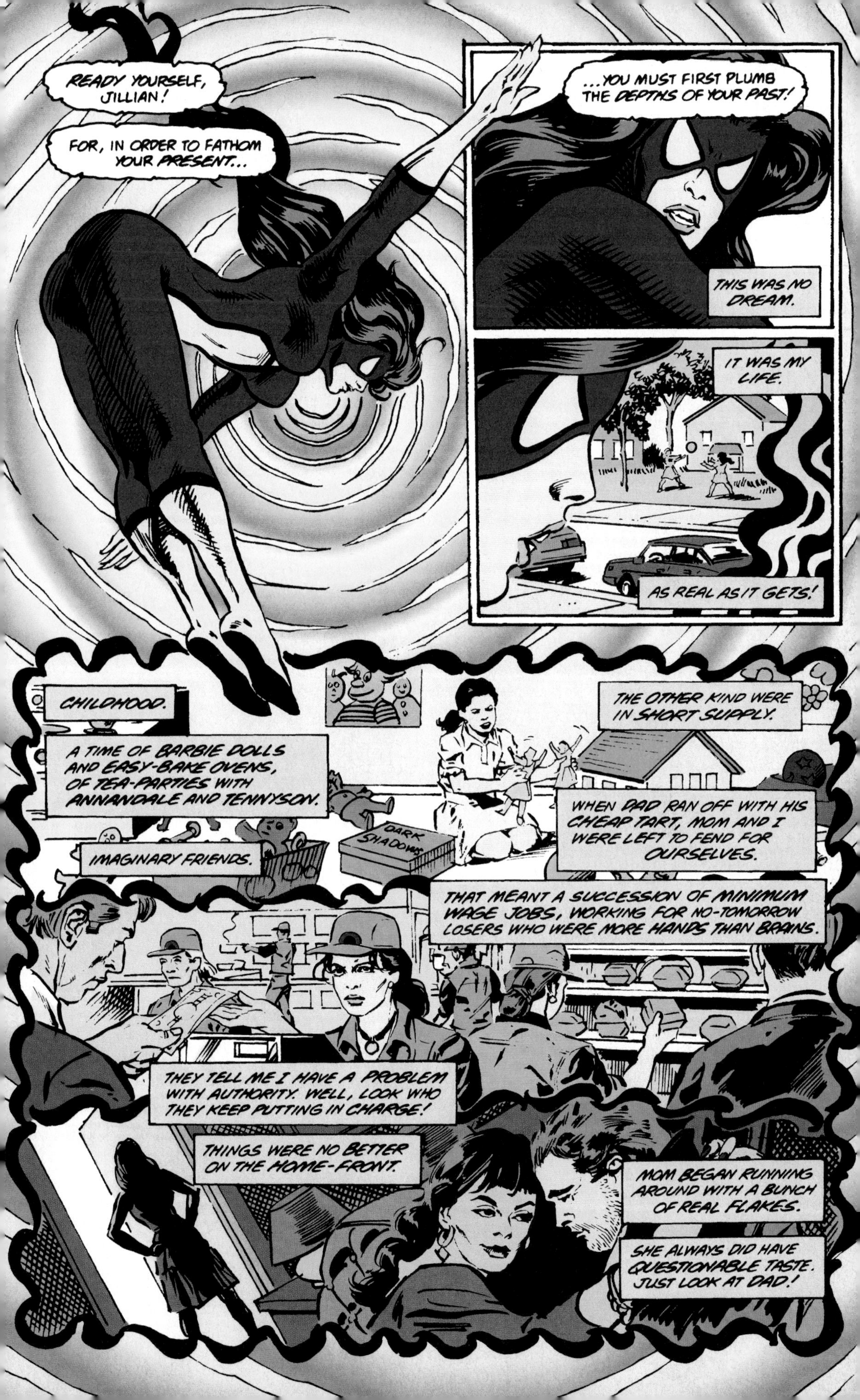

READY YOURSELF, JILLIAN!
FOR, IN ORDER TO FATHOM YOUR PRESENT...
...YOU MUST FIRST PLUMB THE DEPTHS OF YOUR PAST!
THIS WAS NO DREAM.
IT WAS MY LIFE.
AS REAL AS IT GETS!
CHILDHOOD.
A TIME OF BARBIE DOLLS AND EASY-BAKE OVENS, OF TEA-PARTIES WITH ANNANDALE AND TENNYSON.
IMAGINARY FRIENDS.
DARK SHADOWS
THE OTHER KIND WERE IN SHORT SUPPLY.
WHEN DAD RAN OFF WITH HIS CHEAP TART, MOM AND I WERE LEFT TO FEND FOR OURSELVES.
THAT MEANT A SUCCESSION OF MINIMUM WAGE JOBS, WORKING FOR NO-TOMORROW LOSERS WHO WERE MORE HANDS THAN BRAINS.
THEY TELL ME I HAVE A PROBLEM WITH AUTHORITY. WELL, LOOK WHO THEY KEEP PUTTING IN CHARGE!
THINGS WERE NO BETTER ON THE HOME-FRONT.
MOM BEGAN RUNNING AROUND WITH A BUNCH OF REAL FLAKES.
SHE ALWAYS DID HAVE QUESTIONABLE TASTE. JUST LOOK AT DAD!

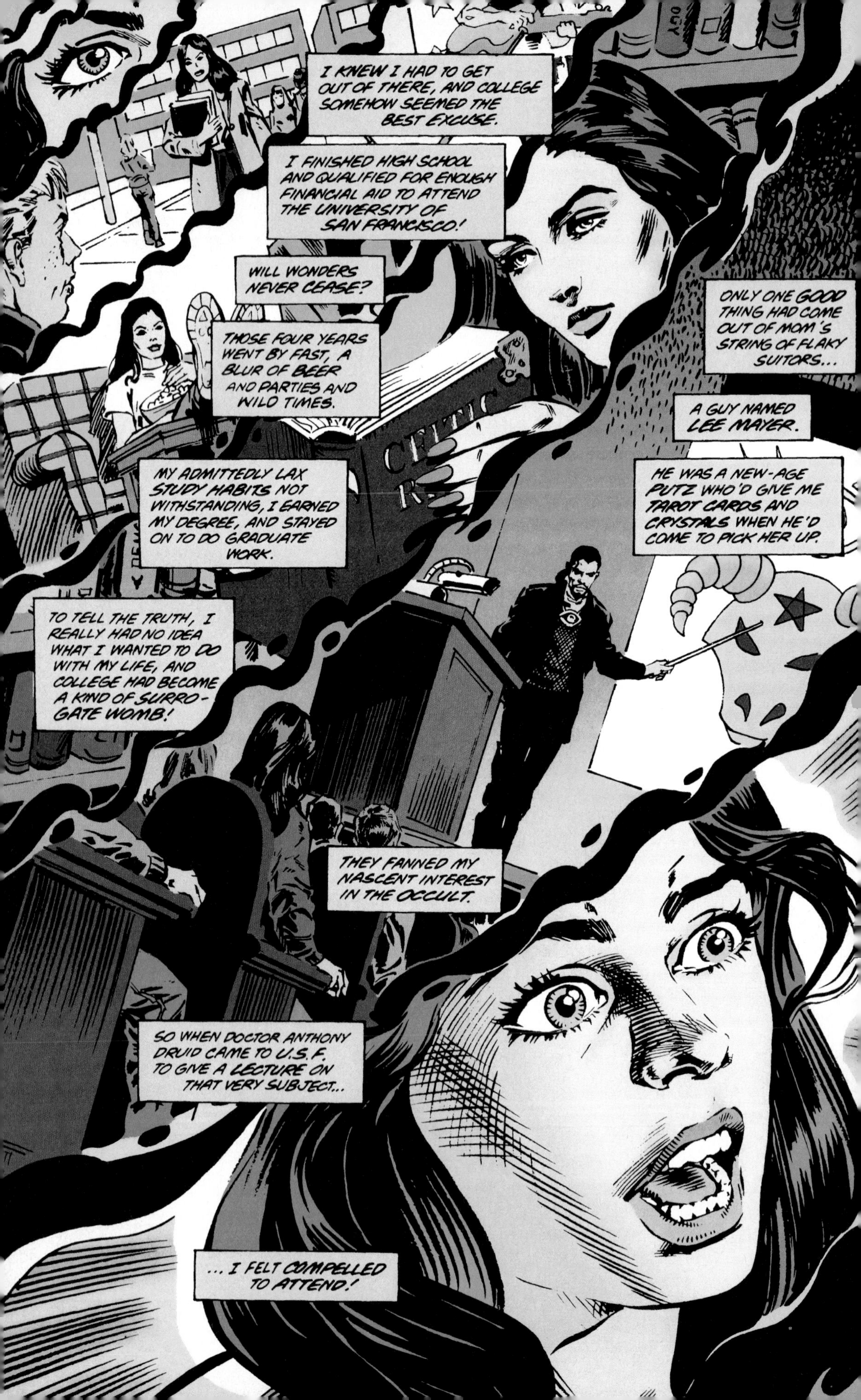
I KNEW I HAD TO GET OUT OF THERE, AND COLLEGE SOMEHOW SEEMED THE BEST EXCUSE.
I FINISHED HIGH SCHOOL AND QUALIFIED FOR ENOUGH FINANCIAL AID TO ATTEND THE UNIVERSITY OF SAN FRANCISCO!
WILL WONDERS NEVER CEASE?
THOSE FOUR YEARS WENT BY FAST, A BLUR OF BEER AND PARTIES AND WILD TIMES.
MY ADMITTEDLY LAX STUDY HABITS NOT WITHSTANDING, I EARNED MY DEGREE, AND STAYED ON TO DO GRADUATE WORK.
TO TELL THE TRUTH, I REALLY HAD NO IDEA WHAT I WANTED TO DO WITH MY LIFE, AND COLLEGE HAD BECOME A KIND OF SURROGATE WOMB!
ONLY ONE GOOD THING HAD COME OUT OF MOM'S STRING OF FLAKY SUITORS...
A GUY NAMED LEE MAYER.
HE WAS A NEW-AGE PUTZ WHO'D GIVE ME TAROT CARDS AND CRYSTALS WHEN HE'D COME TO PICK HER UP.
THEY FANNED MY NASCENT INTEREST IN THE OCCULT.
SO WHEN DOCTOR ANTHONY DRUID CAME TO U.S.F. TO GIVE A LECTURE ON THAT VERY SUBJECT...
... I FELT COMPELLED TO ATTEND!

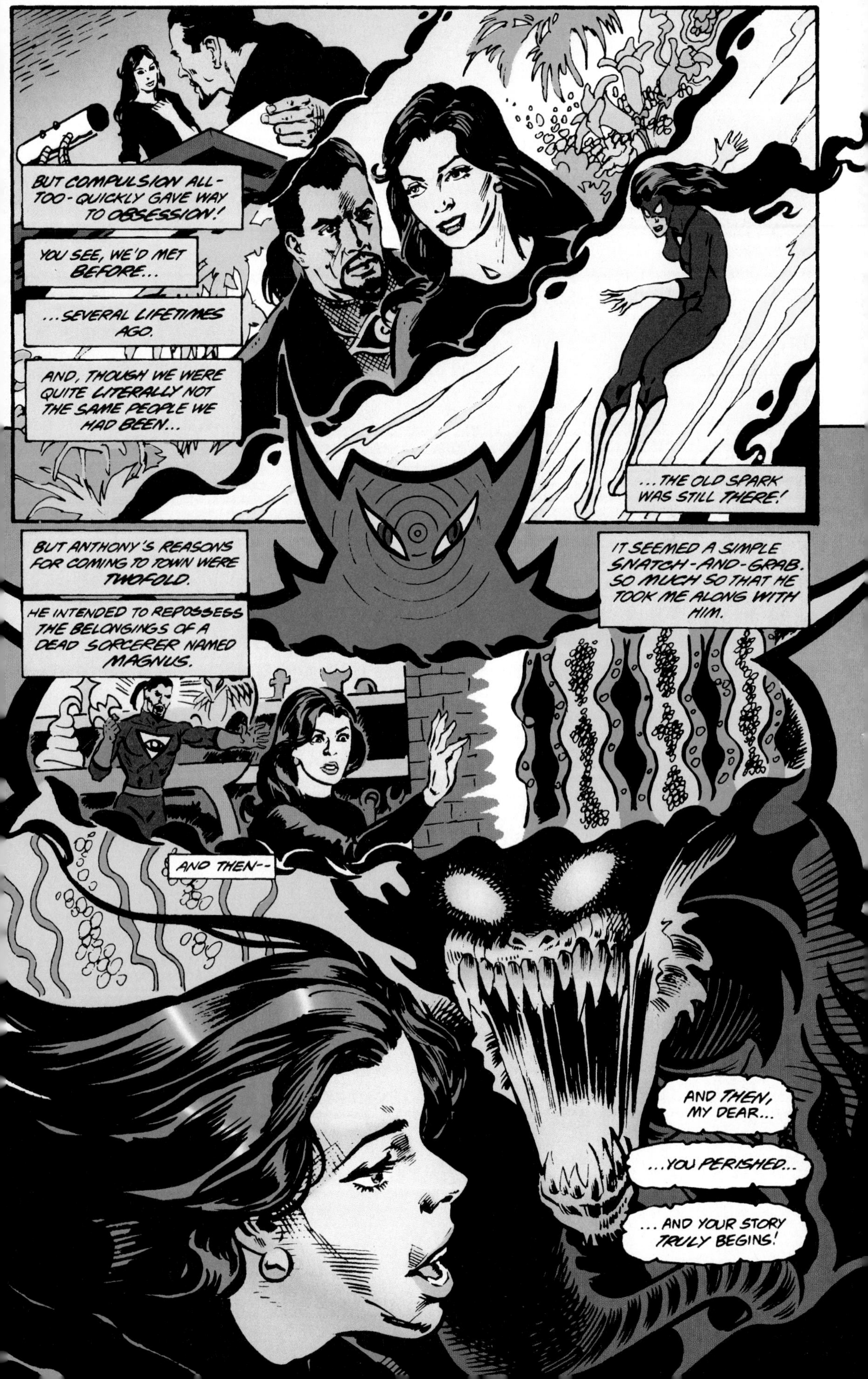
BUT COMPULSION ALL-TOO-QUICKLY GAVE WAY TO OBSESSION!
YOU SEE, WE'D MET BEFORE...
...SEVERAL LIFETIMES AGO.
AND, THOUGH WE WERE QUITE LITERALLY NOT THE SAME PEOPLE WE HAD BEEN...
...THE OLD SPARK WAS STILL THERE!
BUT ANTHONY'S REASONS FOR COMING TO TOWN WERE TWOFOLD.
HE INTENDED TO REPOSSESS THE BELONGINGS OF A DEAD SORCERER NAMED MAGNUS.
IT SEEMED A SIMPLE SNATCH-AND-GRAB. SO MUCH SO THAT HE TOOK ME ALONG WITH HIM.
AND THEN--
AND THEN, MY DEAR...
...YOU PERISHED...
...AND YOUR STORY TRULY BEGINS!

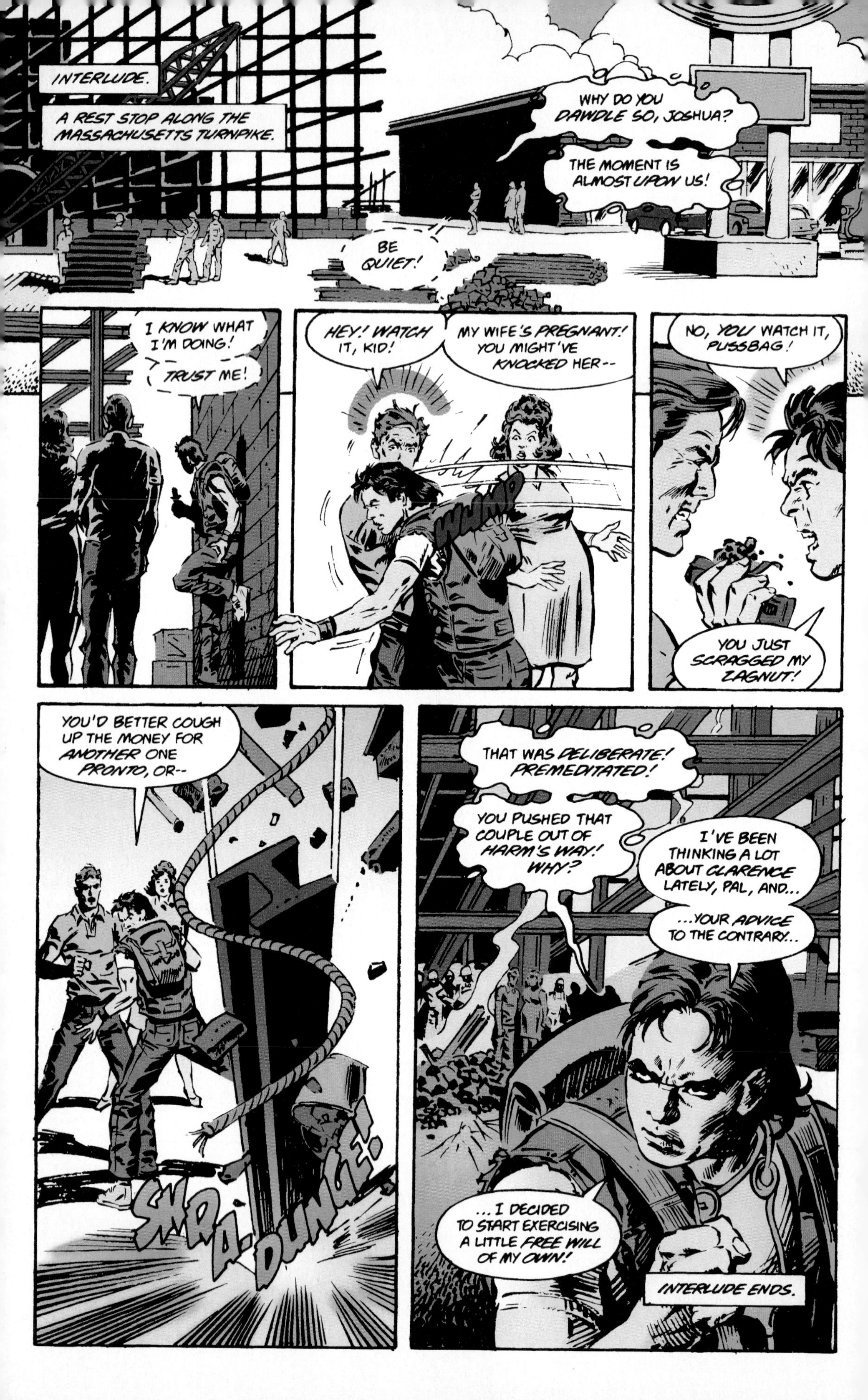

INTERLUDE.
A REST STOP ALONG THE MASSACHUSETTS TURNPIKE.
WHY DO YOU DAWDLE SO, JOSHUA?
THE MOMENT IS ALMOST UPON US!
BE QUIET!
I KNOW WHAT I'M DOING!
TRUST ME!
HEY! WATCH IT, KID!
MY WIFE'S PREGNANT! YOU MIGHT'VE KNOCKED HER--
WHUMP
NO, YOU WATCH IT, PUSSBAG!
YOU JUST SCRAGGED MY ZAGNUT!
YOU'D BETTER COUGH UP THE MONEY FOR ANOTHER ONE PRONTO, OR--
SHRA-DUNGE!
THAT WAS DELIBERATE! PREMEDITATED!
YOU PUSHED THAT COUPLE OUT OF HARM'S WAY! WHY?
I'VE BEEN THINKING A LOT ABOUT CLARENCE LATELY, PAL, AND...
...YOUR ADVICE TO THE CONTRARY...
...I DECIDED TO START EXERCISING A LITTLE FREE WILL OF MY OWN!
INTERLUDE ENDS.

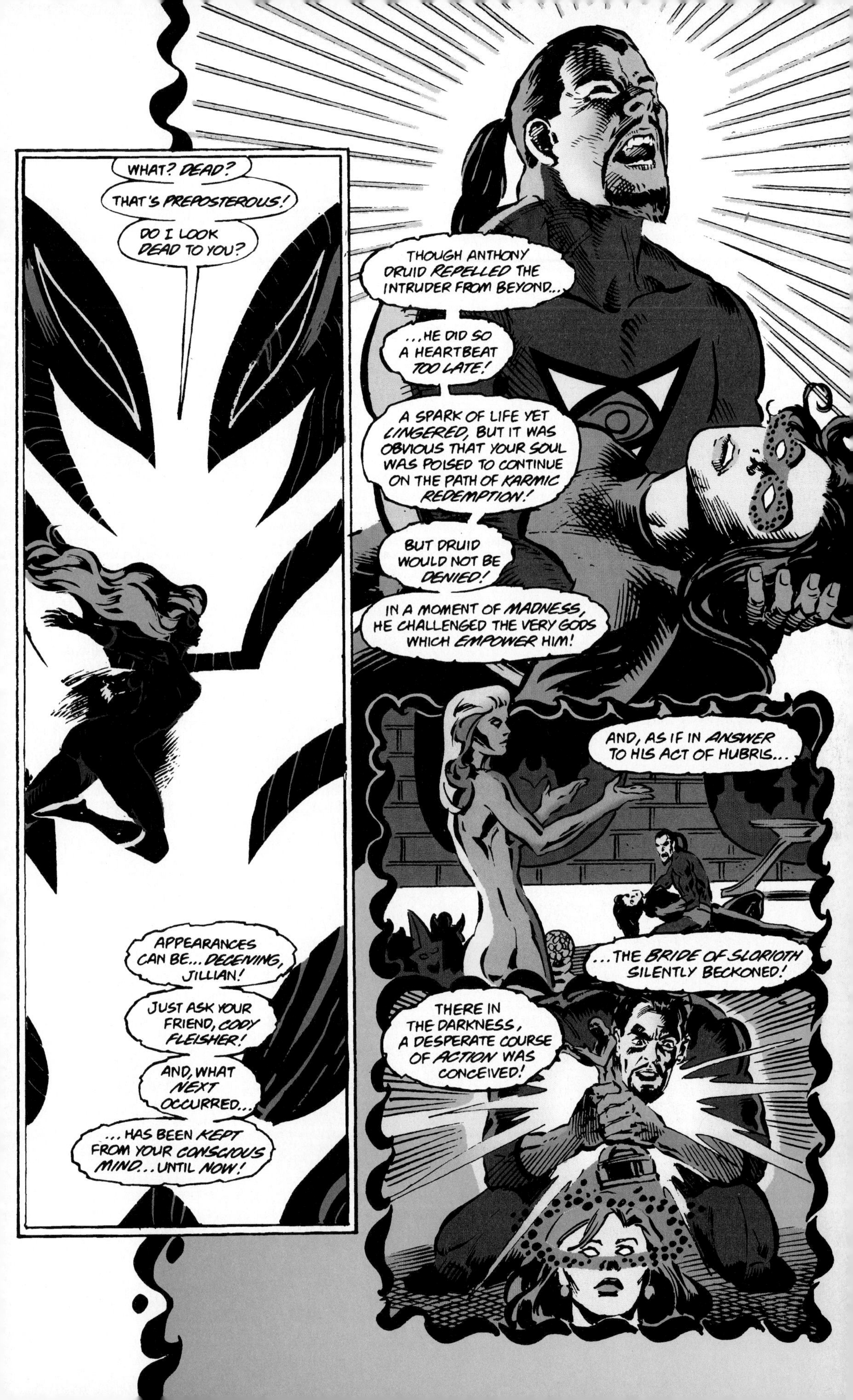
WHAT? DEAD?
THAT'S PREPOSTEROUS!
DO I LOOK DEAD TO YOU?
APPEARANCES CAN BE... DECEIVING, JILLIAN!
JUST ASK YOUR FRIEND, CODY FLEISHER!
AND, WHAT NEXT OCCURRED...
...HAS BEEN KEPT FROM YOUR CONSCIOUS MIND...UNTIL NOW!
THOUGH ANTHONY DRUID REPELLED THE INTRUDER FROM BEYOND...
...HE DID SO A HEARTBEAT TOO LATE!
A SPARK OF LIFE YET LINGERED, BUT IT WAS OBVIOUS THAT YOUR SOUL WAS POISED TO CONTINUE ON THE PATH OF KARMIC REDEMPTION!
BUT DRUID WOULD NOT BE DENIED!
IN A MOMENT OF MADNESS, HE CHALLENGED THE VERY GODS WHICH EMPOWER HIM!
AND, AS IF IN ANSWER TO HIS ACT OF HUBRIS...
...THE BRIDE OF SLORIOTH SILENTLY BECKONED!
THERE IN THE DARKNESS, A DESPERATE COURSE OF ACTION WAS CONCEIVED!

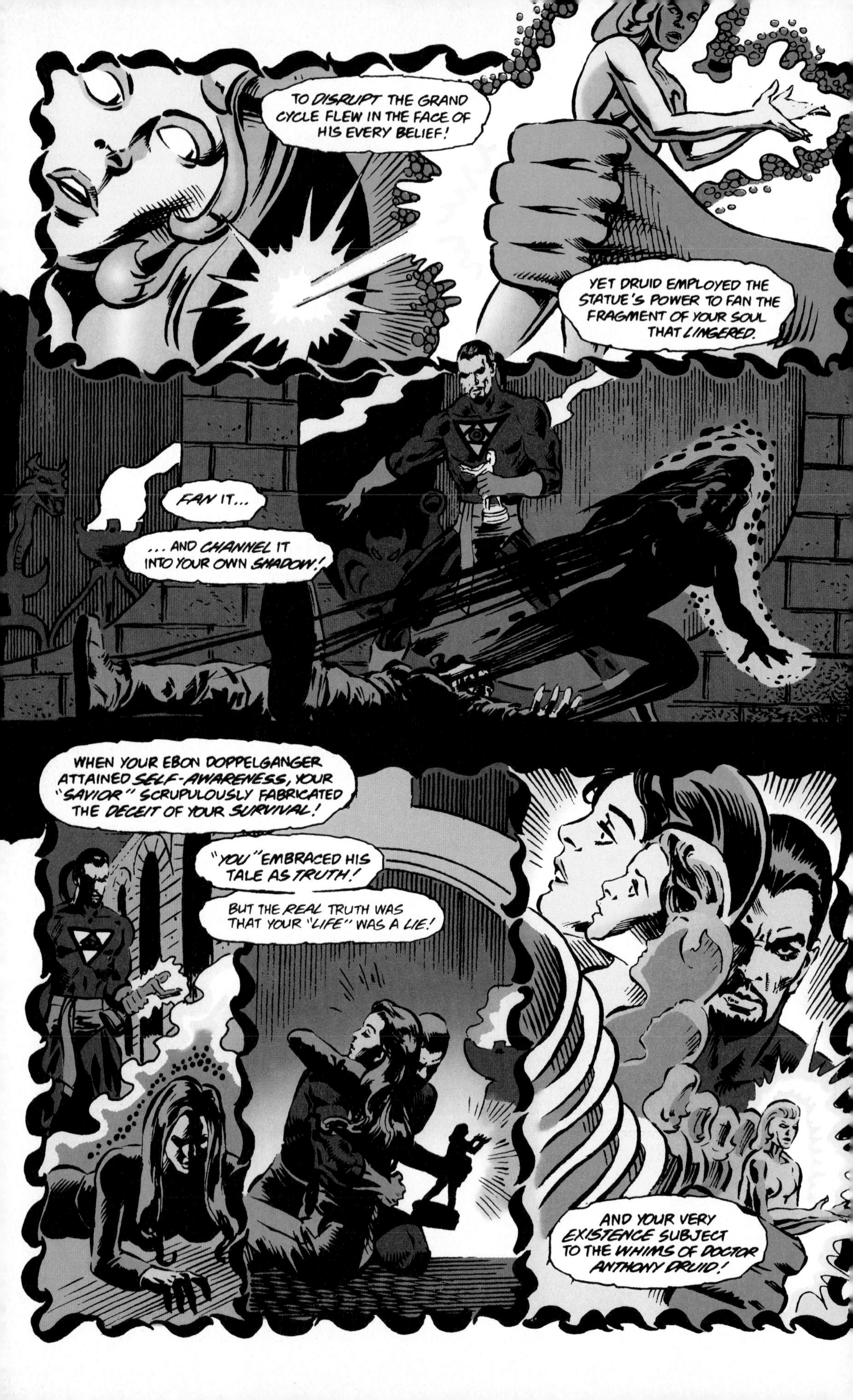
TO DISRUPT THE GRAND CYCLE FLEW IN THE FACE OF HIS EVERY BELIEF!
YET DRUID EMPLOYED THE STATUE'S POWER TO FAN THE FRAGMENT OF YOUR SOUL THAT LINGERED.
FAN IT...
...AND CHANNEL IT INTO YOUR OWN SHADOW!
WHEN YOUR EBON DOPPELGANGER ATTAINED SELF-AWARENESS, YOUR "SAVIOR" SCRUPULOUSLY FABRICATED THE DECEIT OF YOUR SURVIVAL!
"YOU" EMBRACED HIS TALE AS TRUTH!
BUT THE REAL TRUTH WAS THAT YOUR "LIFE" WAS A LIE!
AND YOUR VERY EXISTENCE SUBJECT TO THE WHIMS OF DOCTOR ANTHONY DRUID!

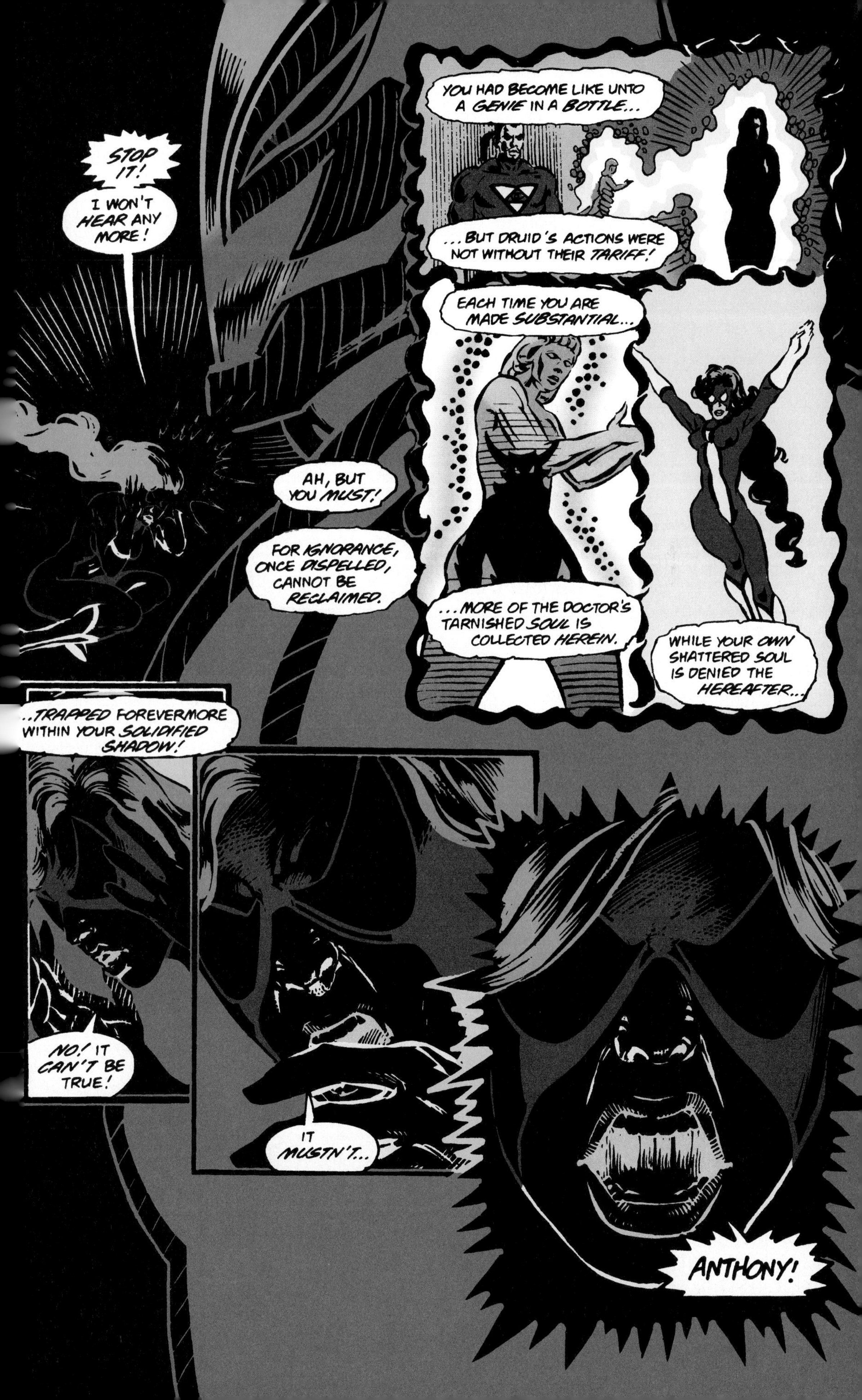

STOP IT!
I WON'T HEAR ANY MORE!
YOU HAD BECOME LIKE UNTO A GENIE IN A BOTTLE...
...BUT DRUID'S ACTIONS WERE NOT WITHOUT THEIR TARIFF!
AH, BUT YOU MUST!
FOR IGNORANCE, ONCE DISPELLED, CANNOT BE RECLAIMED.
EACH TIME YOU ARE MADE SUBSTANTIAL...
...MORE OF THE DOCTOR'S TARNISHED SOUL IS COLLECTED HEREIN.
WHILE YOUR OWN SHATTERED SOUL IS DENIED THE HEREAFTER...
...TRAPPED FOREVERMORE WITHIN YOUR SOLIDIFIED SHADOW!
NO! IT CAN'T BE TRUE!
IT MUSTN'T...
ANTHONY!

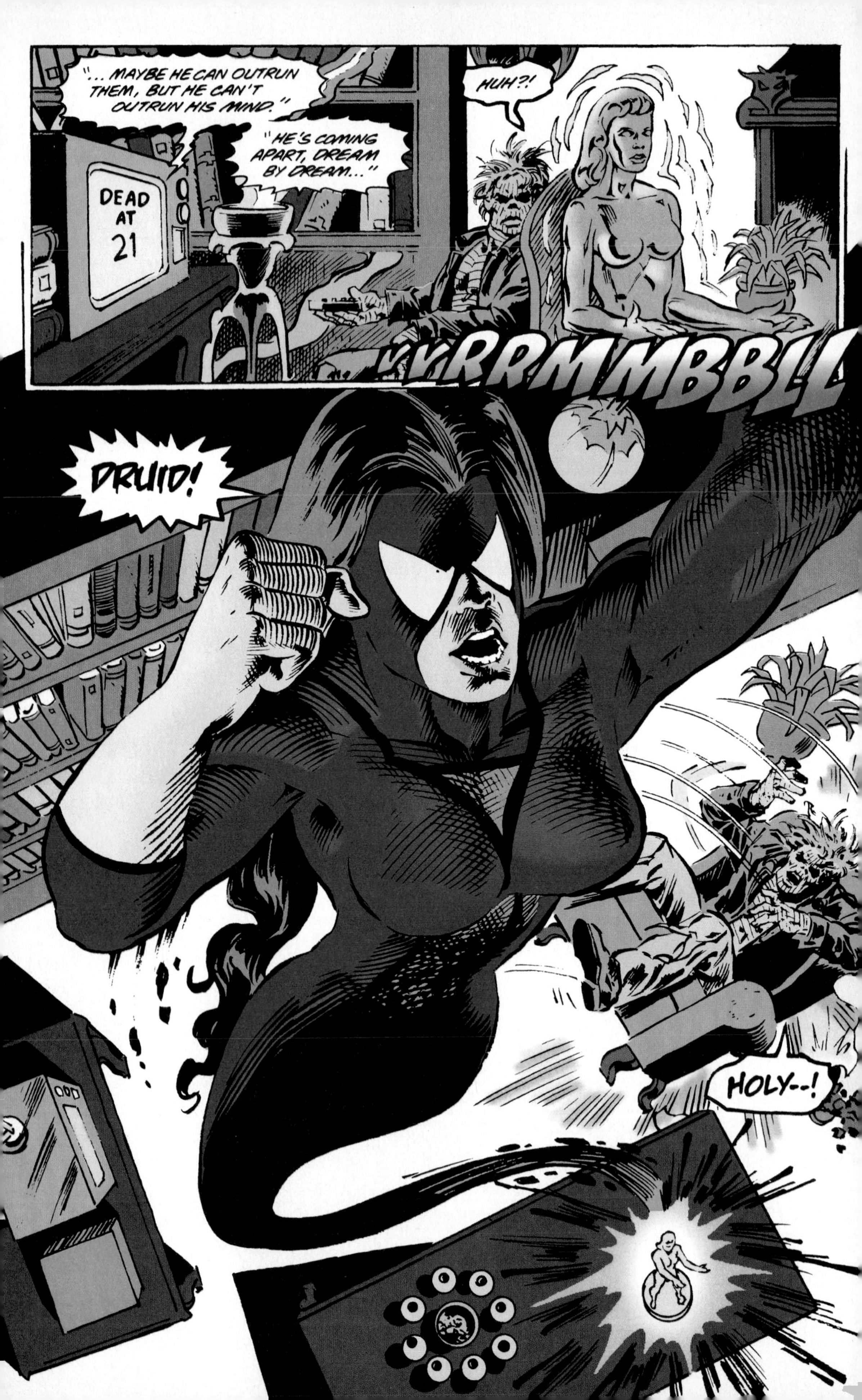
"... MAYBE HE CAN OUTRUN THEM, BUT HE CAN'T OUTRUN HIS MIND."
"HE'S COMING APART, DREAM BY DREAM..."
DEAD AT 21
HUH?!
VRRMMBBLL
DRUID!
HOLY--!

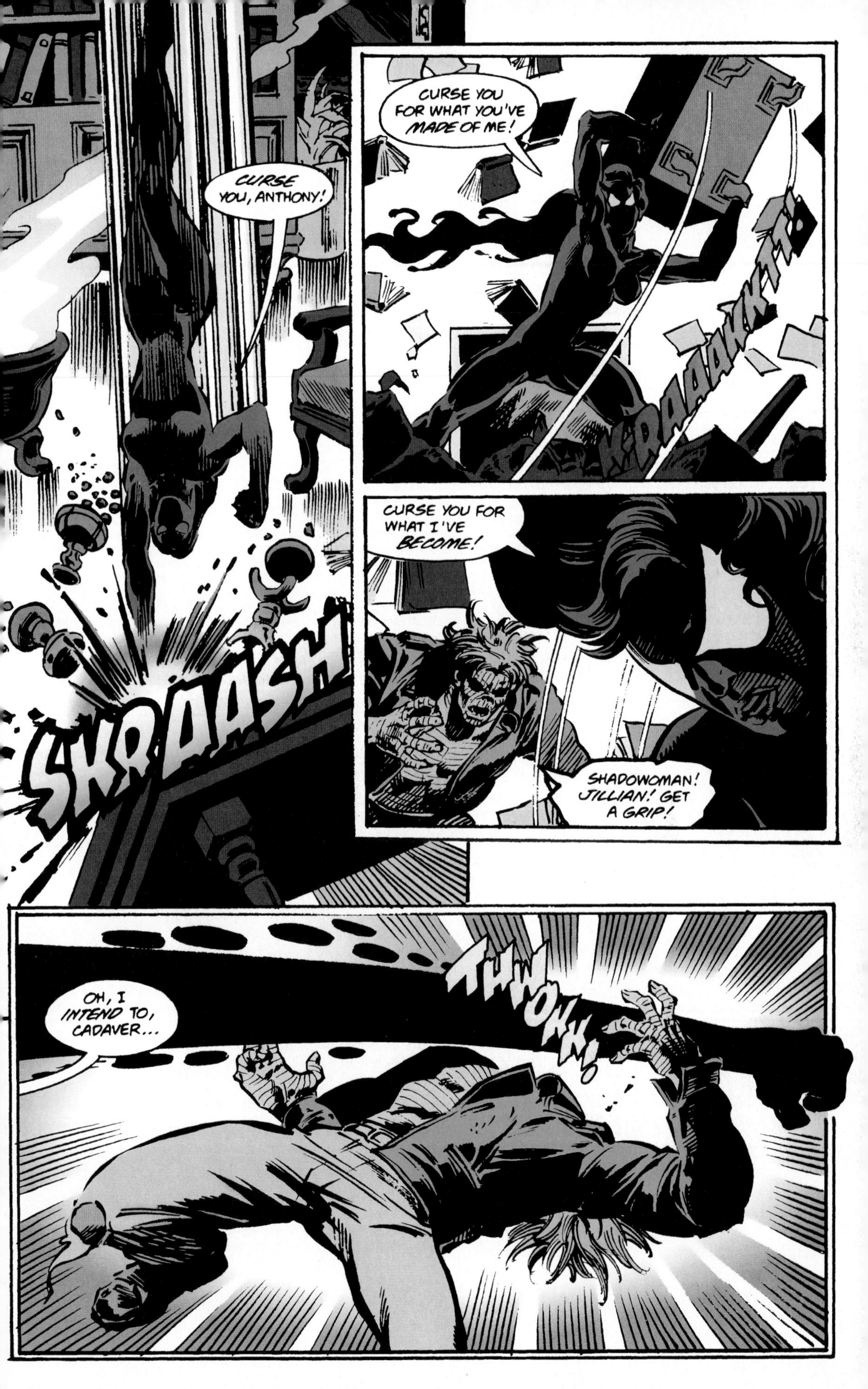
CURSE YOU, ANTHONY!
SKRAASH
CURSE YOU FOR WHAT YOU'VE MADE OF ME!
KRAAAKK
CURSE YOU FOR WHAT I'VE BECOME!
SHADOWOMAN! JILLIAN! GET A GRIP!
OH, I INTEND TO, CADAVER...
THWOKK!

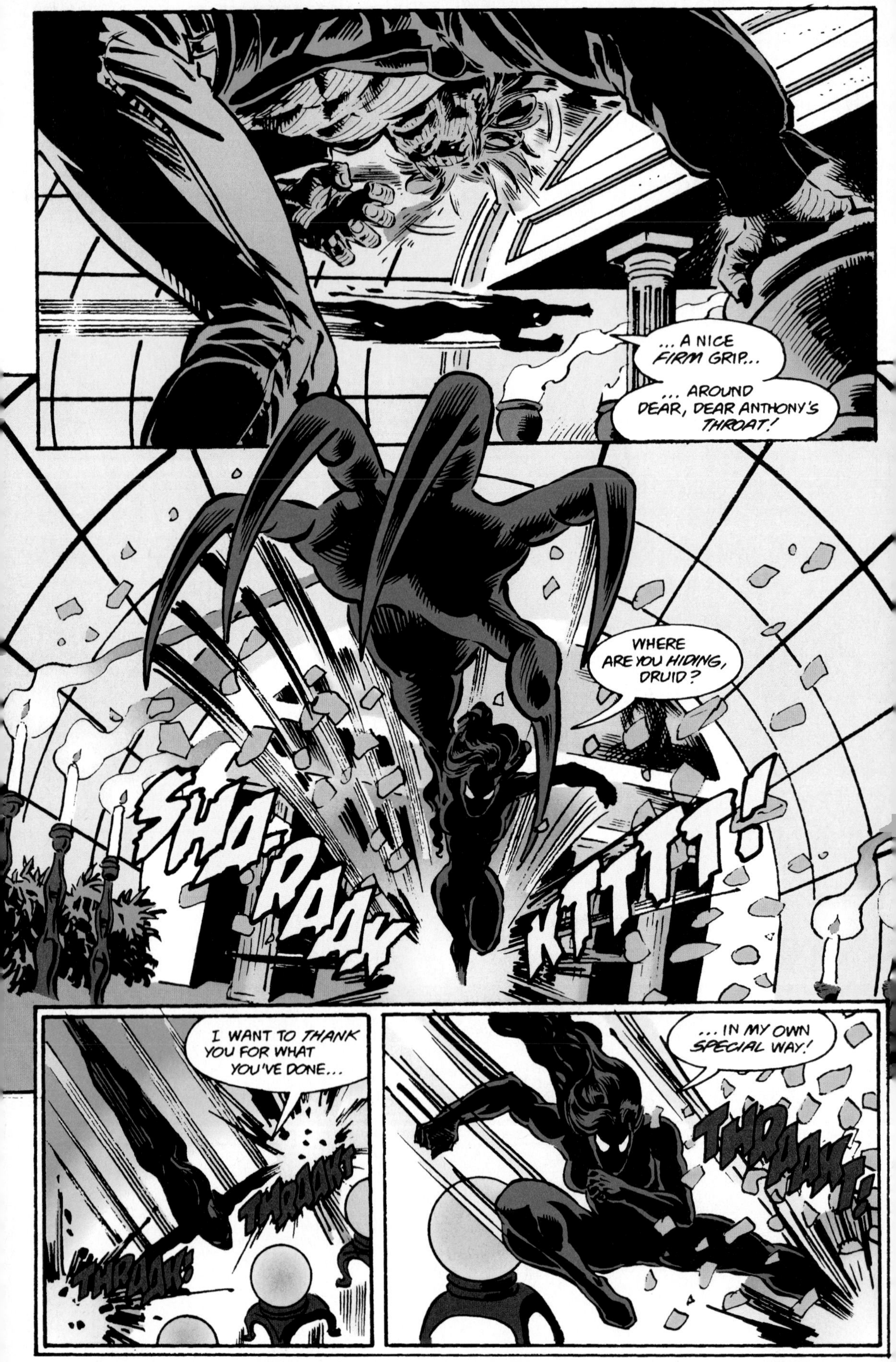
... A NICE FIRM GRIP...
... AROUND DEAR, DEAR ANTHONY'S THROAT!
WHERE ARE YOU HIDING, DRUID?
SHA RAAK KTTTTT!
I WANT TO THANK YOU FOR WHAT YOU'VE DONE...
THRAAK!
THRAAK!
... IN MY OWN SPECIAL WAY!
THRAAKT!

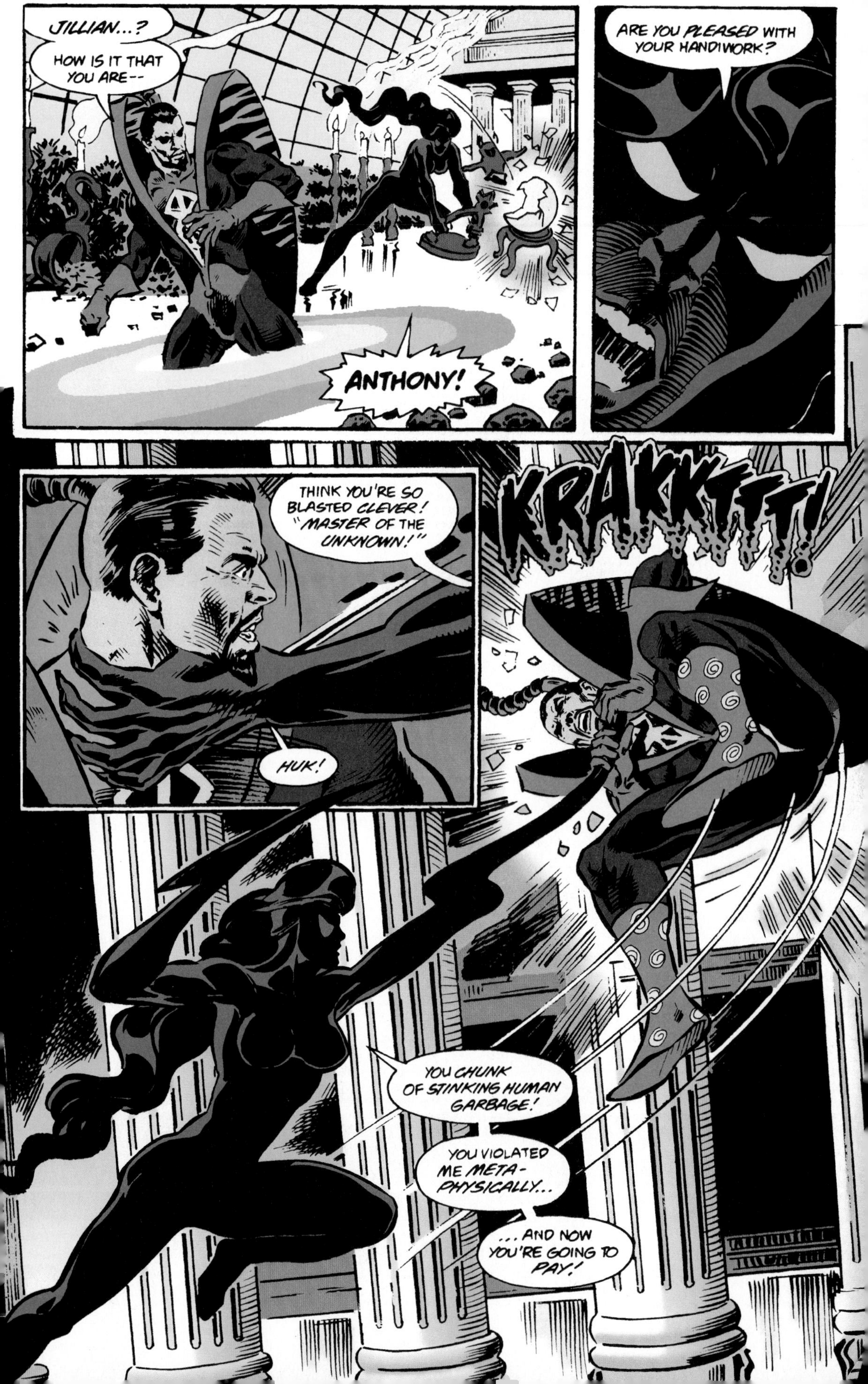
JILLIAN...?
HOW IS IT THAT YOU ARE--
ANTHONY!
ARE YOU PLEASED WITH YOUR HANDIWORK?
THINK YOU'RE SO BLASTED CLEVER! "MASTER OF THE UNKNOWN!"
HUK!
KRAKKTTT!
YOU CHUNK OF STINKING HUMAN GARBAGE!
YOU VIOLATED ME META-PHYSICALLY...
...AND NOW YOU'RE GOING TO PAY!

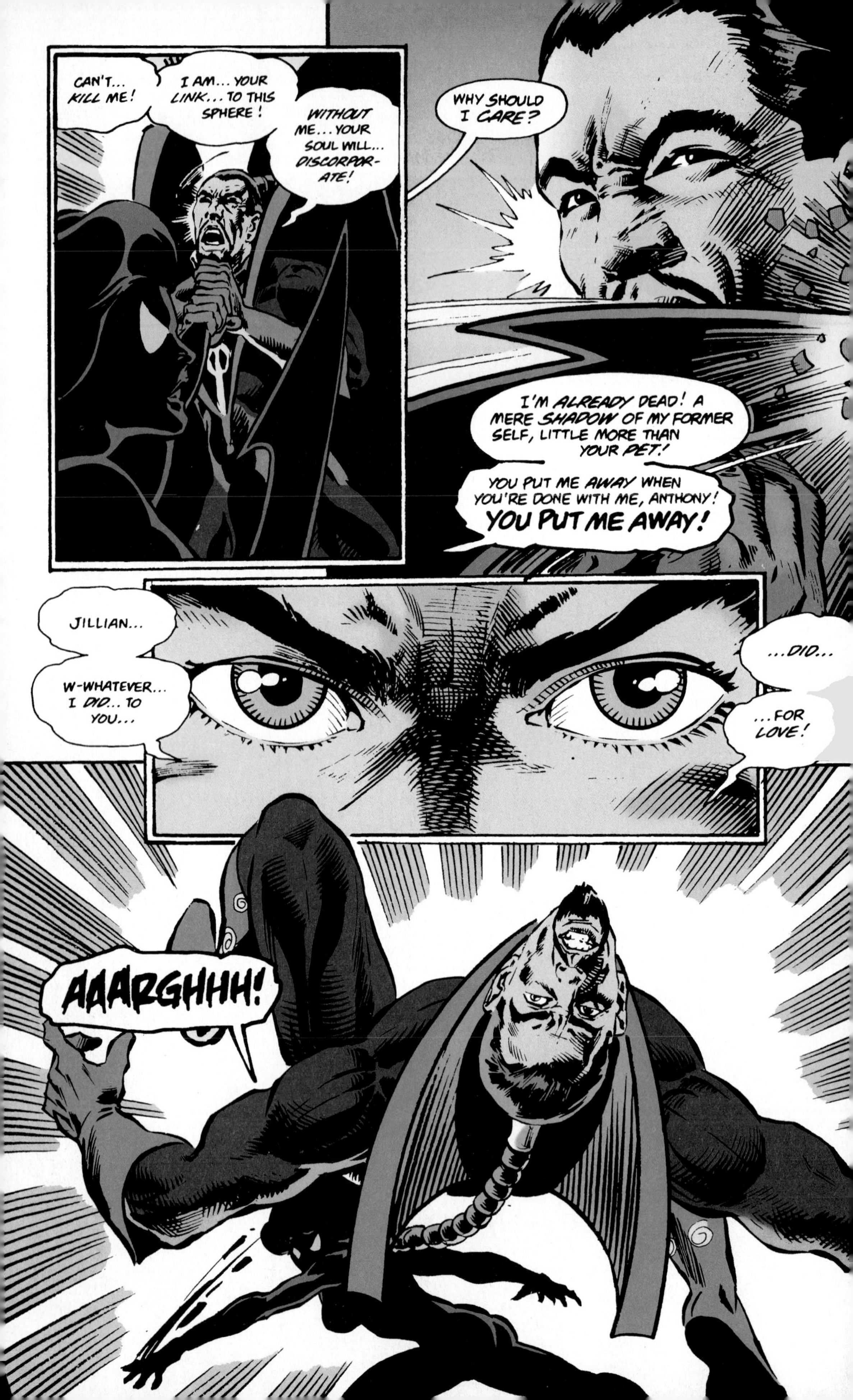
CAN'T... KILL ME!
I AM... YOUR LINK... TO THIS SPHERE!
WITHOUT ME... YOUR SOUL WILL... DISCORPOR-ATE!
WHY SHOULD I CARE?
I'M ALREADY DEAD! A MERE SHADOW OF MY FORMER SELF, LITTLE MORE THAN YOUR PET!
YOU PUT ME AWAY WHEN YOU'RE DONE WITH ME, ANTHONY! YOU PUT ME AWAY!
JILLIAN...
W-WHATEVER... I DID... TO YOU...
...DID...
...FOR LOVE!
AAARGHHH!

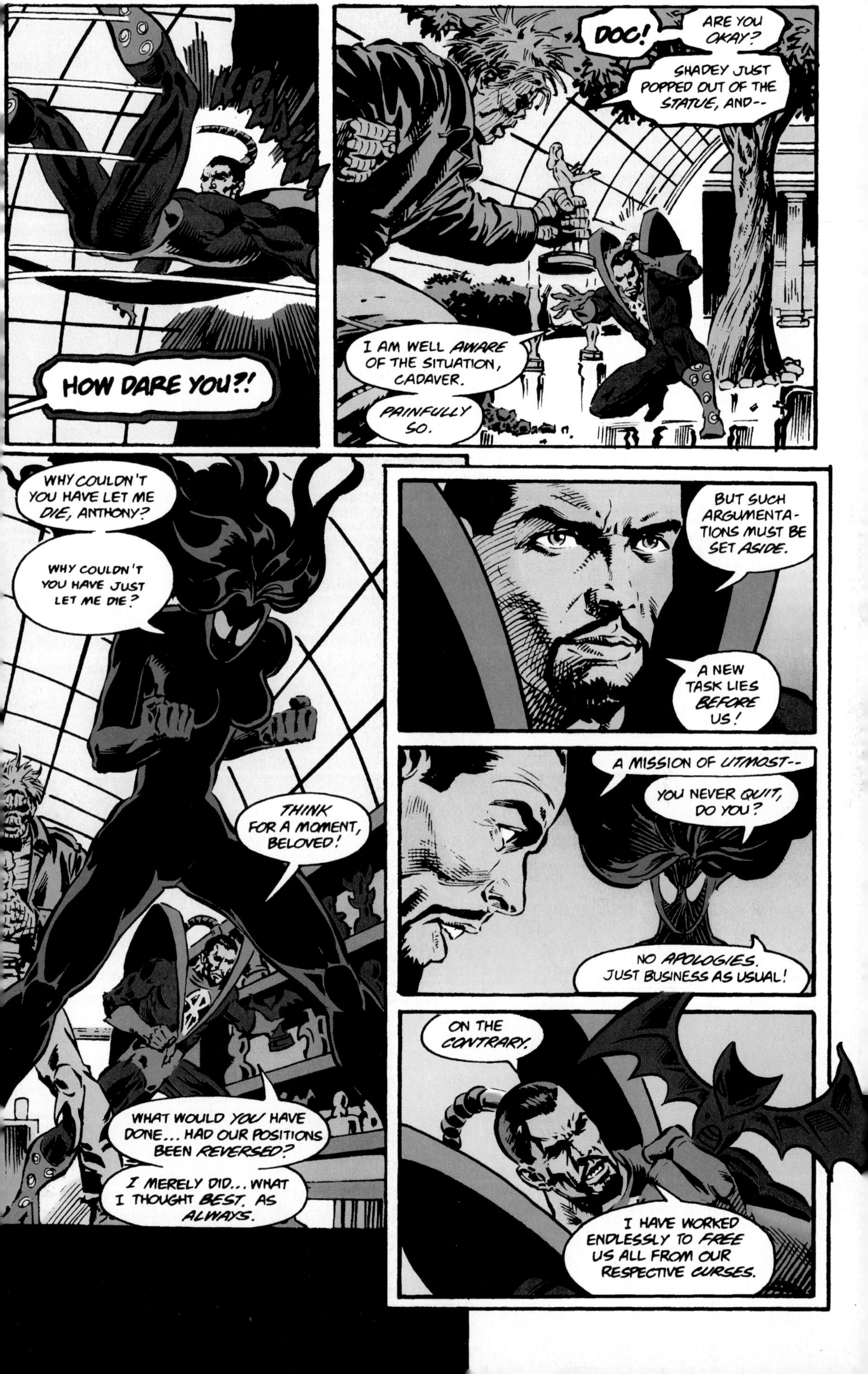
HOW DARE YOU?!
DOC!
ARE YOU OKAY?
SHADEY JUST POPPED OUT OF THE STATUE, AND--
I AM WELL AWARE OF THE SITUATION, CADAVER.
PAINFULLY SO.
WHY COULDN'T YOU HAVE LET ME DIE, ANTHONY?
WHY COULDN'T YOU HAVE JUST LET ME DIE?
THINK FOR A MOMENT, BELOVED!
WHAT WOULD YOU HAVE DONE... HAD OUR POSITIONS BEEN REVERSED?
I MERELY DID... WHAT I THOUGHT BEST. AS ALWAYS.
BUT SUCH ARGUMENTA-TIONS MUST BE SET ASIDE.
A NEW TASK LIES BEFORE US!
A MISSION OF UTMOST--
YOU NEVER QUIT, DO YOU?
NO APOLOGIES. JUST BUSINESS AS USUAL!
ON THE CONTRARY.
I HAVE WORKED ENDLESSLY TO FREE US ALL FROM OUR RESPECTIVE CURSES.

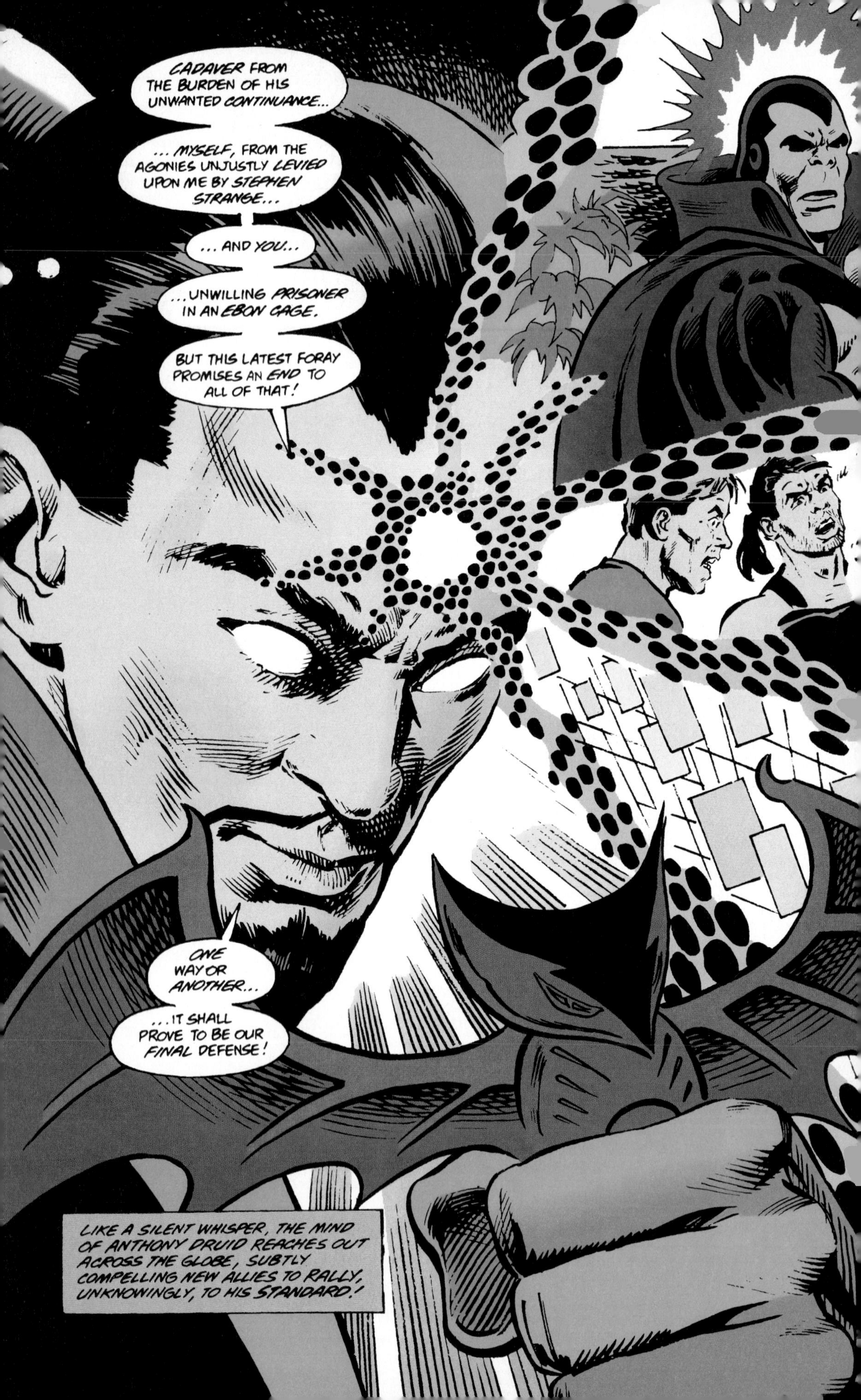
CADAVER FROM THE BURDEN OF HIS UNWANTED CONTINUANCE...
...MYSELF, FROM THE AGONIES UNJUSTLY LEVIED UPON ME BY STEPHEN STRANGE...
...AND YOU...
...UNWILLING PRISONER IN AN EBON CAGE.
BUT THIS LATEST FORAY PROMISES AN END TO ALL OF THAT!
ONE WAY OR ANOTHER...
...IT SHALL PROVE TO BE OUR FINAL DEFENSE!
LIKE A SILENT WHISPER, THE MIND OF ANTHONY DRUID REACHES OUT ACROSS THE GLOBE, SUBTLY COMPELLING NEW ALLIES TO RALLY, UNKNOWINGLY, TO HIS STANDARD!

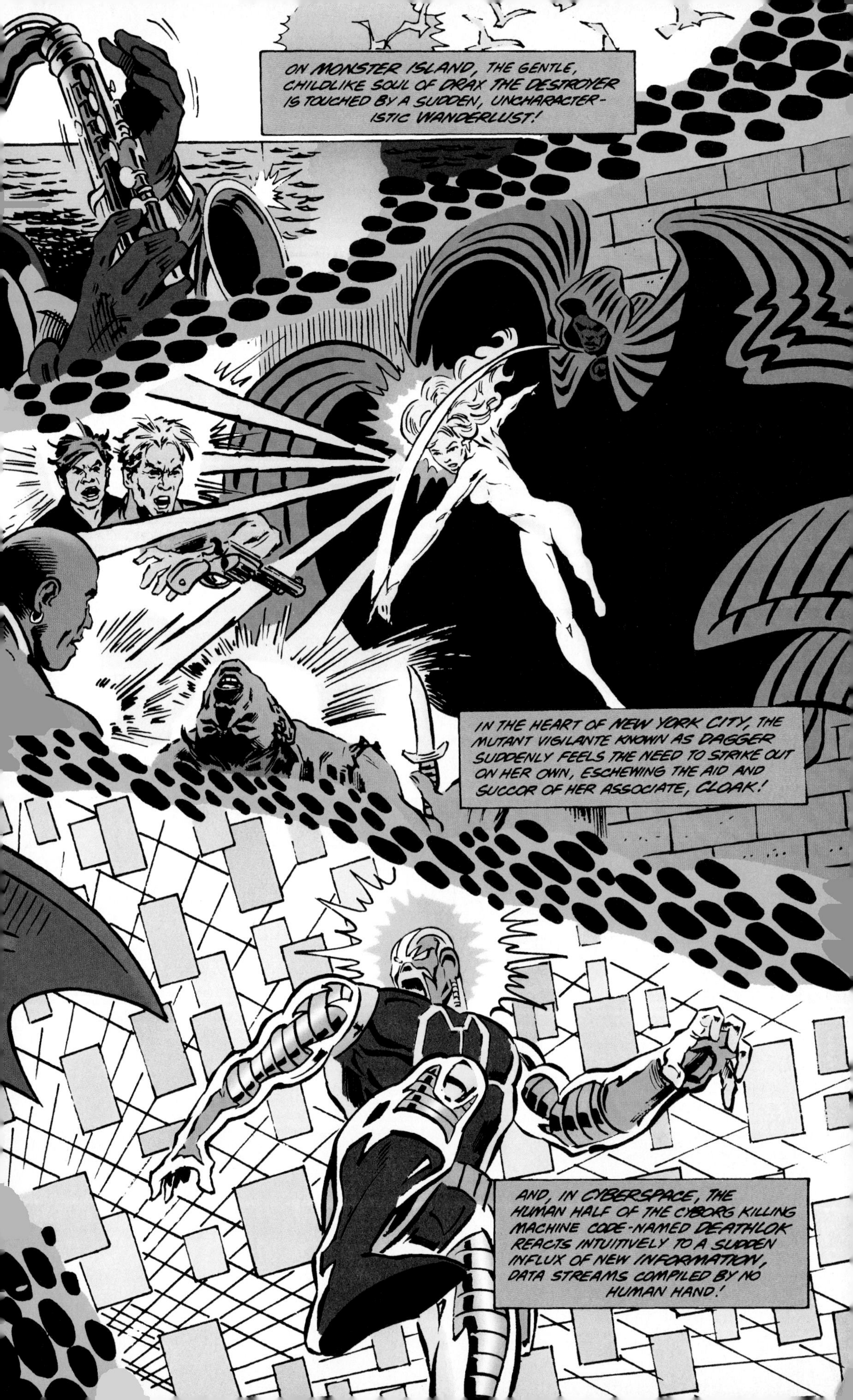
ON MONSTER ISLAND, THE GENTLE, CHILDLIKE SOUL OF DRAX THE DESTROYER IS TOUCHED BY A SUDDEN, UNCHARACTER-ISTIC WANDERLUST!
IN THE HEART OF NEW YORK CITY, THE MUTANT VIGILANTE KNOWN AS DAGGER SUDDENLY FEELS THE NEED TO STRIKE OUT ON HER OWN, ESCHEWING THE AID AND SUCCOR OF HER ASSOCIATE, CLOAK!
AND, IN CYBERSPACE, THE HUMAN HALF OF THE CYBORG KILLING MACHINE CODE-NAMED DEATHLOK REACTS INTUITIVELY TO A SUDDEN INFLUX OF NEW INFORMATION, DATA STREAMS COMPILED BY NO HUMAN HAND!

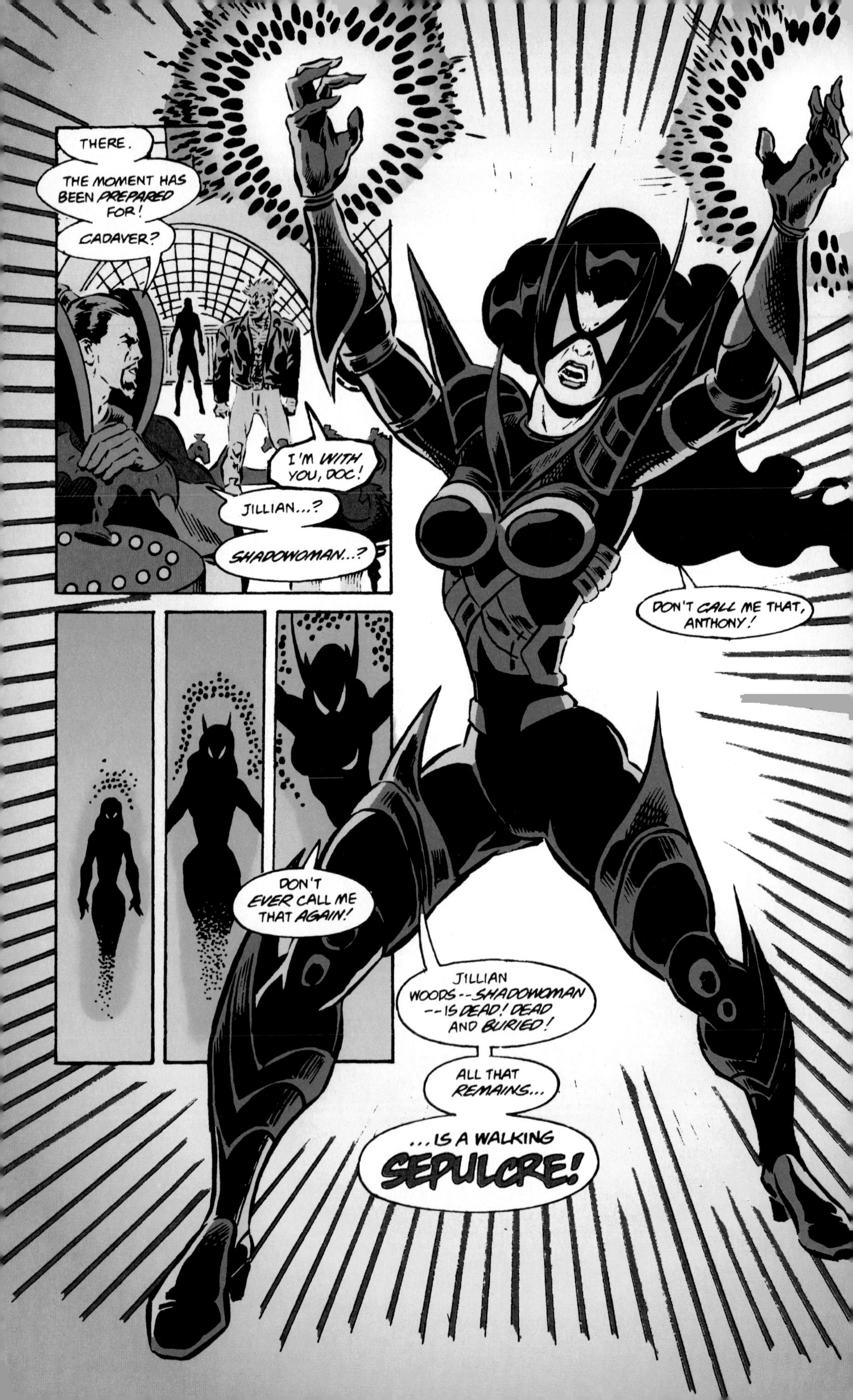
THERE.
THE MOMENT HAS BEEN PREPARED FOR!
CADAVER?
I'M WITH YOU, DOC!
JILLIAN...?
SHADOWOMAN...?
DON'T CALL ME THAT, ANTHONY!
DON'T EVER CALL ME THAT AGAIN!
JILLIAN WOODS--SHADOWOMAN--IS DEAD! DEAD AND BURIED!
ALL THAT REMAINS...
...IS A WALKING SEPULCRE!

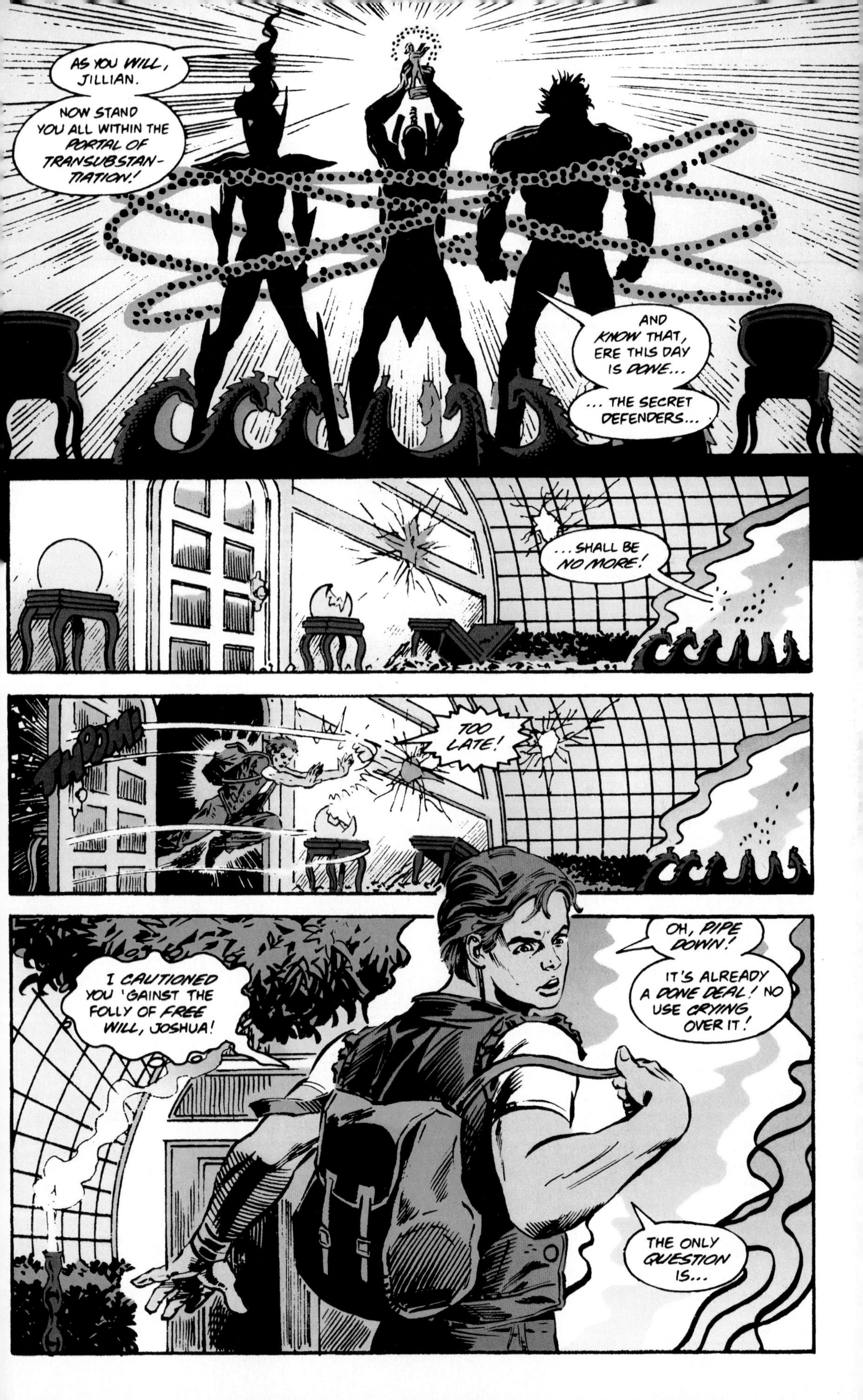
AS YOU WILL, JILLIAN.
NOW STAND YOU ALL WITHIN THE PORTAL OF TRANSUBSTAN-TIATION!
AND KNOW THAT, ERE THIS DAY IS DONE...
... THE SECRET DEFENDERS...
...SHALL BE NO MORE!
THOOMP!
TOO LATE!
I CAUTIONED YOU 'GAINST THE FOLLY OF FREE WILL, JOSHUA!
OH, PIPE DOWN!
IT'S ALREADY A DONE DEAL! NO USE CRYING OVER IT!
THE ONLY QUESTION IS...

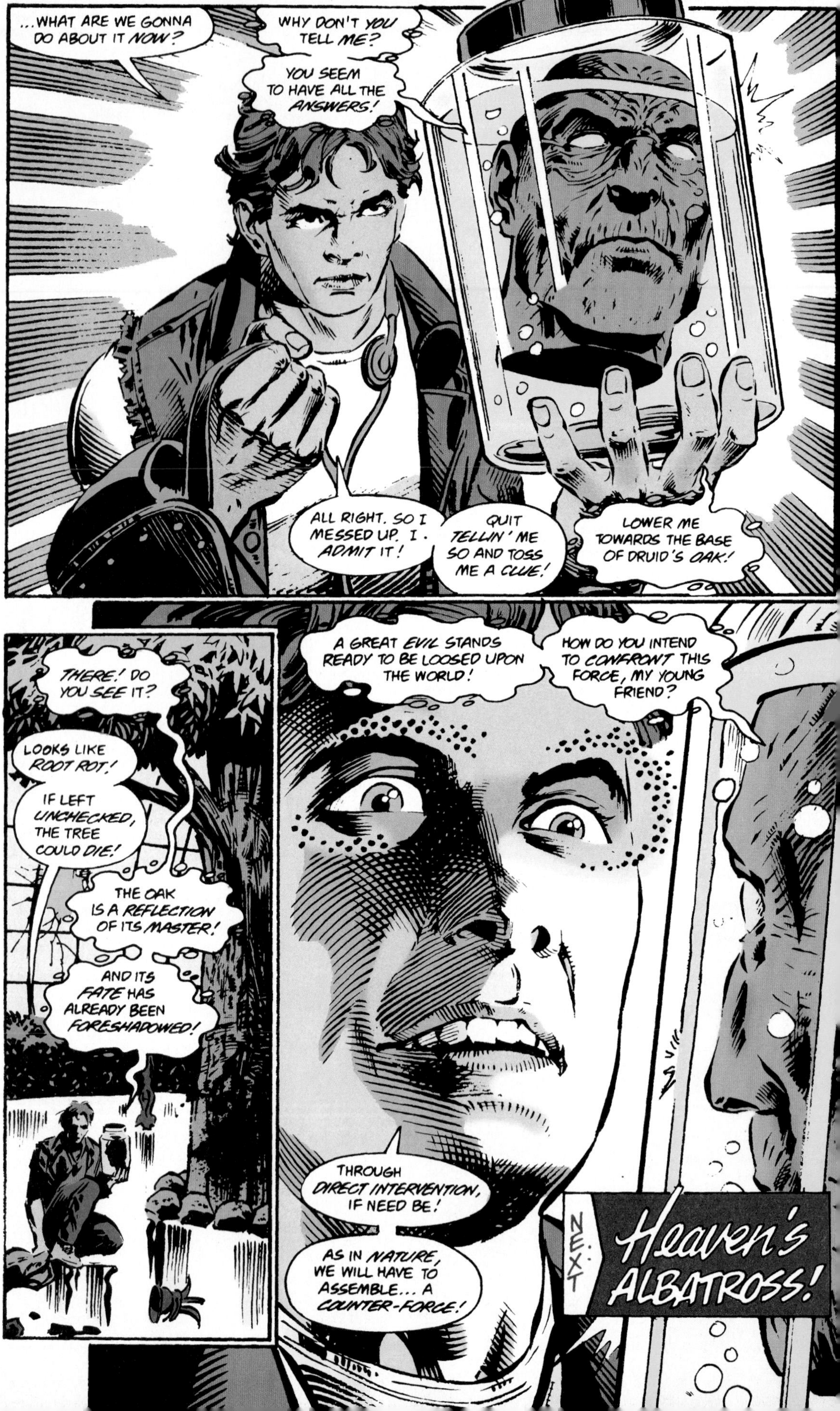
...WHAT ARE WE GONNA DO ABOUT IT NOW?
WHY DON'T YOU TELL ME?
YOU SEEM TO HAVE ALL THE ANSWERS!
ALL RIGHT. SO I MESSED UP. I ADMIT IT!
QUIT TELLIN' ME SO AND TOSS ME A CLUE!
LOWER ME TOWARDS THE BASE OF DRUID'S OAK!
THERE! DO YOU SEE IT?
LOOKS LIKE ROOT ROT!
IF LEFT UNCHECKED, THE TREE COULD DIE!
THE OAK IS A REFLECTION OF ITS MASTER!
AND ITS FATE HAS ALREADY BEEN FORESHADOWED!
A GREAT EVIL STANDS READY TO BE LOOSED UPON THE WORLD!
HOW DO YOU INTEND TO CONFRONT THIS FORCE, MY YOUNG FRIEND?
THROUGH DIRECT INTERVENTION, IF NEED BE!
AS IN NATURE, WE WILL HAVE TO ASSEMBLE... A COUNTER-FORCE!
NEXT: Heaven's ALBATROSS!

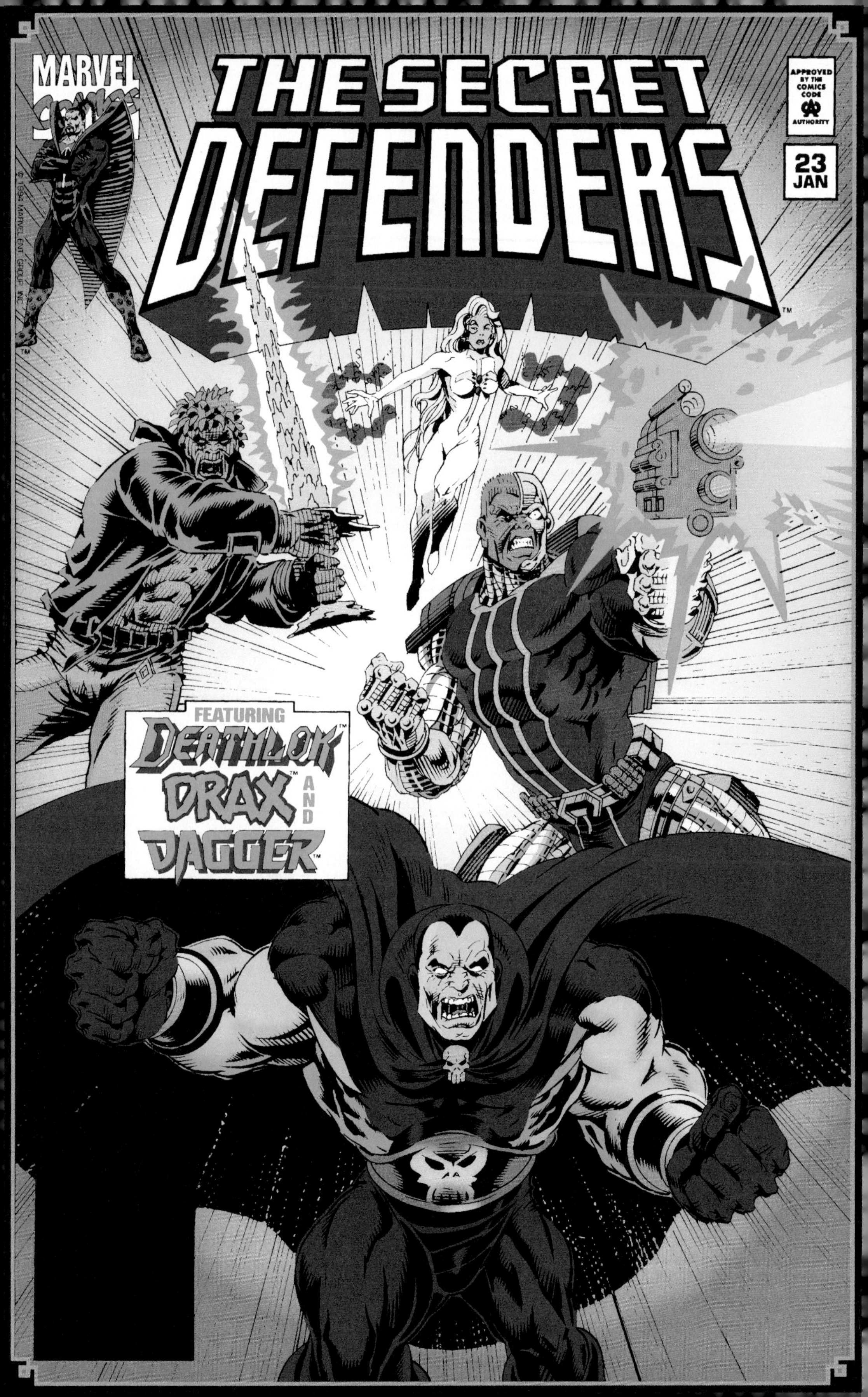
MARVEL
THE SECRET DEFENDERS
APPROVED BY THE COMICS CODE AUTHORITY
23 JAN
© 1994 MARVEL ENT. GROUP, INC.
FEATURING
DEATHLOK
DRAX AND
DAGGER

WHEN DOCTOR ANTHONY DRUID, MASTER OF THE UNKNOWN, RECEIVES A PREMONITION OF IMPENDING DISASTER, HE ASSEMBLES A SQUAD OF SUPERHUMAN OPERATIVES — AGENTS WHO WILL COVERTLY ELIMINATE THE MENACE AT HAND WITH NONE THE WISER!

STAN LEE PRESENTS . .

THE SECRET DEFENDERS

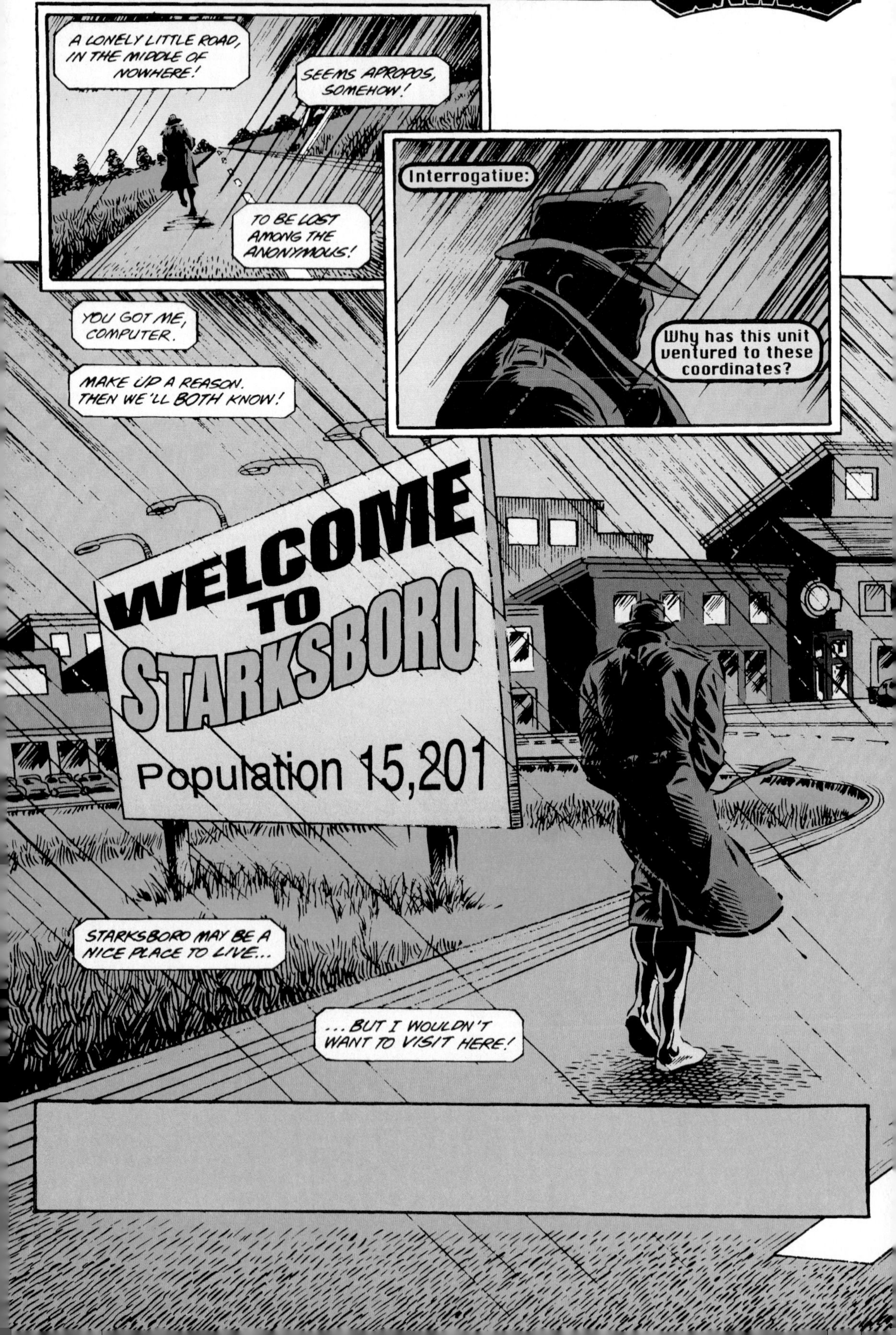
A LONELY LITTLE ROAD, IN THE MIDDLE OF NOWHERE!
SEEMS APROPOS, SOMEHOW!
TO BE LOST AMONG THE ANONYMOUS!
Interrogative:
Why has this unit ventured to these coordinates?
YOU GOT ME, COMPUTER.
MAKE UP A REASON. THEN WE'LL BOTH KNOW!
WELCOME TO STARKSBORO
Population 15,201
STARKSBORO MAY BE A NICE PLACE TO LIVE...
...BUT I WOULDN'T WANT TO VISIT HERE!

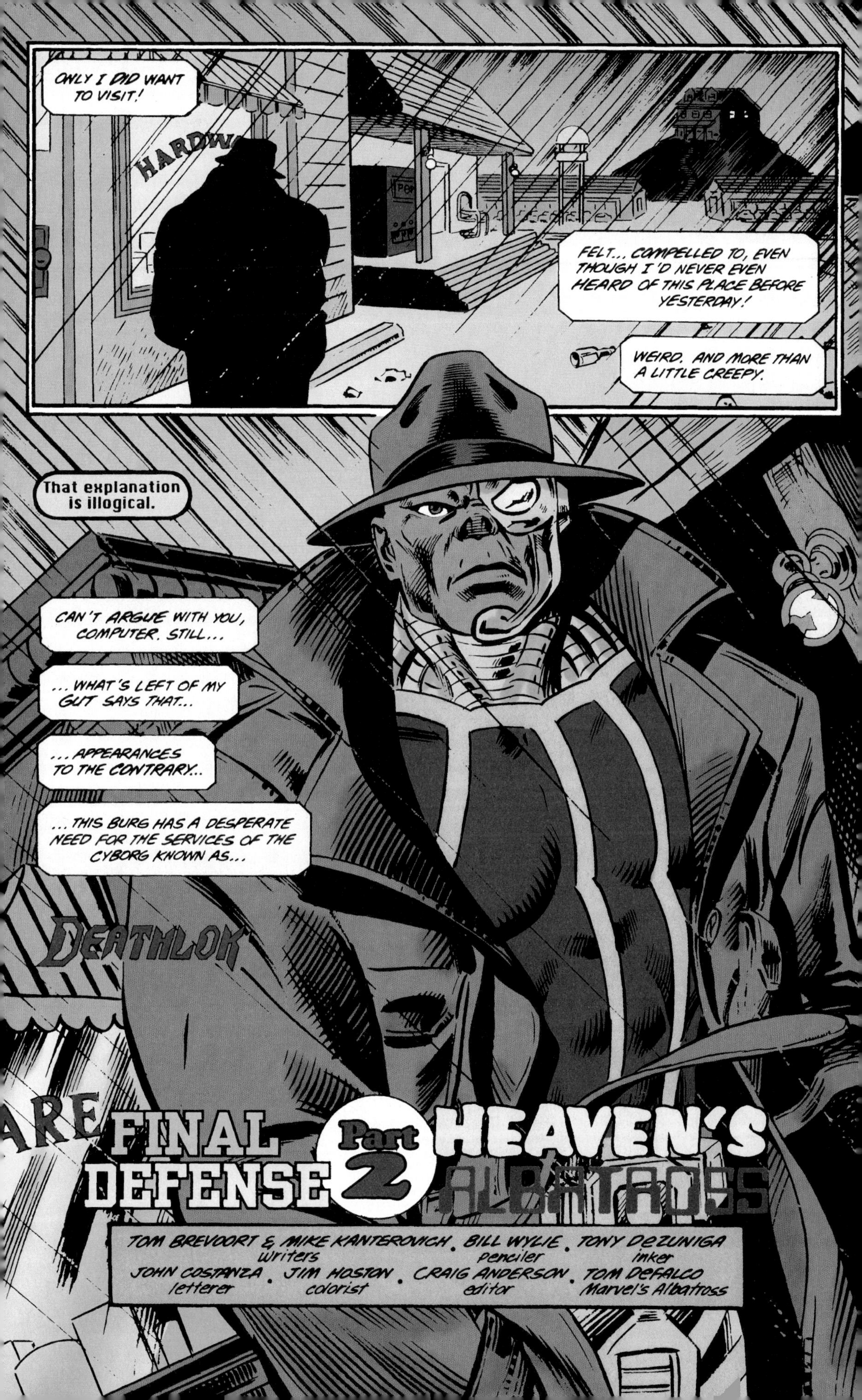

ONLY I DID WANT TO VISIT!
HARDW
FELT... COMPELLED TO, EVEN THOUGH I'D NEVER EVEN HEARD OF THIS PLACE BEFORE YESTERDAY!
WEIRD. AND MORE THAN A LITTLE CREEPY.
That explanation is illogical.
CAN'T ARGUE WITH YOU, COMPUTER. STILL...
...WHAT'S LEFT OF MY GUT SAYS THAT...
...APPEARANCES TO THE CONTRARY...
...THIS BURG HAS A DESPERATE NEED FOR THE SERVICES OF THE CYBORG KNOWN AS...
DEATHLOK
FINAL DEFENSE Part 2 HEAVEN'S ALBATROSS
TOM BREVOORT & MIKE KANTEROVICH . writers BILL WYLIE . penciler TONY DeZUNIGA inker
JOHN COSTANZA . letterer JIM HOSTON . colorist CRAIG ANDERSON . editor TOM DeFALCO Marvel's Albatross

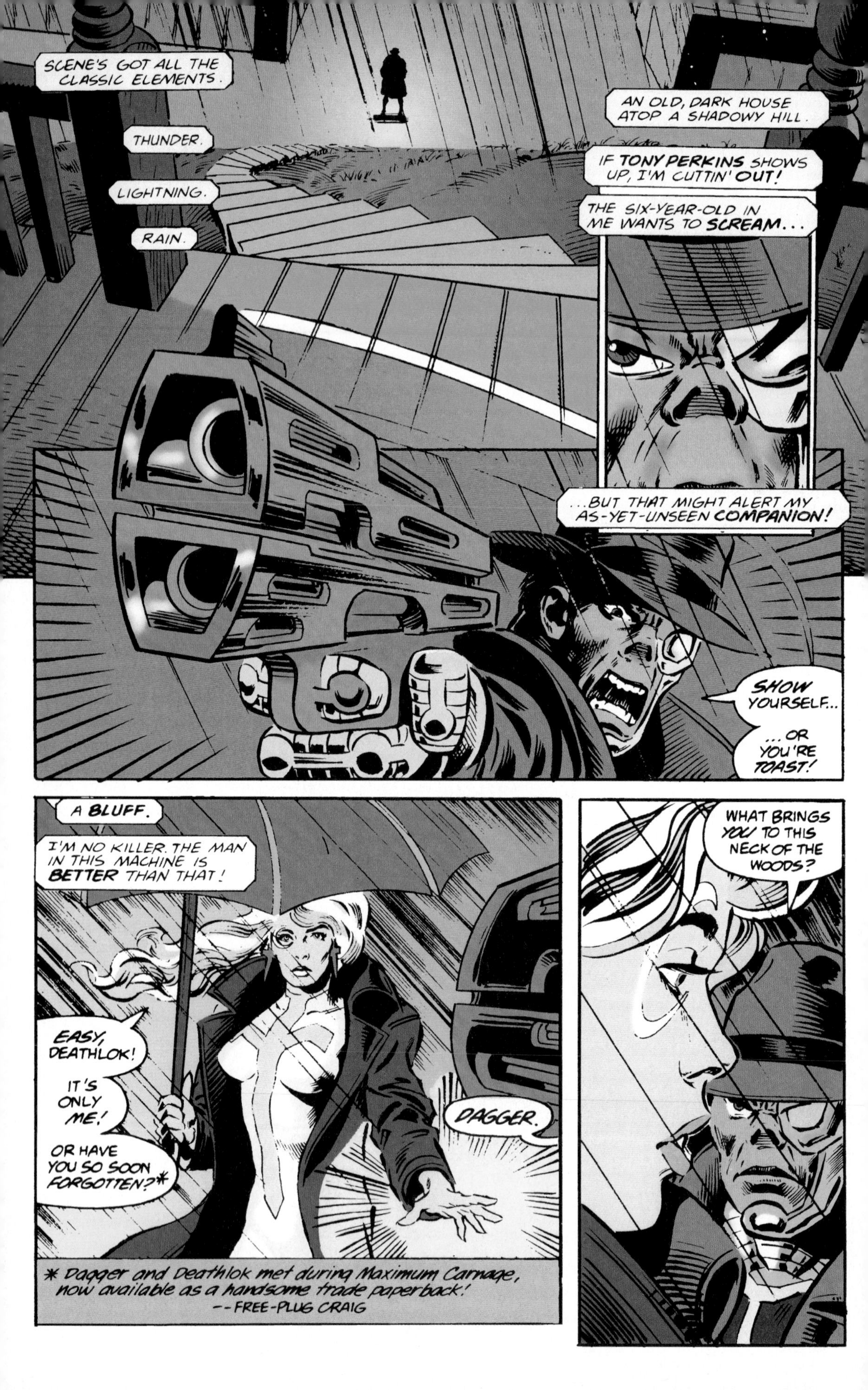
SCENE'S GOT ALL THE CLASSIC ELEMENTS.
THUNDER.
LIGHTNING.
RAIN.
AN OLD, DARK HOUSE ATOP A SHADOWY HILL.
IF TONY PERKINS SHOWS UP, I'M CUTTIN' OUT!
THE SIX-YEAR-OLD IN ME WANTS TO SCREAM...
...BUT THAT MIGHT ALERT MY AS-YET-UNSEEN COMPANION!
SHOW YOURSELF...
...OR YOU'RE TOAST!
A BLUFF.
I'M NO KILLER. THE MAN IN THIS MACHINE IS BETTER THAN THAT!
EASY, DEATHLOK!
IT'S ONLY ME!
OR HAVE YOU SO SOON FORGOTTEN?*
DAGGER.
WHAT BRINGS YOU TO THIS NECK OF THE WOODS?
* Dagger and Deathlok met during Maximum Carnage, now available as a handsome trade paperback!
--FREE-PLUG CRAIG

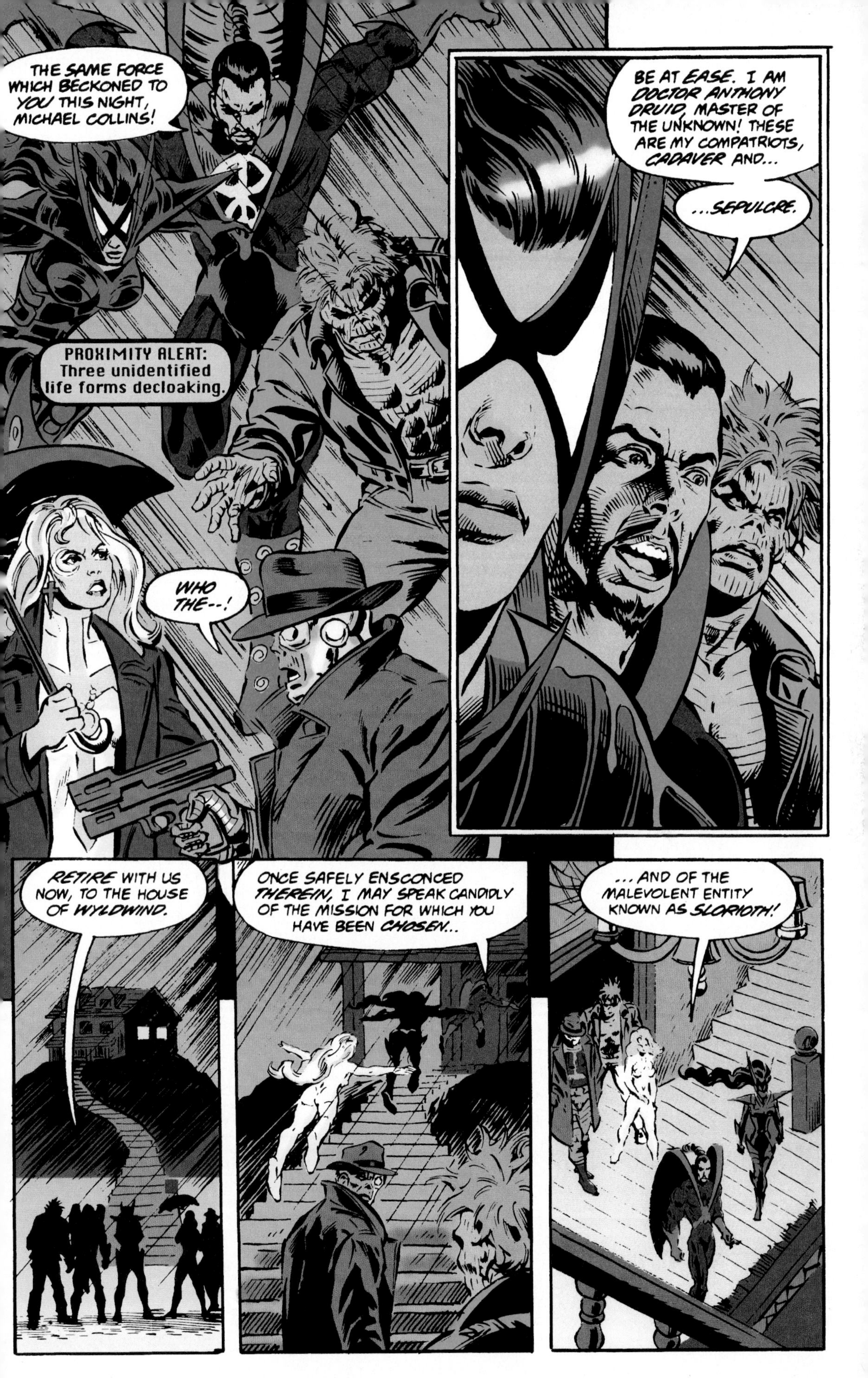
THE SAME FORCE WHICH BECKONED TO YOU THIS NIGHT, MICHAEL COLLINS!
PROXIMITY ALERT: Three unidentified life forms decloaking.
WHO THE--!
BE AT EASE. I AM DOCTOR ANTHONY DRUID, MASTER OF THE UNKNOWN! THESE ARE MY COMPATRIOTS, CADAVER AND...
...SEPULCRE.
RETIRE WITH US NOW, TO THE HOUSE OF WYLDWIND.
ONCE SAFELY ENSCONCED THEREIN, I MAY SPEAK CANDIDLY OF THE MISSION FOR WHICH YOU HAVE BEEN CHOSEN...
...AND OF THE MALEVOLENT ENTITY KNOWN AS SLORIOTH!

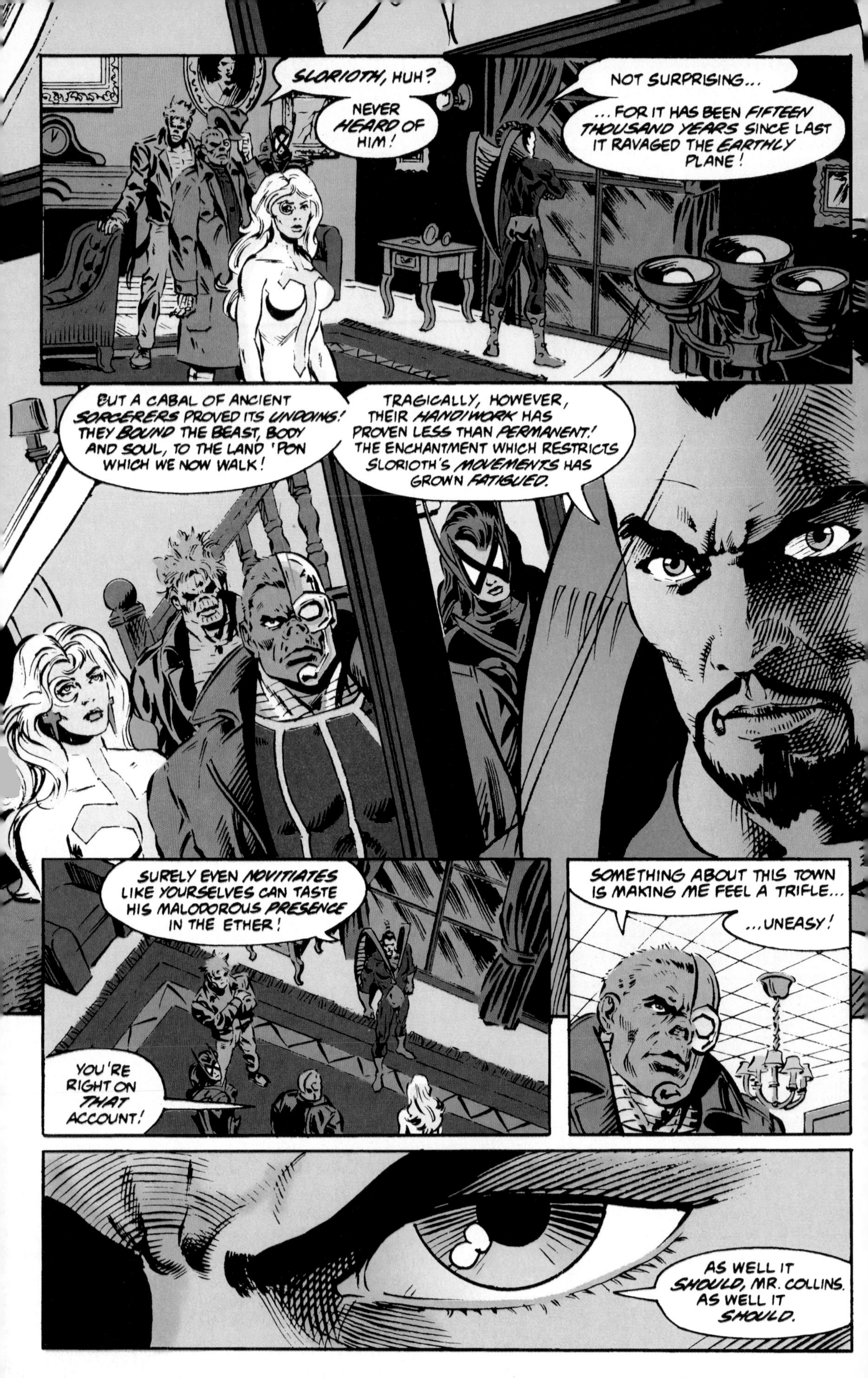
SLORIOTH, HUH?
NEVER HEARD OF HIM!
NOT SURPRISING...
...FOR IT HAS BEEN FIFTEEN THOUSAND YEARS SINCE LAST IT RAVAGED THE EARTHLY PLANE!
BUT A CABAL OF ANCIENT SORCERERS PROVED ITS UNDOING! THEY BOUND THE BEAST, BODY AND SOUL, TO THE LAND 'PON WHICH WE NOW WALK!
TRAGICALLY, HOWEVER, THEIR HANDIWORK HAS PROVEN LESS THAN PERMANENT! THE ENCHANTMENT WHICH RESTRICTS SLORIOTH'S MOVEMENTS HAS GROWN FATIGUED.
SURELY EVEN NOVITIATES LIKE YOURSELVES CAN TASTE HIS MALODOROUS PRESENCE IN THE ETHER!
YOU'RE RIGHT ON THAT ACCOUNT!
SOMETHING ABOUT THIS TOWN IS MAKING ME FEEL A TRIFLE...
...UNEASY!
AS WELL IT SHOULD, MR. COLLINS. AS WELL IT SHOULD.

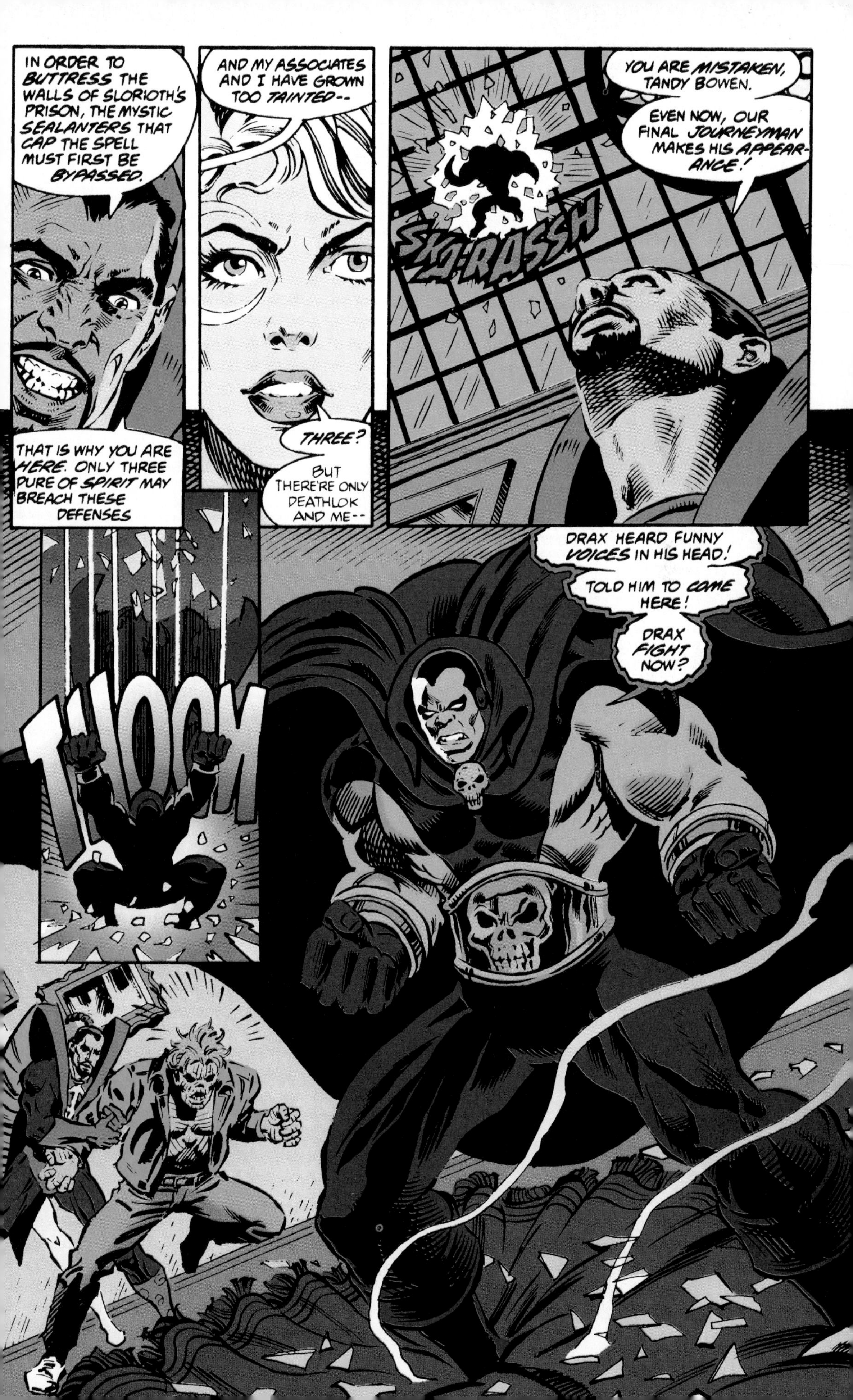
IN ORDER TO BUTTRESS THE WALLS OF SLORIOTH'S PRISON, THE MYSTIC SEALANTERS THAT CAP THE SPELL MUST FIRST BE BYPASSED.
THAT IS WHY YOU ARE HERE. ONLY THREE PURE OF SPIRIT MAY BREACH THESE DEFENSES
AND MY ASSOCIATES AND I HAVE GROWN TOO TAINTED--
THREE?
BUT THERE'RE ONLY DEATHLOK AND ME--
SKA-RASSH
YOU ARE MISTAKEN, TANDY BOWEN.
EVEN NOW, OUR FINAL JOURNEYMAN MAKES HIS APPEARANCE!
THOOM
DRAX HEARD FUNNY VOICES IN HIS HEAD!
TOLD HIM TO COME HERE!
DRAX FIGHT NOW?

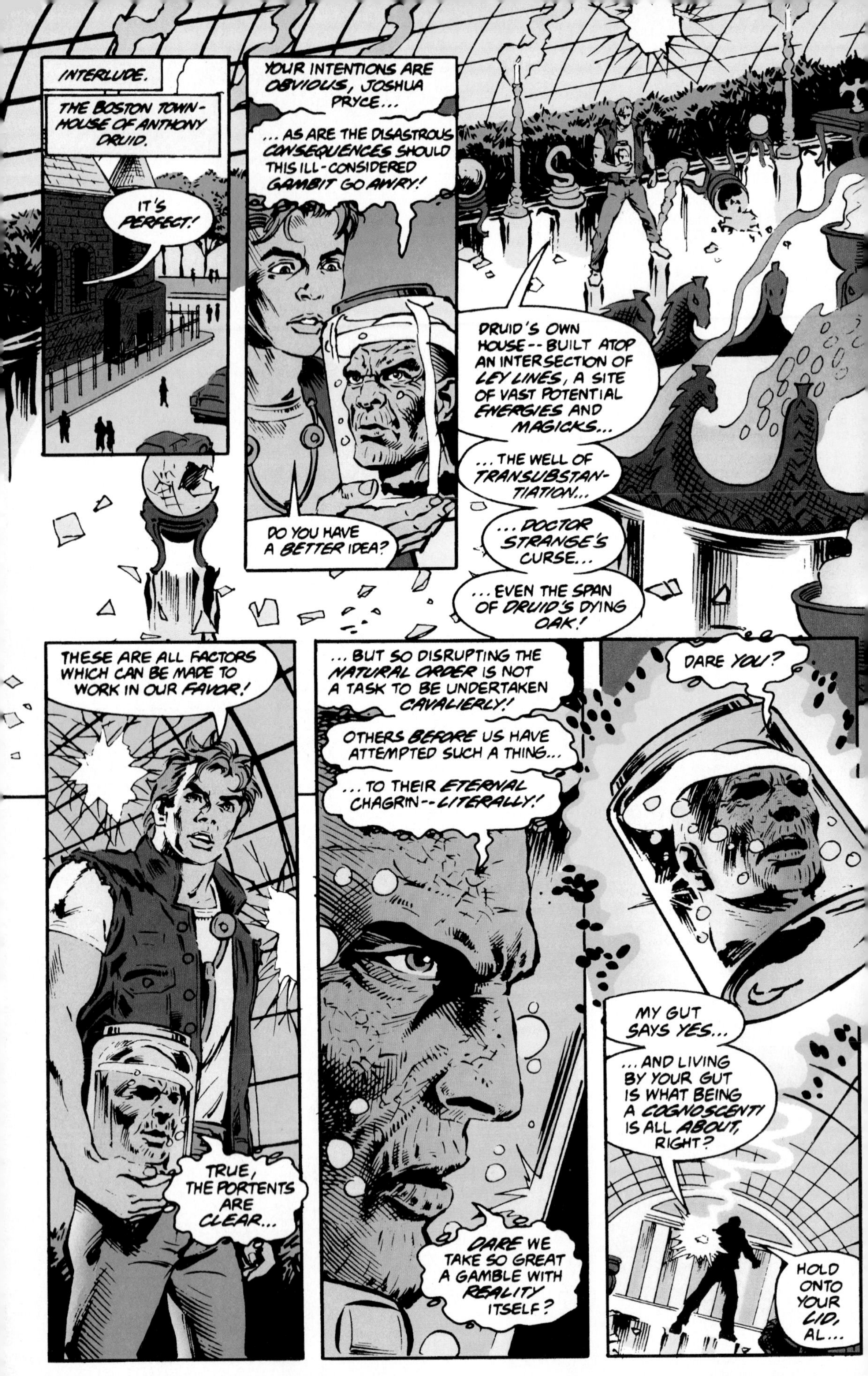
INTERLUDE.
THE BOSTON TOWN-HOUSE OF ANTHONY DRUID.
IT'S PERFECT!
YOUR INTENTIONS ARE OBVIOUS, JOSHUA PRYCE...
...AS ARE THE DISASTROUS CONSEQUENCES SHOULD THIS ILL-CONSIDERED GAMBIT GO AWRY!
DO YOU HAVE A BETTER IDEA?
DRUID'S OWN HOUSE--BUILT ATOP AN INTERSECTION OF LEY LINES, A SITE OF VAST POTENTIAL ENERGIES AND MAGICKS...
...THE WELL OF TRANSUBSTAN-TIATION...
...DOCTOR STRANGE'S CURSE...
...EVEN THE SPAN OF DRUID'S DYING OAK!
THESE ARE ALL FACTORS WHICH CAN BE MADE TO WORK IN OUR FAVOR!
TRUE, THE PORTENTS ARE CLEAR...
...BUT SO DISRUPTING THE NATURAL ORDER IS NOT A TASK TO BE UNDERTAKEN CAVALIERLY!
OTHERS BEFORE US HAVE ATTEMPTED SUCH A THING...
...TO THEIR ETERNAL CHAGRIN--LITERALLY!
DARE WE TAKE SO GREAT A GAMBLE WITH REALITY ITSELF?
DARE YOU?
MY GUT SAYS YES...
...AND LIVING BY YOUR GUT IS WHAT BEING A COGNOSCENTI IS ALL ABOUT, RIGHT?
HOLD ONTO YOUR LID, AL...

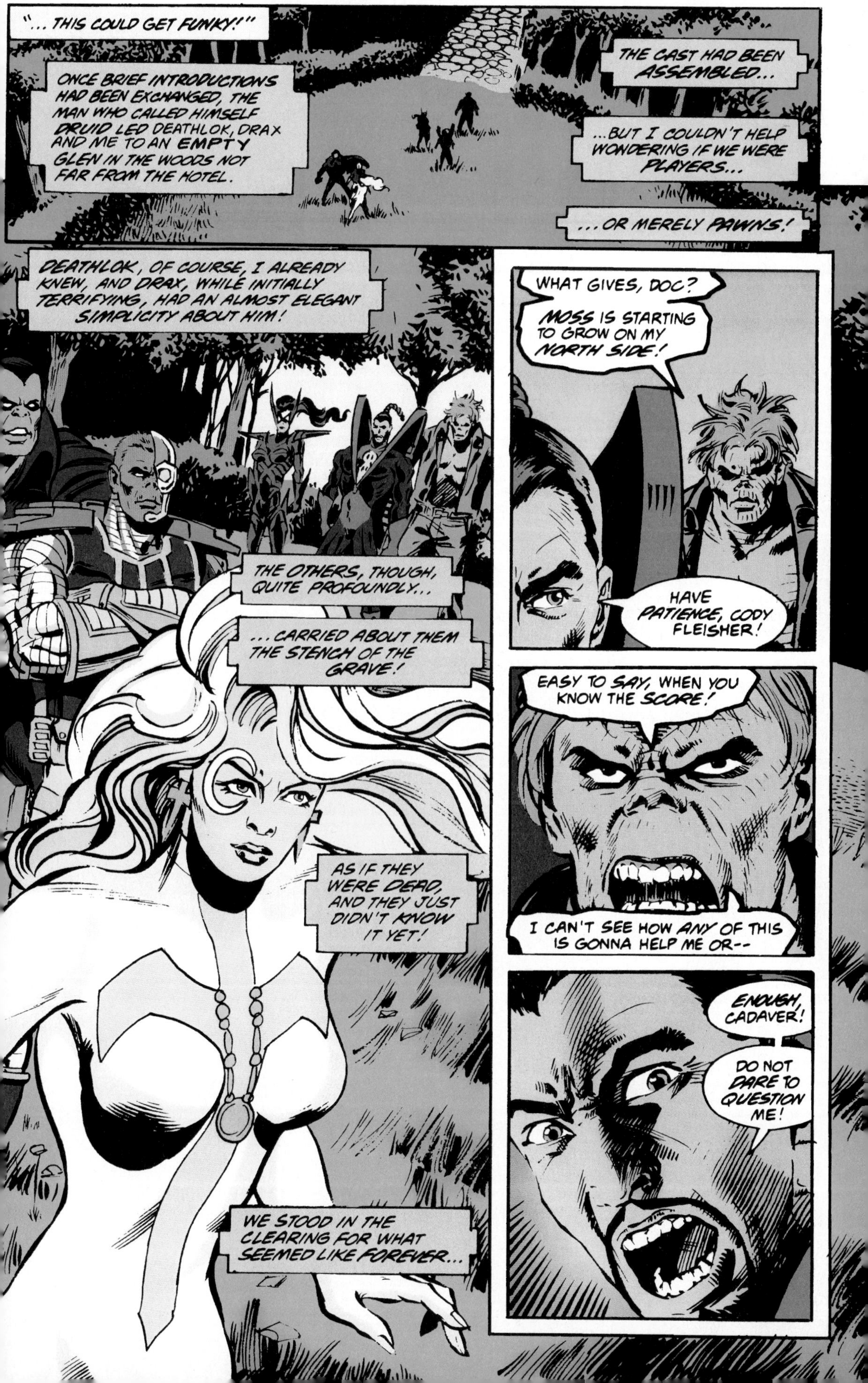
"... THIS COULD GET FUNKY!"
ONCE BRIEF INTRODUCTIONS HAD BEEN EXCHANGED, THE MAN WHO CALLED HIMSELF DRUID LED DEATHLOK, DRAX AND ME TO AN EMPTY GLEN IN THE WOODS NOT FAR FROM THE HOTEL.
THE CAST HAD BEEN ASSEMBLED...
...BUT I COULDN'T HELP WONDERING IF WE WERE PLAYERS...
...OR MERELY PAWNS!
DEATHLOK, OF COURSE, I ALREADY KNEW, AND DRAX, WHILE INITIALLY TERRIFYING, HAD AN ALMOST ELEGANT SIMPLICITY ABOUT HIM!
THE OTHERS, THOUGH, QUITE PROFOUNDLY...
...CARRIED ABOUT THEM THE STENCH OF THE GRAVE!
AS IF THEY WERE DEAD, AND THEY JUST DIDN'T KNOW IT YET!
WE STOOD IN THE CLEARING FOR WHAT SEEMED LIKE FOREVER...
WHAT GIVES, DOC?
MOSS IS STARTING TO GROW ON MY NORTH SIDE!
HAVE PATIENCE, CODY FLEISHER!
EASY TO SAY, WHEN YOU KNOW THE SCORE!
I CAN'T SEE HOW ANY OF THIS IS GONNA HELP ME OR--
ENOUGH, CADAVER!
DO NOT DARE TO QUESTION ME!

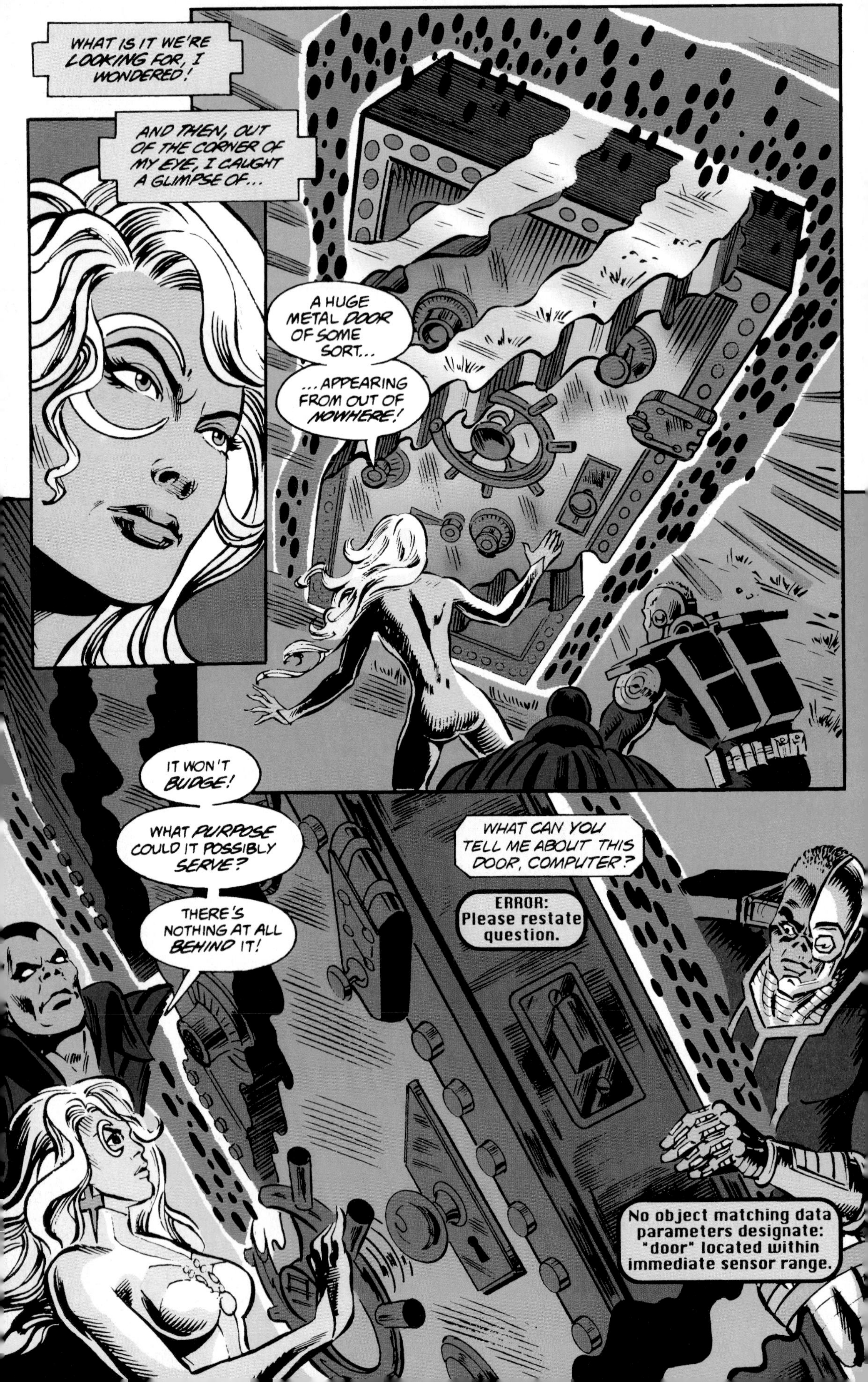
WHAT IS IT WE'RE LOOKING FOR, I WONDERED!
AND THEN, OUT OF THE CORNER OF MY EYE, I CAUGHT A GLIMPSE OF...
A HUGE METAL DOOR OF SOME SORT...
...APPEARING FROM OUT OF NOWHERE!
IT WON'T BUDGE!
WHAT PURPOSE COULD IT POSSIBLY SERVE?
THERE'S NOTHING AT ALL BEHIND IT!
WHAT CAN YOU TELL ME ABOUT THIS DOOR, COMPUTER?
ERROR: Please restate question.
No object matching data parameters designate: "door" located within immediate sensor range.

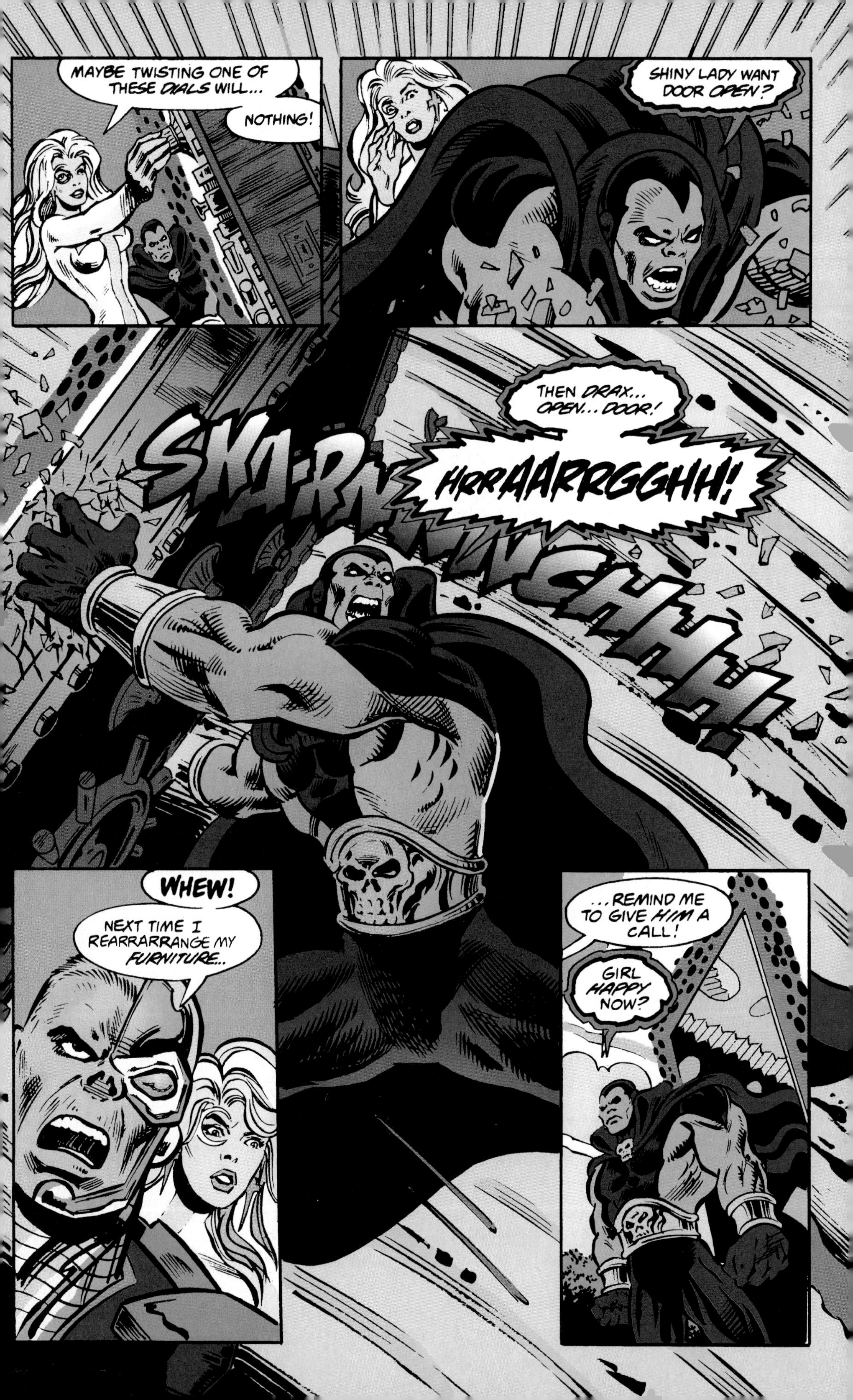
MAYBE TWISTING ONE OF THESE DIALS WILL...
NOTHING!
SHINY LADY WANT DOOR OPEN?
THEN DRAX... OPEN... DOOR!
SKA-RANNNCHHH!
HRRAARRGGHH!
WHEW!
NEXT TIME I REARRARRANGE MY FURNITURE...
...REMIND ME TO GIVE HIM A CALL!
GIRL HAPPY NOW?

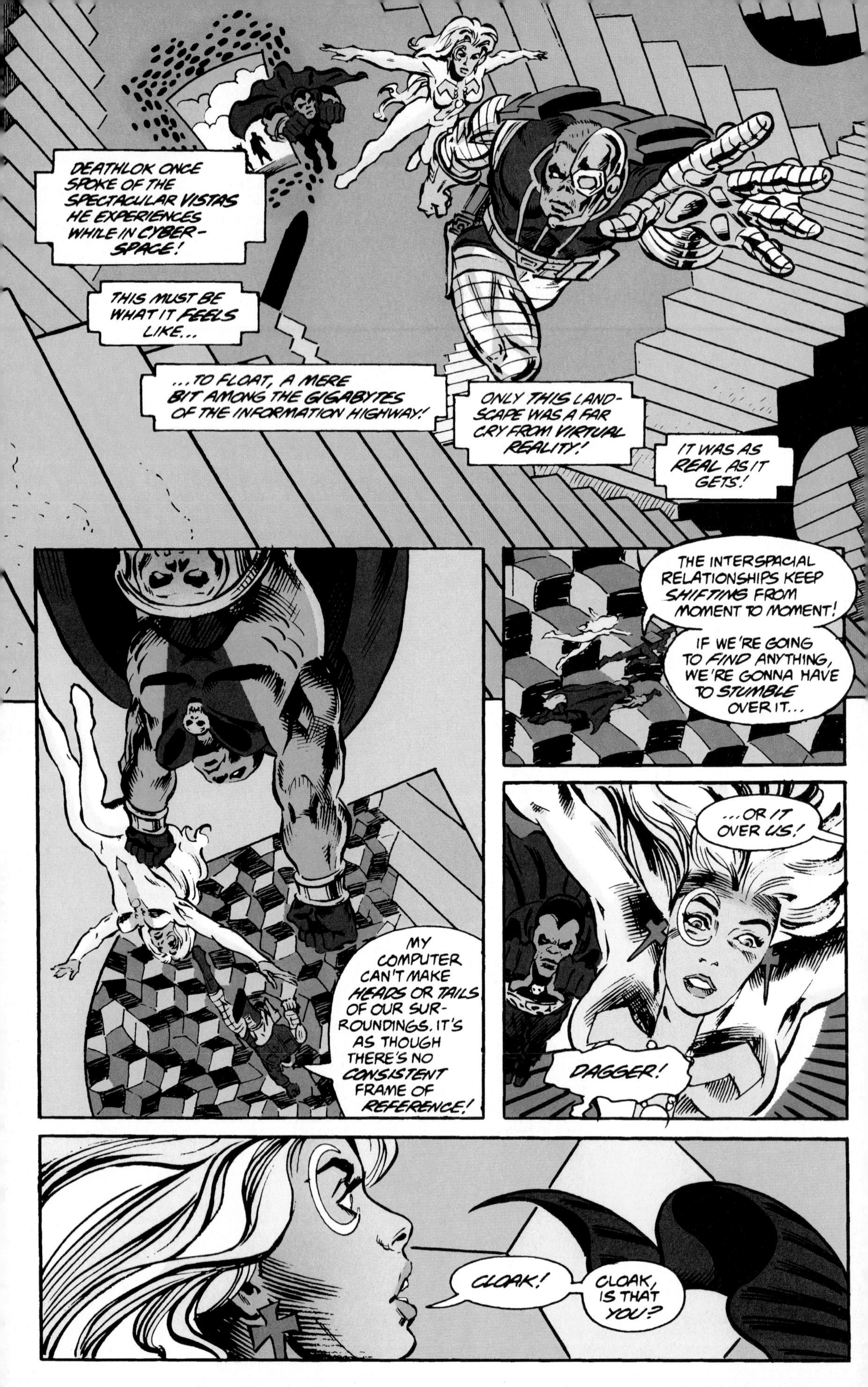
DEATHLOK ONCE SPOKE OF THE SPECTACULAR VISTAS HE EXPERIENCES WHILE IN CYBER-SPACE!
THIS MUST BE WHAT IT FEELS LIKE...
...TO FLOAT, A MERE BIT AMONG THE GIGABYTES OF THE INFORMATION HIGHWAY!
ONLY THIS LAND-SCAPE WAS A FAR CRY FROM VIRTUAL REALITY!
IT WAS AS REAL AS IT GETS!
MY COMPUTER CAN'T MAKE HEADS OR TAILS OF OUR SUR-ROUNDINGS. IT'S AS THOUGH THERE'S NO CONSISTENT FRAME OF REFERENCE!
THE INTERSPACIAL RELATIONSHIPS KEEP SHIFTING FROM MOMENT TO MOMENT!
IF WE'RE GOING TO FIND ANYTHING, WE'RE GONNA HAVE TO STUMBLE OVER IT...
...OR IT OVER US!
DAGGER!
CLOAK!
CLOAK, IS THAT YOU?

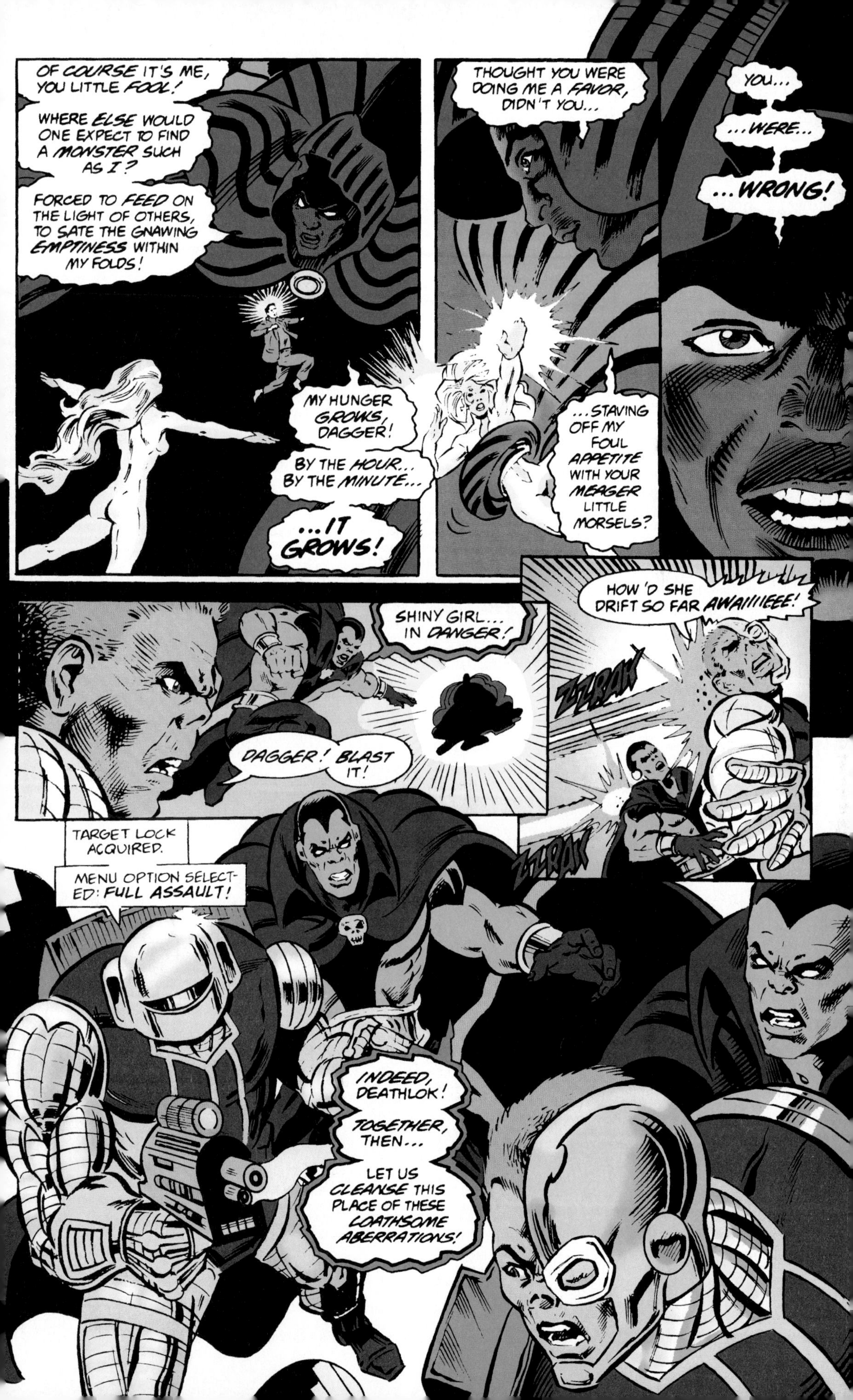
OF COURSE IT'S ME, YOU LITTLE FOOL!
WHERE ELSE WOULD ONE EXPECT TO FIND A MONSTER SUCH AS I?
FORCED TO FEED ON THE LIGHT OF OTHERS, TO SATE THE GNAWING EMPTINESS WITHIN MY FOLDS!
MY HUNGER GROWS, DAGGER!
BY THE HOUR... BY THE MINUTE...
...IT GROWS!
THOUGHT YOU WERE DOING ME A FAVOR, DIDN'T YOU...
...STAVING OFF MY FOUL APPETITE WITH YOUR MEAGER LITTLE MORSELS?
YOU...
...WERE...
...WRONG!
SHINY GIRL... IN DANGER!
DAGGER! BLAST IT!
HOW'D SHE DRIFT SO FAR AWAIIIIEEE!
ZZZBAK
ZZZRAK
TARGET LOCK ACQUIRED.
MENU OPTION SELECTED: FULL ASSAULT!
INDEED, DEATHLOK!
TOGETHER, THEN...
LET US CLEANSE THIS PLACE OF THESE LOATHSOME ABERRATIONS!

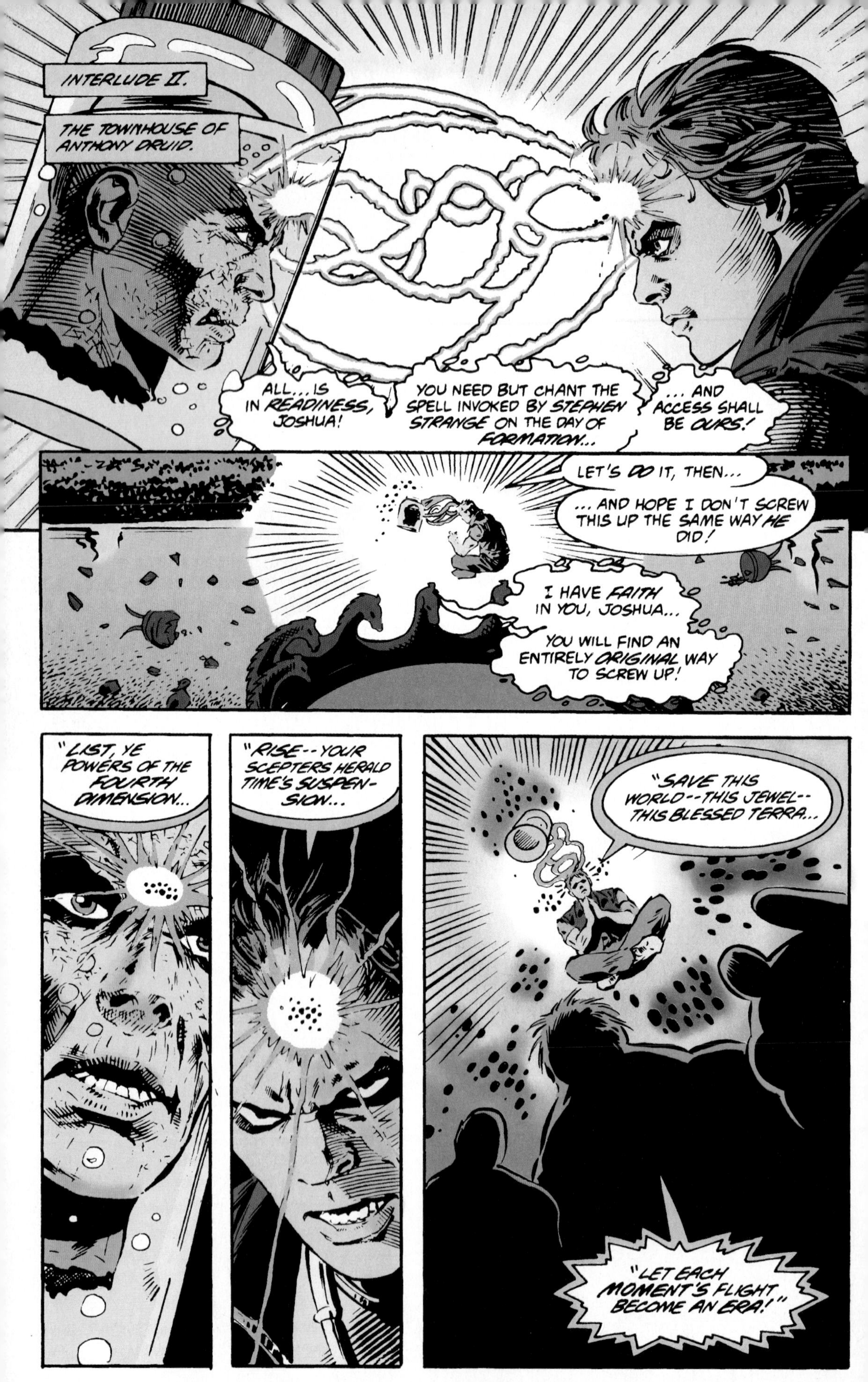

INTERLUDE II.
THE TOWNHOUSE OF ANTHONY DRUID.
ALL... IS IN READINESS, JOSHUA!
YOU NEED BUT CHANT THE SPELL INVOKED BY STEPHEN STRANGE ON THE DAY OF FORMATION...
... AND ACCESS SHALL BE OURS!
LET'S DO IT, THEN...
... AND HOPE I DON'T SCREW THIS UP THE SAME WAY HE DID!
I HAVE FAITH IN YOU, JOSHUA...
YOU WILL FIND AN ENTIRELY ORIGINAL WAY TO SCREW UP!
"LIST, YE POWERS OF THE FOURTH DIMENSION...
"RISE--YOUR SCEPTERS HERALD TIME'S SUSPENSION...
"SAVE THIS WORLD--THIS JEWEL--THIS BLESSED TERRA...
"LET EACH MOMENT'S FLIGHT BECOME AN ERA!"

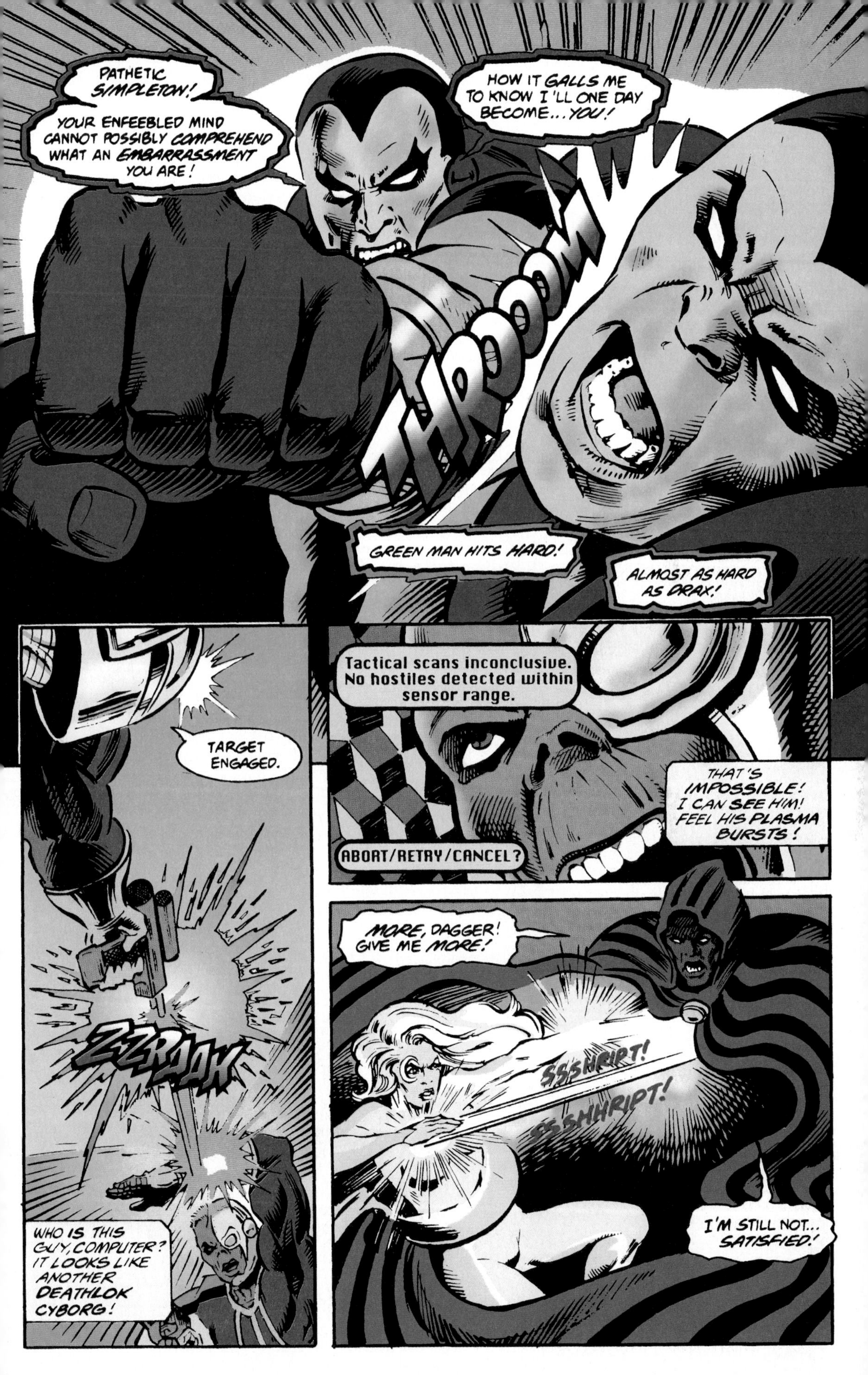
PATHETIC SIMPLETON!
YOUR ENFEEBLED MIND CANNOT POSSIBLY COMPREHEND WHAT AN EMBARRASSMENT YOU ARE!
HOW IT GALLS ME TO KNOW I'LL ONE DAY BECOME... YOU!
THROOOM
GREEN MAN HITS HARD!
ALMOST AS HARD AS DRAX!
TARGET ENGAGED.
ZZRAAK
WHO IS THIS GUY, COMPUTER? IT LOOKS LIKE ANOTHER DEATHLOK CYBORG!
Tactical scans inconclusive. No hostiles detected within sensor range.
THAT'S IMPOSSIBLE! I CAN SEE HIM! FEEL HIS PLASMA BURSTS!
ABORT/RETRY/CANCEL?
MORE, DAGGER! GIVE ME MORE!
SSSHRIPT!
SSSHHRIPT!
I'M STILL NOT... SATISFIED!

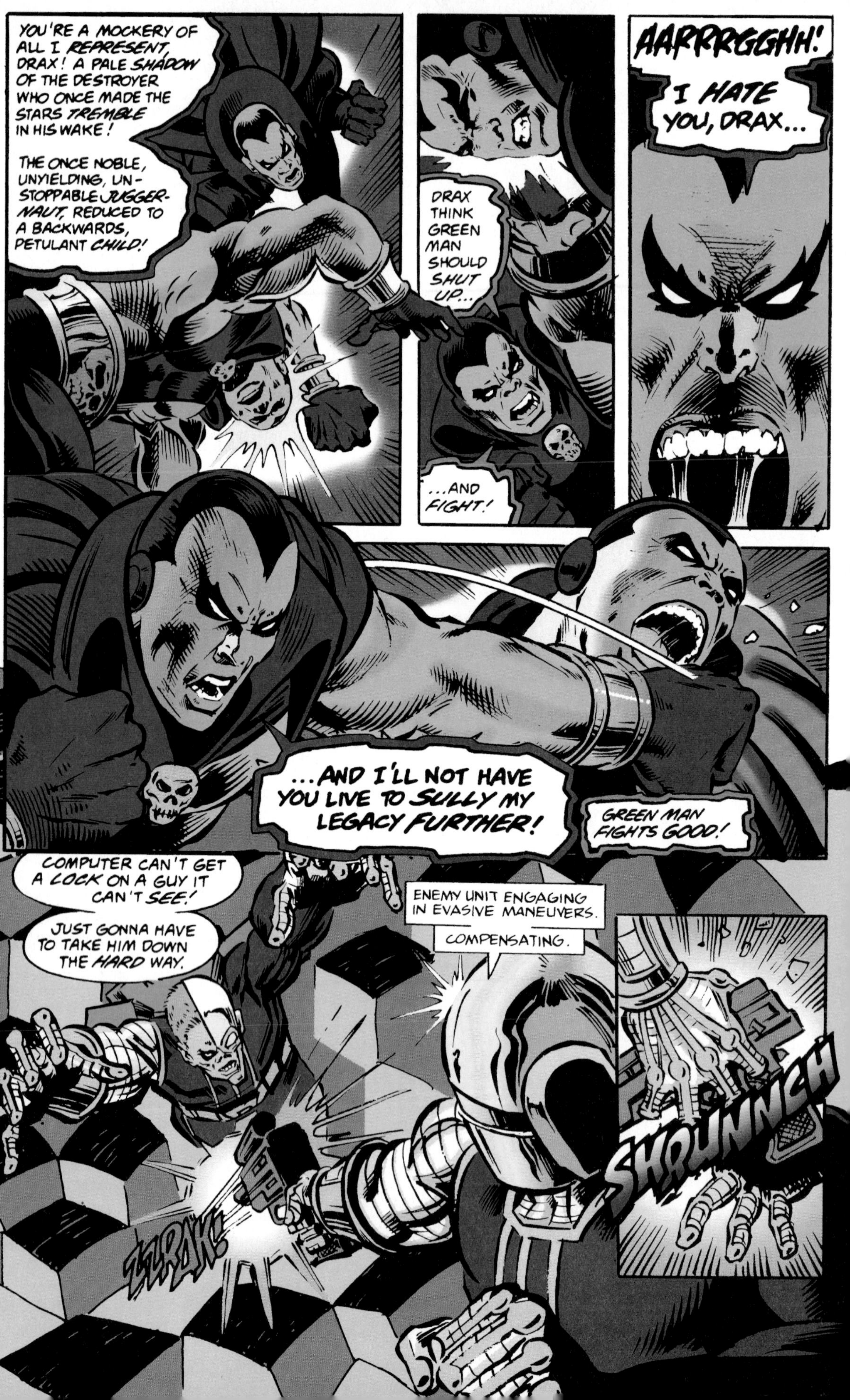
YOU'RE A MOCKERY OF ALL I REPRESENT, DRAX! A PALE SHADOW OF THE DESTROYER WHO ONCE MADE THE STARS TREMBLE IN HIS WAKE!
THE ONCE NOBLE, UNYIELDING, UN-STOPPABLE JUGGER-NAUT, REDUCED TO A BACKWARDS, PETULANT CHILD!
DRAX THINK GREEN MAN SHOULD SHUT UP...
...AND FIGHT!
AARRRGGHH!
I HATE YOU, DRAX...
...AND I'LL NOT HAVE YOU LIVE TO SULLY MY LEGACY FURTHER!
GREEN MAN FIGHTS GOOD!
COMPUTER CAN'T GET A LOCK ON A GUY IT CAN'T SEE!
JUST GONNA HAVE TO TAKE HIM DOWN THE HARD WAY.
ENEMY UNIT ENGAGING IN EVASIVE MANEUVERS.
COMPENSATING.
SHRUNNCH
ZZRAK!

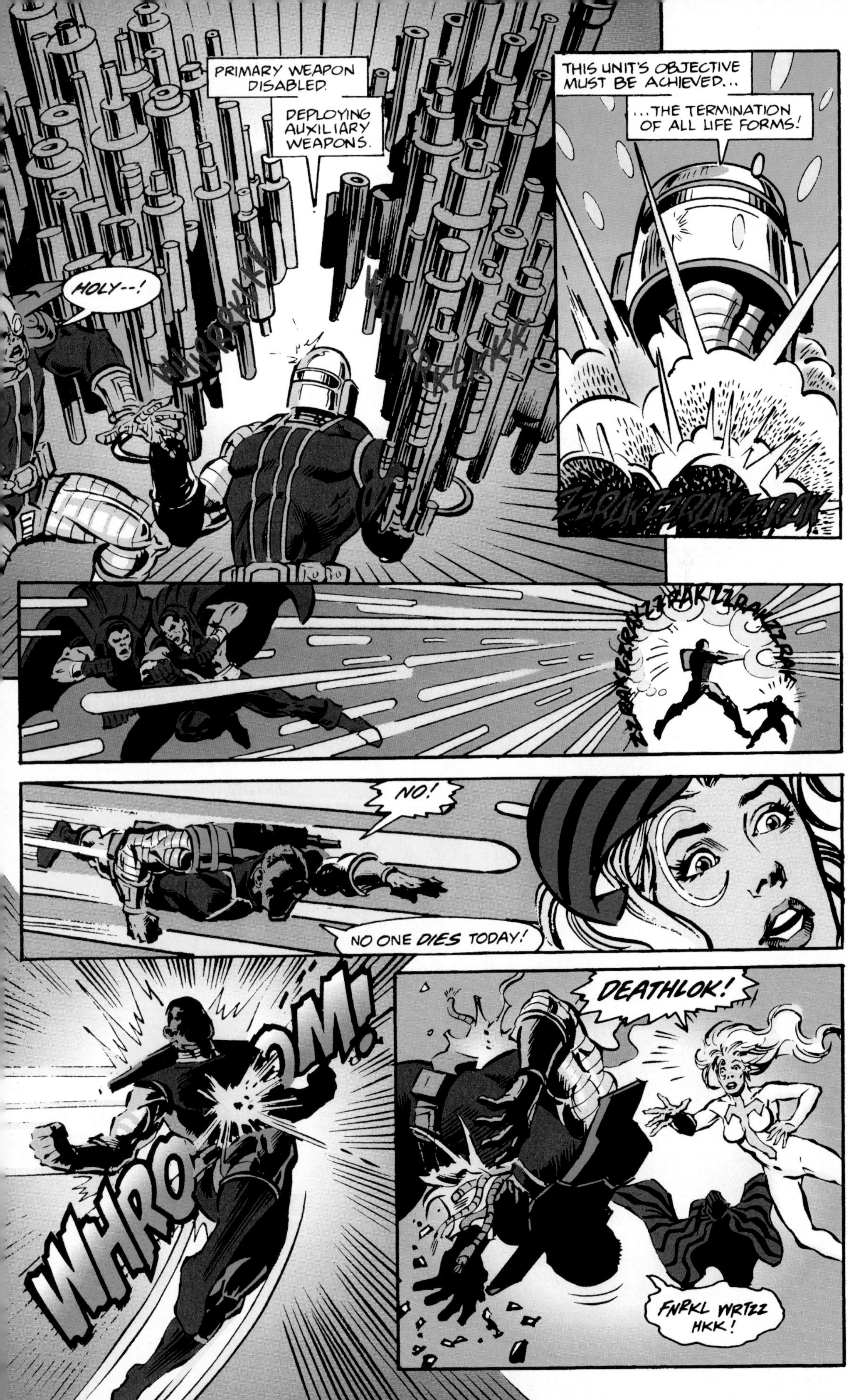
PRIMARY WEAPON DISABLED.
DEPLOYING AUXILIARY WEAPONS.
HOLY--!
WHIRRKLKK
WHIRRKLKKKK
THIS UNIT'S OBJECTIVE MUST BE ACHIEVED...
...THE TERMINATION OF ALL LIFE FORMS!
ZZRAKZZRAKZZRAK
ZZRAKZZRAKZZRAKZZRAK
NO!
NO ONE DIES TODAY!
WHROOOM!
DEATHLOK!
FNRKL WRTZZ HKK!

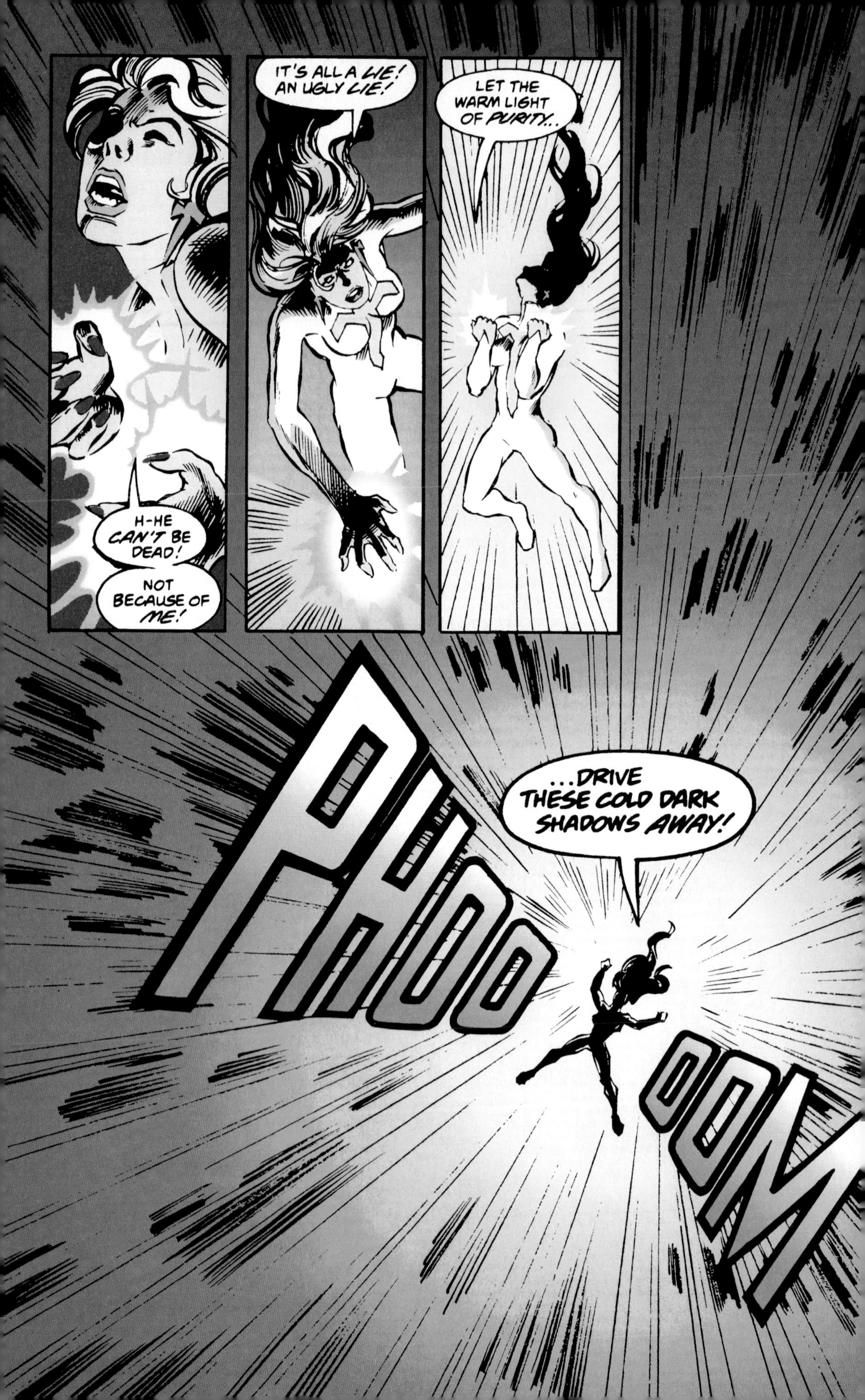
H-HE CAN'T BE DEAD!
NOT BECAUSE OF ME!
IT'S ALL A LIE! AN UGLY LIE!
LET THE WARM LIGHT OF PURITY...
PHOOOOM
...DRIVE THESE COLD DARK SHADOWS AWAY!

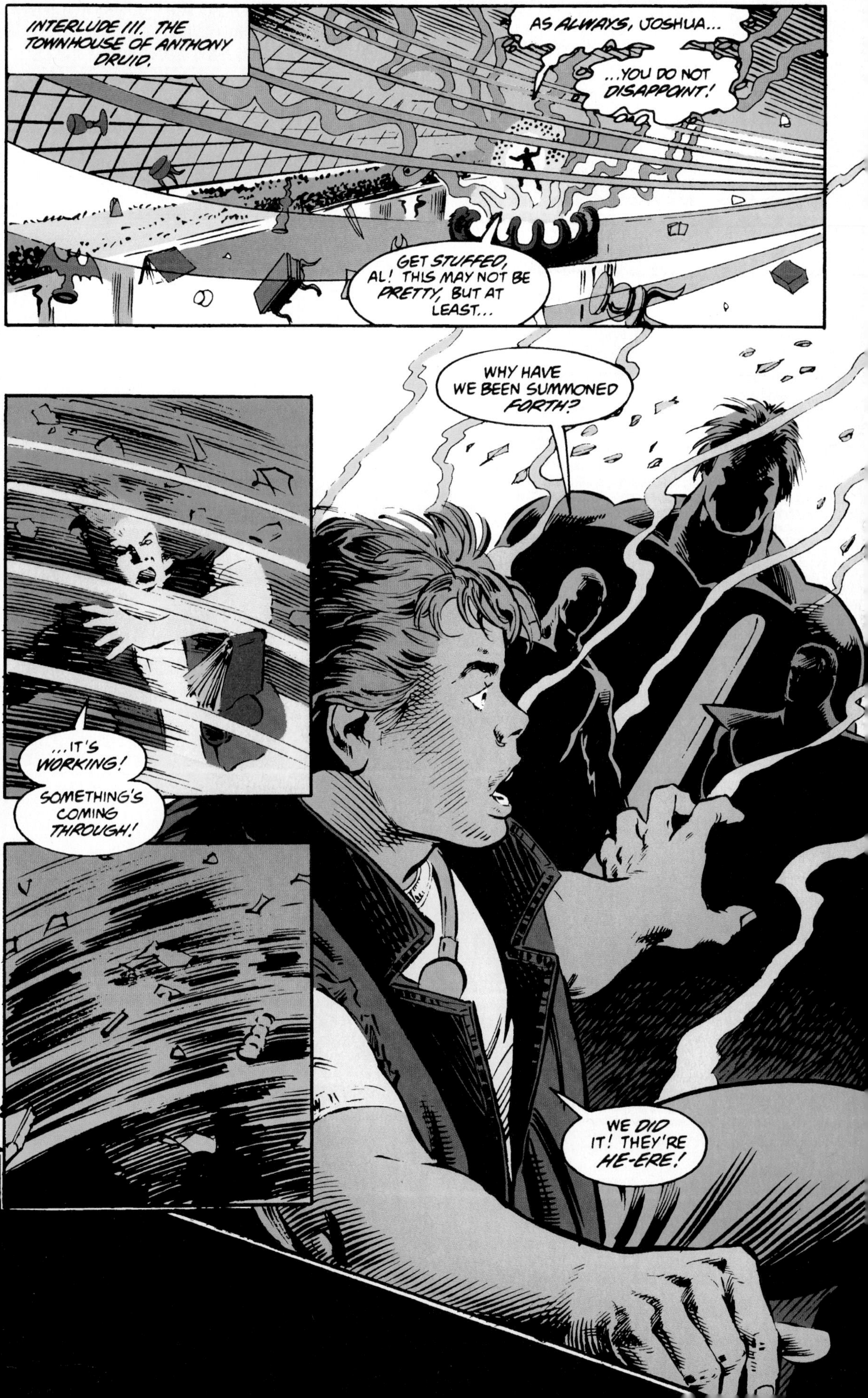
INTERLUDE III. THE TOWNHOUSE OF ANTHONY DRUID.
AS ALWAYS, JOSHUA...
...YOU DO NOT DISAPPOINT!
GET STUFFED, AL! THIS MAY NOT BE PRETTY, BUT AT LEAST...
...IT'S WORKING!
SOMETHING'S COMING THROUGH!
WHY HAVE WE BEEN SUMMONED FORTH?
WE DID IT! THEY'RE HE-ERE!

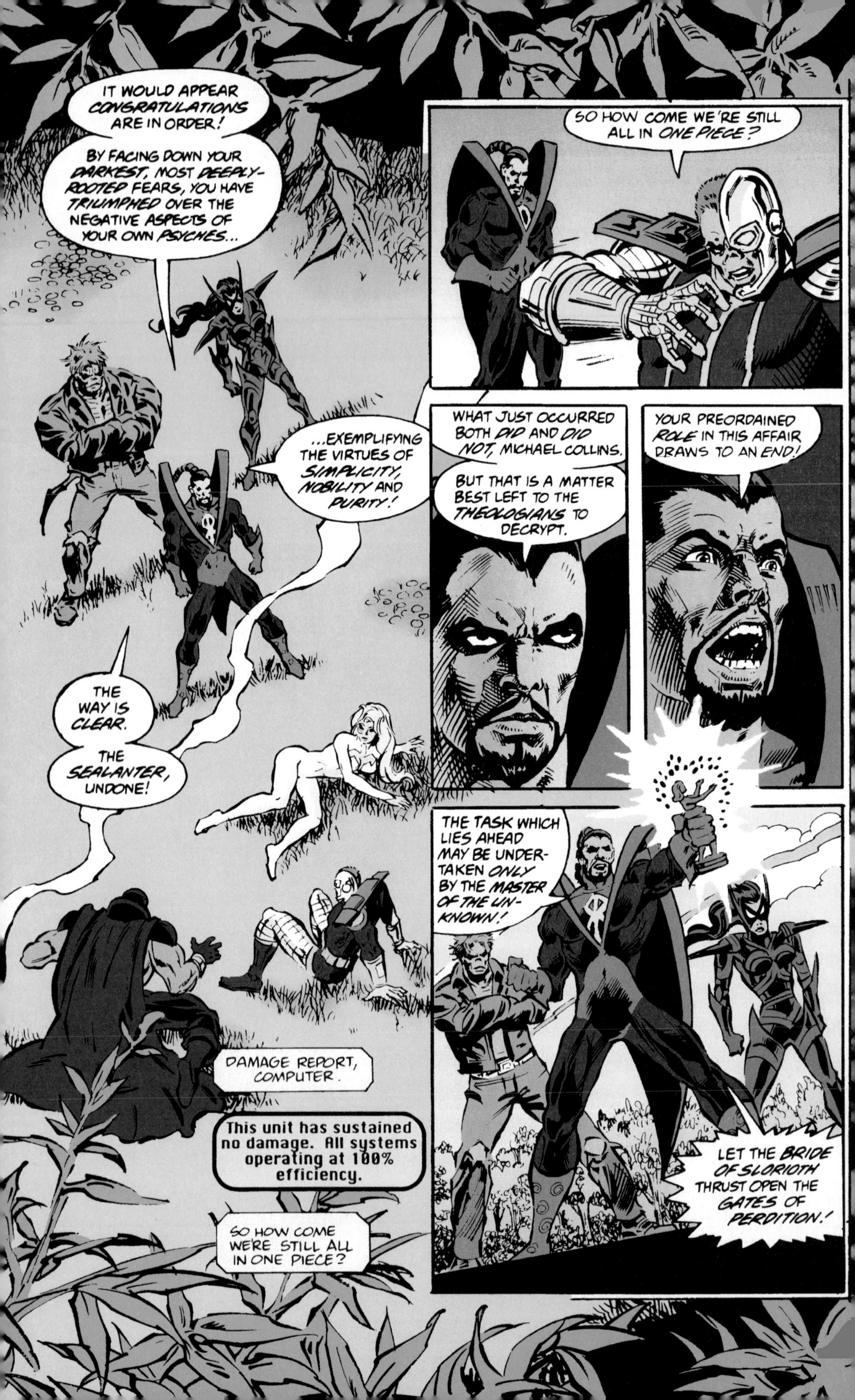
IT WOULD APPEAR CONGRATULATIONS ARE IN ORDER!
BY FACING DOWN YOUR DARKEST, MOST DEEPLY-ROOTED FEARS, YOU HAVE TRIUMPHED OVER THE NEGATIVE ASPECTS OF YOUR OWN PSYCHES...
...EXEMPLIFYING THE VIRTUES OF SIMPLICITY, NOBILITY AND PURITY!
THE WAY IS CLEAR.
THE SEALANTER, UNDONE!
DAMAGE REPORT, COMPUTER.
This unit has sustained no damage. All systems operating at 100% efficiency.
SO HOW COME WE'RE STILL ALL IN ONE PIECE?
SO HOW COME WE'RE STILL ALL IN ONE PIECE?
WHAT JUST OCCURRED BOTH DID AND DID NOT, MICHAEL COLLINS.
BUT THAT IS A MATTER BEST LEFT TO THE THEOLOGIANS TO DECRYPT.
YOUR PREORDAINED ROLE IN THIS AFFAIR DRAWS TO AN END!
THE TASK WHICH LIES AHEAD MAY BE UNDER-TAKEN ONLY BY THE MASTER OF THE UN-KNOWN!
LET THE BRIDE OF SLORIOTH THRUST OPEN THE GATES OF PERDITION!

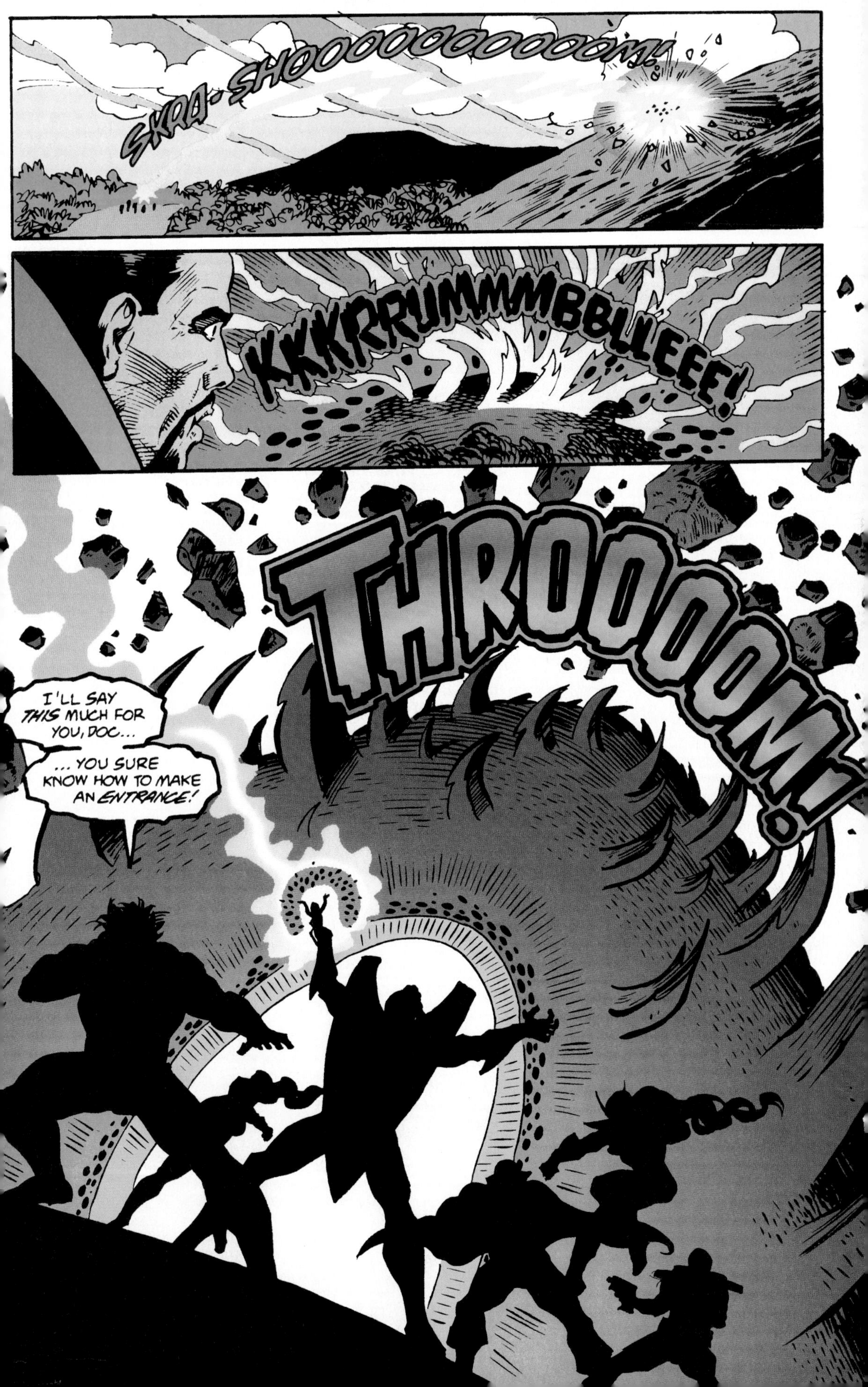
SKRA-SHOOOOOOOOOOOM!
KKKRRUMMMMBBLLEEEE!
THROOOOM!
I'LL SAY *THIS* MUCH FOR YOU, DOC...
... YOU SURE KNOW HOW TO MAKE AN *ENTRANCE*!

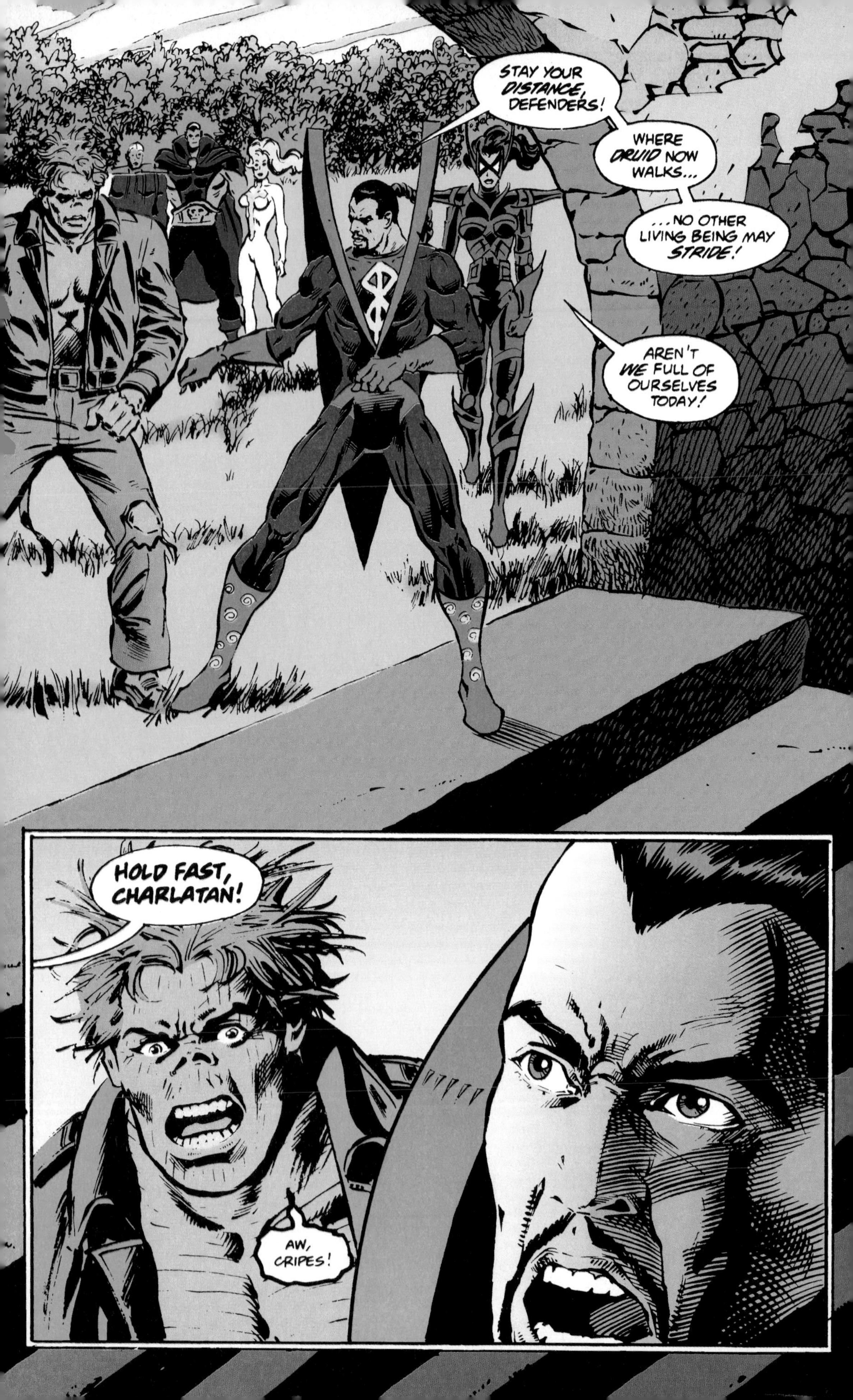
STAY YOUR DISTANCE, DEFENDERS!
WHERE DRUID NOW WALKS...
...NO OTHER LIVING BEING MAY STRIDE!
AREN'T WE FULL OF OURSELVES TODAY!
HOLD FAST, CHARLATAN!
AW, CRIPES!

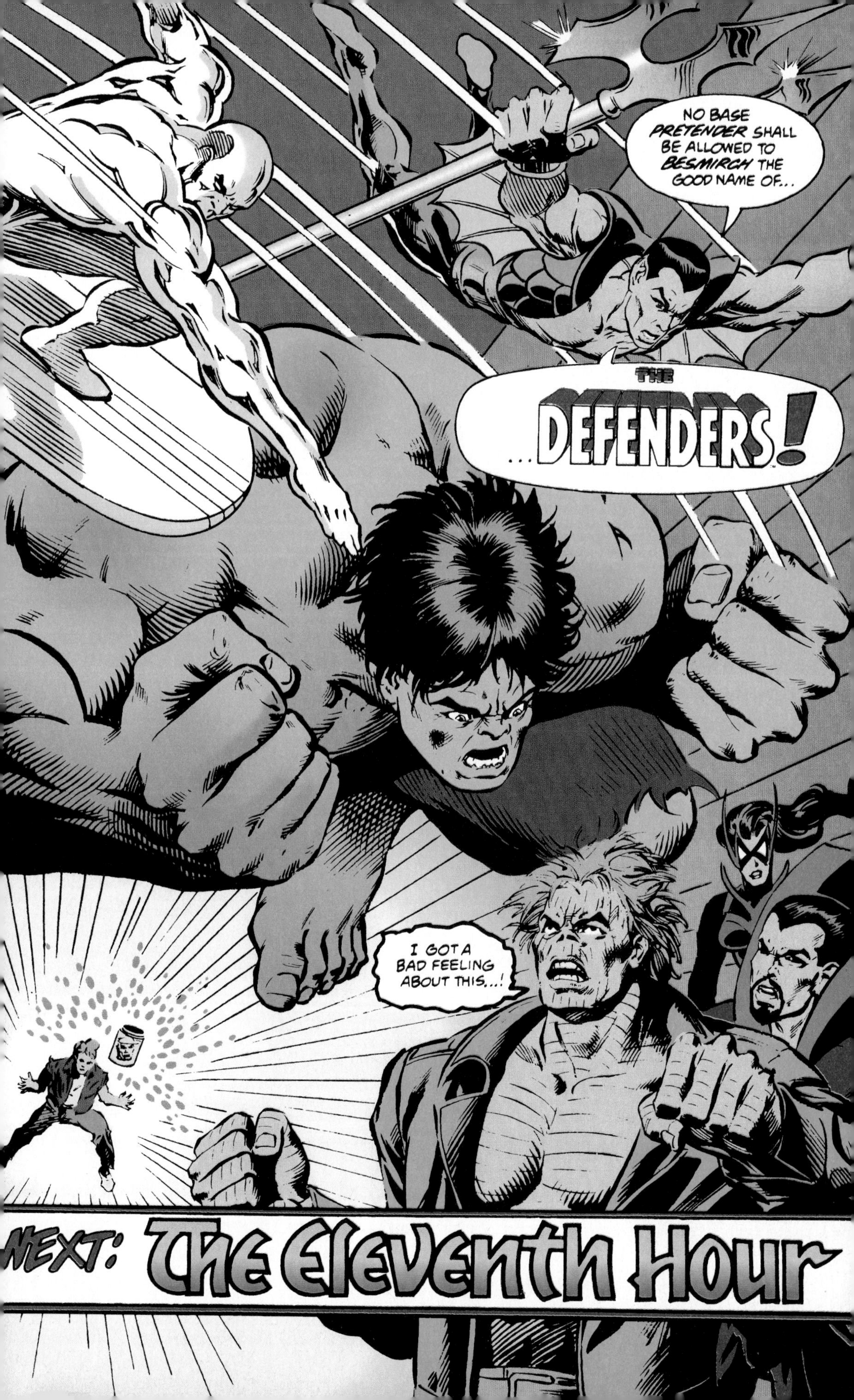

NO BASE PRETENDER SHALL BE ALLOWED TO BESMIRCH THE GOOD NAME OF...
THE ...DEFENDERS!
I GOT A BAD FEELING ABOUT THIS...!
NEXT: The Eleventh Hour

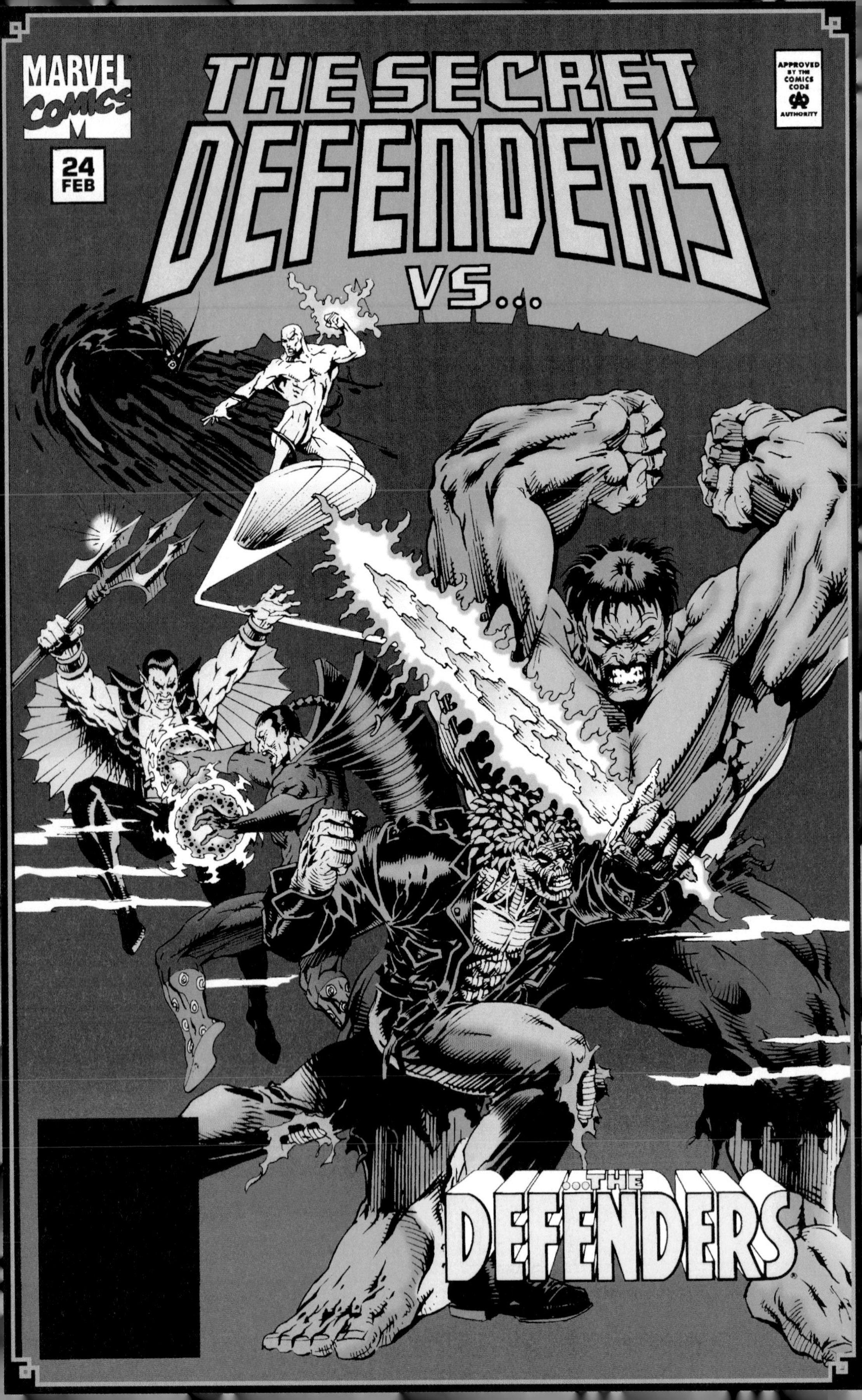
MARVEL COMICS
24 FEB
APPROVED BY THE COMICS CODE AUTHORITY
THE SECRET DEFENDERS
VS...
...THE DEFENDERS

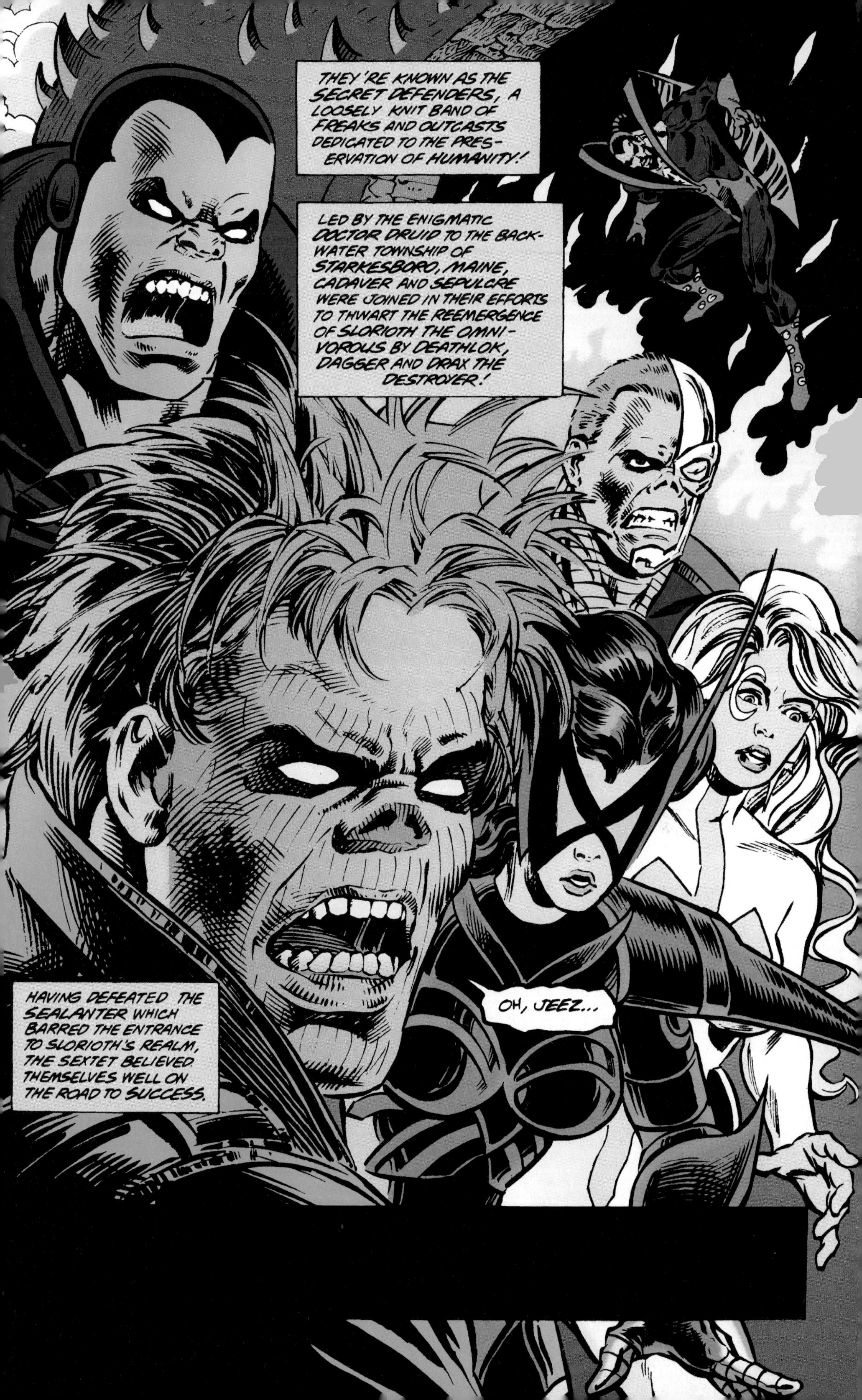
THEY'RE KNOWN AS THE SECRET DEFENDERS, A LOOSELY KNIT BAND OF FREAKS AND OUTCASTS DEDICATED TO THE PRESERVATION OF HUMANITY!
LED BY THE ENIGMATIC DOCTOR DRUID TO THE BACKWATER TOWNSHIP OF STARKESBORO, MAINE, CADAVER AND SEPULCRE WERE JOINED IN THEIR EFFORTS TO THWART THE REEMERGENCE OF SLORIOTH THE OMNIVOROUS BY DEATHLOK, DAGGER AND DRAX THE DESTROYER!
HAVING DEFEATED THE SEALANTER WHICH BARRED THE ENTRANCE TO SLORIOTH'S REALM, THE SEXTET BELIEVED THEMSELVES WELL ON THE ROAD TO SUCCESS.
OH, JEEZ...
[redacted]

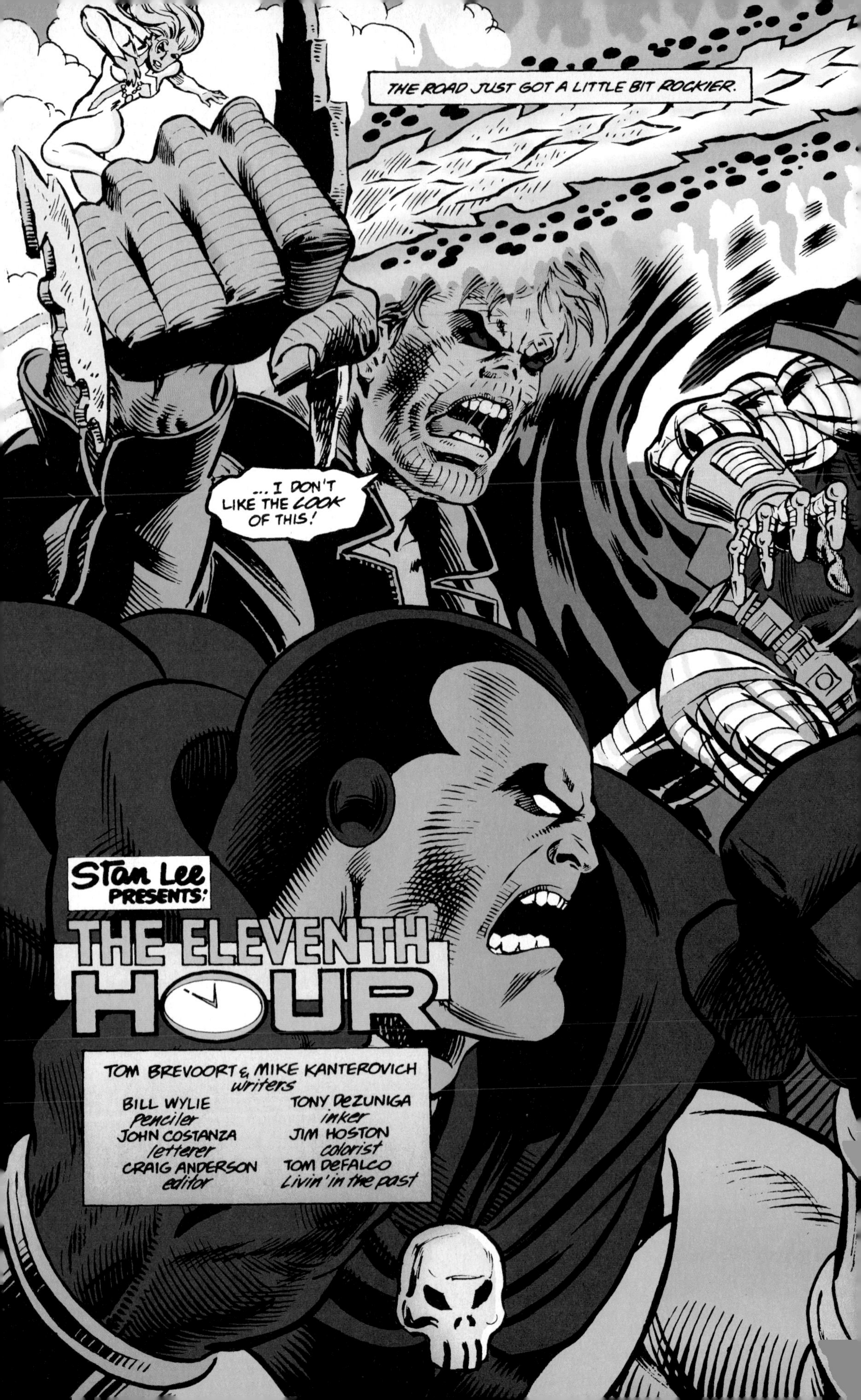
THE ROAD JUST GOT A LITTLE BIT ROCKIER.
...I DON'T LIKE THE LOOK OF THIS!
STAN LEE PRESENTS:
THE ELEVENTH HOUR
TOM BREVOORT & MIKE KANTEROVICH writers
BILL WYLIE penciler
TONY DEZUNIGA inker
JOHN COSTANZA letterer
JIM HOSTON colorist
CRAIG ANDERSON editor
TOM DEFALCO Livin' in the past

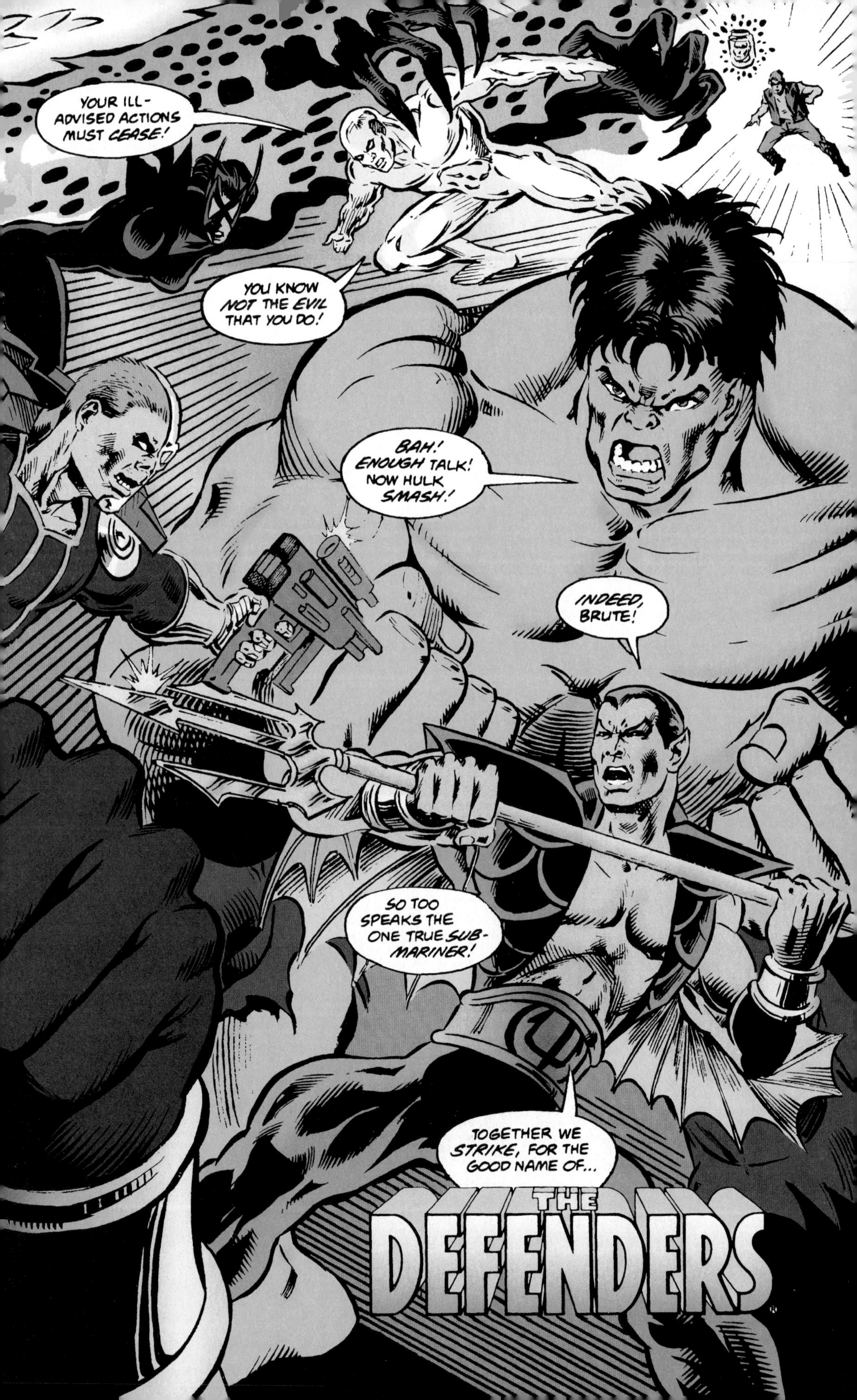
YOUR ILL-ADVISED ACTIONS MUST CEASE!
YOU KNOW NOT THE EVIL THAT YOU DO!
BAH! ENOUGH TALK! NOW HULK SMASH!
INDEED, BRUTE!
SO TOO SPEAKS THE ONE TRUE SUB-MARINER!
TOGETHER WE STRIKE, FOR THE GOOD NAME OF...
THE DEFENDERS

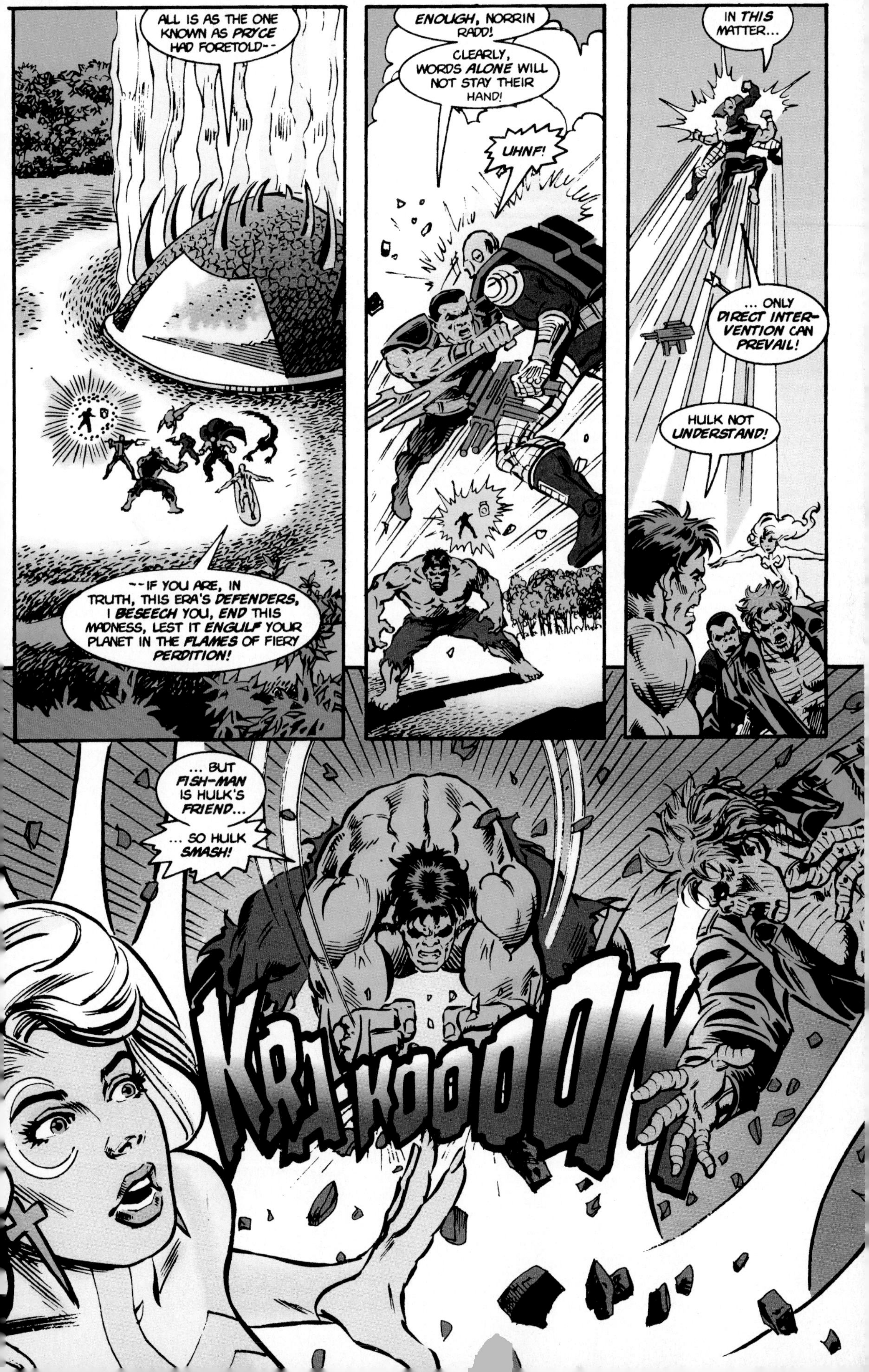

ALL IS AS THE ONE KNOWN AS PRYCE HAD FORETOLD--
--IF YOU ARE, IN TRUTH, THIS ERA'S DEFENDERS, I BESEECH YOU, END THIS MADNESS, LEST IT ENGULF YOUR PLANET IN THE FLAMES OF FIERY PERDITION!
ENOUGH, NORRIN RADD!
CLEARLY, WORDS ALONE WILL NOT STAY THEIR HAND!
UHNF!
IN THIS MATTER...
... ONLY DIRECT INTERVENTION CAN PREVAIL!
HULK NOT UNDERSTAND!
... BUT FISH-MAN IS HULK'S FRIEND...
... SO HULK SMASH!
KRA-KOOOOOM

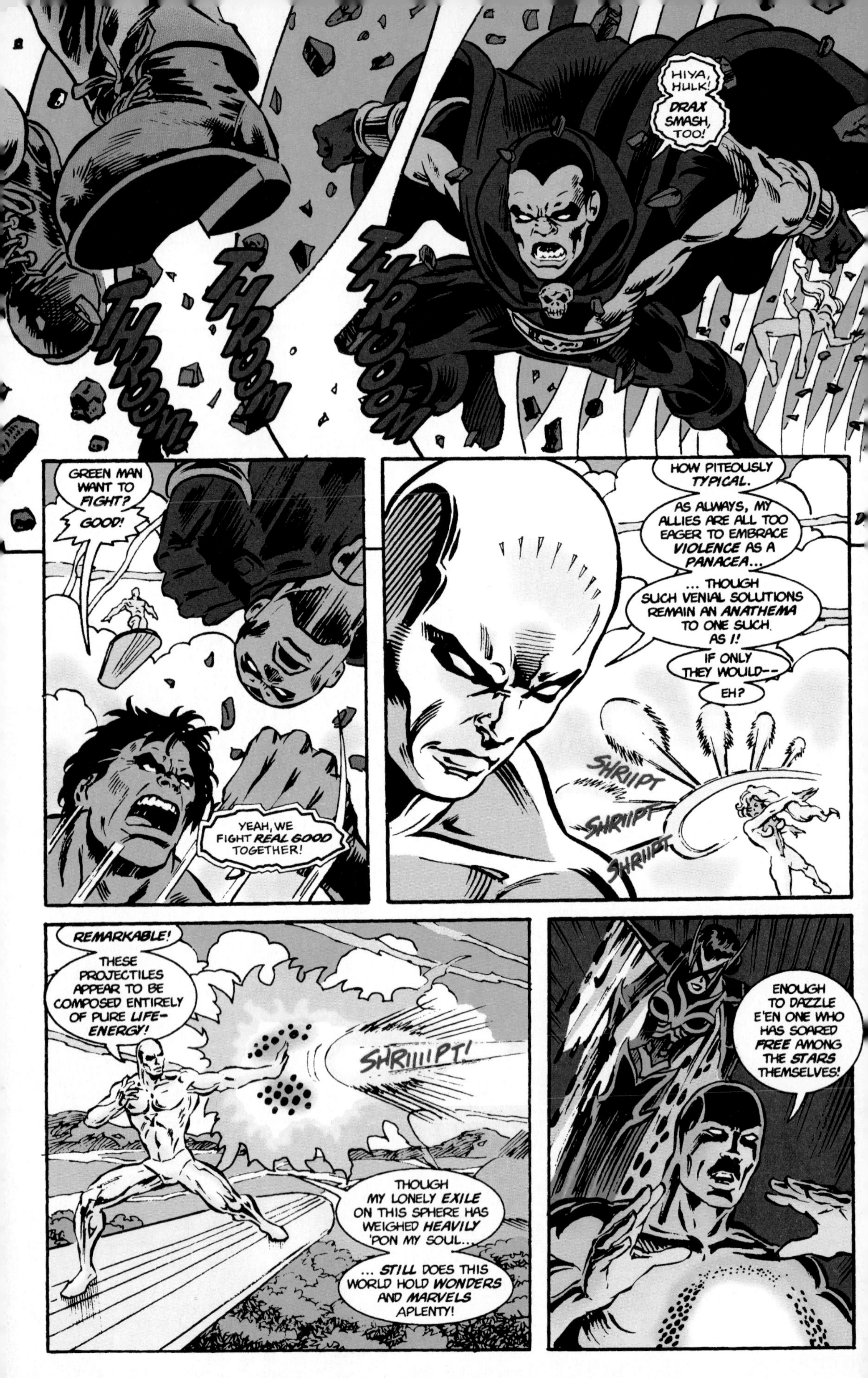
HIYA, HULK! DRAX SMASH, TOO!
THROOM!
THROOM!
THROOOOM!
GREEN MAN WANT TO FIGHT? GOOD!
YEAH, WE FIGHT REAL GOOD TOGETHER!
HOW PITEOUSLY TYPICAL.
AS ALWAYS, MY ALLIES ARE ALL TOO EAGER TO EMBRACE VIOLENCE AS A PANACEA...
... THOUGH SUCH VENIAL SOLUTIONS REMAIN AN ANATHEMA TO ONE SUCH AS I!
IF ONLY THEY WOULD--
EH?
SHRIIPT
SHRIIPT
SHRIIPT
REMARKABLE!
THESE PROJECTILES APPEAR TO BE COMPOSED ENTIRELY OF PURE LIFE-ENERGY!
SHRIIIIPT!
THOUGH MY LONELY EXILE ON THIS SPHERE HAS WEIGHED HEAVILY 'PON MY SOUL...
... STILL DOES THIS WORLD HOLD WONDERS AND MARVELS APLENTY!
ENOUGH TO DAZZLE E'EN ONE WHO HAS SOARED FREE AMONG THE STARS THEMSELVES!

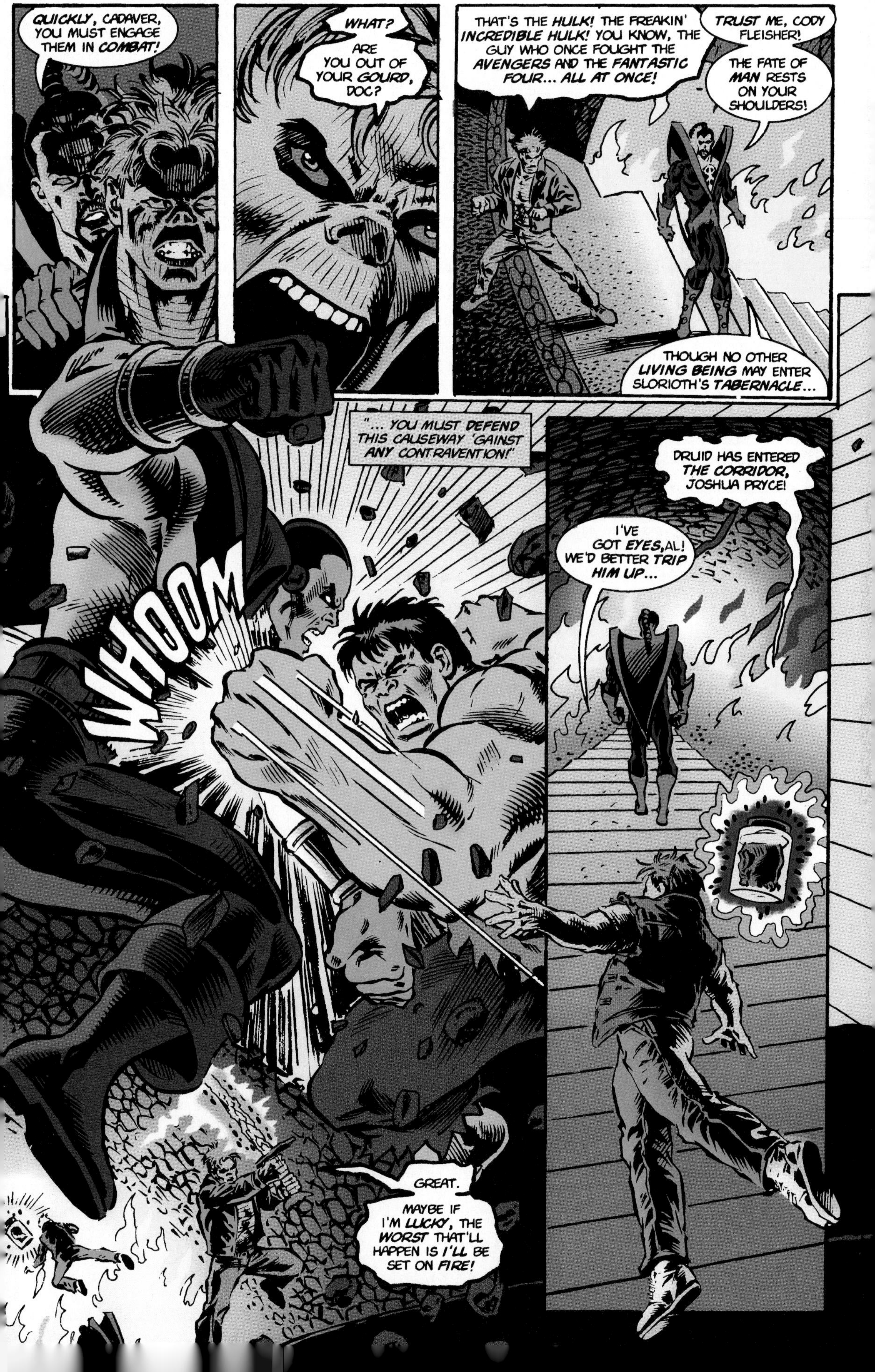
QUICKLY, CADAVER, YOU MUST ENGAGE THEM IN COMBAT!
WHAT?
ARE YOU OUT OF YOUR GOURD, DOC?
THAT'S THE HULK! THE FREAKIN' INCREDIBLE HULK! YOU KNOW, THE GUY WHO ONCE FOUGHT THE AVENGERS AND THE FANTASTIC FOUR... ALL AT ONCE!
TRUST ME, CODY FLEISHER!
THE FATE OF MAN RESTS ON YOUR SHOULDERS!
THOUGH NO OTHER LIVING BEING MAY ENTER SLORIOTH'S TABERNACLE...
"... YOU MUST DEFEND THIS CAUSEWAY 'GAINST ANY CONTRAVENTION!"
WHOOM
DRUID HAS ENTERED THE CORRIDOR, JOSHUA PRYCE!
I'VE GOT EYES, AL! WE'D BETTER TRIP HIM UP...
GREAT.
MAYBE IF I'M LUCKY, THE WORST THAT'LL HAPPEN IS I'LL BE SET ON FIRE!

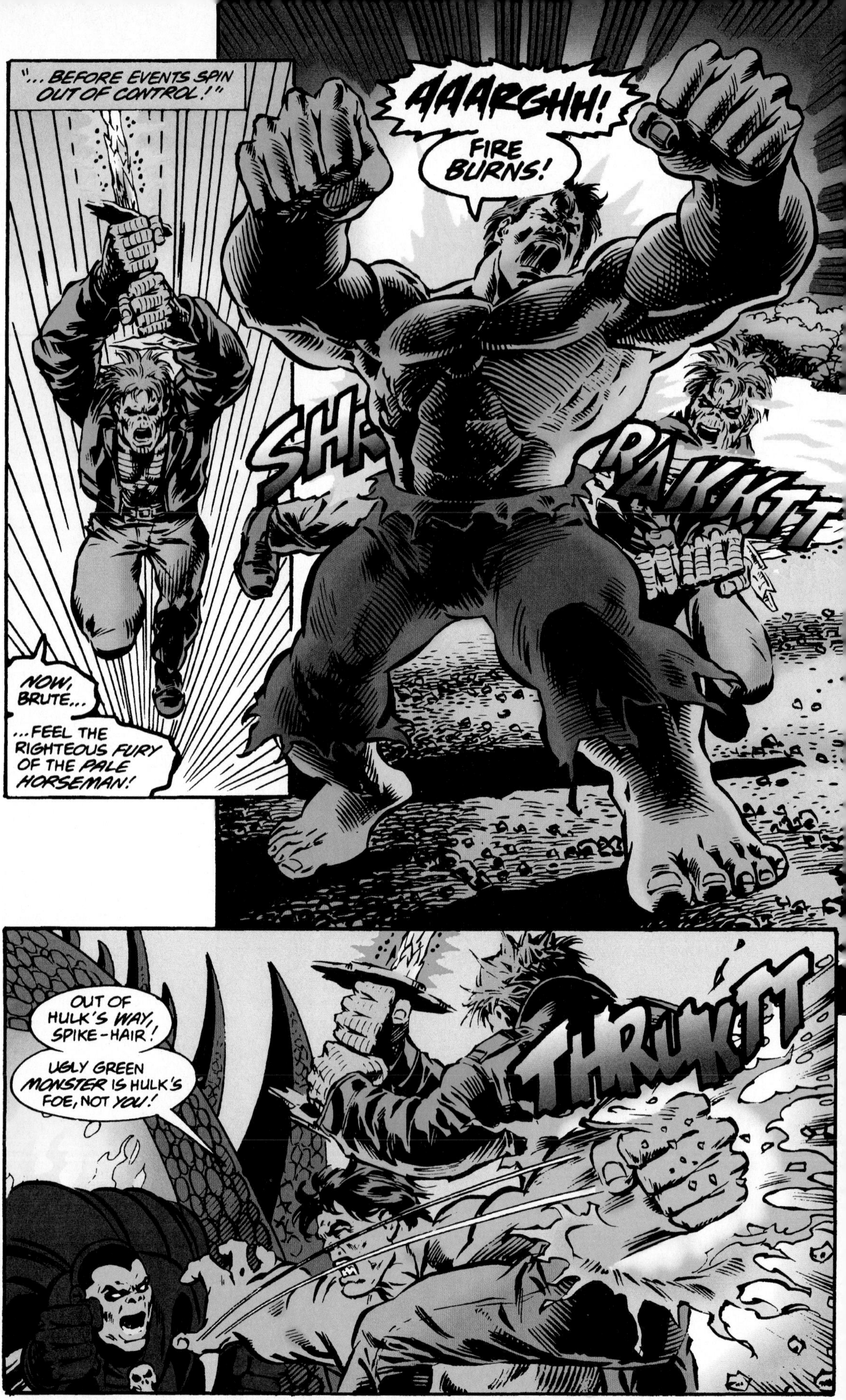
"...BEFORE EVENTS SPIN OUT OF CONTROL!"
AAARGHH!
FIRE BURNS!
NOW, BRUTE...
...FEEL THE RIGHTEOUS FURY OF THE PALE HORSEMAN!
SHH
RAKKTT
OUT OF HULK'S WAY, SPIKE-HAIR!
UGLY GREEN MONSTER IS HULK'S FOE, NOT YOU!
THRUKTT

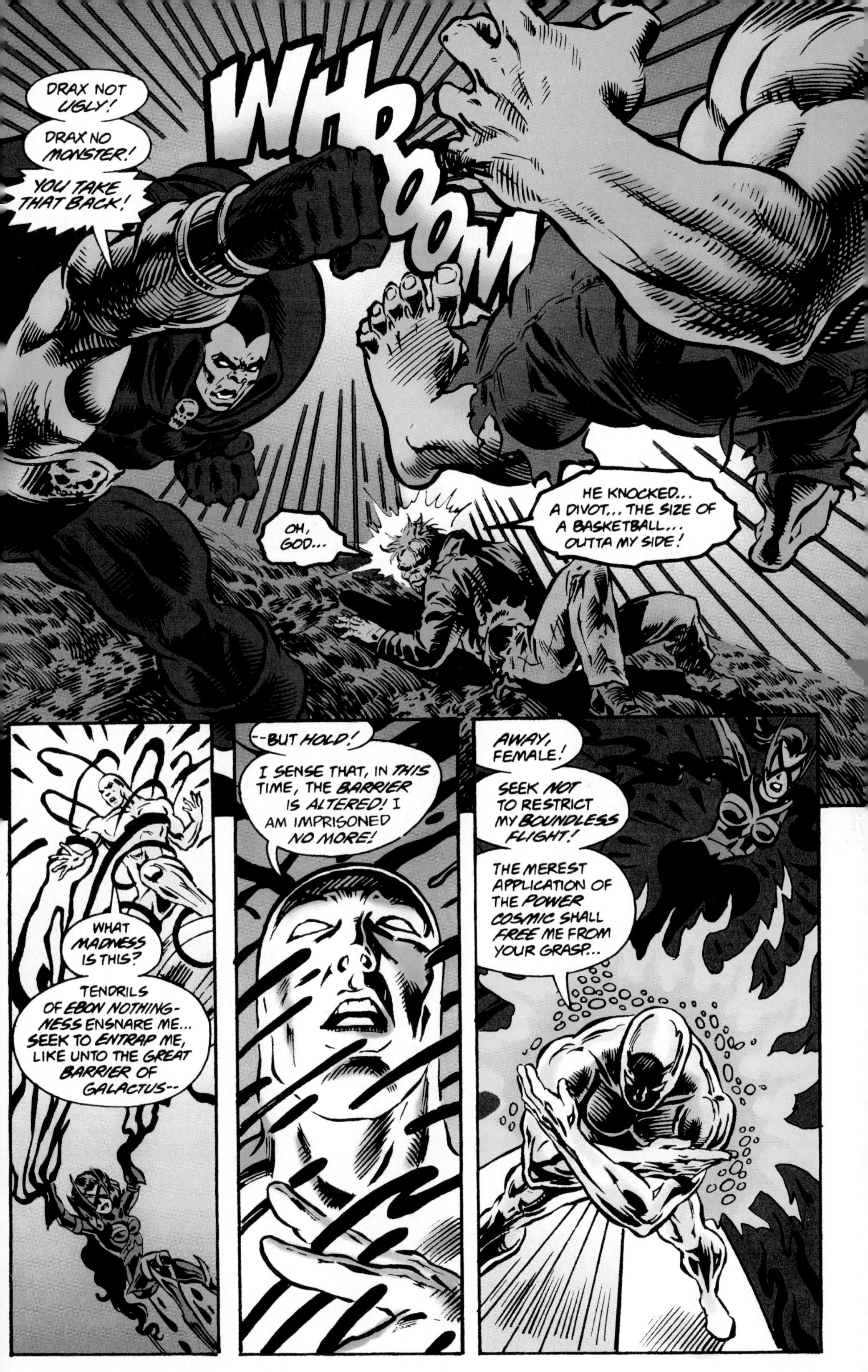
WHOOOOM
DRAX NOT UGLY!
DRAX NO MONSTER!
YOU TAKE THAT BACK!
OH, GOD...
HE KNOCKED... A DIVOT... THE SIZE OF A BASKETBALL... OUTTA MY SIDE!
WHAT MADNESS IS THIS?
TENDRILS OF EBON NOTHING-NESS ENSNARE ME... SEEK TO ENTRAP ME, LIKE UNTO THE GREAT BARRIER OF GALACTUS--
--BUT HOLD!
I SENSE THAT, IN THIS TIME, THE BARRIER IS ALTERED! I AM IMPRISONED NO MORE!
AWAY, FEMALE!
SEEK NOT TO RESTRICT MY BOUNDLESS FLIGHT!
THE MEREST APPLICATION OF THE POWER COSMIC SHALL FREE ME FROM YOUR GRASP...

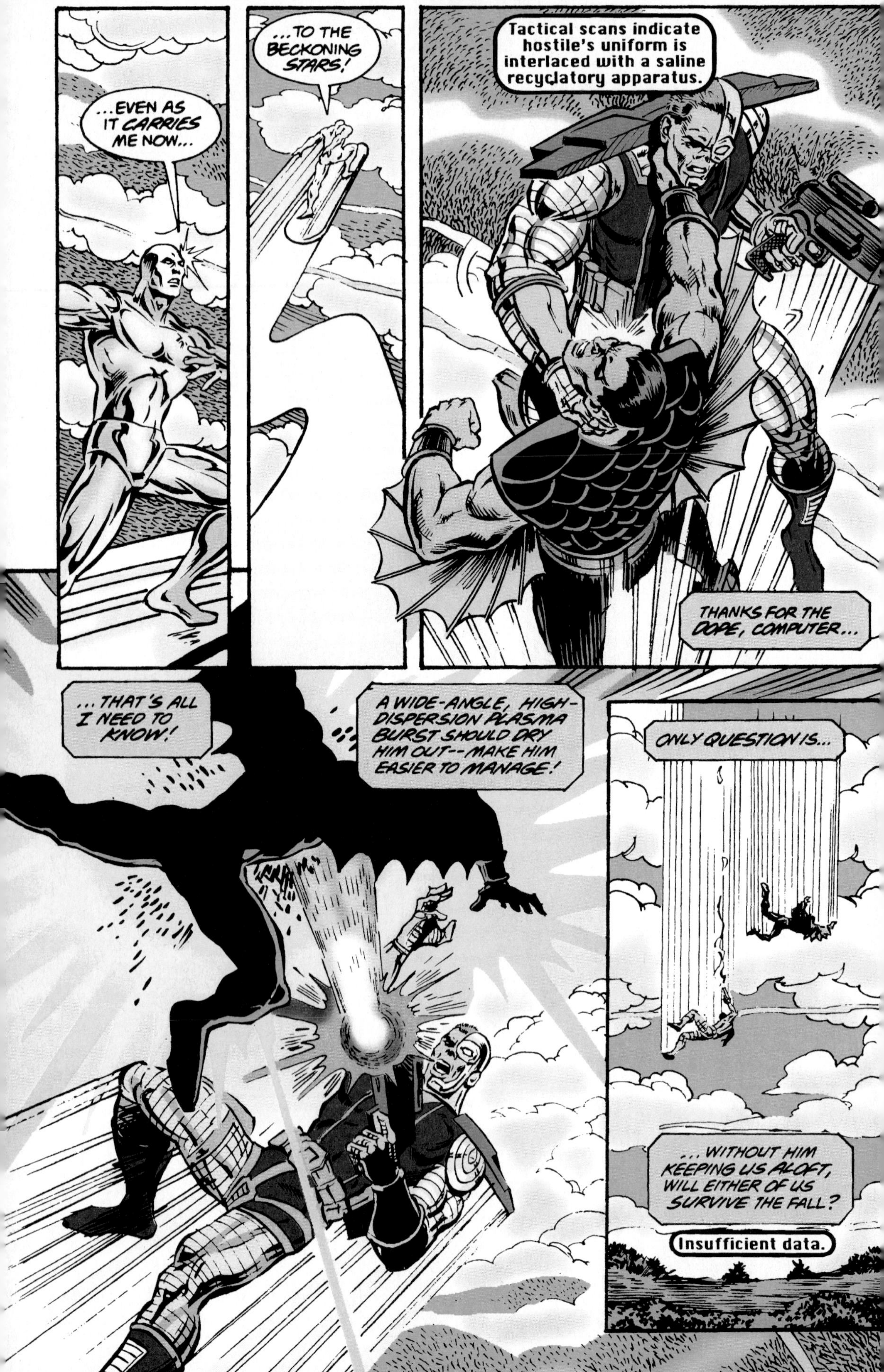
...EVEN AS IT CARRIES ME NOW...
...TO THE BECKONING STARS!
Tactical scans indicate hostile's uniform is interlaced with a saline recyclatory apparatus.
THANKS FOR THE DOPE, COMPUTER...
...THAT'S ALL I NEED TO KNOW!
A WIDE-ANGLE, HIGH-DISPERSION PLASMA BURST SHOULD DRY HIM OUT--MAKE HIM EASIER TO MANAGE!
ONLY QUESTION IS...
...WITHOUT HIM KEEPING US ALOFT, WILL EITHER OF US SURVIVE THE FALL?
Insufficient data.

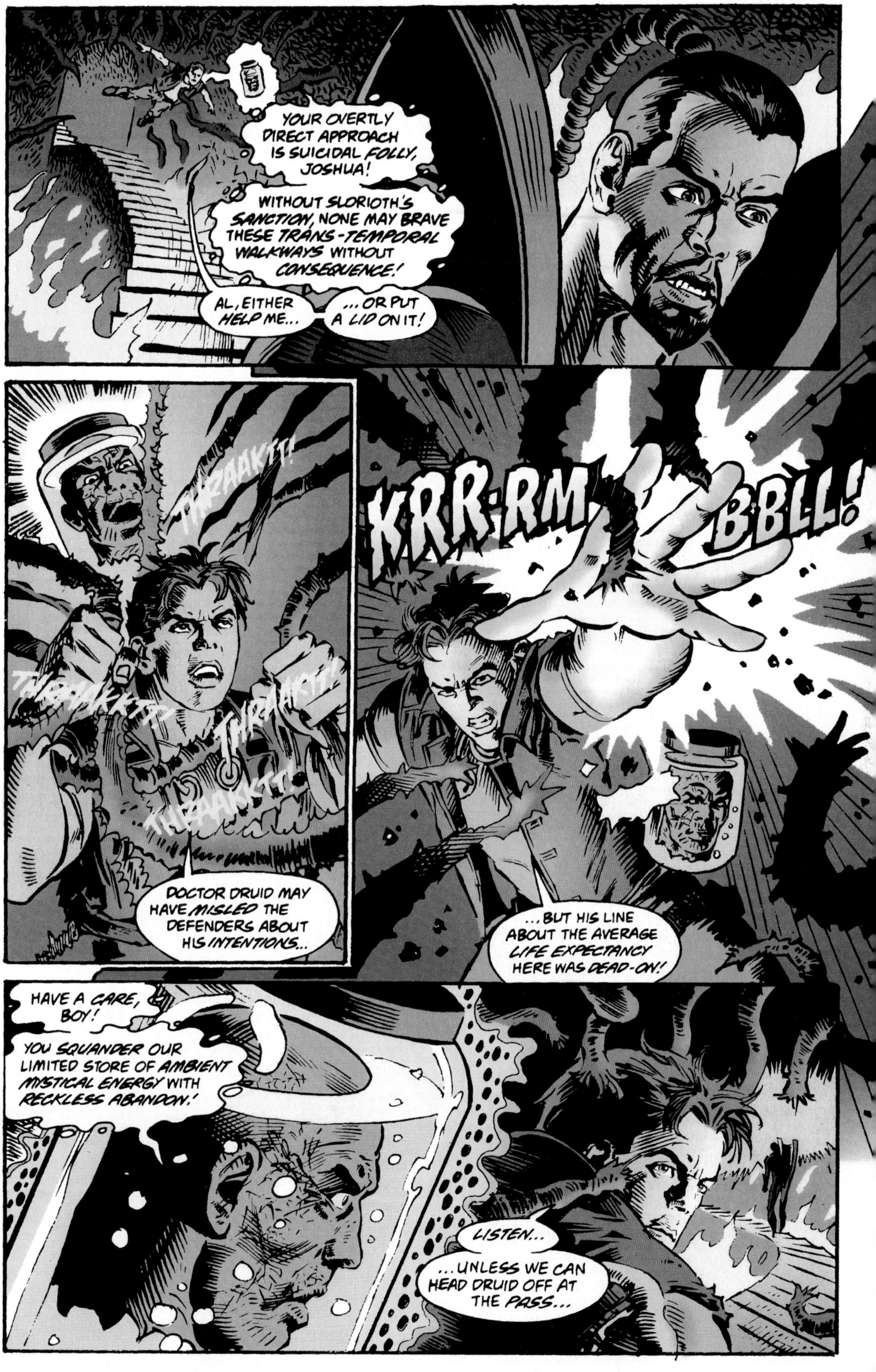
YOUR OVERTLY DIRECT APPROACH IS SUICIDAL FOLLY, JOSHUA!
WITHOUT SLORIOTH'S SANCTION, NONE MAY BRAVE THESE TRANS-TEMPORAL WALKWAYS WITHOUT CONSEQUENCE!
AL, EITHER HELP ME...
...OR PUT A LID ON IT!
THRAAKTT!
THRAAKTT!
THRAAKTT!
THRAAKTT!
THRAAKTT!
DOCTOR DRUID MAY HAVE MISLED THE DEFENDERS ABOUT HIS INTENTIONS...
KRR-RM BBLL!
...BUT HIS LINE ABOUT THE AVERAGE LIFE EXPECTANCY HERE WAS DEAD-ON!
HAVE A CARE, BOY!
YOU SQUANDER OUR LIMITED STORE OF AMBIENT MYSTICAL ENERGY WITH RECKLESS ABANDON!
LISTEN...
...UNLESS WE CAN HEAD DRUID OFF AT THE PASS...

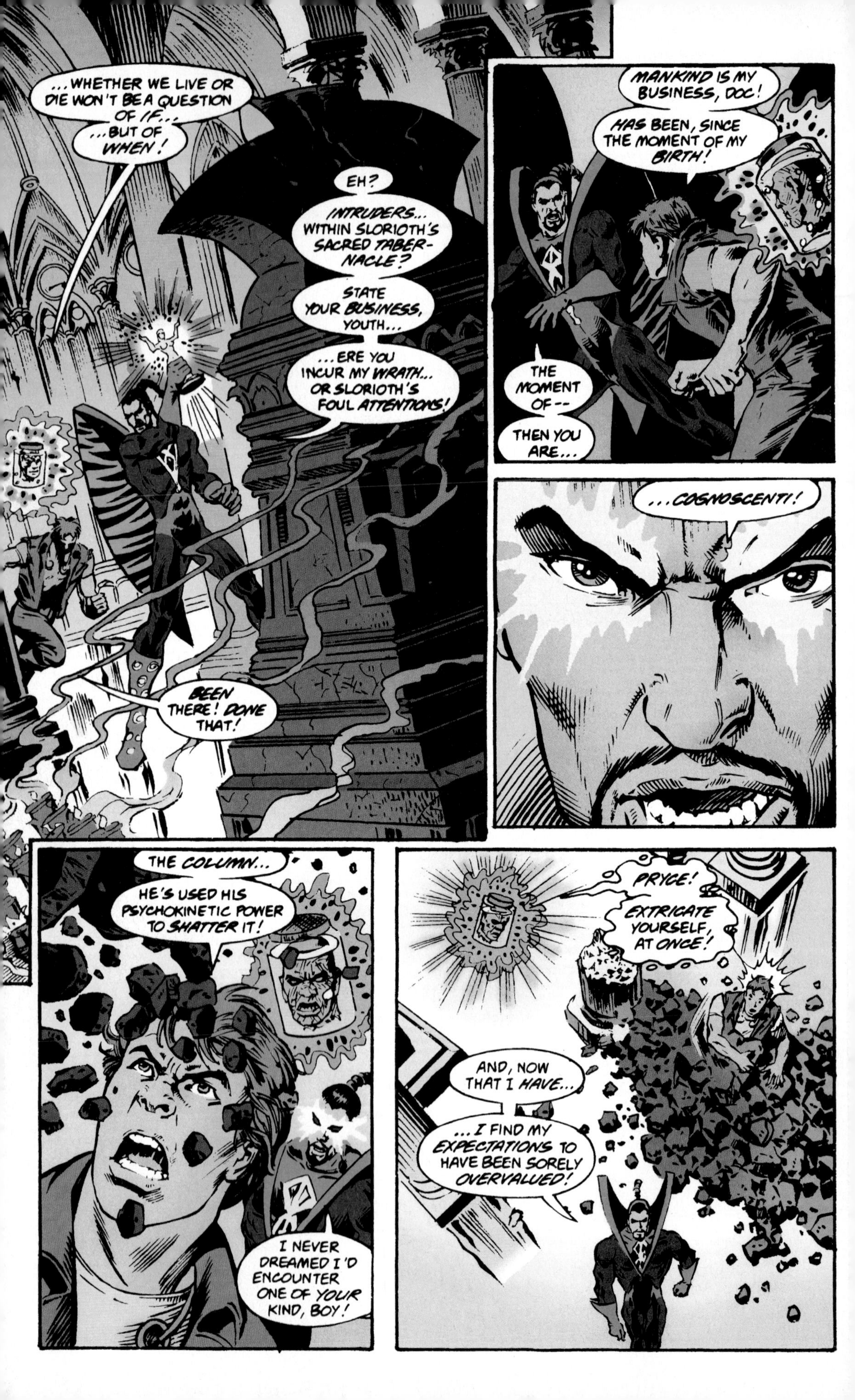
...WHETHER WE LIVE OR DIE WON'T BE A QUESTION OF IF...
...BUT OF WHEN!
EH?
INTRUDERS... WITHIN SLORIOTH'S SACRED TABER-NACLE?
STATE YOUR BUSINESS, YOUTH...
...ERE YOU INCUR MY WRATH... OR SLORIOTH'S FOUL ATTENTIONS!
BEEN THERE! DONE THAT!
MANKIND IS MY BUSINESS, DOC!
HAS BEEN, SINCE THE MOMENT OF MY BIRTH!
THE MOMENT OF--
THEN YOU ARE...
...COGNOSCENTI!
THE COLUMN...
HE'S USED HIS PSYCHOKINETIC POWER TO SHATTER IT!
I NEVER DREAMED I'D ENCOUNTER ONE OF YOUR KIND, BOY!
PRYCE!
EXTRICATE YOURSELF, AT ONCE!
AND, NOW THAT I HAVE...
...I FIND MY EXPECTATIONS TO HAVE BEEN SORELY OVERVALUED!

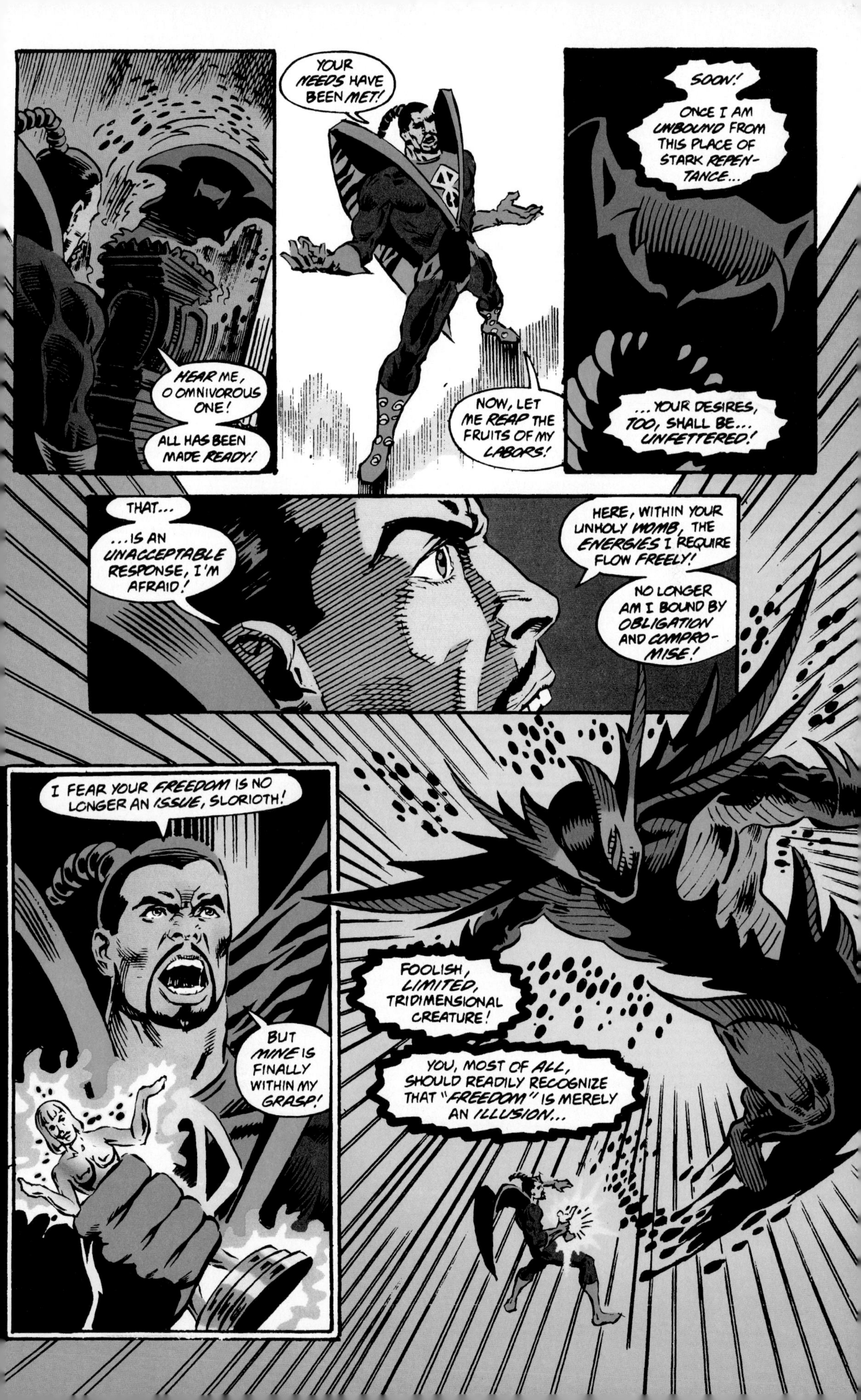
HEAR ME, O OMNIVOROUS ONE!
ALL HAS BEEN MADE READY!
YOUR NEEDS HAVE BEEN MET!
NOW, LET ME REAP THE FRUITS OF MY LABORS!
SOON!
ONCE I AM UNBOUND FROM THIS PLACE OF STARK REPEN-TANCE...
...YOUR DESIRES, TOO, SHALL BE... UNFETTERED!
THAT...
...IS AN UNACCEPTABLE RESPONSE, I'M AFRAID!
HERE, WITHIN YOUR UNHOLY WOMB, THE ENERGIES I REQUIRE FLOW FREELY!
NO LONGER AM I BOUND BY OBLIGATION AND COMPRO-MISE!
I FEAR YOUR FREEDOM IS NO LONGER AN ISSUE, SLORIOTH!
BUT MINE IS FINALLY WITHIN MY GRASP!
FOOLISH, LIMITED, TRIDIMENSIONAL CREATURE!
YOU, MOST OF ALL, SHOULD READILY RECOGNIZE THAT "FREEDOM" IS MERELY AN ILLUSION...

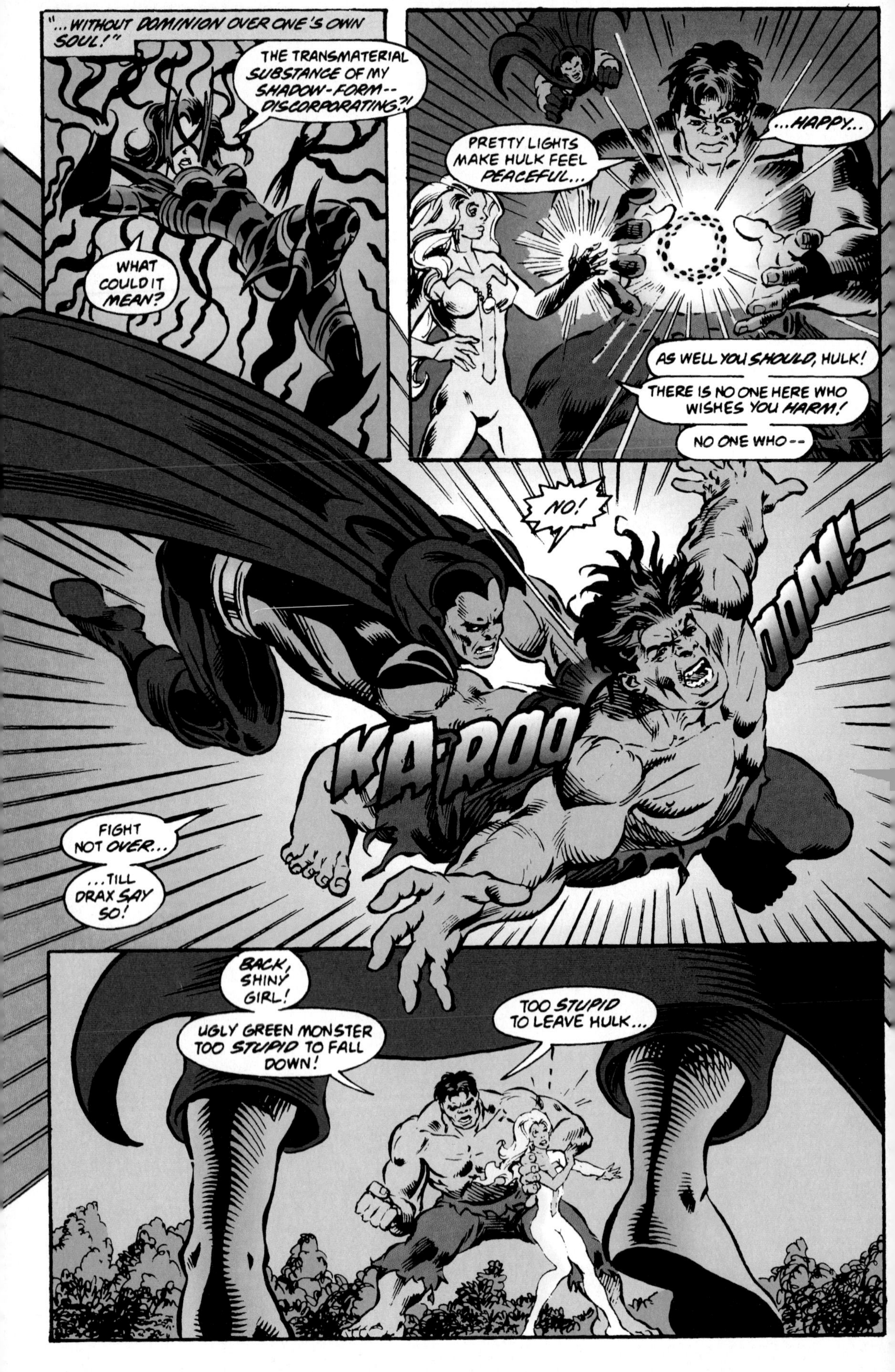
"...WITHOUT DOMINION OVER ONE'S OWN SOUL!"
THE TRANSMATERIAL SUBSTANCE OF MY SHADOW-FORM--DISCORPORATING?!
WHAT COULD IT MEAN?
PRETTY LIGHTS MAKE HULK FEEL PEACEFUL...
...HAPPY...
AS WELL YOU SHOULD, HULK!
THERE IS NO ONE HERE WHO WISHES YOU HARM!
NO ONE WHO--
NO!
KA-ROOOOM!
FIGHT NOT OVER...
...TILL DRAX SAY SO!
BACK, SHINY GIRL!
UGLY GREEN MONSTER TOO STUPID TO FALL DOWN!
TOO STUPID TO LEAVE HULK...

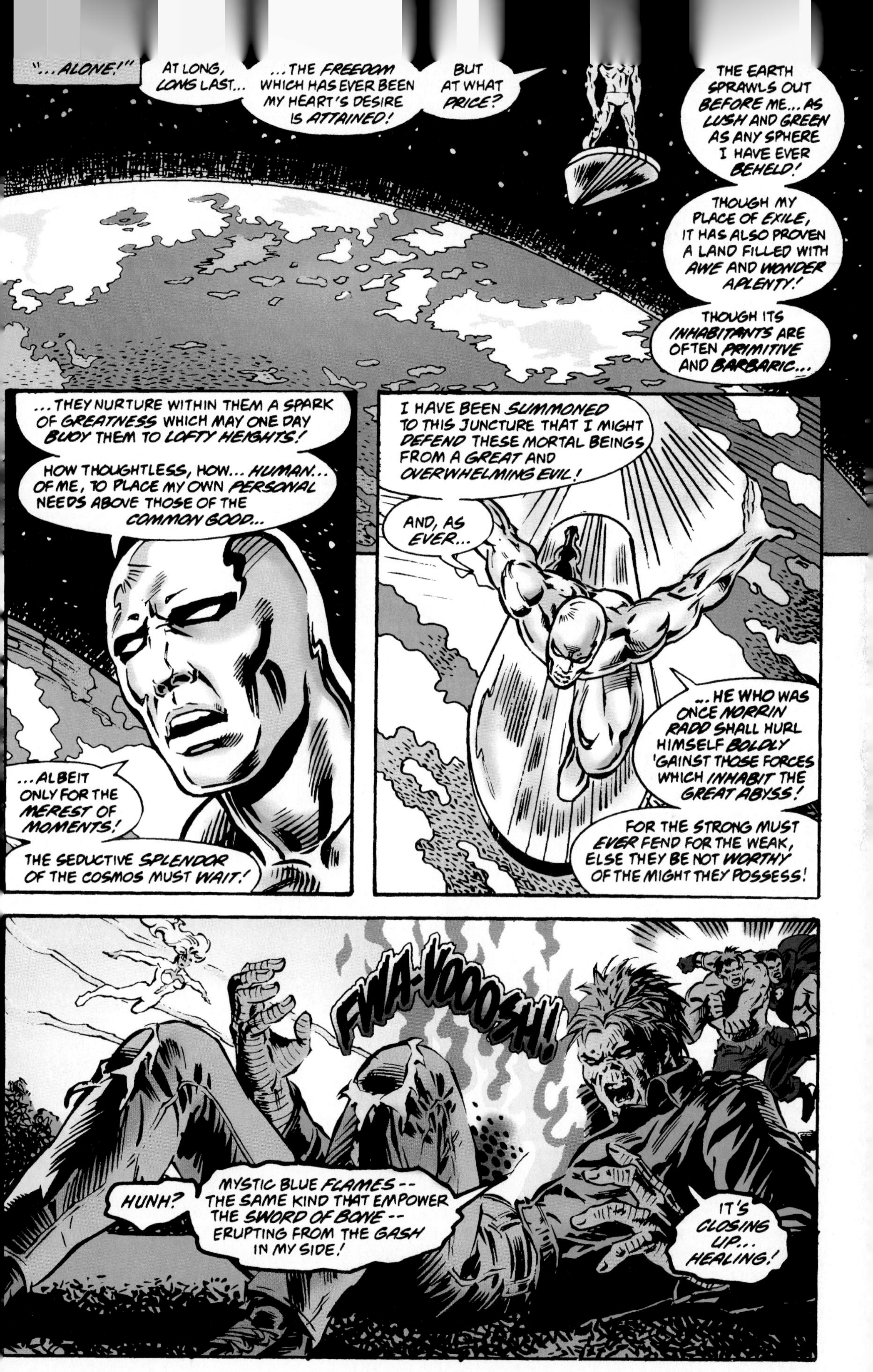
"...ALONE!"
AT LONG, LONG LAST...
...THE FREEDOM WHICH HAS EVER BEEN MY HEART'S DESIRE IS ATTAINED!
BUT AT WHAT PRICE?
THE EARTH SPRAWLS OUT BEFORE ME... AS LUSH AND GREEN AS ANY SPHERE I HAVE EVER BEHELD!
THOUGH MY PLACE OF EXILE, IT HAS ALSO PROVEN A LAND FILLED WITH AWE AND WONDER APLENTY!
THOUGH ITS INHABITANTS ARE OFTEN PRIMITIVE AND BARBARIC...
...THEY NURTURE WITHIN THEM A SPARK OF GREATNESS WHICH MAY ONE DAY BUOY THEM TO LOFTY HEIGHTS!
HOW THOUGHTLESS, HOW... HUMAN... OF ME, TO PLACE MY OWN PERSONAL NEEDS ABOVE THOSE OF THE COMMON GOOD...
...ALBEIT ONLY FOR THE MEREST OF MOMENTS!
THE SEDUCTIVE SPLENDOR OF THE COSMOS MUST WAIT!
I HAVE BEEN SUMMONED TO THIS JUNCTURE THAT I MIGHT DEFEND THESE MORTAL BEINGS FROM A GREAT AND OVERWHELMING EVIL!
AND, AS EVER...
...HE WHO WAS ONCE NORRIN RADD SHALL HURL HIMSELF BOLDLY 'GAINST THOSE FORCES WHICH INHABIT THE GREAT ABYSS!
FOR THE STRONG MUST EVER FEND FOR THE WEAK, ELSE THEY BE NOT WORTHY OF THE MIGHT THEY POSSESS!
FWA-VOOOSH!
HUNH?
MYSTIC BLUE FLAMES -- THE SAME KIND THAT EMPOWER THE SWORD OF BONE -- ERUPTING FROM THE GASH IN MY SIDE!
IT'S CLOSING UP... HEALING!

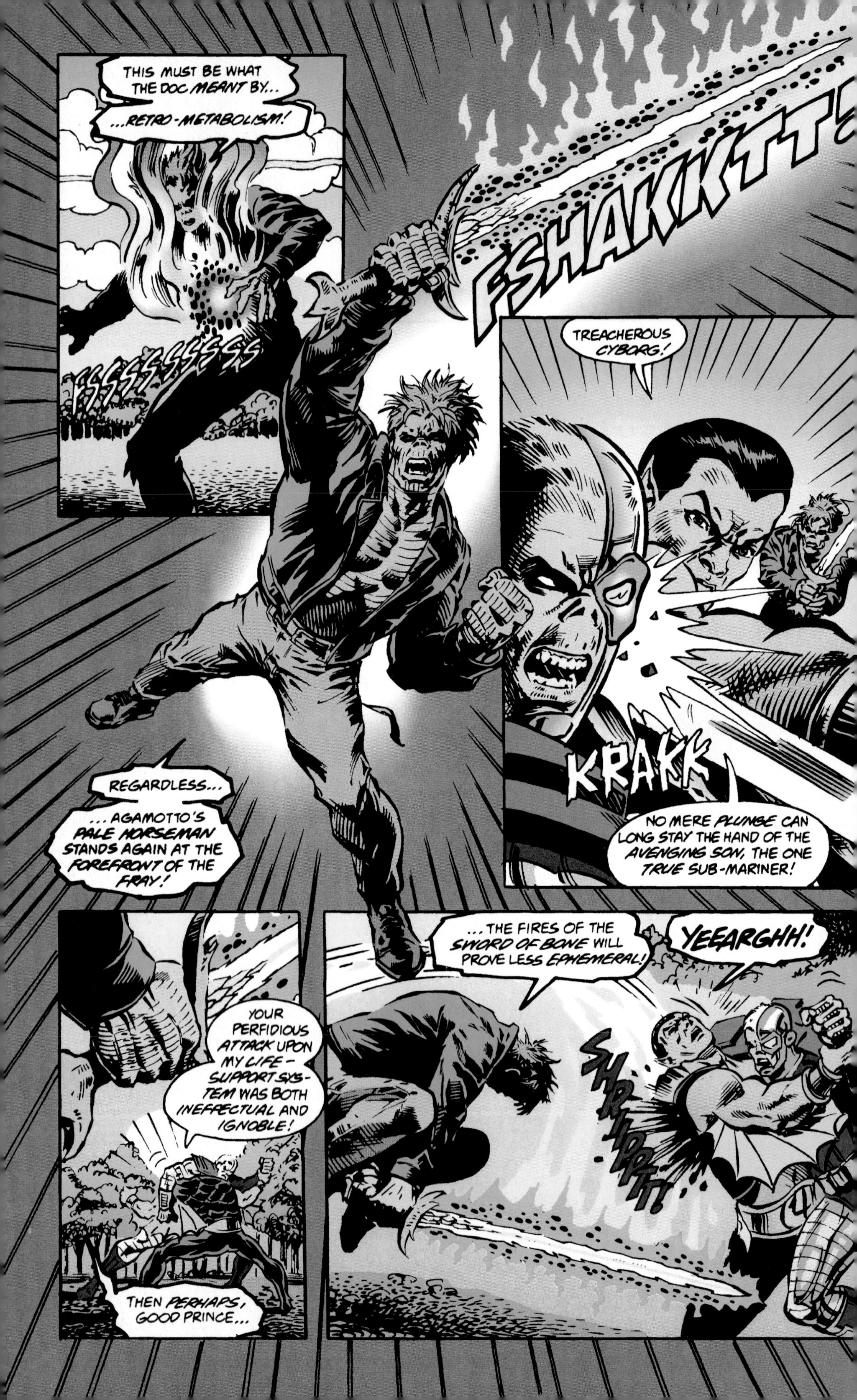

THIS MUST BE WHAT THE DOC MEANT BY...
...RETRO-METABOLISM!
FSSSSSSSSSS
FSHAKKTT
TREACHEROUS CYBORG!
REGARDLESS...
...AGAMOTTO'S PALE HORSEMAN STANDS AGAIN AT THE FOREFRONT OF THE FRAY!
KRAKK
NO MERE PLUNGE CAN LONG STAY THE HAND OF THE AVENGING SON, THE ONE TRUE SUB-MARINER!
YOUR PERFIDIOUS ATTACK UPON MY LIFE-SUPPORT SYSTEM WAS BOTH INEFFECTUAL AND IGNOBLE!
THEN PERHAPS, GOOD PRINCE...
...THE FIRES OF THE SWORD OF BONE WILL PROVE LESS EPHEMERAL!
YEEARGHH!
SHRIPPT!

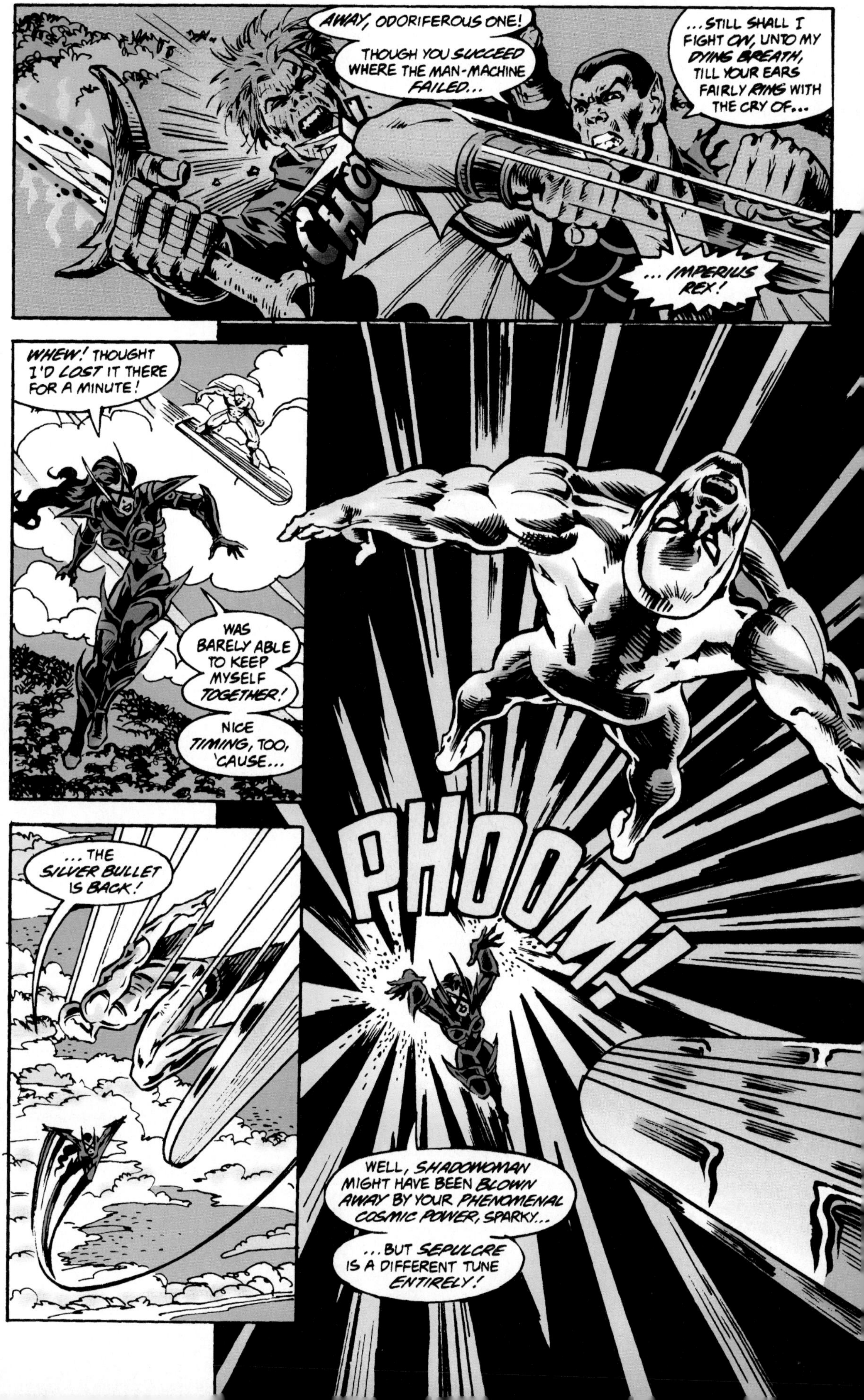
AWAY, ODORIFEROUS ONE!
THOUGH YOU SUCCEED WHERE THE MAN-MACHINE FAILED...
...STILL SHALL I FIGHT ON, UNTO MY DYING BREATH, TILL YOUR EARS FAIRLY RING WITH THE CRY OF...
...IMPERIUS REX!
WHEW! THOUGHT I'D LOST IT THERE FOR A MINUTE!
WAS BARELY ABLE TO KEEP MYSELF TOGETHER!
NICE TIMING, TOO, 'CAUSE...
...THE SILVER BULLET IS BACK!
PHOOM!
WELL, SHADOWOMAN MIGHT HAVE BEEN BLOWN AWAY BY YOUR PHENOMENAL COSMIC POWER, SPARKY...
...BUT SEPULCRE IS A DIFFERENT TUNE ENTIRELY!

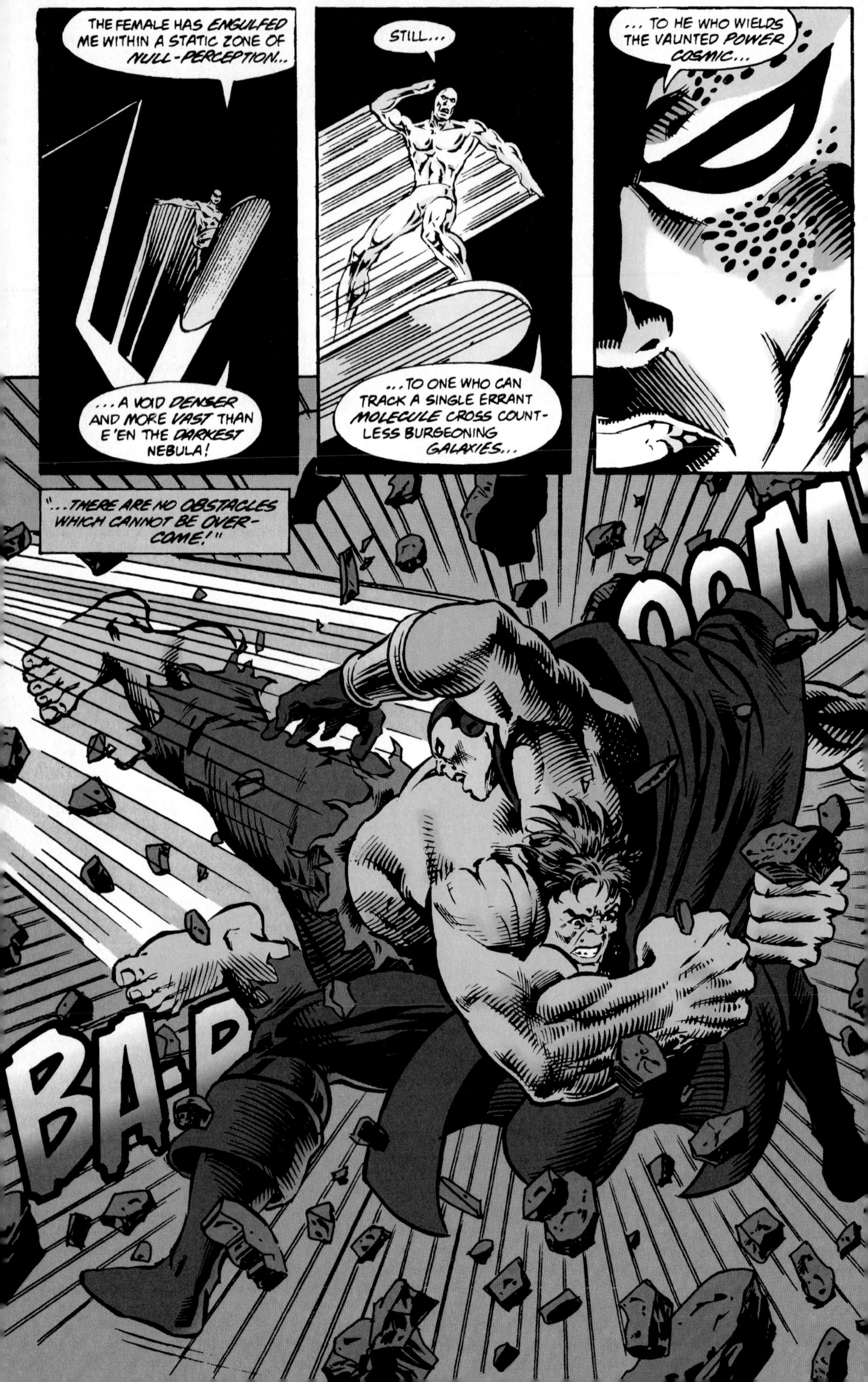
THE FEMALE HAS ENGULFED ME WITHIN A STATIC ZONE OF NULL-PERCEPTION...
...A VOID DENSER AND MORE VAST THAN E'EN THE DARKEST NEBULA!
STILL...
...TO ONE WHO CAN TRACK A SINGLE ERRANT MOLECULE CROSS COUNT-LESS BURGEONING GALAXIES...
... TO HE WHO WIELDS THE VAUNTED POWER COSMIC...
"...THERE ARE NO OBSTACLES WHICH CANNOT BE OVER-COME!"
BA-D
OOM

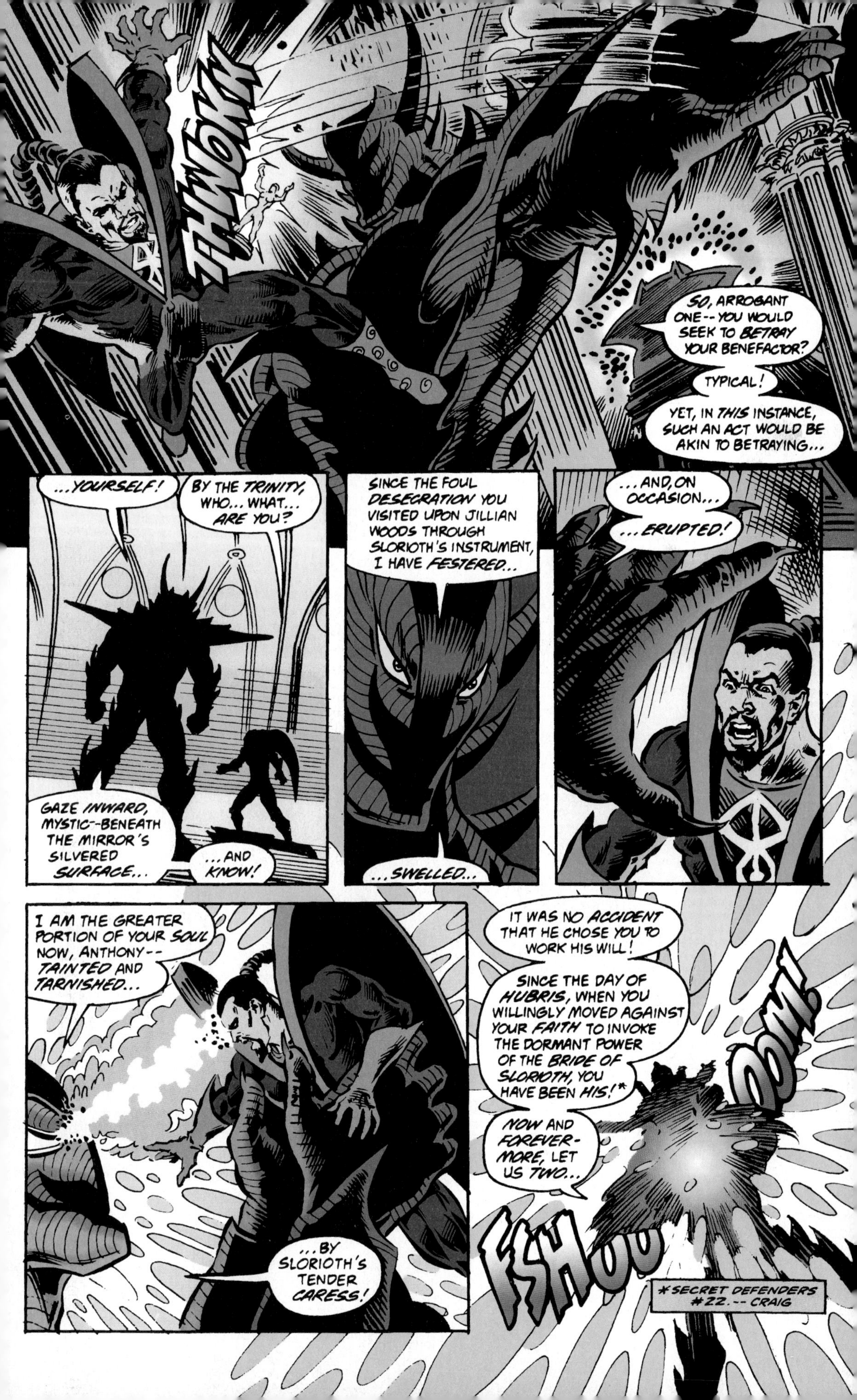
WHOMM!
SO, ARROGANT ONE--YOU WOULD SEEK TO BETRAY YOUR BENEFACTOR?
TYPICAL!
YET, IN THIS INSTANCE, SUCH AN ACT WOULD BE AKIN TO BETRAYING...
...YOURSELF!
BY THE TRINITY, WHO... WHAT... ARE YOU?
GAZE INWARD, MYSTIC--BENEATH THE MIRROR'S SILVERED SURFACE...
...AND KNOW!
SINCE THE FOUL DESECRATION YOU VISITED UPON JILLIAN WOODS THROUGH SLORIOTH'S INSTRUMENT, I HAVE FESTERED...
...SWELLED...
...AND, ON OCCASION...
...ERUPTED!
I AM THE GREATER PORTION OF YOUR SOUL NOW, ANTHONY--TAINTED AND TARNISHED...
...BY SLORIOTH'S TENDER CARESS!
IT WAS NO ACCIDENT THAT HE CHOSE YOU TO WORK HIS WILL!
SINCE THE DAY OF HUBRIS, WHEN YOU WILLINGLY MOVED AGAINST YOUR FAITH TO INVOKE THE DORMANT POWER OF THE BRIDE OF SLORIOTH, YOU HAVE BEEN HIS!*
NOW AND FOREVERMORE, LET US TWO...
FSHOOOOM!
*SECRET DEFENDERS #22.--CRAIG

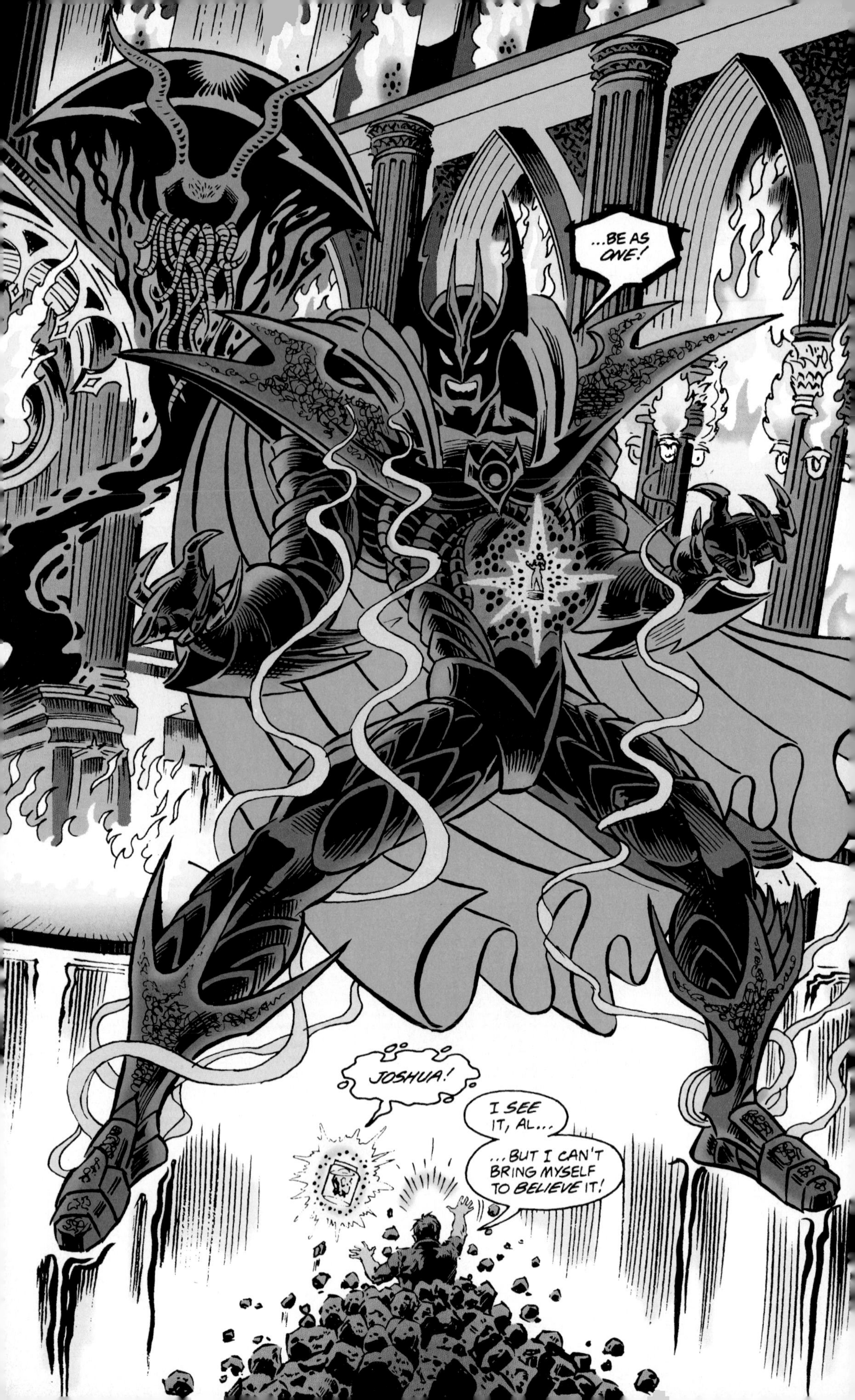
...BE AS ONE!
JOSHUA!
I SEE IT, AL...
...BUT I CAN'T BRING MYSELF TO BELIEVE IT!

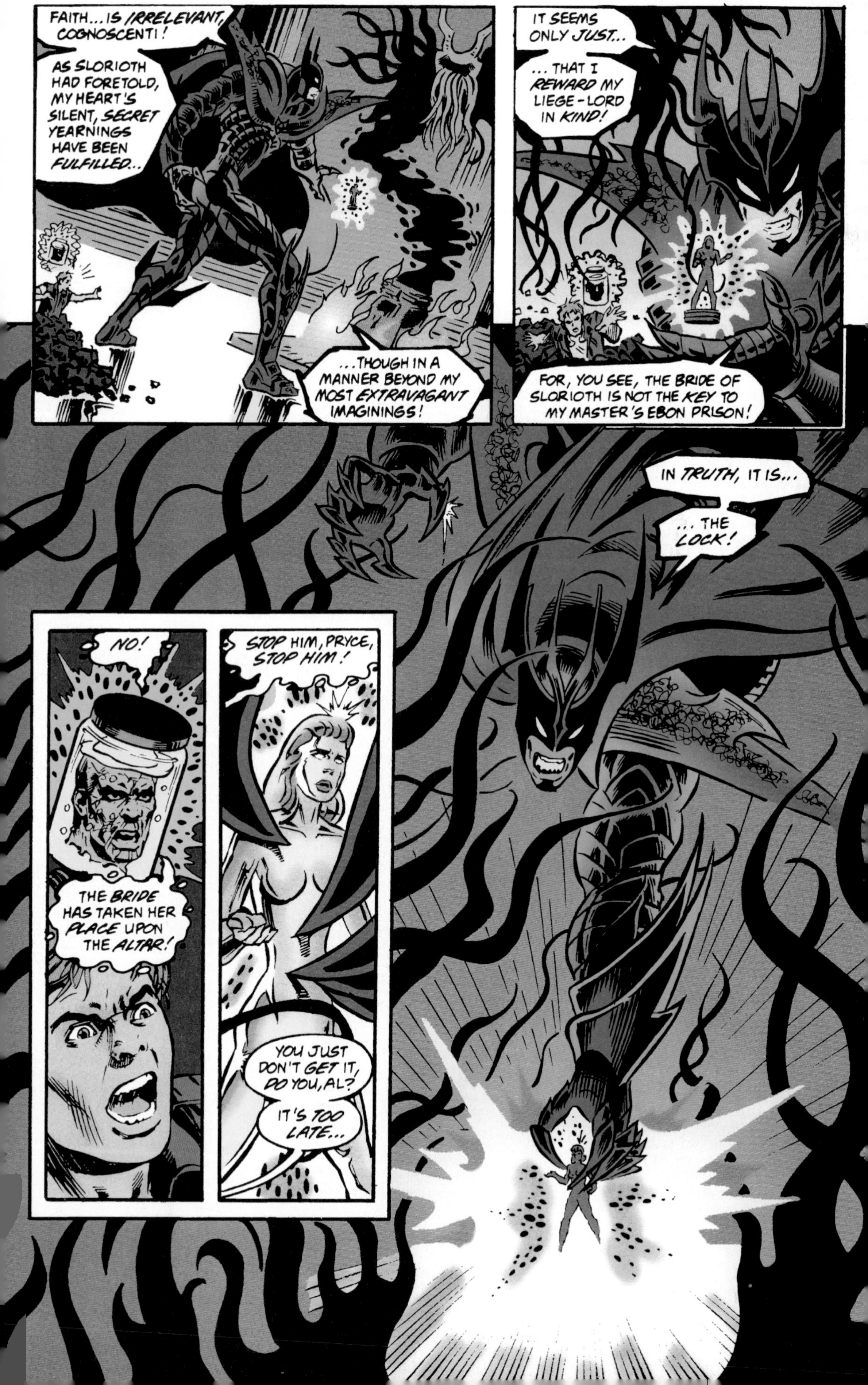
FAITH... IS IRRELEVANT, COGNOSCENTI!
AS SLORIOTH HAD FORETOLD, MY HEART'S SILENT, SECRET YEARNINGS HAVE BEEN FULFILLED...
...THOUGH IN A MANNER BEYOND MY MOST EXTRAVAGANT IMAGININGS!
IT SEEMS ONLY JUST...
... THAT I REWARD MY LIEGE-LORD IN KIND!
FOR, YOU SEE, THE BRIDE OF SLORIOTH IS NOT THE KEY TO MY MASTER'S EBON PRISON!
IN TRUTH, IT IS...
... THE LOCK!
NO!
THE BRIDE HAS TAKEN HER PLACE UPON THE ALTAR!
STOP HIM, PRYCE, STOP HIM!
YOU JUST DON'T GET IT, DO YOU, AL?
IT'S TOO LATE...

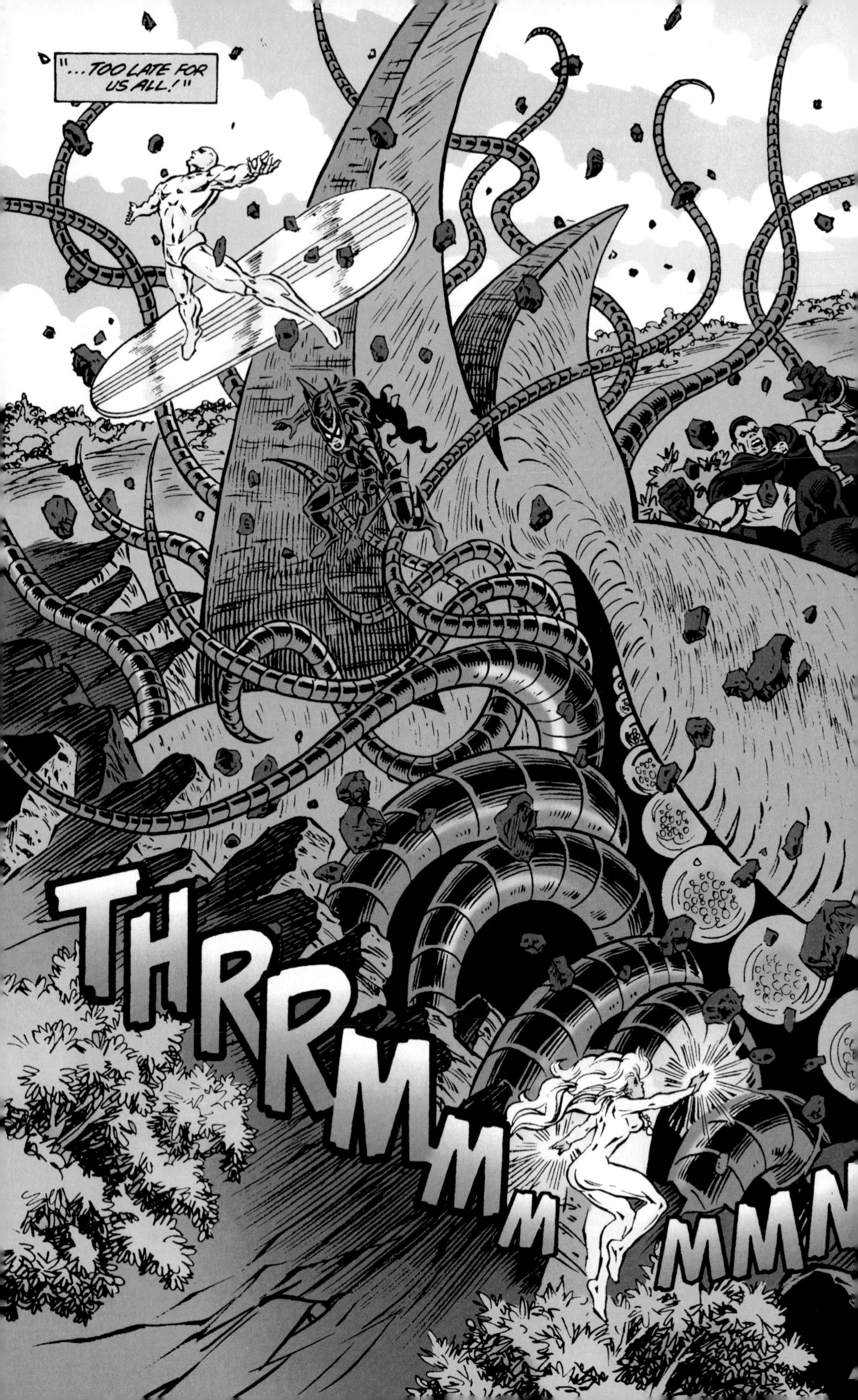
"...TOO LATE FOR US ALL!"
THRRMMMM MMMN

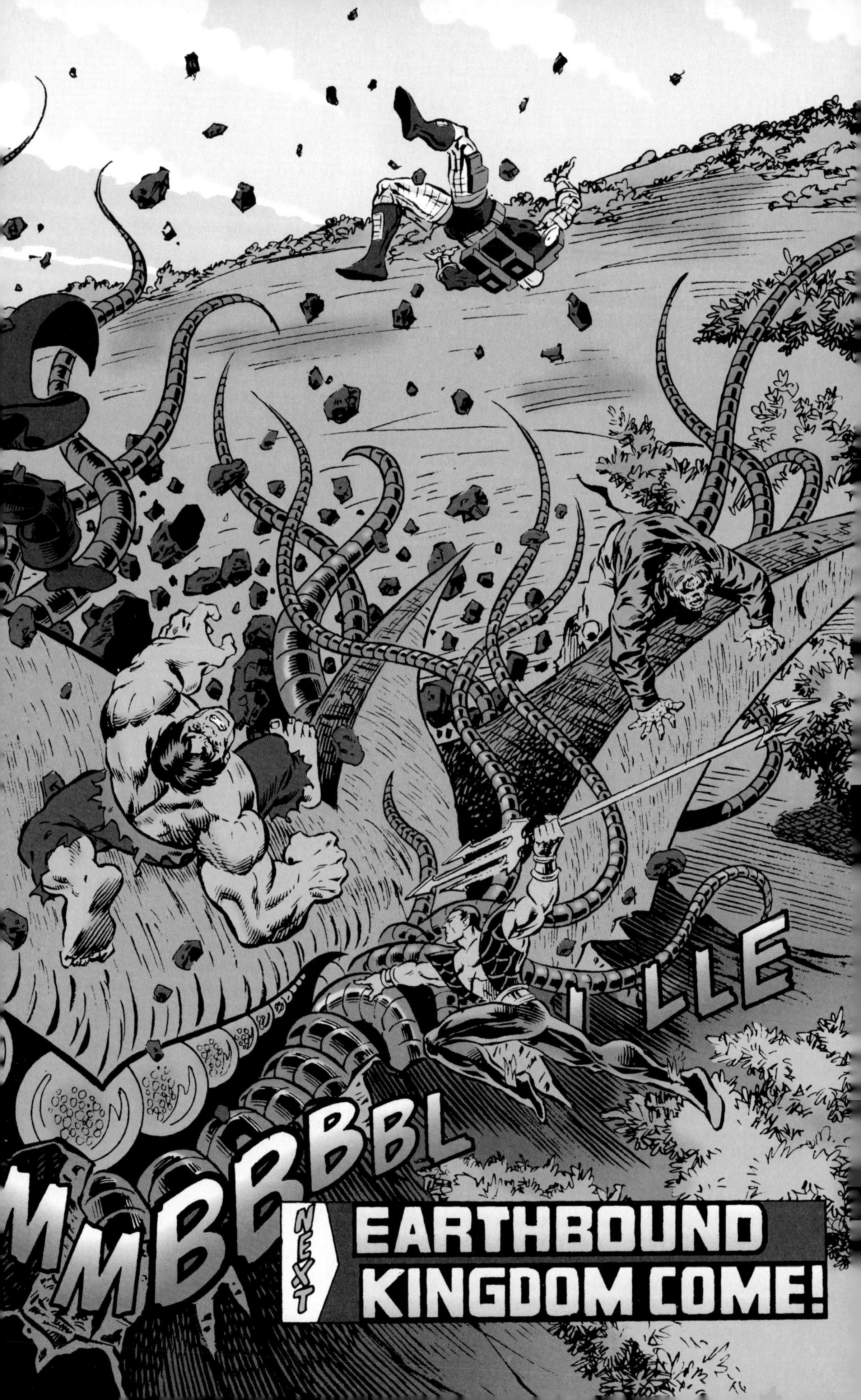
MMBRBBL
LLE
NEXT
EARTHBOUND
KINGDOM COME!

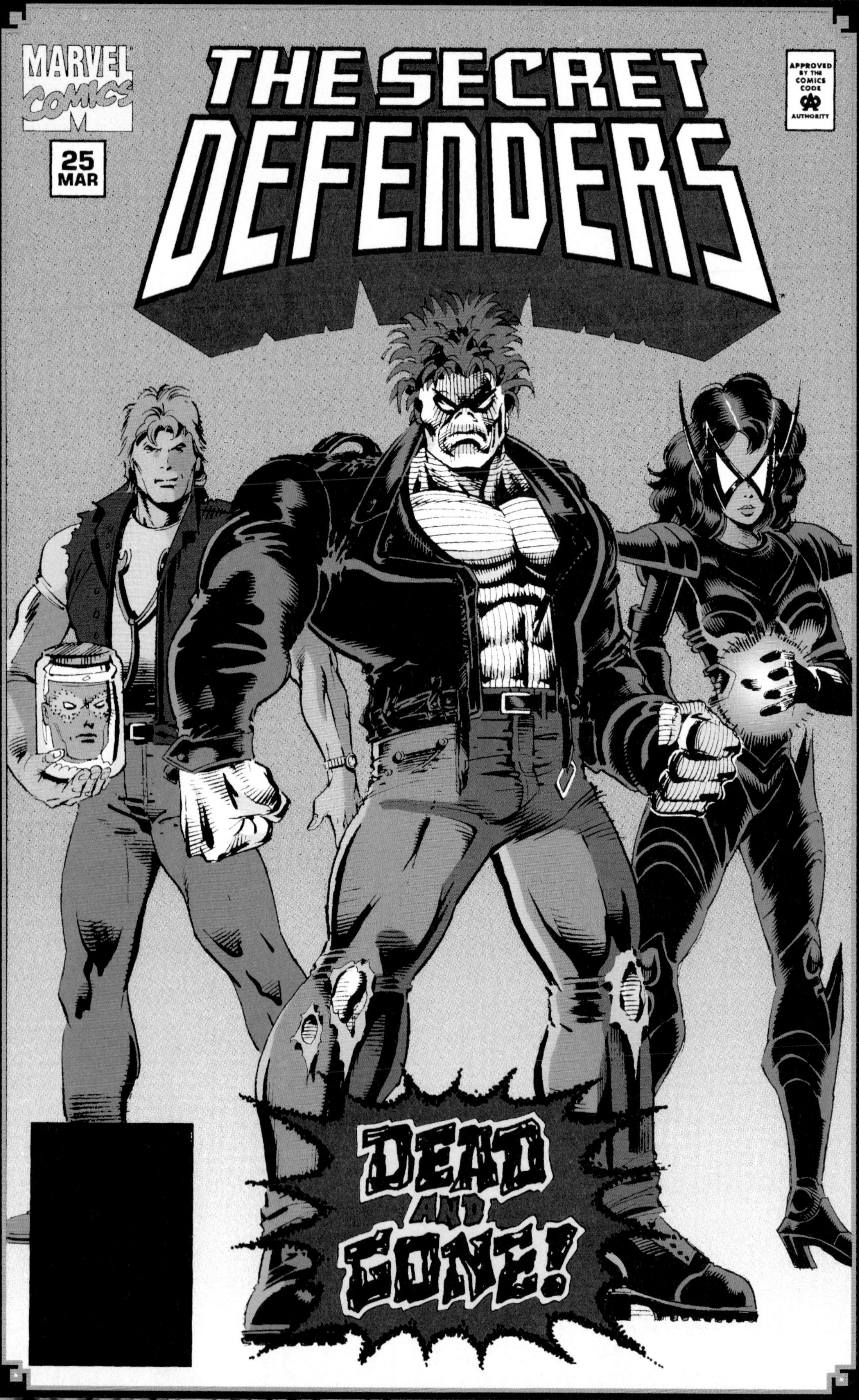
MARVEL COMICS
THE SECRET DEFENDERS
25
MAR
APPROVED BY THE COMICS CODE AUTHORITY
DEAD AND GONE!

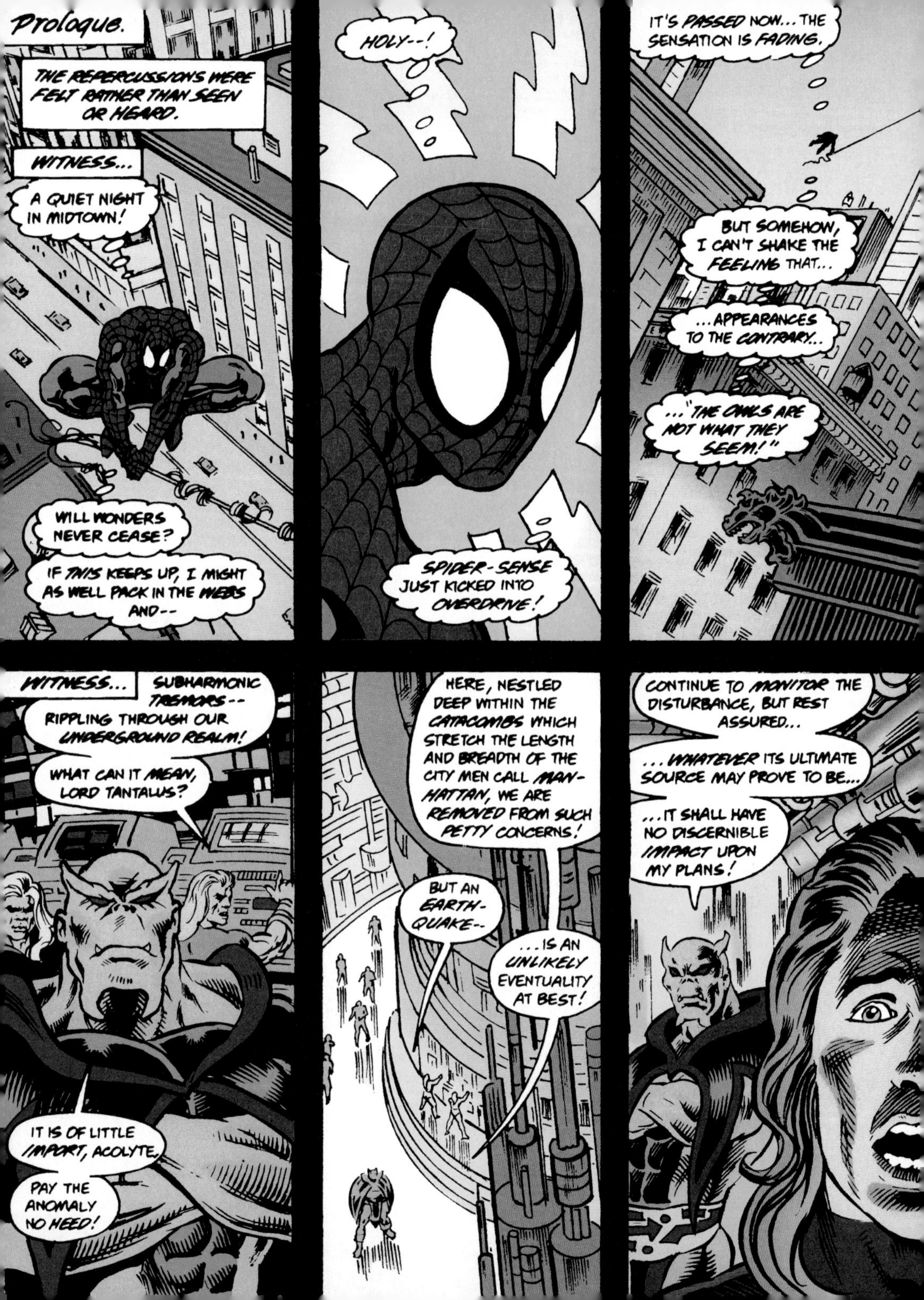
Prologue.
THE REPERCUSSIONS WERE FELT RATHER THAN SEEN OR HEARD.
WITNESS...
A QUIET NIGHT IN MIDTOWN!
WILL WONDERS NEVER CEASE?
IF THIS KEEPS UP, I MIGHT AS WELL PACK IN THE WEBS AND--
HOLY--!
SPIDER-SENSE JUST KICKED INTO OVERDRIVE!
IT'S PASSED NOW... THE SENSATION IS FADING.
BUT SOMEHOW, I CAN'T SHAKE THE FEELING THAT...
...APPEARANCES TO THE CONTRARY...
..."THE OWLS ARE NOT WHAT THEY SEEM!"
WITNESS...
SUBHARMONIC TREMORS-- RIPPLING THROUGH OUR UNDERGROUND REALM!
WHAT CAN IT MEAN, LORD TANTALUS?
IT IS OF LITTLE IMPORT, ACOLYTE.
PAY THE ANOMALY NO HEED!
HERE, NESTLED DEEP WITHIN THE CATACOMBS WHICH STRETCH THE LENGTH AND BREADTH OF THE CITY MEN CALL MAN-HATTAN, WE ARE REMOVED FROM SUCH PETTY CONCERNS!
BUT AN EARTH-QUAKE--
...IS AN UNLIKELY EVENTUALITY AT BEST!
CONTINUE TO MONITOR THE DISTURBANCE, BUT REST ASSURED...
...WHATEVER ITS ULTIMATE SOURCE MAY PROVE TO BE...
...IT SHALL HAVE NO DISCERNIBLE IMPACT UPON MY PLANS!

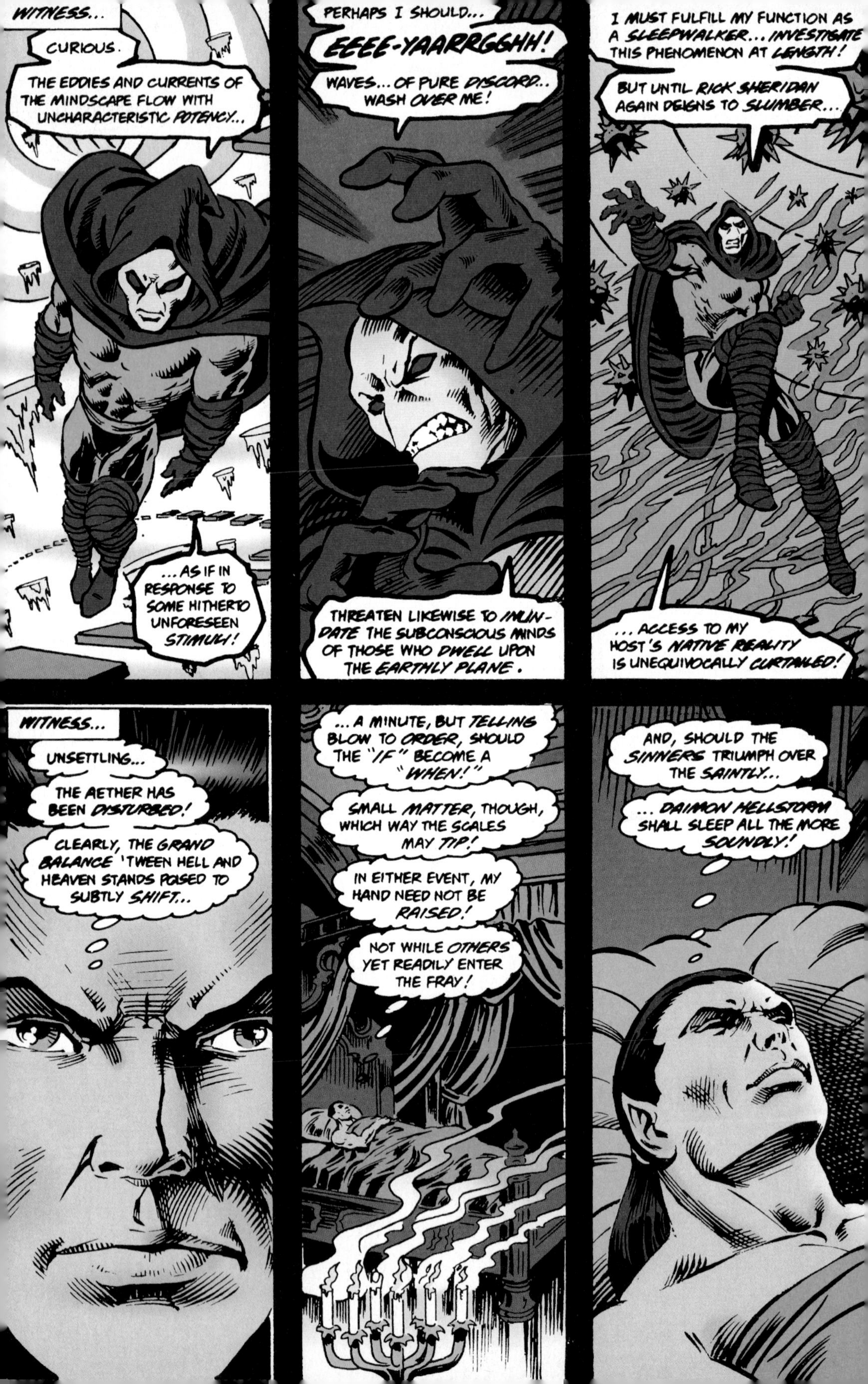
WITNESS...
CURIOUS.
THE EDDIES AND CURRENTS OF THE MINDSCAPE FLOW WITH UNCHARACTERISTIC POTENCY...
...AS IF IN RESPONSE TO SOME HITHERTO UNFORESEEN STIMULI!
PERHAPS I SHOULD...
EEEE-YAARRGGHH!
WAVES... OF PURE DISCORD... WASH OVER ME!
THREATEN LIKEWISE TO INUN-DATE THE SUBCONSCIOUS MINDS OF THOSE WHO DWELL UPON THE EARTHLY PLANE.
I MUST FULFILL MY FUNCTION AS A SLEEPWALKER... INVESTIGATE THIS PHENOMENON AT LENGTH!
BUT UNTIL RICK SHERIDAN AGAIN DEIGNS TO SLUMBER...
...ACCESS TO MY HOST'S NATIVE REALITY IS UNEQUIVOCALLY CURTAILED!
WITNESS...
UNSETTLING...
THE AETHER HAS BEEN DISTURBED!
CLEARLY, THE GRAND BALANCE 'TWEEN HELL AND HEAVEN STANDS POISED TO SUBTLY SHIFT...
...A MINUTE, BUT TELLING BLOW TO ORDER, SHOULD THE "IF" BECOME A "WHEN!"
SMALL MATTER, THOUGH, WHICH WAY THE SCALES MAY TIP!
IN EITHER EVENT, MY HAND NEED NOT BE RAISED!
NOT WHILE OTHERS YET READILY ENTER THE FRAY!
AND, SHOULD THE SINNERS TRIUMPH OVER THE SAINTLY...
...DAIMON HELLSTORM SHALL SLEEP ALL THE MORE SOUNDLY!

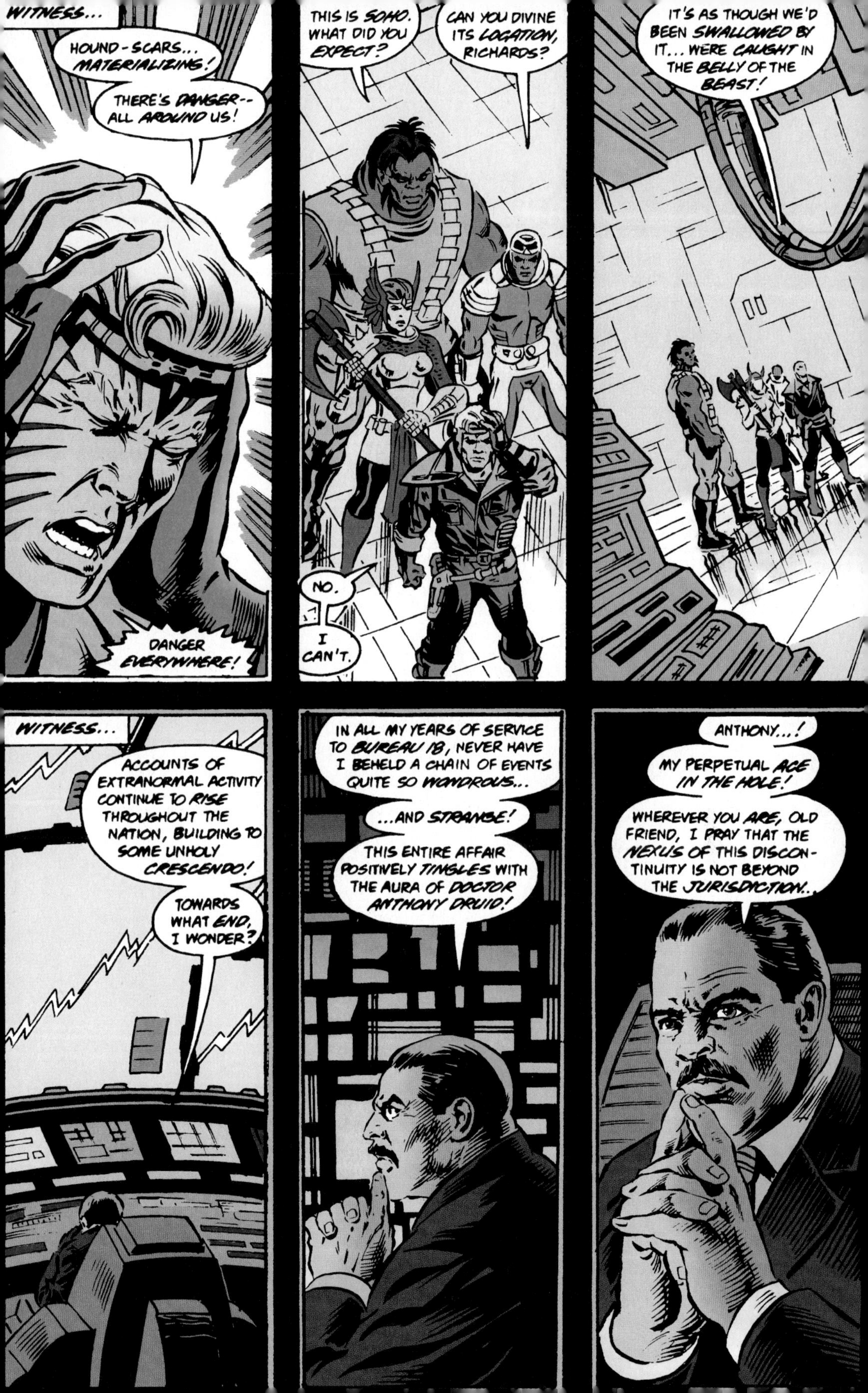
WITNESS...
HOUND-SCARS... MATERIALIZING!
THERE'S DANGER-- ALL AROUND US!
DANGER EVERYWHERE!
THIS IS SOHO. WHAT DID YOU EXPECT?
CAN YOU DIVINE ITS LOCATION, RICHARDS?
NO.
I CAN'T.
IT'S AS THOUGH WE'D BEEN SWALLOWED BY IT... WERE CAUGHT IN THE BELLY OF THE BEAST!
WITNESS...
ACCOUNTS OF EXTRANORMAL ACTIVITY CONTINUE TO RISE THROUGHOUT THE NATION, BUILDING TO SOME UNHOLY CRESCENDO!
TOWARDS WHAT END, I WONDER?
IN ALL MY YEARS OF SERVICE TO BUREAU 18, NEVER HAVE I BEHELD A CHAIN OF EVENTS QUITE SO WONDROUS...
...AND STRANGE!
THIS ENTIRE AFFAIR POSITIVELY TINGLES WITH THE AURA OF DOCTOR ANTHONY DRUID!
ANTHONY...!
MY PERPETUAL ACE IN THE HOLE!
WHEREVER YOU ARE, OLD FRIEND, I PRAY THAT THE NEXUS OF THIS DISCONTINUITY IS NOT BEYOND THE JURISDICTION..

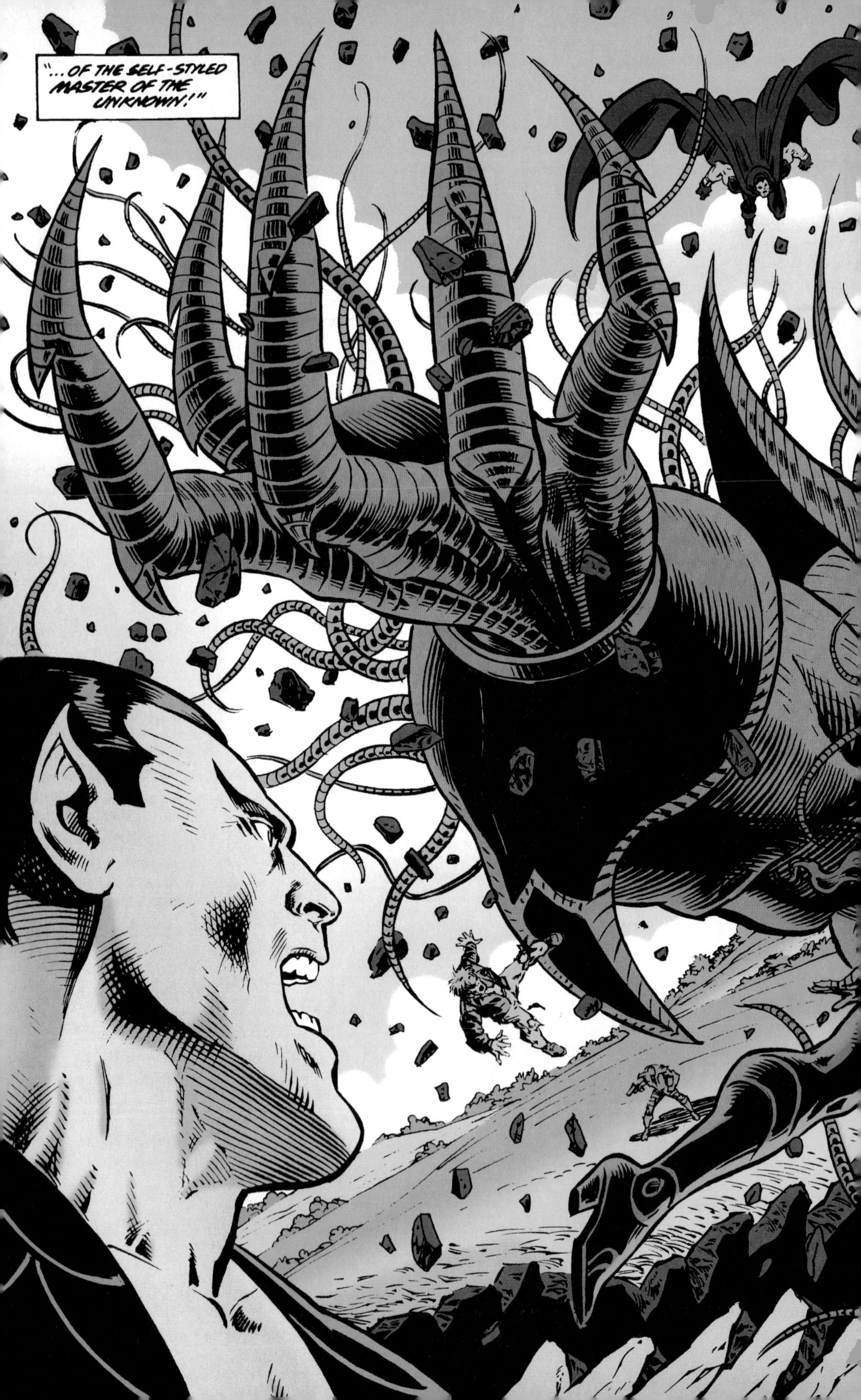
"...OF THE SELF-STYLED MASTER OF THE UNKNOWN!"

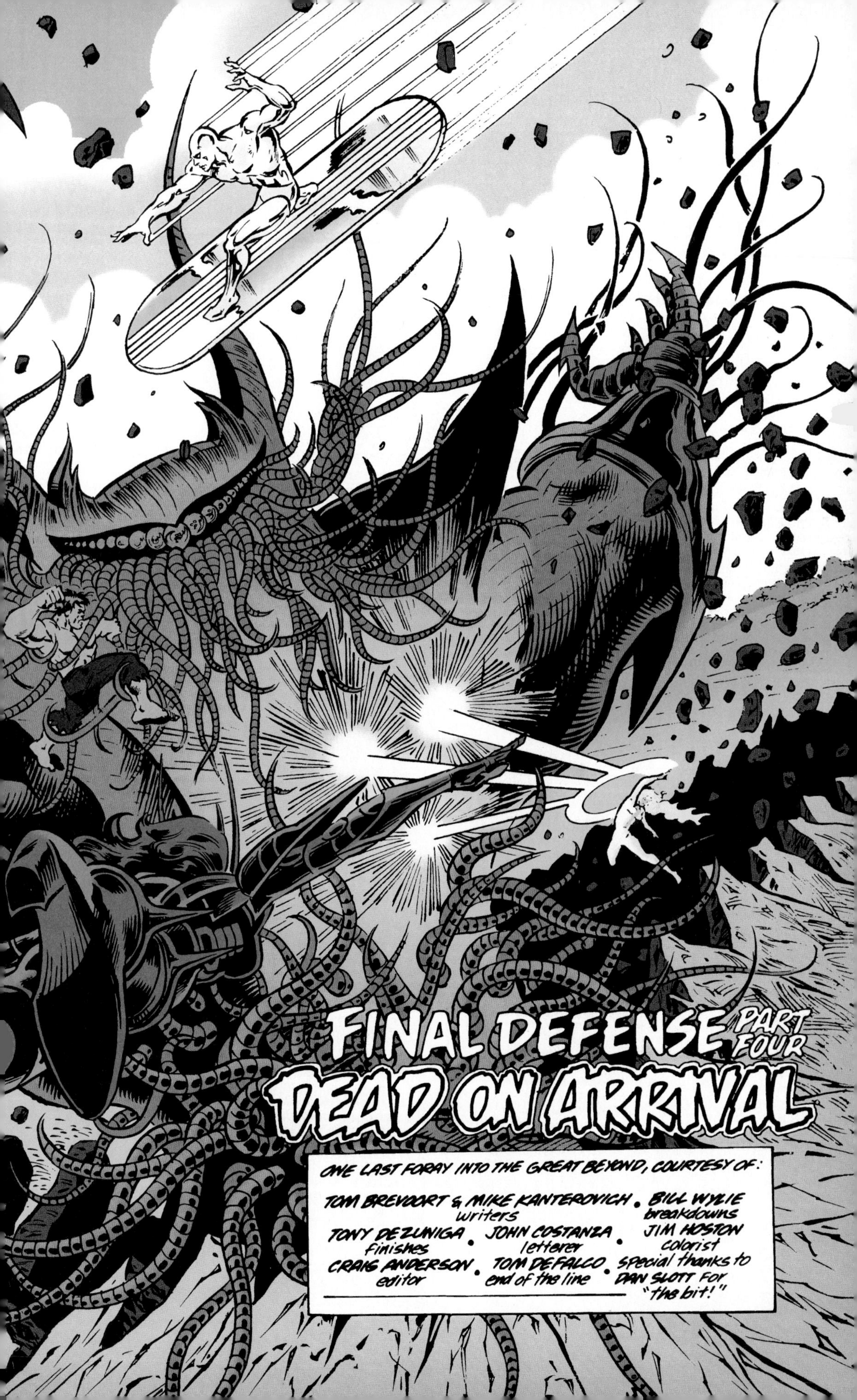
FINAL DEFENSE PART FOUR
DEAD ON ARRIVAL
ONE LAST FORAY INTO THE GREAT BEYOND, COURTESY OF:
TOM BREVOORT & MIKE KANTEROVICH writers • BILL WYLIE breakdowns
TONY DEZUNIGA finishes • JOHN COSTANZA letterer • JIM HOSTON colorist
CRAIG ANDERSON editor • TOM DEFALCO end of the line • special thanks to DAN SLOTT for "the bit!"

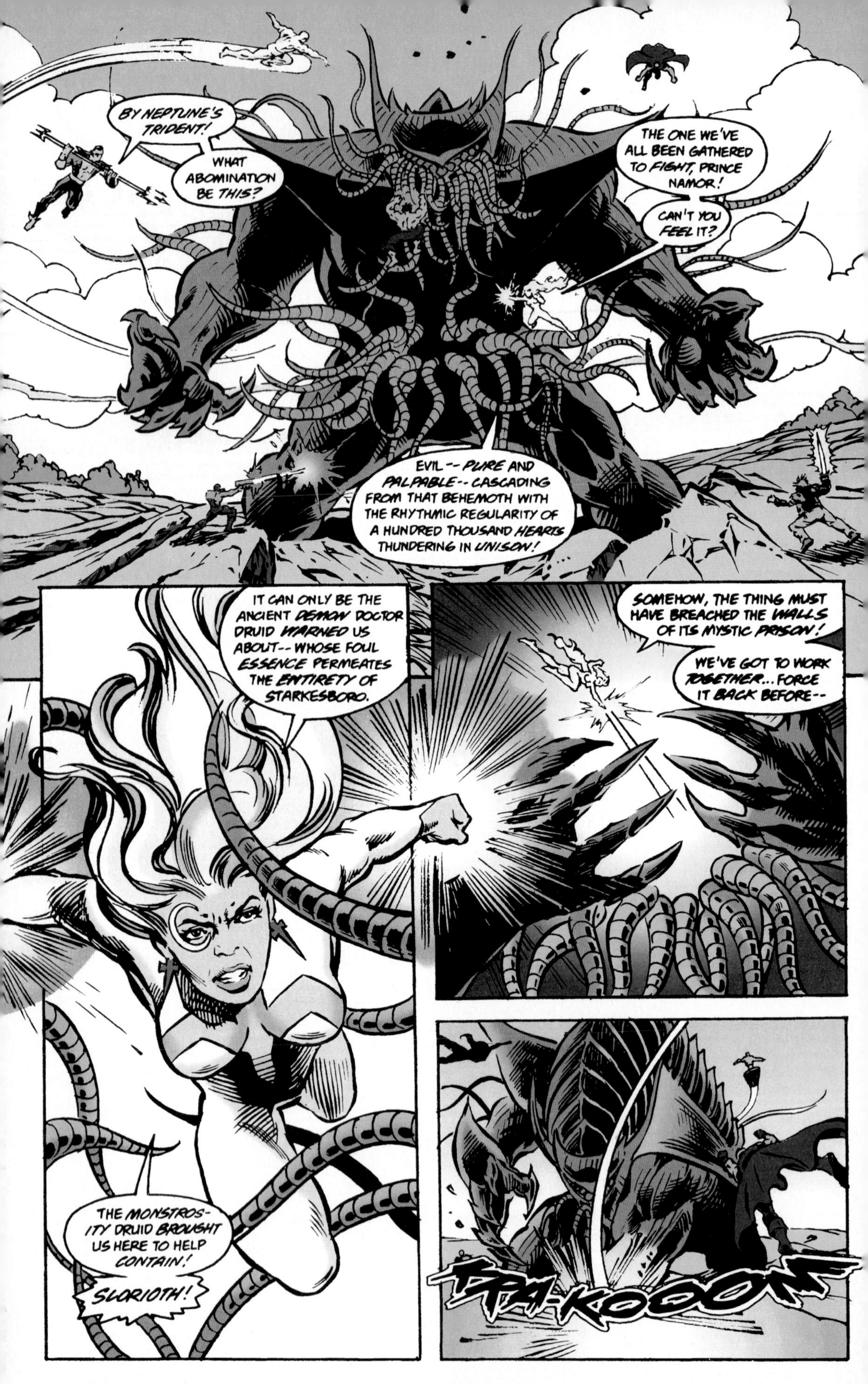
BY NEPTUNE'S TRIDENT!
WHAT ABOMINATION BE THIS?
THE ONE WE'VE ALL BEEN GATHERED TO FIGHT, PRINCE NAMOR!
CAN'T YOU FEEL IT?
EVIL -- PURE AND PALPABLE -- CASCADING FROM THAT BEHEMOTH WITH THE RHYTHMIC REGULARITY OF A HUNDRED THOUSAND HEARTS THUNDERING IN UNISON!
IT CAN ONLY BE THE ANCIENT DEMON DOCTOR DRUID WARNED US ABOUT -- WHOSE FOUL ESSENCE PERMEATES THE ENTIRETY OF STARKESBORO.
THE MONSTROS-ITY DRUID BROUGHT US HERE TO HELP CONTAIN!
SLORIOTH!
SOMEHOW, THE THING MUST HAVE BREACHED THE WALLS OF ITS MYSTIC PRISON!
WE'VE GOT TO WORK TOGETHER... FORCE IT BACK BEFORE--
DDA-KOOOOM

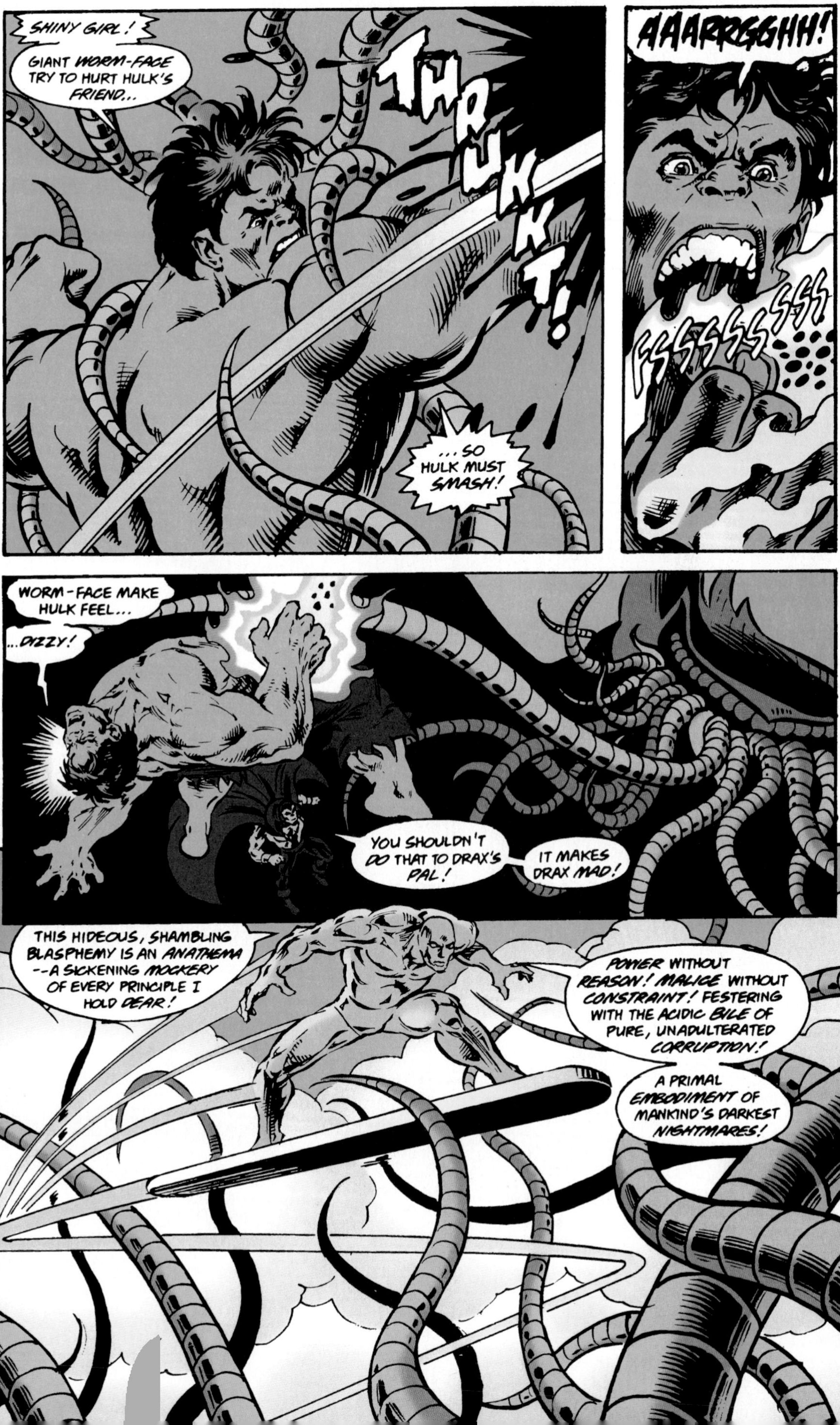
SHINY GIRL!
GIANT WORM-FACE TRY TO HURT HULK'S FRIEND...
THUKT!
...SO HULK MUST SMASH!
AAARRGGHH!
FSSSSSSSSS
WORM-FACE MAKE HULK FEEL...
...DIZZY!
YOU SHOULDN'T DO THAT TO DRAX'S PAL!
IT MAKES DRAX MAD!
THIS HIDEOUS, SHAMBLING BLASPHEMY IS AN ANATHEMA --A SICKENING MOCKERY OF EVERY PRINCIPLE I HOLD DEAR!
POWER WITHOUT REASON! MALICE WITHOUT CONSTRAINT! FESTERING WITH THE ACIDIC BILE OF PURE, UNADULTERATED CORRUPTION!
A PRIMAL EMBODIMENT OF MANKIND'S DARKEST NIGHTMARES!

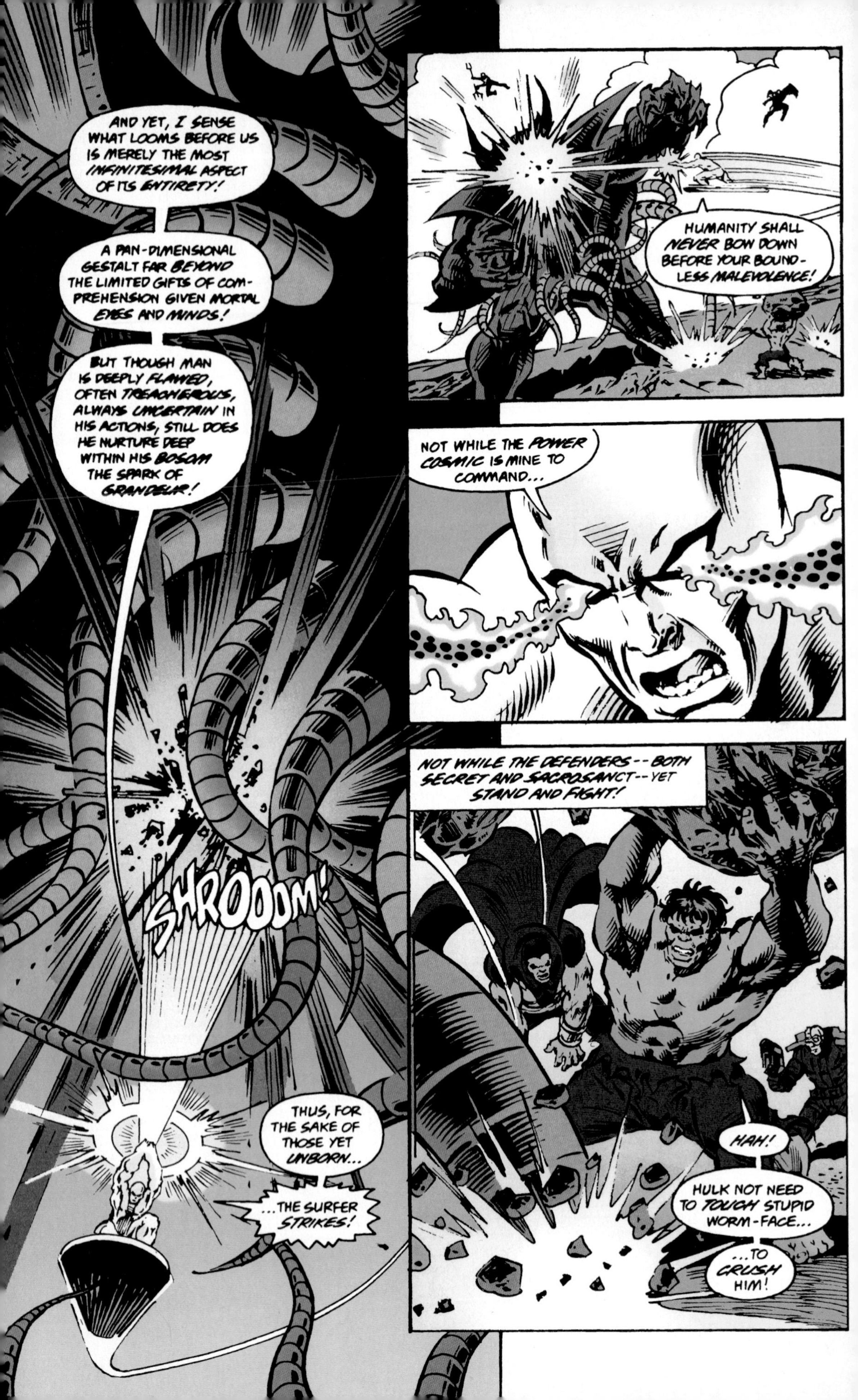
AND YET, I SENSE WHAT LOOMS BEFORE US IS MERELY THE MOST INFINITESIMAL ASPECT OF ITS ENTIRETY!
A PAN-DIMENSIONAL GESTALT FAR BEYOND THE LIMITED GIFTS OF COMPREHENSION GIVEN MORTAL EYES AND MINDS!
BUT THOUGH MAN IS DEEPLY FLAWED, OFTEN TREACHEROUS, ALWAYS UNCERTAIN IN HIS ACTIONS, STILL DOES HE NURTURE DEEP WITHIN HIS BOSOM THE SPARK OF GRANDEUR!
SHROOOM!
THUS, FOR THE SAKE OF THOSE YET UNBORN...
...THE SURFER STRIKES!
HUMANITY SHALL NEVER BOW DOWN BEFORE YOUR BOUNDLESS MALEVOLENCE!
NOT WHILE THE POWER COSMIC IS MINE TO COMMAND...
NOT WHILE THE DEFENDERS--BOTH SECRET AND SACROSANCT--YET STAND AND FIGHT!
HAH!
HULK NOT NEED TO TOUCH STUPID WORM-FACE...
...TO CRUSH HIM!

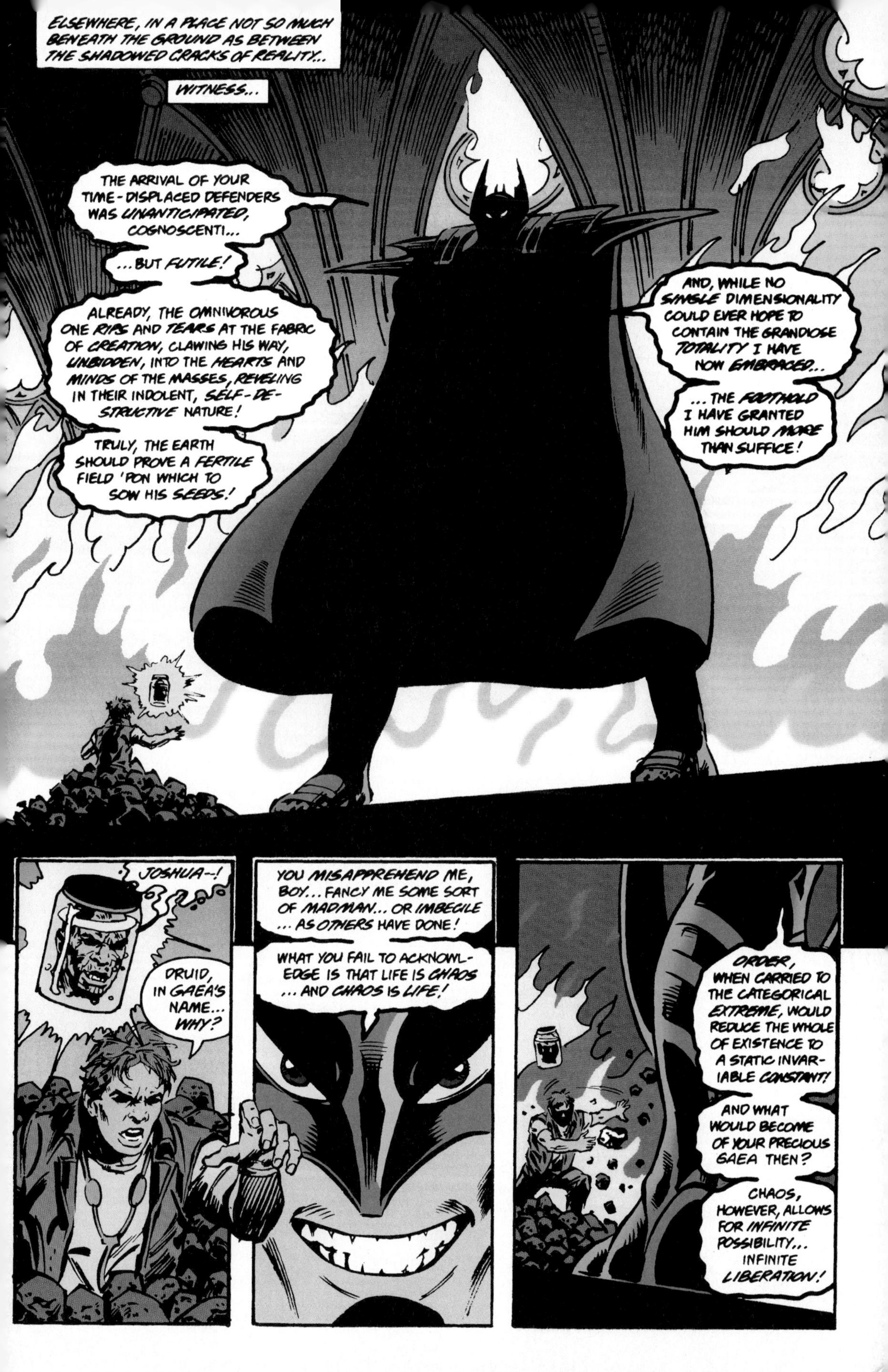
ELSEWHERE, IN A PLACE NOT SO MUCH BENEATH THE GROUND AS BETWEEN THE SHADOWED CRACKS OF REALITY...
WITNESS...
THE ARRIVAL OF YOUR TIME-DISPLACED DEFENDERS WAS UNANTICIPATED, COGNOSCENTI...
...BUT FUTILE!
ALREADY, THE OMNIVOROUS ONE RIPS AND TEARS AT THE FABRIC OF CREATION, CLAWING HIS WAY, UNBIDDEN, INTO THE HEARTS AND MINDS OF THE MASSES, REVELING IN THEIR INDOLENT, SELF-DESTRUCTIVE NATURE!
TRULY, THE EARTH SHOULD PROVE A FERTILE FIELD 'PON WHICH TO SOW HIS SEEDS!
AND, WHILE NO SINGLE DIMENSIONALITY COULD EVER HOPE TO CONTAIN THE GRANDIOSE TOTALITY I HAVE NOW EMBRACED...
...THE FOOTHOLD I HAVE GRANTED HIM SHOULD MORE THAN SUFFICE!
JOSHUA--!
DRUID, IN GAEA'S NAME... WHY?
YOU MISAPPREHEND ME, BOY... FANCY ME SOME SORT OF MADMAN... OR IMBECILE ... AS OTHERS HAVE DONE!
WHAT YOU FAIL TO ACKNOWLEDGE IS THAT LIFE IS CHAOS ...AND CHAOS IS LIFE!
ORDER, WHEN CARRIED TO THE CATEGORICAL EXTREME, WOULD REDUCE THE WHOLE OF EXISTENCE TO A STATIC INVARIABLE CONSTANT!
AND WHAT WOULD BECOME OF YOUR PRECIOUS GAEA THEN?
CHAOS, HOWEVER, ALLOWS FOR INFINITE POSSIBILITY... INFINITE LIBERATION!

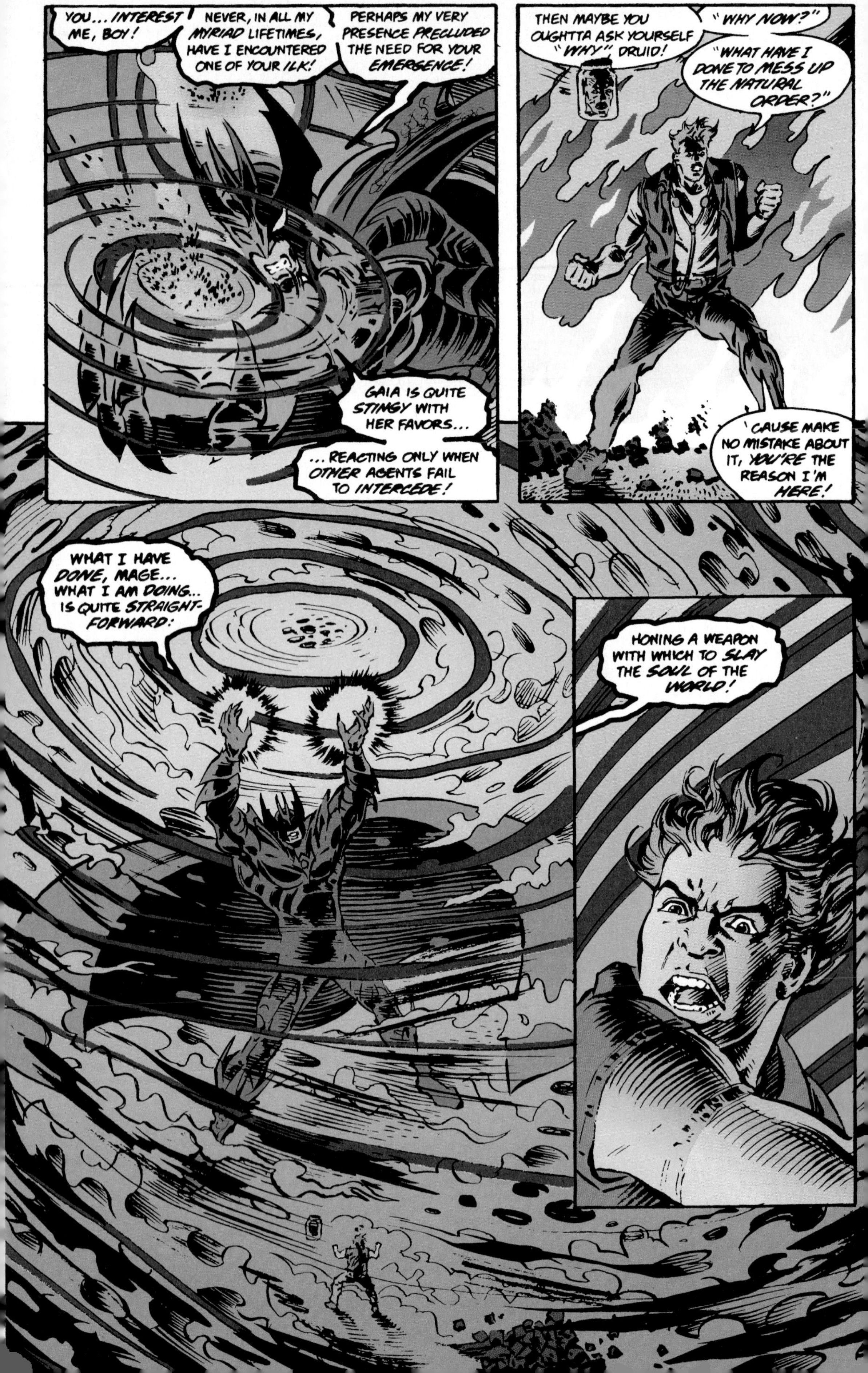

YOU... INTEREST ME, BOY!
NEVER, IN ALL MY MYRIAD LIFETIMES, HAVE I ENCOUNTERED ONE OF YOUR ILK!
PERHAPS MY VERY PRESENCE PRECLUDED THE NEED FOR YOUR EMERGENCE!
GAIA IS QUITE STINGY WITH HER FAVORS...
...REACTING ONLY WHEN OTHER AGENTS FAIL TO INTERCEDE!
THEN MAYBE YOU OUGHTTA ASK YOURSELF "WHY" DRUID!
"WHY NOW?"
"WHAT HAVE I DONE TO MESS UP THE NATURAL ORDER?"
'CAUSE MAKE NO MISTAKE ABOUT IT, YOU'RE THE REASON I'M HERE!
WHAT I HAVE DONE, MAGE... WHAT I AM DOING... IS QUITE STRAIGHT-FORWARD:
HONING A WEAPON WITH WHICH TO SLAY THE SOUL OF THE WORLD!

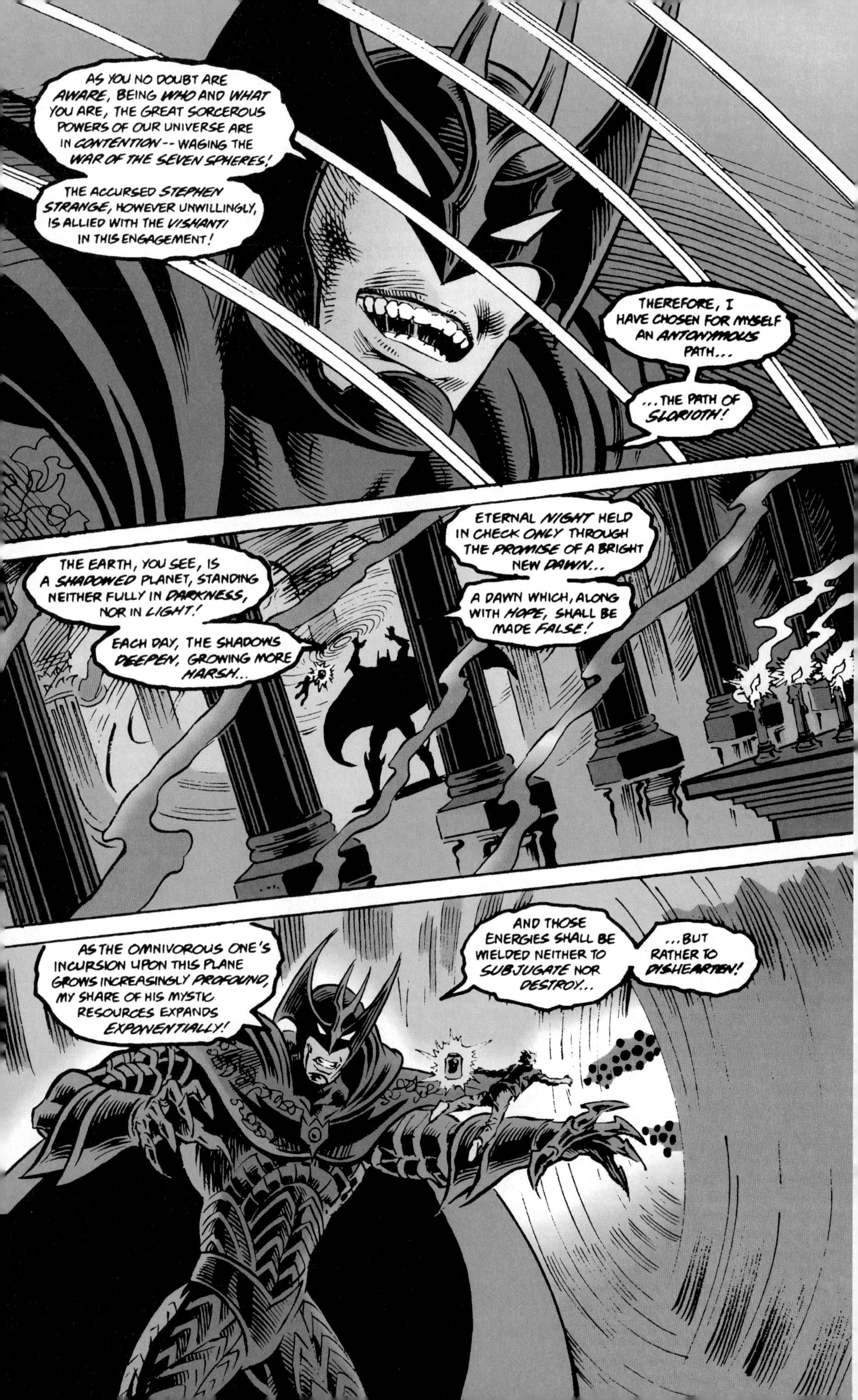
AS YOU NO DOUBT ARE AWARE, BEING WHO AND WHAT YOU ARE, THE GREAT SORCEROUS POWERS OF OUR UNIVERSE ARE IN CONTENTION -- WAGING THE WAR OF THE SEVEN SPHERES!
THE ACCURSED STEPHEN STRANGE, HOWEVER UNWILLINGLY, IS ALLIED WITH THE VISHANTI IN THIS ENGAGEMENT!
THEREFORE, I HAVE CHOSEN FOR MYSELF AN ANTONYMOUS PATH...
...THE PATH OF SLORIOTH!
THE EARTH, YOU SEE, IS A SHADOWED PLANET, STANDING NEITHER FULLY IN DARKNESS, NOR IN LIGHT!
EACH DAY, THE SHADOWS DEEPEN, GROWING MORE HARSH...
ETERNAL NIGHT HELD IN CHECK ONLY THROUGH THE PROMISE OF A BRIGHT NEW DAWN...
A DAWN WHICH, ALONG WITH HOPE, SHALL BE MADE FALSE!
AS THE OMNIVOROUS ONE'S INCURSION UPON THIS PLANE GROWS INCREASINGLY PROFOUND, MY SHARE OF HIS MYSTIC RESOURCES EXPANDS EXPONENTIALLY!
AND THOSE ENERGIES SHALL BE WIELDED NEITHER TO SUBJUGATE NOR DESTROY...
...BUT RATHER TO DISHEARTEN!

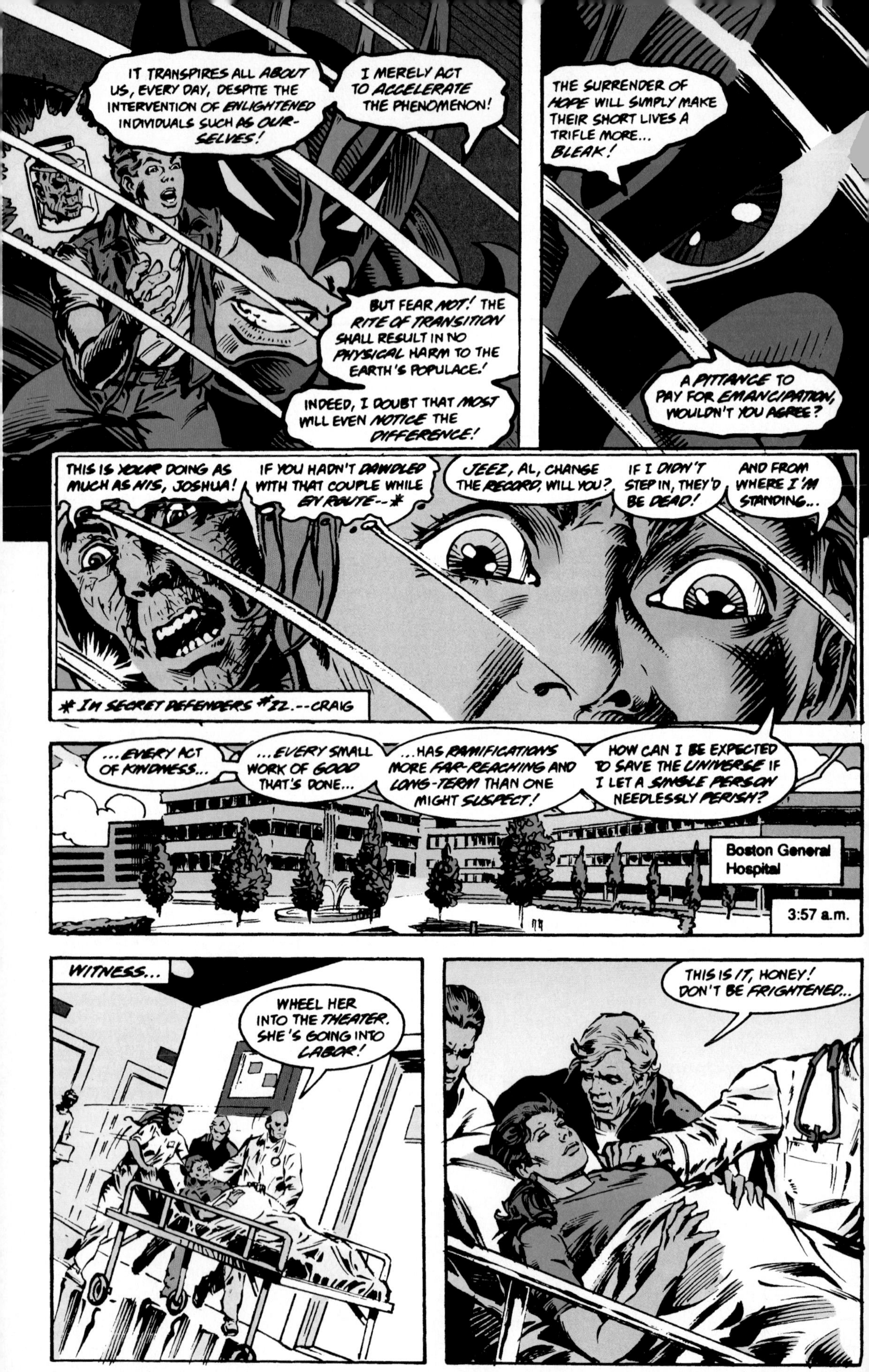
IT TRANSPIRES ALL ABOUT US, EVERY DAY, DESPITE THE INTERVENTION OF ENLIGHTENED INDIVIDUALS SUCH AS OURSELVES!
I MERELY ACT TO ACCELERATE THE PHENOMENON!
BUT FEAR NOT! THE RITE OF TRANSITION SHALL RESULT IN NO PHYSICAL HARM TO THE EARTH'S POPULACE!
INDEED, I DOUBT THAT MOST WILL EVEN NOTICE THE DIFFERENCE!
THE SURRENDER OF HOPE WILL SIMPLY MAKE THEIR SHORT LIVES A TRIFLE MORE... BLEAK!
A PITTANCE TO PAY FOR EMANCIPATION, WOULDN'T YOU AGREE?
THIS IS YOUR DOING AS MUCH AS HIS, JOSHUA!
IF YOU HADN'T DAWDLED WITH THAT COUPLE WHILE EN ROUTE--*
JEEZ, AL, CHANGE THE RECORD, WILL YOU?
IF I DIDN'T STEP IN, THEY'D BE DEAD!
AND FROM WHERE I'M STANDING...
* IN SECRET DEFENDERS #22.--CRAIG
...EVERY ACT OF KINDNESS...
...EVERY SMALL WORK OF GOOD THAT'S DONE...
...HAS RAMIFICATIONS MORE FAR-REACHING AND LONG-TERM THAN ONE MIGHT SUSPECT!
HOW CAN I BE EXPECTED TO SAVE THE UNIVERSE IF I LET A SINGLE PERSON NEEDLESSLY PERISH?
Boston General Hospital
3:57 a.m.
WITNESS...
WHEEL HER INTO THE THEATER. SHE'S GOING INTO LABOR!
THIS IS IT, HONEY! DON'T BE FRIGHTENED...

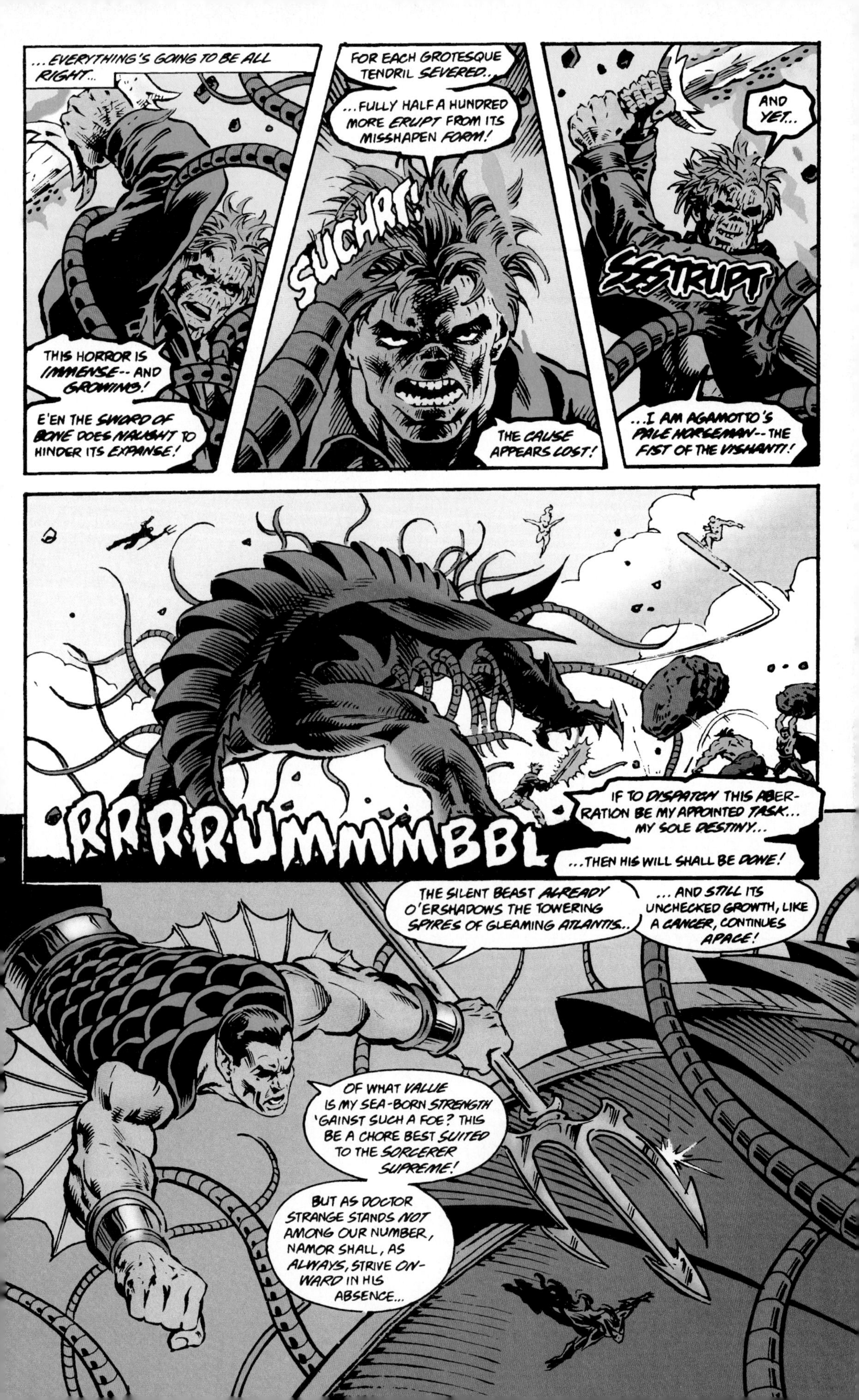

...EVERYTHING'S GOING TO BE ALL RIGHT...
THIS HORROR IS IMMENSE-- AND GROWING!
E'EN THE SWORD OF BONE DOES NAUGHT TO HINDER ITS EXPANSE!
FOR EACH GROTESQUE TENDRIL SEVERED...
...FULLY HALF A HUNDRED MORE ERUPT FROM ITS MISSHAPEN FORM!
SUCHRT!
THE CAUSE APPEARS LOST!
AND YET...
SSSTRUPT
...I AM AGAMOTTO'S PALE HORSEMAN-- THE FIST OF THE VISHANTI!
RRRRUMMMMBBL
IF TO DISPATCH THIS ABER-RATION BE MY APPOINTED TASK... MY SOLE DESTINY...
...THEN HIS WILL SHALL BE DONE!
THE SILENT BEAST ALREADY O'ERSHADOWS THE TOWERING SPIRES OF GLEAMING ATLANTIS...
...AND STILL ITS UNCHECKED GROWTH, LIKE A CANCER, CONTINUES APACE!
OF WHAT VALUE IS MY SEA-BORN STRENGTH 'GAINST SUCH A FOE? THIS BE A CHORE BEST SUITED TO THE SORCERER SUPREME!
BUT AS DOCTOR STRANGE STANDS NOT AMONG OUR NUMBER, NAMOR SHALL, AS ALWAYS, STRIVE ON-WARD IN HIS ABSENCE...

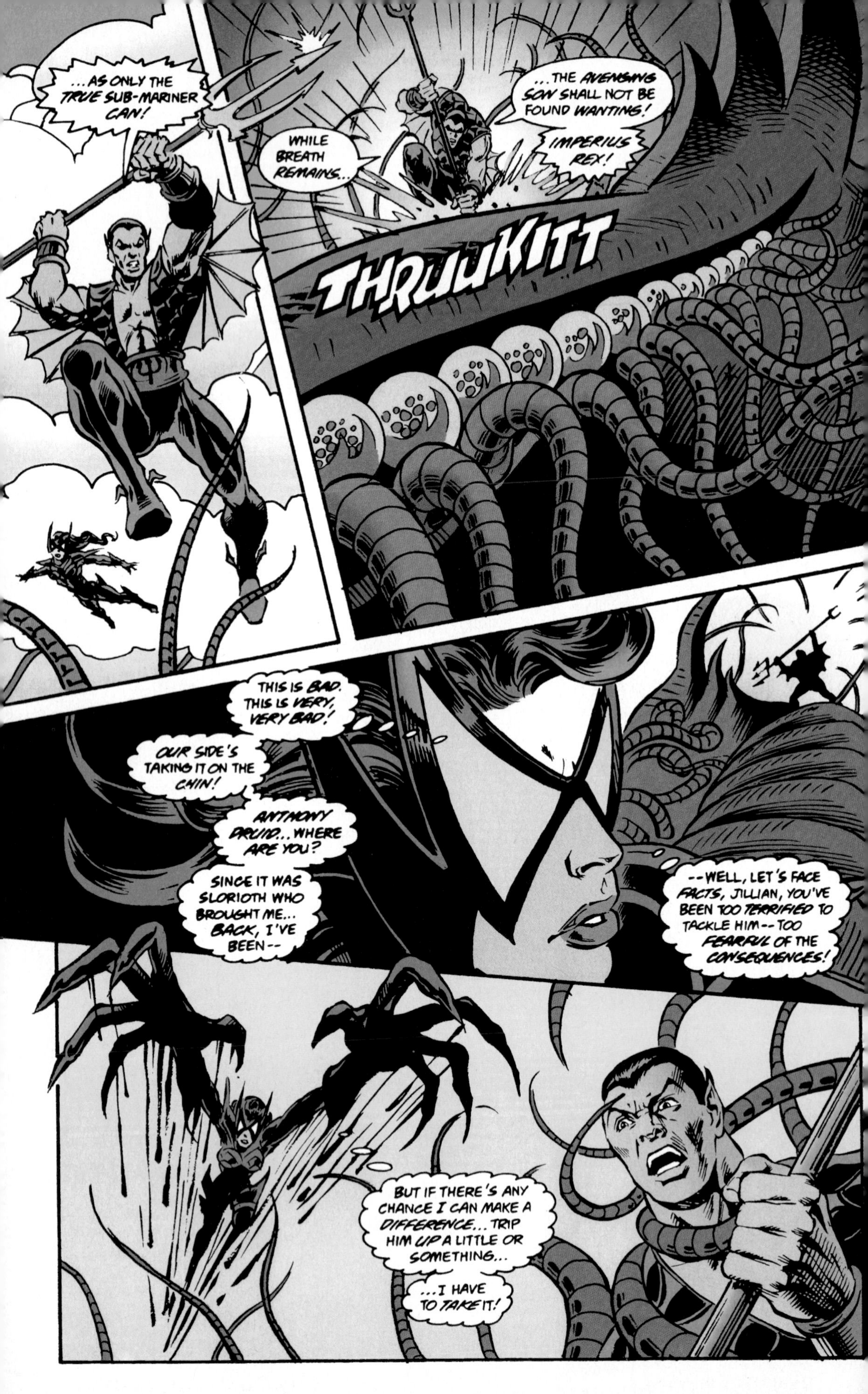

...AS ONLY THE TRUE SUB-MARINER CAN!
WHILE BREATH REMAINS...
...THE AVENGING SON SHALL NOT BE FOUND WANTING!
IMPERIUS REX!
THRUUKITT
THIS IS BAD. THIS IS VERY, VERY BAD!
OUR SIDE'S TAKING IT ON THE CHIN!
ANTHONY DRUID... WHERE ARE YOU?
SINCE IT WAS SLORIOTH WHO BROUGHT ME... BACK, I'VE BEEN--
--WELL, LET'S FACE FACTS, JILLIAN, YOU'VE BEEN TOO TERRIFIED TO TACKLE HIM--TOO FEARFUL OF THE CONSEQUENCES!
BUT IF THERE'S ANY CHANCE I CAN MAKE A DIFFERENCE... TRIP HIM UP A LITTLE OR SOMETHING...
...I HAVE TO TAKE IT!

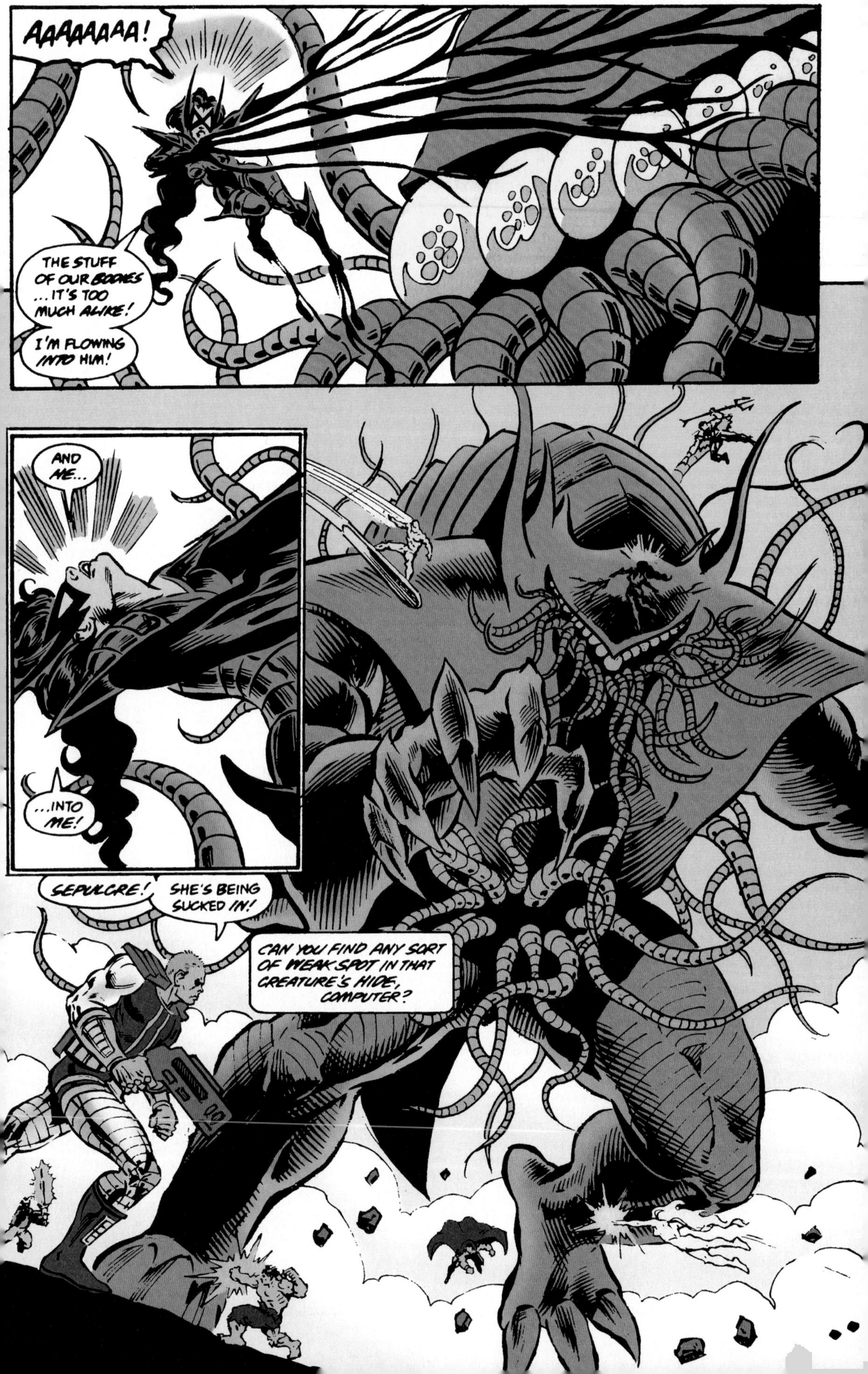
AAAAAAAA!
THE STUFF OF OUR BODIES ...IT'S TOO MUCH ALIKE!
I'M FLOWING INTO HIM!
AND ME...
...INTO ME!
SEPULCRE!
SHE'S BEING SUCKED IN!
CAN YOU FIND ANY SORT OF WEAK SPOT IN THAT CREATURE'S HIDE, COMPUTER?

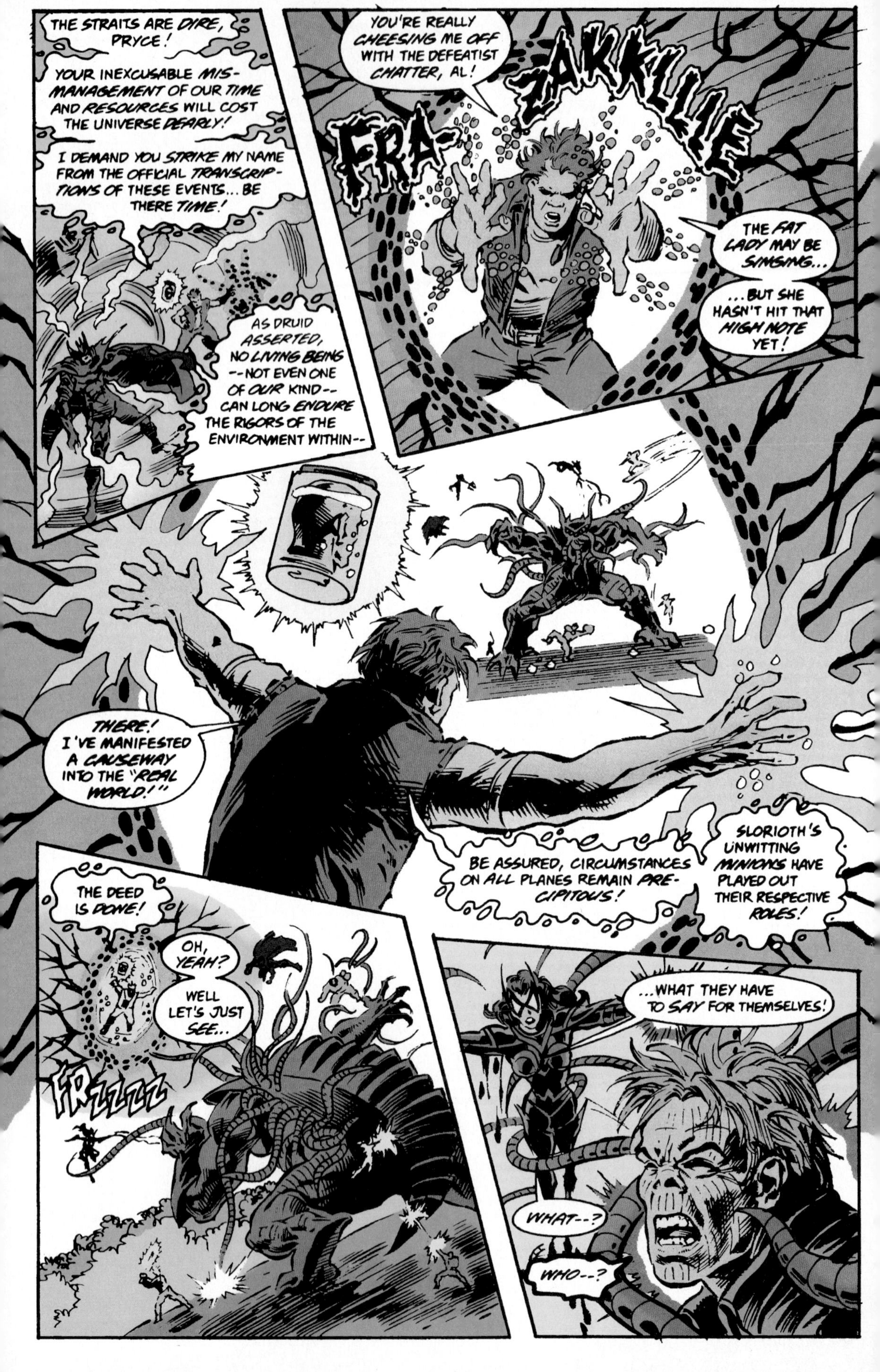
THE STRAITS ARE DIRE, PRYCE!
YOUR INEXCUSABLE MIS-MANAGEMENT OF OUR TIME AND RESOURCES WILL COST THE UNIVERSE DEARLY!
I DEMAND YOU STRIKE MY NAME FROM THE OFFICIAL TRANSCRIP-TIONS OF THESE EVENTS... BE THERE TIME!
AS DRUID ASSERTED, NO LIVING BEING --NOT EVEN ONE OF OUR KIND-- CAN LONG ENDURE THE RIGORS OF THE ENVIRONMENT WITHIN--
YOU'RE REALLY CHEESING ME OFF WITH THE DEFEATIST CHATTER, AL!
FRA-ZAKKLLIE
THE FAT LADY MAY BE SINGING...
...BUT SHE HASN'T HIT THAT HIGH NOTE YET!
THERE! I'VE MANIFESTED A CAUSEWAY INTO THE "REAL WORLD!"
BE ASSURED, CIRCUMSTANCES ON ALL PLANES REMAIN PRE-CIPITOUS!
SLORIOTH'S UNWITTING MINIONS HAVE PLAYED OUT THEIR RESPECTIVE ROLES!
THE DEED IS DONE!
OH, YEAH?
WELL LET'S JUST SEE...
FRZZZZZ
...WHAT THEY HAVE TO SAY FOR THEMSELVES!
WHAT--?
WHO--?

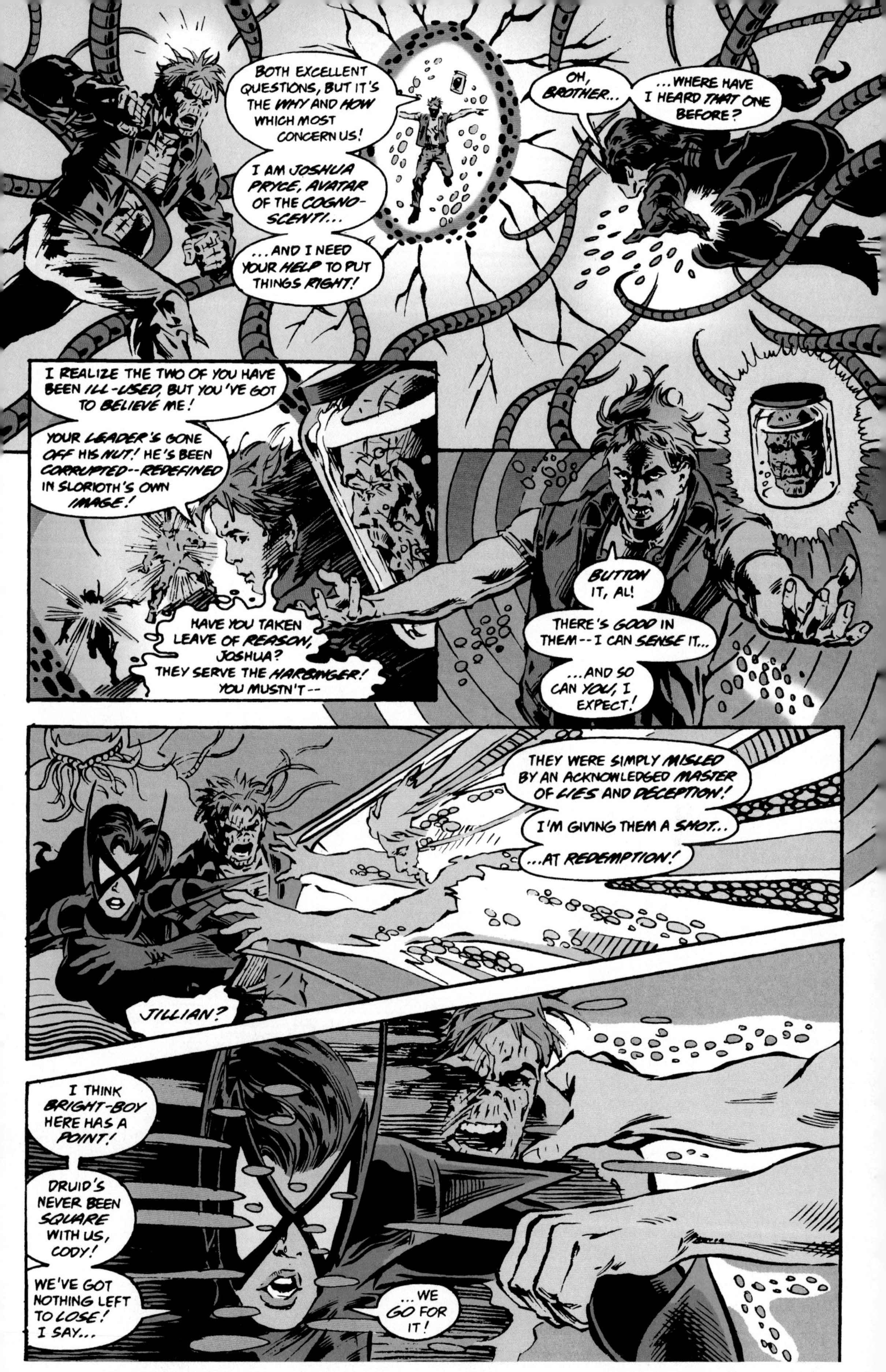
BOTH EXCELLENT QUESTIONS, BUT IT'S THE WHY AND HOW WHICH MOST CONCERN US!
I AM JOSHUA PRYCE, AVATAR OF THE COGNO-SCENTI...
...AND I NEED YOUR HELP TO PUT THINGS RIGHT!
OH, BROTHER...
...WHERE HAVE I HEARD THAT ONE BEFORE?
I REALIZE THE TWO OF YOU HAVE BEEN ILL-USED, BUT YOU'VE GOT TO BELIEVE ME!
YOUR LEADER'S GONE OFF HIS NUT! HE'S BEEN CORRUPTED--REDEFINED IN SLORIOTH'S OWN IMAGE!
HAVE YOU TAKEN LEAVE OF REASON, JOSHUA? THEY SERVE THE HARBINGER! YOU MUSTN'T--
BUTTON IT, AL!
THERE'S GOOD IN THEM--I CAN SENSE IT...
...AND SO CAN YOU, I EXPECT!
THEY WERE SIMPLY MISLED BY AN ACKNOWLEDGED MASTER OF LIES AND DECEPTION!
I'M GIVING THEM A SHOT...
...AT REDEMPTION!
JILLIAN?
I THINK BRIGHT-BOY HERE HAS A POINT!
DRUID'S NEVER BEEN SQUARE WITH US, CODY!
WE'VE GOT NOTHING LEFT TO LOSE! I SAY...
...WE GO FOR IT!

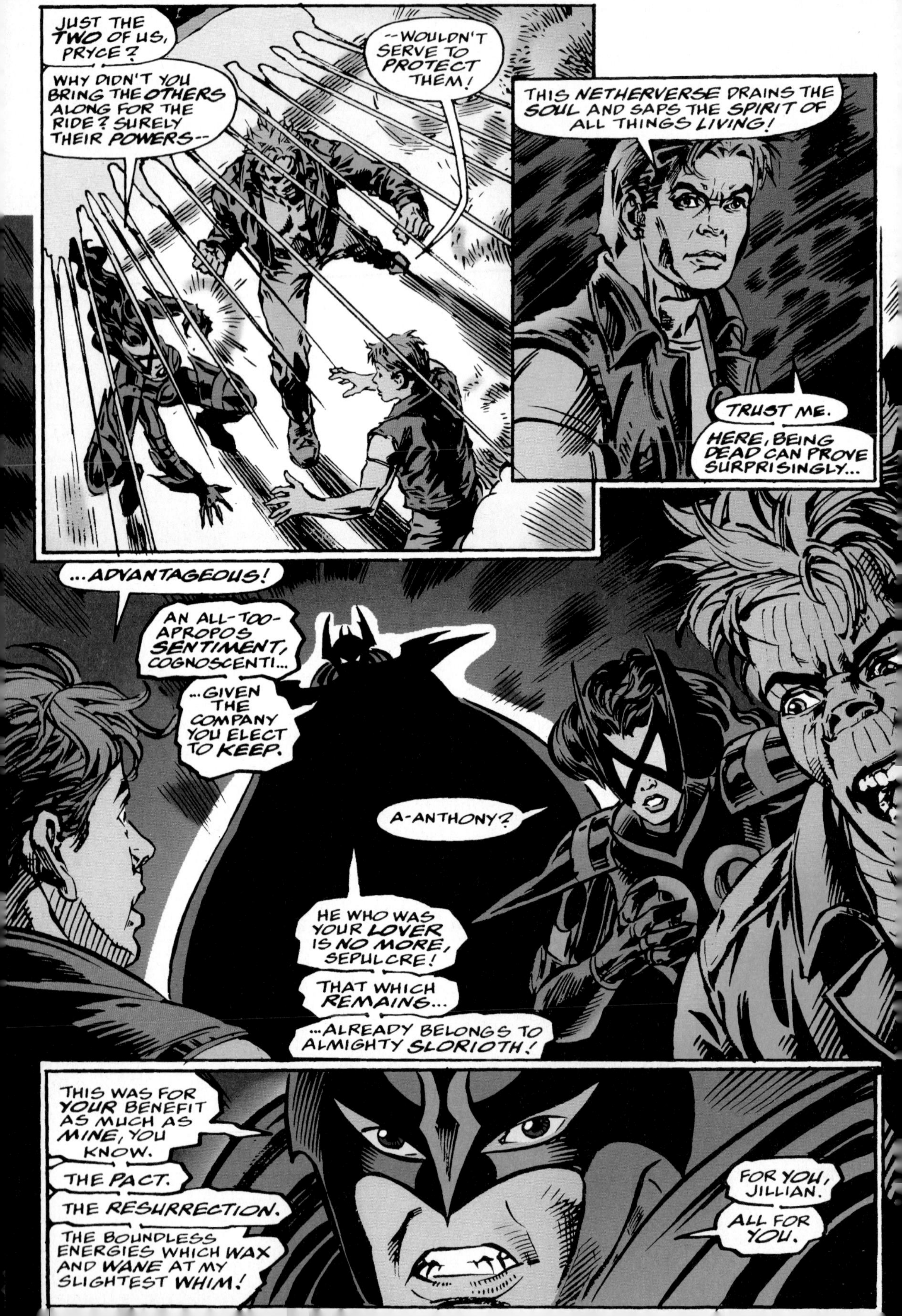

JUST THE TWO OF US, PRYCE?
WHY DIDN'T YOU BRING THE OTHERS ALONG FOR THE RIDE? SURELY THEIR POWERS--
--WOULDN'T SERVE TO PROTECT THEM!
THIS NETHERVERSE DRAINS THE SOUL AND SAPS THE SPIRIT OF ALL THINGS LIVING!
TRUST ME.
HERE, BEING DEAD CAN PROVE SURPRISINGLY...
...ADVANTAGEOUS!
AN ALL-TOO-APROPOS SENTIMENT, COGNOSCENTI...
...GIVEN THE COMPANY YOU ELECT TO KEEP.
A-ANTHONY?
HE WHO WAS YOUR LOVER IS NO MORE, SEPULCRE!
THAT WHICH REMAINS...
...ALREADY BELONGS TO ALMIGHTY SLORIOTH!
THIS WAS FOR YOUR BENEFIT AS MUCH AS MINE, YOU KNOW.
THE PACT.
THE RESURRECTION.
THE BOUNDLESS ENERGIES WHICH WAX AND WANE AT MY SLIGHTEST WHIM!
FOR YOU, JILLIAN.
ALL FOR YOU.

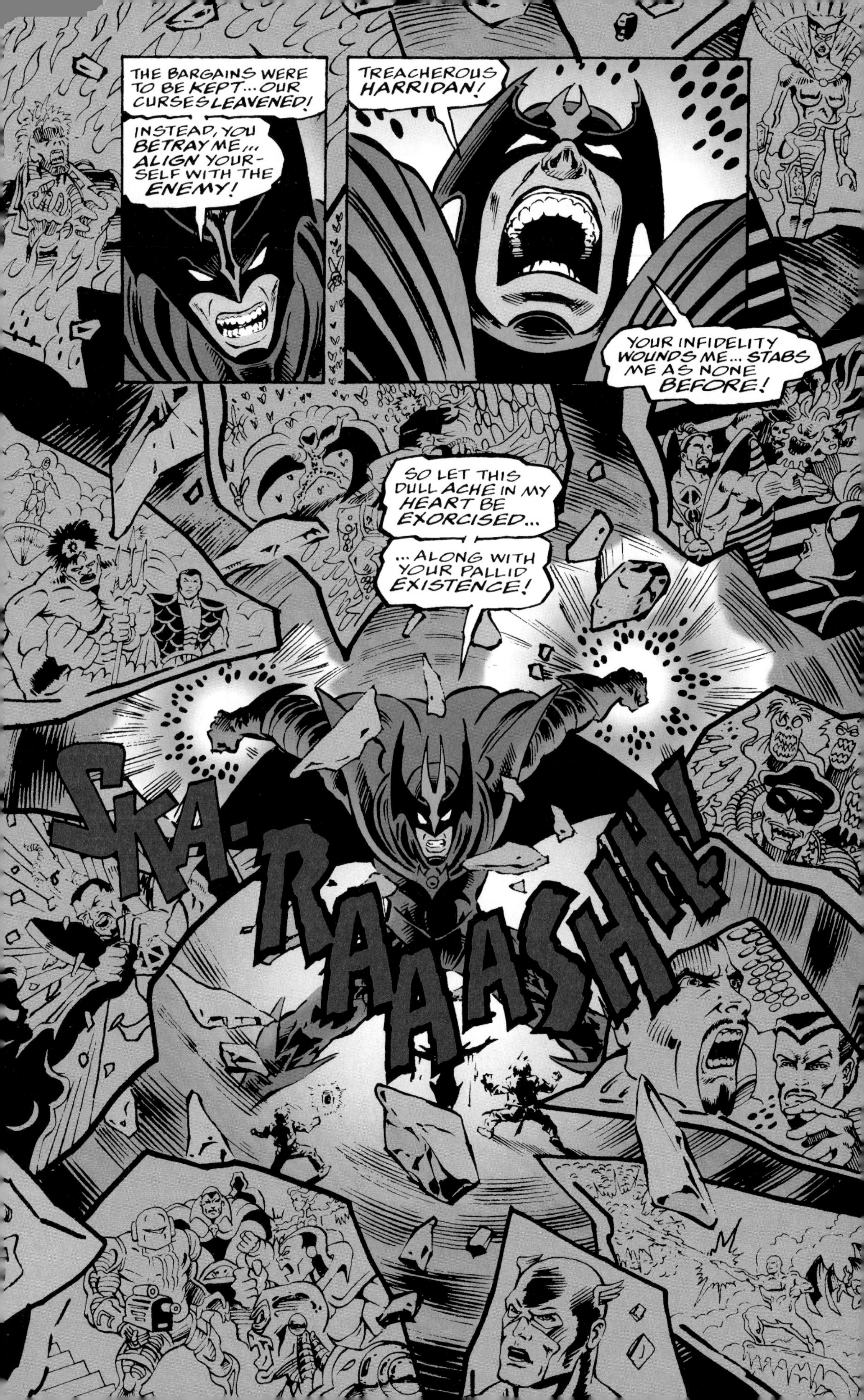
THE BARGAINS WERE TO BE KEPT... OUR CURSES LEAVENED!
INSTEAD, YOU BETRAY ME... ALIGN YOURSELF WITH THE ENEMY!
TREACHEROUS HARRIDAN!
YOUR INFIDELITY WOUNDS ME... STABS ME AS NONE BEFORE!
SO LET THIS DULL ACHE IN MY HEART BE EXORCISED...
...ALONG WITH YOUR PALLID EXISTENCE!
SKA-RAAASHH!

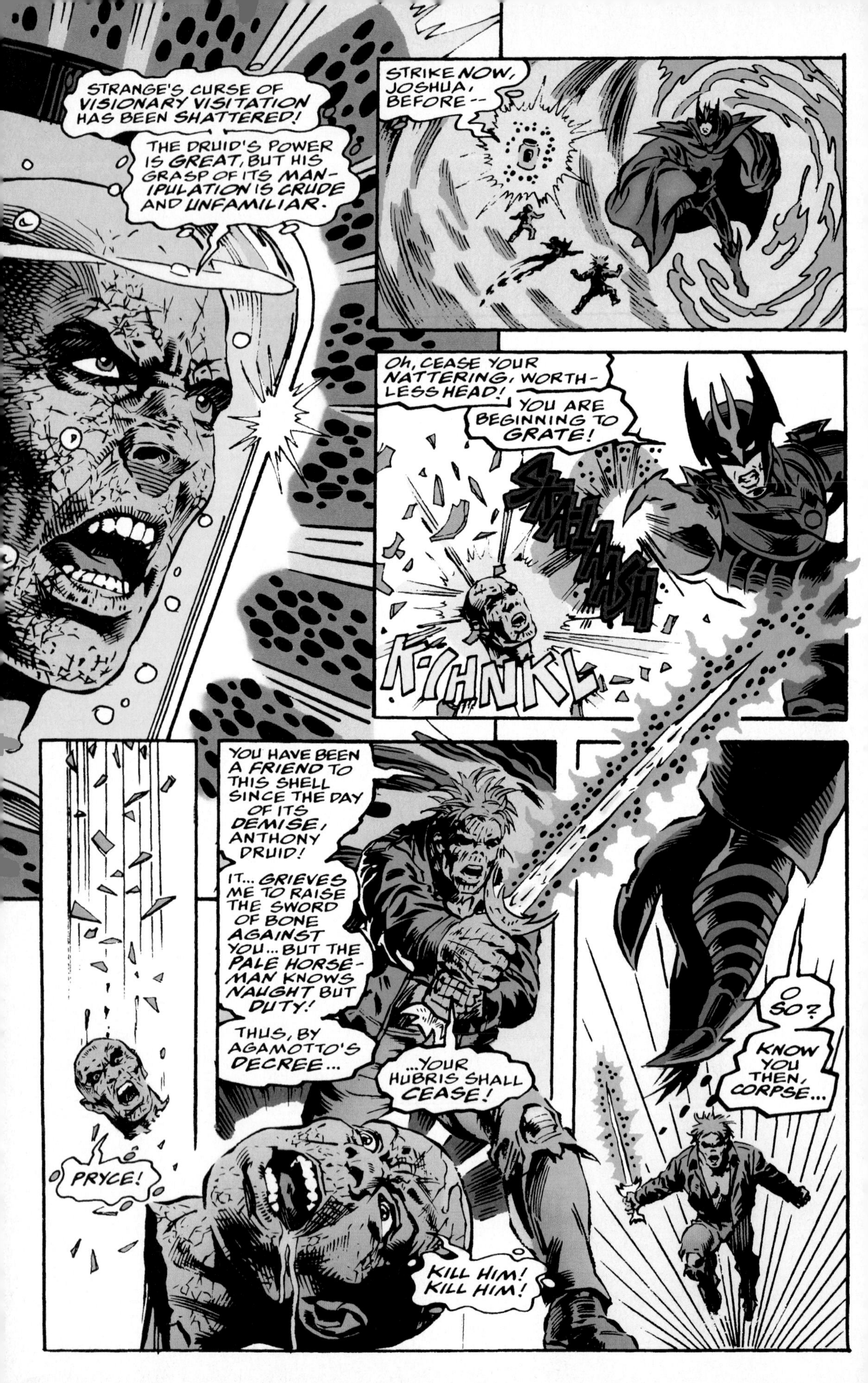
STRANGE'S CURSE OF VISIONARY VISITATION HAS BEEN SHATTERED!
THE DRUID'S POWER IS GREAT, BUT HIS GRASP OF ITS MANIPULATION IS CRUDE AND UNFAMILIAR.
STRIKE NOW, JOSHUA, BEFORE--
Oh, CEASE YOUR NATTERING, WORTHLESS HEAD!
YOU ARE BEGINNING TO GRATE!
SKAH-LAASH
K-CHNKL
PRYCE!
YOU HAVE BEEN A FRIEND TO THIS SHELL SINCE THE DAY OF ITS DEMISE, ANTHONY DRUID!
IT... GRIEVES ME TO RAISE THE SWORD OF BONE AGAINST YOU... BUT THE PALE HORSEMAN KNOWS NAUGHT BUT DUTY!
THUS, BY AGAMOTTO'S DECREE...
...YOUR HUBRIS SHALL CEASE!
KILL HIM! KILL HIM!
O SO?
KNOW YOU THEN, CORPSE...

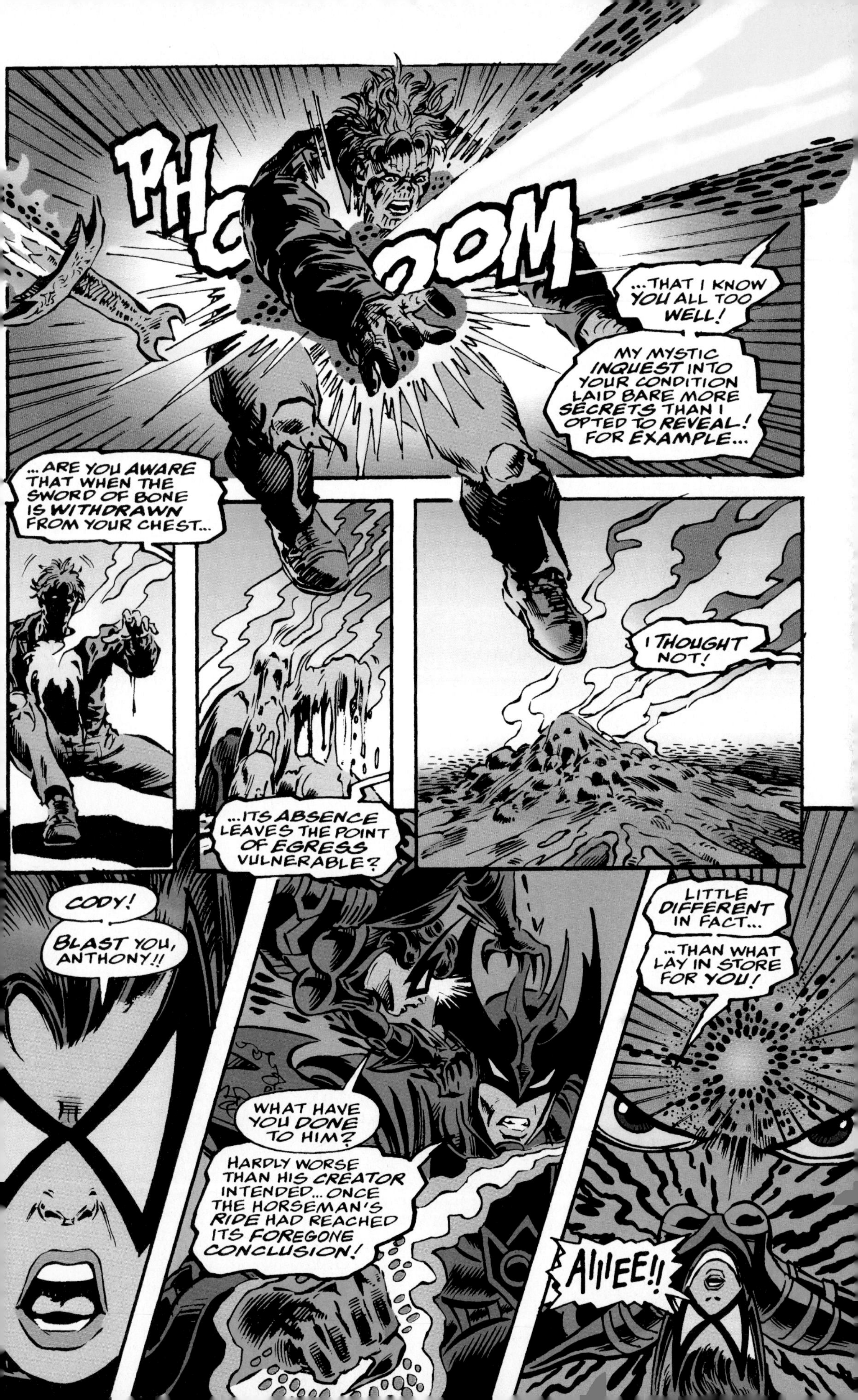
PHOOOOM
...THAT I KNOW YOU ALL TOO WELL!
MY MYSTIC INQUEST INTO YOUR CONDITION LAID BARE MORE SECRETS THAN I OPTED TO REVEAL! FOR EXAMPLE...
...ARE YOU AWARE THAT WHEN THE SWORD OF BONE IS WITHDRAWN FROM YOUR CHEST...
...ITS ABSENCE LEAVES THE POINT OF EGRESS VULNERABLE?
I THOUGHT NOT!
CODY!
BLAST YOU, ANTHONY!!
WHAT HAVE YOU DONE TO HIM?
HARDLY WORSE THAN HIS CREATOR INTENDED... ONCE THE HORSEMAN'S RIDE HAD REACHED ITS FOREGONE CONCLUSION!
LITTLE DIFFERENT IN FACT...
...THAN WHAT LAY IN STORE FOR YOU!
AIIEE!!

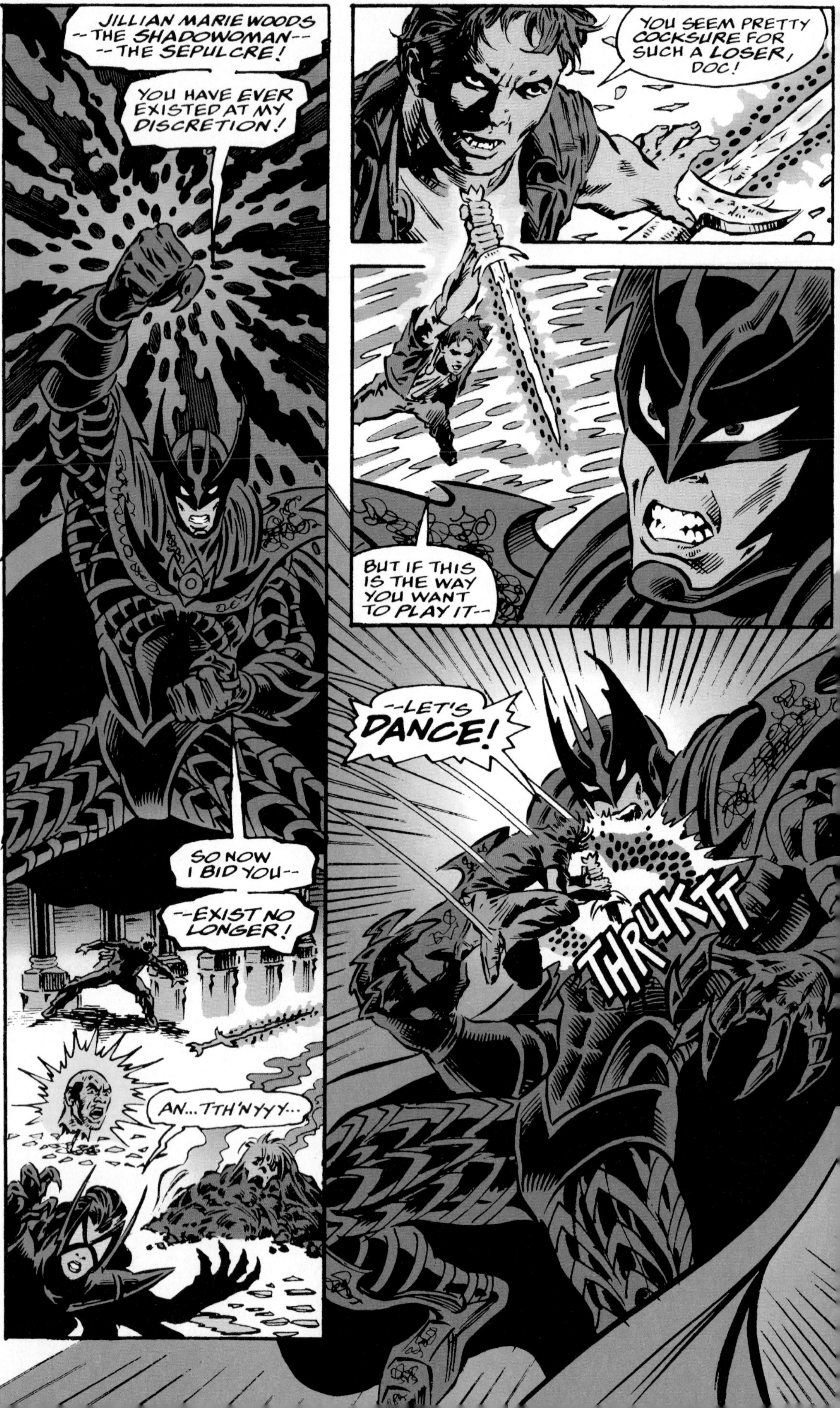
JILLIAN MARIE WOODS --THE SHADOWOMAN-- --THE SEPULCRE!
YOU HAVE EVER EXISTED AT MY DISCRETION!
YOU SEEM PRETTY COCKSURE FOR SUCH A LOSER, DOC!
BUT IF THIS IS THE WAY YOU WANT TO PLAY IT--
--LET'S DANCE!
THRUKTT
SO NOW I BID YOU--
--EXIST NO LONGER!
AN...TTH'NYYY...

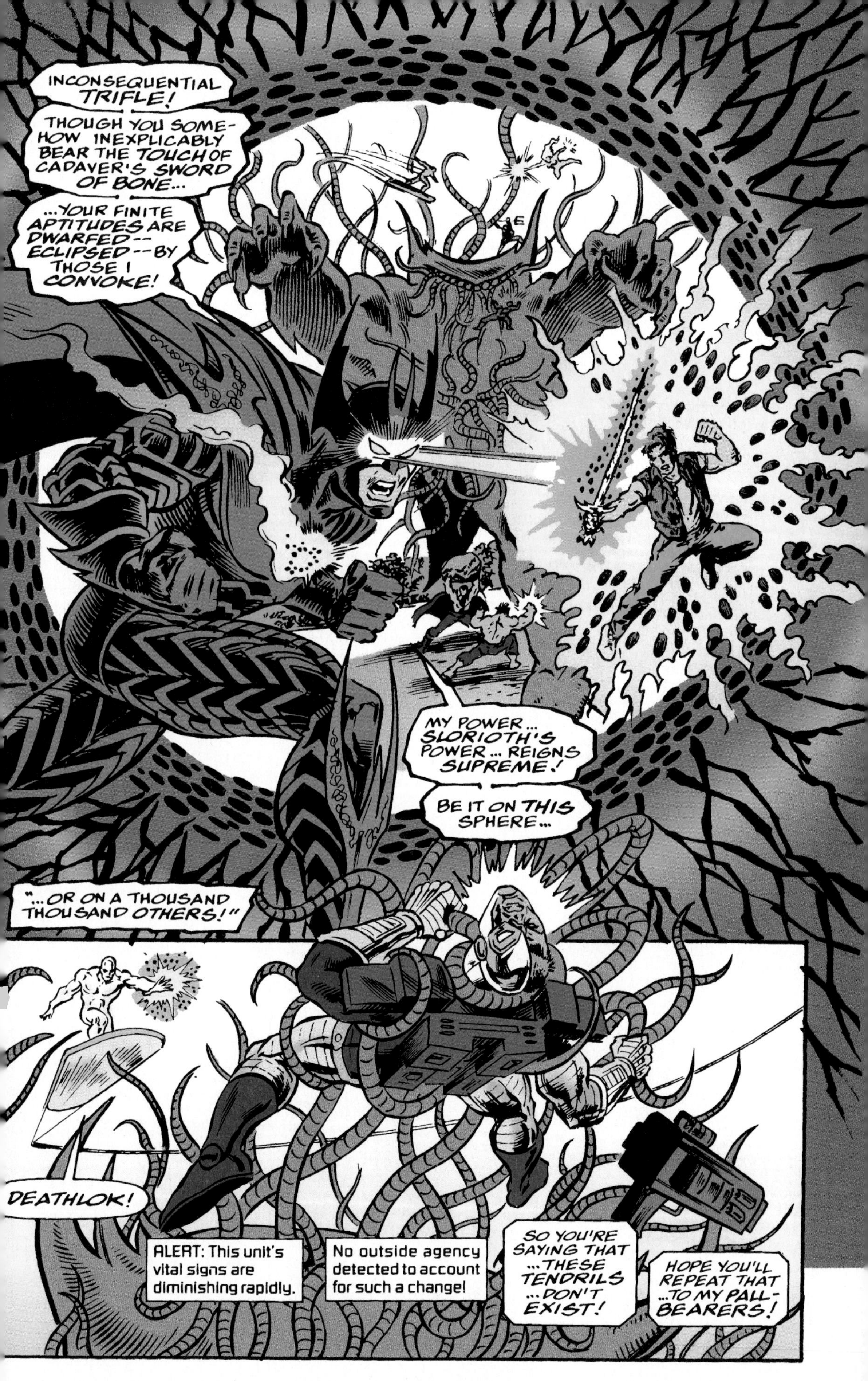
INCONSEQUENTIAL TRIFLE!
THOUGH YOU SOMEHOW INEXPLICABLY BEAR THE TOUCH OF CADAVER'S SWORD OF BONE...
...YOUR FINITE APTITUDES ARE DWARFED-- ECLIPSED--BY THOSE I CONVOKE!
MY POWER... SLORIOTH'S POWER... REIGNS SUPREME!
BE IT ON THIS SPHERE...
"...OR ON A THOUSAND THOUSAND OTHERS!"
DEATHLOK!
ALERT: This unit's vital signs are diminishing rapidly.
No outside agency detected to account for such a change!
SO YOU'RE SAYING THAT ...THESE TENDRILS ...DON'T EXIST!
HOPE YOU'LL REPEAT THAT ...TO MY PALL-BEARERS!

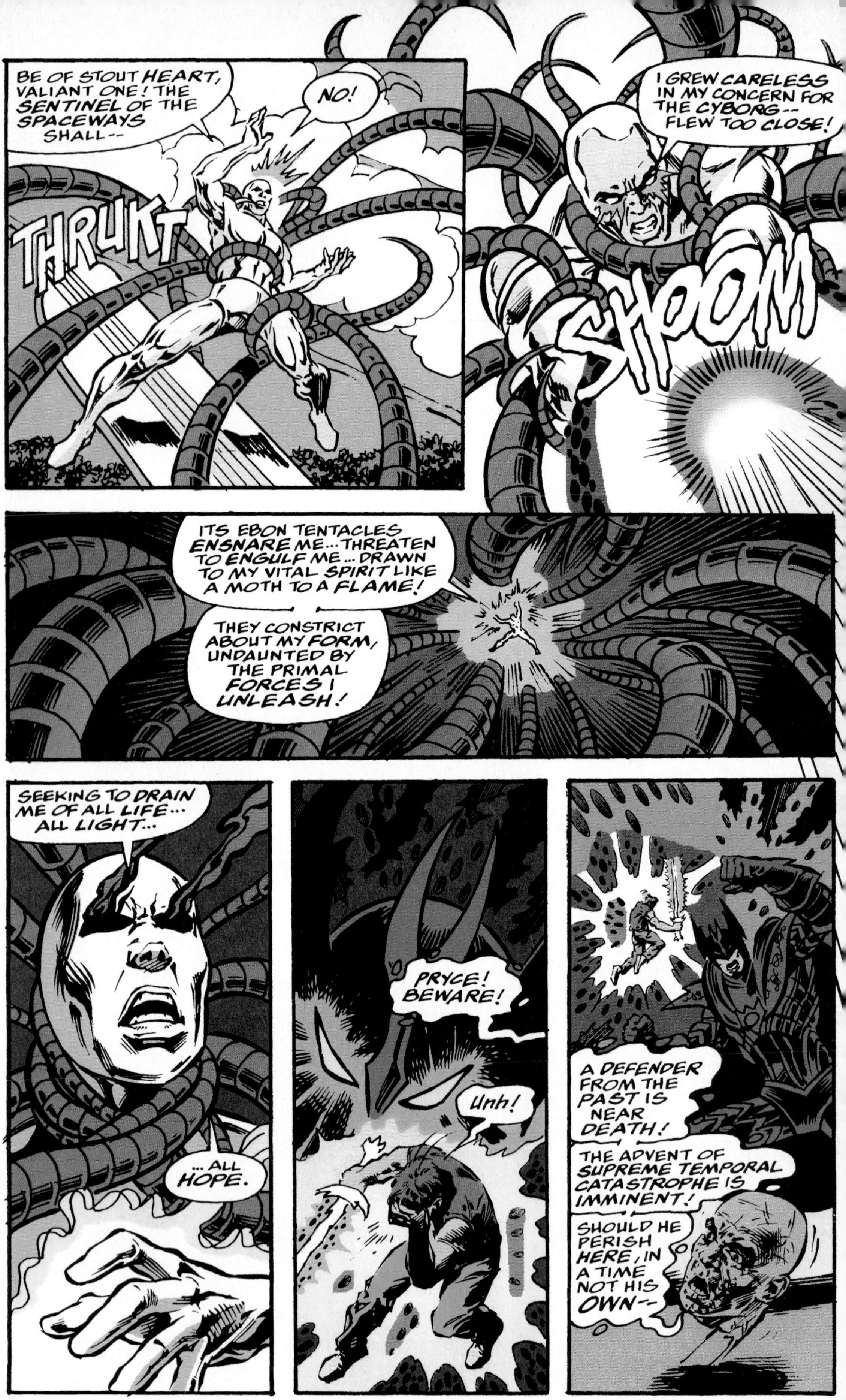
BE OF STOUT HEART, VALIANT ONE! THE SENTINEL OF THE SPACEWAYS SHALL--
NO!
THRUKT
I GREW CARELESS IN MY CONCERN FOR THE CYBORG-- FLEW TOO CLOSE!
SHOOM
ITS EBON TENTACLES ENSNARE ME... THREATEN TO ENGULF ME... DRAWN TO MY VITAL SPIRIT LIKE A MOTH TO A FLAME!
THEY CONSTRICT ABOUT MY FORM, UNDAUNTED BY THE PRIMAL FORCES I UNLEASH!
SEEKING TO DRAIN ME OF ALL LIFE... ALL LIGHT...
...ALL HOPE.
PRYCE! BEWARE!
Unh!
A DEFENDER FROM THE PAST IS NEAR DEATH!
THE ADVENT OF SUPREME TEMPORAL CATASTROPHE IS IMMINENT!
SHOULD HE PERISH HERE, IN A TIME NOT HIS OWN--

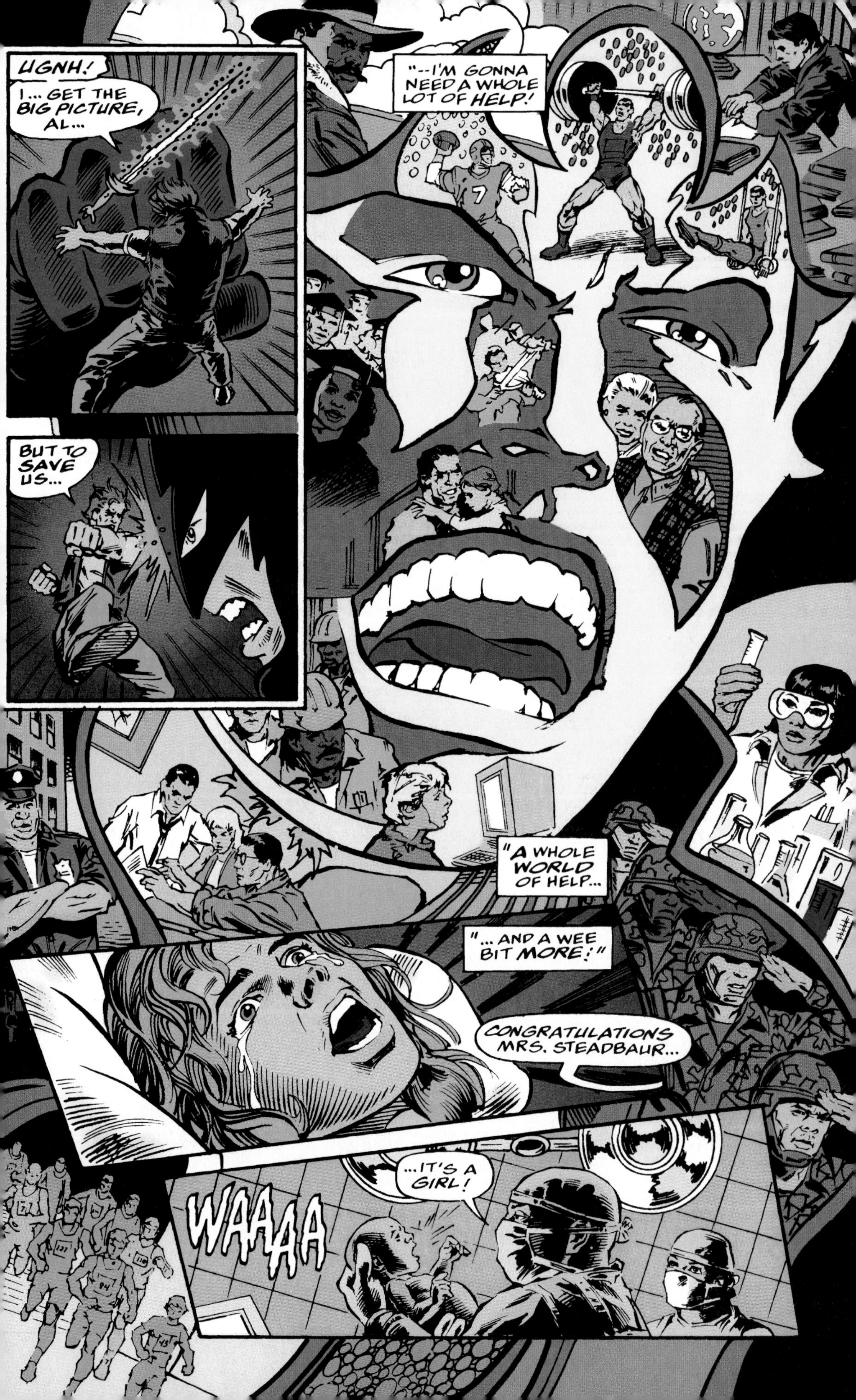
UGNH!
I... GET THE BIG PICTURE, AL...
"--I'M GONNA NEED A WHOLE LOT OF HELP!
BUT TO SAVE US...
"A WHOLE WORLD OF HELP...
"... AND A WEE BIT MORE!"
CONGRATULATIONS MRS. STEADBAUR...
...IT'S A GIRL!
WAAAA

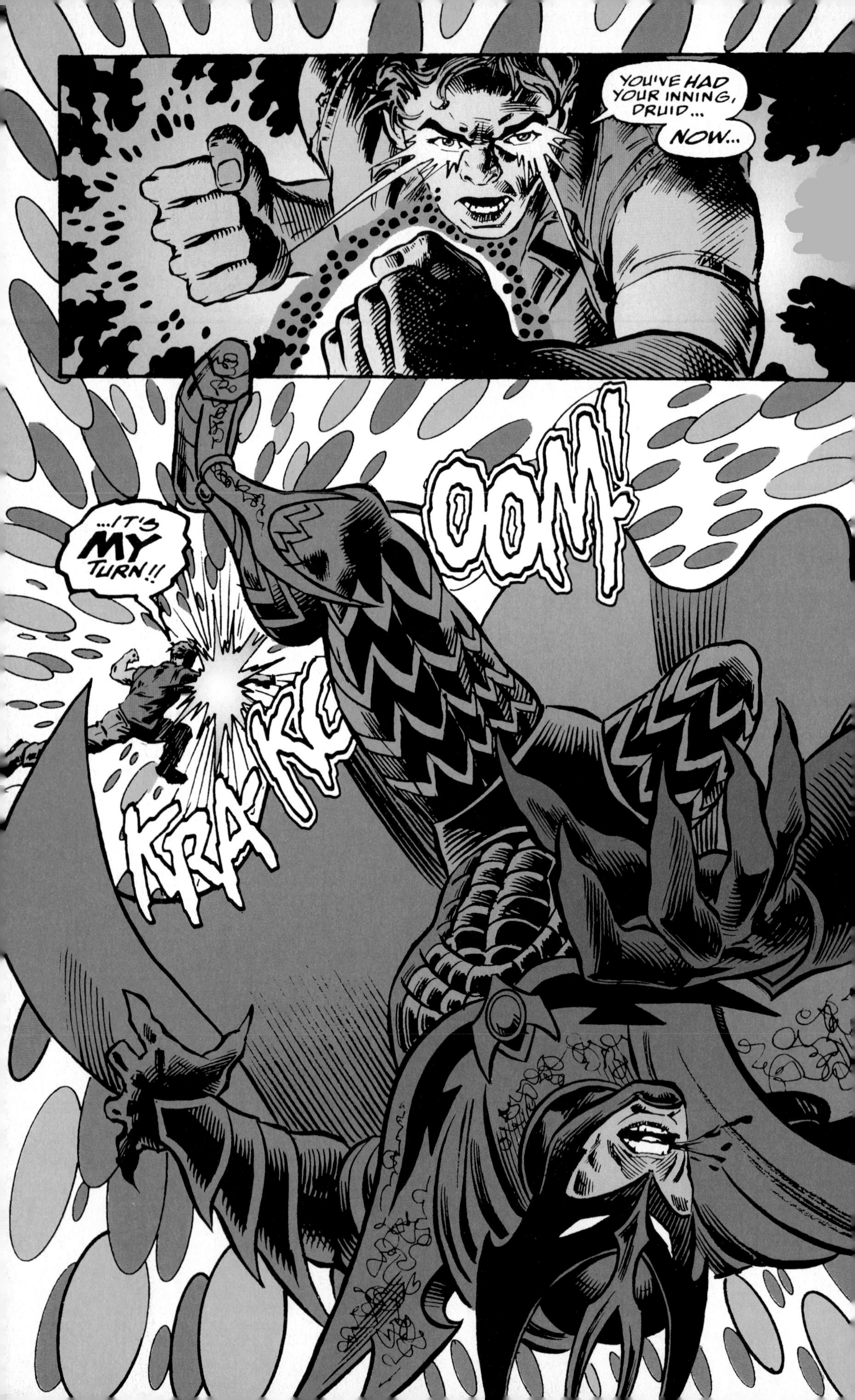
YOU'VE HAD YOUR INNING, DRUID...
NOW...
...IT'S MY TURN!!
KRAKKOOM!

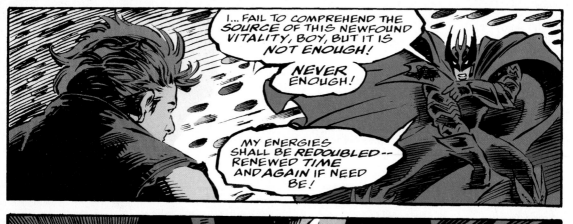

I... FAIL TO COMPREHEND THE *SOURCE OF THIS NEWFOUND VITALITY,* BOY, BUT IT IS *NOT ENOUGH!*

NEVER ENOUGH!

MY ENERGIES SHALL BE REDOUBLED -- RENEWED *TIME AND AGAIN* IF NEED BE!

TOGETHER WE EXTEND BEYOND THE JURISPRUDENCE OF ANY EARTHLY INSTRUMENTALITY!

GAIA'S GRACE NOTWITHSTANDING, YOU *CANNOT...*

...*WILL* NOT...

...*DETER* US!

THE WELL OF SLORIOTH RUNS *DEEP...*

...AND I HAVE YET TO QUAFF MY *LIMIT!*

I *KNOW.*

NEVER *INTENDED* TO.

...TO ATTRACT SOME UNWANTED *ATTENTION!*

A MASTERFUL *STRATAGEM,* MAGE...!

LABYRINTHINE...

...BUT ULTIMATELY *FALLACIOUS!*

JUST WANTED YOU TO MAKE A BIG ENOUGH *"BANG"...*

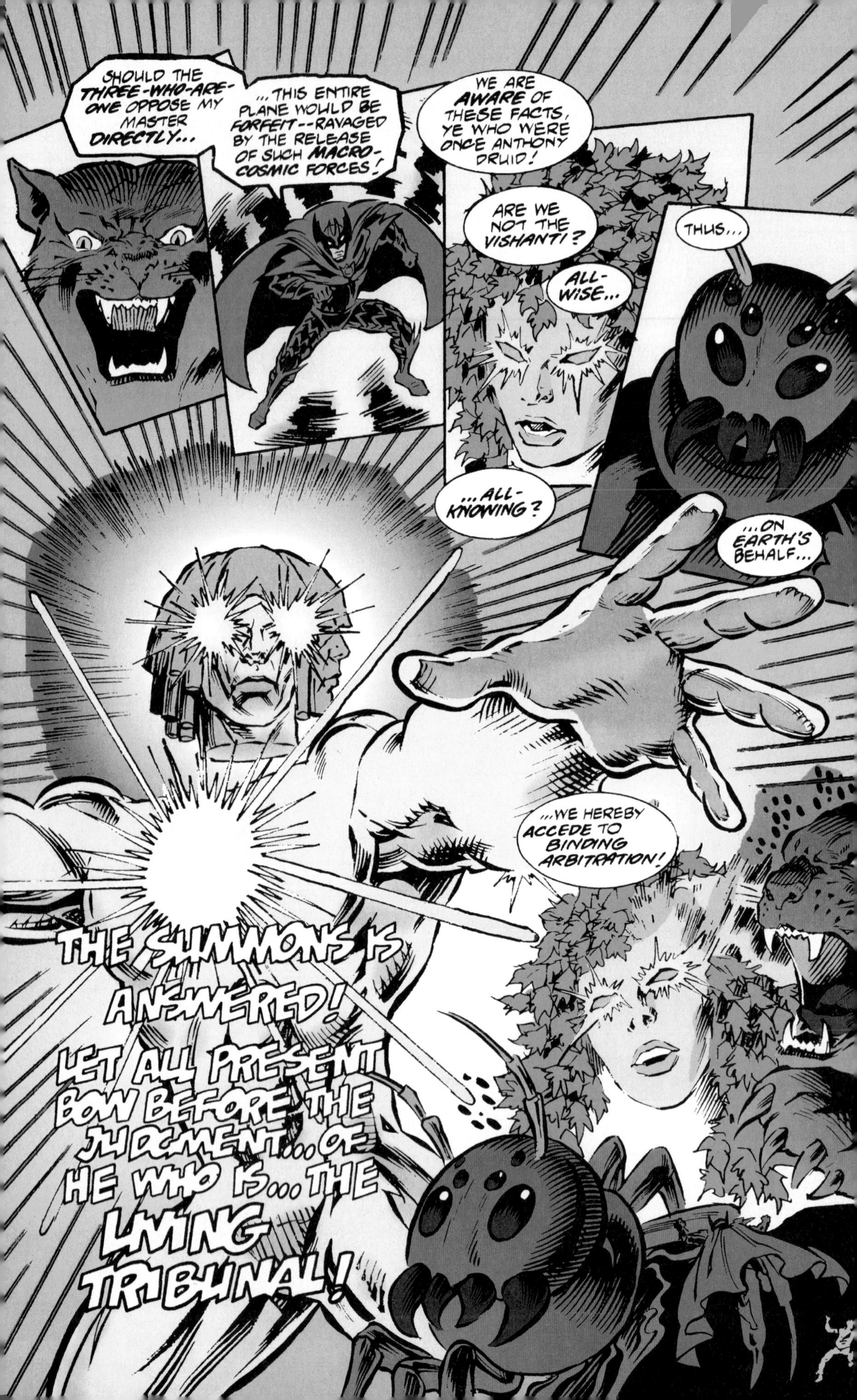
SHOULD THE THREE-WHO-ARE-ONE OPPOSE MY MASTER DIRECTLY...
...THIS ENTIRE PLANE WOULD BE FORFEIT--RAVAGED BY THE RELEASE OF SUCH MACRO-COSMIC FORCES!
WE ARE AWARE OF THESE FACTS, YE WHO WERE ONCE ANTHONY DRUID!
ARE WE NOT THE VISHANTI?
ALL-WISE...
...ALL-KNOWING?
THUS...
...ON EARTH'S BEHALF...
...WE HEREBY ACCEDE TO BINDING ARBITRATION!
THE SUMMONS IS ANSWERED!
LET ALL PRESENT BOW BEFORE THE JUDGMENT...OF HE WHO IS...THE LIVING TRIBUNAL!

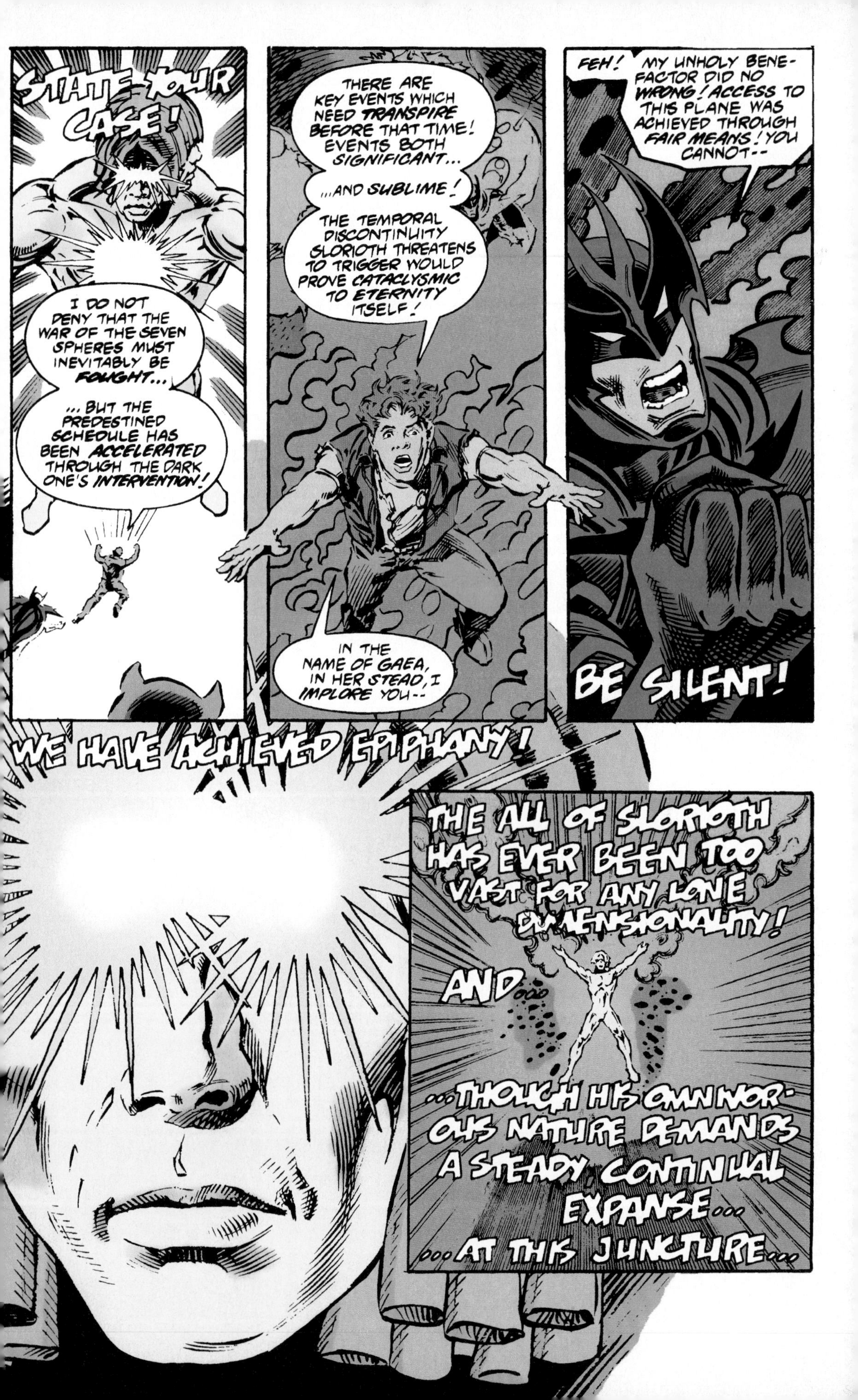
STATE YOUR CASE!
I DO NOT DENY THAT THE WAR OF THE SEVEN SPHERES MUST INEVITABLY BE FOUGHT...
...BUT THE PREDESTINED SCHEDULE HAS BEEN ACCELERATED THROUGH THE DARK ONE'S INTERVENTION!
THERE ARE KEY EVENTS WHICH NEED TRANSPIRE BEFORE THAT TIME! EVENTS BOTH SIGNIFICANT...
...AND SUBLIME!
THE TEMPORAL DISCONTINUITY SLORIOTH THREATENS TO TRIGGER WOULD PROVE CATACLYSMIC TO ETERNITY ITSELF!
IN THE NAME OF GAEA, IN HER STEAD, I IMPLORE YOU--
FEH!
MY UNHOLY BENEFACTOR DID NO WRONG! ACCESS TO THIS PLANE WAS ACHIEVED THROUGH FAIR MEANS! YOU CANNOT--
BE SILENT!
WE HAVE ACHIEVED EPIPHANY!
THE ALL OF SLORIOTH HAS EVER BEEN TOO VAST FOR ANY LONE DIMENSIONALITY!
AND...
...THOUGH HIS OMNIVOROUS NATURE DEMANDS A STEADY CONTINUAL EXPANSE...
...AT THIS JUNCTURE...

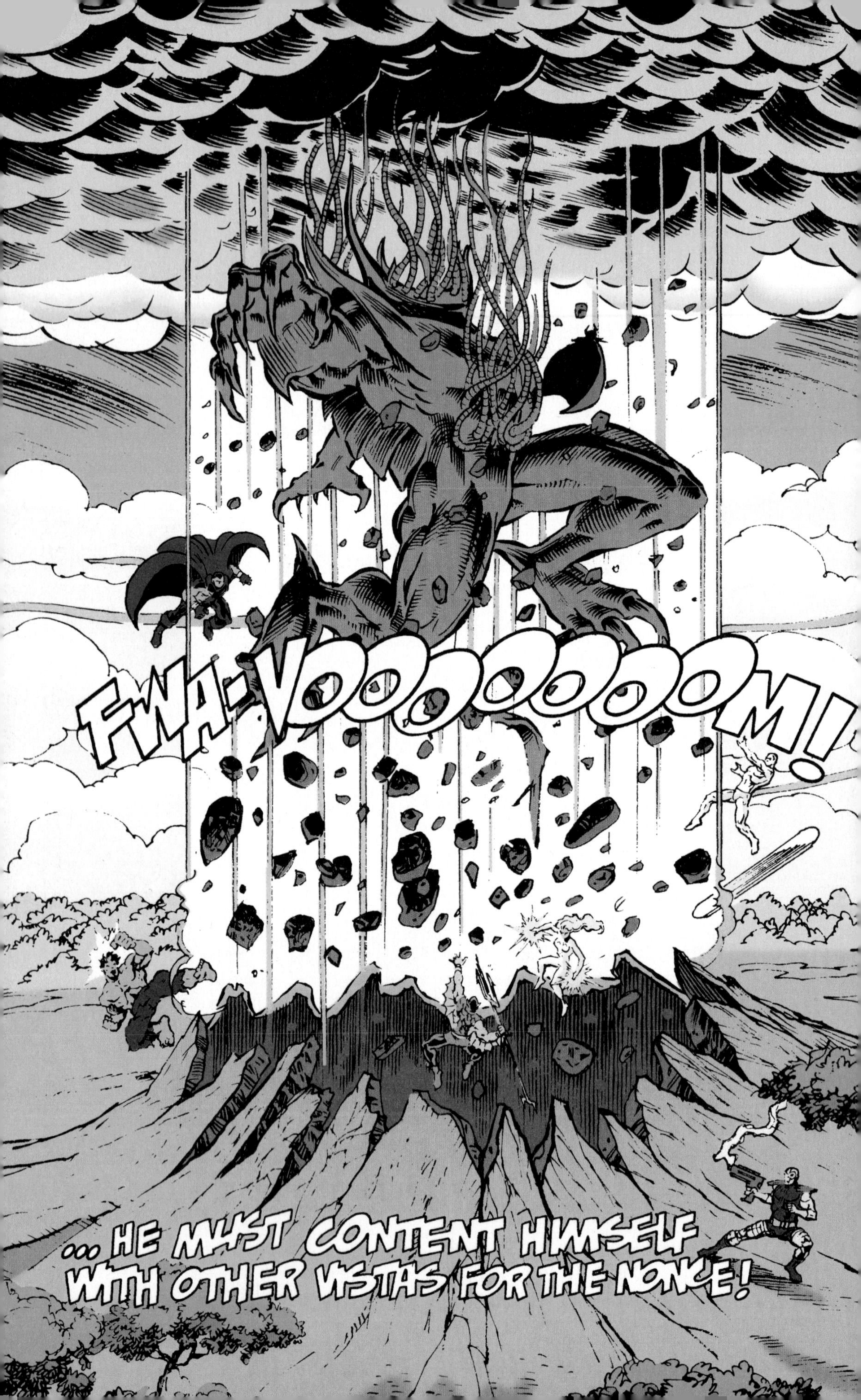
FWA-VOOOOOOOOOM!!
...HE MUST CONTENT HIMSELF WITH OTHER VISTAS FOR THE NONCE!

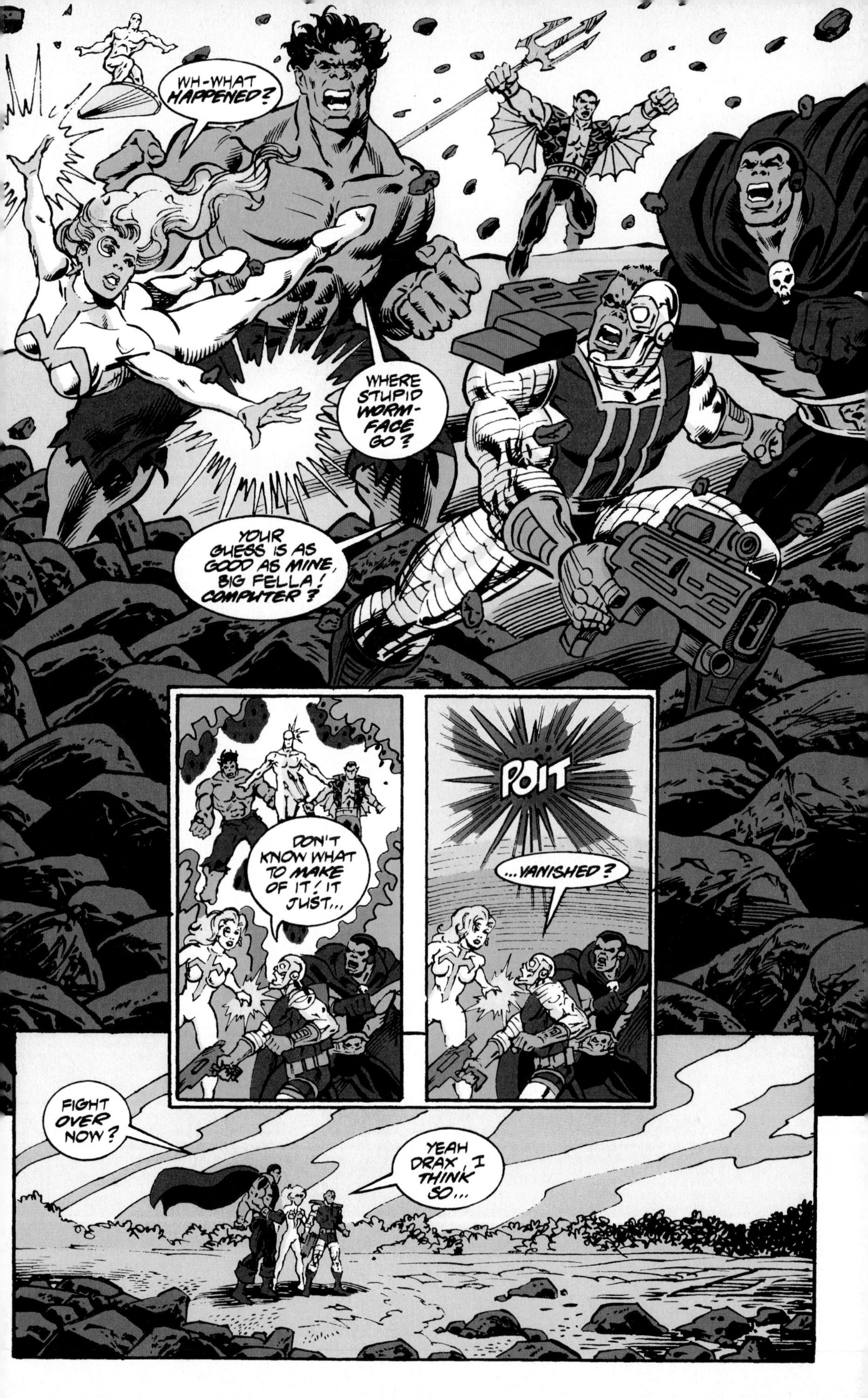
WH-WHAT HAPPENED?
WHERE STUPID WORM-FACE GO?
YOUR GUESS IS AS GOOD AS MINE, BIG FELLA! COMPUTER?
DON'T KNOW WHAT TO MAKE OF IT! IT JUST...
POIT
...VANISHED?
FIGHT OVER NOW?
YEAH DRAX, I THINK SO...

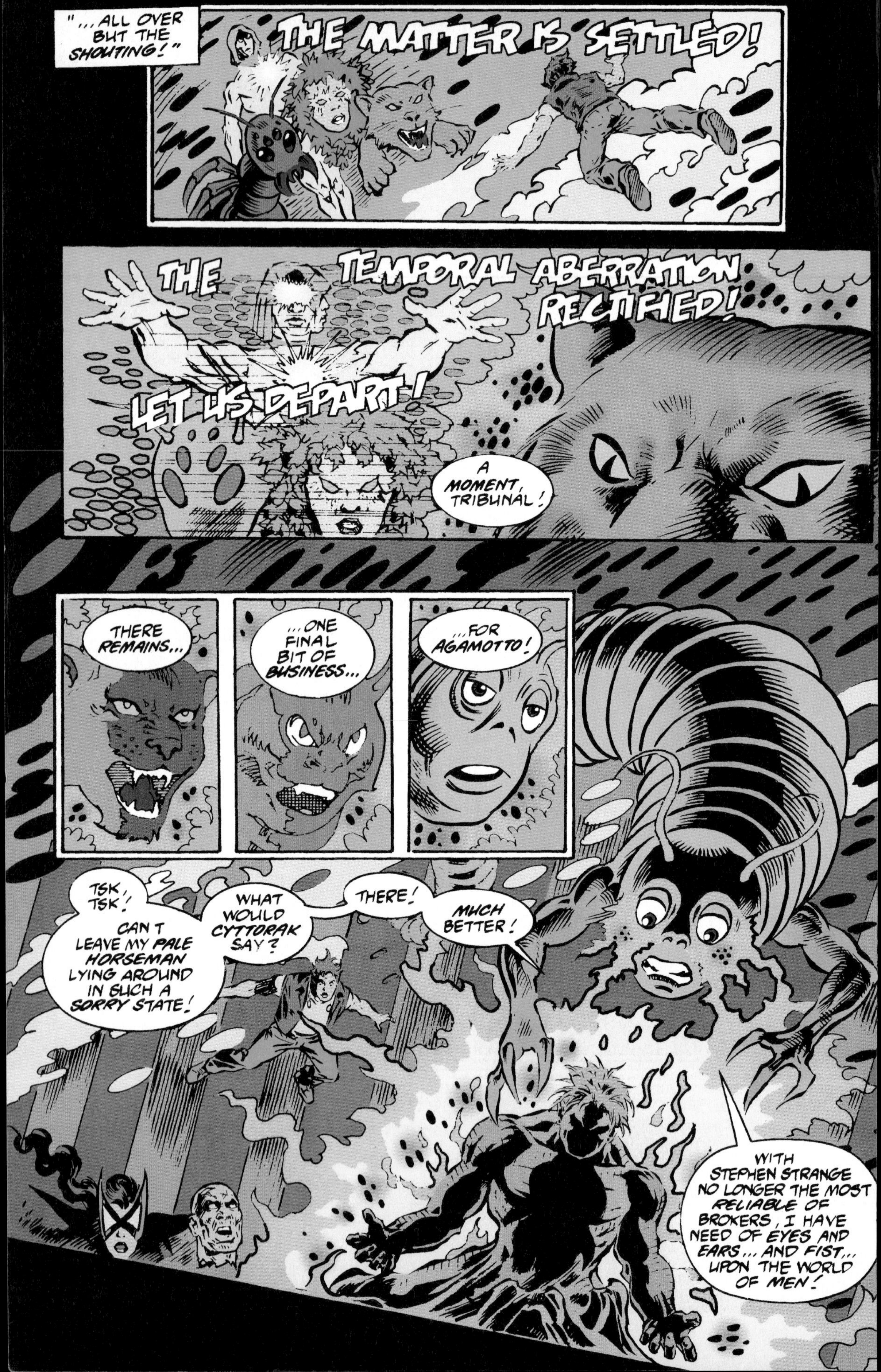
"...ALL OVER BUT THE SHOUTING!"
THE MATTER IS SETTLED!
THE TEMPORAL ABERRATION RECTIFIED!
LET US DEPART!
A MOMENT, TRIBUNAL!
THERE REMAINS...
...ONE FINAL BIT OF BUSINESS...
...FOR AGAMOTTO!
TSK, TSK!
CAN T LEAVE MY PALE HORSEMAN LYING AROUND IN SUCH A SORRY STATE!
WHAT WOULD CYTTORAK SAY?
THERE!
MUCH BETTER!
WITH STEPHEN STRANGE NO LONGER THE MOST RELIABLE OF BROKERS, I HAVE NEED OF EYES AND EARS... AND FIST... UPON THE WORLD OF MEN!

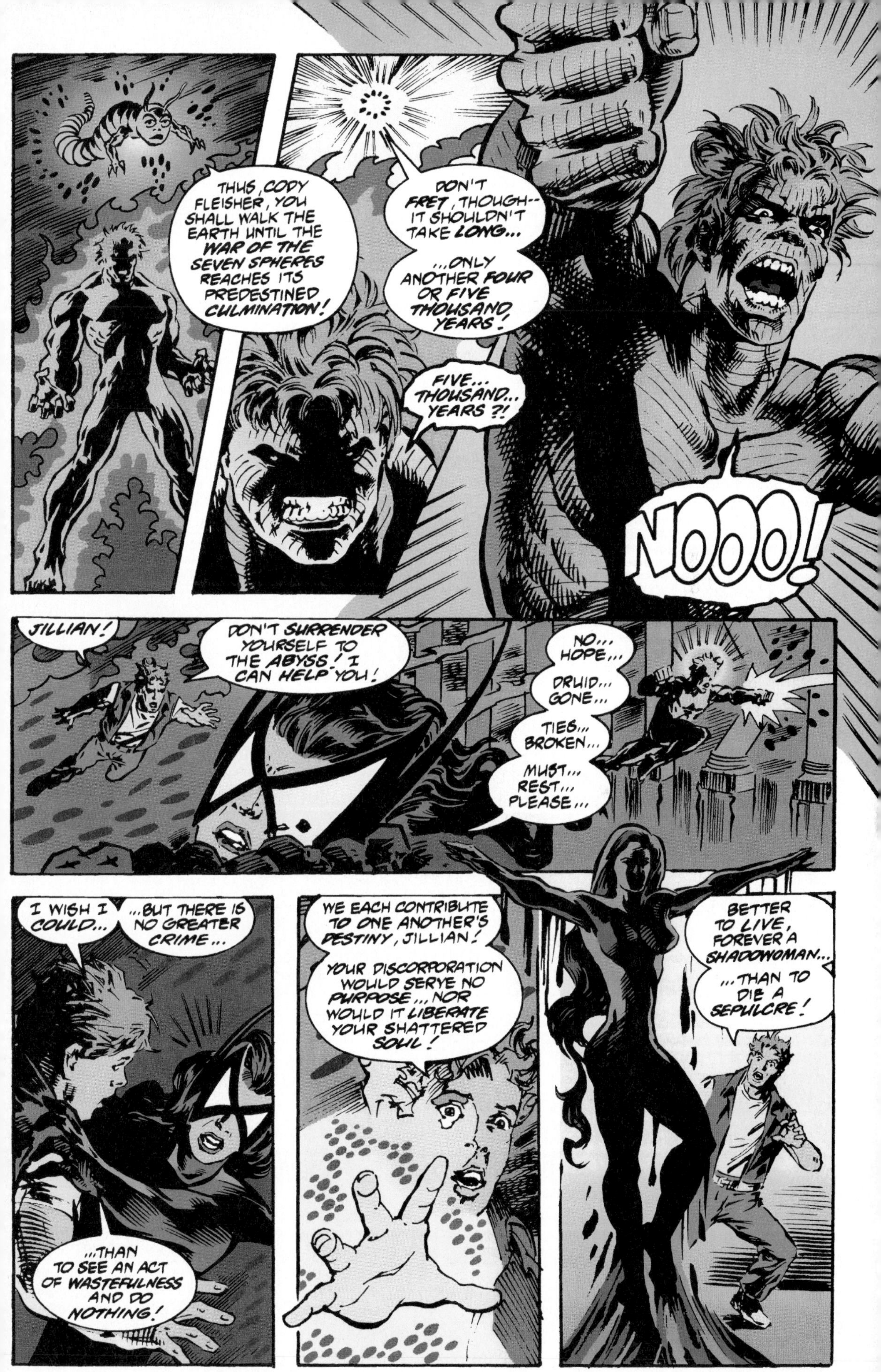
THUS, CODY FLEISHER, YOU SHALL WALK THE EARTH UNTIL THE WAR OF THE SEVEN SPHERES REACHES ITS PREDESTINED CULMINATION!
DON'T FRET, THOUGH-- IT SHOULDN'T TAKE LONG...
...ONLY ANOTHER FOUR OR FIVE THOUSAND YEARS!
FIVE... THOUSAND... YEARS ?!
NOOO!
JILLIAN!
DON'T SURRENDER YOURSELF TO THE ABYSS! I CAN HELP YOU!
NO... HOPE...
DRUID... GONE...
TIES... BROKEN...
MUST... REST... PLEASE...
I WISH I COULD...
...BUT THERE IS NO GREATER CRIME...
...THAN TO SEE AN ACT OF WASTEFULNESS AND DO NOTHING!
WE EACH CONTRIBUTE TO ONE ANOTHER'S DESTINY, JILLIAN!
YOUR DISCORPORATION WOULD SERVE NO PURPOSE... NOR WOULD IT LIBERATE YOUR SHATTERED SOUL!
BETTER TO LIVE, FOREVER A SHADOWOMAN...
...THAN TO DIE A SEPULCRE!

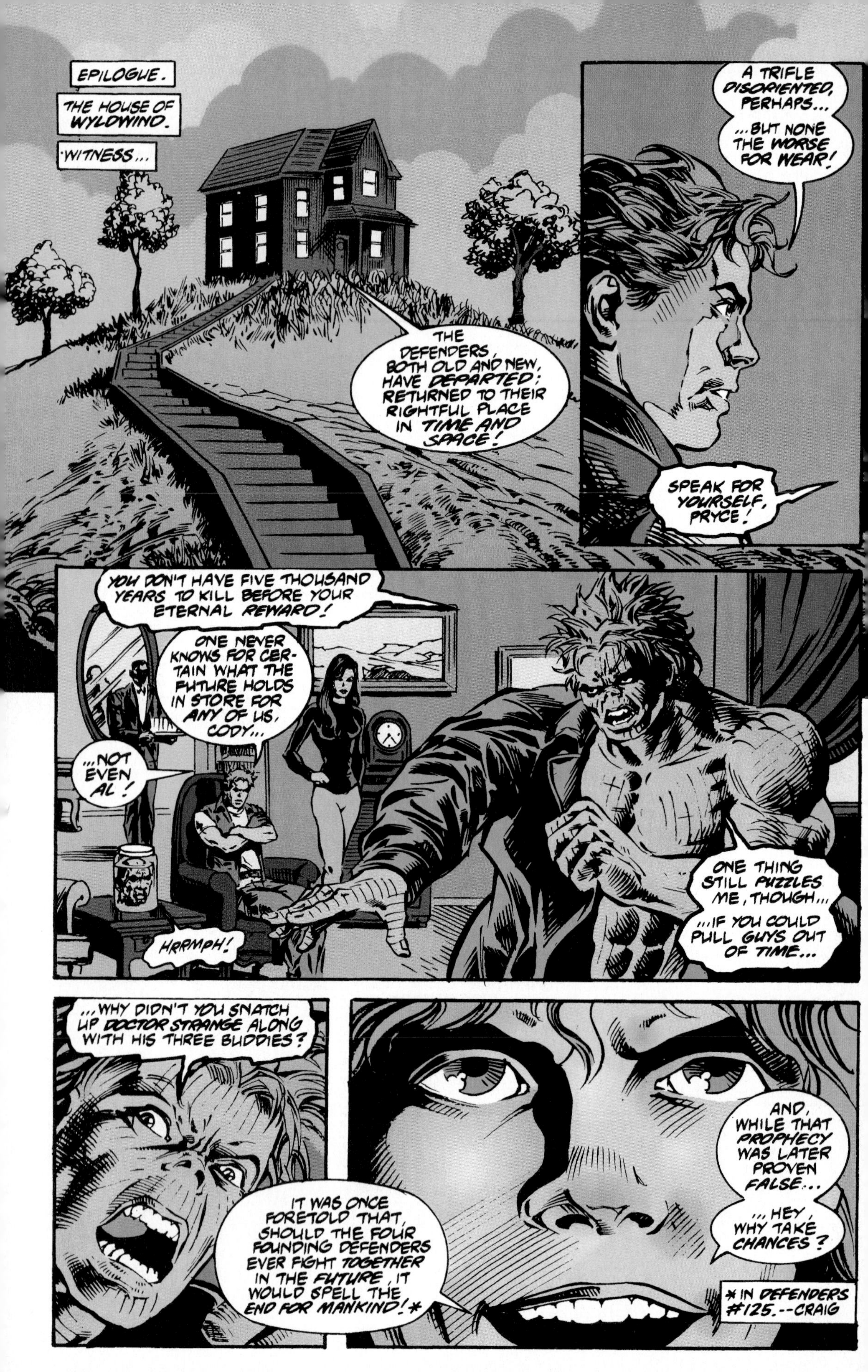

EPILOGUE.
THE HOUSE OF WYLOWIND.
WITNESS...
THE DEFENDERS, BOTH OLD AND NEW, HAVE DEPARTED; RETURNED TO THEIR RIGHTFUL PLACE IN TIME AND SPACE!
A TRIFLE DISORIENTED, PERHAPS...
...BUT NONE THE WORSE FOR WEAR!
SPEAK FOR YOURSELF, PRYCE!
YOU DON'T HAVE FIVE THOUSAND YEARS TO KILL BEFORE YOUR ETERNAL REWARD!
ONE NEVER KNOWS FOR CERTAIN WHAT THE FUTURE HOLDS IN STORE FOR ANY OF US, CODY...
...NOT EVEN AL!
HRRMPH!
ONE THING STILL PUZZLES ME, THOUGH...
...IF YOU COULD PULL GUYS OUT OF TIME...
...WHY DIDN'T YOU SNATCH UP DOCTOR STRANGE ALONG WITH HIS THREE BUDDIES?
IT WAS ONCE FORETOLD THAT, SHOULD THE FOUR FOUNDING DEFENDERS EVER FIGHT TOGETHER IN THE FUTURE, IT WOULD SPELL THE END FOR MANKIND!*
AND, WHILE THAT PROPHECY WAS LATER PROVEN FALSE...
...HEY, WHY TAKE CHANCES?
*IN DEFENDERS #125.--CRAIG

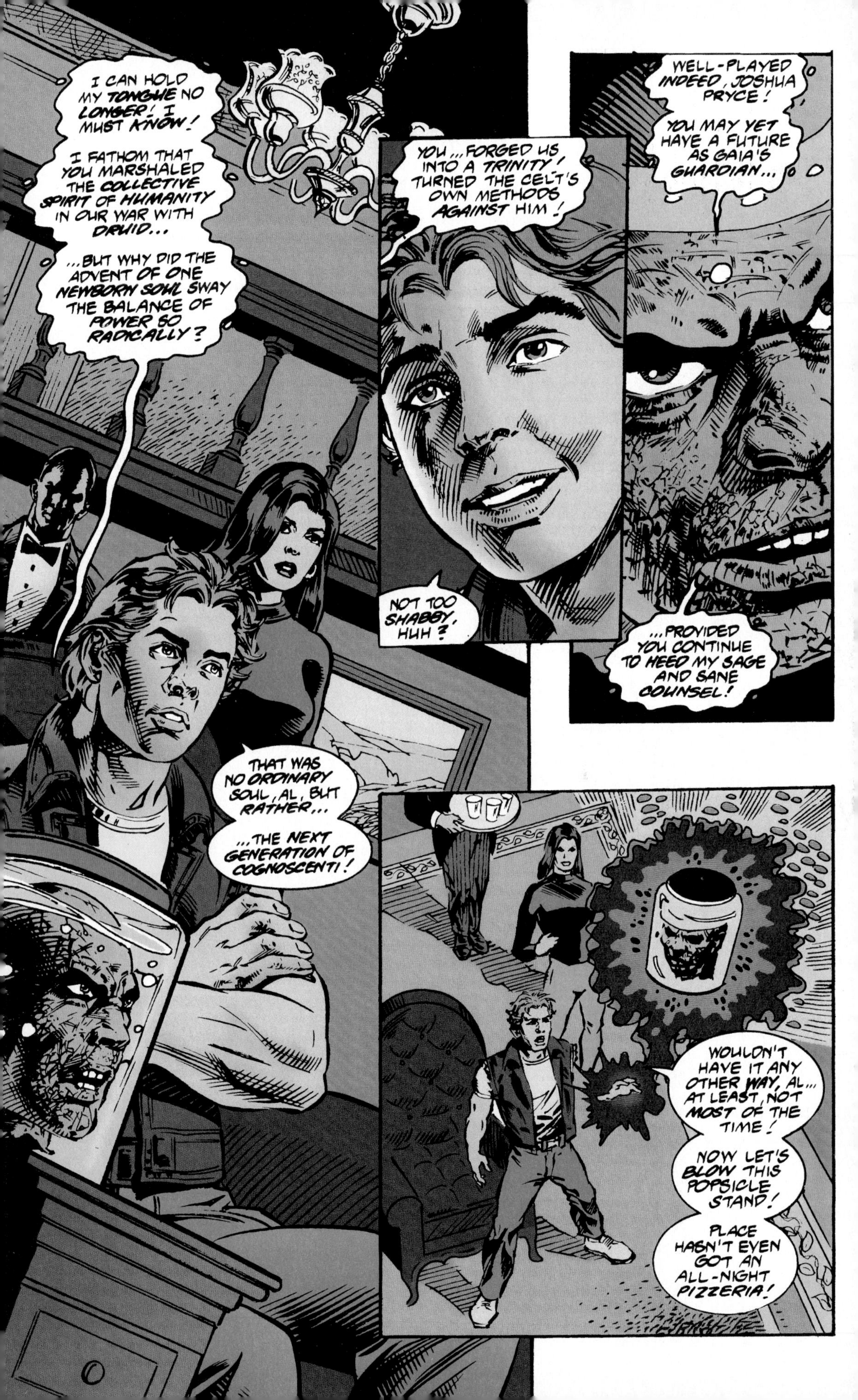
I CAN HOLD MY TONGUE NO LONGER! I MUST KNOW!
I FATHOM THAT YOU MARSHALED THE COLLECTIVE SPIRIT OF HUMANITY IN OUR WAR WITH DRUID...
...BUT WHY DID THE ADVENT OF ONE NEWBORN SOUL SWAY THE BALANCE OF POWER SO RADICALLY?
THAT WAS NO ORDINARY SOUL, AL, BUT RATHER...
...THE NEXT GENERATION OF COGNOSCENTI!
YOU... FORGED US INTO A TRINITY! TURNED THE CELT'S OWN METHODS AGAINST HIM!
NOT TOO SHABBY, HUH?
WELL-PLAYED INDEED, JOSHUA PRYCE!
YOU MAY YET HAVE A FUTURE AS GAIA'S GUARDIAN...
...PROVIDED YOU CONTINUE TO HEED MY SAGE AND SANE COUNSEL!
WOULDN'T HAVE IT ANY OTHER WAY, AL... AT LEAST, NOT MOST OF THE TIME!
NOW LET'S BLOW THIS POPSICLE STAND!
PLACE HASN'T GOT EVEN GOT AN ALL-NIGHT PIZZERIA!

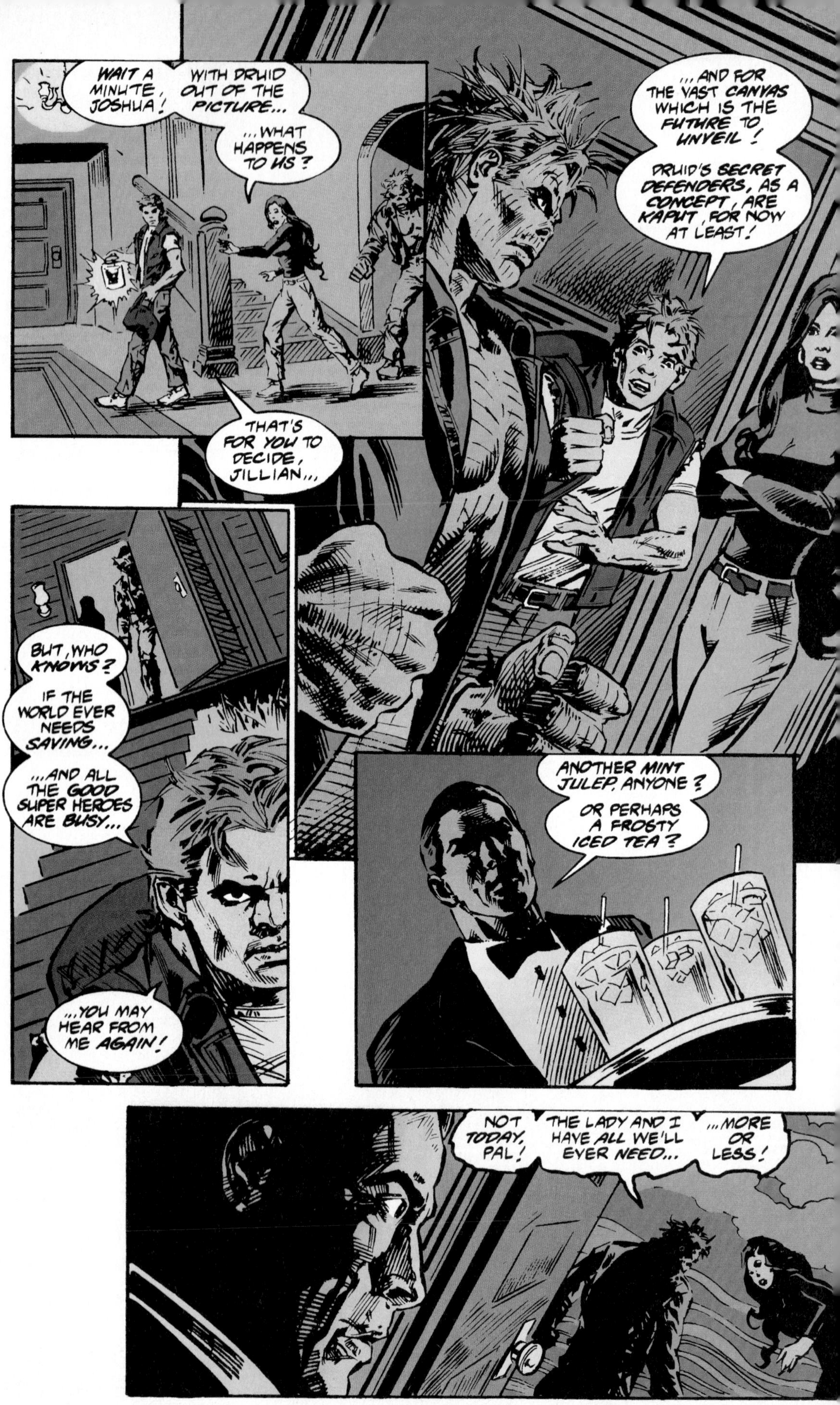
WAIT A MINUTE, JOSHUA!
WITH DRUID OUT OF THE PICTURE...
...WHAT HAPPENS TO US?
THAT'S FOR YOU TO DECIDE, JILLIAN...
...AND FOR THE VAST CANVAS WHICH IS THE FUTURE TO UNVEIL!
DRUID'S SECRET DEFENDERS, AS A CONCEPT, ARE KAPUT, FOR NOW AT LEAST!
BUT, WHO KNOWS?
IF THE WORLD EVER NEEDS SAVING...
...AND ALL THE GOOD SUPER HEROES ARE BUSY...
...YOU MAY HEAR FROM ME AGAIN!
ANOTHER MINT JULEP, ANYONE?
OR PERHAPS A FROSTY ICED TEA?
NOT TODAY, PAL!
THE LADY AND I HAVE ALL WE'LL EVER NEED...
...MORE OR LESS!

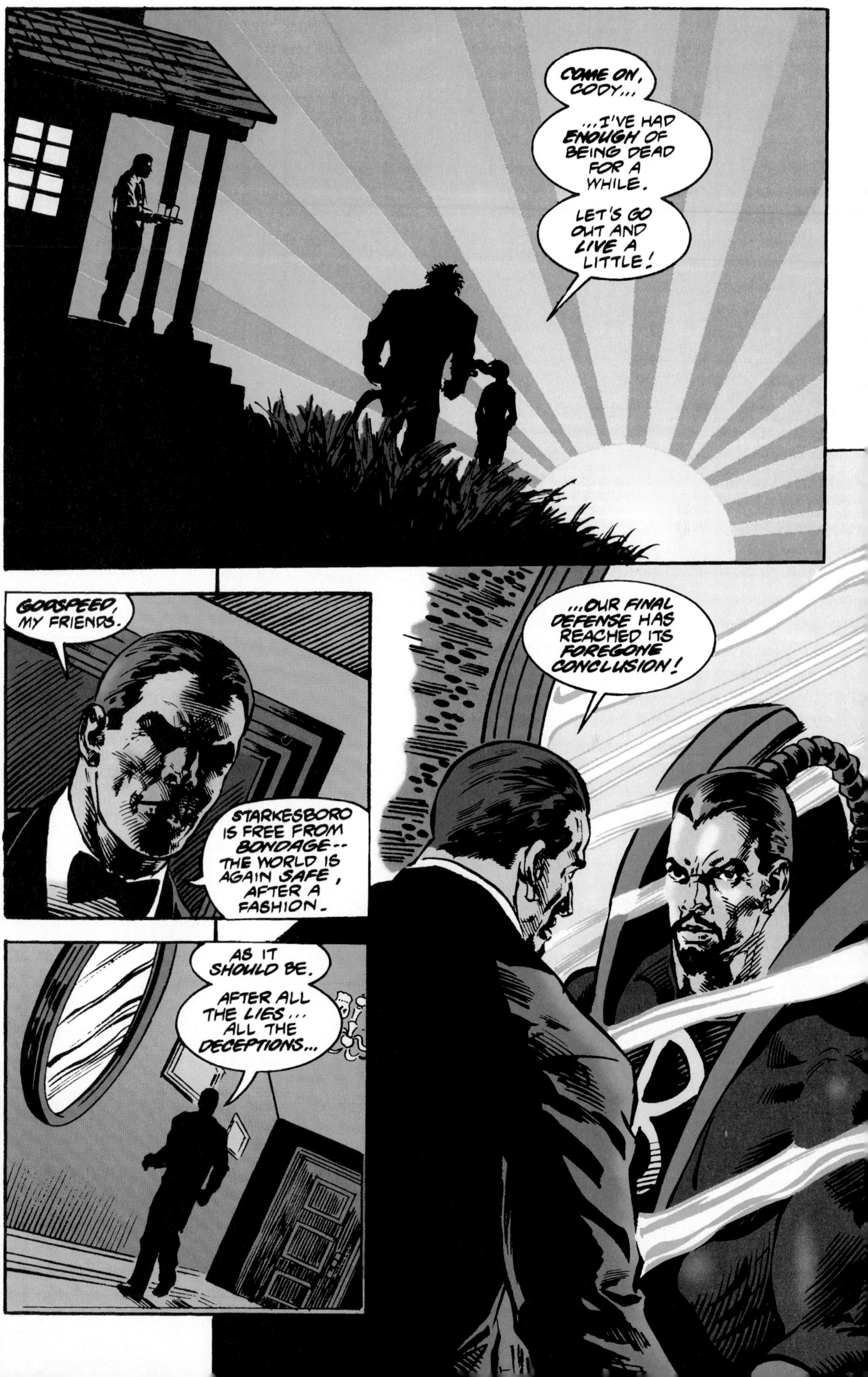
COME ON, CODY...
...I'VE HAD ENOUGH OF BEING DEAD FOR A WHILE.
LET'S GO OUT AND LIVE A LITTLE!
GODSPEED, MY FRIENDS.
STARKESBORO IS FREE FROM BONDAGE-- THE WORLD IS AGAIN SAFE, AFTER A FASHION.
AS IT SHOULD BE.
AFTER ALL THE LIES... ALL THE DECEPTIONS...
...OUR FINAL DEFENSE HAS REACHED ITS FOREGONE CONCLUSION!

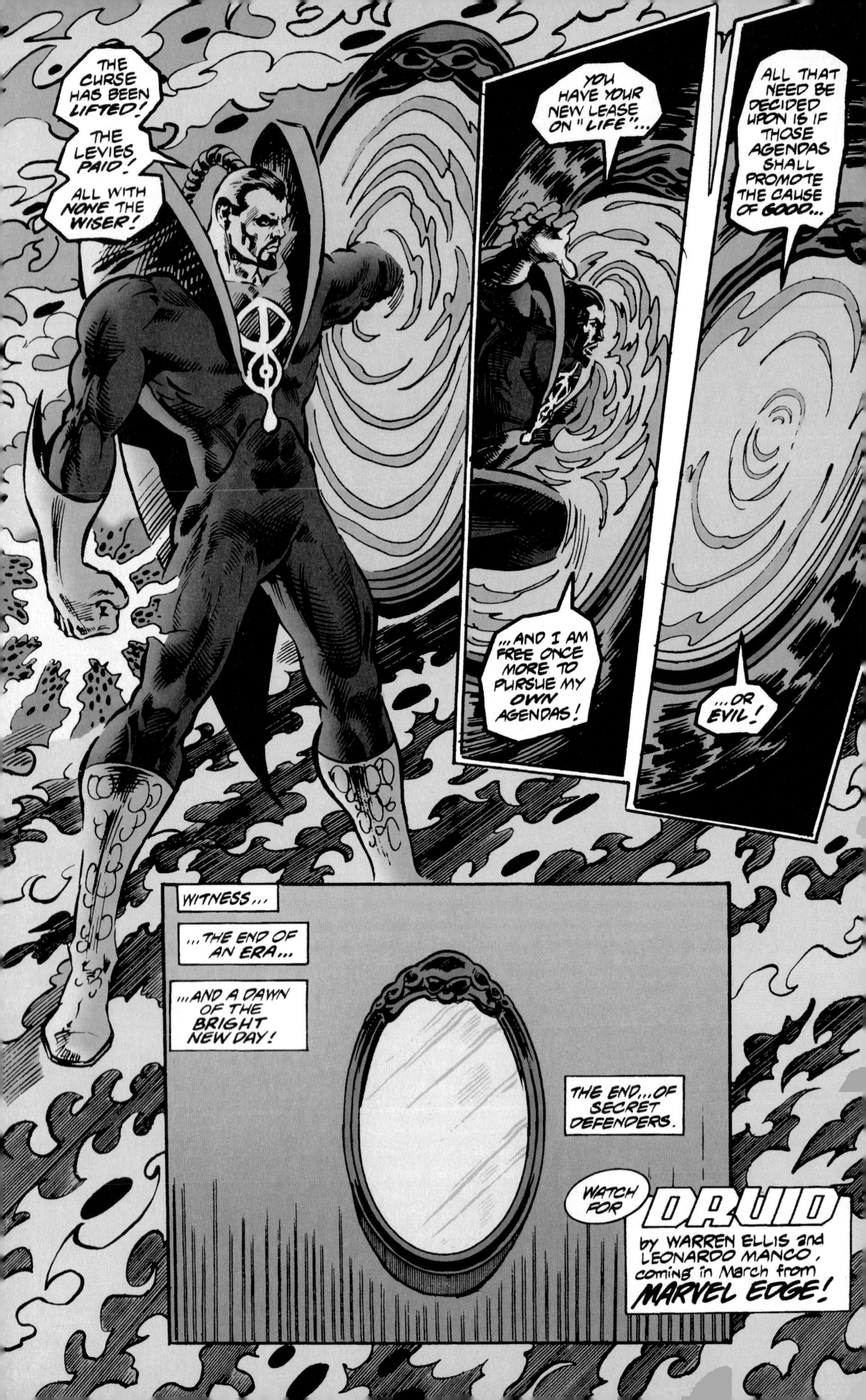
THE CURSE HAS BEEN LIFTED! THE LEVIES PAID! ALL WITH NONE THE WISER!
YOU HAVE YOUR NEW LEASE ON "LIFE"...
...AND I AM FREE ONCE MORE TO PURSUE MY OWN AGENDAS!
ALL THAT NEED BE DECIDED UPON IS IF THOSE AGENDAS SHALL PROMOTE THE CAUSE OF GOOD...
...OR EVIL!
WITNESS...
...THE END OF AN ERA...
...AND A DAWN OF THE BRIGHT NEW DAY!
THE END...OF SECRET DEFENDERS.
WATCH FOR
DRUID
by WARREN ELLIS and LEONARDO MANCO, coming in March from MARVEL EDGE!

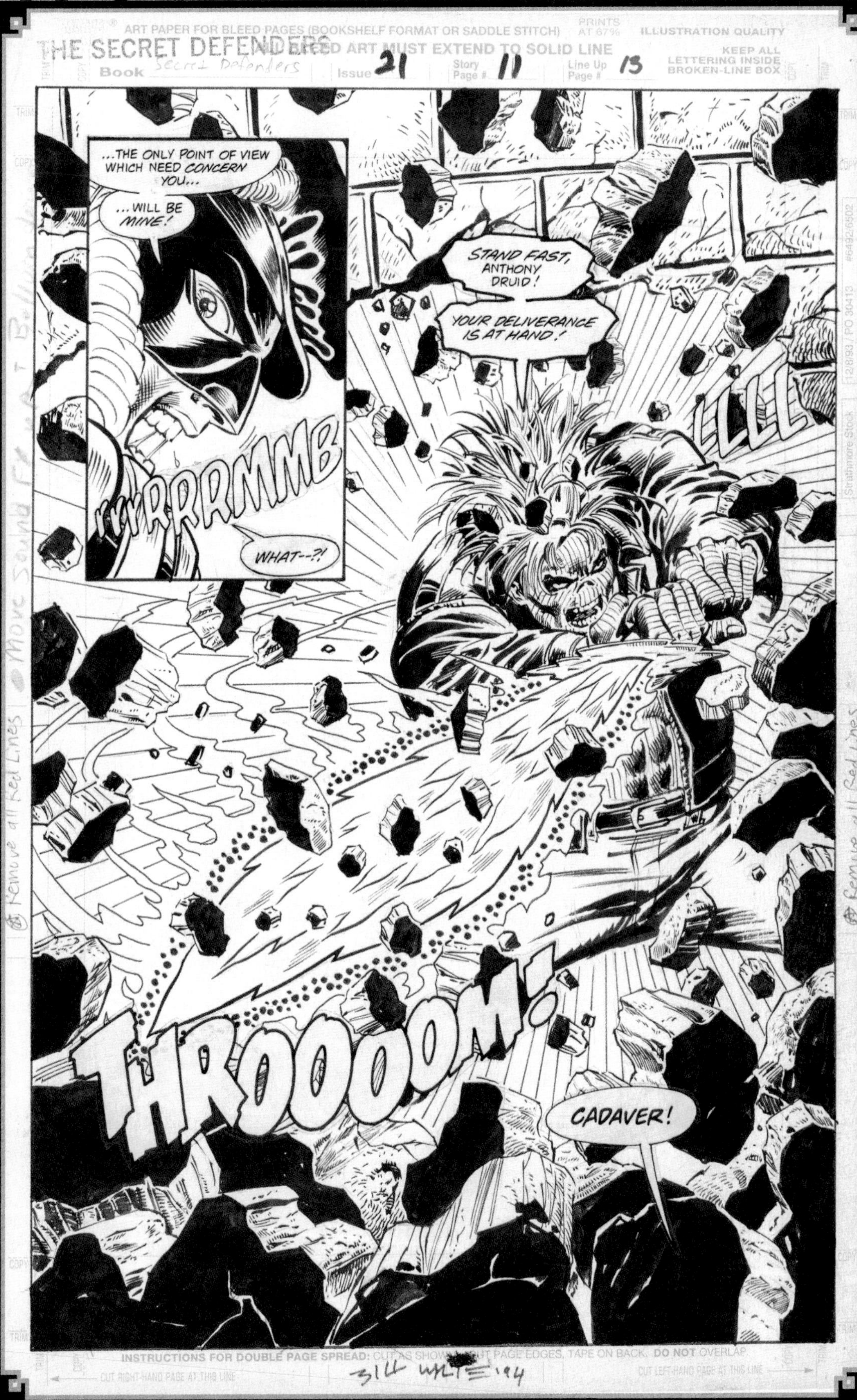
ART PAPER FOR BLEED PAGES (BOOKSHELF FORMAT OR SADDLE STITCH)
PRINTS AT 67%
ILLUSTRATION QUALITY
THE SECRET DEFENDERS
ALL BLEED ART MUST EXTEND TO SOLID LINE
KEEP ALL LETTERING INSIDE BROKEN-LINE BOX
Book Secret Defenders
Issue 21
Story Page # 11
Line Up Page # 13
...THE ONLY POINT OF VIEW WHICH NEED CONCERN YOU...
...WILL BE MINE!
rrrRRRMMMB
WHAT--?!
STAND FAST, ANTHONY DRUID!
YOUR DELIVERANCE IS AT HAND!
THROOOOM!
CADAVER!
Remove all Red Lines
Remove all Red Lines
INSTRUCTIONS FOR DOUBLE PAGE SPREAD: CUT AS SHOWN ... PAGE EDGES, TAPE ON BACK. DO NOT OVERLAP.
CUT RIGHT-HAND PAGE AT THIS LINE
CUT LEFT-HAND PAGE AT THIS LINE
Strathmore Stock
12/8/93 | PO 30413
#6492/6502

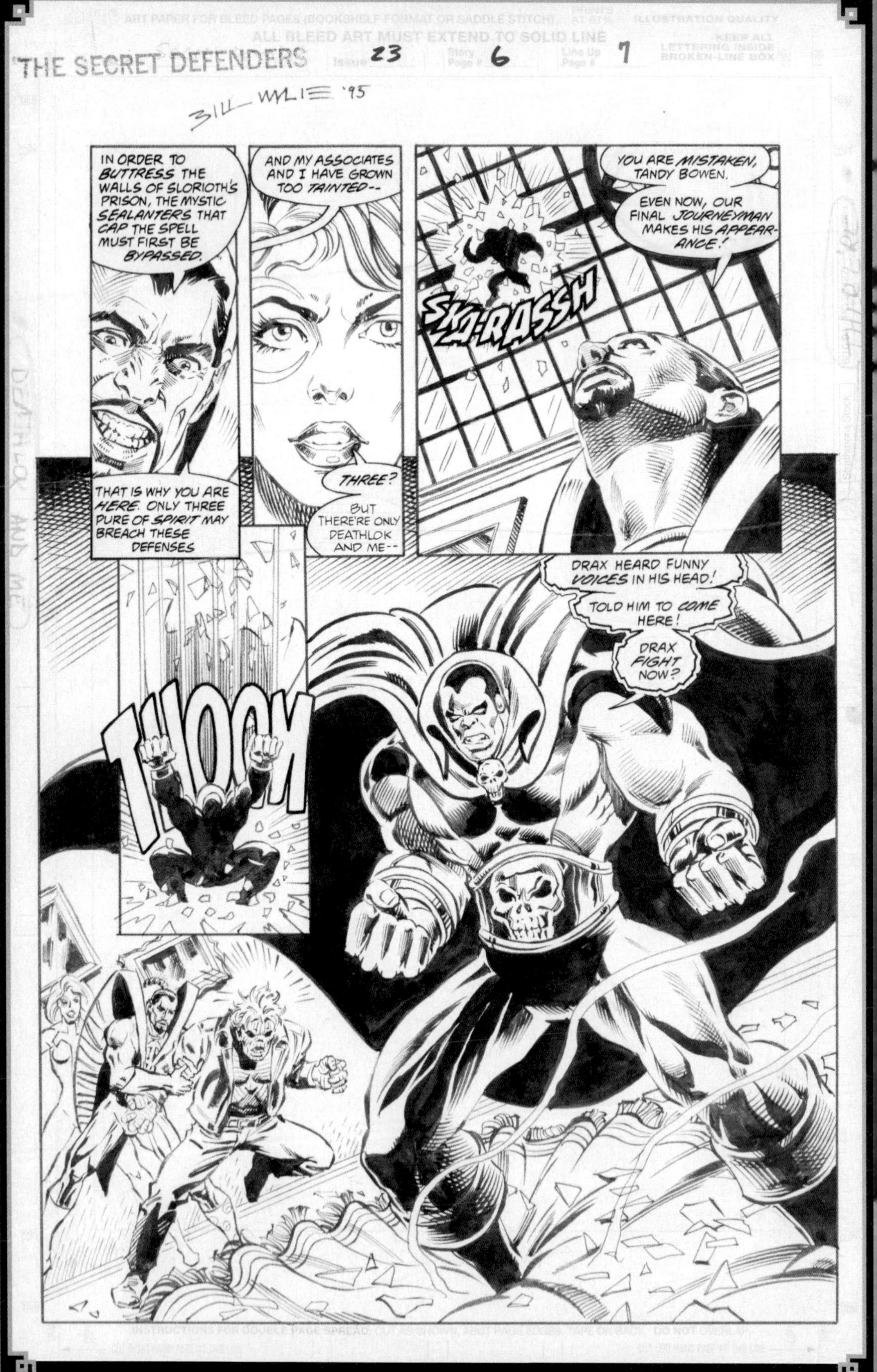
THE SECRET DEFENDERS
Issue 23
Story Page # 6
Line Up Page # 7
BILL WYLIE '95
IN ORDER TO BUTTRESS THE WALLS OF SLORIOTH'S PRISON, THE MYSTIC SEALANTERS THAT CAP THE SPELL MUST FIRST BE BYPASSED.
THAT IS WHY YOU ARE HERE. ONLY THREE PURE OF SPIRIT MAY BREACH THESE DEFENSES
AND MY ASSOCIATES AND I HAVE GROWN TOO TAINTED--
THREE?
BUT THERE'RE ONLY DEATHLOK AND ME--
YOU ARE MISTAKEN, TANDY BOWEN.
EVEN NOW, OUR FINAL JOURNEYMAN MAKES HIS APPEARANCE!
SKA-RASSH
THOOM
DRAX HEARD FUNNY VOICES IN HIS HEAD!
TOLD HIM TO COME HERE!
DRAX FIGHT NOW?
DEATHLOK AND ME

FOLD COPY USE FOR PASTE-UP ONLY COPY TRIM B

TRIM COPY

YELLOW TS

BLACK TS

MARVEL COMICS
THE SECRET DEFENDERS
VS...
24 FEB
APPROVED BY THE COMICS CODE AUTHORITY
...THE DEFENDERS
DIRECT EDITION
$1.95 US $2.65 CAN

RED TS

BLUE TS

COPY TRIM

FOLD COPY TITLE__________ #_____ MONTH_____ MARVEL COMICS COPY TRIM

ARTIST__________

6478

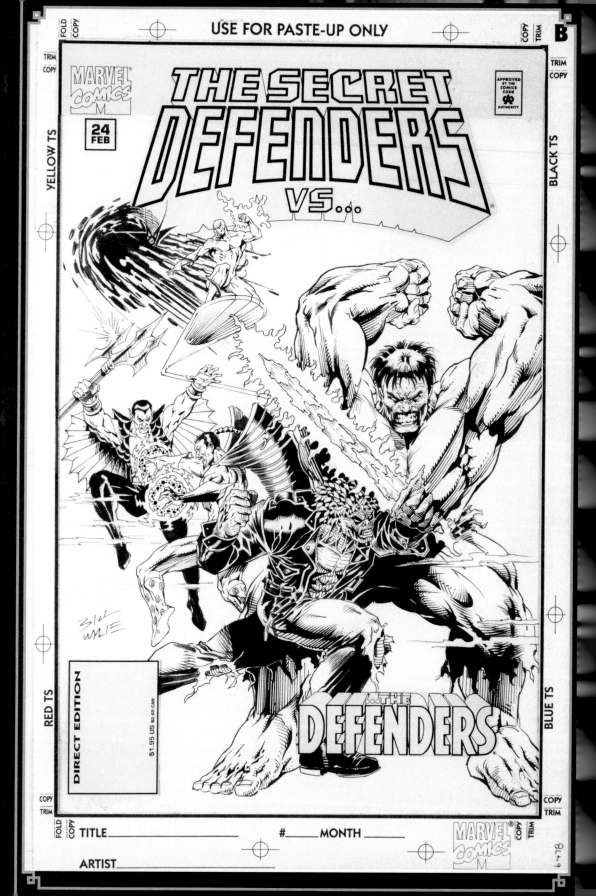

ART PAPER FOR BLEED PAGES (BOOKSHELF FORMAT OR SADDLE STITCH) PRINTS AT 67% ILLUSTRATION QUALITY

ALL BLEED ART MUST EXTEND TO SOLID LINE

KEEP ALL LETTERING INSIDE BROKEN-LINE BOX

Book Secret Defenders Issue 25 Story Page # 30 Line Up Page # 38

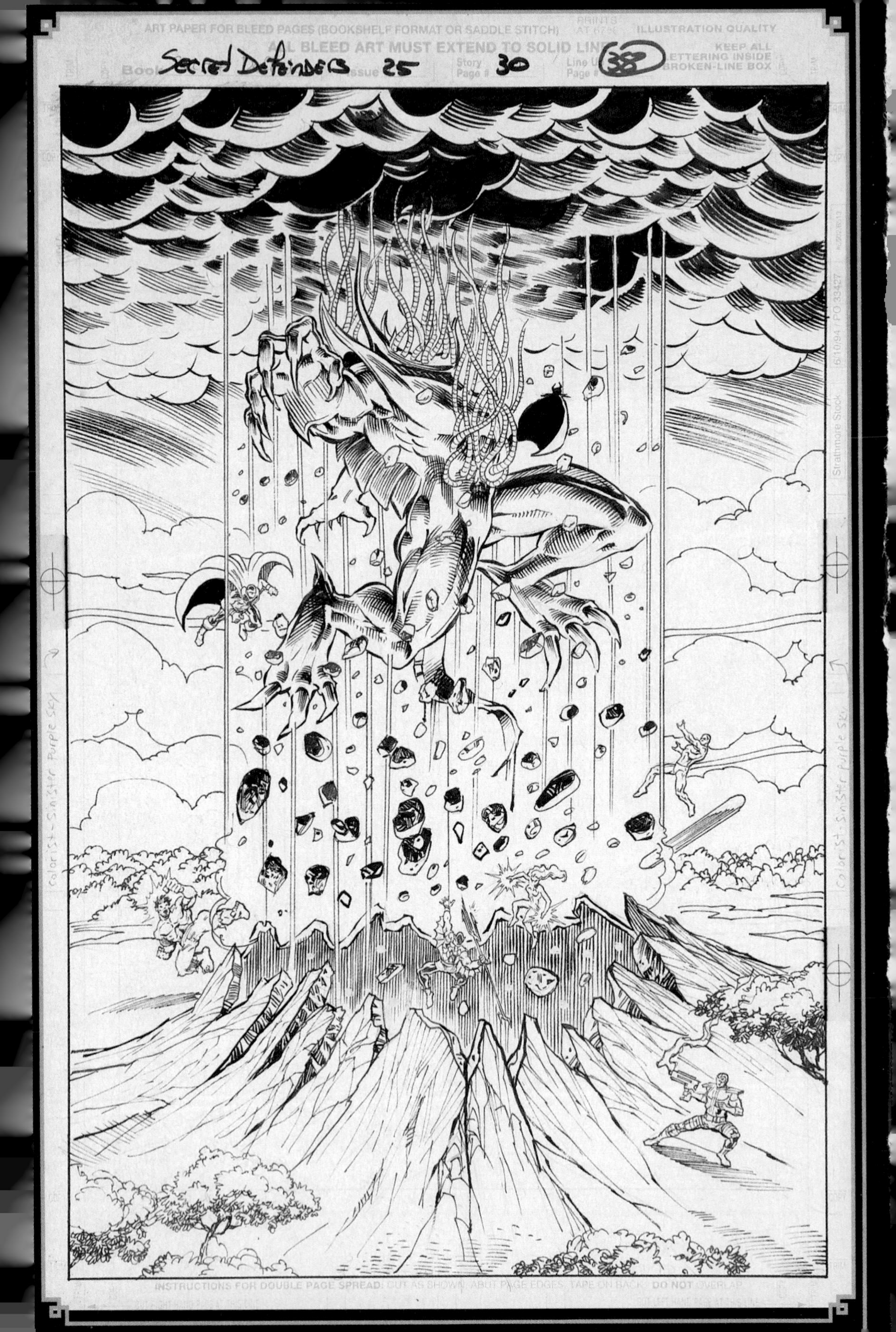

Colorist - Sinister Purple Sky

Colorist - Sinister Purple Sky

Strathmore Stock 6/10/94 PO 33427

INSTRUCTIONS FOR DOUBLE PAGE SPREAD: CUT AS SHOWN, ABUT PAGE EDGES, TAPE ON BACK. DO NOT OVERLAP